INSIDERS' GUIDE® SERIES

INSIDERS' GUIDE® TO THE FLORIDA KEYS AND KEY WEST

ELEVENTH EDITION

VICTORIA SHEARER AND NANCY TOPPINO

INSIDERS' GUIDE®

GUILFORD, CONNECTICUT
AN IMPRINT OF THE GLOBE PEQUOT PRESS

The prices and rates in this guidebook were confirmed at press time. We recommend, however, that you call establishments before traveling to obtain current information.

To buy books in quantity for corporate use or incentives, call **(800) 962–0973, ext. 4551,** or e-mail **premiums@GlobePequot.com.**

INSIDERS' GUIDE®

Previous editions of this book were published by Falcon Publishing, Inc. in 1998, 1999, and 2000.

Text design by LeAnna Weller Smith
Maps created by XNR Productions, Inc. © Morris Book Publishing, LLC

ISSN: 1529-174X
ISBN-13: 978-0-7627-4184-7
ISBN-10: 0-7627-4184-8

Manufactured in the United States of America
Eleventh Edition/First Printing

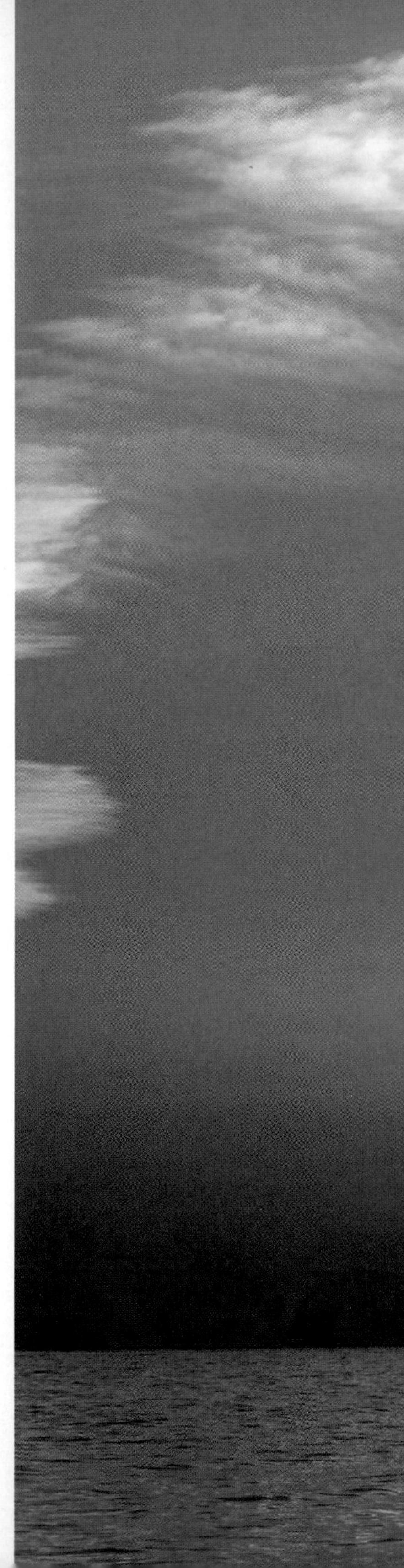

White Street sunset. ROB O'NEAL/*KEY WEST CITIZEN*

A serene Geiger Key sunset. ROB O'NEAL/*KEY WEST CITIZEN*
Key West aerial. ROB O'NEAL/*KEY WEST CITIZEN*

Blow-dart chick. ROB O'NEAL/*KEY WEST CITIZEN*

Fort Jefferson, Dry Tortugas National Park. ROB O'NEAL/*KEY WEST CITIZEN*
Yachting. ROB O'NEAL/*KEY WEST CITIZEN*

Will Soto performing at Mallory Square. ROB O'NEAL/*KEY WEST CITIZEN*
Fantasy Fest Pretenders in Paradise. FLORIDA KEYS & KEY WEST TDC

Hemingway look-alikes. ROB O'NEAL/*KEY WEST CITIZEN*
Bird dog. ROB O'NEAL/*KEY WEST CITIZEN*

Fort Zachary Taylor State Park. ROB O'NEAL/*KEY WEST CITIZEN*

Angler fly fishing. ROB O'NEAL/*KEY WEST CITIZEN*

Sloppy Joe's Bar. ROB O'NEAL/*KEY WEST CITIZEN*
Ready to strut his stuff. ROB O'NEAL/*KEY WEST CITIZEN*

Key West Lighthouse. FLORIDA KEYS & KEY WEST TDC

Duval Street, Key West. FLORIDA KEYS & KEY WEST TDC
Houseboats in Key West. FLORIDA KEYS & KEY WEST TDC

Up, up, and away. ROB O'NEAL/*KEY WEST CITIZEN*

Artist Rick Worth at work. ROB O'NEAL/*KEY WEST CITIZEN*

Home, sweet home. ROB O'NEAL/*KEY WEST CITIZEN*

Coral spawn. FLORIDA KEYS & KEY WEST TDC

Hemingway Home and famous six-toed cats, Key West. FLORIDA KEYS & KEY WEST TDC

CONTENTS

Foreword xxv
Preface xxvi
Acknowledgments xxvii
How to Use This Book 1
Historical Evolution 3
Paradise Found 11
Getting Here, Getting Around 30
Restaurants 43
Seafood Markets and Specialty Foods 85
Nightlife 97
Accommodations 107
Vacation Rentals and Real Estate 166
Campgrounds 179
Boating 188
Cruising 206
Fishing 217
Diving and Snorkeling 243
Recreation 267
Attractions 292
Kidstuff 316
Annual Events 325
Arts and Culture 338
Shopping 348
Retirement 368
Health Care 377
Education and Child Care 384
Media 390
Worship 393

Index 395
About the Authors 411

Directory of Maps

Florida Keys xix
Upper Keys xx
Middle Keys xxi
Lower Keys xxii
Key West xxiii
Key West Old Town xxiv

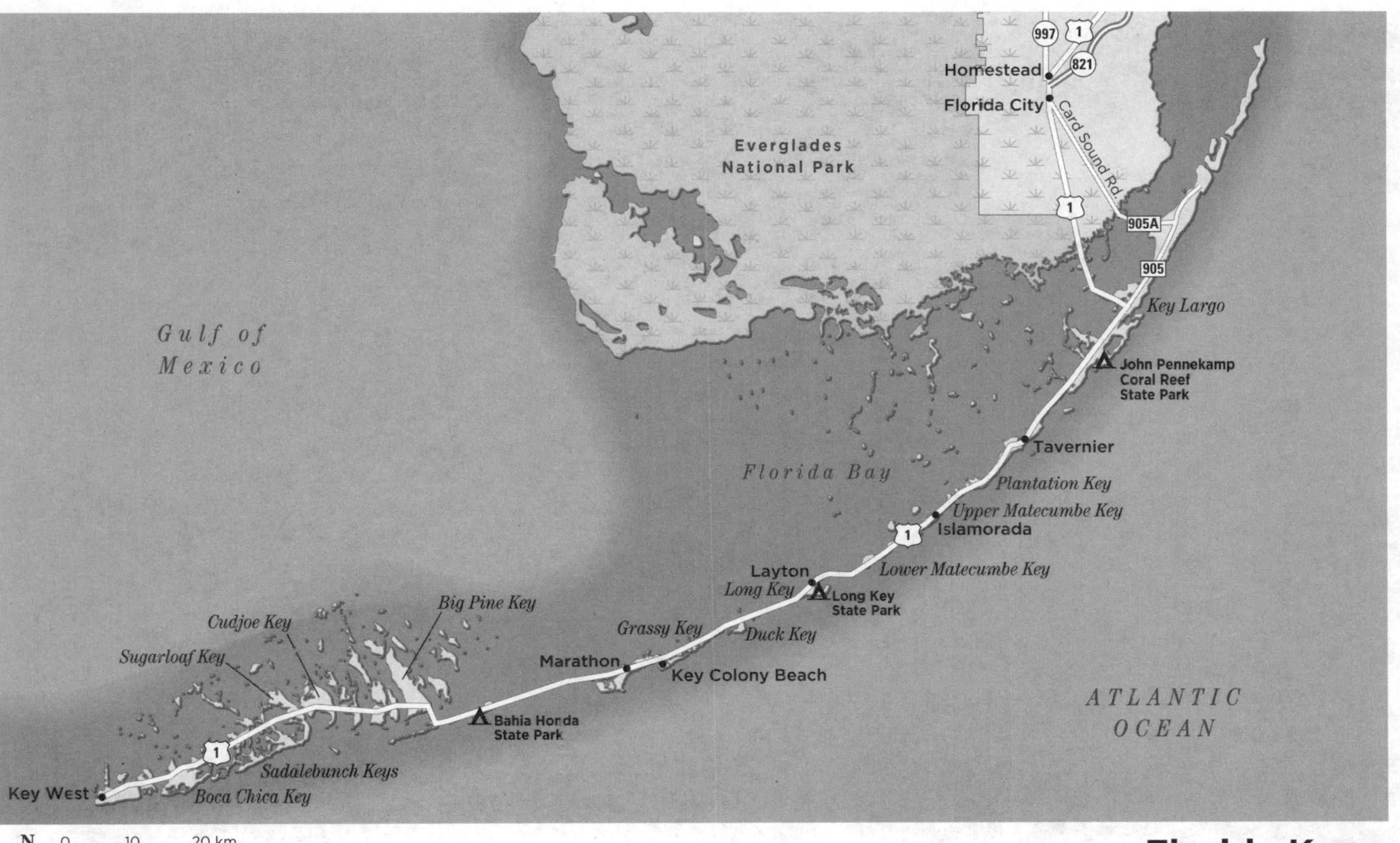

Florida Keys

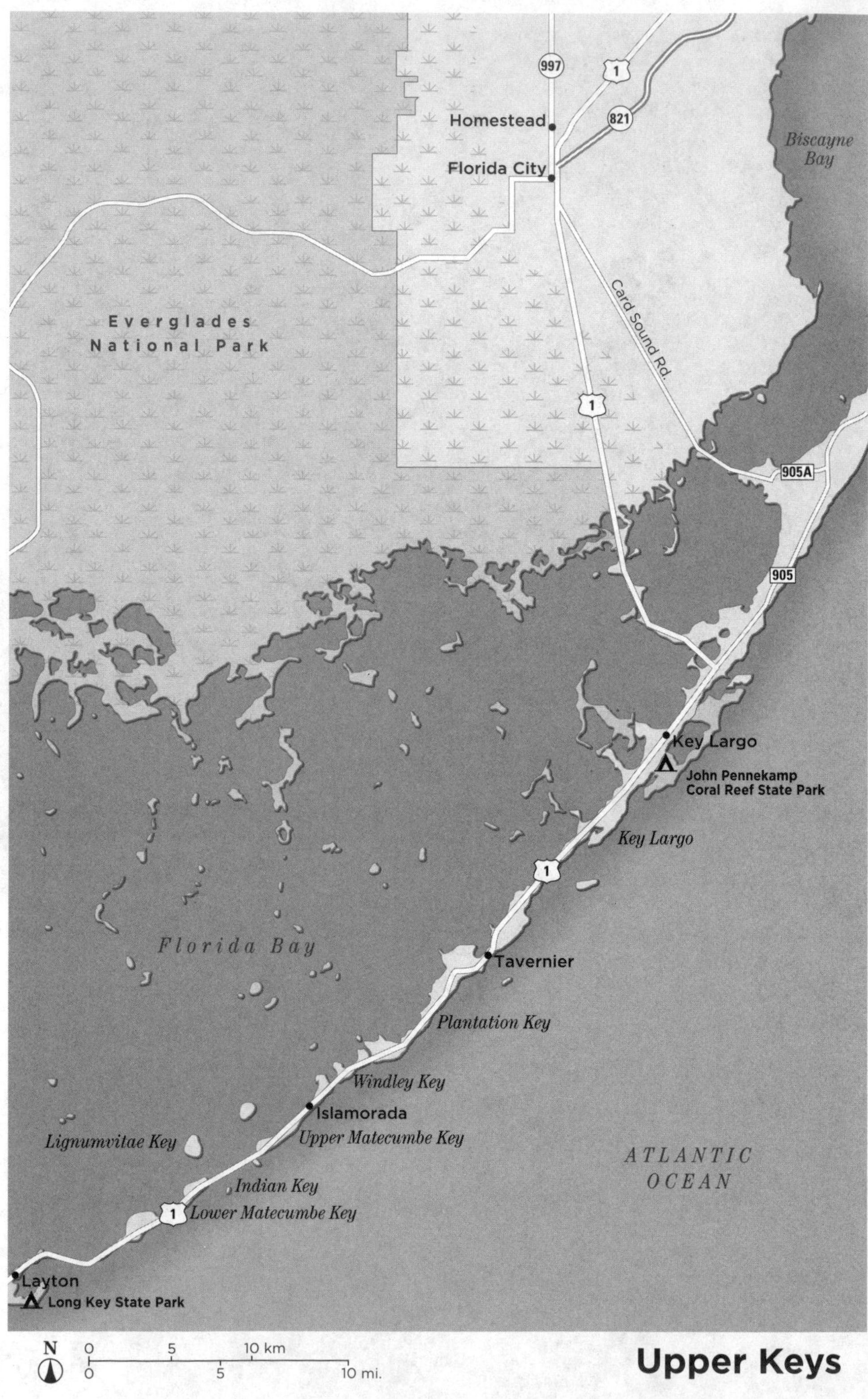
997
1
821
Homestead
Florida City
Biscayne Bay
Card Sound Rd.
Everglades National Park
1
905A
905
Key Largo
John Pennekamp Coral Reef State Park
Key Largo
1
Florida Bay
Tavernier
Plantation Key
Windley Key
Islamorada
Lignumvitae Key
Upper Matecumbe Key
ATLANTIC OCEAN
Indian Key
1
Lower Matecumbe Key
Layton
Long Key State Park
N
0 5 10 km
0 5 10 mi.

Upper Keys

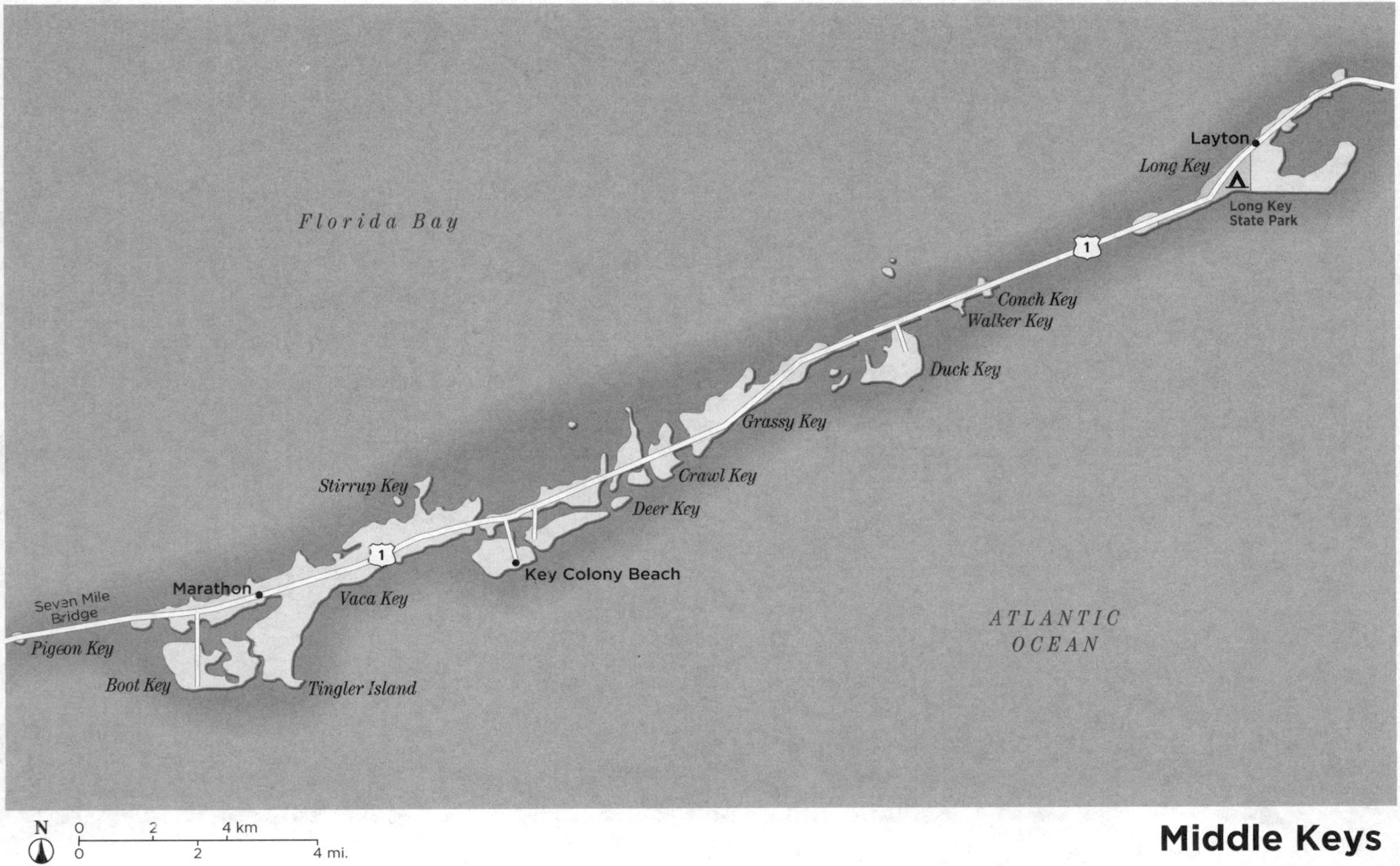

Middle Keys

Florida Bay
Layton
Long Key
Long Key State Park
1
Conch Key
Walker Key
Duck Key
Grassy Key
Crawl Key
Deer Key
Stirrup Key
Key Colony Beach
Marathon
Vaca Key
Seven Mile Bridge
Pigeon Key
Boot Key
Tingler Island
ATLANTIC OCEAN
N
0 2 4 km
0 2 4 mi.

Lower Keys

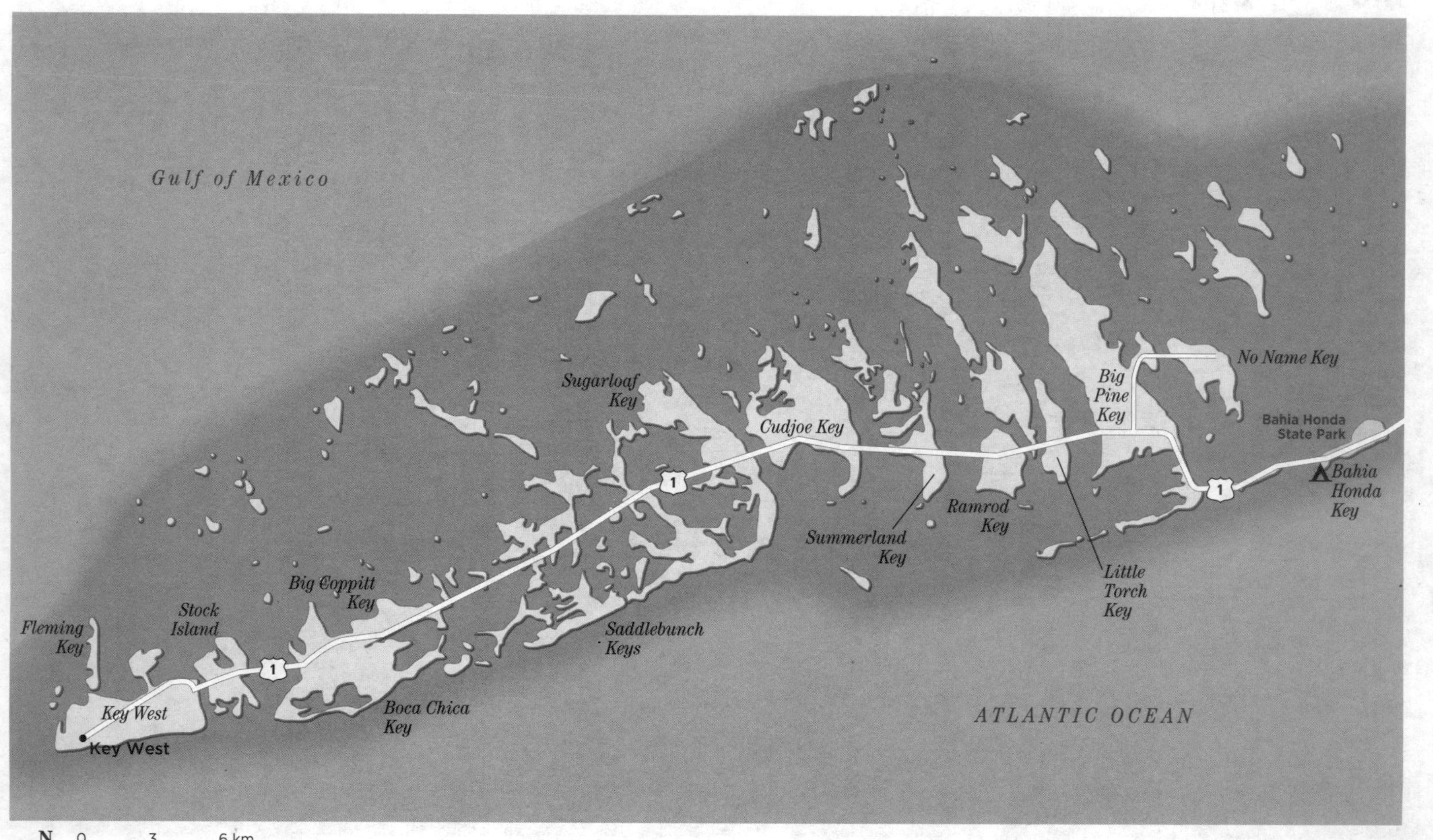
Gulf of Mexico
ATLANTIC OCEAN
No Name Key
Big Pine Key
Bahia Honda State Park
Bahia Honda Key
Little Torch Key
Ramrod Key
Summerland Key
Cudjoe Key
Sugarloaf Key
Saddlebunch Keys
Big Coppitt Key
Boca Chica Key
Stock Island
Fleming Key
Key West
Key West
1
1
1
N
0 3 6 km
0 3 6 mi.

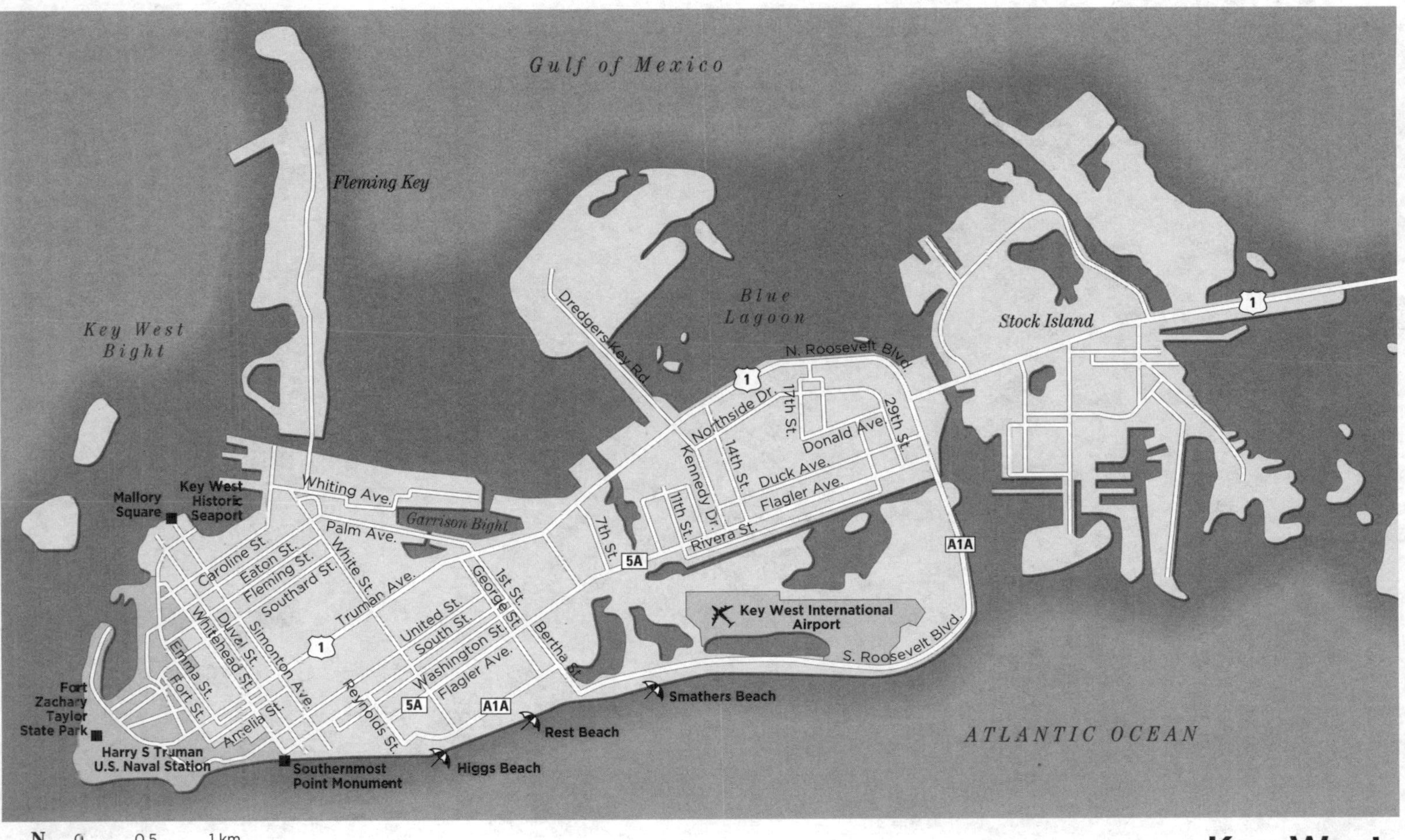
Gulf of Mexico
Fleming Key
Key West Bight
Blue Lagoon
Stock Island
Dredgers Key Rd.
N. Roosevelt Blvd.
Northside Dr.
17th St.
29th St.
Donald Ave.
14th St.
Duck Ave.
Kennedy Dr.
Flagler Ave.
11th St.
Rivera St.
7th St.
Whiting Ave.
Mallory Square
Key West Historic Seaport
Garrison Bight
Palm Ave.
Caroline St.
Eaton St.
Fleming St.
Southard St.
White St.
Truman Ave.
United St.
South St.
George St.
1st St.
Washington St.
Bertha St.
Flagler Ave.
Whitehead St.
Duval St.
Simonton Ave.
Emma St.
Fort St.
Amelia St.
Reynolds St.
Key West International Airport
S. Roosevelt Blvd.
Smathers Beach
Rest Beach
Higgs Beach
Fort Zachary Taylor State Park
Harry S Truman U.S. Naval Station
Southernmost Point Monument
ATLANTIC OCEAN
1
5A
A1A
N
0
0.5
1 km
0.5
1 mi.

Key West

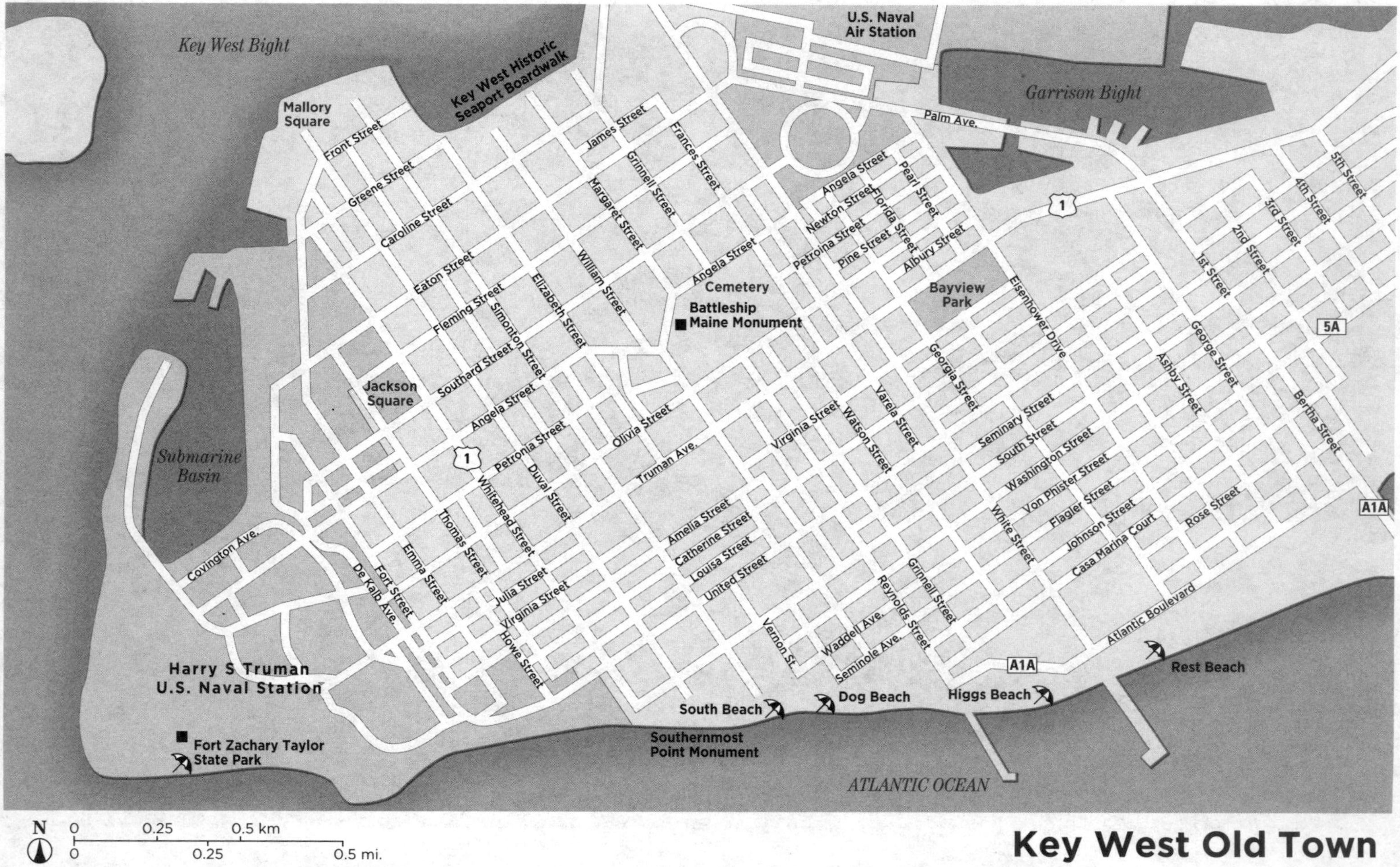

Key West Old Town

Key West Bight
Key West Historic Seaport Boardwalk
Mallory Square
U.S. Naval Air Station
Garrison Bight
Palm Ave.
Front Street
Greene Street
Caroline Street
Eaton Street
Fleming Street
Simonton Street
Southard Street
Elizabeth Street
William Street
Margaret Street
Grinnell Street
James Street
Frances Street
Angela Street
Newton Street
Petroina Street
Pine Street
Florida Street
Pearl Street
Albury Street
Cemetery
Battleship Maine Monument
Bayview Park
Eisenhower Drive
1
5A
A1A
1st Street
2nd Street
3rd Street
4th Street
5th Street
George Street
Ashby Street
Bertha Street
Georgia Street
Seminary Street
South Street
Washington Street
Von Phister Street
Flagler Street
Johnson Street
Casa Marina Court
Rose Street
White Street
Atlantic Boulevard
Jackson Square
Submarine Basin
Angela Street
Petronia Street
Olivia Street
Truman Ave.
Virginia Street
Watson Street
Varela Street
Whitehead Street
Duval Street
Thomas Street
Emma Street
Fort Street
De Kalb Ave.
Covington Ave.
Julia Street
Virginia Street
Howe Street
Amelia Street
Catherine Street
Louisa Street
United Street
Vernon St.
Waddell Ave.
Seminole Ave.
Reynolds Street
Grinnell Street
Harry S Truman U.S. Naval Station
Fort Zachary Taylor State Park
South Beach
Dog Beach
Higgs Beach
Rest Beach
Southernmost Point Monument
ATLANTIC OCEAN
N
0 0.25 0.5 km
0 0.25 0.5 mi.

FOREWORD

If you are on your first visit to our island, or one of the many vacationers who make multiple visits each year—driving, flying, boating, and more recently, bicycling—you may be expecting to see a less vibrant island because of the four hurricanes that threatened our city last summer. I am proud to say that our island's businesses and residents bounced back from the hurricanes' effects, especially Hurricane Wilma, and you can expect to see a lively island lifestyle during your stay.

The City of Key West was well prepared for the hurricane season of 2005. Cleanup began immediately following each hurricane, often while the winds were still blowing steadily at 45 m.p.h., and today business is as usual.

Our island boasts some of the country's best-rated restaurants, and we probably have more great eateries per square mile than any other city in Florida. The countless activities that make Key West attractive to visitors are ready to greet you. Our waters are pristine and hold the only coral reef in the continental United States; Key West sunsets have become so famous that Hollywood comes here to film them. Our art galleries are as diverse as our population and can be found in almost every block of the island. Many artists who call Key West home display locally and nationally. Our museums are known worldwide and you can choose from some the world's best hotels or a small, locally run bed-and-breakfast to stay in.

Walk our island while visiting and see up-close some of the most intriguing architecture in the state. Rent a bicycle and enjoy our many tree-shaded streets. There are bike racks throughout the city for your convenience because we support alternative modes of transportation.
I hope you take advantage of all the activities our island Paradise offers and that you will return often to enjoy our hospitality and uniqueness. After all, there are reasons Key West is often called "America's only Caribbean Island."

—Julio Avael, Key West City Manager

PREFACE

Forget the black-and-white world you leave behind. When you arrive in the Florida Keys, life suddenly turns to Technicolor, and it doesn't take a twister to lead you to the lush Emerald City of Oz. Settle yourself in. Take Toto along, too.

Nowhere else on earth is there an Eden such as ours, where all are admitted freely and via so many varied means. Ours is the land of dreamers, doers, and do-si-doers, of train makers, treasure trovers, and time-honored tranquillity. There are no Munchkins along the yellow brick road that unites each of our magical isles and then appends us to the mainland. In the Florida Keys everyone and everything is larger than life.

Look closely, and the enigmatic view from afar becomes as lucid as the crystalline waters of the Atlantic Ocean and the Gulf of Mexico that envelop us. From coconut palms to cormorants, you'll see that we are more than the Duval Street party scene in Key West. We are angelfish and anemones, gorgonians and groupers, lobsters and lizardfish, sponges and stone crabs. We're a thriving city of marine creatures commuting daily from North America's only barrier reef, approximately 6 miles offshore, to sweeping underwater meadows of turtle grass nearshore where we forage and feed.

By day we are the golden sun that rises over the ocean, glows brightly and then, in ardent shades of red, dips ever-so-gently beneath the Gulf horizon. As darkness enfolds the Florida Keys, we are the cornucopia of stars that seem to gleam more brilliantly here in our endless skies than anywhere else.

We are a necklace of tiny pearl islands tenuously strung together by 42 majestic bridges and the dream of one man, Henry Morrison Flagler. We're divers and diesel mechanics, anglers and archaeologists, sailors and salvagers, cruisers and commercial fishermen, boaters and bartenders, gunkholers and guides, restaurateurs and real estate agents, hoteliers and hostesses. And our heart is in the sea.

We are hardwood hammocks, tropical pinelands, and mangrove islets. Unique in the universe, we are diminutive key deer, sour key limes, and endangered Key Largo wood rats. We are nesting great white herons, communal white pelicans, and showy roseate spoonbills. Creatures great and small, we are bonefish and billfish, sharks and stingrays, sea turtles, manatees, and dolphins. And because we vigilantly guard our copious treasures, we are the Florida Keys Wild Bird Center, Reef Relief, the Turtle Hospital, The Nature Conservancy, and the Reef Environmental Education Foundation. At last we have a brain.

Whether you mistakenly believe that you lack a heart . . . a brain . . . the nerve . . . you're sure to unearth it all, along with a deeply enriched spirit, on your journey through the mysteries, rich history, and legends of the Florida Keys. Experience all the marvels of this awe-inspiring Oz. You'll never want to click your ruby slippers, sandals, or bare feet—or board a plane, boat, or automobile—heading for home. One visit is, after all, what led so very many of us to become Insiders. Welcome to this side of the rainbow. We are the Florida Keys.

i

An infamous bumper sticker seen frequently in the Florida Keys is SLOW DOWN THIS AIN'T THE MAINLAND. ***Things here do have a bit of a mañana attitude. Slow and easy is the way most of the locals live, and that mind-set is part of the required daily dose of living in Paradise.***

ACKNOWLEDGMENTS

The Beatles said it all when they crooned, "I get by with a little help from my friends," and mine rank right up there on the top 40. To my best friend and life partner, my husband, Bob, thank you for undying patience, encouragement, and support from the first edition right through this eleventh update. And my gratitude for translating a lifetime of Florida Keys angling experience for me so that we can all catch the magic of the sport. To my dear friends Wayne and Mary Moccia, thank you for sharing your expansive knowledge of the Keys' cruising waters and for divulging your secret hideaways and favorite dive locations. To Barbara and Dick Marlin, thanks for all the good camping tips. To James and Frankie Hankins, Joe Winter, and John and Louise Skidmore, thanks for the fishing photo ops and the many Insider angling and lobstering tips. To the Lunch Bunch—which grows larger and more dedicated every year—culinary medals of the year to you all for still visiting the restaurants of my choice and critiquing your food. To John Ghee, Dick Adler, and the Everglades houseboat gang, thanks for the green flash, the sunset scale, and years of giggles. To my many friends on Duck Key—you know who you are—thank you for all the unsolicited tips and Insider info that you continue to send my way, and, most important, for never failing to ask, "How's it going?" I am truly blessed. My appreciation to the folks at Globe Pequot Press. And finally, love to my all-grown-up children and their spouses—Kristen, John, Brian, and Lisa—and to my mother, June, for her enduringly patient understanding of my deadline-oriented lifestyle. And love and kisses to the lights of my life, my grandchildren—Brian, Lisa, Ashleigh, Nicholas, Bethany, Bobby, and Christopher. Good job, Insiders. Once again, thanks for the memories.

—VS

My gratitude goes out to my family and friends who help make this writing project so enjoyable and so much fun. My appreciation, also, to the many wonderful people of the Florida Keys who made themselves available to answer the many questions I had and who welcomed the many visits I made to their establishments. The genuine warmth and sincerity of the locals is what makes this beautiful spot a destination that travelers won't forget, and why I remain a permanent Insider in Paradise. A special heartfelt thanks to managing editor Liz Taylor of The Globe Pequot Press for her guidance and support throughout my work on this eleventh edition.

—NT

HOW TO USE THIS BOOK 

Here at the southernmost tip of the continental United States, the serpentine Overseas Highway fuses many of our 800-plus islands with ligaments of vaulted bridges and concrete connective tissue.

Ours is a marriage of land and sea. To merely introduce you to the topside society of the Florida Keys would neglect the flamboyant and fascinating communities living below. This guide lifts the curtain, bringing the many facets of our watery stage to life. We treat you to our unique geology and colorful history. We introduce you to the flora and fauna of the habitats of our tropical ecosystem. And we take you where you may have never been before—fishing, diving, and boating in our waters.

We'll help you sate your appetite with listings of restaurants, seafood markets, and specialty food shops. We'll show you where the action is with the rundown on attractions, recreation sites, festivals and special events, and nightlife of the Keys. We'll offer myriad alternatives for you to rest your weary head: hotels, motels, inns, guesthouses, and condos; campgrounds; even resort marinas and anchoring-out spots for your motor or sailing yacht. Landlubber or seafarer, everything you need to know is in the *Insiders' Guide to the Florida Keys and Key West*.

To navigate this book, begin with the assumption you are traveling "down the Keys," that is, from Key Largo to Key West. We have organized our information by descending mile marker. Mile markers are those small green signs with white numbers you'll see posted at the sides of the Overseas Highway (U.S. Highway 1). We have designated mile-marker addresses as either oceanside (on your left as you travel down the Keys) or bayside (on your right as you go toward Key West). At Key West, which is MM 0, locations are stated using street names.

Most chapters have several parts. A general preface to the subject matter acquaints you with aspects of the topic common to all areas of the Florida Keys. This is followed by specifics for the Upper Keys (MM 106 on Key Largo to MM 70 on Long Key), Middle Keys (MM 70 to MM 39 on Ohio Key), Lower Keys (MM 39 to Stock Island), and finally Key West, the entrance to which is actually about MM 5 on Stock Island, although mile marker appellations are not used in Key West.

When making phone calls from outside the area, note that the area code in the Florida Keys is 305. Since 2002, when you're using the main local carrier, BellSouth, you can call anywhere in the Florida Keys at no charge. Simply dial the 10-digit number, beginning with the area code. For calls to Florida City, Homestead, or Miami that also bear the area code 305, you can expect to pay a flat 25-cent fee, however.

Throughout all the chapters we have sprinkled Insiders' Tips (look for the **i**), extracted from those in the know with a little arm-twisting. You'll find enlightening Close-ups chock-full of information on everything from a recipe for key lime pie to how to make yellowtail chum balls. And just so you will be sure to understand the language, we have included a glossary of Keys-speak.

You hold in your hand a passport to the Florida Keys. We help you hit the road, explore the sea, and speak the language of the natives. Locals call this Paradise. Judge for yourself.

Keys-Speak Glossary

backcountry—shallow sea-grass meadows and mangrove islet waters of Florida Bay

bayside—anything on the opposite coast from the Atlantic; for instance, Florida Bay in the Upper Keys, the Gulf of Mexico in the Middle and Lower Keys

bight—a body of water bounded by a bend or curve in the shore; several are found in Key West

bluewater—deep, offshore waters of the Atlantic Ocean

bubba—slang for best friend, buddy

chickee—an open-sided, thatched-roof hut commonly found near the water's edge that is used as shelter from the sun

coconut telegraph—local gossip about any subject, person, place, or thing

conch—meat of a marine mollusk used in chowder and fritters; once a staple in the diet of early Conchs and Keys-dwelling Native Americans, now an endangered species that may not be harvested in the Keys

Conch (pronounced "konk")—a descendant of the original Bahamians who settled the Keys; a person born in the Florida Keys

conch cruiser—any form of transportation (mainly cars and small trucks) that is painted and decorated with outrageous art work and embellishments

Duval crawl—the notorious bar-hopping Key West scene from one end of Duval Street to the other

Fat Albert—two large, white blimps tethered on Cudjoe Key (MM 23) that the U.S. Government uses to track aircraft, boat traffic (especially for drug enforcement), and weather by radar. Fat Albert is also used to broadcast "TV Marti"—a TV station targeted toward audiences in Cuba.

flats—shallow, nearshore waters of the Atlantic

freshwater Conch—a person who has lived in the Florida Keys for at least seven years

gunkhole—to explore the shallow, nearshore waters and mangrove islets in a shallow-draft craft in search of birdlife and marine species

hammock—an elevated piece of bedrock covered with a hardwood tropical forest; also a woven lounger strung between two palm trees

Keys disease—the party life in the Keys has a tendency to have a lengthy duration. Starting early in the day to late at night, drinks and other vices can be a 24/7 lifestyle.

mile marker or MM—the green-and-white signs along U.S. Highway 1 that mark miles, in descending order, from Florida City (MM 127) to Key West (MM 0)

no-see-ums—tiny, biting flies with a hot, painful stinging bite

oceanside—anything on the Atlantic coast of the Keys

Paradise—The Florida Keys

puddle jumpers—small commercial planes that fly in and out of the Key West airport and take passengers to major airport hubs

the Rock—Slang for the Florida Keys, usually uttered by locals heading for the mainland to vacation, shop, or party: "I need to get off the Rock."

HISTORICAL EVOLUTION 

The saga of the Keys, like the livelihoods of its inhabitants, tethers itself first, foremost, and forever to the sea. Our fragile strand of coral beads, which arcs southwest from the U.S. mainland to within 100 miles of Cuba, has endured for eons at the mercy of the elements. Nature determined, more than humans ever did, the course of our history. That is, until one man accomplished what natural forces could not: He connected the islands to each other and to the mainland United States.

We will chronicle the Florida Keys, therefore, as a man-made triptych, highlighting the eras before, during, and after Henry Flagler's Florida East Coast Railroad Extension refashioned the subsequent history of the region.

PROLOGUE

Native Americans and the Spanish

The earliest recorded evidence of a Native American population in the Keys is estimated to be around A.D. 800, when maritime Indians populated the islands. Kitchen middens, or mounds of fish and sea-turtle bones and conch shells, can be found throughout the Keys. Archaeologists believe that although ancient villages may have existed thousands of years before this time, the rising sea level of the present Holocene epoch (see the Paradise Found chapter) has buried these settlements beneath the ocean.

Historians cannot agree on which tribes of Native Americans inhabited the Florida Keys in the ensuing centuries. The Tequestas, Calusas, Matecumbes, Caribbean Island tribes, and Seminoles from the mainland are all mentioned, although no archaeological evidence is conclusive. Widely accepted, however, is the notion that the Native Americans were seafarers by necessity and initially friendly to the white explorers they encountered.

Ponce de León garnered the credit for naming the Florida Keys *Los Martires* in 1513 during his exploration of the Gulf of Mexico. Legend maintains that the string of rock islands looked to him like suffering martyrs from his vantage point at sea. The Spanish took interest in the Native Americans of *Los Martires* in the centuries that followed but had no desire to seize their rocky islands. Priests from Havana attempted to convert the Native Americans to Catholicism. Some say this was an attempt not to save their souls but to teach them to be friendly to the crews of the Spanish ships and to hate the French and English, Spain's enemies who also were attempting to explore the New World. Spain's overriding interest in the Florida Keys at this time simply was to protect their fleet of treasure ships voyaging past its shores en route from Mexico and Cuba to the mother country.

The Gulf Stream: Treasure Highway

Long before the Overseas Highway became the main road of the Florida Keys, another highway controlled the islands' destiny: the great, blue river-in-the-Atlantic—the Gulf Stream. (The warm water of the Gulf Stream, the temperature of which varies greatly from surrounding waters, flows in a northerly direction between the Keys and Cuba, up the northeast coast of the United States, and then turns toward the east where it crosses the Atlantic Ocean to the European continent.) Conquistadores, explorers, and adventurers capitalized on the pulsing clockwise current (2 to 4 knots) to carry them swiftly back to Europe, where they unloaded the harvested riches of the New World at the feet of greedy monarchs.

The Spanish were the first to send their treasure-laden ships on this precarious route past our island chain, which is protected from the ocean's fury by a barrier coral reef (see the Diving and Snorkeling chapter). The Gulf Stream, which is not a definitive channel, winds an uneven course about 45 miles wide just outside the reef. Bad weather or bad judgment dashed the hopes, dreams, and cargo of hundreds of ships against this unforgiving coral graveyard.

It was the Native Americans who initially took advantage of this unexpected shipwrecked bounty, but salvaging became big business in the Keys with the arrival of the Bahamian Conchs (see The Wrecking Industry in this chapter). The passing ships inspired piracy from many nations, particularly the English, who lurked in the cuts and channels between the islands waiting to raid the ships' caches of gold and silver.

The Native Americans learned the ways of the Europeans, trading with the Spanish in Havana by means of large oceangoing canoes, pirating English ships, and free-diving to salvage the cargo of their wrecked vessels. The white man's diseases, however, greatly reduced Native American numbers. In 1763 Spain gave Florida to England in exchange for Cuba. At this time the last of the indigenous Native American families fled to Havana, fearing retribution for the cruelty they had heaped upon the British sailors found dashed upon the reef and stranded.

The Bahamians

By the early 1700s a group of white settlers from the Bahamas had begun active trading with Havana. Their ancestors, religious dissenters from England, had originally settled on Eleuthera and the Great Abaco Islands in the Bahamas in the 1600s. Experienced seamen and fishermen, these Bahamians harvested the waters of the Florida Keys, selling their catch in Havana. (Many believe the word *key* is derived from the English word *cay*, which in turn is a corruption of the Spanish *cayo*, all meaning "island.") The Keys were considered the pantry of Havana, for our waters supplied Cuba with green-turtle meat, conch, fish, and crawfish. The Bahamians traded their catch for knives, rope, spices, and other much-needed supplies, which they took back to the Bahamas.

When the English took control of Florida in 1763, they proclaimed the waters near the Florida Keys off-limits to residents of the Bahamas, which upset the trade balance between the Bahamas and Havana. This inconvenience was short-lived, however, because Spain regained Florida in 1783, and trade between the Bahamas and Cuba returned to normal. There was some settlement of the Keys by the English during this interval, but colonization of Key West did not begin in earnest until 1821, when Spain ceded Florida to the United States. Before 1821 Key West was just a watering stop for ships traveling the Gulf Stream route from the Gulf to the Atlantic.

A new edict insisting that only U.S. residents could engage in the now-lucrative wrecking operations off the Florida Keys spurred many Bahamian families to emigrate to the settlement of Key West. Many dismantled their entire houses and transported them to our southernmost city (see the Key West Architecture Close-up in the Attractions chapter). Some settlers were freed African-American slaves, dumped throughout the Bahamian islands by the English as they were released from captured slave traders. Ship owners and captains of merchant ships moved to Key West to be close to the trade lanes.

British Bahamians were known as "Conchs" for three legendary reasons: First, a prolific amount of conch flourished in the waters of the Bahamas, and the meat from the conical shells was a staple in the Bahamian diet. Second, it is believed that as a means of early communication, the Bahamian islanders blew into queen conch shells, creating a distinctive wailing cry that could be heard a great distance. Third, during the American Revolution, Tory sympathizers escaped to the Bahamas, where they supposedly said, "We'd rather eat conchs than go to war." Only descendants of the original settlers may legitimately be called Conchs, although today the word generally refers to anyone born in the Florida Keys.

Key West

A time-honored story persists that warring tribes of mainland Seminoles and island Calusas had one final battle on the southernmost island of our chain of keys. Spanish conquistadores purportedly found the island strewn with bleached bones of the Native Americans and called the key *Cayo Hueso* (pronounced *KY-o WAY-so*), or "island of bones." Bahamian settlers pronounced the Spanish name as *Key West*.

Settled long before the other keys in the chain, Key West was very much a maritime frontier town by the 1820s, booming with sea-driven industries. Ships sailing out of Key West Harbor set across the Florida Straits to Havana, their holds filled with the fish, sea turtles, and sponges harvested along the length of the Keys. A lively fishing trade with Cuba continued into the 1870s. The melting pot of Key West included seamen from many cultures: African-American Bahamians, West Indian African Americans, Spanish Cubans, and white Bahamians of English descent.

Key West was incorporated in 1828. Within 10 years it was the largest and wealthiest city in the territory of Florida, even though it could be reached only by ship, a geographic fact of life that continued until Henry Flagler's Florida East Coast Railroad Extension was finished in 1912. But it was the very waters isolating Key West from the rest of the world that contributed to its wealth.

Piracy

When the United States gained possession of Florida and the Florida Keys in 1821, the island of Key West took on a strategic importance as a U.S. naval base. Lieutenant Matthew Perry, who was assigned to secure the island for the United States, deemed Key West a safe, convenient, and extensive harbor. It became the base of operations to fight the piracy that ravaged the trading vessels traveling the Gulf Stream superhighway and those heading through the Gulf of Mexico to New Orleans. English, French, and Dutch buccaneers had threatened the Spanish treasure galleons in the 18th century. In the early days of the 1800s, Spanish pirates, based mainly in Cuba, hid among the islands of the Keys and preyed on all nations, especially the United States. Using schooners with centerboards that drew only 4 to 5 feet of water, the pirate ships dipped in and out of the shallow cuts and channels to avoid capture.

In 1830 Commander David Porter was sent to Key West to head up an antipiracy fleet and wipe out the sea jacking from the region. Commandeering barge-style vessels equipped with oars, Porter and his crews were able to follow the sea dogs into the shallow waters and overtake them. After 1830 the area was safe from banditry once again.

The Wrecking Industry

Whereas the Gulf Stream was once the sea highway carrying Spanish treasure galleons back to Europe, in the 18th and 19th centuries the route was traversed in the opposite direction. Trading vessels sailed from New England ports to the French and British islands of the West Indies and the Antilles, hugging the shoreward edge of the Gulf Stream so as not to have to run against its strong northerly currents. They often ran aground on the reef, giving birth to a lucrative wrecking industry that salvaged silks, satins, lace, leather, crystal, china, silver, furniture, wine, whiskey, and more.

After the United States took possession of Florida in 1821, Key West became an official wrecking and salvage station for the federal government, which sought to regulate and cash in on the lucrative trade that until this time was going to Nassau or Havana. Salvage masters had to get a license from a district court judge, proving that they and their salvage vessels were free of fraud. By 1854 wrecking was a widely practiced profession in the Keys. Fleets of schooners patrolled the Keys from Biscayne to the Dry Tortugas. First they would assist the shipwrecked sailors, then try to save the ship (there was no Coast Guard in those days).

Unlike early unregulated times, the wreckers couldn't just lay claim to the ship's cargo for themselves. They were paid off in shares of the bounty. During peak wrecking years, 1850 to 1860, nearly one ship per week hit the reefs, some with cargo valued in the millions of dollars.

Although by 1826 some of the reefs along the length of the Keys were marked by lighthouses or lightships, most remained treacherous and claimed many cargoes, particularly in the Upper Keys where the Gulf Stream meanders close to the reef. Stories have endured throughout the years that some of the more enterprising and unscrupulous wreckers even changed or removed navigational markers or flashed lights in imitation of a lightship to lure an unsuspecting vessel to its demise on a shallow shoal so they could salvage the cargo. The construction of additional lighthouses along the reef in the mid-1800s improved navigation to the point that the wrecking industry gradually faded away by the end of the 19th century.

The colorful history of the Florida Keys comes alive at www.mile-markers.org in a marvelous virtual road trip. Learn about the people, places, and history of the Keys through photos and postcards. This fascinating presentation of history and legend comes courtesy of the Monroe County Public Library, Florida International University, and the Florida Center for Library Automation.

Sponging

Sponging developed quickly in the Keys after the area became part of the United States, maturing into a commercially important industry by 1850.

Sponge harvesting initially was accomplished from a dinghy: One man sculled while the other looked through a glass-bottomed bucket. The spotter held a long pole with a small, three-pronged rake on one end used to impale the sponge and bring it into the boat. On shore the sponges were laid on the ground to dry in the sun so that the living animal within would dehydrate and die. The sponges then were soaked for a week and pounded on a rock or beaten with a stick to remove a blackish covering. Cleaned of weeds, washed, and hung to dry in bunches, the sponges were displayed for sale.

Cubans, Greeks, and Conchs harvested the sponges as fast and furiously as they could, with little regard for how the supply would be maintained, and it inevitably began to diminish. The Greeks began diving into deeper waters for the sponges, much in demand on the world market by 1900, and eventually moved to Florida's west coast at Tarpon Springs, where the sponging was more bountiful.

By 1940 a blight had wiped out all but about 10 percent of the Keys' sponge population. Although sponges again grow in our waters, commercial sponging is no longer a viable industry as synthetic sponges have absorbed the market.

Cubans and the Cigar Industry

Cuba, closer to Key West than Miami is, has always played a role in the historical evolution of the Keys. Cuban fishermen long frequented the bountiful Keys waters, and in the 19th century Cuban émigrés brought new life and new industry to Key West. William H. Wall built a small cigar factory in the 1830s on Key West's Front Street. It was not until a year after the Cuban Revolution of 1868, when a prominent Cuban by the name of Señor Vicente Martinez Ybor moved his cigar-making factory to Key West from Havana, that the new era of cigar manufacturing began in earnest.

E. H. Gato and a dozen or so other cigar-making companies followed Martínez Ybor. And an influx of Cuban immigrant cigar workers "washed ashore," joining the melting pot in Key West. Tobacco arrived in bales from Havana, and production grew until factories numbered 161, catapulting Key West to the rank of cigar-making capital of the United States. Though the manufacturers moved their businesses to Key West to escape high Cuban tariffs and the cigar-makers' union, the unions reestablished themselves in Key West by 1879, and troubles began anew.

The industry continued to flourish in Key West until its peak in 1890, when the city of Tampa offered the cigar manufacturers lower taxes if they would move to the Gulf Coast swamplands, an area now called Ybor City. With this incentive, the cigar-making industry left the Keys, but many of the Cuban people stayed, creating a steady Latin influence on Key West that has endured to this day.

Key West once was the largest manufacturer of hand-rolled cigars in the United States.

The Salt Industry

Early settlers of Key West and Duck Key manufactured sea salt beginning in the 1830s, using natural salt-pond basins on both islands. Salt was essential for preserving food in those days because there was no refrigeration. Cut off from tidal circulation except during storms, the salt ponds were flooded with seawater and then allowed to evaporate. The resulting salt crystals were harvested.

Capricious weather often flooded the salt ponds with fresh water, ruining the salty "crop." By 1876 the salt industry no longer existed in the Keys. The destructive forces of repeated hurricanes made the industry economically unfeasible.

Homesteading the Keys

Bahamians also homesteaded other Keys in the early 19th century, settling in small family groups to farm the thin soil. Familiar with cultivating the unique land of limestone islands, the Bahamians worked at farming pineapples, key limes, and sapodillas, called "sours and dillies."

Many believe Indian Key was the first real settlement in the Upper Keys. By 1834 it had docks, a post office, shops, and a mansion belonging to the island's owner, Jacob Housman. It became the governmental seat of Dade County for a time, but attacks from mainland Native Americans proved an insurmountable problem for this little key (see the Attractions chapter). Through the ensuing decades, Bahamian farmers homesteaded on Key Vaca, Upper Matecumbe, Newport (Key Largo), Tavernier, and Planter. By 1891 the area that is now Harry Harris Park in Key Largo had a post office, school, church, and five farms (see the Recreation chapter).

The census on any of these keys varied widely over the course of the century, and little is known as to why. For instance, Key Vaca had 200 settlers in 1840, according to Dr. Perrine of Indian Key, but by 1866, a U.S. census revealed an unexplained population of zero for Key Vaca.

FLAGLER'S FOLLY: THE FLORIDA EAST COAST RAILROAD EXTENSION

The dream of one man changed the isolation of the Florida Keys for all time. Native New Yorker Henry Flagler, born in 1830 and educated only to the eighth grade, established the Standard Oil Company with John D. Rockefeller in 1870 and became a wealthy, well-respected businessman. In 1885 he purchased a short-line railroad between Jacksonville and St. Augustine and began extending the rails southward toward Miami, then only a small settlement.

Flagler's vision of his railroad project went beyond Miami, however. He wanted to connect the mainland with the deep port of Key West, a booming city of more than 10,000 people, in anticipation of the growing shipping commerce he thought would be generated by the opening of the Panama Canal in the early years of the 20th century. He may even have set his sights on eventually connecting Key West with Cuba.

By 1904 the railroad extended to Homestead, at the gateway to the Keys. The year 1905 saw the commencement of what many perceived as an old man's folly: a railroad constructed across 128 miles of rock islands and open water, under the most nonidyllic conditions imaginable, by men and materials that had to be imported from throughout the world. Steamships brought fabricated steel from Pennsylvania, and cement from Germany and Belgium was used to create concrete supports below the waterline. Cement for above-water concrete came from New York State, sand and gravel from the Chesapeake, crushed rock from the Hudson Valley, timbers and pilings from Florida and Georgia, and provisions, from Chicago. Barges carried fresh water from Miami to the construction sites. Nothing was indigenous to the Keys except the mosquitoes and the sand flies.

By 1908 the first segment, from Homestead to Marathon, was completed, and Marathon became a boomtown. Ships brought their cargoes of Cuban pineapples and limes here, where they were loaded onto railway cars and sent north. (The railroad turnaround was at the present site of Knight's Key campground.) Railroad workers used Pigeon Key (see the Attractions chapter) as a base for further railway construction.

The 7-mile "water gap" between Marathon and Bahia Honda took some engineering prowess to overcome, and the completion of the project was severely hampered by several devastating hurricanes in 1909 and 1910. But on January 22, 1912, Henry Flagler—by then age 82—finally rode his dream from Homestead to Key West. He traveled across 42 stretches of sea, more than 17 miles of concrete viaducts and concrete-and-steel bridges,

i

At MM 31 on Big Pine, in front of Big Pine Liquors, there is an unimpressive stone marker. What makes it memorable is that this plain stone sign is the original post that guided railroad conductors on Flagler's Overseas Railroad as they passed Big Pine. Going north on U.S. Highway 1 it reads, JAX 492 (Jacksonville, Florida); going south it reads KW 30 (Key West).

and more than 20 miles of filled causeways, ultimately traversing 128 miles from island to island to the fruition of his vision. He entered Key West that day a hero. He died the following year probably never knowing that his flight of fancy changed the course of the Florida Keys forever.

Flagler's railroad, called the Key West Extension, made Key West America's largest deepwater port on the Atlantic Coast south of Norfolk, Virginia. Trade with the Caribbean increased, and Key West flourished for 23 years, recovering from the loss of the sponge and cigar industries.

The railroad stop on Key Largo was called Tavernier, and it developed into a trading center for the Upper Keys. Pineapple farming faltered in Key Largo and Plantation Key from a combination of tapping out the nourishment in the thin soil and market competition from the shiploads of Cuban pineapples transported by railway car from the docks of Key West to the mainland. The railroad company built a fishing camp on Long Key that attracted sportfishing aficionados from all over, including writer Zane Grey, a camp regular. Real estate boomed for a time, as people came to the Keys to homestead. The Florida East Coast Railroad Company completed construction of Key West's first official tourist hotel, the Casa Marina, in 1921. La Concha was built in 1928.

In 1923 Monroe County appropriated funds to construct a road paralleling the railroad. The bumpy rock road crossed Card Sound with a long area of fill and a wooden bridge. Half a dozen humpback bridges crossed the creeks and cuts on Key Largo. Extending the length of Key Largo, the road continued across Plantation Key, Windley Key, and Upper Matecumbe. At the southern end of our island chain, a narrow, 32-mile road connected Key West with No Name Key off Big Pine Key. A car ferry service provided the waterway link between the two sections of roadway by 1930, which traversed what we now call the Upper and Lower Keys.

Still, the journey across this 128-mile stretch from Homestead to Key West proved a rugged, dusty, insect-ridden, costly, all-day affair, and tourism did not flourish as hoped and expected. Fresh water remained a coveted, scarce resource in the Florida Keys. Cisterns saved the funneled rainwater, which was parsimoniously meted out. Salt water was used whenever possible, and wash days were also always bath days. This was hardly a tourist mecca.

The Great Depression delivered a near-fatal blow to the Florida Keys with a one-two punch. The cigar industry had moved to Tampa, sponging went to Tarpon Springs, and lighthouses had put an end to wrecking long before. The population of Key West dropped from 22,000 to 12,000. By 1934, 80 percent of the city's residents relied on government assistance. The Federal Emergency Relief Administration stepped in and commenced development and promotion of Key West as a magnet for increased tourism in the Keys.

To that end, developers began building bridges to connect the Middle Keys to each other and to the two sections of finished roadway. A "bonus army" of World War I veterans was employed to accomplish this momentous task. However, in 1935 Mother Nature reasserted her authority and once again charted the destiny of our islands. On Labor Day, what today we would call a Category Five hurricane hit the Upper and Middle Keys, destroying much of Flagler's Railroad. Hundreds of lives were lost when the 17-foot storm surge hit the bridge-building crew working on a bridge at Islamorada.

Because of mismanagement and lack of foreign freight heading northward from Cuban and Caribbean ports, the railroad was already in receivership. The railroad chose not to rebuild, citing financial difficulties. By this time it had become cheaper to haul cargo by truck than by train. The county's Overseas Road and Toll Commission purchased the right-of-way from the Florida East Coast Railroad and converted the single-track railway trestles, which remained intact after the hurricane, into two-lane bridges for automobiles. The highway from Homestead to Key West opened for traffic in 1938.

EPILOGUE

In the late 1930s, the U.S. Navy, stationed in Key West, began construction of an 18-inch pipeline that carried fresh water from wells in Homestead to Key West. The naval presence in Key West grew with the beginning of World War II, when antisubmarine patrols began surveillance of surrounding waters. The navy also improved the highway to better accommodate the transfer of supplies for its military installation. The Card Sound Road was bypassed. The new road, which followed the old railroad bed, now is known as the "18-mile stretch." By 1942 the Keys enjoyed fresh water and electricity service, and the Overseas Highway (U.S. Highway 1) officially opened in 1944, ushering in a new era of development that continues to this day.

After World War II the Florida Keys became more and more popular as a sportfishing destination, and fishing camps dotted the shores from the Upper Keys to Key West. Still a rather remote, primitive spot to visit, the Keys nevertheless continued to evolve into a desirable tourist terminus, and Key West burgeoned as a port of call. Also contributing to Key West's rebirth was the discovery of pink gold: shrimp. Fishermen who had caught a shark in the waters between Key West and the Dry Tortugas found the fish's stomach filled with large pink shrimp. This led to the discovery of a bountiful shrimping area off the Tortugas, and the Key West "pinks" shrimping industry was spawned in the Florida Keys. It is still a viable occupation as far up the Keys as Marathon.

From 1978 to 1983 the old railbed conversion bridges were retired. Modern concrete structures, some four lanes wide, now span our waters. Most mind-boggling as an engineering feat is the seemingly endless Seven Mile Bridge, which connects the once insurmountable watery gap between Marathon and Bahia Honda Key. Many of the old bridges have been recycled as fishing piers, but others still stand, abandoned and obsolete alongside their successors, crumbling reminders of the Keys' not-so-distant past.

By the 1980s the Florida Keys had emerged as a tourist-driven economy. Tourism remains the major industry of the Keys today, with fishing, scuba diving, boating, and the attractions of Key West topping the list of popular agendas.

Of growing concern is the effect the influx of visitors will ultimately have on the delicate balance of habitats within the tropical ecosystem of the Florida Keys (see the Paradise Found chapter). The jury is still out. Will humans or Mother Nature determine the postscript for Paradise?

i

The Florida Keys get some drinking water pumped from the freshwater Biscayne Aquifer in Miami-Dade County. Key West gets its water supply from the Stock Island desalinization plant. This plant is the only one in the country currently extracting pure salt water and turning it into household drinking water.

PARADISE FOUND 

Make no mistake, the sea is in charge here and always has been. About 100,000 years ago during the Sangamon Interglacial period of the Pleistocene epoch, the Florida Keys flourished under the waters of the Atlantic Ocean as a string of living coral patch reefs at the edge of the continental shelf. Deposits of oöids (small calcareous spheres resembling fish roe) accumulated on the lower portion of the reef. Sea level was some 25 feet higher than it is today. But with the onset of the last glacial period, the Wisconsin, the oceans receded and the sea dropped more than 150 feet.

The reef emerged as a landmass, exposing the corals and oöids to the atmosphere, rain, and pounding surf. The onslaught of the elements killed the corals, and the fossil remnants cemented themselves together, creating coral bedrock. This bedrock, called Key Largo limestone, now comprises the basis of the Upper and Middle Keys from Soldier Key near Miami to Big Pine Key. When the waters receded, the oöids compacted into rock called oölite. Now referred to as Miami oölite, this rock forms the foundation of the Lower Keys and Key West, cut through by tidal channels from the Gulf of Mexico to the Florida Straits. At the lowest sea level of the Wisconsin period, Florida Bay and Hawk Channel unfolded as dry land.

About 15,000 years ago the climate began to warm and sea levels rose again. This present interglacial period is called the Holocene epoch. As the sea once again claimed portions of the coral bedrock, living corals attached themselves to the limestone and began to grow anew. These growths now form the living coral reef tract that is presently submerged 4 to 5 miles offshore, extending from Fowey Rocks to the Dry Tortugas (see our Diving and Snorkeling chapter). The higher elevations of bedrock became isolated above sea level, a sparkling chain of islands dividing the seas.

Throughout the ages, the fluctuation of the sea has determined the fate of the coral islands we call the Florida Keys and will dictate its future as well. Put into simple perspective, sea level has been rising for the past 15,000 years, and the rate appears to be increasing due to the long-range effects of global warming. Just imagine: A 6-foot rise in sea level would eliminate all of the Lower and Middle Keys except Key West. The Upper Keys, being somewhat higher, would escape extinction for a time. But if sea level increases by 15 feet, the string of islands known as the Florida Keys will be reduced to a couple of tiny islets, and the majority of Paradise will be lost once again to the sea.

To be in the Florida Keys is to become one with nature, for the Keys offer unparalleled opportunities to be in direct daily contact with her substantial bounty. You'll know what we mean the moment you crest the first of the 42 bridges now spanning our islands and feel the vast power of the surrounding seas. Gaze down on our string of coral pearls from the air and you'll see that the Keys look insignificant juxtaposed against the encompassing Atlantic Ocean and Gulf of Mexico.

Insiders' Guides to other locales will introduce you to the lay of the land. But to gain an understanding of our world, which we reverently refer to as "Paradise," you must be forearmed with the scope of our waters, for all things revolve around the sea here. We will acquaint you with our climate, weather, and the multiple interrelated habitats of our tropical ecosystem—the only such ecosystem in the continental United States.

The word *tropical* generally refers to plants and animals living in the latitudes between the Tropic of Cancer in the Northern Hemisphere and the Tropic of

Capricorn in the Southern Hemisphere. The Florida Keys are somewhat north of the Tropic of Cancer, but the warming influence of the nearby Gulf Stream assures us the benefits of a tropical climate. Our natural flora grows nowhere else in North America, and the combination of our eight interrelated habitats and the creatures dwelling therein is truly unique. Come, join us for a sneak preview of Paradise. We're one of a kind—here, there, or anywhere.

HABITATS OF THE FLORIDA KEYS

The Land

HARDWOOD HAMMOCKS

When the coral reef emerged from the sea eons ago and calcified into limestone bedrock, floating debris accumulated on it, decomposed, and gradually evolved into a thin layer of soil. Seeds from the hardwood forests of the Yucatan, Honduras, Nicaragua, South America, and the Caribbean Islands were carried to the Florida Keys by the winds of hurricanes, the currents of the Gulf Stream, migrating birds, and eventually even humans. Thus, the vegetation of the Florida Keys is more common to the tropical Caribbean Basin than to the adjoining temperate areas of mainland Florida.

Found throughout the Keys, these West Indian tropical hardwood hammocks nurture highly diverse communities of rare flora and fauna—more than 200 species—some found nowhere else in the United States. The hammocks (originally an Indian word meaning "shady place") also shelter a variety of endangered species.

Most of the hardwood hammocks of the Keys were cleared years ago to supply the wood for shipbuilding and home building and to clear the land for planting pineapples or citrus as a commercial venture. But several good examples of West Indian hardwood hammocks still flourish in the Keys. The largest contiguous hammock in the continental United States is on North Key Largo. Known as the Key Largo Hammock State Botanical Site, it encompasses 2,700 acres. You will find a virgin hardwood hammock on Lignumvitae Key, which is preserved as a state botanical site. You can access the island only by boat. State park naturalists offer guided tours of the hammock. The Crane Point hammock in Marathon offers self-guided tours (see the Attractions chapter). You'll find other stands of hardwood hammocks sprinkled throughout the Keys.

A hardwood hammock has a layered structure much like other forests, with a tall overstory, a midstory, and an understory. Many of the trees and plants will be unfamiliar to you, and some carry with them a colorful past. In the next paragraphs we describe four of our hammocks' more infamous residents: lignum vitae, gumbo-limbo, Jamaica dogwood, and poisonwood trees.

Probably the most sought-after tree in the virgin hammock was the lignum vitae (Latin for "wood of life"). It is so valuable, heavily harvested, and slow-growing that it now tops the endangered list. Most visible today sprinkled throughout the hardwood hammock on Lignumvitae Key, the tree has a resin content of 30 percent.

The wood cannot be kiln-dried or glued because of the gum content of this resin, called guaiac gum. Lignum vitae was used in the hinges and locks on the Erie Canal, which have been functioning now for more than 100 years. Mythical tales surround the tree: Old texts suggest

> i
>
> ***With 42 bridges connecting the Florida Keys, 15 percent of travel time is spent on bridges. The longest bridge is seven Mile Bridge and the shortest is Harris Gap Bridge, a mere 37 feet long.***

lignum vitae, often called the "holy wood," was the tree referred to in the Biblical Garden of Eden and was used to fashion the Holy Grail.

Bold and brazen, the gumbo-limbo trees, often reaching 40 feet, cop the moniker "tourist trees" because their reddish, peeling bark brings to mind sunburned visitors to our islands. The tree hides a checkered past. In early times, settlers stripped off a piece of bark from the gumbo-limbo, revealing the tree's gluelike oozing sap. When birds landed on this particular branch, they stuck tight and could not fly away. Gathered by human predators, the birds were sold for 5 cents each to the Cuban cigar industry for the entertainment of the cigar rollers. Florida law forbids this practice of bird capture today. On a more respectable note, the resin from the gumbo-limbo was once used in the manufacture of varnish.

Also contributing to antics on the wrong side of the law is the Jamaica dogwood tree, called the fish poison tree. The roots, twigs, leaves, and gray-green scaly bark were used to stupefy fish and aid in their capture. When ground into a sawdust chum and placed in the shoreline waters, the vegetation emitted a chemical similar to an invertebrate poison that paralyzed the gills of the fish, affected their air bladders, and caused them to float to the surface, where they were easily harvested.

Belonging to the same family as poison ivy, the poisonwood tree masquerades as a beautiful, harmless canopy but contains a poisonous sap that causes severe dermatitis in humans. Native Americans of the Keys would tie their captives beneath the foliage of the 30-foot poisonwood tree. When it rained, the fresh water passing through the leaves carried the urushiol oils with every drop, causing a raging rash and slow torture.

Beneath the wide awning of the overstory, the smaller trees of the midstory flourish with less drama. Many of the trees bear fruits favored by the feathered tenants of the hardwood hammock habitat.

A dense understory of plants, shrubs, and vines adapts to the shady conditions on the hammock floor. And wildflowers must reach for the sky under the shady foliage top hat of the hammock, often turning into creeping vines.

The Key Largo wood rat, an endangered species that looks more like a big-eared Disney mouse than a London sewer rat, joins the Key raccoon, the Key cotton mouse, opossums, gray squirrels, and an assortment of migratory birds amid the flora of the hammocks. The 16-inch-long rodent, found only in the hammocks of North Key Largo, has been dubbed a "pack rat," because it likes to collect empty shells, aluminum pop-top tabs, and the colorful rings from plastic milk bottles.

THE PINELANDS

Pinelands in the Lower Florida Keys differ from the vast forests you may have seen in other areas of the United States. Adapting to growing conditions atop Miami oölite with limited fresh water, the tall, spindly trees are small in girth and sparsely foliated. Primarily found on Big Pine Key, these South Florida slash pines mingle with an understory of silver palms and brittle thatch palms, both of which are rare outside the Keys and protected under the Preservation of the Native Flora of Florida Act. Among the 7,500 protected acres in the Lower Keys, other pinelands grace No Name Key, Little Pine Key, Cudjoe Key, Sugarloaf Key, and Summerland Key.

The most famous pineland resident in the Lower Keys is undoubtedly the key deer, a subspecies of the Virginia white-tailed deer, found nowhere else in the world. These tiny deer, each about the size of a large dog, attempt to coexist with human inhabitants who have taken over much of the unpreserved woodlands of the Lower Keys. However, the diminutive animals frequently venture out of the woods and onto the Overseas Highway, where they are often struck and killed by vehicles. For that reason, speed limits

CLOSE-UP

Geckos

Look! Up on the wall! Down on the ground! Look everywhere! It's a gecko!

These tiny creatures with large eyes and tiny feet are nothing to fear, they are really a welcome sight in buildings and homes. You see, they are insect destroyers. At one time it was popular to buy and release geckos in buildings to control roaches and moths. They are insatiable night stalkers of small insects and can be seen on exterior walls near lights. They are also very shy and hide when folks are near.

The only native Florida gecko is the reef gecko, found in the southeastern part of Florida and the Keys. All other geckos in the state are descendants of introduced species. The Indo-Pacific (or house gecko) has spread quickly because it is unisexual. Usually tan or gray with light spots and smooth skin, sometimes if captured, a house gecko will turn a ghostly white and throw off part of its tail.

Some residents in the Keys say if you find a gecko in the house it brings good luck! Maybe that is because your home will be bug free! As you travel the Keys and look on the outside of homes and inside gift shops and art galleries, you'll see many brightly painted geckos as an art form. We want visitors to know how much we like having them here.

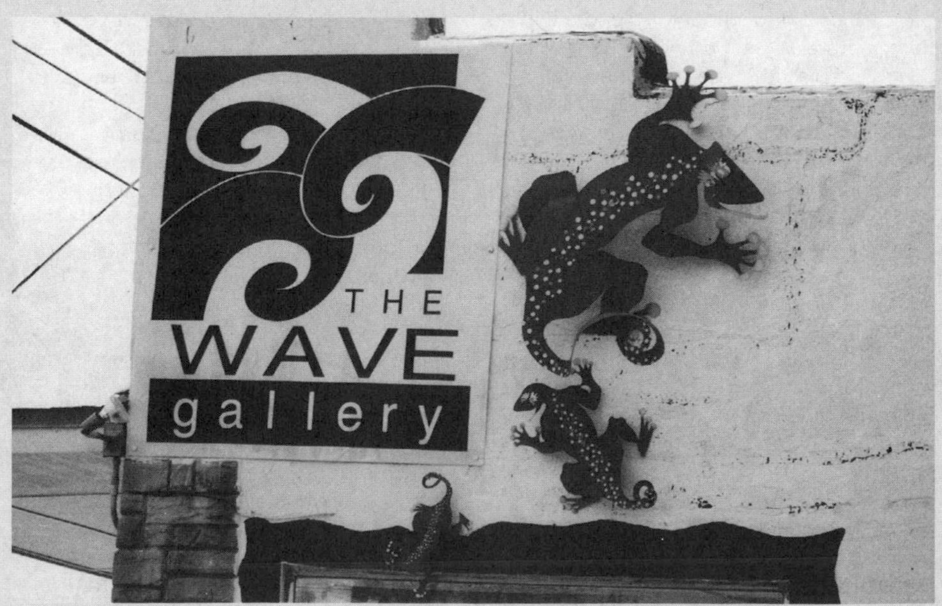

Bigger than life, geckos hang on a wall for all to see. PHOTO: LINDA STEDMAN

through Big Pine Key are reduced (45 mph daylight, 35 mph nighttime) and strictly enforced by law enforcement officials.

In 1957 the National Key Deer Refuge was established in Big Pine Key to ensure a sheltered natural habitat for the endangered species. About 800 key deer exist in the Lower Keys today. The key deer feed on red and black mangroves, thatch palms, and a variety of native berries. While they can tolerate small quantities of salt in brackish water, fresh water is essential to their survival. No official records document the origin of the key deer in the Florida Keys, but it is widely believed they migrated from the mainland as white-tailed deer when the seas receded in the Wisconsin glacial period. When sea level rose again during the present interglacial epoch, the deer were trapped in their pineland habitat. Over time their diminutive stature evolved as an adaptation to their sparsely vegetated environment.

The Shoreline

MANGROVE HABITATS

Called the island builders, mangroves comprise the predominant shoreline plant community of the Florida Keys, protecting the landmass from erosion. Able to establish itself on the coral underwater bedrock or in the sand, the mangrove's root structure traps, holds, and stabilizes sediments. Over time the infant mangrove habitats establish small islets such as those you'll see peppering Florida Bay and the oceanside nearshore waters. Mangrove habitats bordering the Keys filter upland runoff, maintaining the water quality of our seas.

The leaf litter that falls from the red mangroves decomposes in the tangle of its prop roots, forming a critical base in the food chain that supports the myriad species of the marine community inhabiting shoreline waters. Important as a breeding ground and nursery for juvenile spiny lobster, pink shrimp, snook, mullet, tarpon, and mangrove snappers, the mangroves also shelter these sea creatures from their predators. (See the Diving and Snorkeling chapter and the Fishing chapter for more on the fascinating underwater creatures living here.)

Great rookeries of wading and shorebirds roost and nest on the canopy of broad leaves of the mangrove habitats, creating a virtual aviary in every uninhabited islet (see the Gunkholing Close-up in this chapter for our bird-watching primer). Three kinds of mangroves thrive in the Florida Keys. The distinctive high-arching prop roots of the red mangrove enable the plants to exchange gases and absorb oxygen from the seawater. Long, pencil-like seedpods, called propagules, develop during the summer and drop off the mangroves in the autumn, floating upright hither and yon with the tides. Eventually snagged on a branch or caught against a rock, the seedling establishes itself by growing prop roots, and a key is born.

The black mangrove, with dark, scaly bark, grows in the high-tide zone. The white mangrove, smallest of the three species, looks like a shrub with broad, flat, oval leaves and grows above the high-tide line along with stands of buttonwood trees.

SAND BEACH HABITATS

Most of the islands of the Florida Keys have a limestone rock shoreline, but Long Key, Bahia Honda Key, and small portions of the shoreline of Lower Matecumbe have beaches of sand consisting not of quartz but of tiny fossils. These minuscule remains of calcareous, lime-secreting marine plants and animals are broken down by wave action upon the sea bottom. Only keys that have a break in the offshore reef line or are near a deep tidal

i

Cuba is closer to Key West than Miami is. Cuba sits only 90 miles off the southern tip of Key West, while Miami is 130 miles north off "the rock."

channel receive enough sediment to build a natural beach. Fronted in most cases by beds of sea grass, the Keys' beaches always have a "weed line" on shore made up of remnants of turtle grass, manatee grass, or sargassum weed washed up with the tide.

The natural beaches of the Keys don't have sand dunes but rather more bermlike mounds. Sea oats grow in the sand, helping to hold the particles together. State law mandates that you may not pick sea oats at any time.

The Sea

SEA-GRASS HABITATS

In the shallow nearshore waters of the ocean or Florida Bay, sediments build up on the limestone bedrock sea bottom, supporting a variety of sea grasses that perform an integral function in our tropical ecosystem. Sea grasses grow entirely under water, one of the few flowering plants to do so. Most prevalent of the sea grasses in the Florida Keys are the sweeping meadows of turtle grass, which have interlocking root systems that burrow as deep as 5 feet into the sediment. The wide, flat blades, often more than 12 inches long, break the force of the waves and slow current velocity.

The turtle grass traps marine sediments and silt carried in and out on the tides, allowing them to settle to the bottom. This natural filtration system clarifies the water and enhances coral growth in the nearby reef habitat. The sunken pastures of turtle grass and the less abundant shoal grass and manatee grass, which have rounded leaves and weaker root systems, become very dense, providing food and shelter for marine life at all levels of the food chain (see the Fishing chapter for more on the species dwelling within).

More than 80 species of resident and migratory coastal birds forage the sea grasses, feeding on fish and invertebrates of the habitat (see the Gunkholing Close-up in this chapter for our bird-watching tips).

Boat propellers and personal watercraft can easily scar the shallow turtle-grass meadows, effectively destroying that portion of the habitat. These scars do not heal because the sea grass will not grow back. The drastic reduction in fresh water from the Everglades also threatens the sea-grass habitat, for it is believed to have contributed to the sea-grass die-off in Florida Bay. Because of their pivotal position among the habitats, ill health of the turtle-grass meadows will ultimately affect the entire Florida Keys ecosystem.

A shark sighting is a common occurrence while gunkholing.

HARDBOTTOM HABITATS

Wave action and tidal currents sweep the limestone bedrock of the nearshore sea-bottom habitats nearly clean, permitting no sediment buildup. Algae, sponges, gorgonian corals, and stony corals attach themselves directly to the bedrock. The most common sponge you will see from your small skiff or while snorkeling in these waters is the loggerhead sponge, a barrel-shape sponge easily identified by the dark holes in its upper surface.

Snapping shrimp often make their homes within the sponges; they make a popping sound with their large snapping claw to repel predators.

More seaward of the nearshore waters, colonies of soft corals dominate the underwater hardbottom landscape. A feathery fairyland blooms like a backstage theater costume room.

Tentacled anemones also call the hardbottom habitat home and peacefully coexist with conchs and tulip snails, the spiral-striped spindle-shaped mollusks. The much-sought-after stone crabs and juvenile spiny lobsters try to stay out of sight here (see the Diving and Snorkeling chapter). Boat wakes, anchor damage, and collection of sea creatures by divers and snorkelers threaten the hardbottom habitats.

CLOSE-UP

A Gunkholing Primer

Rachel Carson may have said it all in *The Edge of the Sea:* "I doubt that anyone can travel the length of the Florida Keys without having communicated to his mind a sense of the uniqueness of this land of sky and water and scattered mangrove-covered islands."

Nowhere will you be more aware of our quintessence than when you are gunkholing. Here in the Florida Keys, *gunkholing* simply means slipping off land in a small dinghy, canoe, sea kayak, or shallow-draft skiff equipped with a push pole and tranquilly gliding through our shallow, mangrove-lined inshore waters in search of sightings of indigenous birds and aquatic creatures.

Though the dedication to spotting feathered friends may be referred to as "birding" or "bird-watching" in some areas of the country, here in the Keys another arena of fascinating marine creatures presents itself in the shallow waters of our flats. You can easily gunkhole on your own without a guide, or you can sign up for a guided ecotour (see the Recreation chapter).

Hundreds of virgin mangrove islets sprinkle the inshore waters of the inhabited Keys, often serving as giant rookeries for shorebirds and wading birds that are attracted to the abundant chow wagon beneath the surface of the water. Look to our Recreation chapter for information on renting a kayak, canoe, or small skiff. See the Attractions chapter for descriptions of the wildlife refuges of the Florida Keys, many of which encompass myriad outlands. And most important, read on for a primer of the most frequently encountered species on a gunkholing expedition in our tropical ecosystem.

Nature's Aviary

When gunkholing around the mangrove islets in search of wild birdlife, be sensitive to the presence of nesting birds. Do not anchor within 200 feet of an island, and keep noise to a minimum so as not to frighten the birds. If you do happen to flush a bird from its nest, move away from the nest area so that the bird will swiftly return to guard its young.

Here are several species you can expect to spot:

• **Brown Pelican—**Some say the brown pelican's mouth can hold more than its stomach can, but this common resident of the Florida Keys will push this theory to the limit given half a chance. The brown pelican will dive from 20 to 30 feet above the sea, entering the water like a competing Olympian and scoring with freshly caught fish every time. You'll see these cute, personality-packed fish-beggars everywhere, especially hanging out at fishing marinas. Look for them on their favorite gravity-defying perches atop mangroves or feathery Australian pines.

• **American White Pelican—**With a wingspan of 10 feet, the white pelican is more than a bird of a different color. These winter visitors to the Florida Keys (they are frequently spotted in Montana in the summer months) live a much different lifestyle than their brown cousins.

White pelicans live in flocks of 500 or more and are cooperative feeders who herd fish into an ever-narrowing circle. PHOTO: VICTORIA SHEARER

Completely white except for black-tipped wings and long yellow beaks, white pelicans live together in flocks in the uninhabited wild of the backcountry keys. The white pelicans, far from the panhandling ways of the browns, are cooperative feeders, congregating as a team on the water's surface and herding fish into an ever-narrowing circle where the group will dine. Look for white pelicans at Little Arsnicker or Sandy Keys in the Upper Keys backcountry.

• **Cormorant—**Cormorants by the thousands inhabit rookeries in the mangroves of the unpeopled islands. These large-bodied, hook-billed black birds, consummate fish-catchers all, will launch themselves in attempted flight at the first inkling of an approaching gunkholer, often hitting the water in a brief belly flop before gaining momentum to become airborne. Like the lesser-seen anhinga, or water turkey (more prevalent in the Everglades), the cormorant's plumage becomes waterlogged, which facilitates diving and swimming skills in its endless search for fish. You'll often see the birds perched on poles and buoy markers, wings outstretched in a drying maneuver. Cormorants swim with only their necks and heads visible above the water.

• **Snowy Egret and Great Egret—**Plume hunters nearly eradicated the egret population at the turn of the 20th century, for the birds' magnificent snow-white aigrettes were high fashion in the millinery industry. The egrets achieve

The osprey can be distinguished by a black streak behind each eye. PHOTO: WAYNE MOCCIA

their feathery plumage only in breeding season, so it was easy for the hunters to kill the birds in their nests. Both snowy and great egrets thrive once again in the Florida Keys. Distinguished from their cousins the great white herons, which also grace the shorelines of the Keys, the white egrets have black legs with yellow feet and black bills. Though both egrets display magnificent white plumage, the snowy egret is about half the size of the great egret.

• **Great White Heron**—Formerly considered a separate species from the great blue heron encountered in many parts of the United States, what we commonly call the great white heron is actually the white "morph," or color phase, of the great blue. Found only in the tropical ecosystem, this large white heron, more than 4 feet tall, is not as fearful of humans as other species, and is often seen in backyards and other inhabited areas. You'll be able to tell a great white heron from a great egret because the heron has long yellow legs and a yellow beak. The heron still-hunts for its food: Standing stiffly at full alert, the heron stalks a prey of fish, frogs, or lizards; it then stabs the prey with its beak, flips the prize whole into its narrow throat, and swallows it in one long neck-expanding

Look for the bald eagle's distinctive white head and tail high in the mangroves of uninhabited keys in the Florida Bay, where they build their nests. PHOTO: MARY MOCCIA

gulp. Herons and egrets build their lofty stick nests atop the mangroves of remote rookery keys.

• **Roseate Spoonbill—**A rare sighting in the Florida Keys, the roseate spoonbill, or pink curlew, is more common in the upper Florida Bay near Flamingo in Everglades National Park. Like the great white heron and egret, it also was slaughtered to near extinction in the early 1900s for its brilliant pink plumage, which was used for ladies' hats. The roseate spoonbill moves its large spatulate bill from side to side under water in the shallows, searching for minnows and small aquatic creatures. This distinctive bird is costumed like a vaudeville dancer—pink body accented by an orange tail, a bare greenish head, bright red shoulder and chest patches, and a black-ringed neck.

• **White Ibis—**Common in the Florida Keys, the white-plumed ibis bears black-tipped wings, most apparent when spread in flight, a distinctive scarlet, down-curved bill, and red legs. You'll often see young ibises, which are brown, in a flock of their white brethren, searching for aquatic insects, crabs, shrimp, and small snakes. The ibis was once worshipped in Egypt as a bird-headed god, and the pharaohs were buried alongside a mummified ibis. Killing an ibis for any other purpose was an offense punishable by death.

• **Osprey—**The high platform-topped poles you may see along the Overseas Highway have been erected for the osprey, which builds its bulky nest atop, laying three eggs out of harm's way each breeding season. Look up when trying to spot these fish-eating birds in the wild as well, for their nests will be constructed on the very pinnacles of the trees. Resembling a bald eagle, the osprey can be distinguished by a black streak behind each eye.

- **Magnificent Frigatebird—**The graceful, effortless flight of the frigatebird, or man-o-war bird, often heralds fish below, for this coastal forager is constantly on the lookout for finned pleasures. Often known to harass other seabirds until they drop their catch, the piratical frigatebird catches the spoils midair. Having a wingspan greater than 7 feet, the frigatebird inflates its throat sac and floats on air currents, its deeply forked, scissorlike tail a distinctive sight.

- **American Bald Eagle—**Once endangered nearly to the point of extinction, American bald eagles have made a recovery all across the United States due to preservation efforts. Look for the bald eagle's distinctive white head and tail high in the mangroves of uninhabited keys in Florida Bay, where they build their nests. Fish dominate their diet, and it is not uncommon for the bald eagle to steal the catch of a neighboring osprey.

Nature's Aquarium

As you gunkhole through our shallow sea-grass, mud, sand, and hardbottom habitats surrounding mangrove areas of our uninhabited keys, you may observe life below the surface of the water. Be sure to wear polarized sunglasses and proceed in a shallow-draft craft.

- **Starfish—**Commonly adorning the sandy bottom areas or sea-grass meadows of the shallow waters are cushion sea stars, often referred to as "starfish." These heavy-bodied, orange-brown creatures with five thick, starlike arms don't look alive, but they are.

- **Sponges—**See Hardbottom Habitats in this chapter for a description of the sponges you'll see growing on the seafloor.

- **Stingray—**This unusual creature, shaped like a diamond or disk, often lies motionless on the ocean bottom, partially buried in the sand. The ray has eyes and breathing holes on its topside, with its mouth positioned on the underside to feed off the seafloor. When frightened, the stingray will swim away, its huge, winglike fins flapping in gentle undulation.

- **Horseshoe Crab—**You'll quickly spot the distinctive spikelike tail and smooth, horseshoe-shaped body shell of this 300-million-year-old species as the crab forages the sea-grass habitat for algal organisms.

- **Sea Turtle—**Keep a close lookout for the small head of the giant sea turtle as it pops out of the water for a breath of air. Loggerheads can remain submerged for as long as three hours. Green turtles, once commonplace here but overharvested for use in soup, for steaks, in cosmetic oils, and for leather, are rarely encountered today. The sea turtles' front appendages have evolved into flippers.

- **Manatee—**On a lucky day, you may catch a rare glimpse of the timid West Indian manatee, or sea cow, a docile aquatic mammal that likes to graze on the turtle-grass flats. The brownish gray manatee has armlike flippers, a broad, spoonlike tail, and an adorable wrinkled face. It can grow to 15 feet long, weighing in at nearly a ton. Protected as an endangered species, the manatee often rolls on the water's surface for air and cannot swim rapidly enough to avoid collision with oncoming boaters, a constant

A shark sighting is a common occurrence while gunkholing. PHOTO: MARY MOCCIA

source of peril (see the Boating chapter for regulatory information).

• **Bottlenose Dolphin**—A more frequent sight on a gunkholing excursion is that of bottlenose dolphins, which you probably remember as the "Flipper" performers of marine parks. Seen in free-swimming pods in open waters, the graceful dolphins undulate through the waves with rhythmic regularity, and they are sometimes curious enough to approach your boat.

• **Fish of the Flats**—Alert attention to underwater movements in the sea grass of the flats may net you a sighting of a baby black-tip or bonnethead shark, a nurse shark, barracuda, bonefish, and more. See The Flats section of the Fishing chapter for descriptions of the finned treasures lurking beneath the shallows.

CORAL REEF

Extending 200 miles, from Fowey Rocks near Miami to the Dry Tortugas, our living coral reef habitat—the only one in the continental United States—is a national treasure. The reef, composed of the limestone remains of colonies of individual animals called polyps, plays host to an unbelievable assortment of marine creatures, fish, and vegetation (see the Diving and Snorkeling chapter and our Fishing chapter). The coral reef habitat, together with the mangrove and sea-grass habitats, is the breeding ground for 70 percent of the commercial fishing industry's catch.

This wave-resistant barrier, which protects the sea-grass meadows from erosion and heavy sedimentation, is particularly beautiful off the Upper Keys. The landmass of Key Largo shields the coral habitat from changing water temperatures and sediments that emanate from Florida

Bay through the tidal channels of the Middle and Lower Keys. Though it rigidly protects the shoreline of the Florida Keys from tropical storms, the coral reef itself is a fragile habitat. Field studies since 1984 have indicated some coral die-off and the sometimes fatal bleaching or discoloration of the corals in select areas of the Keys' barrier reef. Excessive nutrients in the water due to land-based pollution will degrade water quality and foster the growth of algal blooms, which screen the sunlight, robbing the coral of the oxygen that is necessary for healthy development.

Humans constitute one of the reef's most destructive threats. Anchor damage, boat groundings, and snorkelers and divers touching, collecting, or stepping on the delicate organisms can cause injury and certain death to the reef.

BARE-MUD AND BARE-SAND BOTTOM HABITATS

Along the barrier reef, skeletons of reef plants and animals form areas of open, bare-sand sea bottom, inhabited by species of algae, sea urchins, snails, clams, and worms that serve as the food train for visiting starfish, conch, and finfish. Similar belts or patches of bare-mud bottom habitats, both oceanside and in Florida Bay, support a like assemblage of marine creatures. Joining this group are burrowing shrimp, whose tunneled dwellings leave telltale mounds in the mud.

WEATHER AND CLIMATE

The mild tropical climate of the Florida Keys has no equal in the United States. Neither frost, nor ice, nor sleet, nor snow visits our islands. In fact, Key West is the only city in the continental United States below the frost line.

Temperature

The proximity of the Keys to the Gulf Stream in the Straits of Florida and the tempering effects of the Gulf of Mexico guarantee that average winter temperatures vary little more than 14 degrees from those of the summer months. Average year-round temperature is about 75 degrees. Cold, dry air moving down from the north in the winter is greatly modified by the Gulf waters over which it passes. And southeasterly trade winds and fresh sea breezes keep summer temperatures from ever reaching the triple-digit inferno experienced by the Florida mainland. The water and land heat and cool at different rates, creating thermal currents that air-condition the Keys.

Weather in Key West is always chamber-of-commerce perfect. The temperature has never reached 100 degrees and there has never been a frost. No wonder folks call this "Paradise."

Rainfall

The Florida Keys experiences two seasons: wet and dry. From November through April, the sun shines abundantly and less than 25 percent of the year's precipitation falls, usually associated with a cold front in the dead of winter. May through October is the rainy season, when nearly three-quarters of our annual rainfall occurs during brief daily showers or thunderstorms. But these percentages are deceiving; our climate is really quite dry. Average rainfall in the winter is less than 2 inches a month; summer months see closer to 4 to 5 inches of rain.

Hurricanes

The piper must be paid for this idyllic climate, and hurricanes have always been a key ingredient in our tropical mix. The potentially deadly weather systems move

The Marl Lands

While in Florida you might hear someone use the term "marl lands." Marl is calcitic mud beneath the water of the Everglades and it's commonplace in and around Florida City and Homestead. This gateway to the Florida Keys proved fertile ground for growing crops as far back as the early 1900s, when portions of the Everglades were drained. The Florida East Coast Railroad Extension provided a means to ship the produce north to market. Today the area burgeons with an extensive network of fruit and vegetable growers, nurseries, and landscaping operations.

westerly off the African coast during hurricane season (officially June 1 to November 30 but most prevalent in August and September) and generally turn northward near the Lesser Antilles islands, often heading our way.

Hurricanes have been harassing visitors to our shores for centuries. In 1622 at least five ships of the Spanish *Tierra Firma* Fleet wrecked as a result of a hurricane west of the Dry Tortugas. One of the most famous of these ships, the *Atocha,* was discovered and salvaged in 1985 by Mel Fisher (see Mel Fisher Maritime Heritage Society and Museum in the Attractions chapter). The New Spain Armada suffered a fatal blow by a hurricane in 1733, when 17 of 21 galleons struck the reefs of the Upper Keys, spewing treasure cargo amid the coral.

Key West suffered a devastating hurricane in 1835, but the hurricane of 1846 is considered the city's most severe. Key West residents pluckily rebuilt after these hurricanes and through the repeated hammerings of 1909, 1910, 1914, and 1919. On Labor Day 1935, a Category Five hurricane tore through the Upper Keys and Lower Matecumbe, totally destroying the area, including Flagler's Florida East Coast Railroad Extension. Five hundred people lost their lives in the high winds and 7-foot tidal surge in Lower Matecumbe alone. Experts estimate that the Labor Day hurricane packed winds of between 200 and 250 miles per hour. In comparison, Hurricane Andrew's winds, which hit the Miami area in 1992, peaked at an intensity of 175 miles per hour.

On August 29, 1960, an African storm caused an airplane crash near Dakar, Senegal, Africa, killing 63 people. Three days later this storm system was officially named Donna by the National Hurricane Center, which was formed in 1955 in Miami. By September 9, Donna's eye, which stretched 21 miles wide, passed over the region, bringing horrendous winds that effectively leveled the area from Marathon to Lower Matecumbe. Tides in Marathon were more than 9 feet high, and the surge in Upper Matecumbe topped 13 feet. Tea Table Bridge washed out, the freshwater pipeline broke in six places, and electricity was out. Donna ranks among the most destructive storms in U.S. history.

T.hree hurricanes have hammered the Florida Keys in recent years. Hurricane Georges, a strong Category Two hurricane with sustained winds of 105 mph, wreaked havoc from the Middle Keys to Key West on September 25, 1998. The massive cleanup and repair effort took residents nearly a year, but courtesy of La Niña, a wet summer in 1999 restored most of the lost foliage to its former glory. Then on October 15, 1999, Hurricane Irene battered the Keys with 75 mph winds and dumped 10 to 20 inches of rain on the still-recovering islands. And on October 24, 2005, the Lower Keys had an uninvited tourist by the name of Wilma. This Category

Five hurricane, with winds of 125 mph, inundated a large portion of the Lower Keys. A storm surge of 10 feet from the Gulf of Mexico flooded and destroyed everything in its path (see Foreword).

Visitors to the Florida Keys during hurricane season should heed official warnings to evacuate our islands in the event of a potential hurricane. Because we have only one main artery linking our islands to the mainland (the Overseas Highway), it takes 22 to 26 hours of crawling, bumper-to-bumper traffic to clear residents and visitors out of the Florida Keys. Officials warn that storm-watching during a hurricane is not a diversion to be considered here. A sizable hurricane will cut all services in the Keys and communications to the outside world.

i

Since 1941 the U.S. Navy has operated the Boca Chica Naval Air Station. (Boca Chica means "small mouth" in Spanish.) The Navy selected this location because the weather conditions for flying are the best in the nation, not to mention that living in this tropical location isn't bad, either!

PROTECTORS OF PARADISE

The natural wonders that make up the Florida Keys have good friends in the following organizations, which oversee efforts to protect the region's environment as best they can.

Florida Keys National Marine Sanctuary

In 1990 President. George H. W. Bush signed into law the Florida Keys National Marine Sanctuary and Protection Act, designed to protect our spectacular marine ecosystem. The resulting Florida Keys National Marine Sanctuary encompasses 2,800 square nautical miles, incorporating within its boundaries the previously formed Key Largo National Marine Sanctuary (1975) and the Looe Key National Marine Sanctuary (1981). The Florida Keys National Marine Sanctuary engulfs all of the Florida Keys, including the Marquesas Keys and the Dry Tortugas, and surrounding waters. In an effort to provide a secure habitat for the marine flora and fauna that make the Florida Keys so special, the protection act immediately prohibited oil drilling within the sanctuary and created an "area to be avoided" (ATBA) for large ships in our waters.

Ecologists hope that the access restrictions and activity regulations in select areas of the Florida Keys National Marine Sanctuary will help protect sensitive areas of the ecosystem. Furthermore, professionals feel that, with minimal human contact, areas of high ecological importance will evolve naturally and those areas representing a variety of habitats will be sustained. This zoning program will be monitored for revision every five years (see the Boating chapter for more information on specific regulations and restrictions). For more information, call the Florida Keys National Marine Sanctuary offices at (305) 743-2437 or log on to www.fknms.nos.noaa.gov.

The Nature Conservancy of the Florida Keys

The Nature Conservancy established a Florida Keys program in 1987 to protect the health and extraordinary diversity of our tropical ecosystem. This nonprofit conservation group states its mission as "preserving plants, animals, and natural communities that represent the diversity of life on Earth by protecting the lands and waters they need to survive." The Conservancy's work includes monitoring, management, and stewardship actions in the water and on the land; advocacy efforts; and support for volunteer programs. To date it has helped preserve

CLOSE-UP

Sunrise, Sunset

In the Florida Keys we justifiably lay claim to the most spectacular sun awakenings and finales in the universe. Anglers rise early enough to witness the brilliant fireball burn its way out of the ocean, its igneous shafts dramatically piercing the clouds overhead. Divers relish the midday sun's intense rays, which light up the ocean waters like a torch, illuminating the colorful corals below. Sunbathers lie prone on pool decks and man-made beaches, soaking the solar rays, storing up some much-needed vitamin D.

But our sunsets take center stage in the twilight hours. Both visitors and residents jockey for an unobstructed vantage point from which to watch the smoldering orange ball ooze into the sea like a sphere of molten lava. Flotillas of small boats drift anchorless in the Gulf waters . . . waiting. Travelers pull their autos off the Overseas Highway and stand at the water's edge, their awestruck attention riveted on the setting sun. Key West even has a daily sunset celebration ceremony at Mallory Square, complete with fire-eaters, jugglers, and Keys buskers of every shape and description.

If you are vigilant, you may see the green flash, a brilliant, emerald-colored spark of light that occasionally appears just as the sun melts into the sea. The rare sighting lasts only a second or less and has inspired legends the world over. According to the *Boston Globe,* "The green color results from the refraction, or bending, that sunlight undergoes as it passes through the thick layers of atmosphere near the horizon. Blue and green wavelengths of light are refracted the most, just like in a prism, so the setting sun appears to have a very thin blue-green fringe on its top edge. This fringe is hidden by the glare from the rest of the sun until all but the last of the sun's rim is blocked by the horizon."

In the Florida Keys the sun sets over the Gulf of Mexico. The day must be clear, and the sun must meet the horizon through a cloudless sky to see the green flash.

Although sighting a green flash is a singular phenomenon akin to spotting a comet or a shooting star, every sunset is reason for celebration in the Florida Keys. So allow us to share with you our little-known and much-guarded 10-point secret rating scale for the ceremonial Keys sunset watch:

The Gee-Whiz Sunset Rating Chart
Score five points if the sun sets at all because that means you are alive.

Score a point for this sunset's preglow and look for the green flash because the horizon is unobstructed. PHOTO: VICTORIA SHEARER

Add:

- One point for preglow (reflection of sun and streaks across the water).
- One point if you see the bottom of the sun touch the horizon.
- One point if the top of the sun touches the horizon.
- One point for an afterglow (the sky turns pastel colors).
- One point for the company you keep while you are watching the sunset.
- Score a bonus point if a sailboat, bird, or cloud moves in front of the sun as it sets.
- Sighting of the green flash is an automatic 10.

more than 6,000 acres in the Keys and 27,600 acres in the Everglades.

Green Sweep, the Conservancy's volunteer-based invasive-plant control program, started in 2000, removes invasive plants on public lands and privately owned buffer lands and replants native species. In 2002, work took place on 260 acres at 47 sites from Key Largo to Key West. To find out about volunteer workdays call (305) 745-8402.

The Nature Conservancy is a leader in the Lower Keys Wildland Fire Hazard Reduction Initiative, a multiagency effort to reduce the threat of wildfires and to maintain the rare pine rockland forest through increased application of prescribed fire.

In 2002, the Conservancy launched Florida Keys Watch, a program that tests canal water quality in the Keys in an effort to scientifically document bacterial and viral contamination and their sources. Keys Watch volunteers and staff collect canal water samples at 17 sites throughout the Keys and test these for bacteria. Sites demonstrating continuous high levels of the enterococci bacteria are screened further for the presence of viral pathogens, which will determine the source of the contamination.

Also in 2002, the Conservancy launched a new initiative under its volunteer Sea Stewards program in the Keys. The *Diadema* Restoration Project is an innovative plan to restock coral reefs with the long-spined sea urchin, *Diadema antillarum.* Once plentiful throughout the Caribbean, the *Diadema* population was decimated in 1982 due to an unidentified pathogen. These urchins eat the algae that can smother coral and prevent settlement of juvenile corals. The urchins' grazing capability makes them critical to maintaining healthy coral reefs.

For more information about The Nature Conservancy, please call the Keys program office at (305) 745-8402 or visit their Web site at www.nature.org.

Reef Relief

Reef Relief, a Key West-based nonprofit group of volunteers founded in 1986, works toward the preservation and protection of the coral reef habitat of the Florida Keys. The group has installed more than 100 mooring buoys, which, when used properly, eliminate anchor damage at the reef. The Florida Keys National Marine Sanctuary maintains the mooring buoys.

Another part of Reef Relief's mission is public awareness and education regarding the living coral reef habitat. To this end, each year the organization sponsors a cleanup campaign that attracts hundreds of volunteers. They comb shorelines and out-islands and dive the reef, collecting trash and storm-driven debris. For more information, contact Reef Relief Environmental Education Center, 201 William Street, Key West, (305) 294-3100, www.reefrelief.org.

Turtle Hospital

The grounds of the Hidden Harbor Motel—MM 48.5, Bayside, Marathon (see the Accommodations chapter)—shelter the famed Turtle Hospital, a turtle rapid-care center and recovery room run as a labor of love by Ritchie Moretti since 1986. The reptilian effort, which is financially supported by the income generated from Hidden Harbor Motel, has drawn the attention and cooperation of the University of Florida. In 2005, the Turtle Hospital released 81 endangered green baby sea turtles back into the wild.

Local veterinarians volunteer their time, often performing complicated turtle surgery on fibro-papilloma tumors, impactions, and shell fractures caused by hit-and-run boating injuries. After surgery, the turtles are moved to the recovery room, the property's original saltwater pool.

More than 5,000 schoolchildren visit the Turtle Hospital every year, learning about the fascinating reptilian order Chelonia. The general public visits too. The Turtle Hospital offers a 45-minute guided educational experience three times daily. The tour requires reservations and, since this is a working hospital, cancellations occur due to turtle emergencies and/or weather. For more information, visit the Turtle Hospital's Web site at www.turtlehospital.org or call (305) 743-2552.

Reef Environmental Education Foundation

A sort of Audubon Society for fish, the Reef Environmental Education Foundation's mission is "To educate, enlist, and enable divers and non-divers alike to become active stewards in the conservation of coral reefs and other marine habitats." To that end, the foundation offers educational programs and informational seminars for divers and snorkelers on the wonders of our coral reef as well as those in the waters of North and South America and the Caribbean. The foundation also maintains an ongoing data-collection program whereby underwater aficionados record what types of marine life they see, where these creatures are spotted, and how many of each species are seen. Each summer the Great American Fish Count, from July 1 to July 14, focuses particular attention on this program with a series of educational seminars that prepare volunteer divers and snorkelers for undersea survey excursions with local Keys dive shops. For more information, contact the Reef Environmental Education Foundation, MM 98, Center Median, Key Largo, (305) 852-0030, or check out their Web site at www.reef.org.

i

All sea turtles in U.S. waters are considered to be either threatened or endangered species; it is therefore illegal to handle or transport them without the proper permit. Always contact the proper authorities if you find a sea turtle. If you find a sick, injured, or dead sea turtle in Florida Keys waters, contact the Marine Patrol at (800) DIAL-FMP.

GETTING HERE, GETTING AROUND

You are headed for the Florida Keys. Whether you travel by land, by sea, or by air, you must conform to some strict, uncompromising standards that your travel agent may have neglected to tell you.

"Ha!" you say.

"Ah, but true," say we.

First, remove your socks. You won't need them here. Don your shorts. They are de rigueur. Slip on those shades. How else can you see? And reset your watch. The pace is slower here; you're on Keys time now.

Things really are different here. Our single main street stretches 126 miles—from Florida City to Key West—and dead-ends at the sea. Our 42 bridges span the kissing waters of the Atlantic Ocean and the Gulf of Mexico, from Key Largo to Key West. And our Keys communities resound as distinctively as the ivories of a piano.

So come on down. We're playing your song.

BY AIR

Commercial Flights

Florida Keys Marathon Airport
MM 52 Bayside, Marathon
(305) 743-2155, (305) 289-6060
www.floridakeysairport.com

The Florida Keys Marathon Airport is an FAA-certified facility that would make Flagler's railway journey seem a bad dream—if only it offered commercial air service. The $7.5-million, 20,000-square-foot building opened in February 1995.

There are no major carriers flying out of the middle keys. At the present time several small commuter airlines are providing limited service from Marathon to various locations in Florida where you could connect with a major carrier. Florida Coastal Airlines (www.flyfca.com, 888-322-0077) and Paradise Air (www.flyparadiseair.com, 305-743-4222) fly between Marathon and Fort Lauderdale.

Avis, Budget, and Enterprise rental cars are still available at the airport. Make reservations for a vehicle in advance whenever possible (see our By Land section in this chapter). The airport terminal is also a regular Greyhound Bus stop on the way to Miami.

Key West International Airport
3491 South Roosevelt Boulevard, Key West
(305) 296-5439
www.keywestinternationalairport.com

Although Key West is the Florida destination of choice for thousands of visitors each year, do not expect to arrive here via commercial jetliner. Air service to this island in the sun is of the commuter variety. The planes are small, and flights are often overbooked during peak seasons, especially in January and February, so be sure to arrive early to check in for your flight.

If you are meeting a flight, short-term metered parking is available. You may also park in the long-term lot. Weekly rates are available.

Avis, Budget, Dollar, and Hertz rental cars are available at the airport terminal; Alamo and Enterprise are just a courtesy call away (see listings in our Rental Cars section in this chapter). Whenever possible, make reservations for your vehicle in advance. Taxis stand by in front of the airport awaiting each flight, and many hotels offer complimentary shuttle service.

Commercial flights into and out of Key West are provided by the following airlines:

- American Eagle (American Airlines, 800-433-7300, www.aa.com): American Eagle offers connecting service to a multitude of American Airlines flights via Miami.
- Cape Air (305-293-0603, 800-352-0714, www.flycapeair.com): Cape Air provides scheduled service between Key West and Fort Lauderdale as well as southwest Florida airports in Naples and Fort Myers.
- Continental Connection, operated by Gulfstream International Airlines (305-294-9460; 800-523-3273, domestic; 800-231-0856, international; www.gulfstreamair.com): Gulfstream provides feeder service to Key West for both Continental Airlines and United Airlines. Flights from Key West connect through Miami, Tampa, and Fort Lauderdale.
- Delta Air Lines (800-221-1212, www.delta.com): Comair, the Delta Connection, offers service between Key West, Atlanta, and Orlando, where you can pick up any number of connecting flights on Delta Airlines
- USAir Express (800-428-4322, 800-943-5436, www.usair.com): USAir Express offers flights from Key West to Miami and Tampa, where you can connect with many USAir flights.

Miami International Airport
LeJeune Road, Miami
(305) 876-7000
www.miami-airport.com
An international airport offering flights on most major airline carriers, Miami International Airport is accessible from either Interstate 95 or Florida's Turnpike via Highway 836 and LeJeune Road. You can rent a car (see the listing in this chapter for 800 numbers) and drive the distance to the Keys. Miami to Key Largo is approximately 60 miles; to Islamorada, 80 miles; to Marathon, 115 miles, to Big Pine, 130 miles; to Key West, 160 miles.

Fort Lauderdale-Hollywood International Airport, Interstate 595 East Fort Lauderdale
(954) 359-1200
www.fll.net
Smaller than Miami International, this airport off Interstate 595 offers fewer flight options but is hassle-free compared to Miami's. To drive to the Keys from Fort Lauderdale-Hollywood International Airport, follow signs to Florida's Turnpike via I-595. Driving from Fort Lauderdale-Hollywood International Airport will add about 45 more minutes to your total trip.

Gotobus
Various Locations
(617) 354-2101
www.gotobus.com
In 2005, the Gotobus company started offering luxury bus service as an alternative to flying or driving between Florida destinations. The company now offers service between Key West, Marathon, Fort Lauderdale, Miami, and Orlando. Steward, beverage, and meal service are available, along with, onboard entertainment.

SeaCoast Airlines
3471 South Roosevelt Boulevard, Key West

MM 52 Bayside, Marathon
(866) 302-6278
www.seacoastairlines.com
Enjoy flightseeing trips in a relaxed atmosphere on SeaCoast Airlines from Key West to St. Petersburg/Clearwater and Zephyrhills airports. SeaCoast Airlines offers a great way to get to connecting flights, with the bonus of beautiful coastal scenery along the way.

Private Aircraft

Paradise Jet Support
MM 52 Bayside, Marathon
(305) 743-4222
www.flyparadiseair.com
Paradise Aviation is a flight-based opera

Directions to the Keys

Directions from Miami International Airport via Florida's Turnpike: Take LeJeune Road south to Highway 836 West. As you approach the ramp, get in the right-hand lane. Be aware, however, that a frontage-road access just before the sign and arrow often lures confused first-timers into turning too soon. The ramp is actually just after the sign and arrow. Follow Highway 836 West to Florida's Turnpike South, Homestead. Continue on Florida's Turnpike until it ends in Florida City at U.S. Highway 1. Continue south on US 1 to the Keys.

tion at the east end of the Florida Keys Marathon Airport runway. If you wish to land your private aircraft or jet in Marathon, call Marathon UNICOM on frequency 122.8. Paradise Aviation will issue a wind and a runway advisory. After you land, they will contact you by tail number and advise you where to tie down. No landing fee is charged, but a tie-down fee is levied. Paradise Aviation offers both 100 low-lead (LL) fuel and Jet A fuel. Jet charter service is available to most locations.

Paradise Aviation also offers charter flights to any airport in Florida. A 24-hour appointment is necessary.

Marathon Jet Center
MM 52 Bayside, Marathon
(305) 743-1995
www.marathonjetcenter.com
Located at the west end of Florida Keys Marathon Airport, Marathon Jet Center is a flight-based operation that caters to general aviation and light aircraft. It offers a maintenance facility on the premises and sells 100 low-lead (LL) and Jet A fuel. Tie-down fees are charged per overnight or per month. Marathon Jet Center offers aircraft for rent and also gives aerial tours of the Middle Keys and the reef.

Island City Flying Service
3471 South Roosevelt Boulevard, Key West
(305) 296-5422
Island City Flying Service is a flight-based operation at the Key West International Airport. If you want to land your private aircraft or jet in Key West, call Island City UNICOM on frequency 122.95. There is no reserved parking—you may take any available space you see on the ramp. No landing fee is charged, but daily parking and overnight tie-down fees are assessed depending on the size of your aircraft. The daily parking fee is waived with a fuel purchase.

Island City Flying Service offers both 100 low-lead (LL) fuel and Jet A fuel and rents life vests and life rafts as required by law for flying to the Bahamas or the Caribbean. Flight instruction is available.

BY SEA

Visit the Florida Keys as the pirates and buccaneers did before you—by sea. Revel in the beauty of these sea pearls, strung together by the wisp of the Overseas Highway. Your perspective of the Keys will be different when viewed from our waters. Navigate your motor or sailing craft through the Intracoastal Waterway, which extends from Miami through Card Sound and Barnes Sound and down the length of the Keys in the Florida Bay/Gulf of Mexico. Or parallel the oceanside shores following Hawk Channel, a well-marked route protected by the reef.

Long a bustling port, Key West Harbor is still busy—full of commercial traffic, tourist-filled tour boats, and visiting cruise

ships. If you choose to navigate your motor or sailing craft to Key West from the Atlantic, come in through the main ship channel, which is marked "S.E. Channel" on the charts. From the Gulf take the N.W. Channel until it intersects with the main ship channel. You can anchor out in protected areas of the harbor or put into one of the comprehensive Key West marinas.

For complete information on arriving and vacationing on your pleasure craft, see our Cruising chapter.

Sea Key West Express
Land's End Marina, Key West
(239) 394-9700, (888) 539-2628
www.keywestshuttle.com

Offering daily service between Marco Island and Fort Myers Beach and Key West, the Key West Shuttle combines a pleasure voyage at sea with getting there. A new high-speed catamaran has recently joined the fleet, which also consists of the 110-foot *Captain Red* and 130-foot *Whale Watcher. Captain Red* leaves from Marco River Marina in Marco Island at 8:30 A.M. and departs Key West at 5:30 P.M. *Whale Watcher* departs from Salty Sam's Marina in Fort Myers Beach at 8:30 A.M. and leaves Key West at 5:30 P.M.

Ships include full galleys and bars, air-conditioned enclosed cabins, and sundecks. *Captain Red* even has slot machines! The trip takes about four hours.

X-Press to Key West
Key West Historic Seaport
(941) 765-0808, (800) 283-4496
www.keywestferry.com

X-Press to Key West is the only high-speed ferry from the southwest Florida coast to Key West. The ferry leaves Fort Myers Beach daily at 8:00 A.M. and arrives in Key West at 11:30 A.M. The return trip leaves the dock at the Hilton Resort and Marina, right in the heart of Key West, at 5:00 P.M. and arrives back in Fort Myers Beach at 8:30 P.M. A free continental breakfast and free parking in Fort Myers Beach are included in the round-trip fee. You can return the same day or stay several days in Key West. Reservations are suggested. The ferry dock in Fort Myers Beach is located under the San Carlos Sky Bridge on the Fisherman's Wharf on the Fort Myers side.

BY LAND

The Overseas Highway tethers our islands to the mainland like a long umbilical cord. Addresses along this common main street are issued by mile markers, designated as MM. Commencing with MM 126 in Florida City and culminating with MM 0 in Key West, small green markers with white numbers are posted every mile.

The Overseas Highway actually curves and drifts toward the southwest, rendering it all but impossible to refer to directions as "north to here" or "south to there." Here in the Keys everything is grounded by a mile marker, and you'll note that we orient most of the addresses we give in this book by mile marker.

As you head toward Key West, mile marker numbers descend in order. Anyplace on the right side of the road bordering Florida Bay or the Gulf of Mexico is referred to as bayside. The opposite side of the road, bordering the Atlantic Ocean, is therefore called oceanside. So addresses on the Overseas Highway will usually be referred to by both mile marker number and a bayside or oceanside distinction.

The old saying, "All roads lead to the sea," could very well have been written about the Keys. The occasional side street you might encounter on one of our wider islands—such as Key Largo, Marathon, or Big Pine Key—will terminate at the bay, the Gulf, or the ocean after only a few blocks.

Key West, the southernmost point in the continental United States, slumbers closer to Havana than it does to Miami—when it sleeps, that is, which is not all that often. In Keys-speak, this is where the action is.

Although nearly 25,000 people make Key West their home, this island still retains a small-town charm. The quaint Old Town area remains essentially a charming, foliage-canopied grid of streets lined with gingerbread-trimmed frame structures that evoke a succession of bygone eras and a cache of simmering secrets. This area, by the way, boasts the largest collection of frame structures in a National Register historic district of any city in Florida—nearly 3,000—and some architectural elements that are found nowhere else in the world.

The Mid Town area is predominantly residential. New Town takes in the shopping centers and fast-food and hotel chains along North Roosevelt Boulevard on the Gulf side and across the island to the airport and beaches along South Roosevelt Boulevard on the Atlantic side.

Old Town, destination of choice for most visitors to Key West, is accessed from the Overseas Highway by either North Roosevelt Boulevard (U.S. Highway 1) to Truman Avenue or South Roosevelt Boulevard (A1A) along the beach to White Street. From White Street, Southard Street runs one way toward the heart of Old Town. Fleming Street is one way leading the opposite direction.

Old Town is anchored by Duval Street, which has been dubbed "the longest street in the world" because it runs from the Atlantic to the Gulf of Mexico. It is actually only a little more than a mile long. Although finding your way around Key West is not difficult, the narrow, often one-way streets—combined with a proliferation of tourist-driven rental cars and scooters in peak seasons—can make driving around this island both frustrating and time-consuming. Old Town is best explored on foot or by bicycle.

Key West provides public bus service and several other unique modes of transportation, which we describe in this chapter.

Rental Cars

Public transportation in the Keys (except for Key West) is practically nil. You really need a car to get around. Most rental car agencies are at the airports in Marathon or Key West, as well as at airports in Miami and Fort Lauderdale. Some pick up and deliver vehicles. Reserve your automobile before you arrive in the Keys—availability in peak seasons is often limited—at one of the following agencies:

Alamo Rent A Car
2516 North Roosevelt Boulevard, Key West
(305) 294-6675, (888) 426-3304
www.alamo.com

Avis Rent A Car
MM 52 Bayside, Florida Keys Marathon Airport
(305) 743-5428, (800) 831-2847

3491 South Roosevelt Boulevard, Key West International Airport, Key West
(305) 296-8744, (800) 831-2847
www.avis.com

Budget Car & Truck Rental
MM 52 Bayside, Florida Keys Marathon Airport
(305) 743-3998, (800) 527-0700

3495 South Roosevelt Boulevard, Key West International Airport, Key West
(800) 527-7000 (local), (800) 527-0700
www.budget.com

Dollar Rent A Car
3491 South Roosevelt Boulevard, Key West International Airport, Key West
(305) 296-9921, (800) 800-4000
www.dollar.com

Enterprise Rent-A-Car
MM 100.2 Oceanside, Key Largo
(305) 451-3998, (800) 736-8222

MM 52 Bayside, Florida Keys
Marathon Airport
(305) 289-7630, (800) 736-8222

2834 North Roosevelt Boulevard, Key West
(305) 292-0220, (800) 325-8007
www.erac.com

Enterprise has locations serving the Keys from top to bottom, including Key West. The Key Largo office offers pickup of vehicles from Key Largo to MM 70, Fiesta Key. The Marathon Enterprise office is in the Florida Keys Marathon Airport terminal. This office will pick up your rental car as far up the Keys as MM 70 or as far down the Keys as Little Palm Island. Key West pickup and delivery also is offered.

Hertz Rent A Car
3491 South Roosevelt Boulevard, Key West International Airport, Key West
(305) 294-1039, (800) 654-3131
www.hertz.com

Taxi Service

If you don't have your own automobile or haven't rented a car for the duration of your visit, you may find yourself in need of ground transportation within the Keys. Be aware that the fare could get pricey (sometimes approaching the cost of a daily rental vehicle), especially if you are traveling any distance. But if you need a lift, call one of the following:

In the Upper Keys, Key Largo Cabs (305-451-9700, 305-852-8888) or Mom's Taxi (305-852-7999, 305-453-4049).

In the Middle Keys (Marathon), try Action Taxi (305-743-6800) or Sunset Taxi (305-289-7422, 888-919-8294, www.sunsettaxi.com).

In the Lower Keys, you can call Sugarloaf Key Taxi (305-745-2319) or Sunset Taxi (305-872-4233).

Key West taxis include: A Airport Cab Company (305-292-1111); Five 6's Cab Company (305-296-6666, www.keywesttaxi.com); and Friendly Cab Company (305-292-0000, 305-295-5555).

The island of Key West is only 8 square miles in size, and thanks to the ready availability of taxicabs and shuttle services, you really don't need a car to get around it. In fact, you may be better off without wheels. Our streets are narrow and almost always congested, and parking is expensive and often not readily available.

Airport Limousine and Shuttle Service

In the event you are stranded without transportation to either of the mainland airports, alternative transport is available. These companies offer a variety of services, often also catering to private groups and functions. Prices and services vary, so call around and compare. The following options are available in the Florida Keys: Cadillac Jack (305-853-5550, 888-233-5550, www.cadillacjackinc.com), Keys Shuttle (305-289-9997, 888-765-9997, www.floridakeysshuttle.com).

Bus Service

Greyhound Bus Lines
3535 South Roosevelt Boulevard, Suite 104, Key West International Airport, Key West
(305) 296-9072,
(800) 410-5397 (tricounty),
(800) 231-2222 (nationwide)
www.greyhound.com

Greyhound bridges the gap in mass

CLOSE-UP

I Don't Believe What I Just Saw

A lot of folks buy outlandish clothes or elaborate jewelry to make a social statement. That's okay if you live any place else except the Florida Keys. Here, when you want to make a declaration—loud and clear—you embellish a vehicle. In the Keys these vehicles are know as "Conch Cruisers." Anything that moves is fair game. You will see bicycles painted in bright colors with beads, feathers, Christmas lights, and anything else that strikes a happy mood to their owners. Sometimes these fun and unbelievable land yachts are used as lawn ornaments. Owners here will say, "You can't miss my house. It's the one with the bicycle all lit up parked at the garden gate or the purple car with my dog at the steering wheel!"

One antiquated van advertising children's furniture for rent has a baby carriage on the top, a doll in the seat, and balloons and flags fluttering in the wind. Another car has seagulls glued on the top, sides, doors, and hood, with a blue background, fluffy clouds, and bird "droppings" painted on in strategic spots for a touch of realism. One Jeep in particular has plants that are alive and flourishing on the front seats, back seats, and flowing out of all the open areas of the vehicle. Can't imagine where the driver sits. And then there is the fellow who drives the Keys in a '60s-era car with his pet iguanas along for the ride. They are hanging not only on him, but also all over the back dash, seats, and front dashboard! You will do a double take when you see that for the first time.

At a store on Duval Street, there is a small sports car that has been totally covered with pieces of mirrors, beads, and jewels. It is a showstopper. Another business, Peppers of Key West (see the Seafood Markets and Specialty Foods chapter), uses one giant chili pepper to envelope a car. When the owners aren't driving it around town, the car is parked in front of the shop. What better way to advertise!

The colorful four-wheel vehicles are legal here and they do have Florida license tags, but few owners ever go beyond MM 10 because of the age of the

ground transit from Key West to Miami and beyond. Greyhound departs the Key West depot, which is housed in the Adam Arnold Annex at the airport, usually four times a day, seven days a week, bound for Miami International Airport, the Miami Amtrak station, and downtown Miami, with convenient connections for the Tri-Rail system. (Schedules vary during the off-season.) Four of the Greyhound stops in the Keys sell tickets: Big Pine Motel, Big Pine, MM 30.7 Bayside; chamber of commerce, MM 53 Bayside, Marathon (tickets only—pickup spot is at Florida Keys Marathon Airport, MM 52); Burger King, Islamorada, MM 83.5 Oceanside; and Howard Johnson Hotel, Key Largo, MM 102 Bayside.

Additional boarding locations are

Turtle painted on truck. PHOTO: LINDA STEDMAN

vehicles and the fragile nature of the decorations. Each year at the Schooner Wharf Bar (see the Nightlife chapter), they hold a Conch Cruiser Car Show that really brings out the pros in the craft. There is something to be said for the people who own these mobile pieces of art. You may chuckle when you see one, but you can also appreciate the talent that went into creating it. Isn't that what art is suppose to do? "Move" you in more ways than one?

sprinkled along the Overseas Highway, marked by signs with the Greyhound logo. They are at the corner of Virginia and Simonton Streets (in Key West); Boca Chica, MM 7; Big Coppitt, MM 10.6; Sugar Loaf, MM 17; Cudjoe Key, MM 22; Ramrod Key, MM 27.8; Florida Keys Marathon Airport, MM 52; Layton, MM 69; Islamorada, MM 82.5; and Tavernier, MM 92. The bus also stops at MM 126 in Florida City.

The trip will take 4 hours, 15 minutes from Key West to Miami International by Greyhound Bus. Fares to Miami International Airport depend on embarking and disembarking sites. Greyhound schedules and fares are subject to change. Be sure to confirm your specific travel arrangements when purchasing tickets.

Florida Keys Commuter Bus Service
Various Locations
(305) 292-4500
www.monroecounty-fl.gov

JGT Bus Company from Miami-Dade County provides a Florida Keys commuter bus service throughout Monroe County. The buses run from Florida City and Homestead to Marathon. In September 2005, a new bus service, Lower Keys Shuttle Service, began operating between Key West and Marathon. The bus service arose from a partnership between the cities of Key West and Marathon and Monroe County designed to alleviate traffic on the Overseas Highway. The bus stops in Marathon are timed to coordinate with the existing bus line that operates between Marathon and Florida City.

City of Key West Department of Transportation
627 Palm Avenue, Key West
(305) 292-8160, (305) 293-6435
www.keywestcity.com

Public transport city buses, many of which are brightly decorated with the works of local artists, circle the island of Key West several times a day along color-coded routes. Buses on the blue/gold/red routes travel clockwise, while buses on the orange/purple/green routes run counterclockwise. Signs at all of the bus stops sport colored dots to indicate the routes they serve.

Buses on all routes travel to Old Town as well as to the hospital on Stock Island and to the shopping plazas along North Roosevelt Boulevard (US 1) in New Town. However, only the green and blue routes serve the airport, Smathers Beach, and other stops along South Roosevelt Boulevard (Route A1A). The orange and red routes, which traverse the interior of the island along Flagler Avenue, serve Key West High School. The red and blue routes are the only ones to serve Bahama Village (via Emma and Angela Streets). The gold route goes from Stock Island to the Overseas Market, via North Roosevelt Boulevard. The purple route connects Searstown on North Roosevelt with the perimeter of Old Town, via Palm Avenue.

Although this may sound confusing, the buses in Key West are actually quite easy to use as long as you keep one basic rule in mind: If you took the blue route to your destination, take the green route home; red route out, orange route home. And if all else fails, just take the same route to and from your destination. Remember that this is an island where the buses traverse in a great big circle. You simply cannot get lost if you stay on a particular bus since it will eventually return to the stop where you boarded it. For more information call the Key West Department of Transportation (KWDOT) for directions.

On weekdays, bus service starts as early as 6:00 A.M. and continues until 11:30 P.M.; on weekends and holidays, the hours may be shorter and the stops less frequent, depending on the route. The green route, for example, operates Monday through Friday only. Buses on each route make their complete rounds once an hour. At any given stop, however, you can expect a bus to appear, going one direction or the other, every half hour throughout the day. A complete timetable and route map is available from KWDOT.

The fare is $1.00 for adults. Children younger than age five ride free with a paying adult. Senior citizens pay 50 cents, but they must first obtain an identification card for $2.00 at the KWDOT office (see address previously listed). Students also may ride for 50 cents if they display their school ID card upon boarding. The bus drivers do not carry change, so you must have exact fare. Monthly passes may be purchased from the bus driver or at the KWDOT office. One-, three-, and seven-day passes can be purchased from the bus driver for unlimited use.

"BOB" is the Bikes on Buses program. This allows customers to take their bicycles on the bus, for free, by securing them onto a bike rack attached to the front of the bus.

Alternative Key West Transportation

TROLLEY TOUR

Old Town Trolley Tours of Key West
Key West Welcome Center
3840 North Roosevelt Boulevard
(305) 296-6688
www.historictours.com

Listen to a narrative of historic Key West on this continuous loop tour, learning as you go. Although this transportation option is promoted and sold as a 90-minute tour, you can hop on and off the trolley as many times per day as you wish. It's one hassle-free way to shop, dine, or take in the myriad attractions Key West has to offer.

You can park your car free at the Key West Welcome Center, where you can also buy tickets and board the trolley. Day-trippers will find the welcome center readily accessible upon entry into Key West. Bear right and follow the signs for US 1. The welcome center is on the left side of the road. Park your car, then grab a trolley and let your conductor spirit you around Key West. You can disembark at Mallory Square, Historic Key West Seaport, Crowne Plaza La Concha, Angela Street Depot (corner of Angela and Duval), Bahama Village Market, Key West Welcome Center, The Casa Marina Resort, the Southernmost Point Trolley Stop, and Truman Avenue and Duval Street. Trolleys stop at each location every 30 minutes.

Cost of the trolley tour is $22 per day for adults and teens, $11 for children ages 4 through 12. Children age 3 and younger ride free.

NOTE: The Conch Trains that you see chugging around town are bona-fide touring vehicles; you cannot get on and off a Conch Train at will. See our Attractions chapter for further information on this and other tours.

SHUTTLE SERVICES

Bone Island Shuttle
Various locations around Key West
(305) 293-8710
www.boneislandshuttle.com

On an island with too many cars and not enough places to put them, the idea of a shuttle service specifically designed to cart tourists from one end to the other is such a no-brainer we wonder why someone didn't think of it sooner. At just $8.00 per adult (kids age 12 and younger ride for free) for a full day of unlimited transportation, Bone Island Shuttle provides an inexpensive, worry-free way to get around Key West—several times a day if you like. Multiple-day discounted passes are also available.

Bone Island's easy-to-spot vehicles—handpainted with tropical designs by local artists—operate from 9:00 A.M. to 11:00 P.M., seven days a week along two routes. Shuttles on the red route travel in a clockwise direction around the island; shuttles on the blue route travel counterclockwise. On any given day there are always at least four, and sometimes six, Bone Island Shuttles in operation between the tourist attractions in Old Town. A shuttle going one way or the other stops at the Key West Welcome Center and the Key West Historic Seaport, Mallory Square, Bahama Village Market, Fairfield Inn, Days Inn, and Radisson Key West. Route maps and schedules are available at the Key West Chamber of Commerce, Mallory Square, and in brochure racks all across the island.

Individual shuttle tickets may be purchased at the Key West Welcome Center, 3840 North Roosevelt Boulevard, from Trolley and Conch Train ticket vendors, at several Old Town attractions, or from the concierge or front-desk staff at any of the hotel stops. Group charters are available, too.

The official Web site for the Florida Keys is www.fla-keys.com. You can also find information at these sites: www.thefloridakeys.com and www.fabulousvacations.com.

MOPEDS, SCOOTERS, AND ELECTRIC CARS

Key West is the perfect place to explore by moped, although we wouldn't recommend riding in the Mallory Square/lower Duval Street area or along North Roosevelt Boulevard, which are heavily congested with people, automobiles, and delivery trucks. Many places rent a choice of either mopeds or bicycles by the hour, day, overnight, or week (see our Recreation chapter for information on bicycle rentals).

Some companies consider a daily moped rental to be 24 hours; others cap the day at 8 hours. Inquire when you call. Some moped rental agencies even rent double scooters that seat two; it is illegal to carry a passenger on any other kind. The following Key West companies rent a full range of vehicles: Adventure Scooter & Bicycle Rentals, 2900 North Roosevelt Boulevard (and five other locations), (305) 293-9933; The Bicycle Center, 523 Truman Avenue, (305) 294-4556; Moped Hospital, 601 Truman Avenue, (305) 296-3344; Randall J's Scooter Rentals, 505 Greene Street (and five other locations), (305) 296-0208; Bone Island Cycle, 1910 North Roosevelt Boulevard, (305) 293-9877; and Tropical Rent-A-Car, 1300 Duval Street, (305) 294-8136.

The newest addition to the Key West self-propelled transportation scene is Electric Cars of Key West, 500 Truman Street, (305) 294-4724, (888) 800-8802. These egg-shaped electric vehicles are eerily quiet and understandably slow. They seat two or four, have no doors, and top out at 25 mph, making them ideal for an island where the speed limits never go above 35. You can rent one of these electric cars from two hours to overnight.

Paradise Pedicab
401 Southard Street, Key West
(305) 292-0077

Take a tour of Key West the slow-and-easy way in a *velotaxi,* better known as a pedicab. These bicycle-powered vehicles are a great way to feel the warm breeze on your face and breathe in the tropical air as your cyclist narrates the sights. A most unique mode of transportation in this most unique town.

FOOT POWER

Strolling Key West is a great way to work off the pounds you'll be packing on by grazing the tempting kiosks, juice bars, ice-cream shops, restaurants, and, of course, bars of Key West. The sidewalk-lined streets in Old Town often front little-known lanes where unusual shops or galleries hide beneath ancient foliage. You'll miss these—and much of the mystery and charm of this southernmost city—if you don't get out of your car and walk a bit.

You can explore on your own or take advantage of one of the many guided tours that are available (see our Attractions chapter for several options). Perhaps the best-documented self-guided walking tour of Key West has been compiled by Sharon Wells. Her *Walking & Biking Guide to Historic Key West* is free for the asking at the Key West Chamber of Commerce (open 8:30 A.M. to 5:00 P.M. daily) at Mallory Square. You can also find copies at several shops around town. Wells guides you along 10 routes, identifying the buildings of architectural or historical significance you will pass along the way.

While at the chamber, you may also want to pick up a copy of the Pelican Path map-brochure. Originated by the Old Island Restoration Foundation, the Pelican Path is a self-guided walking tour that takes you past some of Key West's most historically and architecturally significant buildings.

Getting Around on Two Wheels

A few words of caution about two-wheeled transportation: Bicycle, moped, and scooter riders are subject to the same traffic laws as those who operate four-wheeled vehicles. That means you must have lights at night, obey all traffic signals and signs, stay off the sidewalks, and travel in the correct direction on one-way streets. Keep in mind, too, that you operate these vehicles at your own risk. In a collision with a car, a scooter or moped almost always loses. If you wreck your rental scooter, you will be personally liable for the damages. The rental agents are not required to offer insurance. They are, however, required to provide instruction and to offer helmets.

You should be aware that riding a motor scooter on the streets of Key West can be dicey. The streets are narrow, and many a rider has taken a spill. Although some rental locations may not require helmets, we recommend you wear one. Riding the motorized vehicles on main highways is not recommended, as they cannot maintain the posted speed limit of cars and trucks.

Key West Parking

Parking is plentiful and free of charge in the Keys, until you visit Key West. Ask any Key West local if there's a downside to living in Paradise and he or she will almost always complain about parking. There are simply too many cars in Old Town Key West and too few places to put them. And because the permanent population of this tiny island keeps growing and most visitors either arrive by car or rent a vehicle when they get here, the parking problem isn't going away anytime soon.

Patrons of the shops and restaurants in Duval Square (1075 Duval Street) will find free parking available in an adjacent lot accessed from Simonton Street. Free parking for patrons of some Duval Street restaurants, shops, and bars may also be available in designated lots off either Whitehead or Simonton Streets, both of which run parallel to Duval. Metered curbside parking is, of course, available on several downtown streets, including Duval, Whitehead, and Simonton, as well as along most of the streets that intersect them. Special curbside parking areas are designated for scooters and mopeds; do not leave vehicles on the sidewalk.

In the past, tourists who wanted to avoid feeding meters and didn't mind a little extra walk could simply secure a free curbside parking spot in the many residential Old Town neighborhoods several blocks off Duval. No more. In an effort to appease Key West residents who complained about having to park several blocks from their homes because tourists had taken their curbside spots, the city of Key West inaugurated a resident parking program in early 1998. We're sorry to say it's not very visitor-friendly.

Here's how parking in residential Old Town works: Curbside spots along many Old Town streets have been ruled off with white paint and marked with the large yellow letters RP. In order to park your vehicle in one of these spots, your car must display either a Monroe County license plate or a residential parking permit (available from the city of Key West with proof of residence).

If you park in one of the RP spaces and your car does not show the proper proof of residence, you may return to find it gone. Your illegally parked vehicle will have likely been towed to the city's

> ***Be sure to park your vehicle only in designated areas, pay attention to the signs, and never, never block a driveway or park alongside a yellow curb. If the sign says that unauthorized vehicles will be towed, believe it.***

impound lot on Stock Island. To retrieve it, you will have to have cash (about $85)—no checks or credit cards are accepted.

If you want to be right in the thick of things, you will either have to feed a meter or pay to park in a lot. The meters cost $1.50 per hour, and they run until midnight daily, including Sunday and holidays. Meter maids (and men) regularly patrol the streets of Key West, and tickets are liberally distributed. All-day parking is available for more reasonable prices at several privately owned lots on either side of Duval Street; watch for the lot attendants holding cardboard signs. You might also consider one of the convenient parking facilities described below.

Caroline Street Parking Lot
Corner of Caroline and Margaret Streets
(305) 293-6421
Adjacent to the attractions at Key West Historic Seaport, this open-air lot offers full-day parking for a maximum of $16.25.

> ***Don't park in the curbside parking marked RESIDENTIAL PARKING unless your automobile has Monroe County, Florida, license plates, or your car will be towed. These spaces are reserved for Key Westers and other Florida Keys locals.***

If you just need to run a quick errand, you can park here for an hourly charge. The lot is accessible 24 hours to cars, motorcycles, and scooters only; no RVs, trailers, or buses permitted.

Mallory Square Parking Lot
Corner of Wall and Front Streets
(305) 292-8158
www.keywestcity.com
This parking lot abuts the cruise-ship dock off Wall Street in the Mallory Square area and is convenient to all the west-end attractions and the sunset celebration. Through the years, however, it has been reduced in size to accommodate the enlarged and improved Mallory Square, so parking space is limited. Rates run $4.00 per hour, day and night. The lot is open from 8:00 A.M. until midnight. Cars, motorcycles, small trucks, and vans are welcome; campers, RVs, buses, and trailers are not.

Old Town Parking Garage
Key West Park N' Ride,
300 Grinnell Street
(305) 293-6426
www.keywestcity.com
The Old Town Parking Garage offers you the chance to find one of 250 covered parking spaces at a reasonable rate anytime, day or night. Cars, small trucks, and motorcycles are welcome here. For $2.00 an hour ($13.00 maximum), you can park and then ride one of the shuttles to the downtown area several blocks away. There is no extra charge for the shuttle when you show your ticket; a shuttle ride will cost 50 cents per person without the ticket. If your stay will be long-term, choose the monthly rate of $75, plus tax.

RESTAURANTS 

Take in the glorious sights in the Florida Keys, then treat your taste buds to a culinary holiday they will never forget. Stone crabs, yellowtail snapper, cracked conch, ropa vieja, picadillo, queen of all puddings, and Key lime pie are yours for the asking.

Surrounded by water, the Florida Keys yields a bounty that easily could qualify as the eighth wonder of the world. We confidently can boast that nowhere else in the continental United States—oh, why not say it, the universe even—will you find fresher, more innovatively prepared fish and seafood than in our restaurants.

Be sure to sample our special natural resources, served any way you like. We import a few raw materials in the feather and flesh categories as well, so your palate will be truly well rounded. (For preparing your own fare, see the Seafood Markets and Specialty Foods chapter.)

Enjoy the relaxed atmosphere of our restaurants, where even the most upscale dining carries a laid-back apparel code. Be it a roadside cafe or a resort dining room, you need dress no more formally than "Keys casual," typically an ensemble of shirt and shorts, shoes, or sandals. Men may leave their sport jackets at home, and don't even think about bringing a suit to the Keys unless it is the swimming variety. The same code applies to women; we don't discriminate here. The occasional restaurant, such as Cheeca Lodge, Pierre's, or Little Palm Island, affords you the chance to dress up a bit more if you like—long slacks for the gentlemen, perhaps an island-style dress for the ladies. But the choice is yours.

The appearance of a restaurant's decor doesn't hold to the strict expectations of other parts of the country, either. You'll find that the most unassuming hole in-the-wall cafe, diner, or bistro may serve the best food in town. Don't drive by.

---

i

Leave those sport coats, ties, and cocktail clothes behind. This is the Florida Keys and the dress code is Keys Casual. Rule of thumb: If you need a reservation, you need a collared shirt, shorts, and shoes. Even when formal weddings are held on the beach, the brides and grooms often go barefoot!

Some of our culinary treasures are hidden away off the beaten track. We'll help you find them.

You may find our specialties, from fish to fowl, a trifle confusing. We will translate the Keys-speak. We have organized the restaurants of the Keys from Key Largo to Key West by descending mile marker and have located them as oceanside or bayside. In the Key West section, we offer a cuisine-oriented arrangement with restaurants listed alphabetically.

Free on-site parking is available at virtually all our recommended establishments in the Upper, Middle, and Lower Keys. However, most restaurants in Key West do not have on-site parking. Most restaurants suggest that you make reservations, especially during the high season. Those that do not take reservations will be noted.

Many restaurants serve limited alcoholic beverages. You may infer that unless we specify that an establishment offers a full-service bar—usually the larger restaurants or resort facilities—only beer and wine will be served.

Accessibility for the physically challenged varies greatly in restaurants throughout the Keys. While many of our establishments are at ground level, and some second-story locations within large resorts may have elevators, steps sometimes must be negotiated and some bathrooms may be too tiny to accommodate a wheelchair. If this is of particular concern to you, be sure to call the restaurants to see exactly what arrangements might be made to fit your needs.

Unless otherwise specified, you may assume that our recommended restaurants are air-conditioned. Those that provide outdoor seating or accessibility by sea will be highlighted. Children are generally welcome in Florida Keys restaurants. The odd exceptions or age restrictions will be stated.

The dollar sign price code indicated in each restaurant listing will help you gauge the cost of your dining experience. Each code category is based on dinner for two, without starters, dessert, alcoholic beverages, tax, or tip. Some of our restaurants include soup or a house salad with an entree; at others, entrees are strictly a la carte. Most of our restaurants accept major credit cards but rarely a personal check. If plastic is not acknowledged, we alert you in advance so you won't be caught short of cash.

PRICE-CODE KEY

Our price-code rating reflects the cost of dinner entrees for two, without cocktails, appetizers, wine, dessert, tax, or tip.

$	**Less than $25**
$$	**$25 to $40**
$$$	**$41 to $60**
$$$$	**More than $60**

THE FLORIDA KEYS

Upper Keys

Crack'd Conch **$$**
MM 105 Oceanside, Key Largo
(305) 451-0732
www.keysconch.com

Inside this 1930s white Conch house, trimmed in bright lime green and lavender, is some of the tastiest seafood in all the Florida Keys. Wallpapered with business cards, the Crack'd Conch has been operated by the Peterson family since the 1970s . . . from all appearances with a hearty sense of humor as well as talent in the kitchen. They note on the menu: "This establishment is run by a very close staff and family . . . close to broke, close to insanity, and close to killing each other!"

The conch chowder is loaded with conch and fresh vegetables and packs a bit of a spicy punch; conch salad contains just enough tangy juice to give it the right kick. The seafood combo basket, consisting of shrimp, cracked conch, and fried fish, is a hefty enough portion to feed two. Fried 'gator tails—not a local catch of the day in the Keys—are a popular appetizer and dinner. Crack'd Conch features more than 100 different types of beers.

The restaurant is open for lunch and dinner every day except Wednesday. Reservations are accepted. In addition to cash, traveler's checks, and credit cards, Crack'd Conch gladly will accept "gold, pirate treasure, or the keys to expensive sports cars" as payment for your dining adventure.

Hobo's Café **$**
MM 102 Oceanside, Key Largo
(305) 451-5888

Hobo's has done what hobos do—travel. This place use to look like a hobo on the outside, but now there's nothing but a "homey" feeling about their new digs. Hobo's moved down US 1 in the summer of 2006 and has maintained the same casual atmosphere. Shirts and shoes are required dress, but if you have socks on, you are overdressed. They want you relaxed so you can wolf down their home-cooked burgers, fish, salads, black beans, and corn and finish things off with a slice of their mouth-pleasing key lime pie. An "insider's" secret is out about one of the best locals place in the upper Keys.

Sundowners on the Bay **$$**
MM 104 Bayside, Key Largo
(305) 451-4502
www.sundownerskeylargo.com

One of Key Largo's most popular places to enjoy the sunset, this open and airy—yet cozy and intimate—establishment overlooks the azure expanse of Blackwater Sound. On the light side, Sundowners' fish sandwich wins raves—fresh fish grilled and topped with sautéed onions and American cheese on a kaiser roll. If you prefer a more elaborate meal, try the locals' favorite, Blackened Tuna Alfredo—fresh yellowfin tuna seared in Cajun spices, and tossed with linguine—or the Mermaid's Delight—jumbo shrimp and scallops served with Sundowners' seafood stuffing. The Key's famed yellowtail snapper is served seven ways, including the secret Nassau style. Wednesday and Saturday are prime rib nights, and Friday night is an all-you-can-eat fish-fry extravaganza.

All tables are set with fresh flowers for evening dining. A large bar, adjoining the indoor dining area, is available for dinner service as well, and busy evenings tend to run on the loud side. The patio and deck afford more privacy. Sundowners offers a full bar and is open for lunch and dinner. Reservations are recommended. The restaurant is accessible by boat.

Señor Frijoles $
MM 103.9 Bayside, Key Largo
(305) 451-1592

Don your sombrero for a taste of Mexico by the sea—Keys style. Señor Frijoles nestles on Florida Bay next to Sundowners and offers the usual popular Tex-Mex fare, such as burritos, enchiladas, and quesadillas. But you'll also find some jazzed-up Conch Republic versions, such as Grilled Shrimp and Pineapple Pizza and Enchiladas del Mar, which are filled with shrimp, crabmeat, and fish in a red sauce.

You don't have to look for Jimmy Buffett to find Margaritaville. Señor Frijoles offers five different margaritas as well as a potpourri of other tropical libations and Mexican beers with which you can toast the fabulous Keys sunset. Señor Frijoles is accessible by boat and open for lunch and dinner daily.

Gus' Grille $$
MM 103.8 Bayside, Marriott Key Largo Bay Beach Resort, Key Largo
(305) 453-0000
www.marriottkeylargo.com

This award-winning restaurant serves dinner specialties such as grilled dolphin served with Asian mango and papaya salsa and yellowtail snapper with an almond crust, topped with avocado, orange, and chive sweet-butter sauce. The executive chef creates his "Floribbean" specialties before your eyes in an open kitchen, an upmarket grill-style presentation reminiscent of a tony trattoria.

Unobstructed views of Florida Bay and the famous Keys sunset are available from virtually every seat in the house. Booths line the window walls of the light and airy dining room; outdoor patio dining is also available.

Open daily for breakfast, lunch, and dinner, Gus' has wheelchair-accessible facilities and an elevator. You can dock your boat at the Marriott while you enjoy your meal at Gus', but reservations for both slips and tables are recommended.

Num Thai Restaurant & Sushi Bar $$
MM 103.2 Bayside, Key Largo
(305) 451-5955

If your taste for Asian food hovers around Thailand or Japan, Num Thai can offer you the best of both worlds: Spicy Thai curries and noodle dishes or sushi, sashimi, and traditional Japanese dishes. The restaurant basks in the glow of deep-teal-colored walls covered with Asian accents. Three tatami tables, which seat two to four people, complement the wood-laminate tables peppering the interior. A sushi bar affords one and all the opportunity to watch the masters at work. Japanese offerings include temaki, cone-shaped hand rolls; hosomaki, medium rolls cut into bite-size pieces; a wide assortment of sushi, by the piece or in dinner combos; and tempura. Or enjoy Thai satays; spicy beef salad; seafood, chicken, or beef curries; or Volcano Jumbo Shrimp, grilled and fired with chili sauce. Pad Thai proves to be a hefty portion.

Open for lunch Monday through Friday and dinner every day, Num Thai accepts reservations for parties of more than five. American and Oriental beers, wine, plum wine, and sake all are offered.

The Fish House **$$**
MM 102.4 Oceanside, Key Largo
(305) 451-4665, (888) 451-4665
www.fishhouse.com

The scent of freshly prepared seafood lures patrons into this campy nautical establishment, which is bedecked with fishnets, mounted fish, buoys, and twinkling fish lights. Seafood is the name of the game here, and the food doesn't disappoint. The extensive menu features smoked fish (done on premises), Jamaican Jerk, Conch salad, and ceviche. The Fish Matecumbe, a mouth-watering combo of the fresh catch of the day topped with tomatoes, shallots, capers, fresh basil, olive oil, and lemon juice and broiled to perfection, is always a favorite. The Fish House food is as memorable as "The Fish House Gang" that serves it.

The Fish House is open for lunch and dinner daily. Reservations are not accepted.

Encore **$$$**
102.4 Oceanside, Key Largo
(305) 451-0650

The owners of the perennially popular The Fish House, C. J. Berwick and Doug Prew, have outdone themselves this time. In the building next door they have opened Encore, an upscale fine-dining restaurant that tingles the taste buds and scintillates the senses. From the baby grand piano to the long mahogany bar, Encore plays the gustatory scene to much applause. And although the decor is elegant, you do not need to be similarly attired to dine here.

You will need to make dinner reservations during high season and holiday weekends. Our popular restaurants attract hungry crowds.

Keys casual is good enough! An outdoor patio invites dining amid lush tropical vegetation in all seasons (unobtrusive heaters warm things up on those occasional cool nights in December and January).

You'll find plenty of fish on the menu, such as the wildly popular Fish Matecumbe from sibling restaurant The Fish House. But Encore offers a great selection from the land, too, such as New Zealand lamb and Angus beef. Appetizers, soups, and salads are inventive and the signature dessert, White Chocolate Baby Grand, will finish you off.

After dinner, stop at the piano bar, where you can enjoy tunes from Sinatra to Billy Joel. And, on some lucky evenings, you might even catch a local or two playing along on their own instruments. All in all, this is a night out not to be missed. Encore is open daily for dinner only. Reservations are suggested for Friday and Saturday nights.

Upper Crust Pizza **$$**
MM 101.6 Oceanside, Key Largo
(305) 451-4188

Long a favorite pizza restaurant in Marathon, Upper Crust moved up the Keys several years ago and is now winning raves in Key Largo. You can build your own thick-crust pizza with an array of ingredients, but the House Deluxe is a combination you won't want to miss—pepperoni, sausage, mushroom, green pepper, onion, black olives, and extra cheese. Upper Crust also serves pasta and subs and offers daily specials that are difficult to pass up.

Upper Crust is open daily for lunch and dinner.

Tower of Pizza **$**
MM 100.5 Bayside, Key Largo
(305) 451-1461, (305) 451-3754

MM 81.9 Bayside, Islamorada
(305) 664-8216, (305) 664-8246

Antipasto, Greek salad, minestrone, and a potpourri of great pasta dishes vie with fantastic pizza at both Tower of Pizza establishments. Sauces and dough here are homemade, and cheeses are fresh. Locals particularly like the Sicilian-style pie, but you can build your own from a long list of tantalizing ingredients. Delivery is free with a minimum order.

Both Towers are open every day for lunch and dinner.

Coconuts Restaurant & Lounge $$
MM 100 Oceanside, Marina Del Mar Resort and Marina, 528 Caribbean Drive, Key Largo
(305) 453-9794
www.coconutsrestaurant.com

This vibrant outdoor restaurant, cornered between Key Largo Harbor and the swimming pool of Marina Del Mar Resort and Marina, offers fine cuisine and lively after-hours entertainment. Ceiling fans cool patrons, who enthusiastically devour Coconuts' many specialties, among them conch egg roll, which is the best of both the Orient and Caribbean, served over honey mustard sauce; dolphin Lorenzo, a mouthwatering dish with blue-crab meat and lobster sauce; and scallop brochette, prepared with giant scallops and grilled on brochette. Coconuts' signature dish is Yellowtail Largo style, yellowtail snapper sautéed with artichoke hearts, shrimp, and capers in a lemon white-wine sauce.

After dinner, head for Coconuts' indoor nightclub and dance the night away or sit back and enjoy the live entertainment (see the Nightlife chapter). The establishment has a full bar and offers weekday happy hours from 5:00 to 7:00 P.M. Coconuts is accessible by boat. Reservations are accepted for parties of more than nine. To reach Coconuts, head toward the ocean on Laguna at MM 100; the restaurant is about a quarter mile in on the left.

Snook's Bayside Restaurant $$$
MM 99.9 Bayside, Key Largo
(305) 453-3799
www.snooks.com

Exquisitely nestled amid towering palms at the very edge of Florida Bay, Snook's secretes itself away down a narrow, winding driveway off the Overseas Highway. Virtually every seat in the house affords a view of the water, be it from the elegant dining room or from a seat on the patio. Expect linen cloths and napkins, fresh flowers, and candlelight—not always an ambience found accompanying great food in the Keys. And great food it is.

Snook's signature fish, yellowtail snapper, is seared in oregano with shrimp, tomato, almonds, and Pernod for one popular specialty. You'll find Seafood Dieppoise, a rich combination of shrimp, scallops, and mussels in a lobster cream sauce. Carnivores will find Angus beef here, and chicken lovers appreciate Snook's Hazelnut Chicken, which is prepared with a delectable Frangelico orange-thyme sauce.

Snook's pastry chef prepares all breads and desserts, which challenge the waistline with decadence. Two full bars are on premises, one sporting a pounded copper top, and an extensive wine list includes more than 175 selections from throughout the world. Enjoy happy hour Monday through Friday from 5:00 to 7:00 P.M.

Snook's offers live entertainment nightly in season and on weekends during the off-season. The restaurant is open for lunch and dinner Monday through Saturday; brunch is served on Sunday. Snook's is accessible by boat.

If you're a bride-to-be, Snook's offers the services of attentive wedding experts who will assist you in planning all the details for an unforgettable Keys wedding event.

Cafe Largo $$
MM 99.5 Bayside, Key Largo
(305) 451-4885
www.yp.bellsouth.com/sites/cafelargo

Third-generation owned, Cafe Largo greets you with bistro tables atop terra-cotta tile floors, a setting that evokes a continental flair, the interior punctuated with a swirl of stark white, hunter green, and peach and wall murals featuring local scenery.

House specialties at this Italian trattoria include a vast array of pasta, chicken, veal, and eggplant dishes as well as Angus beef, individual hand-tossed pizzas, and homemade sausage. Fresh fish and seafood offerings round out the diverse menu.

The restaurant has a full bar. It is open every day for lunch and dinner.

Bayside Grille **$$**
MM 99.5 Bayside, Key Largo
(305) 451-3380
www.yp.bellsouth.com/sites/cafelargo
Situated at the end of a winding drive behind Cafe Largo and perched on the very edge of Florida Bay, Bayside Grille commands one of the premier waterfront vistas in the Keys. Small, casual, and bistroish, the open-air Bayside Grille's layout of tables fronted by glass pocket doors enables all diners to drink in the shimmering blue sea while partaking of a palate-tingling selection of offerings. Seafood reigns here—Key West Garlic Shrimp, Island Seafood Curry, and Seafood Enchiladas are favorites. But landlubbers will also find a good selection of beef, chicken, and lamb entrees. Italian dishes with flair are also on the menu, such as rigatoni with vodka sauce and frutta de mar, assorted seafood steamed in a marinara sauce.

Bayside Grille offers a full bar and the restaurant serves lunch and dinner daily.

DJ's Diner and Coffee Shop **$**
MM 99.4 Oceanside, Key Largo
(305) 451-2999
Established in 1958, DJ's relocated to the Overseas Highway in Key Largo in 2005. Now old regulars drive over and DJ's new clientele continues to grow, so the place that serves "the best breakfast in town" is likely to be bustling with activity when you come by. DJ's serves daily lunch specials, too, but no dinners. So, get up early, have a BIG appetite, and enjoy this bright spot in the Upper Keys.

Harriette's **$**
MM 95.7 Bayside, Key Largo
(305) 852-8689
This popular roadside diner-style restaurant offers reasonably priced home-style meals in a simple setting. Tables and chairs surround counter dining; local arts and crafts on consignment provide the decor.

Harriette's specialty? Ensuring that no guest leaves the restaurant hungry. Open only for breakfast and lunch, Harriette's serves filling omelets, oversize homemade biscuits with sausage gravy, burgers, and hot and cold sandwiches. The restaurant caters primarily to a repeat local crowd, so lunch specials change daily. Look for comfort food at Harriette's: meat loaf, pork chops, stuffed peppers, roast pork, and chicken and dumplings.

Harriette's is open seven days a week from 6:00 A.M. to 2:00 P.M. Reservations are not accepted; no credit cards.

Snapper's Waterfront Saloon & Raw Bar **$$**
MM 94.5 Oceanside
139 Seaside Avenue, Key Largo
(305) 852-5956
www.thefloridakeys.com/snappers
The best part of Snapper's is sitting out on the deck near the water overlooking Snapper's Marina . . . next to the food, that is, which is Old Florida and Bahamian cuisine at its best. You can graze on blackened dolphin fingers, nut-encrusted baked Brie with strawberry sauce, or a seafood burrito (mahimahi, shrimp, and scallops sautéed in tomato sauce, wrapped in a tortilla, and topped with Monterey Jack and cheddar cheese). Or for a "reel meal," choose selections from the Florida Keys piscatory pantry: Try onion-encrusted yellowtail or grouper roulade. Key Largo Crab Cakes are a specialty of the house. Snapper's offers an extensive raw bar as well as sandwiches, burgers, and a few selections for landlubbers. On Sunday they serve a champagne jazz brunch from 10:00 A.M. to 2:00 P.M.

Weekends feature live entertainment in season. The restaurant is accessible by boat. Reservations are accepted.

Craig's Restaurant **$$**
MM 90.5 Bayside, Tavernier
(305) 852-9424

A 1977 graduate of the Culinary Institute in Hyde Park, New York, chef-owner Craig Belcher opened his namesake establishment in 1981 with his signature sandwich, which he bills "World Famous Fish Sandwich."

A simply appointed, diner-style restaurant with an all-day menu, Craig's tries to please every palate, be it down-home or gourmet. Specialties of the chef include Fish Tropical (grouper or dolphin sautéed with bananas, pineapples, oranges, and strawberries and topped with sliced almonds) and Fish Seminole (baked grouper or dolphin with sautéed shrimp and mushrooms, scallops, scallions, tomatoes, and hearts of palm in lemon-butter sauce). The Jon Chicken Sandwich, a grilled chicken breast with Dijon mustard, Cajun seasoning, melted cheese, grilled onions, grilled mushrooms, and bacon, puts a little pep in the ubiquitous poulet. And, best of all, you'll get a free piece of key lime pie with your entree.

Open seven days a week for breakfast, lunch, and dinner, Craig's does not accept reservations.

Old Tavernier Restaurant **$$**
MM 90.3 Oceanside, Tavernier
(305) 852-6012

One of the Upper Keys' most popular establishments, the Old Tavernier marries the Mediterranean and the Caribbean with a continental flair to create a singular cuisine.

Diners enjoy traditional Italian pasta favorites such as pasta primavera, angelhair marinara, baked ziti, fettuccine Alfredo, or eggplant, chicken, and veal parmigiana. Or they can opt for a culinary adventure with Yellowtail Provençal (pan-sautéed and served with fresh tomatoes, button mushrooms, scallions, garlic, white wine-lemon butter sauce, and fresh basil); Cioppino (fresh seafood stewed in a zesty tomato sauce with white wine and served over fettuccine); Grill-seared Greek Rack of Lamb, rubbed with kosher salt and oregano in a lemon glaze; or yellowtail snapper with a toasted almond-banana-berry-rum glaze.

Guests have the option of dining indoors—where white linen tablecloths are aglow with candles and watercolor sailboat scenes dot the walls—or outdoors on a balcony overlooking a narrow canal. Old Tavernier has a full bar and is open daily for dinner only. The restaurant is accessible by boat.

Pizza in the Mangroves **$**
MM 88.8 Bayside, Tavernier
(305) 853-3800

Pizza, handmade and baked in a stone-lined pizza oven, is the claim to certain fame here at Tavernier's newest pizza establishment, aptly named Pizza in the Mangroves. Locals rave about the crust, characterized as neither thick nor thin, but light, fluffy, and tender. You'll also find sub sandwiches and calzones here as well as tuna or crab salad in an edible bowl, which draws accolades as well. This pizzeria is open daily.

Marker 88 **$$$**
MM 88 Bayside, Islamorada
(305) 852-9315, (305) 852-5503
www.keysdining.com/marker88

This famous Islamorada culinary landmark combines bayside ambience with innovative preparation of the Keys' freshest bounty. Marker 88 was established in 1978 by German-born, Swiss-trained André Mueller, who made the cuisine legendary. Mueller sold the restaurant in 2003 to the Stokey family, owners of Señor Frijoles and Sundowners in Key Largo (see listings in this chapter) The restaurant is popular with presidents—such as George H. W. Bush—and local patrons alike.

Marker 88's cuisine is legendary. Favorite dishes include Key West pink shrimp "Calabrese"—sautéed shrimp in virgin olive oil, chopped garlic, roasted red pepper, and broccoli tossed with penne. Another swoon dish is tuna steak "Au Poivre"—pan-seared yellowfin tuna flambéed with brandy and served with green-peppercorn sauce.

Java Jolt

Expect Florida Keys java jolt when you have your first taste of the Cuban coffees served here. Café con Leche is a delightful blend of rich coffee made with hot milk and usually served with sugar. Buche, a Cuban thunderbolt of caffeine served in a tiny shot glass and gulped in one hearty swallow, is definitely not for the faint of heart! Most restaurants and establishments serve these versions, and they're a must try if you love coffee. *Mucho Gusto!*

Dessert hits the mark also. Try the key lime baked Alaska, with ice cream and key lime filling topped in meringue. Then there is the oh-la-la Rangoon. This dessert is sautéed, laced with currant gelée and cinnamon, and garnished with diced fresh mangoes, papayas, pineapples, and bananas.

As sophisticated as the Marker 88 cuisine may be, decor here is charmingly rustic: Wood tables are made of hatch covers lifted from boats. Tiffany lighting provides a soothing romantic setting, and views of Florida Bay abound. Marker 88 is surrounded by heavy tropical vegetation and rambling docks, and a deck laden with wood outdoor tables and chairs provides the perfect setting for a predinner sunset libation or a starlit after-dinner drink.

This boat-accessible restaurant maintains a full bar and is open daily from 11:00 A.M. to 11:00 P.M. Reservations are recommended.

Picchi's 88 Ristorantino $$
MM 88 Oceanside, Islamorada
(305) 852-5051

Argentinean cuisine makes a spectacular addition to the Florida Keys at Picchi's 88 Ristorantino, a tiny yet classy bistro that modestly sits in a small strip mall in Islamorada. Or, if take-away is what you prefer, the adjoining open kitchen accommodates this option as well. Either way, feast on Argentinean beef or tingle your taste buds with such native specialties as morcilla, empanadas, churrasco, or Parrillada Chacarera for two or four. If you prefer a more tropical twist, try these local favorites: Caribbean baby back ribs cooked in a delicate mango-chutney sauce or the shrimp and mushroom bisque, which is loaded with fresh mushrooms and shrimp. Dessert choices include Flan with Chantilly Cream, Torta Mimosa, and Sflogia Chocolatto. Picchi's 88 is open daily for lunch and dinner.

Smuggler's Cove $$
MM 85.5 Bayside, Islamorada
(305) 664-5564, (800) 864-4363
www.thefloridakeys.com/smugglerscove

If you want to find a good place to eat, ask a local. Smuggler's Cove, a locals' favorite in Islamorada, puts on no pretensions. What they do put on, however, is a great fish sandwich, among other entrees, that draws raves. You'll find St. Louis-style hickory-smoked ribs, crab cakes, and even a 20-ounce rib-eye steak. What Smuggler's lacks in decor and ambience, they make up for in taste. Smuggler's Cove is boat accessible.

Island Grill $$-$$$
MM 85.5 Oceanside, Islamorada
(305) 664-8400

Don't pass up the opportunity to stop here if you see the parking area full. Cruise the parking lot to find a spot because this is one of those "don't judge a book by its cover" places. If the hostess tells you there is a little wait, go to the bar and play a couple of ring-toss or pirate-dice games and have a cold, tall Key West Sunset Ale.

If you are seated inside at the Island Grill, ask for a table near the ceiling-to-floor window area, which will put you right along the canal facing Snake Creek. Outdoor tables are the best choice because you are actually on the dock area of the restaurant. The menu is swimming with seafood, and Island Grill is one of the best places to try an appetizer of spicy seared tuna nachos served over fried wontons with a seaweed salad amid ginger and sweet soy dressing. This dish is so mountainous that it could pass for an entree! Fish tacos made with mahimahi are equally filling, as are conch fritters and the Caesar salad with grilled shrimp. Entrees include crunchy yellowtail snapper with sweet chili sauce served with green beans and rice. Youngsters might like the chicken sandwich or fried fish selections. Open for lunch and dinner but early arrival, for either meal, is suggested due to parking limitations.

Ziggie's Gumbo and Crab Shack $$
MM 83 Bayside, Islamorada
(305) 664-3391

A taste of New Orleans awaits you at Ziggie's Gumbo and Crab Shack. Sitting in funky booths surrounded by fishing buoys and memorabilia, you can feast on crab cakes, oysters, po'boys, gumbo, crab and corn bisque, jambalaya, shrimp creole or étouffée, and red beans and rice with bayou sauce. And if you're hankering for a Cajun crab fix, you have a lot of choices: garlic blue crabs, Maryland blues, queen crab, Canadian stone crab, king crab, and certainly not least, Florida stone crabs. Add a side of fried okra or hush puppies, if you are able. Ziggie's signature cocktail is called The Hurricane; its secret recipe came direct from New Orleans.

Lorelei Restaurant $$$
Cabana Bar $
and Grand Slam Lounge $
MM 82 Bayside, Islamorada
(305) 664-4656
www.loreleifloridakeys.com

The legend of Lorelei—a nymph of the Rhine—maintains that her sweet, lyrical singing lured sailors to shipwreck on a rock. Today's Lorelei lures you to a primo perch on the very edge of Florida Bay, where you'll relish breakfast, lunch, or dinner daily as well as those other munching hours in between. Come by boat, if you like, because the Lorelei also maintains a marina where you'll be able to rub shoulders with some of the Keys' renowned fishing guides.

The Cabana Bar breaks the day starting at 6:00 A.M., then serves a casual lunch menu from 11:00 A.M. to 9:00 P.M. The Cabana Bar offers live entertainment nightly from just before sunset until late at night. Reservations are not taken at the Cabana Bar.

The air-conditioned Lorelei Restaurant's expansive seafood-inspired menu makes a gustatory decision a difficult task. The shrimp or the catch of the day can be enjoyed six different ways. Or mix it up with a combination platter of shrimp, fish, scallops, conch, and crab cakes. Landlubbers are accommodated with steak, chicken, and pasta offerings.

The Lorelei Restaurant is open daily for dinner. Early-bird specials are offered from 5:00 to 6:00 P.M. Lorelei's family menu offers seven complete meals for $15.95 each, a real value.

Atlantic's Edge $$$
MM 82 Oceanside
Cheeca Lodge & Spa, Islamorada
(305) 664-4651
www.cheeca.com

The fine-dining room at Cheeca Lodge and Spa has panoramic vistas of the Atlantic Ocean, with seating indoors and out. Chef Andy Niedenthal delights in serving only fresh, indigenous foods, and many are inspired by the resort's Avanyu Spa. Some of the selections are jumbo sea scallops with goat cheese potatoes; Bahamian blue-crab fritters with key lime sauce; and shrimp curry with cocitos, coconut milk, plantains, and jasmine rice. Also available to tempt your palate is tempura lobster combined with sesame-soy glaze and lemongrass. Atlantic's Edge hosts a delightful Sunday brunch during the winter season.

The Cheeca children's menu is the result of consultations with local Plantation Key elementary schoolchildren; it includes all their favorites, such as pizza, chicken fingers, fish fingers, popcorn shrimp, even a child-size filet mignon. A dessert highlight is "The Dirt Cup"—chocolate pudding with crumbled Oreo cookies topped with a candy Gummi Worm.

The indoor dining atmosphere at Atlantic's Edge features casual elegance—linen tablecloths, crystal goblets, and bud vases—highlighted by a panoramic view of the Atlantic through floor-to-ceiling glass walls.

Atlantic's Edge is open for dinner nightly, offering libations from a full bar.

Squid Row **$-$$**
MM 81.9 Oceanside, Islamorada
(305) 664-9865
www.keysdining.com/squidrow

This unassuming roadside diner will surprise you. The food is good, portions are hearty, and the prices are reasonable. And you'll find a $3.00 margarita here! You'll also find an extensive array of appetizer offerings such as a conch chowder, called Bahamian Borscht, squid rings and "things," as well as oysters Moscow (made with caviar). A number of the seafood dishes are fried, but you can also find sautéed fish, such as Catch of the Day Almondine, which is coated with bread crumbs and sliced almonds and served with key lime butter. A selection of beef, chicken, and pasta dishes is offered as well.

Homemade desserts include such yummy concoctions as Jeanne's Toll House Pie a la Mode, chocolate-covered oysters, and caramel-covered squid. Yep, you're in the Keys. Squid Row is open daily for lunch and dinner.

Kaiyo **$$**
MM 81.7 Oceanside, Islamorada
(305) 664-5556
www.kaiyokeys.com

Kaiyo's delightful blend of "Florida Asian" results in an exciting presentation of sushi and Keys-inspired dishes. Ones to try are tempura-fried whole bass or tuna tataki, which is seared in peppercorns and orange ponza. Also not to be missed are Kaiyo's sakes. One that is very quaint is sake margarita, served with a salt rim and key lime, on the rocks or frozen. Sake to me! Kaiyo's has 12 types of saki, Kirin beer, and special teas.

From the menu (fastened to a wooden board held by a bamboo rod), to the amenities (hot towels served before dining), to the decor (the restaurant is awash in varying hues of blues and purples punctuated by upscale Asian accents), Kaiyo pays exquisite attention to the details. A massive mosaic depicting the tropical reef and its creatures, based on Sieber's love of sea glass, dominates the sushi bar room.

And where did the restaurant's unusual name come from? In Japanese *kai* means "small body of water" and *yo* means "large body of water." In its cuisine and its ambience, Kaiyo, situated in Islamorada between the Atlantic Ocean and the Gulf of Mexico, successfully marries the mystique of Asia with the mystery of the sea.

Kaiyo is open for lunch and dinner daily. The restaurant does not accept reservations or large groups, but you can call ahead for preferred seating.

Morada Bay Café **$$-$$$**
MM 81.6 Bayside, Islamorada
(305) 664-0604

Leading the Purple Isle's lineup, Morada Bay Café restaurant in Islamorada delivers a tapas-style selection of appetizers and eclectic entrees in the most seductive of atmospheres. From the bark-chip parking lot, past a huge copper urn filled with bougainvillea petals, to the cobblestone brick entrance under a thatched-roof canopy—Morada Bay Café neglects no detail of ambience. Pastel beach tables and low Adirondack-style chairs pepper a wide expanse of sandy beach (imported from the Bahamas) that fronts the gentle waters of Florida Bay. Curving palms and tiki torches complete the outdoor illusion. The white Key West–style restaurant building itself sparkles with raspberry shutters and periwinkle trim. Design detailing on light fixtures, wall sconces, and artistic renderings is exquisite. Funky painted pine tables sit outdoors under a canopy and inside beneath a vaulted whitewashed ceiling.

You'll be happy to know the food at Morada Bay Café is as imaginatively designed as the decor. Thai Dolphin Fingers or chicken with a jerk rum glaze, tuna tartare, stuffed Anaheim chile, Thai ribs, and to-die-for mussels shine from the tapas menu. The four designer salad creations—Mediterranean, Sunshine, Morada Bay, and Caesar—tempt even the most ardent meat-and-potatoes lover. If you prefer a traditional dining entree instead of the wonderful array of light noshes, any of Morada Bay Café's fresh fish selections—all imaginatively prepared—will more than satisfy your taste for the sea. Morada Bay Café finishes you off with some calorie-loaded ammunition. Save room for dessert if you are able. Morada Bay Café is open for lunch and dinner daily.

This is the perfect place to watch the sunset, as Morada Bay Café perches at the edge of Florida Bay. Recognizable musicians often stop by for a lively impromptu set while vacationing in the Keys.

Pierre's Restaurant **$$$$**
MM 81.6 Bayside, Islamorada
(305) 664-3225

Magazine shoots and movie stars can be seen here, but the real star attraction at Pierre's is the cuisine. Sharing the same beach, sunset, and ambience with the more casual Morada Bay Café, Pierre's is the place to go for a romantic, deep-pocket dining experience. Flickering candlelight and comfy leather sofas greet you in the downstairs lounge area for predinner libations, and a covered porch welcomes you to sit a spell on cushioned wicker chairs and watch the famed Keys sunset. Walk up the sweeping curved staircase, however, and your dining adventure begins. The decor, tropically British colonial, is elegant yet casual. Dine indoors or out on the covered porch. Check your almanac and join in the upscale monthly full-moon beach party held here. Torches, live music, and special tropical drinks are a sure bet to get you moonstruck or howling at the moon!

The culinary stars shine with such signature dishes as Lotus-root-crusted Yellowtail, Tempura Lobster tail, and a constantly changing rota of the chef's creative offerings. Pierre's is open every evening for dinner only.

Islamorada Fish Company **$–$$**
MM 81.5 Bayside, Islamorada
(305) 664-9271, (800) 258-2559
www.ifcstonecrab.com

Islamorada Fish Company, primarily a seafood market that opens at 9:00 A.M., also serves lunch and dinner daily until 9:00 P.M. Eat indoors at the Island Conch House Eatery or outside under umbrella tables that perch on a peninsula jutting into Florida Bay. Renowned for fish and stone crabs so fresh they almost jump out of the water and onto your plate, Islamorada Fish Company's restaurant is so popular that it is not unusual to wait an hour or more for a table. But don't worry. The restaurant abuts World Wide Sportsman's cavernous sports emporium, so you can browse your wait away or sit in a rocking chair on the store's porch, look at the sunset, and wait for your name to be called. This is the perfect place for a light, casual meal on a fine day. (See the Seafood Markets and Specialty Foods chapter for more information.)

Uncle's Restaurant **$$$**
MM 80.9 Oceanside, Islamorada
(305) 664-4402
www.keysdining.com/uncles

Mexican tiles, ceiling fans, stained glass, candlelit tables, soft music, and original paintings of Keys flora and fauna set the stage for fine dining at Uncle's. And if you'd prefer to sit under the stars, Uncle's will accommodate you, for it also serves dinner at tables sprinkled on an outdoor deck.

Uncle's cuisine sparkles with a decidedly Mediterranean flair. Seafood selections are many, including fish du jour prepared seven different ways, and there are lamb, veal, beef, pasta, and vegan selections as well.

Uncle's offers a full bar and is open daily, except Sunday, for dinner only. They will happily cook your catch for a fraction of the normal dinner price.

Lazy Days Oceanfront Bar & Seafood Grill **$$**
MM 79.9 Oceanside, Islamorada
(305) 664-5256

Lazy Days provides the ideal setting for kicking back, gazing over the sparkling blue Atlantic, and dining on a revolving selection of seafood offerings. The elevated plantation-style building with turquoise roof, French doors, and wraparound balcony is, indeed, designed for lazy days, for it perches directly on the shoreline of the ocean. During the winter season all doors are open, and Bahama fans circulate the fresh ocean air inside and out. Brass hangings and rich tropical foliage enhance the dining room.

New owners in 2003, Lupe and Michelle Ledesma, have kept some of the menu favorites, such as Caribbean Bouillabaisse or Dolphin with Tropical Fruit Salsa, which is served with a mango-rum sauce, while adding some specialties of their own.

Lazy Days serves lunch and dinner daily. Lazy Days is accessible to boats with a 2- to 3-foot draft.

Papa Joe's Landmark Restaurant **$$**
MM 79.7 Bayside, Islamorada
(305) 664-8109

Built in 1937, Papa Joe's is a historical landmark and the site of Islamorada's very first fishing tournament. The restaurant has a no-nonsense, no-frills ambience that is perennially popular with visiting anglers and locals alike.

Papa Joe's specializes in lobster and catches of the day. Try Papa Joe's Seafood Stew—Key West shrimp, clams, mussels, crab, fresh fish, and scallops in a seasoned tomato broth over linguine. If you've had a lucky day fishing, Papa Joe's will cook your catch any way you like it. Steaks, prime rib, chicken, and veal dishes are available for carnivores.

Open daily for lunch and dinner, Papa Joe's is accessible by boat and features an on-premises marina. The restaurant maintains a full bar. A waiting list takes the place of reservations; when you call, you're put at the top of the waiting list.

Little Italy **$$**
MM 68.5 Bayside, Layton, Long Key
(305) 664-4472

If good, hearty Italian cooking is what you're after, Little Italy rates a hearty molto buono. This family-style restaurant offers an extensive menu of pasta, veal, chicken, and seafood dishes and a selection of steaks for red-meat lovers. Favored by locals who appreciate the huge portions, Little Italy garners particular accolades for its Veal Parmesan, Linguine with Red Clam Sauce, and Mermaid's Delight, a savory concoction of scallops layered with crabmeat stuffing topped with shrimp, mushrooms, butter, and sherry and finished with a light cream sauce.

Little Italy is open for breakfast, lunch, and dinner seven days a week. It offers libations from a full-service bar.

Middle Keys

WatersEdge **$$$**
MM 61 Oceanside,
Hawk's Cay Resort, Duck Key
(305) 743-7000
www.hawkscay.com

Flanking Hawk's Cay Marina, WatersEdge provides the option of dining on the open-air porch or indoors in air-conditioned comfort in the Caribbean-style dining room or in the low-lit Truman's Bar. Nightly specials center on fresh local fish prepared many ways, and the stuffed Florida lobster—stuffed with shrimp, scallops, and crabmeat—is one of the best you'll find in the Keys. All dinner entrees include the soup and salad bar, which rates as a meal in itself. WatersEdge serves dinner nightly. If you plan to come by boat, be sure to call the marina in advance to secure a slip (see the Cruising chapter).

The Wreck & Galley Grill and Sports Bar **$–$$**
MM 59 Bayside, Grassy Key
(305) 743-8282

Nautically decked out with photos of some of the dive wrecks in the Keys, Wreck & Galley Grill ranks as a top-notch Middle Keys watering hole. Buffalo wings here—billed as the largest in the Keys—live up to their hype. Burgers are made from Black Angus beef, and Jamaican jerk chicken and grilled or blackened fish sandwiches have won raves from the locals. All-you-can-eat nights include fried grouper on Wednesday, prime rib on Friday, and frog legs on Saturday. This is the perfect place for a beer and a bite.

Hideaway Cafe **$$$–$$$$**
MM 58 Oceanside, Rainbow Bend Resort, Grassy Key
(305) 289-1554
www.hideawaycafe.com

The only thing rivaling the direct ocean vistas at Hideaway Cafe is the cuisine. Sure to please the gourmand, the Hideaway also will intrigue the diner who likes to pig out: The Hideaway Rib Steak is large enough to serve a family of four. Other favorites include seafood crepes—a seafood combo rolled in a homemade crepe—topped with flamingo sauce, and seafood puttanesca—shrimp, scallops, and shellfish in a red, spicy sauce. Top off your dinner with bananas a la Hideaway—what a gourmet surprise.

Hideaway Cafe is open daily for lunch and dinner. The service is "relaxed," so plan to drink in the view along with your libations. Reservations are recommended.

i

Papa Joe's, MM 79.7 Bayside, was built in 1937. One of the few "watering holes" on the Overseas Highway, this bar and restaurant became a community gathering place as well as a hurricane shelter.

Quarterdeck Restaurant **$–$$**
400 Key Colony Beach Causeway, Key Colony Beach
(305) 289-0141

Perched on the canal waters of Key Colony Beach, the Quarterdeck offers casual dining on picnic and patio tables and great food. Quarterdeck's primarily seafood-laden menu runs the gamut from raw bar (oysters, shrimp, and wings cost only a quarter each from 4:00 to 6:00 P.M.) to really tasty entrees. Specialties abound: Monday night is Mexican; Tuesday, pasta; Wednesday, all-you-can-eat grouper; and Thursdays, prime rib.

Of course, you can get fish sandwiches, fried seafood baskets, burgers, steak, and chicken, too.

You can motor up to Quarterdeck's dock, tie up, and enjoy your repast. The Quarterdeck is open daily for lunch and dinner.

Key Colony Inn **$$**
MM 54 Oceanside, 700 West Ocean Drive, Key Colony Beach
(305) 743-0100

The Key Colony Inn is a favorite dining haunt of residents and visitors alike. Besides the varied menu selections—75 entrees—of Italian-style pasta, veal, and chicken dishes, Key Colony Inn offers innovative presentations of Florida Keys seafood, steaks, and interesting daily specials. Diners agree, portions here are large, and you'll get a lot of bang for your buck.

If dinner conversation is important, request a corner table, which may be a bit quieter, because ceiling acoustics in Key Colony Inn do not filter the noise of a room full of chattering diners. Or if the weather is fine, and it usually is, sit outside on the covered veranda. The restaurant features a full-service bar. Key Colony Inn is open for lunch and dinner daily. This place is always packed, lunch or dinner. Reservations are suggested year-round.

The Island Tiki Bar & Restaurant $-$$
MM 54 Bayside, Marathon
(305) 743-4191
www.keysdining.com/theisland

Perched on a narrow spit of land jutting out into the Gulf of Mexico, The Island provides one of the most scenic sunset spots in the Middle Keys and some doggone great food to boot. Whether you feel like a margarita and some nachos, a grilled grouper sandwich, a bowl of conch chowder, or a more substantial meal, the Island doesn't disappoint. Try the conch ceviche, tender, marinated, and unforgettable pieces of conch with onions and peppers in a lime vinaigrette, or the seafood burros, with shrimp, scallops, spinach, black bean salsa, and sauce verde.

Tables are of the picnic or patio varieties, supercasual. Kids love playing in the open-air terrain. You can come to the Island in a shallow-draft boat and dock alongside the restaurant. The Island is open for lunch and dinner daily.

Don Pedro's Restaurant $
MM 53 Oceanside, Marathon
(305) 743-5247

Savor the fine cuisine of our neighbor to the south, Cuba, at Don Pedro's. Specialties at this storefront cafe include a tasty whole-fried yellowtail snapper, ropa vieja, churrasco with chimichurri sauce, and Argentinian steak. All the especialidades Cubanas are served with yellow rice, black beans, sweet plantains (a member of the banana family), and Cuban bread. Top off your meal with a traditional Cuban dessert, such as flan de leche or arroz con leche. Unless you like your coffee espresso-style, be sure to select cafe con leche when you order coffee, because Cuban coffee is very strong, like espresso. Don Pedro's also serves homemade sangria.

Don Pedro's serves lunch Monday through Friday, and dinner Monday through Saturday. All menu prices include sales tax.

Leigh Ann's Coffee House & Antipasti Bar $
MM 52 Oceanside, Marathon
(305) 743-2001

This popular coffeehouse is quaintly closeted in a pale-peach and white Key West-style building on the Overseas Highway. With French doors flung open wide, tile floors, tropical plants, and an eclectic array of rustic furniture and Keys art, this is coffeehouse a la Keys. Chic, clean, and packed with personality, Leigh Ann's food is pretty good, too. Homemade soups rival sandwiches on bagels, croissants, and sub rolls. Specials are made in small batches to ensure freshness. You can get an upscale pizza and a selection of salads as well. And don't forget the coffee. Choose among cappuccino, mocha coolers, muddy mocha, or macchiato.

Leigh Ann's is open from 7:00 A.M. to 7:00 P.M. Monday through Friday; 8:00 A.M. to noon on Saturday. The restaurant is closed on Sunday. During the winter months Leigh Ann's is open for dinner six nights a week. Specialty nights feature poetry readings and music jam sessions. And Leigh Ann's now serves beer and wine as well. This is a happening place!

Shucker's Raw Bar & Grill $
MM 50.5 Bayside, Marathon
(305) 743-8686
www.keysdining.com/shuckers

Established in 1987, Shucker's is a Marathon landmark. The menu is Keys eclectic, offering everything from burgers, conch chowder, and grilled fish sandwiches to full dinners with a bevy of seafood, beef, chicken, or pasta dishes. Some menu offerings, like the Chef's Salad, mirror those of Shucker's sister restaurant, The Island Tiki Bar & Restaurant (see separate listing in this chapter).

The spacious restaurant, with vaulted ceilings, pale yellow walls, and green carpeting, creates an indoor island feeling.

You'll find a great kids' menu, and the little ones are served a coloring book and crayons to occupy themselves during the wait for their meal.

This is a good choice for lunch or a light dinner with the family. Shucker's is open daily.

Village Cafe **$$**
MM 50.5 Bayside, Gulfside Village, Marathon
(305) 743-9090

Generous portions and tasty Italian pasta and pizza entrees distinguish the extensive menu of the Village Cafe, a bustling place at breakfast, lunch, or dinner. Murals of scenes from Venice to Rome grace the walls of this trattoria, a vision of white-latticed simplicity. The outstanding pizza at the Village shines amid a number of perennial pasta favorites: ziti with broccoli, blue crab with spaghetti in red sauce, penne with fresh tomato and basil, and gnocchi. You'll find the traditional Italian renditions for veal, chicken, and seafood, as well as a changing rota of daily specials.

Village Cafe is open for all three meals from Monday through Saturday. Sundays it serves a breakfast buffet until 2:00 P.M. and then reopens at 5:00 P.M. for a dinner buffet. You'll find entertainment and dancing here on weekends.

Herbie's **$-$$**
MM 50.5 Bayside, Marathon
(305) 743-6373

Ask anyone: Herbie's is classic Keys. This roadhouse-style watering hole—two simple rooms and a porch with a large bar area and picnic tables—attracts a loyal contingent of locals and snowbirds alike. The conch chowder here is outstanding—packed with conch and chunks of potato. You can order fried shrimp, clam, oyster, or fish baskets or platters, or opt for burgers, dogs, and conch or fish sandwiches. Dinner specials are surprisingly sophisticated, and portions are generous. Herbie's will also cook your catch if you've had a lucky day on the water.

Herbie's is open for lunch and dinner from Tuesday through Saturday. The restaurant is not air-conditioned and does not accept reservations or credit cards.

53rd Street Dock & Deli **$**
MM 50.3 Oceanside, 71 53rd Street, Marathon
(305) 743-0500

Though this tiny restaurant-delicatessen does actually sit alongside a Marathon canal, it isn't vital to maintaining its quirky island charm. The brightly painted interior re-creates the dockside experience—in air-conditioned indoor comfort. You really need to visually take in all the decorative details here before you ever glance at the menu. The floor of Dock & Deli is painted as a dock, with sharks and manatees swimming alongside. Twinkling lights ornament artificial palm trees. Tables, chairs, and accent furniture are eclectically painted, and bright buoys and Caribbean dolls hang over the edge of an actual boat that is suspended from the ceiling. Local art adorns the walls, and there's even a mermaid on the back door.

Once you're sated with funky island ambience, order salad, soup, or a sandwich, such as a Cuban Press, Muffuletta, or Richie's Rubin, along with a side or two. The portions are enormous. You may want to sample a few selections and share. And save room for ice cream; it's the old-fashioned kind. The Dock & Deli is open Monday through Saturday from 10:00 A.M. to 3:00 P.M.

Marathon Pizza and Pasta **$**
MM 50 Oceanside, 19 Sombrero Boulevard, Marathon
(305) 743-9993

If you like REALLY good pizza, then head to this locals' favorite. They offer a regular smorgasbord of toppings, including Buffalo chicken—you have to taste it to believe it! Their thin Greek-style crust makes you almost want to order just the pizza shell. And the salads are luscious and fresh; especially memorable is the Caesar. Marathon Pizza and Pasta also serves soups, appetizers, hot and cold

Florida Keys chefs use mixed elements of Asian, Latin American, and traditional American cuisine to create a unique style they call Floribbean cuisine.

sandwiches, and pasta. Sadly, they only deliver within the city limits of Marathon.

Barracuda Grill **$$–$$$**
MM 49.5 Bayside, Marathon
(305) 743-3314
www.barracudagrill.com

Imaginative preparation and presentation showcase the entrees at the Barracuda Grill, a small, lively, Zagat-rated bistro in the heart of Marathon. Chef-owners Jan and Lance Hill invest their considerable talents in an exquisite selection of culinary offerings, assuring that Barracuda Grill retains its coveted place in the hearts—and tummies—of locals and visitors alike. Tantalizing stars of the menu are often the char-grilled veal chop, a 22-ounce rib-eye steak, roasted rack of lamb with black raspberry sauce or a sauté of portobello mushrooms, and mangrove snapper with mango salsa. A daily changing menu of the chefs' creative interpretations rivals the old favorites.

Barracuda also offers a great children's menu with kid-friendly dishes such as Oodles of Noodles, Fish Have Fingers, and One Big Fish. Not your typical family restaurant, at Barracuda Mom and Dad can dine sumptuously and keep their kids happy, too.

Barracuda Grill is open for dinner Monday through Saturday. Reservations are not taken. This popular spot fills up quickly, especially in high season, so come early if you don't want to wait for a table.

The Stuffed Pig **$**
MM 49 Bayside, Marathon
(305) 743-4059
www.thestuffedpig.com

During high-season mornings you'll see a line of hungry diners outdoors reading newspapers and patiently awaiting admittance to the inner sanctum of the Stuffed Pig. This popular cafe packs 'em in for hearty country breakfasts. Try the Pig's Breakfast: two eggs, two pancakes, two sausages, two slices of bacon, potatoes, and toast. Or a Pig's Omelet, a four-egg wonder with the works. You'll find grits-and-grunts, which includes fish, two eggs, and potatoes; country-fried steak; gravy and biscuits; and alligator tail and eggs. If you adhere to less porcine standards, the veggie-and-egg-substitute omelet will hold the cholesterol. The Stuffed Pig also serves lunch.

The Stuffed Pig is open seven days a week at the crack of dawn (5:00 A.M.; an hour later on Sunday). They close at 2:00 P.M. Monday through Saturday and at noon on Sunday. No reservations or credit cards are accepted.

Annette's Lobster & Steak House **$$–$$$**
MM 49 Bayside, Marathon
(305) 743-5516

An extensive menu and hearty portions distinguish this Marathon steak-and-seafood restaurant. Annette's sports a nautical decor with dark paneling, wood-plank floors, and memorabilia from the sea. The restaurant offers a smoking and a nonsmoking room, which are separated by a huge salad bar. You'll enjoy choosing from the vast selection of pastas, steaks, seafood, and, of course, lots of lobster. Signature dishes include Horseradish Grouper and an 18- to 20-ounce Cowboy Steak, which is an Angus bone-in rib eye. Annette's will also cook your catch for you. Ask for the macadamia nut–encrusted rendition. A new addition is the "stone grill." Your food is cooked on granite stones and brought tableside, stones and all.

Libations from the full bar include creative tropical rum concoctions, such as a Raspberry Rita or a Bushwacker. Annette's places dessert selections on the menu's first page, so you are sure to be tempted and forewarned to save room.

Annette's Lobster & Steak House is open daily for lunch and dinner.

Keys Fisheries Market & Marina **$-$$**
MM 49 Bayside, at the end of 35th Street, Marathon
(305) 743-4353, (866) 743-4353
www.keysfisheries.com

Vaguely reminiscent of the famed Islamorada Fish Company, for more than 30 years Keys Fisheries Market & Marina has been the Middle Keys' answer to the quaint, picturesque, eat-the-seafood-right-off-the-boat dining experience. Diners order their selections from an outdoor window, then carry trays to picnic tables overlooking a small marina harbor. You must help yourself to soft drinks, fast-food style.

Though the place is rustic and informal, the fish doesn't get any fresher than this, because Keys Fisheries is just that, a working fishery and fish market (see the Seafood Markets and Specialty Foods chapter). Your wisest choices here will be local Keys seafood—such as grouper, yellowtail snapper, or mahimahi—lobster bisque or chowder, Key West shrimp, and stone crabs and Florida lobster in season. You can enjoy an all-you-can-eat fish fry on Tuesday night.

Keys Fisheries Market & Marina is open for lunch and dinner daily.

Butterfly Café **$$$**
MM 48.5 Oceanside, Marathon
(305) 289-7177
www.tranquilitybay.com/dining.htm

Butterfly Café, which opened in 2006, is one of the newest eateries in the Middle Keys. Housed in the main building of the lovely Tranquility Bay Beach House Resort (see Accommodations chapter), this fine new restaurant is truly "Keys casual" with a traditional flare. Its chic but casual design, with white tablecloths and open, airy, high ceilings flowing out onto a large veranda with breathtaking views of Gulf sunsets, only enhances the fare. Tropical world cuisine blended with exotic spices and fresh local catches is in evidence on the menu. The Sunset Sweet Potato Bisque, the Mango BBQ Quail, and the horseradish-crusted grouper served with leeks and citrus salad, are all excellent choices. A fitting finish would be the TDF (to-die-for) sticky toffee pudding. Don't count the calories—this is why you are on vacation!

The Butterfly Café and its staff have positioned themselves to offer the high quality from first-class restaurants, and they are making this a reality. Open for breakfast, lunch, dinner, and Sunday buffet. A children's menu is available and reservations are required for all seatings.

Burdine's Chiki Tiki Bar and Grill **$**
MM 47.5 Oceanside, Marathon
(305) 743-9204

Take a break and go to this fun-to-be-in-the-Keys eatery. Burdine's sits on a channel into Boot Key Harbor, and the view is as good as the food. You enjoy ocean breezes with a true Keys decor. The ceiling is covered in palm fronds, and nautical items finish out the lively atmosphere. The service is friendly and you are made to feel welcome and appreciated. The menu holds a bountiful selection, from chicken caesar pita to Joe Mama's biker sausage, fish sandwiches, and cheeseburgers. They also dish out some great Cuban selections, such as black beans and rice served with a flour tortilla. If you order nothing else, be sure to get the skinny French fries. They are hand cut and are served with their famous "fry dust." Save room to sample a twist on a local favorite: key lime pie that is deep-fried! The outside is a crisp pastry, and the cool key lime filling inside tingles your taste buds. This will put a smile on your tan face.

Cabot's on the Water **$$-$$$**
MM 47.5 Oceanside
725 11th Street, Marathon
(305) 743-6442

Tucked on Sister's Creek at the entrance to Boot Key Harbor by water and at the end of 11th Street by land, Cabot's (formerly the original Shucker's) affords a pelican's-eye view of the sunset from its expansive dining deck. Opened early in 2003 and totally renovated to be light, bright, and upmarket, Cabot's offers open-air, waterside dining in a casual and congenial

The Lime of the Keys

Key lime fruit is very small (1 to 2 inches), round, and a greenish-yellow color at maturity. The tart juice extracted from the limes goes on and into almost everything edible, from fish to salads, drinks, meats, and, of course, desserts. The key limes were grown in southern Florida and the Florida Keys until the 1926 hurricane wiped out the citrus crop. The trees were replaced with a Persian lime, and most remaining key lime trees were found throughout backyards in the Florida Keys. But commercial production of the key lime trees is once again happening on a small scale, and key limes do seem to be making a slight comeback as a Florida crop in recent years. Once you have tasted a true key lime, any other lime will pale in comparison.

atmosphere. The ambitious all-day menu presents varied offerings from raw bar, appetizer noshes, salads, and seafood sandwich baskets (the sushi-grade ahi tuna sandwich is great!) to pastas and upscale (and pricey) fish, seafood, and prime-grade beef offerings.

Cabot's is open daily for lunch and dinner. You can enjoy libations from a full-service bar. Signature drinks include the Dock Walker, Sitting Duck, and Dirty Parrot. Live entertainment starts at sunset. With its unobstructed view across the water, Cabot's is a great place to look for the green flash (see the Paradise Found chapter).

Porky's Bayside **$**
MM 47.5 Bayside, Marathon
(305) 289-2065

Looks aren't everything! This tiny, open-air restaurant sits on the water with a picturesque setting among the lobster traps on the commercial fishing docks. Porky's is known for humdinger barbecue and a "Chuck Wagon Special" for breakfast that includes three of everything—eggs, bacon, sausage, pancakes, and a heap of potatoes. Touted as "Swinin and Dinin," Porky's serves breakfast, lunch, and dinner every day beginning at 6:00 A.M. Reservations for large parties only are accepted. No credit cards.

Lower Keys

Rob's Island Grill **$**
MM 31.5 Bayside, Big Pine Key
(305) 872-3022

To locals this is a watering hole where everyone knows your name, what you like to eat, and what you like to watch on the sports channel. To Keys visitors, it's a great restaurant offering sports, spirits, and dynamite eats. You can get local seafood, pasta, and prime rib, or come on Mexican Night or Key West Shrimp Night and try the evening special. If you only want a sandwich, how about the Dolphin Reuben made with rye bread and topped with Swiss cheese and coleslaw? Or maybe you have a taste for portobello mushrooms stuffed with blue crab and topped with mozzarella cheese? If your favorite team is losing and you're too depressed to be social, call ahead for takeout. This food could restore your good mood!

No Name Pub **$**
MM 31 Bayside, North Watson Boulevard, Big Pine Key
(305) 872-9115

This funky, one-of-a-kind establishment bills itself as "a nice place . . . if you can find it." And you might not find it without a little Insider knowledge. The No Name Pub—a pale yellow building with teal trim that looks like a house in a residential neighborhood—is topped with a small sign declaring its beginnings in 1936. And North Watson Boulevard is off the beaten track, too. Turn right at the traffic light at MM 31 in Big Pine (the only light from Marathon to Stock Island) onto Key Deer Boulevard. Proceed to Watson Boulevard and take another right. At the fork in the road, bear left, heading toward No Name Key. Go across a humpback bridge and past a residential subdivision. Just before the No Name Bridge across Bogie Channel, the pub will be on your left, all but hidden under a canopy of large trees.

Although the pizza is a star culinary attraction at No Name Pub, the decor and local Keys characters distinguish it from other pizza establishments. The interior is literally wallpapered with dollar bills autographed by diners of years past. Be sure to scope out the barstools; no two of them stand at the same height. Those that are too short for the bar have 4-by-4-inch blocks of wood nailed to the bottoms of their legs. The management brags: "Friendly people, lousy service, great food!"

The famous pizza is deep dish and arrives at your picnic table steaming hot; let it cool a bit to avoid burning your palate. You'll taste a jolt of oregano, and the cheese is so thick it will drip down your chin with every bite. Yummm!

No Name Pub is open seven days a week for lunch and dinner from lunchtime until "whenever."

Big Pine Restaurant & Coffee Shop $
MM 30 Bayside, Big Pine Key
(305) 872-2790

The Big Pine Restaurant, sitting next to Big Pine Key's post office, has served this community since the 1950s. Now new owners have given the restaurant a face lift and enlarged the menu, which still highlights traditional American fare: breakfasts of eggs, pancakes, or cereal; lunches of sandwiches or swell burgers; and classic dinners featuring steak, chicken, or fish. New choices include smoked fish, chicken, or ribs. Stop in and sit awhile, visit with the Big Pine Key regulars—and enjoy the food!

Parrotdise Bar and Grill $
MM 28.5 Bayside, 183 Barry Avenue, Little Torch Key
(305) 872-9989

Situated high above Big Pine Channel on the Gulf, the pavilion-like interior is true Keys atmosphere for a casual feast. A local favorite is the dolphin fingers, lightly broiled and served with fruit chutney. The seared tuna with sesame seeds served with ginger, wasabi, and soy is a real crowd pleaser. The Parrotdise offers beer and wine for their bar service. The bar and grill is open 11:00 A.M. to 10:00 P.M.

Little Palm Island Resort & Spa $$$$
MM 28.5 Oceanside, Little Torch Key
(305) 872-2551
www.littlepalmisland.com

Dining at Little Palm Island is pure magic . . . romance with a capital R. You step into a fairy tale the moment you check in at the mainland substation on Little Torch Key to await one of the Grand Craft launches. The *Truman* or *Miss Margaret* will spirit you to the island. The 15-minute boat ride to Little Palm Island simply heightens the anticipation. As you arrive at the island's dock, you'll spot the Great House nestled amid towering coconut palms. Once a rustic fishing-camp retreat, the Great House now houses Little Palm Island's world-renowned restaurant.

You may dine beneath the stars under a palm tree, at water's edge alongside the beach, on the outside wood deck, in the covered open-air porch, or indoors in air-conditioned comfort. Wherever you choose to partake of Little Palm's gourmet repast, you will be pampered with exquisite food and unobtrusive service. Classic European preparations fused with Floridian, Caribbean, and Pan-Asian flavors are the tantalizing offerings from the chef. Insiders know this translates into the meal of a lifetime.

Little Palm Island accepts a limited number of reservations from the general public for lunch and dinner daily. Sundays a tropical buffet-style brunch from 11:30 A.M. to 2:30 P.M. replaces the luncheon offerings. Call well in advance to secure a booking.

Little Palm offers libations from a full-service bar and maintains an extensive wine list. The launch leaves the Little Torch Key substation for luncheon dining at 11:30 A.M. and 12:30 P.M.; for dinner at 5:30 and 6:30 P.M. You will be seated immediately upon disembarking. You may come to Little Palm Island on your own boat, but be sure to make slip reservations in advance (see our Cruising chapter). Children must be age 16 or older to dine at Little Palm Island.

The Square Grouper Bar and Grill **$$**
MM 22.5 Oceanside, Cudjoe Key
(305) 745-8880

Since its opening in 2003, The Square Grouper Bar and Grill has created a reputation for outstanding Keys cuisine. Located midway between Key West and Big Pine, this establishment sets out to satisfy your hankering for memorable seafood. Conch and lobster fritters with oriental dipping sauce are a crowd pleaser, and be sure to try the seared sesame-encrusted tuna. After 5:00 P.M. the catch of the day is prepared in a different manner nightly. A children's menu is available, and a dessert certain to bring out the fun in dinner for everyone is chocolate fondue with fresh fruit, marshmallows, and pound cake. Open wide and say a-a-a-h!

Mangrove Mama's Restaurant **$$**
MM 20 Bayside, Sugarloaf Key
(305) 745-3030

From US 1 you might miss Mangrove Mama's if you blink, because it looks tiny. What awaits you is a colossal culinary treat inside. This brightly hued Caribbean-style roadhouse offers a rustic old garden in the back where you can nosh or dine amid the banana trees. The old chairs are painted in a barrage of drizzled primary colors; ceramic fish sculptures adorn the walls. Bright tropical tablecloths cover the simple tables, and painted buoys hang from the trees and suspend from the rafters.

You'll find that shrimp and seafood get special treatment—scampi, tempura, stuffed with crabmeat, barbecued on a skewer, or rolled in coconut and deep-fried. Ribs are spicy, and scallops, chicken, steaks, and fresh fish march to a different drummer here, too.

The restaurant serves lunch and dinner daily and brunch on Sunday. Indoor dining is air-conditioned. In addition to a full-service bar, Mangrove Mama's has an extensive wine list. Reservations are suggested for dinner.

Bobalu's Southern Cafe **$**
MM 10 Bayside, Big Coppitt Key
(305) 296-1664

Appearances can be deceiving. Bobalu's may look a little shabby on the outside, but the food and portions are anything but. The cuisine at Bobalu's is home-style, hearty, and southern. The menu includes such entrees as pot roast, pork chops, and authentic fried chicken. Side dishes include sweet potatoes, okra, and turnip greens. The mashed potatoes are the made-from-scratch kind, and desserts such as blackberry cobbler and bread pudding will take you back to the days when families sat down together over Sunday dinner. New to the menu is New Haven–style pizza, a Neapolitan-style pie with a crispier crust.

Even though it's located 10 miles outside Key West, Bobalu's is famous enough to garner intense loyalty in many locals who willingly make the drive. Key West's favorite native son Jimmy Buffett has been known to dine here on occasion; he even mentioned this place in his book *Where Is Joe Merchant?*

If inexpensive, stick-to-your-ribs food is what you're looking for, then look no more—you have come home. Bobalu's is open Tuesday through Saturday for lunch and dinner and for Sunday brunch from 11:00 A.M. to 3:00 P.M. Bobalu's serves beer and wine coolers only, in addition to soft drinks.

KEY WEST

Some have called Key West the most successful melting pot in the United States. And no wonder. The southernmost city has a vibrant spirit that sparkles nowhere more brilliantly than in its cuisine. With restaurants as diverse and creative as a miniature Manhattan, Key West reflects the enduring ethnic traditions of generations past as well as the cutting-edge composition and presentation you would expect to find in major cosmopolitan cities worldwide. Add to all this gustatory wonder a dash of plain old Key West party and pizzazz, and you have a combination that is difficult to beat—anywhere! You can graze the sidewalk cafes of Duval Street or drink and nosh at Key West's panoply of saloons. Sit beneath a canopy of poinciana trees to sample the upscale, up-to-the-minute cuisine or eat your way around the world without ever leaving our 8-square-mile island.

But while it's tough to find a bad meal in Key West, it isn't tough to find an expensive one. When it comes to dining out, our small town leans toward big-city prices. Even a simple hamburger can be costly here. But hey—you're on vacation. Just sit back, relax, and enjoy!

Whatever your pleasure, remember this is still the Keys. Dress code is always Keys casual; just make sure you wear a shirt and shoes with your shorts, and you're dressed for any occasion.

Key West has more than 150 restaurants, some say the most per capita in the United States. Many line the famed Duval Street; others are tucked away down tree-lined alleys or in unassuming residential-looking buildings. We will not highlight the national restaurant chains, most of which are in the newer sections of Key West along North Roosevelt Boulevard, because you are probably already familiar with

i

Real key lime pie is pale yellow in color. If you are served a green key lime pie, it is an impostor.

their offerings. But we will assist you in finding those treasures known to locals—Insiders who keep their collective culinary finger on the pulse of the restaurant scene in Key West.

Our restaurants, like our people, defy easy classification. But we have divided the establishments into four categories to help you choose your dining preference: Key West Classics, those inimitable restaurants that the locals love and that you won't want to miss; Surf and Turf, primarily casually presented, simply prepared red meat and/or seafood; Island Eclectic, upscale gourmet dining of the modern American or new American cuisine genre, created with a tropical flair; and The Melting Pot, a potpourri of diverse ethnic offerings that spirit your taste buds to the far corners of the globe—The Americas, South of the Border, The Continent, The Far East, and The Islands. Restaurants are listed in alphabetical order in each category.

You will find that reservation policies vary in Key West. The more upscale the restaurant, the more likely you will need a reservation, especially in high season. If it's something you need to consider, we mention the restaurant's reservation policy in its description.

Unlike many restaurants in the rest of the Keys, most of those in Key West have full-service bars. We will highlight the ones that serve beer and wine only. On-site parking is a rarity among our recommended restaurants, most of which are in Old Town, where land is at a premium. In most cases you will need to park curbside on one of Key West's side streets or in a municipal or private lot (see our Getting Here, Getting Around chapter).

Unless stated otherwise, you may assume that restaurants are air-conditioned. Major credit cards and traveler's checks are widely accepted, but personal checks

> ***Conch fritters, made from imported conch (harvesting this shellfish in our waters is not permitted), are seasoned with garlic and spices and then deep-fried. They do not resemble true southern fritters you may have encountered elsewhere.***

are not. And there is no restriction as to children dining in most establishments. Because restaurants in Key West's Old Town are often situated in 19th-century frame buildings that were formerly houses, accessibility for the physically challenged varies greatly. Sometimes steps must be negotiated, some bathrooms may be too tiny to accommodate a wheelchair, and separate nonsmoking sections may not always be available. If any of these anomalies is of particular concern to you, be sure to call the establishment to see exactly what arrangements might be made to fit your needs.

Our price code mirrors that of the rest of the Florida Keys and is based upon dinner for two, without starters, dessert, alcoholic beverages, tax, or tip.

PRICE-CODE KEY

$	**Less than $25**
$$	**$25 to $40**
$$$	**$41 to $60**
$$$$	**More than $60**

Key West Classics

A&B Lobster House **$$**
700 Front Street
(305) 294-5880

A&B Lobster House, named for its original owners Alonzo and Berlin, is considered a Key West institution among seafood connoisseurs. Situated beside the water at the foot of Front Street, A&B offers a sumptuous selection of seafood as well as terrific views of the yachts moored at the Key West Historic Seaport.

In addition to Maine and Florida lobster, the classic menu includes traditional oyster and clam stews as well as pan roasts prepared by slow-roasting oysters, clams, mussels, and lobsters, then adding them to a broth of fresh herbs and vegetables with a touch of cream and sherry. Steaks and pasta dishes are also available.

Dine inside or outside; in either case, reservations are suggested. After dinner, retire to Berlin's Bar to sample the fine selection of cigars and after-dinner drinks.

A&B Lobster House is open daily from 6:00 P.M.; Berlin's opens at 5:30 P.M. for predinner cocktails.

Alonzo's Oyster Bar **$-$$**
700 Front Street (downstairs)
(305) 294-5880

If you like oysters, Alonzo's is the place to go. You can order them up raw, on the half shell, baked, or batter dipped and fried. This casual seaside eatery, situated downstairs from A&B Lobster House, also serves freshly shucked clams, lobster, conch, mussels, and a variety of dishes made with the native shrimp known as "Key West pinks." If you're in the mood for a seafood soup besides chowder, try a bowl of the white clam chili. It's plenty filling but not as rich as its creamier cousin.

Alonzo's is open daily from 11:00 A.M. to 11:00 P.M. There's plenty of indoor and outdoor seating; reservations are not necessary. Free parking is available.

Blue Heaven **$$**
729 Thomas Street
(305) 296-8666
www.blueheavenkw.com

Blue Heaven—at various times a bordello, a pool hall, a railroad water tower, a cockfighting arena, a boxing ring (frequented by Papa Hemingway himself), an ice-cream parlor—is now a popular restaurant at the corner of Petronia and Thomas Streets. This throwback to the hippie era offers Caribbean and vegetarian cuisine in an unhampered island setting. Situated in historic Bahama Village, Blue Heaven's ambience is as legendary as its cuisine.

Roosters, hens, and chicks strut all around the picnic tables that fill Blue Heaven's backyard; so do the resident kitties. Jimmy Buffett's 1995 song "Blue Heaven Rendezvous" was inspired by this diamond in the rough.

Indeed, the magic is alive and well at Blue Heaven, where patrons enjoy specialties such as jerk chicken, Caribbean shrimp, and locally caught seafood entrees. A dessert must-have is Banana Heaven, served with homemade vanilla ice cream. Sunday brunch at Blue Heaven, with diverse preparations of eggs, waffles, and pancakes—including the famous beer-batter and pecan varieties—draws crowds that line themselves up 'round the corner. Shrimp and grits are a highlight of brunch.

This is a place where kids are actually encouraged to run around and play; there's even a rope for them to swing on.

Blue Heaven has a full bar and serves liquor, wine, and beer. Blue Heaven serves breakfast with roosters, lunch under the shade, and dinner under the stars daily. Reservations are accepted for parties of 10 or more and besides the fowl, they have live entertainment.

BO's Fish Wagon **$**
801 Caroline Street
(305) 294-9272

Almost any restaurant in Key West can make you a fish sandwich, but no one can make you a fish sandwich like Buddy Owen. He starts with Cuban bread, then piles the fresh fish and grilled onions so high, we dare you to try to get your mouth around it.

Belly up to the counter and place your order for a fish sandwich grilled (yellowtail) or fried (grouper); add sides like fries or onion rings only if you're really hungry. The portions here are huge. The menu also features squid rings (what every other restaurant in town politely calls calamari), fish-and-chips, the ubiquitous conch fritters, burgers, and hot dogs. To quench your thirst, select from bottle or draft beer, wine by the glass (plastic, that is), sodas, or key limeade.

While you're waiting for your sandwich to be delivered to your table, take a look around. The decor here can only be called Key West eclectic—fishing nets, lobster traps, a muffler shop sign, even an old pickup truck. BO's is closed on Sunday.

Camille's Restaurant **$-$$**
1202 Simonton Street
(305) 296-4811
www.camilleskeywest.com

Their motto is "Exotic family cooking with no boundaries," and Camille's means it. The reasonably priced menu at this eclectic local favorite features a wide array of gourmet breakfast, lunch, and dinner specials; it changes daily and nightly. Stone-crab claw-meat cakes are grilled and served with spiced rum-mango sauce. A real crowd pleaser is Paradise Pasta—Key West pink shrimp, lobster, asparagus, and red and yellow peppers in a garlic Alfredo sauce.

Weekend breakfast at Camille's is a particular treat, offering pecan waffles, an orgy of eggs Benedict, and eggs galore or eggs whatever. And for lunch, the hand-pulled chicken salad sandwich is always a delicious choice.

Liquor and wine are offered, and the ambience is so friendly that tourists are treated like locals. Happy hour with "happy prices" is a favorite with Camille's patrons from 4:00 to 6:00 P.M. daily. Expect a wait—especially for breakfast. Camille's is open daily for breakfast, lunch, dinner, and happy hour. Reservations are a good idea.

---

i

If you like to choose a restaurant by its bill of fare, grab a copy of* The Menu. *This quarterly restaurant guide, published by the* Key West Citizen, *features menus from more than 60 Key West eateries. You'll find free copies at hotels, attractions, grocery stores, and newsstands all around Key West. You can also visit their Web site: www.keywest.com/themenu.

The Deli Restaurant **$**
531 Truman Avenue
(305) 294-1464

Enter through the double portals of the Deli Restaurant, each of which sports a giant seahorse-shaped window, and you will be welcomed home.

This, the oldest family-run restaurant in Key West, has been greeting locals with good cheer and affordable home-style cookin' since 1950. Established by John and Joan Bernreuter as a corner delicatessen where Aunt Mamie and John's grandmother, Poppy, made the salads, the Deli Restaurant today serves up generations of vintage Conch dishes under the supervision of Bobby Bernreuter. His daughter Patty is in charge of baking the pies and keeping track of the orders and paperwork.

Try roast turkey (the real thing) or fried chicken, franks and beans, or sugar-cured ham, roast beef, or pork. You'll find Key West shrimp or yellowtail grilled or fried and conch chowder made from the secret family recipe. Allow some room for dessert, because Toll House Cookie Pie, Apple Crumb Pie, or Sweet Potato Pie are sure to bring on a wave of nostalgia.

The Deli Restaurant is open daily from 7:30 A.M. to 10:00 P.M. Beer and wine are available. The Deli Restaurant does not take reservations.

Harpoon Harry's **$**
832 Caroline Street
(305) 294-8744

Harpooned and hanging from the ceilings of this hometown-style diner is everything—including the kitchen sink. Across from Key West Historic Seaport, on the site of what was a small hospital-turned-barbershop, Harpoon Harry's combines Tiffany light fixtures with old roller skates, sleds, and carousel horses. Framed advertisements recall the days of Lucky Strike cigarettes, Mennen Toilet Powder, knee-highs, and antique cars. The restaurant's movie-star wall boasts Elvis, Sophia, and Lucy and Desi. A case contains a collection of Mickey Mouse glasses, which are probably worth a fortune. It is, in fact, this original decor that drew The Travel Channel to Harpoon Harry's in 1995. Restaurateur Ronald Heck is the creative genius responsible for it. The owner of Michigan's Lighthouse Inn, Heck informed his Midwestern employees and patrons of the interior design plans he had for his new establishment, and they came bearing all sorts of amusements.

The luncheon menu at Harpoon Harry's is much less eccentric than the decor: meat loaf or roast turkey with mashed potatoes, breaded veal cutlets, homemade chicken potpie, and melt-in-your-mouth roast pork chops with gravy. Breakfast is highlighted by Harry's Special: eggs, sausage, bacon, ham, and toast and jelly served with home fries or grits.

Two counters, booths, and tables are available daily for breakfast and lunch. Reservations are not accepted.

Hog's Breath Saloon **$**
400 Front Street
(305) 292-2032
www.hogsbreath.com

The name of this establishment may not be appealing, but its fish sandwiches—blackened or grilled with lemon—are. They're served up by the ton. Built to resemble an authentic surfer bar, Hog's Breath features lots of wood, including an African mahogany bar at which some guests are fortunate enough to land a seat. Mounted fish and surfboards hang from the walls, along with active water-related photographs. Not surprisingly, owner Jerry Dorminy of Alabama is a water-sports enthusiast. He originally established a Hog's Breath Saloon in Fort Walton Beach, Florida, in 1976, as a place where he and his friends could retreat after a day of fishing and sailing.

In 1988 Dorminy opened Hog's Breath Key West. Here, nautical charts of Caribbean waters are lacquered onto wood tables, and patrons dine indoors or outside on a brick patio from which large trees sprout. In addition to the fish sandwich, Hog's Breath's smoked-fish dolphin dip and raw bar with oysters, shrimp, and stone crabs (in season) are extremely popular.

The restaurant's full-service bar features the medium-bodied Hog's Breath beer, brewed in the Midwest. In case you were wondering, the name of the joint comes from an old saying of Dorminy's grandmother, that "hog's breath is better than no breath at all."

The restaurant is open for lunch and dinner, and live bands play folk rock, rock, blues, and jazz throughout the day and evening. Reservations are not accepted.

Jimmy Buffett's Margaritaville Cafe $
500 Duval Street
(305) 292-1435
www.margaritaville.com/keywest

Lunch really could last forever at Jimmy Buffett's Margaritaville Cafe, and patrons who steer here quite often remain throughout much of the day, regardless of whether or not they have amended their carnivorous habits. Margaritas are de rigueur, but bartenders also serve up the performer's personal favorite: a Cajun martini infusion of Smirnoff vodka and potent jalapeño and Scotch bonnet peppers. "Parrothead" and other island music plays in the background, and decorations include oversize props from stage settings of Buffett tours, including stuffed iguanas from "Off to See the Lizard," a mock-up version of his seaplane, a flying goose, and a big warm bun and a huge hunk of meat. The fixin's—lettuce and tomato, Heinz 57, and french-fried potatoes—are not forgotten. The casual and friendly Margaritaville, Buffett feels, combines his great love for music and food, both of which satisfy the soul.

Specialties of the house include Cheeseburgers in Paradise, blackened hot dogs, Delta catfish Reuben, and fried Key West shrimp baskets.

Margaritaville is open for lunch and dinner daily. Live music is offered nightly, beginning at 10:30 P.M. Reservations are not accepted, but those on the waiting list may shop for souvenirs in Buffett's adjacent store.

The restaurants in Key West are as eclectic as the culture. Even for an Insider, choosing a restaurant is difficult, but if you go to www.keywestmenu.com, it will help you narrow down the delectable temptations!

Kelly's Caribbean Bar, Grill & Brewery $$
301 Whitehead Street
(305) 293-8484
www.kellyskeywest.com

Named after actress Kelly McGillis, this Caribbean restaurant is on the site of the original Pan American World Airways offices. In 1927 Pan Am launched its first international air service from Key West, when mail was flown from the island's Meacham Field to Havana. The following year Pan Am began providing passenger service to Havana.

A display of early photographs and memorabilia of Pan Am service from Key West line the elegant violet-and-blue library room on the first floor. Clever decorating details fit the theme. When you dine in the front room of the first floor, you settle your tail feathers into old airplane seats, some of which offer views of a triangular bar designed to resemble the wing of a plane. Ceiling fans in the first-floor lounge (known as the Crash Room Bar) are miniature reproductions of an airplane motor.

Outdoor dining is available on a stone patio with gardens. On the second floor Kelly's Clipper Club Lounge invites patrons to relax in an open-air gazebo-style setting.

Among the house specialties here are Caribbean Apple Chicken—smothered in Kelly's special apple glaze—and Camarones Curaçao—grilled shrimp first marinated in coconut milk, lime juice, ginger, and teriyaki.

Kelly's Caribbean also is home to the Southernmost Brewery, which whips up an all-natural selection including Key West

Golden Ale, Havana Red Ale, Southern Clipper Wheat Beer, and Black Bart's Root Beer.

The restaurant is open for lunch and dinner seven days a week. Reservations are accepted for parties of more than six. Key West hotel guests receive preferred seating.

McGillis and Fred Tillman have opened another restaurant in Key West: On the beach, Duval Beach Club, 1405 Duval Street, (305) 295-6550, offers drinks and dining, inside and out. You can even reserve your own beach chair here.

Lobo's Grill **$**
5 Key Lime Square
(305) 296-5303

Lobo's is where locals love to lunch. The menu includes burgers, nachos, quesadillas, and salads. But the real standouts are the roll-up sandwiches—a mix of meats, cheeses, fresh veggies, and spreads tucked tightly, then rolled, in a giant flour tortilla. Choose from such selections as the Delhi Chicken—curried chicken salad, Swiss cheese, sprouts, mango chutney, avocado, lettuce, and pineapple; or Porky's Nightmare—honey-baked ham, roast pork, bacon, cheddar, Swiss, lettuce, tomato, onions, and honey mustard.

You can eat in or take out; call ahead for quick pickup or free delivery in Old Town. Lobo's is open from 11:00 A.M. to 6:00 P.M. Monday through Saturday, and on Sunday in season. No credit cards.

Paradise Cafe **$**
1000 Eaton Street
(305) 296-5001

The sign outside reads HOME OF THE ISLAND LEGEND MONSTER SANDWICH. Indeed. It would be tough to find a bigger, better sandwich anywhere in Key West. Choose from 15 lunchtime varieties—everything from ham and cheese, sliced turkey, and hot Italian beef to chicken salad, tuna salad, and BBQ pork—all made to order on Cuban bread with the fixins you select. Paradise Cafe also serves up breakfast sandwiches—hearty combinations of egg, cheese, ham, and/or steak, on Cuban bread, of course.

Eat in, take out, or phone for delivery. Paradise Cafe is open Monday through Friday from 6:00 A.M. to 4:00 P.M. and on Saturday from 6:30 A.M. to 2:00 P.M. No credit cards.

Pepe's Cafe & Steak House **$$**
806 Caroline Street
(305) 294-7192

Billed as the "Eldest Eating House in the Florida Keys, established 1909," Pepe's is as beloved to Conchs and Key Westers as the Mallory Square sunset celebration. In the old commercial waterfront area of Old Town, Pepe's touts its Apalachicola Bay oysters, when available, as among its specialties: raw, baked, Florentine, Mexican, or Rudi style. But you will find a bit of the hoof available at Pepe's as well: New York strip steaks at 8, 12, and 15 ounces, filet mignon, pork chops, even barbecue. And Pepe's burgers sound as intriguing as they taste: White Collar Burger, Blue Collar Burger, Slit Ray Burger, and Patty Melt. Be sure to try a margarita here (the lime juice is squeezed fresh) and, for dessert, the brownie pie, served warm with ice cream—ask for Cuban coffee flavor instead of vanilla. Mmmmm! Pepe's serves early (mainly breakfast, 6:30 A.M. to noon), late (primarily dinner, after 4:30 P.M. to closing), and in between, predominantly oysters, soups, and sandwiches.

One thing is for certain: No matter when you visit Pepe's, you will not leave hungry. The restaurant is open every day. Patio dining is also available. Reservations are not accepted.

Turtle Kraals Waterfront Seafood Grill and Bar **$-$$**
231 Margaret Street
(305) 294-2640
www.turtlekraals.com

Offering Southwestern food with a definite seafood influence, Turtle Kraals occupies the site of a former turtle cannery, hence the name—which essentially means "turtle pen." Turtle Kraals has an immense affection for wildlife, which is evidenced by the large saltwater enclosure behind the restaurant, where many kinds of injured sea life recover. Lobster Chili Rellenos—lobster-stuffed poblano peppers, crispy fried, served with tomatillo sauce, sour cream, yellow rice, and black beans, and grilled Churrasco steak with mojo served with grilled onions, roasted corn flan, and fried plantains are two favorite dishes. Turtle Kraals offers a huge selection of beer, and a full bar is available as well. Turtle Kraals is open daily for lunch and dinner.

Believe it or not, in a town like Key West that rocks until well into the wee hours, late-night dining is hard to come by. With few exceptions, most restaurants do not serve past 11:00 P.M. As a general rule: Eat early, party late.

Surf and Turf

Captain Run Aground Harvey's Floating Pub and Grub **$**
Garrison Bight Marina/Charter Boat Row/US 1
City Marina, Key West
(305) 296-9907

Captain Run Aground tells it like it is. Every table is *on* the water because you are *on* the water, literally. This locals' hangout is perched on the top deck of a boat anchored in the Garrison Bight Marina. Now, this is true Keys atmosphere and this is a true floating restaurant. Come to eat, or just sit awhile and have a few drinks. The dress is casual, all the better to enjoy good seafood, good service, and a million-dollar view. You can also purchase fresh seafood to prepare at home. They will even pack your catch after a day of fishing.

Commodore Waterfront Steakhouse **$$$**
700 Front Street at Key West Historic Seaport
(305) 294-9191

Tables covered in white linen are surrounded by mahogany paneling, brick walls, and lush greenery. Ceiling fans gently whirl and window walls look out onto the charming harbor of Key West Historic Seaport. The Commodore exudes the elegance of a fine ship, and the establishment offers some top-notch meat and seafood to match the refined ambience.

Signature dishes abound. Oysters Commodore are lightly breaded, flash-fried, and topped with remoulade. The New York Steak Roquefort is a prime New York sirloin strip topped with melted Roquefort cheese. The broiled veal chop is thick and served in its own juices. Steamed mussels are lightly steamed in white wine, garlic, and ginger.

Commodore Waterfront Steakhouse serves dinner nightly. Free parking is available at A&B Marina.

Conch Republic Seafood Company **$$**
631 Greene Street
(305) 294-4403
www.conchrepublicseafood.com

From the look of this place—with its old wooden railings, weathered tin roof, and lazy, wobbly ceiling fans—you'd swear it had been in Key West for decades. Not so. The Conch Republic Seafood Company opened for business in the newly renovated Key West Historic Seaport in 1999.

As you've no doubt surmised, the menu here is heavy on seafood. Entrees include grilled or fried Key West pinks (shrimp), grilled tuna steak, Bahamian-style cracked conch, and pan-seared grouper fillet. For starters, try a bowl of callaloo soup—a blend of island greens and crabmeat in a spicy lobster stock.

The full-service, 80-seat bar boasts one of the best rum selections around—more than 80 varieties are available, along with 25 kinds of beer. The full menu is available daily from noon until 11:00 P.M. Live music is offered nightly, and happy hour is from 4:00 to 7:00 P.M. daily.

Reservations are not necessary, and you need not ask for a waterfront table. Every seat has an open-air view of the harbor action. Check out the 80-foot aquarium stocked with local seafood that is the centerpiece of the restaurant, and don't miss the 1,200-pound antique still that stands behind the bar in honor of the rumrunners of yesteryear.

Before the era of Styrofoam and paper cups, the Key West version of coffee "to go" was an empty, clean, evaporated milk can with the lid removed and your favorite Cuban coffee inside. To hold the heat of the beverage, a slice of toasted Cuban bread was placed on top!

Crabby Dicks' Seafood Restaurant and Lounge $-$$
712 Duval Street (upstairs)
(305) 294-7229
www.crabbydickskeywest.com

Note the apostrophe placement in the name of this restaurant—it refers to the two owners, Dick Cami and Richard First. Though they were newcomers to Key West when they opened this establishment in 1996, they are not newcomers to the restaurant business. Cami was owner of the famed Peppermint Lounge in New York City.

The specialty here is—you guessed it—seafood. The menu boasts everything from crab legs to catfish to freshly shucked oysters and clams. The prices are reasonable, the sauces are made from scratch, and the portions are plentiful.

In addition to some of the freshest seafood on the island, Crabby Dicks' has a couple of other things going for it, too. You get a great view from the second-story veranda overlooking the 700 block of Duval Street, and there is ample free parking for diners behind the restaurant.

Crabby Dicks' is open daily from 11:30 A.M. to 10:00 P.M. The daily happy hour is from 4:00 to 7:00 P.M.

Duffy's Steak & Lobster House $$
Corner of Simonton Street and Truman Avenue
(305) 296-4900

The beginnings of this structure date from the late 1890s, but it wasn't until 1948 that the building actually became Duffy's Tavern. Today the interior has been updated with deep green paint and the original glass block set off by neon lighting. Bulky wood booths, a wood floor, and high ceilings lend a rustic atmosphere. The entertainment is found through Duffy's abundant windows, for the restaurant proves ideal for people-watching.

Owned by Timothy Ryan, proprietor of Pisces (see separate restaurant listing in this chapter) next door, Duffy's specializes in prime rib, steaks, and lobster. All dishes are simply prepared and served with a salad, freshly baked bread, and a choice of potato. Daily specials, such as Angel-hair Pasta with Gulf Shrimp in a brochette or Chicken San Bernardino, a breaded breast of chicken sautéed and then covered in eggplant and mozzarella in a tomato-basil sauce, satisfy more intricate taste buds.

Lunch and dinner are served here daily. Reservations are not accepted.

Half Shell Raw Bar $$
231 Margaret Street
(305) 294-7496
www.halfshellrawbar.com

The Half Shell Raw Bar is inches from the water and beyond casual. When the owners opened this seafood establishment in 1980, they dotted the all-wood walls with amusing license plates.

Always consistent at Half Shell Raw Bar is its fresh seafood served on the casual, open-air waterfront. Located in Land's End Village at the Key West Historic Seaport, the restaurant is known for local seafood. The center of the action is Shucker's station, where mountains of oysters, clams, shrimp, and stone crabs are simply prepared, reasonably priced, and served with plastic utensils on paper plates at picnic tables. Half Shell carries stone crabs in season and Maine lobster. Its full bar offers beer, wine, and frozen drinks.

Patrons may opt for outdoor dining on either a waterfront deck or a patio. Reservations are accepted for parties of more than six. Half Shell Raw Bar is open daily for lunch and dinner. Off-street parking is abundant.

Hurricane Joe's Bar and Grill **$$**
MM 4.5 Oceanside, Stock Island
(305) 294-0200

Situated upon pilings overlooking Cowkey Channel, Hurricane Joe's is one of the best restaurants in the Keys. The location may look informal because it is inside the Hurricane Hole Marina compound, but what awaits the diner is one fine restaurant. The atmosphere and dress code is Keys comfortable. The ample tables and room size of Hurricane Joe's gives it an airy feel even when the place is packed with folks. The menu is varied enough that it will please everyone's palate. The appetizers range from imperial stuffed clams, to scallop St. Jacques, to conch fritters. The catch of the day is served six different ways, and the entrees are very creative—scallops wrapped in bacon, lobster ravioli, crawfish étouffée. All are served with potato casserole, cole slaw, Caesar salad, or Hurricane Joe's house salad. The other interesting items they offer are "wraps"—mounds of perfectly seasoned seafood wrapped in a gourmet tortilla, with lettuce and remoulade sauce. Yum yummy! Don't forget the homemade desserts that are delivered to the restaurant each day. Mango monsoon cheesecake is delectable, as is the muddy water apple pie. Unhook your belt buckle at least two notches before you sit down to partake of your delightful meal.

Michaels **$$$**
532 Margaret Street
(305) 295-1300
www.michaelskeywest.com

Tucked away in a quiet Old Town neighborhood several blocks off Duval, this casual yet elegant little gem of a restaurant would be easy to miss, but we urge you not to. Since January 1997, owners Melanie and Michael Wilson have been serving up some of the best food on the island.

Michael, the former corporate chef for the Chicago-based Morton's Steakhouses, knows how to cook a piece of beef. His prime beef is flown in fresh via FedEx from Allen Brothers in Chicago and his Filet al Forno, rubbed with roasted garlic and Roquefort, has garnered rave reviews and numerous awards. The menu also includes seafood and pasta specialties; for theatergoers, a specially priced, two-course dinner is offered nightly. And a good selection of fondues is available in the Garden Bar. No matter which entree you select, be sure to save room for dessert. The Chocolate Volcano is a house specialty—it erupts at the touch of your fork!

Martini drinkers will appreciate the wide selection of vodkas and olives—they're stuffed with everything from the traditional pimientos to blue cheese, anchovies, and prosciutto. And if martinis aren't your forte, there are plenty of other liquors to choose from as well as a wide selection of fine wines.

Michaels is open nightly from 5:30 P.M. Reservations are recommended for both indoor and outdoor seating.

Prime 951 **$$$**
951 Caroline Street, Key West
(305) 296-4000
www.MontysStoneCrab.com

What a delightful surprise to enter the "Keys swank" atmosphere of Prime 951. The decor is nothing like the Technicolor offerings of other bars and restaurants in the Keys. What you notice first is the cool sensation of dark mahogany and richly upholstered booths. The tables are covered with crisp white linen cloths and tall drinking vessels. The staff is dressed all in black and the hushed atmosphere takes everyone down about two notches. Even though Prime 951 has a limited menu, each and every selection is superb. They offer a local seafood special prepared Keys style, and their beef steak selections are outstanding.

Turtle Kraals Museum

In 1849 Armand Granday opened the Key West Turtle Cannery on the Key West docks and successfully operated it until 1890. The sea turtles were kept in *kraals,* or water corrals, until they went to the cannery, where they were decapitated and cut into steaks or used in soup. The turtle cannery operated under a succession of owners until the 1970s, when a diminished population of green turtles led to the 1973 Endangered Species Act, which placed them under federal protection. In 1999, charter-fishing captain Tina Brown founded the nonprofit Turtle Kraals Museum adjacent to Turtle Kraals Waterfront Seafood Grill (see listing in this chapter), on the site of the original cannery, as a means of educating the public about sea turtles. This free museum offers exhibits and photographic displays depicting the history of the industry and the plight of Florida's sea turtles—hawksbill, Kemp's ridley, loggerhead, green, and leatherback—all of which are still endangered. For more information, contact Turtle Kraals Museum, 200 Margaret Street, Key West, (305) 294-0209.

One of the house specialties is home-fried potatoes that are mashed and then fried. A feat in itself! Desserts are homemade key lime pie with a nut-based piecrust and a to-die-for chocolate cake that is worth the calories. Enjoy the food and the loveliness of this elegant restaurant.

Rusty Anchor Restaurant $$
MM 5 Oceanside, 5510 Third Avenue, Stock Island
(305) 296-2893
www.rustyanchorseafood.com

Weigh anchor for a satisfying seafood meal at the Rusty Anchor, a casual seafood haven for the piscatorially inclined. You won't find fresher fish and seafood anywhere, for in the back of the Rusty Anchor is a commercial seafood market that supplies many of Key West's restaurants. The fish, lobsters, shrimp, and stone-crab claws are delivered right from the boat (see our Seafood Markets and Specialty Foods chapter). The restaurant exudes a casual nautical atmosphere punctuated by rope-edged tables, wood buoys, nautical art prints, and photographs of the fishing fleets of old Key West. A 400-plus-pound marlin is mounted at one end of the dining room, and a couple of 15-pound lobsters grace the other walls.

Lunch and dinner are simply prepared. The saltwater fish is caught daily in the Key West area and generally is served broiled or fried. Try the teriyaki-grilled tuna sandwich on Cuban bread if it is offered as a special. You can nosh on conch fritters or slurp chowder, peel steamed shrimp, or nibble a salad. If seafood is not your favorite, Rusty Anchor also serves burgers, steaks, and ribs. Food is presented picnic style on plastic plates, drinks in plastic cups, and beer out of the can.

Open Monday through Saturday, the Rusty Anchor does not require reservations. It's a great place to bring the kids.

Seven Fish $$
632 Olivia Street
(305) 296-2777
www.7fish.com

Don't be fooled by the name; this is a bistro you'll love to call your own. Although the seafood here is excellent, this restaurant, which is located at the corner of Olivia and Elizabeth Streets, has much more to recommend it. In addition to the freshest fish, the menu includes grilled chicken, meat loaf with mashed potatoes, and a New York strip steak cooked the way you like it. Salads—three-cheese Caesar, mixed greens with balsamic vinegar, or roasted red pepper and goat cheese—are available in two sizes. And for an additional charge, you can add grilled chicken or a crab cake to your greens if you like.

The environment at Seven Fish is cozy and friendly, the food flavorful and inexpensive. On the downside, Seven Fish is small—go early or you may have to wait—and the tables are quite close together. The restaurant is open nightly 6:00 to 10:00 P.M. except Tuesday. That's when the staff goes fishing. Reservations are recommended.

Island Eclectic

Alice's at La Te Da **$$$**
1125 Duval Street
(305) 296-6706, ext. 39
www.lateda.com/Alices

Eclectic means "selected from various doctrines, methods, and styles," and Alice's rightly bills itself as "eclectic cuisine" with a menu you won't find anywhere else.

Alice's creations—which chef Alice Weingarten has dubbed "Fusion-Confusion"—have earned her awards . . . and rightfully so. Her breakfast menu features the likes of a magic mushroom and goat cheese omelet created from shiitake and porcini mushrooms and Sonoma County goat cheese. Luncheon choices include a Monte Cristo sandwich that is beyond even the heartiest appetite. Dinner offerings range from Macadamia-coconut-crusted Shrimp with honey wasabi to Cuban-style marinated ostrich with black beans, corn avocado salsa, and coconut rice. And to cap it off, Alice makes a Cappuccino Bread Pudding with Russian Chantilly Cream that is beyond delicious.

Relocated from the corner of Duval and Amelia Streets to La Te Da, Alice's is open daily for breakfast and dinner. Lunch is served from Tuesday through Sunday. Reservations are strongly recommended.

Bagatelle **$$-$$$**
115 Duval Street
(305) 296-6609
www.bagatelle-keywest.com

Incongruous amid the tourist trappings of lower Duval, Bagatelle sits reservedly amid the fray. Situated on two floors of a gracious old Key West home, Bagatelle serves fresh local ingredients with island inventiveness. Try the Pecan Dolphin or the Bahamian Cracked Conch Steak, if offered, for something different. Or enjoy avocado fan salad or a seafood puff pastry stuffed with the catch of the day.

Wraparound balconies on both levels afford outdoor dining, or you may choose to dine indoors where the decor favors that of a first-rate art gallery. Bagatelle is a premier spot from which to view the Fantasy Fest Parade (see the Annual Events chapter). Reservations for the evening of Fantasy Fest should be made well in advance of the event, even up to a year.

Bagatelle serves lunch and dinner daily. Reservations are suggested for dinner in all seasons at this popular restaurant, but at least a day in advance in high season.

Big John's Pizza **$**
1103 Kmart Shopping Center
(305) 293-9576

610 Greene Street
(305) 293-0377
www.bigjohnspizzakw.com

If you don't feel like going out to a full-fledged restaurant, Big John's Pizza is an eatery located in a New Town shopping center where all the locals go to partake of the best pizza this side of Rome. Sure, there are the usual pizza-chain operations here, but this place is "where the locals know it's good." The couple who owns Big John's takes great pride not only in their food but also in their friendly and cheerful help. The establishment is bright and pristine, and the booths remind you of a set on *Happy Days.* The menu offers such fab choices as their homemade garlic knots, buffalo chicken salad, 20-inch pizzas, calzones, strombolis, and their world-class-famous "Stuffed John," a double-crusted pizza stuffed with more ingredients than is allowed! Big John's is open daily for lunch and dinner and offers free delivery anywhere in the city limits of Key West. A minimum order amount is needed beyond Mile Marker 2.

Café Marquesa **$$$$**
600 Fleming Street
(305) 292-1919, (800) 869-4631
www.cafemarquesa.com
Golden walls covered with paintings, pastel tile floors, large mirrors, and a panoramic country-kitchen mural set the scene for one of the finest dining encounters in Key West. Long a front-runner in the panoply of establishments plying to please your palate, Café Marquesa, situated in the historic Marquesa Hotel, remains a consistent winner.

Gracing the white linen tablecloths is an eclectic assortment of innovative dishes. Specialties of the house have included Peppercorn Dusted Seared Yellowfin Tuna, Feta and Pine Nut Encrusted Rack of Lamb, and Grilled, Marinated Key West Shrimp.

Café Marquesa, reminiscent of a European brasserie, oozes style. Reservations are highly recommended in all seasons. Café Marquesa serves dinner nightly.

Hot Tin Roof **$$$**
Zero Duval Street at Ocean Key Resort
(305) 296-7701, (800) 328-9815
www.oceankey.com
The Hot Tin Roof name comes from Tennessee Williams's (a past resident of Key West) most famous play, *Cat on a Hot Tin Roof.* The dining room and outdoor deck enjoy panoramic views of Key West Harbor and its famed sunset. The chef has combined elements of South American, Asian, and French cuisine in an interpretation of flavors and attitudes of Key West he calls "Conch-fusion." Prime examples of this gustatory philosophy include Seafood Paella with Lobster, and an ahi tuna ceviche appetizer. The Stage Door Lounge serves themed signature cocktails and offers live jazz music some evenings as well. Hot Tin Roof is open for dinner nightly.

Latitudes Beach Cafe **$$$**
Sunset Key
(305) 292-4313
www.keywest.com/themenu/latitudes
When you think of dining seaside somewhere on a secluded island, this is the kind of place that comes to mind. Just five minutes across the water from the hustle and bustle of Mallory Square, Latitudes might just as well be half a world away. It is that peaceful, that serene. And as near as we can tell, still largely undiscovered. Granted, it takes some planning to get here. You have to make a reservation, and you have to board a boat. But if what you seek is a quiet evening escape from the craziness of Key West, dinner at Latitudes on Sunset Key is well worth the effort.

The cuisine here could best be described as eclectic. Dinner entrees include the likes of Pan-seared Chilean Sea Bass, Coconut-and-macadamia-encrusted Grouper, Key Lime Chicken Piccata, and Beef Tenderloin with Gorgonzola-scallion butter and a marinated portobello mushroom. A full bar offers exotic frozen island drinks as well as beer and wine.

Sunset Key is a private island, half of which is devoted to guest cottages, the other to pricey waterfront homes (see the Accommodations chapter and Vacation Rentals and Real Estate chapter for additional information). Island access is thus largely limited to residents. Launches for Sunset Key leave regularly throughout the day from the pier at the Westin Key West Resort and Marina at 245 Front Street. If you are not living or staying on the island, you must make a reservation for your meal at Latitudes with the Westin concierge to secure a boarding pass.

Latitudes is open daily for breakfast, lunch, and dinner.

Louie's Backyard **$$$$**
700 Waddell Avenue
(305) 294-1061
www.louiesbackyard.com

An enduring favorite among locals and visitors alike, Louie's Backyard combines island manor house ambience with cutting-edge cuisine. And though the exquisitely prepared, complex combination of ingredients that marks Louie's is often imitated elsewhere in Key West, this restaurant continues to shine. A sweeping veranda, for outdoor dining, overlooks Louie's "backyard," which is actually a prime piece of Atlantic oceanfront property. In the '70s this spot was a favorite with next-door-neighbor Jimmy Buffett, who often played for his supper.

Dinner entrees span the globe, with fresh local seafood garnering center stage. An equally innovative cuisine is offered on the lunch menu for nearly half the price of evening dining. Try lunch offerings such as Bahamian conch chowder with bird-pepper hot sauce, spicy fried chicken salad with a citrus-sesame-peanut dressing, or a fish and shellfish pan stew with bacon, mushrooms, and cheddar grits. Sample dinner offerings include sautéed Key West shrimp with bacon, mushrooms, and stone-ground grits or sautéed grouper with Asian vegetables, or grilled veal chop with stewed sweet onions and mustard seeds. Top off lunch or dinner with one of Louie's truly decadent desserts.

Louie's Backyard serves lunch and dinner daily. Reservations are recommended in all seasons but especially in winter and on weekends. The Afterdeck outdoor oceanside bar is open all day and into the wee hours (see our Nightlife chapter).

Mangoes **$$**
700 Duval Street
(305) 292-4606
www.mangoeskeywest.com

Patrons enjoy one of the best views of

If your dream dinner is a sunset lobster feast with your own personal chef aboard a 43-foot trimaran, hop aboard **Dreamchaser,** ***berthed at Key West Historic Seaport marina, for a four-course gourmet dinner topped off with one of our special Key West sunsets. You can make reservations by calling (305) 292-8667 or logging on to www.dreamchaser charters.com.***

Duval Street at Mangoes, where fresh Caribbean-style seafood is served in an outdoor, corner cafe setting of white-umbrella-covered tables. Indoor dining is equally sophisticated, with candlelight and fresh flowers on every table and original artwork lining the walls.

Open daily for lunch, dinner, and late-night pizza (15 varieties cooked in a wood-fired oven), Mangoes' specialties include pan-seared yellowtail snapper with passion fruit, on the sweet side, and a lobster, scallops, and shrimp dish known as Gueddengo, served with a slightly spicy tomato sauce. Reservations are accepted during peak season for parties of more than five.

Nicola Seafood **$$$**
601 Front Street
At the Hyatt Key West Resort and Marina
(305) 296-9900, ext. 54

Nicola Seafood offers indoor and outdoor dining with a stunning ocean view through two walls of floor-to-ceiling windows. Located at the corner of Simonton and Front Streets at the Hyatt Key West Resort and Marina, Nicola specializes in island fare—fresh fish and seafood blackened, grilled, or sautéed and served with a sauce on the side. Popular dishes include Sweet Potato Pecan Crusted Yellowtail, topped with rum-basted bananas; Moroccan Rubbed Sea Bass with cucumber-yogurt slaw and Israeli couscous; and the appetizer Wild Mushroom Crespelle, which is a crepe stuffed with Boursin cheese and wild mushrooms, draped in Chardonnay sauce.

Nicola Seafood is open for breakfast, lunch, and dinner daily.

nine one five **$$**
915 Duval Street
(305) 296-0669
www.915duval.com
Snappy concept with gastronomical success! The chefs at nine one five have created dishes meant to mix and match and be served with wine. Upscale without being pretentious and loaded with atmosphere, this restaurant, housed in a stately Victorian home, is the talk of the town. While you're waiting for your meal, try an appetizer like tuna dome made with Dungeness crab and diced Granny Smith apples in lemon miso, wrapped with sushi-grade Ahi tuna. Don't miss the seared sea scallops with black truffle butter and sautéed rapini. And for dessert, how about Earl Grey crème brûlée? Open for lunch and dinner. Reservations suggested.

Rooftop Cafe **$$$**
310 Front Street
(305) 294-2042
High amid the treetops, Rooftop Cafe looks down on the tourist mecca along Front Street near Mallory Square. And although the restaurant bustles with dining activity, the atmosphere remains unhurried and removed from the fray. Diners may sit on a second-floor balcony, which extends on two sides of the building, under the canopy of ancient leafy trees. Inside, ceiling fans mounted on the white vaulted ceiling gently move the air about the open-air, pavilion-style dining room.

The cuisine, innovative in both composition and presentation, combines local piscatory resources with an international flair. Dinner creations have included: Sautéed Pepper Tiger Tuna, a tuna steak with black pepper and sesame seeds served with soy-wasabi sauce and mung sprouts; Savory Shrimps, Key West pinks marinated in shallots, herbs, and oil, then grilled and served on roasted corn and fennel risotto; and Shellfish Lasagna, a chef's selection of seafood under a blanket of lemon-pepper pasta served on a lobster and oregano coulis. Luncheon selections transcend the norm as well. Rooftop Cafe is open daily for breakfast, lunch, and dinner. Reservations are strongly suggested for dinner in all seasons, especially at sunset.

Square One **$$$**
1075 Duval Street
(305) 296-4300
www.squareonerestaurant.com
Enjoy a touch of class and a bit of craziness, Manhattan style, at Square One, a casually sophisticated uptown bistro in Duval Square. Two enormous tropical floral murals flank the walls, offsetting the highly polished wood decor. The green carpet is mirrored in the green-rimmed chargers, which sit upon white linen tablecloths in the rich-looking dining room.

Diners are treated to light piano music as they try these signature dishes: roast rack of lamb encrusted with Pommery mustard and served with honey shallot confit and minted bordelaise sauce, or sautéed sea scallops served on a bed of poached spinach with a light champagne mustard-cream sauce. And there is always a chef's choice pasta selection and other daily specialties.

Now open for breakfast every morning is Café Square One, and one item to swoon over is stuffed French toast with raspberries and cream cheese. Square One offers the option of outdoor dining in their tree-lined courtyard. Ample free parking is available. Square One serves lunch and dinner, and breakfast is served at the Café Square One. Reservations are recommended for breakfast, lunch, and dinner.

Melting Pot

Dion's Quick Mart **$**
1127 Truman Avenue, Key West
(305) 294-7572

3228 Flagler Avenue, Key West
(305) 294-4574

5350 US 1
Stock Island, Key West
(305) 296-9901
Locals call Dion's Quick Mart a one-stop-shopping experience for your immediate needs. They sell everything from gas for your car to bread, milk, magazines, and the best fried chicken you have ever tasted. Forget about all the other brands of fried chicken you might have experienced in your travels, Dion's prides itself in quality, fresh, juicy, hot, crunchy, memorable chicken. You can smell the aroma of the fryers when you get near the place. It might be 6:00 A.M. by your watch, but your nose knows your taste buds are screaming "gimme some of that chicken" by the time your body reaches the counter. They also offer such other eats as fried okra and corn dog on a stick, but chicken is the code of the road here. Call ahead for large orders. The location on Truman Avenue is open 24 hours, the shop on Flagler Avenue is open 6:00 A.M. to 11:00 P.M., and the Stock Island mart is open 6:00 A.M. to 12:00 P.M.

Meteor Smokehouse **$-$$**
404 Southard Street
(305) 294-5602
www.greenparrot.com/meteor
American
Nestled tight against the Green Parrot bar, one of Key West's oldest and most popular watering holes (see the Nightlife chapter), this unassuming eatery is easy to find—just follow the enticing smell of hickory-smoked meats sizzling on the island's only authentic pit barbecue.

Meteor specializes in ribs—the Memphis-style, dry-rubbed, baby back variety and St. Louis–style spareribs, to be exact—as well as pulled pork and Texas beef brisket, all smoked low and slow for 16 hours. Opt for a platter if you're especially hungry—you get the meat, plus a corn-bread muffin and two sides—or just have a sandwich if you're not. And be sure to ask for plenty of napkins. These ribs are the lip-smackin', mouthwatering, and up-to-your-elbows-in-barbecue-sauce kind.

Remember, the dolphin you see offered on the menu is not the cute bottlenose variety that cavorts in our seas. You will be ordering dolphinfish, commonly marketed outside the Keys as mahimahi.

If you'd rather not eat in, phone ahead and carry out. Either way, the full menu is available daily, for lunch, dinner, and all times in between. Free parking for diners is available next door.

PT's Late Night Bar and Grill **$**
920 Caroline Street
(305) 296-4245
American
PT's (short for Paul Tripp, the owner) is a friendly neighborhood grill that lives up to its motto—"large plates, small prices." And the portions are ample.

Choose from such all-American favorites as meat loaf, Yankee pot roast, smothered pork chops, and country-fried steak. Or chow down on a plate of fajitas. The choices include steak, chicken, shrimp, and veggie, or a combination thereof. Salads and sandwiches appease lighter appetites, too.

The full menu is served until 3:00 A.M. nightly; the bar remains open until 4:00 A.M.

Sarabeth's **$$**
530 Simonton Street, Key West
(305) 293-8181, (800) 773-7378
www.sarabeths.com
There is a real Sarabeth, and she is an award-winning jam maker, pastry chef, and restaurateur. Not only does her "empire" include four locations in New York City and now Key West, but her legendary spreadable fruits and pastries can be purchased on her Web site as well as in her establishments. The restaurant group is well known for fresh, updated classic American cooking. The James Beard award-winning menus include from-scratch pancakes, salads, sandwiches, meatloaf, grilled meats, and fish. The coffee is served in cups so large they are

called bowls. When you partake of any item, you are made to feel as though you are sitting in Sarabeth's personal kitchen where everything is created just for you. Seating, indoors or out, in this historic 1800s clapboard building is a wonderful way to make a Keys memory. Reservations are suggested for parties of four or more.

South of the Border

Chico's Cantina **$$**
MM 4.5 Oceanside, Stock Island
(305) 296-4714
www.chicoscantina.com
Mexican

Sit among giant cacti, Mexican tapestries, and a selection of south-of-the-border folk art at Chico's Cantina, a perennial favorite for Mexican cuisine. This small cantina—only 12 tables—knocks itself out with the freshest ingredients fashioned into off-the-charts homemade Mexican dishes. The food at Chico's is not your ordinary Mexican fare. Complimentary salsa is prepared with fresh tomatoes, onions, and peppers, creating the perfect balance between sweet and sassy. The salsa is so popular among locals that the restaurant sells the stuff in bulk. The sizzling fajitas—with a choice of vegetarian, chicken, beef, chicken-and-beef combo, shrimp, or shrimp-and-beef combo—are accompanied by fresh vegetables, cooked just until crispy. And the Fish Adobado, grilled in corn husks, packs just the right spicy zing. Daily specials usually highlight local seafood such as yellowtail snapper.

Chile peppers rule the roost at Chico's Cantina. Not only is their subtle presence notable in the cuisine, but their icons appear on the curtains, as lights around the windows, even on ceramic pots. Chico's serves the same menu for both lunch and dinner. It's open daily. Beer and wine are served; takeout is available.

If you're driving, order a nonalcoholic beer or wine. Most of our restaurants stock a good selection of alcohol-free choices and tempting straight-arrow tropical concoctions.

El Meson de Pepe **$$**
410 Wall Street
(305) 295-2620
www.elmesondepepe.com
Cuban

Situated just off Mallory Square, the original El Meson de Pepe draws a large post-sunset crowd. A salsa band plays nightly as the sun sinks into the Gulf of Mexico, which adds to the festive and welcoming atmosphere.

Look for Cuban-Conch classics on the menu—Mollete a la Pancho; Cuban bread stuffed with picadillo, a spicy combination of ground beef, capers, raisins, olives, and seasonings; and ropa vieja. Quench your thirst with a mojito—a rum concoction made with mint and sugar syrup that is similar to a mint julep.

Both locations are open for breakfast, lunch, and dinner daily. Large groups are welcome, and reservations are appreciated but rarely necessary.

El Siboney **$**
900 Catherine Street
(305) 296-4184
Cuban

A cascade of bilingual chatter washes over the enthusiastic diners at El Siboney restaurant, an informal restaurant specializing in Cuban cuisine. The words *el siboney* refer to a Cuban Indian, and artwork depicting el siboney adorns the white walls of the restaurant. Red vinyl covers the simple cafe chairs, and your cutlery is served in a white paper bag. The food is top drawer all the way, though. Hot, buttery Cuban bread is immediately whisked to your table, and then begins the difficult decision of which taste-tempting delicacy to order. Portions are enormous at El Siboney; the same menu is offered at lunch or dinner.

We recommend one of the combination platters, especially if trying Cuban cuisine is a new experience for you: A platter of roast pork, black beans, yellow rice, and cassava is served heaped with raw onions. The pork melts in the mouth. Or try the roast pork accompanied with yucca and tamale; sounds similar, tastes totally different. You'll find myriad Cuban twists with beef, including the popular ropa vieja (shredded beef) and boliche (Cuban pot roast). Crab, shrimp, and chicken all get the wonderful Cuban garlic treatment, and you can choose paella for two persons. You can order an array of sandwiches or sides of tamale, yucca, black beans, platanos, and tostones. Wash it all down with homemade sangria, beer, or house wines, and try rice pudding, flan, or natilla for dessert if you have room.

El Siboney is closed on Sunday. No credit cards.

Jose's Cantina $
800 White Street
(305) 296-4366
Cuban

Step inside this little neighborhood diner and you might believe you'd just walked in from the streets of Havana. The owners are Cuban, and so are most of the customers. But even if you don't speak Spanish, you're sure to receive a hearty bienvenida (welcome) here. The menus are in English, the waitstaff is bilingual, and the food is plentiful, delicious, and cheap.

Jose's has one of the best Cuban mixes on the island—that's a sandwich combination of ham and shredded pork on Cuban bread with lettuce, tomato, mayo, mustard, onions, and pickles. The dinners—Cuban variations on chicken, pork, and beef—come with the traditional black beans, yellow rice, and plantains. Beer, wine, and homemade sangria are available.

Jose's is open for breakfast, lunch, and dinner, 365 days a year—yes, even Christmas. This restaurant is very small and, judging from the lack of parking spaces in the surrounding neighborhood at 8:00 A.M., high noon, and 7:00 P.M., quite popular. To avoid the congestion, plan to arrive a little ahead or well after peak dining periods. Reservations are not accepted.

i

A Florida state law banning smoking in restaurants was passed in 2002. The restaurants in the Florida Keys are smoke free; the only exception is if an establishment is open on three sides.

The Continent

Abbondanza $
1208 Simonton Street
(305) 292-1199
Italian

At last, a place to enjoy casual Italian fare in Old Town. The specialty here is pasta, of course, in a variety of shapes and with sauces that range from marinara to Alfredo. You'll also find such main dishes as chicken Marsala and veal Parmesan, plus daily specials.

The food is quite tasty, the atmosphere is comfortable, and you're sure to discover that the portions at this restaurant live up to its name, which is Italian for "plenty."

Abbondanza is a choice place to have dinner for two or a crowd. There is a full bar, and the menu selections are more reasonably priced than some other Italian restaurants in town.

Abbondanza is open daily for dinner. No reservations are accepted.

Antonia's Restaurant $$
615 Duval Street
(305) 294-6565
www.antoniaskeywest.com
Italian

Stroll by this Northern Italian restaurant on any afternoon, and you can watch pasta in the making along the marble window-front table. Stringy mozzarella also is made fresh on the premises. Elegant, yet understated, Antonia's is a great place to go if you want to dress up. The menu changes every evening. Past offerings include grilled filet of beef tenderloin, served with mushrooms, brandy, and cream; pan-seared yellowtail braised with watercress, endive, radicchio, and white wine; and Linguine Cousteau, a variety of shellfish served in a fresh tomato sauce.

Virtually all the restaurant's veal dishes are popular, and even with all these spectacular entrees, patrons simply cannot pass up the homemade desserts. Panna Cotta features Italian vanilla ice cream with fresh berries and strawberry sauce. Chocolate Fondant is served warm with two sauces—raspberry and mango. And of course key lime pie, which won raves in the *New York Times. Bellissimo!*

Antonia's maintains an extensive Northern Italian and American wine list. The restaurant is open daily for dinner only.

Banana Cafe **$$$**
1211 Duval Street
(305) 294-7227
French

Settle into this quiet open-air bistro, and choose from more than 40 breakfast and lunch crepes. The exterior of Banana Cafe resembles a quaint Caribbean cottage; the airy interior says French bistro, with pinkish pine wood, artistic black-and-white photography, ceiling fans, and a small piano bar. Dining also is offered on the front balcony or along the side on a wood deck shaded by large tropical trees.

Thin, pancakelike crepes are stuffed with veggies, fish, and meat, and they are designated either sweet or savory. The most desirable crepe among patrons is the ratatouille, overflowing with sautéed eggplant, zucchini, peppers, extra-virgin olive oil, and garlic and topped with a fried egg sunny-side up. Past dinner selections have included such offerings as Salmon Paupiette, served with sautéed spinach and leeks in shallot jus; sliced duck breast served with a sweet-and-sour currant sauce; and yellowtail snapper and crab roulade with tropical mango sauce. Desserts, such as tarte tatin and crème brûlée, are, oh, so French and decadent.

Banana Cafe is open for breakfast, lunch, and dinner daily. Reservations are recommended, particularly on weekends. Live jazz is offered here on Wednesday and Thursday nights.

Finnegan's Wake Irish Pub & Eatery **$**
320 Grinnell Street
(305) 293-0222
Irish

No need to kiss the Blarney stone at Finnegan's Wake, whose staff guarantees this is one wake you won't want to miss. This Irish pub and eatery sails your spirit across the Big Pond, as you toast the legend of the miraculous resurrection of mythical Tim Finnegan. Try authentic Irish fare: bangers and mash (sausages and mashed potatoes, to those of you not wearing the green), shepherd's pie, corned beef and cabbage, Finnegan's Irish Stew, potato pancakes, or the Dublin Chicken Pot Pie. The lip-smacking lovely Irish Potato-leek Soup, a house specialty, is thick and chunky and served with grated cheddar, chopped scallions, and bacon. And be sure to try a black and tan—half Guinness, half lager—or a pint of bottled cider. They also offer 26 draft beers.

Like any good Irish wake, the merriment goes on all day and into the wee hours. Finnegan's Wake is open from lunchtime until 4:00 A.M. (serving dinner until 10:30 P.M., bar menu until 3:00 A.M.). You'll find two happy hours here—from 4:00 to 7:00 P.M. and from midnight to 2:00 A.M. Patio dining is available. Reservations will be honored but usually are not necessary. Weekends feature live Irish music.

The Grand Café **$$$**
314 Duval Street, Key West
(305) 292-4740
www.grandcafekeywest.com

Southern French cuisine of Provence in a

tropical setting is the ambience of The Grand Café. A gracious wait staff orchestrates a fine dance from kitchen to table. The ultimate maestros are the owners and chef who demand nothing short of the best from themselves and whose food is consequently at the same level. The sauces are light and represent the flavors of southern French cooking, with fresh herbs and olive oil. The Grand Café takes reservations and prides itself on excellent wine selections and simply grand martinis. C'est bon.

La Trattoria $$
524 Duval Street
(305) 296-1075
www.latrattoriakeywest.com
Italian

This upscale SoHo-style New York bistro rates as a Key West treasure. A romantic taste of old Italy favored by locals, visitors, and Keys residents from as far away as Key Largo, La Trattoria redefines the traditional pasta, veal, chicken, lamb, and seafood dishes of the mother country. The sophisticated decor (linen cloths top intimate tables encircled with black lacquered chairs) belies the fact that you are a stone's throw from the sidewalks of busy Duval Street.

Try Agnello alla Griglia (lamb with fresh rosemary) or Cheese Tortellina alla Romana, with smoked ham and peas in a parmigiana cream sauce. Penne all' Arabbiata, quill-shaped pasta, delivers a bit of a bite, and the traditional Linguine alle Vongole does not disappoint. The Insalata Mista will transport your taste buds to Venice for sure. And don't forget dessert—the tiramisu is to die for here. La Trattoria serves dinner nightly.

Reservations are suggested, especially in high season. After dinner, retire to Virgilio's, the charming little cocktail lounge with live music just around the corner.

Mangia Mangia $$
900 Southard Street
(305) 294-2469
www.mangia-mangia.com
Italian

The Key West Restaurant and Bar Association has an impressive membership representing most of the bars and restaurants in Key West. Before you arrive or while staying in the Keys, go to www.kwrba.com or call (305) 292-2092 and check out their calendar of events. Various restaurants and bars host these events and they are open to the public. It's a great way to meet new people and have an entertaining and educational evening.

Off the main drag but definitely on the right track is the pasta lovers' nirvana, Mangia Mangia. Meaning "eat, eat" in Italian, Mangia Mangia bestows a passel of homemade fresh pasta (made daily on the premises) and finely seasoned sauces that would excite any palate.

The chefs work their macaroni magic in plain view. You can always order the basic sauces—marinara, Alfredo, pesto, meat, and red or white seafood—but for something out of the ordinary, try Bollito Misto di Mare—fresh scallops, shrimp, conch, salmon, and local fish in a garlicky clam sauce. The daily specials will prove difficult to pass up.

Outdoor seating is delightful where the patio area is enclosed with palm trees and flowers. Mangia Mangia serves dinner daily. The restaurant does not take reservations; plan to arrive before 6:00 P.M. to avoid a wait. You can enjoy selections from Mangia Mangia's extensive wine list. Beer also is served.

Martin's Cafe Restaurant $$
416 Applerouth Lane
(305) 296-1183
German

Put on your lederhosen, for Martin's treats you to German cuisine with an island flair. Tucked a few steps off the 500 block of Duval Street on Applerouth Lane, Martin's expansive menu all but guarantees *guten appetit*. Begin with Pilze a la Martin, toasted bread rounds topped with sautéed mushrooms and herb garlic butter. You'll find classic German dishes such as pepper steak, sauerbraten with spaetzle and red cabbage, and Wiener schnitzel, but Martin's also prepares island seafood creations *a la deutsch.* Grouper Dijon arrives on a bed of champagne kraut with rosemary potatoes. Sea Scallops Wunderbar is baked with spinach encased in puff pastry and is served with a light brown sauce. Choose from a large selection of fine German wines and beers.

Martin's Cafe Restaurant serves dinner nightly and offers Sunday brunch. Reservations are suggested.

Opera Italian Restaurant **$$$**
613 Duval Street
(305) 295-2705
www.operarestaurant.com
Italian

Chef Andrea Benatti brings a bit of Ferrara to Key West, putting his own innovative twist on classic Italian dishes. You'll find such seafood offerings as Filletto di Tonno in Crosta—pan-seared tuna mignon with sesame seeds on chick peas in a spicy tomato sauce; meat selections such as Filetto di Manzo—pan-seared filet mignon served over roasted portobello mushroom and mashed potatoes in a red wine and cranberry sauce; and pasta dishes such as Lasagne Opera—a classic Italian lasagna made of handmade pasta, beef ragout, and béchamel sauce. You can top off your meal with some belly-busting desserts such as crème brûlée, tiramisu, and *crema bavarese*—creme bavarese flavored with white chocolate, creme de menthe, and almonds. Altogether a stunning gastronomic encounter.

Opera is open for dinner Tuesday through Sunday.

Pisces **$$$$**
1007 Simonton Street
(305) 294-7100
www.pisceskeywest.com
French

This enduring tropical French establishment has won awards and accolades from *Gourmet, Bon Appétit,* and *Wine Spectator* magazines, and the recognition is well deserved. At Pisces, creativity culminates in such delicacies as Lobster Tango Mango and Raspberry Duck. One of its finest treasures is Yellowtail Atocha, snapper sautéed in tarragon butter with shrimp and scallops. Specials are available nightly.

Each of two dining rooms has a distinctive character. The decor features wainscoting, subdued lighting, and local acrylic, watercolor, and oil paintings. Fresh flowers decorate every table.

The extensive wine list features some of the best of the vineyards of France and California. Pisces is open every day for dinner. Reservations are recommended.

The Far East

China Garden West **$**
531 Fleming Street
(305) 296-6177

3300 North Roosevelt Boulevard/
Searstown Shopping Center
(305) 296-5618
Chinese

China Garden West is a quiet, unassuming restaurant with two locations in Key West. One is located in Old Town on a corner off Duval. There you will find a peaceful atmosphere and delightful service. They aim to please. The China Garden West is great for lunch, with chef's specials of pressed duck, subgum wonton, or seagrass salad. They also have dynamite combo platters offering oriental delights.

The China Garden West in Searstown has the same menu with a vast choice to select from. They are both open seven days a week; takeout is offered and free delivery is available in Key West with a minimum order of $10.

Kyushu Japanese Restaurant **$$**
921 Truman Avenue
(305) 294-2995
Japanese

Take off your shoes! Kyushu provides an authentic Japanese dining experience in tatami rooms, or individual low-to-the-ground tables and benches secluded by bamboo screens. As a courtesy, your Asian waitress removes her slippers in unison with you. The open entranceway at Kyushu takes patrons out of Key West and into an exotic garden with a bridged koi pond and views of royal poinciana trees. Hand-painted Japanese sheets stretch from floor to ceiling, and saltwater aquariums, fresh flowers, and Japanese paintings of geisha women are found throughout. Crepe-paper box lights add soft lighting.

The menu includes sashimi, sushi rolls, tempura, katsu, and stir-fry and teriyaki dishes. An extensive selection of sushi—including eel, conch, octopus, yellowtail, tuna, and snapper—is most popular, and patrons are offered the option of dining at the informal sushi bar.

The full-service bar features sake and plum wine, along with Japanese beers such as Sapporo, Kirin, and Asahi. Off-street parking is available at the restaurant lot on Packer Street. Reservations are recommended during high season; Kyushu is open for lunch and dinner seven nights a week.

Origami Japanese Restaurant **$$**
1075 Duval Street
(305) 294-0092
Japanese

The stark white decor of Origami provides a backdrop for the brightly colored tropical fish adorning the walls. And like the Japanese art of folding paper into decorative or representational forms—origami—the restaurant fashions fresh, local seafood into exquisite sushi and sashimi. Rumor has it that the dragon roll must not be missed. Origami also offers traditional Japanese cuisine, such as teriyaki, chicken katsu, steak yakiniku, and tempura.

Sit at the cafe-style tables or at the sushi bar and watch the masters at work. Origami is situated in Duval Square. Free parking is available in the adjoining lot off Simonton Street. Origami is open for dinner daily. Smoking is not permitted inside, but smokers may sit in Origami's lovely outdoor seating area. Beer, wine, and sake are served. Reservations are suggested in high season.

In the off-season many restaurants limit their hours; some even close altogether. To avoid disappointment, phone ahead.

Thai Cuisine **$**
513 Greene Street
(305) 294-9424
www.thaicuisinekeywest.com
Thai

The salubrious cuisine of Thailand tingles your palate with the afterglow of Thai curries. Thai curry is a fiery Southeast Asian stew that's not even a kissing cousin to the bland Indian-style powder we Americans associate with the moniker. Thai curry is actually a cooking method, not an ingredient. Together with spices, herbs, and aromatic vegetables, hot chile peppers are ground into a dry paste that infuses Thai curries with heat and passion. At the same time, coconut milk, fish sauce, sugar, and kaffir lime leaves—ubiquitous to every variation of Thai red and green curry—confuse the palate with a riot of sweet-and-sour sensory stimuli.

For another traditional delight, try Pad Thai, spicy rice noodles sauteed with shrimp, chicken, and egg, or frog legs with garlic and black pepper. The portions are enormous. Enjoy a selection of Thai and Japanese beers, house wines, plum wine, and sake. Outdoor seating is available in the evening. Thai Cuisine serves lunch Monday through Friday and is open for dinner every night. Takeout is available, and Thai Cuisine offers free delivery in Key West.

Two other Far Eastern restaurants in Key West are under the same ownership—Kozuchi Japanese Restaurant (512 Greene Street, 305-292-0009) and Thai Cuisine Continental (918 Duval Street, 305-295-8808).

The Islands

Bahama Mama's Kitchen **$-$$**
324 Petronia Street
(305) 294-3355
www.keywest.com/themenu/bahamamamas
Bahamian

If it's island food and atmosphere you seek, you can't get any more authentic than Bahama Mama's Kitchen. Owner Cory Sweeting is a fourth-generation Bahamian on both sides. For a logo, he chose a drawing of Grandma Sweeting wielding a wooden spoon (most of the recipes have come from her kitchen), and for location, he picked the Key West neighborhood known as Bahama Village.

The menu here is limited but tasty. Conch is the obvious seafood choice, but you'll also find grouper, shrimp, and red snapper. The lamb chops are blackened, the chicken is curried with ginger, and collard greens are a must. Dinners come with plantains and hush puppies and two sides—pigeon peas and rice.

Bahama Mama's serves breakfast, lunch, and dinner daily. Reservations are not necessary. You'll find free parking in the rear of the restaurant.

Jamaican Me Hungry **$**
Coco Palms Café
300 Front Street, Key West
(305) 296-0046
Jamaican

Half a block from Mallory Square, climb a set of unassuming stairs and be welcomed into the world of Jamaican Me Hungry, a restaurant with a tree-house atmosphere overlooking the sights and sounds of Key West. You'll be treated like a "local" here, with Jamaican family food to comfort you. Try the Jamaican meat patties served warm and sweetly spicy, or roasted whole snapper smothered in a wealth of fresh veggies. Other tempting items include the curried goat, oxtail, jerk chicken, and jerk pork. For the vegan appetite there is a hearty dish of Jamaican spiced cabbage served with a mound of rice and a broad selection of fresh salads. Don't forget to indulge in Abby's famous rum cake to finish off your meal. Jamaican Me Hungry offers reggae, calypso, jazz, and limbo nights too, so you can enjoy live music while you dine.

SEAFOOD MARKETS AND SPECIALTY FOODS

Here in the Florida Keys, we think our fish is pretty special. It's certainly the freshest—sometimes only minutes from line to linen. Its pedigree is elite; most species are not marketed outside South Florida. And the abounding variety of innovative culinary presentations is astounding. Visitors to the Florida Keys, accustomed back home to choosing among cod, halibut, haddock, swordfish, and tuna, are often overwhelmed when confronted with the bountiful selections from our underwater treasure trove.

When you stop at one of our many seafood markets, you will undoubtedly meet the three royal families of our tropical waters: snapper, grouper, and dolphin. The famed yellowtail or the equally desirous mangrove or mutton snapper most often represents the moist, sweet snapper dynasty. The firm, mild-flavored grouper clan, members of the sea bass family, competes in popularity with the large-flaked and sweetly moist dolphinfish (not to be confused with the porpoise dolphin, which is a mammal).

You won't want to miss our Florida lobster, a delicacy any way you look at it (see the Diving for Lobster Close-up in the Diving and Snorkeling chapter). And if you have never tasted a stone-crab claw, you are in for a treat (see the Close-up in this chapter).

To round out your palate, we have provided you with a rundown of delicatessens and shops selling specialty foods. If you're eating in tonight or tomorrow, you'll want to know what we know: the out-of-the-way shops that help you make Martha Stewart look like an also-ran.

We have listed our recommended seafood markets and specialty food shops by mile marker (MM) from the top of the Keys in Key Largo to Key West. Key West businesses are listed in alphabetical order.

Most places remain open until at least 5:00 P.M., with the exception of bakeries, which usually open early and often close in the early afternoon. During high season, December through April, many of these markets and stores extend their hours. The off-season often brings abbreviated hours, so you may want to call before you shop.

UPPER KEYS

Alabama Jack's
1500 Card Sound Road (Oceanside), Key Largo
(305) 248-8741

There are a couple of reasons why one drives the back door into the Florida Keys. Card Sound Road, north of Key Largo, offers incentives to take this scenic excursion. The traffic is not as heavy, the wildlife are more prolific (crabs run across the road, crocs occasionally appear, and the birds are bountiful), and you can eat at Alabama Jack's. No trip to the Florida Keys is complete without stopping at this Caribbean honky-tonk. Key West may have Margaritaville, but the rest of us can boost about this local favorite. Don't be turned off by the outside of the place; it's what's inside that makes this a true Keys treasure. Alabama Jack's is rated to have the best Conch fritters and key lime pie by everyone who manages to find the place. It sits on the water where you can feed the fish, check out the mangroves, and enjoy the friendly Keys attitude of the staff.

Dockside Cakes Bakery & Deli
MM 103 Bayside, Key Largo
(305) 451-7060, (800) 813-2253
www.docksidecakes.com
You won't lose any weight indulging here, but it's definitely worth it. All cakes, breads, pastries, muffins, and bagels are made on the premises, and they taste as good as they smell. Enjoy a potpourri of deli sandwiches or freshly brewed specialty coffees, too. Dockside Cakes also caters deli and breakfast platters.

The Fish House Restaurant & Seafood Market
MM 102.4 Oceanside, Key Largo
(305) 451-4665, (888) 451-4665
www.fishhouse.com
Primarily a seafood restaurant (see the Restaurants chapter), the Fish House also offers fresh catch of the day from their small seafood market so that you can be the chef of the day if you like. You'll find just-off-the-boat local favorites such as snapper, dolphin, and grouper, as well as other seasonally caught species.

Remedy's Health Foods
MM 100.6 Bayside, Plaza 101, Key Largo
(305) 451-2160
If your idea of a pick-me-up requires vitamins, herbs, and healthful foods, you'll find all this plus berries, dried fruit-and-nut mixes, and more at this health food store. The shop stocks food supplements, herb cheese, and protein supplements as well as a wide range of natural products for face and body—soaps, shampoos, conditioners, toothpaste, moisturizers, and face creams.

Key Largo Coffee House
MM 100.2 Oceanside, Key Largo
(305) 453-4844
If you're a coffee connoisseur in Key Largo, you'll want to find your way to the Key Largo Coffee House, which is housed in a Conch-style house that sits on a lush wooded lot. This shop opened to fill a local demand for a coffee shop, and it fills it well! Choose from among house-blend coffee, gourmet flavors of the day, and espresso drinks. If you prefer a cool drink, how about an iced coffee or a fruit smoothie made with a green-tea base? After making your choice, pick a seat on the wide porch and savor your cup of joe in the fresh air. If you're hungry, the Coffee House serves freshly baked pastries as well as breakfast sandwiches and omelets. In the afternoon (before 5:00), you can choose from Panini sandwiches and wraps to tame those hunger pangs.

Key Largo Fisheries
MM 99.5 Oceanside, 1313 Ocean Bay Drive, Key Largo
(305) 451-3782, (800) 432-4358
www.keylargofisheries.net
The family-run Key Largo Fisheries ships wholesale to hundreds of clients throughout the country and also offers retail sales at their Key Largo store and via overnight delivery. At Key Largo Fisheries, customers will find choice seafood, including snapper, grouper, shrimp, and, in season, Florida lobster and stone-crab claws. Conch here is imported from the Bahamas and the West Indies. Key Largo Fisheries is open Monday through Saturday.

Chad's Deli and Bakery
MM 92.3 Bayside, Tavernier
(305) 853-5566
Lots of good food at reasonable prices and quick service! That is not only a winning combo (just like some of their menu items), it is also what makes Chad's Deli and Bakery a success in the Upper Keys. The wait staff is very friendly and knows all the regulars by name. That goes a long way in a small place like Tavernier and the Keys. In 2005, they added additional seating by expanding into the space next door, and a dinner menu was included as well. Their specialities are four-way sandwiches, speciality pizzas (try the Mombo Combo), calzones, pasta, goulash, and

salads. They also serve beer and wine to round out your meal.

Sunshine Supermarket
MM 91.8 Oceanside, Tavernier
(305) 852-7216
There isn't a Tavernier resident who doesn't know about the rotisserie chicken and Cuban bread here. Family owned and operated, Sunshine Supermarket offers some tasty Cuban specialties as well: roast pork, ribs, yellow rice, and black beans and rice, all at reasonable prices. The pork is marinated in mojo sauce—a Cuban concoction of oil, vinegar, garlic, and other spices. It is available for chicken as well, upon request, and you can buy it by the bottle here.

The Garden Cafe
MM 86.7 Bayside at the Rain Barrel, Islamorada
(305) 852-6499
For those locals long-addicted to Jose Palomino's famed vegetarian wraps at the former Garden Gourmet in Marathon and for all visitors to the Keys, good news! Jose and wife Teddy Thompson have moved up the Keys to the Rain Barrel complex, where they now run the Garden Cafe. You'll love your veggies even more with the creative selection of salads, sandwiches, and wraps. You'll find smoothies, fresh-squeezed juices, coffees, and iced teas as well. And can enjoy your repast at a table set in a tropical garden under the tall trees of a hardwood hammock.

Village Gourmet
MM 82.7 Oceanside, Islamorada
(305) 664-4030
Village Gourmet bills itself as "creative cuisine," and that it is. This gourmet-to-go shop (or eat in at one of a handful of tables if you like) offers a selection of unusual sandwiches—such as a marinated portobello mushroom with fresh spinach and tomato with wasabi mayonnaise on your choice of specialty breads—in addition to 18 other deli sandwich and sub offerings. You'll find salads—such as Greek, antipasto, blackened chicken, or curried chicken—and even entrees, including stuffed shells, chicken parmigiana, or lasagna. You can create your own pasta special by choosing among four pastas, five sauces, and four toppings, such as meatball or sausage. Or order a gourmet pizza—unbelievable combinations of ingredients atop a homemade hand-tossed crust. The bakery case holds some tantalizing specialty breads—sun-dried tomato, olive, rosemary—and don't forget desserts. Chocolate pizza or peanut butter pie is sure to get your attention. Village Gourmet is open daily.

Islamorada Restaurant and Bakery
MM 81.6 Bayside, Islamorada
(305) 664-8363
The banner out front proclaims, BEST BUNS IN TOWN, and these oversize cinnamon rolls live up to the hype. Topped with cream-cheese icing, the buns are undoubtedly one of the local favorites. Also available are "gooey" or sticky buns, bagels, muffins, scones, and croissants. As you might imagine, this restaurant is a wildly popular Islamorada breakfast spot.

---

i

You can bring a little Florida Keys sunshine home or send some to a friend. Keywestseafood.com packs up fresh Keys seafood with tropical treats such as local sauces, seasonings, marinades, and key lime pie. Then they festively wrap it and send it "off the rock." (www.keywestseafood.com)

Islamorada Fish Company
MM 81.5 Bayside, Islamorada
(305) 664-9271, (800) 258-2559
www.ifcstonecrab.com
This Islamorada legend operates out of a state-of-the-art, 5,000-square-foot facility in the totally renovated former Green Turtle Cannery building next door to the Islamorada Fish Company's original location. Ten thousand pounds of superfresh fish and seafood find their way through

CLOSE-UP

Florida Stone-Crab Claws

Now, you Yankees can brag about your blue crabs, and you West Coasters may boast of Dungeness. But here in the Florida Keys we crow about crab claws like none other—those of the Florida stone crabs.

The stone crabs, large nonswimming crabs found in deep holes and under rocks in the waters surrounding the Keys, have the unusual ability to release their legs or pincers if caught or when experiencing extreme changes in temperature. The separation always occurs at one of the joints to protect the crab from further injury. What is unique about this situation is that the stone crab regenerates the severed appendage, a feat it can accomplish three or four times during its lifetime.

The stone crab's two claws serve distinct purposes: The larger claw, or crusher, is used to hold food and fight predators. The smaller claw, known as the ripper, acts as a scissors for cutting food.

The crabs are harvested commercially in the Florida Keys with baited traps. One or both of the crab's claws are removed (it greatly improves the crab's chances of survival if only one claw is taken). The forearm must measure at least 2¾ inches to harvest it legally. The live stone crabs must then be returned to the water, where in 18 months a new claw will have grown to legal size. It is illegal in the state of Florida to harvest whole stone crabs. They are one of our precious resources.

the cutting rooms here, much displayed in a showy 31-foot display case. Everything is temperature controlled at Islamorada Fish Company, so the fish stays extra fresh. You can watch the cutters in action from a glassed-in cutting room.

You'll find all the local favorites, such as dolphin, Florida lobster, grouper, snapper, swordfish, stone-crab claws, blue crab, Key West pink shrimp, and tuna. Conch here is offered either ground or in steaks and is flown in from the Turks and Caicos Islands. Sea and bay scallops come from Boston, oysters from Apalachicola, and the market carries clams and mussels. You can liven things up with their extensive selection of hot sauces.

If you prefer to dine in this charming seafood market ambience, the store has a full-service restaurant (see the Restaurants chapter). Its fried grouper sandwich is an award winner.

The Trading Post
MM 81.5 Bayside, Islamorada
(305) 664-2571

This is definitely Islamorada's "super" market. Here you'll discover super grocery selections, supergood deli items, a super meat market, super wine offerings, and super hours. The Trading Post is open 24 hours a day, seven days a week! The store also offers customized catering.

A stone-crab claw has a hard, heavy, porcelainlike shell with a black-tipped pincer. Seafood markets sell stone-crab claws fully cooked. When cooked, the meat inside the shell is sweet and firm-textured. A mild sweet odor indicates freshness.

The shells must be cracked before serving. If you plan to eat your stone-crab claws within an hour of purchase, have the seafood market crack them for you. It is not recommended that you crack the claws until you are ready to eat them. If you crack the claws yourself, lightly tap the crockerylike shells with a hammer, a small wooden mallet (available at seafood markets), or the back of a tablespoon. The shells also will crack like a fine china teacup if you hit one claw against the other. Pick the meat from the shell using a small cocktail fork and serve with mustard sauce (cold claws) or clarified butter (resteamed claws).

Stone-crab claws are in season from October 15 until May 15. They do not freeze particularly well, but most seafood markets listed in this chapter will ship iced, fresh stone-crab claws anywhere in the United States.

Florida stone crabs have the unusual ability to regenerate a severed claw, a feat they can accomplish three or four times during their lifetime, making it a delightfully delicious, renewable resource. PHOTO: HAWK'S CAY RESORT

MIDDLE KEYS

Nichols Seafood of Conch Key
MM 63 Bayside, Conch Key
(305) 289-0900
www.upperkeys.com/nichols

At Nichols Seafood, the back door is Florida Bay and the front door is the seafood counter. You can't get any fresher than that! Nichols employs more than 40 commercial fishing families who bring seafood directly from their boats to you. Nichols is the largest spiny lobster fishery in the United States, so you can be assured of a good supply of lobster here! Buy them whole, tails, live, or frozen. You can buy fresh fish here, too.

Captain's Three
MM 54 Oceanside, Coco Plum Drive, Marathon
(305) 289-1131

Captain's Three maintains its own fishing, crabbing, and lobstering crews, guaranteeing the freshest catches of the day. The shop always has plenty of Key West shrimp. The staff will special-order oysters and cherrystone clams for you with advance notice. Be sure to try the homemade cocktail sauce. Captain's Three is closed May through August.

Fish Tales Market & Eatery
MM 53 Oceanside, Marathon
(305) 743-9196, (888) 662-4822

For those who despaired the day Grassy Key Dairy Bar closed its doors, cheer up. Johnny, George, and Jackie Eigner have opened Fish Tales in the location of the former Island City Fish Market and still serve up some of the piscatory delights locals and visitors love. The tiny eatery offers fish and seafood baskets and sandwiches, along with a few heartier specials daily. And you'll find Johnny's famous salad and George's popular wasabi and honey/mustard sauces as well. You can even try one of the brothers' homemade bratwurst, which is made with smoked mackerel. Fish Tales will cook your catch if you've had a productive day on the water.

The well-stocked seafood market offers Key West shrimp, stone crabs, tuna, swordfish, the Keys trio—snapper, grouper, and dolphin—and more. Fish Tales is open Monday through Saturday from 11:00 A.M. to 6:30 P.M. and will ship seafood anywhere in the United States. A choice-grade meat counter offers aged steaks, pork tenderloin, and rack of lamb as well.

Food for Thought
MM 51 Bayside, Gulfside Village, Marathon
(305) 743-3297, (800) 338-9495
www.foodforthoughtinc.com

If you are in the market for health food products, you'll find them tucked in Food for Thought, a shop that is also half bookstore. It carries wheat-free, fat-free, and sugar-free staples, organic foods, vitamins, and homeopathic remedies. Pick up your favorite novel or magazine in the book section to treat your mind as well.

Keys Fisheries Market & Marina
MM 49 Bayside, at the end of 35th Street, Marathon
(305) 743-4353, (866) 743-4353
www.keysfisheries.com

Fish here is fresh, fresh, fresh, because Keys Fisheries' fishing fleet works out of the marina. You'll find Key West pinks (shrimp), Florida lobster, stone crabs, and all varieties of local fish here, as well as clams, oysters, scallops, squid, conch, and more. Take home homemade soups and seafood salads or spreads if you like. You can also order from the menu of the adjoining eatery (see the Restaurants chapter). They also offer you an experience on board a working lobster or stone-crab boat for the day (see the Fishing chapter) and will fillet, pack, and ship your catch so you can take your Keys bounty home with you.

LOWER KEYS

Big Pine Bagel Island
MM 30 Bayside, Big Pine Shopping Center
(305) 872-9912

In a shopping center on Big Pine Key sits a great little bakery and sandwich shop. The folks at Big Pine Bagel Island bake delectable everyday cakes as well as special-occasion ones, like wedding cakes. For breakfast or morning coffee-break eating, try their homemade bagels, pastries, and Danish. If breakfast is not your thing, stop in for lunch. Try their tuna on a fresh bagel, hot soup, or salads. Sometimes parking is tight, but your search for a space will be well worth the effort.

Good Food Conspiracy
MM 30 Oceanside, Big Pine Key
(305) 872-3945

A full assortment of health foods, homeopathic remedies, vitamins, organic poultry, and organically grown produce is offered at the Good Food Conspiracy. If you browse the shelves, you'll find interesting specialty foods as well. Part of the Conspiracy is a juice and sandwich bar, which features an "outgoing menu" of healthful selections.

Key West Fish Cutters Restaurant and Fish Market
MM 25 Bayside, Summerland Key
(305) 744-3335

This restaurant and fish market is right on the water, so as you pull into the parking lot, you see the boats hauling in the catch

of the day. Call ahead to see what is in season. You can dine in or take out, and the food is Florida Keys fresh!

E Fish and Seafood
MM 22.5 Oceanside, Cudjoe Key
(305) 745-3887
Shelves and shelves of marinades and seafood sauces will inspire you to try your culinary skills in a new creation when you stop in at E Fish. The very complete fish and seafood selection lets you choose among the usual Keys finfish (grouper, snapper, and dolphin) and golden crab, stone-crab claws, lobsters, blue crabs, oysters, and mussels.

Baby's Coffee
MM 15 Oceanside, Key West
(800) 523-2326
www.babyscoffee.com
It's the hottest coffee craze in the Florida Keys, but just who is Baby? The legend lives on: "Late, last century (circa 1991), Gary & O. T. left the Big Bad Apple (NY), looking for a home for their new coffee-roasting company. They set up shop in a small building on the uptown side of Key West's famed Duval Street. In the 1920s an old Cuban family had owned this building and christened it 'Baby's Place,' after the family's youngest son. 'Baby' Rodriguez grew up and ran a cantina there where, legend has it, Ernest Hemingway indulged in the occasional crapshoot with locals, known as 'conchs.' Inspired, Gary and O. T. adopted the Baby's name and let the dice roll one more time."

Lucky for us Gary and O. T. rolled those dice, 'cause Baby's Coffee is great. And their business grew so large they had to relocate up the Keys on a no-name stretch at MM 15 (Baby's mailing address is Key West even though MM 15 is not Key West). Baby's roasts only 100 percent Arabica coffee. They ship their coffee fresh within 48 hours; it is not vacuum-packed or freeze-dried. You'll find all their Key West roasts, Hawaiian roasts, specialty roasts, flavored coffees, and decaf roasts on their Web site.

KEY WEST

The Art of Baking by Henrietta
316 Petronia Street, Bahama Village, Key West
(305) 295-0505
www.henriettakeywest.com
Hankering for a sugar rush? Head to Bahama Village and follow your nose to The Art of Baking by Henrietta. The owner is famous for her cookies; key lime, coconut, and sweet potato pies; wedding, birthday, and holiday cakes; cinnamon rolls and homemade key lime/orange marmalade. As for her Jamaican black rum cakes, pumpkin rolls, and coconut strips, well, one taste leads to another . . . and another . . . If celebrities like John Waters of *Hair Spray* and *Divine* fame select Henrietta for their birthday cakes when in Key West, shouldn't you?

Bama Sea Products
6840 Front Street, Stock Island
(305) 294-0684
Bama Sea Products, "where shrimp boats unload," is on Stock Island, and it's a great place to get seafood as fresh as if you caught it yourself. You can go watch the boats unload their catch and choose from the day's bounty of fresh shrimp, fish, lobster, conch, stone crabs, and other seafood items. They are open six days a week (closed on Sunday) and prices are retail.

Blond Giraffe
1209 Truman Avenue
(305) 293-6667

629 Duval Street
(305) 293-6998, (888) 432-6283

MM 49.5 Oceanside, Marathon Plaza, Marathon
(305) 743-4423
www.blondgiraffe.com
Key lime pie is indigenous to the Florida Keys. Ask the locals and they'll be happy to tell you their favorite recipe. Rating right up there at the top of the list is the superb blend of flavors produced at the Key Lime Pie Factory and sold by the Blond Giraffe

at two locations in Key West and one in Marathon. The supertart custard filling and sweet, fluffy meringue sit on a sinfully rich yet delicate pastry crust, reminiscent of an English butter cookie. This recipe won the 1999 Key West Key Lime Pie Festival. You can order pies and have them shipped anywhere in the United States from Blond Giraffe's Web site.

The Coffee and Tea House of Key West
1218 Duval Street
(305) 295-0788
One look at the broad porch and big, shaded yard will have you stepping inside for your coffee, then back out to sip it. Select from a plain old cup of joe or treat yourself to a latte, con leche, espresso, cappuccino, iced mocha, or fresh-brewed iced or hot tea in a variety of flavors. And how about a fresh-baked muffin, croissant, bagel, or slice of key lime pie to accompany that beverage? Mmmm . . . now grab a seat outside. Sit a spell and watch the world go by.

Damn Good Food To-Go
700 Front Street
(305) 294-0011
It's 4:00 A.M. The bars on Duval Street just called it quits, but your appetite won't. Where can you go for a bite to eat . . . or better yet have that bite delivered right to your door? Damn Good Food To-Go, that's where. This always-open, never-closed, eat-in, take-it-out, have-it-come-to-you emporium has everything you need to appease your late-night munchies. You can get breakfast from midnight to 11:00 A.M., plus hot or cold sandwiches, soups, salads, burgers, dogs, and rotisserie chicken the rest of the time. You can even satisfy your sweet tooth with a slice of New York–style cheesecake or a wedge of chocolate suicide layer cake. It's all good and all prepared fresh from recipes the owners have collected across the country. Delivery is free to Old Town, but you'll need to spend at least $15 minimum for a free delivery to New Town.

i

Harvesting conch (pronounced konk) in Florida waters is illegal. Therefore, most seafood markets import conch from the Turks and Caicos Islands. Firmer in texture than that from most other waters, conch from Turks and Caicos waters is some of the best in the world.

Fausto's Food Palace
522 Fleming Street
(305) 296-5663

1105 White Street
(305) 294-5221
www.faustos.com
"Not just a grocery, a social center" reads the slogan in the ads for this gourmet food emporium, which has been serving Key West since 1926. The Fleming Street site is its largest and oldest. Here, in addition to the usual bread, milk, produce, canned goods, and kitchen staples, you will find fresh local seafood, premium meats and poultry, and more than 700 varieties of wine as well as Beluga caviar, pâtés, rare cheeses, and desserts. A sushi chef is on duty every day, and party platters are available with as little as one hour's notice. The deli counter is especially busy at noontime when the folks who work downtown line up for their daily ration of hot soup, fresh-made sandwiches, and specials like home-made meat loaf and mashed potatoes, Cuban pork, or black beans and rice. The White Street site is more like a neighborhood grocery, with a smaller deli counter and a more limited selection of produce, bread, frozen foods, and canned goods.

5 Brothers
930 Southard Street
(305) 296-5205
If you're headed downtown along Southard Street any weekday morning between 7:30 and 8:00, expect to encounter a traffic jam at the corner of Grinnell Street. It's just the locals pulling over to pick up their "fix" at 5 Brothers. This is where Key West goes for buche,

that tiny cup of industrial-strength Cuban coffee that satisfies your caffeine habit with a single swig and gets your juices flowing. This tiny corner grocery also makes a mean Cuban mix—that's a combination ham/pork/salami/Swiss/lettuce/pickle sandwich served on Cuban bread—and great conch chowder (Friday only). For you early birds, 5 Brothers opens at 6:00 A.M. (closed Sunday).

Flamingo Crossing
1107 Duval Street
(305) 296-6124

Since 1987 this has been a favorite with locals and visitors alike. Flamingo Crossing is the place to pause for refreshment as you make your way up and down Duval. Fresh homemade ice cream is the business here, and it's the closest thing to Italian gelato this side of the Mediterranean. You can choose from such flavors as Cuban coffee, raspberry cappuccino, coconut piña colada, key lime, passion fruit, and green tea, among others. Or try the ice cream called guanabana/sour sop—two names for the same tasty, delicate fruit. Flamingo Crossing also makes its own sorbet and yogurt. If you're just in the mood for a thirst-quencher, try a key limeade. (See the Kidstuff chapter.)

Flora & Flipp on Fleming
811 Fleming Street
(305) 296-1050

Don't be fooled by appearances. This unassuming little neighborhood deli attracts everyone from the movers and shakers of Key West to tourists who just happen on it. Why? Because the folks at Flora & Flipp really know how to make a sandwich. There's a special concoction on the menu each day, but you can enjoy a perennial favorite, the Very Veggie, anytime. The sandwich has avocado, tomato, leaf lettuce, daikon, watercress, beets, and red onion with tamari dressing on Cuban bread; it's presented like a gift—wrapped in floral wrapping paper and topped with a candy kiss. To give your repast the respect it deserves, walk one block up Fleming toward Duval to the brick patio garden beside the pale pink Monroe County Public Library and sit on a park bench under the palms.

Shucked oysters are plump and have a natural creamy color and clear liquid. There should be no more than 10 percent liquid, by weight, when shucked oysters are purchased in a container.

Goldman's Bagel Deli
2796 North Roosevelt Boulevard, Overseas Market
(305) 294-3354

If not for the palm trees outside the door of this full-service restaurant-deli in the Overseas Market, you'd swear you just walked in from the streets of New York or Chicago. Here, the hot corned beef and pastrami sandwiches are sliced thin and piled high in traditional deli style, the bagels are baked fresh daily, and the cans of Dr. Brown's black cherry and cream sodas are icy cold. You can carry out such delicacies as chopped liver, potato knishes, smoked whitefish, and kosher franks, along with the bagels and an array of flavored cream cheeses sold by the pound. Try our favorite—the everything bagel "schmeered" with smoked-salmon cream cheese. Breakfast and lunch are served at tables along one side and at the counter. Deli platters and catering are also available.

Kermit's Key West Key Lime Shoppe
200 Elizabeth Street
(305) 296-0806, (800) 376-0806
www.keylimeshop.com

You can't miss this place because the key lime chef is outside waving you in to key lime heaven. Everything inside is made with key lime juice, including oils, cookies, candy kisses, salad dressings, juice concentrate, pie filling, and sweets of all sorts. You'll also find key lime soaps and lotions here. And be sure to look outside for the authentic key lime tree—the source of all this pleasure and a rarity these days in the Florida Keys.

Key West Key Lime Pie Company
701 Caroline Street
(305) 294-6567
Key lime pie, a Florida Keys tradition, is the primary business at this Old Town company, established in 1985. Each handmade, 9-inch pie (also sold by the slice) is frozen, literally melting in your mouth, bite by bite. The company will ship the pies anywhere in the continental United States overnight or provide you with a frozen travel pack, so you can take a pie on the road with you or back home by airplane. If a fork isn't your style, how about key lime pie on a stick, dipped in dark chocolate? Messy to eat, but, oh, so yummy.

Key West Tea & Coffee
608 Front Street, Key West
(305) 292-7998, (888) 840-1280
www.keywesttea.com
Drink a little sun-glow when you visit Key West—Sun-glow tea, that is. Made with apple, hibiscus, rosehips, papaya, pineapple, and orange, this brightly flavored beverage is just one of many fruit-infusion teas you can find at Key West Tea & Coffee. If fruit infusions aren't your cup of tea, how about a powerful and malty black tea, like Mallory Square, or a green tea like Pirate's Gunpowder, or the classic Key West tea? You won't be left out here if you prefer a cup of joe: Try the French Roast or Columbian Supremo. If you fall in love with a flavor you can't buy back home, you can order it from the Web site.

---

i

Why are shrimp caught in Key West waters called "Key West Pinks?" Shrimp take on the color of the bottom of the sea. Shrimp harvested off a sandy seafloor are an amber color. Those harvested off a coral bottom, such as surrounds Key West, are light pink in color.

La Dichosa Bakery
1206 White Street
(305) 296-6188
If you've had anything on Cuban bread anywhere in Key West, chances are that bread came from this bakery. La Dichosa supplies just about all of Key West's restaurants with these long loaves of flat, flavorful, crusty bread. But that's not all you'll find here. The cases are filled with all kinds of baked goodies—cupcakes, éclairs, napoleons, and chocolate chip cookies so buttery rich they crumble at the touch. La Dichosa also makes wedding cakes. You can even grab a con leche or buche to complement your sweet treat. Sit inside or take it to go.

Mattheessen and Magilner's Candy Kitchen
419 Duval Street
(305) 296-8014
No tourist destination is complete without at least one fudge shop. In Key West you'll find more than your fill of this melt-in-your-mouth confection at this Duval Street emporium. Traditional chocolate is always a favorite, of course, but the key lime and maple-pecan varieties are equally tasty and sinful.

Mattheessen's 4th of July
Ice Cream Parlor
1110 White Street, Key West
(305) 294-8089
The original 4th of July Restaurant opened its doors in the 1950s and didn't close them until the 1980s. Now this Key West tradition has been revived by the Mattheessen family, who have remodeled the old eatery with sparkling, new, red, white, and blue décor and are now offering ice cream, marble-slab fudge, cookies, and BBQ to old aficionados and enthusiastic newcomers. Gleaming new glass cases let your little ones look at their choices of ice cream. Bright blue booths tempt those who want to linger for a while. Slide in and treat yourself to a Cuban sundae, made with Cuban coffee, mocha chips, and Dulce de Leche ice cream topped with

hot fudge and caramel sauce, chocolate-covered espresso beans, whipped cream, and of course, a cherry on top.

Peppers of Key West
602 Greene Street
(305) 295-9333, (800) 597-2823
www.peppersofkeywest.com
Peppers, where chile peppers are the name of the game, bills itself as "the hottest spot on the island." More than 300 varieties of hot sauces already grace the shelves, and more arrive from all over every day. Peppers always has a basket of chips and a few open bottles at the front counter so you can have a taste, if you dare. In addition, the folks here will open any bottle in the store if you ask for a sample. Best-sellers include Big Bubba's Rubba Jerk Rub, Crazy Jerry's Lizard Eyes, Goin' Bananas, Hog's Ass Barbecue Sauce, Hot n' Honey, and JC's Midnight Salsa. Peppers bottles their own brands of "hot"— #1, #2, and Goin' Bananas. Look for their key lime juice as well. And be sure to look around the neighborhood for the chile pepper car. It belongs to one of the owners and can usually be found parked near the shop.

Planet Smoothie
1075 Duval Street
(305) 294-4604
For a breakfast charge or to kick an afternoon slump, head for Planet Smoothie, where the drinks are made from the freshest ingredients. Try the Chocolate Elvis, made with peanut butter, bananas, yogurt, and chocolate, of course. Or maybe you'd prefer the Road Runner, a whirl of perfection made from blueberries, strawberries, bananas, and OJ. On request, they'll slip in a protein supplement too, to really keep you going. Planet Smoothie also offers health foods: bars, dried foods, and snacks.

Rusty Anchor Fisheries
5510 Third Avenue, Stock Island
(305) 296-2893
www.rustyanchorseafood.com
Where's the fish? A little Insider help is needed to negotiate for fish at this place, known to locals as having the freshest at the best prices. The fish market is directly behind Rusty Anchor Restaurant, which is on Third Avenue (see our Restaurants chapter), although no sign on Third Avenue indicates the fishmonger's presence. Your safest bet is to enter the restaurant and look for brown double doors at the far end of the room. Exit through these portals, and you will find yourself outside, directly in front of a fish-cleaning building. Find out about the catch of the day, and then it's "Let's make a deal!" Rusty Anchor is known for some of the best prices on jumbo stone-crab claws and colossal shrimp ("under 15s"). Alternately, but not as much fun, you can call and get the daily fish report.

Fresh fish has practically no odor at all. The fishy odor becomes more pronounced with time. If you notice a strong disagreeable odor when making your purchase, the fish is not fresh.

Stock Island Lobster Co.
6639 Maloney Avenue, Stock Island
(305) 296-5844
This wholesale fishery and lobstering operation doesn't have a showcase retail shop, but it will sell to the general public. Call for prices and availability of the catch of the day (sold as whole fish only), stone-crab claws, and whole Florida lobsters in season.

Sugar Apple Natural Foods
917 Simonton Street
(305) 292-0043
A longtime favorite of health-conscious Key Westers, Sugar Apple stocks organic and hard-to-find groceries, vitamins, beauty aids, homeopathic remedies, books, and herbs. A juice bar and deli serve up sandwiches, smoothies, specials, and teas. The owners and staff are very knowledgeable about their products and the benefits of healthy living.

Waterfront Market
201 William Street
(305) 296-0778

The serious cooking aficionado and the robust eater will have a ball in this market, now located between the Caroline Street side of the Key West Historic Seaport and William Street (parking entrance). Browsing the shelves reminds us of perusing an international library. All the difficult-to-find ingredients for Japanese, Thai, Chinese, or even Middle Eastern dishes dress the shelves here, often scrutinized by Key West's top professional chefs. A dried-bean emporium showcases bins of baby limas, black beans, pintos, and even black-eyed peas. A similar rice case offers sushi rice, winter wheat, and bulgur (and those are just the ones we recognize).

Waterfront Market features a complete fish market, sushi by Origami (see listing in the Restaurants chapter), bakery, deli, coffee-bean center, and produce counter.

NIGHTLIFE

In the Florida Keys, what to do after our famous sunsets is a choice as individualistic as our residents and visitors.

But for those revelers who like to party until the wee hours, we take you on a club crawl, tavern tromp, saloon slog—call it what you like. Come promenade our pubs, bars, and nightclubs from Key Largo to Key West, our southernmost city, where a night on the town redefines the cliché.

As a general rule, bars are open later the farther down in the Keys you go, with many establishments in Key West open until 4:00 A.M. Taverns and pubs in the Upper and Middle Keys are more likely to close between midnight and 2:00 A.M.

We encourage you to have fun and enjoy our casual Keys pubs, but keep in mind that the DUI limit here is .08, less than some other states. Remember, too, that driving-under-the-influence laws apply to all vehicles—scooters and bikes included. So if you drink, don't drive. Or pedal. Take a cab or take along a designated driver.

You'll find the majority of these places open seven nights a week. Exceptions are noted. Remember, however, that hours and entertainment may vary depending on the season or whim of the owners. To avoid disappointment, it is always best to phone ahead.

UPPER KEYS

Caribbean Club
MM 104.5 Bayside, Key Largo
(305) 451-4466

Bogey and Bacall are alive and well in this famous Key Largo bar and restaurant. The walls are filled with memorabilia from the 1948 classic movie, *Key Largo,* which was filed here. Great sunset views and live entertainment draw late-night crowds, making this a popular locals' hangout. They have come into the 21st century by offering karaoke one night a week and, oh, yes, the popular Beach Boys tune, "Kokomo," which mentions Key Largo, is sometimes on the request list.

Breezer's Tiki Bar
MM 103.8 Bayside, Marriott Key Largo Bay Beach Resort, Key Largo
(305) 453-0000
www.marriottkeylargo.com/restaurants

Breezer's is an elegant, elevated gazebo-sheltered bar overlooking the showy property and wondrous waters of the Marriott Key Largo Bay Beach Resort. This fantasy island setting provides the perfect backdrop for the accompanying live island-style music on Friday and Saturday. Having a drink here is soothing to the soul.

Coconuts Restaurant & Lounge
MM 100 Oceanside, Marina Del Mar Resort and Marina, 528 Caribbean Drive, Key Largo
(305) 453-9794
www.coconutsrestaurant.com

A perennial nightclub favorite with a percolating dance floor, Coconuts has theme nights that keep 'em coming: Monday, disco night; Tuesday, blues; Wednesday, ladies' night, with free drinks to all females from 9:00 to 11:00 P.M.; Thursday, Friday, and Saturday, live Top-40 dance bands; and Sunday, karaoke. See our Restaurants chapter for dining options here.

Holiday Inn Key Largo Resort and Marina
MM 99.7 Oceanside, Key Largo
(305) 451-2121
www.holidayinnkeylargo.com

You'll discover a couple of options at the Holiday Inn Key Largo. Bogie's Cafe has a piano lounge where you can enjoy the

Many Florida Keys watering holes have a happy hour, which often coincides with the daily sunset celebration.

tinkling of the ivories. Picking up the pace a bit with live music Thursday through Saturday, a mix of reggae, rock, and pop attracts an equal mingling of locals and tourists to the outdoor tiki bar.

Snapper's Waterfront Saloon & Raw Bar
MM 94.5 Oceanside, Key Largo
(305) 852-5956
www.thefloridakeys.com/snappers

Snapper's oozes Keys atmosphere, especially on the cypress-and-palm-frond chickees on the outside waterside deck. Menu items are innovative (see the Restaurants chapter), and patrons enjoy live entertainment on weekends.

Hog Heaven Sports Bar
MM 85.3 Oceanside, Islamorada
(305) 664-9669
www.keysdining.com/hogheaven

The congenial outdoor saloon of Hog Heaven Sports Bar sits unassumingly on the waterfront. You can amuse yourself with televised sports, talk with the locals, or head to the point, where a chickee yields seclusion that may foster romance. As you might expect, the pork here is heavenly.

Lorelei Cabana Bar
MM 82 Bayside, Islamorada
(305) 664-4338
www.loreleifloridakeys.com

This bar not only serves great drinks, but the Lorelei offers one of the best views of stunning sunsets in the Florida Keys. The bar is a laid-back waterside watering hole and lunch spot all day long, and the views of Florida Bay cannot be beat. See our Restaurants chapter for dining options here.

Woody's Saloon & Restaurant
MM 82 Bayside, Islamorada
(305) 664-4335
www.keysdining.com/woodys

Woody's hand-tossed, Chicago-style pizza is great, but this saloon's claim to fame just has to be its regular entertainment offering: Big Dick and the Extenders (Thursday through Saturday). A suggestive play on words, Big Dick is most certainly a tall man, and his schtick—making rude fun of audience members—makes Howard Stern look like a choirboy. The Extenders do play some music, but the audience-participation dirty joke contest allows Dick, who wears a very big top hat, to sharpen his barbs. Sit in the back unless you have a thick skin or a penchant for verbal abuse. And now Woody's has the Keys' answer to Las Vegas Showgirls—"The Sassy But Classy All Female Dance Revue," Tuesday through Saturday.

MIDDLE KEYS

Truman's at WatersEdge
MM 61 Oceanside, Hawk's Cay Resort & Marina, Duck Key
(305) 743-7000
www.hawkscay.com

An intimate dance floor heats up the action with live entertainment during high season, but all year long this watering hole, just off the Hawk's Cay Marina, finds guides, island residents, and hotel guests trading fish stories. The bar area is adjacent to the popular family-style restaurant, the WatersEdge (see the Restaurants chapter).

Dockside Lounge
MM 53 Oceanside, 35 Sombrero Road Sombrero Marina, Marathon
(305) 743-0000
www.keysy.com/dockside

The dock rocks during Sunday-night jam sessions, when bands from throughout

Florida showcase their talents. This laid-back, open-air harborside lounge is a hub for Boot Key live-aboards who ride dinghies to shore and park their bicycles and cars nearby. Live entertainment is offered nightly at Dockside.

Brass Monkey
MM 50 Oceanside, Kmart Plaza, Marathon
(305) 743-4028, (305) 743-5737
This long-established bar and liquor store is a regulars' hangout in Marathon. The Brass Monkey serves up not only lunch and dinner but also live music six nights a week. The lounge opens early and closes in the wee hours. "That Funky Monkey" is still going strong after all these years!

Seven Mile Grill
MM 46 Oceanside, Marathon
(305) 743-4481
You can't miss this watering hole, as it sits off U.S. Highway 1 at the beginning of the Seven Mile Bridge heading south to Key West. When it opens in the morning, you see the many folks lining the bar to sip their favorite beverage and toast the local color that is the Florida Keys. Lite fare is on the menu, as are the many drinks of choice.

LOWER KEYS

No Name Pub
MM 31 Bayside, North Watson Boulevard, Big Pine Key
(305) 872-9115
Wallpapered with dollar bills and full of good cheer and local color, No Name Pub is a must-do, night or day (see the Restaurants chapter for menu offerings and directions). Off the beaten path about as far as you can go in Big Pine, this small saloon sports a funky bar and a pool table.

Parrotdise Bar and Grill
MM 28.5, Bayside, 183 Barry Avenue, Little Torch Key
(305) 872-9989

You must be 21 years of age to purchase or consume alcohol in Florida, including beer. Be sure to carry ID as most establishments will card you. Remember to drink responsibly and don't drink and drive. There are plenty of modes of transportation available to get you home.

Perched high above the Big Pine Channel, on the Gulf, sits this local haunt. New owners may have changed the name, but the Parrotdise is still a fun, casual meeting hangout for drinks and eats. Easily accessible by car or boat, this bar and grill offers wine and beer along with fabulous water views.

KEY WEST

Renowned for its nightlife, Key West boasts of having more bars per capita than anywhere else in the United States. With many of the establishments open seven days a week until 4:00 A.M., this tiny island lives up to its slightly eccentric reputation. An age-old tradition in Key West is called the "Duval Crawl"—a sampling of libations from all the nightspots on Duval Street, until the only means of moving is to crawl.

In this section we recommend a road map for such a crawl. We start at the Atlantic end of Duval Street, where the pubs are more sparsely located, and move toward the Gulf of Mexico, where the kegs flow freely. *NOTE:* We do not recommend trying to take in every establishment listed here in one night, but if you do, please take a taxi when you finish (see the Getting Here, Getting Around chapter).

Of course, not all the bars in Key West are on Duval Street. We have also included a section called Local Favorites—Key West classics that are a little more off the beaten path but definitely worth checking out. Cheers!

The Quintessential Duval Crawl

La-Te-Da
1125 Duval Street
(305) 296-6706
www.lateda.com

The La-Te-Da is a combination hotel, cabaret, restaurant, and bar that has been an icon of the party scene since 1978. They not only offer a bar that faces lively Duval Street but also live entertainment in their Cabaret Lounge as well as the By George Bar. There is also a Terrace Bar overlooking the beautiful tropical pool. With the great island drinks and delicious food being served here, you may find it difficult to leave this adult party scene.

801 Bourbon Bar
801 Duval Street
(305) 294-4737
www.801bourbon.com

With a clientele consisting of primarily gay patrons and tourists, the 801 offers a first-floor bar with billiards. A second floor offers live entertainment with drag shows nightly, beginning at 11:00 P.M.; if you've never seen a drag show, you may be pleasantly surprised. The professionally choreographed productions here are loads of fun.

Bourbon Street Pub
724 Duval Street
(305) 296-1992
www.bourbonstreetpub.com

Live entertainment at the predominantly gay Bourbon Street includes bands, drag shows, comedians, and, on weekends, male dancers. Key West's only VJ plays tunes, mixing videos with songs for dancing. The emphasis here is on high-energy dance music. Happy hour is noon to 8:00 P.M. daily, and Friday is the Drag Your Ass to Bourbon Street party, when all bartenders dress in drag and the bar sees its largest crowd of the week.

Green Parrot
601 Whitehead Street
(305) 294-6133
www.greenparrot.com

Not exactly on Duval Street, but close enough and so quintessentially Key West, the Green Parrot rates a stop on any Duval Crawl. Frequented primarily by locals, this eclectic bar is housed in an 1890s-era building half a block off Duval, down Southard Street. Walls are adorned with unusual oversize portraits and a wall mural of the Garden of Eden. Weekends feature local and national bands playing blues and zydeco, and the large dance floor is usually crowded. The bar also sports video games, billiard tables, darts, a pinball machine, and a jukebox. And if you're hungry, the Meteor Smokehouse next door has great ribs (see the Restaurants chapter).

Virgilio's
524 Duval Street
(305) 296-8118
www.latrattoriakeywest.com

This classy little New York-style bar is not really on Duval; it's actually situated on Applerouth Lane, just around the corner from La Trattoria, one of Key West's best Italian eateries (see the Restaurants chapter). Martinis and their cousins—Gibsons, Manhattans, and cosmopolitans—are the specialty here. Grab a seat at the bar or in one of the overstuffed easy chairs while you sip your cocktail and listen to live light jazz and contemporary music from some of Key West's finest musical talent.

Rum Barrel
524 Front Street, Key West
(305) 292-7862
www.rumbarrel.com

Owners of the Pirate Soul Museum have made another tremendous addition to their legacy by opening the Rum Barrel. This active, fun bar and restaurant is located right next to the museum (see Attractions chapter) so it is a no-brainer to have lunch, dinner, or just drinks here on your jaunt in and around Key West. The interior has the aura of a 300-year-old tavern, and the seating is terrific; you can sit outside overlooking Old Town or inside at the Quarterdeck bar, listening to live music. Rum Barrel is proud to serve more than 30 different beers by the bottle or on draught. Their food is described as "get-your-hands-dirty" and they equally boast of having the biggest burgers and turkey legs found anywhere. Yo ho ho!!!

Jimmy Buffett's Margaritaville Cafe
500 Duval Street
(305) 292-1435
www.margaritaville.com/keywest
Yes, the big man himself does play here once in a while, as do some of the Coral Reefers and bands that have opened for Jimmy on tour. Props from past concerts decorate the walls and ceiling. Beginning at 10:30 each night and continuing well into the wee hours, a variety of bands and solo artists perform everything from rock 'n' roll to reggae to rhythm and blues. Margaritas are just one of the many frozen drinks offered at the air-conditioned yet open-air bar. You can nosh on a Cheeseburger in Paradise with all the fixin's or pick up some Buffett clothing, recordings, books, and memorabilia at the shop next door (see the Restaurants and Shopping chapters).

The Top
Crowne Plaza Key West La Concha
430 Duval Street
(305) 296-2991
www.laconchakeywest.com
High above the city of Key West, with views of the Key West harbor as well as up and down Duval Street, this eagle's-eye perch is one of the most famous bars in all the Keys. The Crowne Plaza Key West La Concha (see Accommodations chapter) was the first upscale lodging facility in the area, and to accommodate its infamous and famous clientele, this bar was developed. Rumor has it Hemingway romanced Ava Gardner and Marlene Dietrich at La Concha and spent many romantic nights high in the sky (in more ways than one) here at this bar. It offers a great view of Fantasy Fest revelers (see Annual Events chapter) or just a superb sunset aerie. They also have nightly entertainment, which changes weekly. Call to check out the lineup.

For the latest listing of which bands are playing where in Key West, check* Paradise, *the entertainment section in Thursday's edition of the* Key West Citizen. *Free copies of* Paradise *are available throughout the Keys at hotels, restaurants, and wherever newspapers are sold.

Hard Rock Cafe
313 Duval Street
(305) 293-0230
www.hardrock.com
A world-renowned classic, Hard Rock Cafe joined the Conch Republic in the summer of 1996. Situated in a renovated, three-story, Conch-style house on Duval Street, Hard Rock Cafe Key West celebrates historic Key West, the preservation of the Florida Keys' fragile environment, and, of course, rock 'n' roll. This 235-seat Hard Rock is open seven days a week and serves up all-American fare.

Fat Tuesday
305 Duval Street
(305) 296-9373
Stop in at Fat Tuesday and choose from one of 26 flavors of frozen drinks, including margaritas, piña coladas, and 190-octane rum runners. Our favorite is the Pain in the Ass, a combination piña colada and rum runner. The motto here is "One daiquiri, two daiquiri, three daiquiri, floor," and you can even buy a T-shirt that says it.

Bull & Whistle
224 Duval Street
(305) 296-4565
www.thebullandwhistle.com

Take a guided walking tour of the most famous and interesting drinking establishments in Key West, beginning in Old Town and ending on Duval Street. Led by your "professional" guide, you'll be treated to jokes, antics, contests, and stories (Best of the Bars, 305-292-9994; www.keywesthunt.com).

This local favorite is actually three bars in one. The Bull is downstairs and features live music in an open-air setting. The Whistle is upstairs and offers pool and video games, along with a great view of Duval Street from the balcony. The Garden of Eden, on the very top, has a great view of Key West . . . and more. It's the only clothing-optional roof garden in town. The Bull & Whistle complex is located at the corner of Duval and Caroline Streets.

Rick's Key West
202–208 Duval Street
(305) 296–4890, (877) 659–9719
www.rickskeywest.com
Rick's Key West offers four nightspots in one complex. Rick's Downstairs Bar offers live professional entertainment from 3:00 P.M. until midnight. Then the amateurs take over until 4:00 A.M. at the karaoke bar. The Tree Bar allows you to sit and sip a spell, all the while watching the sights of Duval Street pass by. Durty Harry's opens at 8:00 P.M. and plays live rock 'n' roll until 4:00 A.M. This bar also has a television wall, which shows all major sporting events. And for a little more risqué entertainment, the Red Garter Saloon is a mirror-and-brass adult club. Pick your pleasure.

Captain Tony's Saloon
428 Greene Street
(305) 294–1838
www.capttonyssaloon.com
Just half a block off Duval, this watering hole is the site of Key West's first hanging tree, still in evidence inside the bar. Captain Tony's is the original location of Sloppy Joe's. Once owned by Capt. Tony Tarracino, a friend of Jimmy Buffett and a former Key West mayor, the saloon features walls covered with undies and business cards. Live entertainment is offered nightly.

Sloppy Joe's Bar
201 Duval Street
(305) 294–5717
www.sloppyjoes.com
It's no wonder this was Hemingway's favorite watering hole. The upbeat atmosphere of Sloppy Joe's is contagious. The bar opened in 1933 on the site of what is now Captain Tony's Saloon. In 1937 it moved to its current location. Some say that Hemingway did some writing in the back rooms of the bar and kept a few of his manuscripts locked up here. Photos of Hemingway line the walls. Live entertainment is offered from noon to 2:00 A.M. daily. Among the brews offered here is Sloppy Joe's beer, which is actually made by Coors. A gift shop sells T-shirts, boxer shorts, hats, and other souvenirs with the Sloppy Joe's logo.

Hog's Breath Saloon
400 Front Street
(305) 292–2032
www.hogsbreath.com
"The Hog," as locals know this place, features an open-air mahogany bar surrounded by water-sports-related memorabilia, including mounted fish and surfboards. You can try the medium-bodied Hog's Breath beer and sample one of the saloon's famed fish sandwiches. The restaurant (see the Restaurants chapter) is open for lunch and dinner. Live bands play rock, folk rock, blues, and jazz throughout the day and well into the evening. You can purchase T-shirts, hats, and sundry other items emblazoned with the saloon's slogan: "Hog's Breath is better than no breath at all."

Pier House Resort
1 Duval Street
(305) 296-4600, (800) 327-8340
www.pierhouse.com
Pier House offers a little something for everyone. The view of the famous Key West sunset is beautiful from the Havana Docks Bar, and the intimate Beach Bar & Grille has great entertainment nightly. If you like things a little quieter, settle in and enjoy the piano bar in the dimly lit Wine Galley. The tiny Chart Room Bar, which is filled with peanut shells, is a favorite hangout with the locals.

Local Favorites

The Afterdeck Bar at Louie's Backyard
700 Waddell Avenue
(305) 294-1061
www.louiesbackyard.com
The deck is large and right on the water. And we do mean right on the water. One false step, a few cocktails too many, and . . . splash! Service is friendly and courteous, and the setting is exactly what you were thinking of when you first thought of coming to the Florida Keys. The adjoining restaurant is one of Key West's finest (see the Restaurants chapter under Louie's Backyard).

Atlantic Shores Pool Bar & Grille
510 South Street
(305) 296-2491, (800) 526-3559
www.glresorts.com
The weekly tea dance at Atlantic Shores—Key West's own version of Miami's South Beach-style art deco joints—draws Sunday-night partygoers in droves. A poolside disc jockey plays dance tunes, and wait-staff serve cocktails. The pool area at Atlantic Shores is clothing-optional and tends to be mostly frequented by gays. On Thursday night Atlantic Shores also shows artistic independent and foreign films not found at the big cinemas as well as some popular recent flicks you may have missed; call for details.

Finnegan's Wake Irish Pub & Eatery
320 Grinnell Street
(305) 293-0222
www.keywestirish.com
Exactly like a good Irish public house ought to be, Finnegan's keeps the merriment going until nearly dawn (4:00 A.M.) and is among a mere handful of Key West establishments serving food into the wee hours (see the Restaurants chapter). You're sure to find your Guinness here, and you can even down a black and tan. Order one and the barkeep will think you just returned from the Emerald Isle. Enjoy live Irish music on weekends.

PT's Late Night Bar and Grill
920 Caroline Street
(305) 296-4245
This local gathering spot offers billiards, darts, trivia games, and the opportunity to catch up with friends over a variety of home-style meals or drinks. The pot roast here is legendary. Televised sports provide most of the entertainment, but live bands do occasionally perform.

Schooner Wharf Bar
202 William Street
(305) 292-9520
www.schoonerwharf.com
Dockside at the Key West Historic Seaport is the open-air, thatched-palm Schooner Wharf, which bills itself as "the last little bit of old Key West." The place offers outdoor thatched-umbrella tables, a covered bar, grill, and indoor games, including billiards and darts. Live jazz, rhythm and blues, and island music are featured nightly.

Stick and Stein Sports Rock Cafe
Key Plaza Shopping Center,
North Roosevelt Boulevard
(305) 296-3352
With 11 pool tables, air hockey, darts, and video and pinball games, Stick and Stein earns its reputation as the biggest sports bar in Key West. Watch the game of your choice on one of 80 TV screens or satisfy

CLOSE-UP

See You in the Movies

Lights, camera, action! The Florida Keys is an ongoing movie, of sorts. We have glorious weather, Technicolor tropical scenery, and the most interesting people! No wonder the Keys attracts not only tourists but also a steady stream of filmmakers. Ever since the forties, in fact, moviemakers have been coming to the Keys, using our landmarks as backdrops to some of motion pictures' most memorable scenes.

True Lies (1993) starring now-governor Arnold Schwarzenegger, was one of the most memorable. Can you remember Jamie Lee Curtis dangling high over the Seven Mile Bridge? Or Anna Magnani, standing in the door of St. Paul's church on Duval Street, pleading her case to the priest in *Rose Tattoo* (1959)? The James Bond thriller, *License to Kill* (1988) was shot in and around the Hemingway House in Key West. *PT 109* (1962) had Cliff Robertson portraying John Kennedy on Little Palm Island Resort near Little Torch Key. And the 2004 flick, *The Pacifier,* followed macho actor Vin Diesel off Mallory Square in Key West, near Sunset Key.

The list goes on—right here. Rent a few—or all of these films—and see if you can guess the Keys' locations where they were shot.

Cuba Gooding, Jr. on set. PHOTO: ROB O'NEAL

1944	*To Have and Have Not*	Humphrey Bogart & Lauren Bacall
1948	*Key Largo*	Humphrey Bogart & Lauren Bacall
1954	*Beneath the Twelve Mile Reef*	Robert Wagner & Terry Moore
	Rose Tattoo	Anna Magnani & Burt Lancaster
1956	*Carib Gold*	Ethel Waters & Cicely Tyson
1959	*Operation Petticoat*	Tony Curtis & Cary Grant
1960	*All Fall Down*	Warren Beatty & Angela Lansbury
1962	*PT 109*	Cliff Robertson
1974	*92 in the Shade*	Peter Fonda
1979	*The Last Resort*	Eartha Kitt
	The Final Countdown	Martin Sheen & Kirk Douglas
1985	*Running Scared*	Billy Crystal
1988	*License to Kill*	Timothy Dalton
1991–92	*Criss-Cross*	Goldie Hawn
1992–93	*Matinee*	John Goodman
1993	*True Lies*	Arnold Schwarzenegger & Jamie Lee Curtis
1994	*Drop Zone*	Wesley Snipes
1995	*Up Close and Personal*	Michelle Pfeiffer & Robert Redford
	Blood and Wine	Jack Nicholson
	Executive Decision	Steven Seagal
1996	*Spanish Prisoner*	Steve Martin
	Speed 2	Sandra Bullock
1997	*Assault on Devil's Island*	"Hulk" Hogan
	Tomorrow Never Dies	Pierce Brosnan
	Murder of Crows	Cuba Gooding, Jr.
1998	*Office Space*	Jennifer Aniston
2000	*The Crew*	Burt Reynolds
	Heartbreakers	Sigourney Weaver & Jennifer Hewitt
2002	*Red Dragon*	Ralph Fiennes
	2 Fast 2 Furious	Paul Walker
2004	*The Pacifier*	Vin Diesel

That's a wrap! And "you'll be back" . . . to the fabulous Florida Keys.

*Monroe County Tourist Development Council

your appetite with some chicken wings or peel-and-eat shrimp.

Turtle Kraals Waterfront Seafood Grill and Bar
231 Margaret Street
(305) 294-2640
www.turtlekraals.com

The lounge portion of this turtle-cannery-turned-restaurant rocks throughout the evening, offering live entertainment (in season) and billiard tables in an open-air, waterfront setting (see the Restaurants chapter). Turtle Kraals's full bar is known for its frozen margaritas, microbrewed beers, and imported beers on tap.

ACCOMMODATIONS 

From luxury resorts to little-known hideaways, the Florida Keys' myriad accommodations suit every vacation fantasy and budget.

What began in the 1930s as a small assortment of fishing camps experienced a renaissance after World War II ended. Henry Flagler's Railroad and the creation of the Overseas Highway had made our islands more accessible, but residents still relied on cisterns for fresh water until water lines were installed to service the Key West naval base during World War II. The availability of fresh water made our region a more civilized and desirable vacation destination, and, in the 1950s and 1960s, when motoring became a popular means of travel, hotels and motels sprang up throughout our islands.

LOCATION AND AMENITIES

Like our Conchs—those of us born in the Keys—and Keys characters—those of us who were not—accommodations in the Florida Keys are highly individualistic. Most are situated on the Florida Bay, the Gulf of Mexico, or the Atlantic Ocean. We commonly refer to the Atlantic as "oceanside." For simplicity's sake in this chapter, we refer to the bayside and gulfside as "bayside."

You can enjoy swimming and water sports in either the bay or the ocean. Expect to find our coastline waters calmer than those you may have encountered in the rest of South Florida. The waters of the Gulf of Mexico and Florida Bay cover shallow sea-grass flats, and the barrier reef, some 4 to 5 miles offshore in the Atlantic, breaks the surf, thereby keeping waters inside the reef from 1 to 3 feet most of the time. The oceanside coastline is also fronted with shallow flats in places. The interruption of wave action by the coral reef dictates that the Florida Keys does not have an abundance of natural beaches. Most of our beaches are made with imported sand and are unsupervised.

Oceanside accommodations offer exotic sunrises and proximity to dive sites, oceanside flats, and blue-water locations for sportfishing. Water access is generally deeper on the oceanside than in the bay, affording boaters and sailors more options. Bayside lodgings can boast of our spectacular Keys sunsets, which sink into the placid skinny waters of the Gulf like a meltdown of molten lava. Some hotels, motels, resorts, and inns sit alongside inland canals or marina basins, and many of our waterfront facilities are accessible by boat.

Many of our small mom-and-pop lodgings you will see lining the Overseas Highway were primarily built in the 1950s and 1960s as fishing camps. These facilities offer basic, affordable rooms and efficiencies, some with screened patios. Mom-and-pop motels often draw cost-conscious families, last-minute travelers, anglers, and scuba divers—those active, outdoorsy types seeking nothing more than a bed and a shower. These motels have a high return rate.

Also individually owned, but often with more expansive waterfront properties and recreational amenities, are facilities that offer a potpourri of accommodation options, ranging from sleeping rooms to efficiencies to multiple-bedroom apartments, often within one property. Many sleeping rooms provide mini-refrigerators and have balconies, while efficiencies offer abbreviated kitchens as well. Suites, villas, and cottages will allow you the space to spread out a bit and to cook a meal or two "at home" when the mood hits. They usually have a sleeper sofa in the living space and a full kitchen. These accommodations often maintain freshwater swimming pools, hot tubs, and guest laundry facilities. If they don't offer on-premises water sports, these recreational activities are almost always located nearby. Since all of these properties have evolved throughout the decades with a multitude of owners, ask whether your accommodations have been updated recently. Most owners renovate when the budget allows, so some rooms or cottages may be more desirable than others.

Our large comprehensive resorts offer all the amenities of a mom-and-pop facility and then some. From fitness to child-care centers and concierge to room service, these hotels cater to families and honeymooners, business travelers and sports enthusiasts, power players and movie stars. You'll find tennis courts and water sports, fishing charters and dive excursions. Some offer optional conference rooms or a variety of travel/sport packages. Couples often opt for romantic weddings and honeymoons amid our tropical breezes, lush foliage, crystalline seas, and magnificent sunsets.

And when spring break rolls around, college students from across the country flood our hotels, beaches, tiki bars, and nightspots.

Whether the accommodations are large, small, or somewhere in between, all of our guest properties exude a casual, barefoot ambience. To one degree or another, all bestow the uninterrupted escape for which the Florida Keys has always been known.

RATE INFORMATION

Rate structures for Keys lodgings vary nearly as much as the accommodations themselves, but you can draw a few generalizations. Rates fluctuate by season and depend largely upon the size of the accommodation and its proximity to the water.

High season (December through April) supports the highest rates. High-season rates usually prevail during sport lobster season in July (a near holiday in the Keys; see the Diving chapter), Fantasy Fest in the autumn (our southernmost decadent version of Mardi Gras; see our Annual Events chapter), and most national holiday weekends. You must make reservations well in advance of your visit during any of these times. Many facilities fully book available accommodations one year in advance for high season and the holidays.

A second season commences in May and continues through the summer months, attracting vacationers seeking to escape the steamy heat of the rest of Florida and the Deep South. Rates during this period are generally slightly less than high season.

Low season is September and October, bringing a savings of about 20 percent off high-season rates. Some facilities maintain low-season rates into November as well.

Rates for motel or sleeping rooms, which typically hold two double beds, are based on single or double occupancy. Additional guests are charged a supplementary fee, but motels impose a maximum occupancy for each room.

Children younger than age 13 frequently are permitted to stay for free when accompanied by an adult. Cribs and cots often are provided at no charge or at a minimal additional cost.

Condominiums, villas, and cottages generally establish a weekly rate per unit, but many also offer a three- or four-night package as well, which is priced per night.

Accommodations of like rating will command differing prices, depending upon how close they are to the waterfront and what kind of view they offer. If you prefer accommodations overlooking the bay or ocean, ask for a bayfront or oceanfront room. Sometimes waterfront means a canal or lagoon. Be sure to query. Water view does not necessarily mean that your room will be on or facing the water, but as a general rule, water view is less expensive and provides at least a glimpse of the bay or ocean. Garden views and nonwaterfront accommodations, often just a short walk to water's edge, are priced even lower.

We suggest you shop around for exact daily or weekly rates and vacancies. Be sure to ask if the facility offers any discounted rates. Sometimes you can luck into a short-term discount or sport package that will be just what you are seeking.

In all cases, rates are quoted for the high season. Prices for motel- or sleeping-room facilities are figured on a double-occupancy average rate per night. Villas, efficiencies, and condominium units, which generally establish rates per unit rather than per person, will be quoted as such. And even though these units traditionally are rented by the week, we have computed our code on an average daily rate so that you can compare apples with apples.

It is not uncommon to find accommodations that run the gamut of several price-code categories all at the same place. The code will indicate if you can expect a range of space and pocketbook possibilities. (Accommodations in Key West generally are more expensive than the rest of the Keys; therefore, we have established a separate pricing key for Key West accommodations.)

Price codes are high-season rates figured without additional fees, such as room service and calls, and without the 11.5 percent room tax. Our recommended accommodations accept major credit cards unless otherwise specified.

PRICE-CODE KEY

$	**$55 to $99**
$$	**$100 to $150**
$$$	**$151 to $250**
$$$$	**$251 and higher**

RESERVATION AND CANCELLATION POLICIES

Typically, you confirm your room by holding it with a major credit card. If you do not have a major credit card, you may often hold a room with an advance check or money order. The balance—always paid with a credit card, traveler's checks, or cash—will be collected either upon check-in or check-out. Be aware that cancellation policies vary.

If you do not cancel your room within a property's specified advance time, you will likely be charged a sizable fee whether or not you arrive. And when you pay for a room when you check-in, most facilities do not provide refunds or credits if you pay for more days than you are able to stay.

During high season and special events, our facilities almost always are full. You might benefit from a no-show on a walk-in basis late at night, but we suggest reserving and confirming dates, accommodations, and prices three to six months in advance. More desirable facilities fill up more rapidly, and special events sometimes require one-year advance planning.

To avoid potential complications, be sure to inquire about all details of your accommodations when making reservations and confirmations. Obtain a confirmation number and the full name of the person who takes your reservation.

If you are planning to arrive at one of our resort marinas by sailing or motor yacht, be sure to read our Cruising chapter first. Dockage space for transient cruisers is at a premium at these desirable establishments and is often booked a year in advance during high season. Be sure to ascertain water depth and size restrictions of the marina before you venture here in your vessel. Many of our recommended accommodations offer marina facilities where you may bring your own trailered boat and, for a small daily fee, secure dockage of your craft for the duration of your stay. The boat basins of these facilities are usually not as deep as the resort marinas that accommodate large vessels and therefore are more suitable for shallow-draft boats. Those accommodations offering accessibility by boat have been noted throughout.

Check-in time typically is after 2:00 P.M., and check-out is between 10:00 and 11:00 A.M. Some facilities levy an extra charge if you occupy your room after check-out time. But in some cases, the management is prepared to keep your luggage safe while you soak in a few extra rays before catching that flight home. They may even have a room designated for you to shower and change in before you leave. It is always better to inquire than to ignore posted check-out times.

In this chapter we escort you through some of the Florida Keys' more outstanding facilities. Our selections are based on attributes of rooms, service, location, property, and overall ambience. Listed by descending mile marker number beginning with Key Largo in the Upper Keys and heading down the Keys to Big Coppitt, these facilities encompass a wide assortment of styles and rates. We have included directions for those establishments located off the Overseas Highway that may be difficult to find. In the Key West section, we switch to alphabetical order; we also provide a separate section of inns and guesthouses in our southernmost city, with a corresponding pricing code for those accommodations.

THE FLORIDA KEYS

Upper Keys

At the top of the Keys, Key Largo, home of John Pennekamp Coral Reef State Park, bustles with an energetic crowd of divers and snorkelers in all seasons. The orientation here is definitely geared toward the underwater treasures of the coral reef that lies just 4 miles offshore. Many motels and resorts in this area offer diving and snorkeling packages.

The settlement of Tavernier snuggles between Key Largo and Islamorada. This quiet area is known for its historic qualities. Dubbed the Sportfishing Capital of the World, Islamorada stretches from Plantation Key at mile marker 90 to Lower Matecumbe Key at mile marker 73. This village of islands, incorporated in 1998, is renowned for its contingent of talented game-fishing guides (see the Fishing chapter) and prestigious fishing tournaments.

The Upper Keys pulsates with tiki bars and watering holes as well as an array of fine restaurants (see the Restaurants and Nightlife chapters). Excursions to historic Indian Key and Lignumvitae Key and visits to Theater of the Sea, which offers dolphin and sea mammal shows and allows guests to swim with the dolphins, rate high on the list of things to do for families and sports enthusiasts alike (see the Attractions chapter).

Amy Slate's Amoray Dive Resort $$–$$$
MM 104.2 Bayside, Key Largo
(305) 451-3595, (800) 426-6729
www.amoray.com

About 80 percent of the guests at Amy Slate's Amoray Dive Resort are divers. An eclectic collection of plantation-style villas springs to life daily as the undersea enthusiasts rustle about, eager to embark on the resort's 45-foot *Amoray Diver* for the half-hour ride to John Pennekamp Coral Reef State Park (see the Diving and Snorkeling chapter).

Amy Slate's Amoray owes its name in part to *People* magazine. The publication sent a writer to Key Largo to cover an Amy Slate underwater wedding "crashed" by a moray eel, and thus coined the term "That's Amoray."

The rooms here are named for tropical fish. Varying in size, amenities, and price, the rooms range from the standard motel variety to small apartments with full kitchens. The accommodations all have ceiling fans and feature tile floors, queen-size beds, and daybeds. Two-story, two-bedroom, two-bath duplexes accommodate as many as eight guests; they offer full kitchens and screened porches with personal hammocks. Some accommodations afford partial water views.

A pool and hot tub front Florida Bay, and a bayfront sundeck and small sandy area at the water's edge sport a picnic table, barbecue grill, and hammock, allowing for swimming, snorkeling, and fishing.

Continental breakfast is included in the room rate. Boat slips are available.

Marriott Key Largo Bay Beach Resort $$$–$$$$
MM 103.8 Bayside, Key Largo
(305) 453-0000, (800) 932-9332
www.marriottkeylargo.com

Bayside sunset views and a primo location near John Pennekamp Coral Reef State Park mark only two of a multitude of pluses at the Marriott Key Largo Bay Beach Resort. The 132 hotel rooms of this Key West–style resort vary in view (bay view and deluxe bay view cost more), but all include a room safe, minibar, pay-per-view in addition to free cable television, hair dryer, coffeemaker, iron, and ironing board. All but 20 rooms have patios.

Rooms are equipped with voice mail and a dataport. For more spacious quarters but more dearly priced, 20 suites—1,200 square feet apiece—have a full kitchen, a full bathroom, a queen-size sleeper sofa in the living room, and two bedrooms, one with a king-size bed and one with two double beds. Wraparound patios provide panoramic views of Florida Bay and its famed sunsets. For the royal treatment, the resort also offers one 1,400-square-foot penthouse suite, which, in addition to the amenities of the other suites, features a Roman tub in the master bedroom as well as a bath and a half.

Treat yourself to libations or dining at one of Marriott Key Largo Bay's restaurants or bars—Gus' Grille (see the Restaurants chapter); Breezer's Tiki Bar (see the Nightlife chapter); or Flipper's Pool Bar, beside the pool, hot tub, and beach area. The beat heats up on weekend evenings with late-night live entertainment at Gus' After Dark nightclub.

The resort also features a fitness area with state-of-the-art equipment and offers a full-service complete day spa as well as therapeutic sea-breeze-kissed massage in a private open-air tiki hut. A nine-hole "putting challenge" golf course, "hot clock" basketball, table bowling, Ping-Pong, horseshoes, and Velcro target toss stand ready to amuse you. Marriott Key Largo Bay Beach Resort also has a tennis court. A boutique shop in the lobby called By the Way will lure the shopaholics. It's A Dive provides on-premises water-sports selections ranging from diving, snorkeling, parasailing, and glass-bottomed boat excursions to boat or personal watercraft rentals.

Fishing charters can be booked through the hotel as well. Guests receive unlimited passage aboard a casino gaming ship. Boat dockage is available for guests' vessels at no extra charge. Marriott also offers a full activities program for children ages 5 to 13, from Wednesday through Sunday.

Jules' Undersea Lodge $$
MM 103.2 Oceanside, 51 Shoreline Drive, Key Largo
(305) 451-2353
www.jul.com

For a unique experience that is one to write home about, Jules' Undersea Lodge has to be near the top of the list. You actually dive 21 feet beneath the surface of the sea to enter this lodge. This only underwater hotel in the world is under the surface of a tropical mangrove of the Emerald Lagoon. The cottage-size building has hot showers, a well-stocked kitchen (with refrigerator and microwave), books, music, and video movies. As you snuggle in your bed, you can view the sea life that appear at the windows of this aquatic habitat.

Dive certification is offered at the facility and individuals must meet the requirements of PADI and Discover Dive in order to stay in the lodge. The minimum age for guests is 10 years old.

Largo Lodge $$
MM 101.7 Bayside, Key Largo
(305) 451-0424, (800) 468-4378
www.largolodge.com

A secluded, romantic, rain-forest setting greets you at this old-island-style, adults-only hideaway. At Largo Lodge a collection of three rustic duplex cottages is nestled among lush, tropical gardens

Accommodating Info

The following Florida Keys chambers of commerce can provide information about most area accommodations: Key Largo, MM 106 Bayside, (305) 451-1414, (800) 822-1088, www.keylargo.org; Islamorada, MM 82.5 Bayside, (305) 664-4503, (800) 322-5397, www.islamoradachamber.com; Marathon, MM 53.5 Bayside, (305) 743-5417, (800) 262-7284, www.floridakeysmarathon.com; Lower Keys, MM 31 Oceanside, (305) 872-2411, (800) 872-3722, www.lowerkeyschamber.com; Key West, Mallory Square, (305) 294-2587, (800) 648-6269, www.fla-keys.com.

overflowing with bromeliads, orchids, and trickling water fountains. A quiet and spacious sandy pier faces the waters of Florida Bay, where you can relax and read, swim, picnic, or simply worship the sun. And you may meet one of the wild-bird contingents that frequent the premises.

Each one of the lodge's six ground-level, concrete-block-style units features one bedroom, a living-dining combination, full kitchen, terrazzo floors with area rugs, beamed cathedral ceilings with fans, and French doors opening to spacious screened patios. Bedrooms feature two queen-size beds; some units have sleeper sofas, and rollaway beds are provided. The private, tiled baths are small and somewhat dated, but functional. Maximum capacity in each unit is four occupants.

Largo Lodge's owner, Harriet Stokes, collects ceramic memorabilia from the 1940s and 1950s, which you'll see decorating the rooms. Boat dockage is available, but you should launch your boat at a public ramp (see our Boating chapter) and bring it around to Largo Lodge, because the lush tropical plantings make it difficult to maneuver a trailer.

Marina Del Mar Resort and Marina **$$-$$$$**
MM 100 Oceanside, 527 Caribbean Drive, Key Largo
(305) 451-4107, (800) 451-3483
www.marinadelmarkeylargo.com

The Marina Del Mar Resort and Marina, on a quiet, dead-end street along an ocean-fed canal and boat basin, draws an active boating, fishing, and diving crowd. This facility shares the same marina as its sister properties—Holiday Inn Key Largo Resort and Ramada Resort and Marina.

The rooms are bright and modern with tile floors, ceiling fans, white wicker furnishings, and bold tropical accents and feature king-size beds or two double beds. Some also have whirlpool tubs, complete kitchens, and private waterfront balconies. All are equipped with ironing boards and irons. A complimentary continental breakfast is offered daily, and restaurants and attractions are nearby.

Deep-sea charter fishing boats are docked behind the Marina Del Mar. The hotel also maintains two tennis courts and a small fitness room with Nautilus equipment.

Overlooking the heated swimming pool, complete with brick sundeck and hot tub, is Coconuts, a casual indoor-outdoor restaurant (see the Restaurants and Nightlife chapters). Coconuts features a raw bar and serves lunch and dinner throughout the week; the place heats up with live entertainment nightly.

The resort's marina attracts long-term and transient cruisers (see our Cruising chapter). A snorkeling excursion vessel and a glass-bottomed tour boat, which both offer daily trips to the coral reefs, are berthed here as well. Next door a full-service dive center offers resort and open-water diving instruction and certification.

Holiday Inn Key Largo Resort and Marina **$$-$$$$**
MM 99.7 Oceanside, Key Largo
(305) 451-2121, (800) 843-5397
www.holidayinnkeylargo.com

If action is what you seek on your vacation, the 132-room Holiday Inn, situated on a busy boat basin, bustles with activity from dawn until dark. You'll find charters for snorkeling, diving, fishing, sunset cruises, and sailing excursions and even a Las Vegas-style gambling boat emanating from the docks that run between the Holiday and its sister hotels, the Ramada Key Largo Resort and Marina Del Mar Resort and Marina (see separate listings). Together they compose the Key Largo Resorts.

Bogie's Cafe offers indoor or outdoor dining for breakfast, lunch, or dinner. The Tiki Bar serves light fare all day while live music percolates poolside on weekend evenings. You'll find a small "marketessen" in the lobby for sandwiches, pastries, juice, soda, and bottled water.

Rooms at the Holiday Inn face lush tropical gardens or the harbor, and the colorful appointments in each room reflect the flora that flourishes outside the tinted glass doors. Rooms feature modern bathrooms, king-size beds, floor-to-ceiling beveled mirrors, and great vacation amenities such as coffeemakers, hair dryers, mini-refrigerators, ironing boards and irons, cable TV with HBO guest choice movies, and voice mail.

Palm trees, frangipani, and bougainvillea weave a foliage trail between the two heated pools and the hot tub, and chickees and tropical waterfalls pepper the property. Docked canalside at the Holiday Inn are two famous boats: the original *African Queen* from the legendary movie of the same name and the *Thayer IV* from the motion picture *On Golden Pond*.

The Holiday Inn maintains a fitness room, children's playground, and a changing rota of children's activities. Guests receive complimentary passes for the casino cruise.

Ramada Key Largo Resort and Marina **$$-$$$$**
MM 99.7 Oceanside, Key Largo
(305) 451-3939, (800) 843-5397
www.ramadakeylargo.com

Sister hotel to the Holiday Inn and Marina Del Mar Resort and Marina, the Ramada exudes a quieter, more laid-back ambience. Reciprocal privileges exist among the three facilities, so guests may enjoy dining at or room service from Bogie's Cafe and Coconuts, as well as all the chartered action.

The 88 rooms and 5 Jacuzzi suites of this boutique hotel have all the same amenities as the Holiday Inn (see the previous listing) and are decorated in island rattan. The spacious rooms have king-size, queen-size, or two double beds; some also have sleeper sofas. Each room opens onto a private patio or balcony. The king suites feature two bathrooms, two televisions, and a Jacuzzi bath as well as a shower and a private sundeck. The Ramada wraps around a small, private, kidney-shaped swimming pool. All room rates include a complimentary continental breakfast and tickets for the casino cruise.

Bayside Resort **$-$$$$**
MM 99.5 Bayside, Key Largo
(305) 451-4450, (800) 242-5229
www.baysideresort.us

Formerly known as the Marina Del Mar Bayside Resort, now simply Bayside Resort, this West Indies style retreat is situated on a sandy beach astride Florida Bay. This family-owned hotel features 54 rooms and villas. The villas overlook the heated swimming pool or the bay, and three of the king rooms also have a view of Florida Bay. Rooms are bright and modern with tile floors, ceiling fans, cable television, air-conditioning, and wicker furnishings. King-size beds or two double beds are available. Diving, snorkeling, and fishing excursions are nearby.

Sunset Cove Motel **$-$$**
MM 99.3 Bayside, Key Largo
(305) 451-0705, (877) 451-0705
www.sunsetcovebeachresort.com

Concrete camels, elephants, lions, tigers, and leopards lurk on the grounds of the Sunset Cove Motel, incongruously poised among the 9 scattered sleeping rooms and the 10 freestanding cottages. Don't worry, they are only life-size painted statues of the African beasts, remnants of a former owner's travels and hobbies.

All the units at Sunset Cove are individually decorated, most still sporting '50s and '60s decor and furnishings, and offer a variety of bedding options, tile floors, and dated but clean, functional private baths. The cottages also have full kitchens. Each unit showcases wall murals of exotic flora and fauna, painted by area artists.

Down at the waterfront on Florida Bay, you'll enjoy free use of paddleboats and canoes. The beach is peppered with lounge chairs and barbecue grills if your idea of recreation is more reclined. A large thatched chickee with a stone waterfall in the middle of the property creates an island ambience. Guests are welcome to use Sunset Cove's boat ramp, and boat dockage for vessels up to 20 feet in length is available at no extra charge. Maid service is not available; fresh towels must be obtained at the office. Sunset Cove does not have a swimming pool. Guests enjoy a free continental breakfast.

Hungry Pelican Motel **$-$$**
MM 99.3 Bayside, Key Largo
(305) 451-3576
www.hungrypelican.com

Murals of manatees, pelicans, and wading birds decorate the outside walls of the one-story "old Keys" buildings at Hungry Pelican, which are linked by masses of bougainvillea. New ownership in 2006 brought a revival to the 23 units and the grounds of the Hungry Pelican Motel. All the accommodations have bright new furniture and paint. The grounds of the property have been redone to give a crisp look to the once-dated motel. Each unit is air-conditioned and has a small refrigerator, private bathroom with a shower, tile floors, and internet access. Some have kitchens as well. The duplex unit by the water features two queen-size beds and screened porch on one side and one queen-size bed, a kitchen, and screened porch on the other. These units are more expensive and cannot be connected.

Situated on Florida Bay, Hungry Pelican has two fishing piers. You'll be able to swim or snorkel between the piers, but the facility does not have a swimming pool. You may launch your boat from Hungry Pelican's boat ramp, and dockage for small boats is free for guests. Use of paddleboats, canoes, and kayaks is complimentary. Continental breakfast is offered daily. The property sports a large chickee for lounging, and barbecue pits are scattered about.

Kona Kai Resort **$$$$**
MM 97.8 Bayside, Key Largo
(305) 852-7200, (800) 365-7829
www.konakairesort.com

Lost in a cluster of mom-and-pop motels toward the southern end of Key Largo sits a truly intimate, adults-only gem known as Kona Kai. Owner-operators Joe and Ronnie Harris have created a small, quiet tropical resort hermitage, sure to dissolve your city cares. Near the facility's tennis court, the owners have planted an exotic tropical fruit garden of lichis, guava, starfruit, sapote, Florida pistachios, jackfruit, and more. Guests are free to help themselves to samplings of the tropical fruits.

Gardens throughout the two-acre property of winding walkways showcase 20 varieties of palm trees, 30 varieties of hibiscus, 30 species of bromeliads, plus heliconia and birds-of-paradise. The owners collect and plant rare and endangered species of flora. An orchid shadehouse features 250 species of exotic blooms. The gardens were featured on HGTV's *Secret Garden Show* in 2001.

An elevated swimming pool and a hot tub are accented by a magnificent circular staircase and paver-stone deck, as well as a thatched-palm chickee; a glass-block wall shelters a saltwater pond with a waterfall. Lounge chairs, picnic tables, barbecue grills, a hammock, and a fiberglass Ping-Pong table sit close to Kona Kai's white-sand beach, which is guarded by a stone alligator. You'll be able to snorkel, swim, and fish off a platform at the end of a dock, and a paddleboat, kayak, and other water "toys" are available free of charge.

Kona Kai's 11 cottage-style suites and guest rooms are decorated with flair, style, and attention to every detail. All units feature double-, queen-, or king-size beds. Suites have ceiling fans, tile baths and floors, glass-block showers, antiques, CD players and VCRs, and eclectic design accents. Many also have a full-size sleeper sofa or futon, and some units have full kitchens complete with Noritake china and matching flatware. Those without kitchens have small refrigerators and coffeemakers. Each room is named for a tropical fruit. Just look for the corresponding icon on the tile under the outside lantern to your room. Keeping with this theme, the Harrises place fruit-scented soaps, shampoos, and skin lotion in each bathroom. Rooms, some of which are connected, offer either courtyard or full waterfront views. Kona Kai is a nonsmoking establishment.

A small, lovely fine-art gallery on the property exhibits the work of South Floridian Clyde Butcher and other world-renowned artists (see the Arts and Culture chapter). Many of the original paintings from the gallery are hung in the individual guest suites as well and can be purchased. An outdoor dive station with rinse and soak tanks, an outdoor shower, and open-air lattice lockers are just down the walkway. Kona Kai can accommodate five boats with up to a 2-foot draft.

Sheraton Beach Resort
Key Largo $$$–$$$$
MM 97 Bayside, Key Largo
(305) 852-5553, (800) 539-5274
www.keylargoresort.com

Orchids, bromeliads, towering palms, and gas torches set the stage for tropical ambience at Sheraton Beach Resort Key Largo, a four-story, tin-roofed enclave painted in shades of beige and featuring walls of windows. The three-story open lobby showcases a Mexican-tile floor, mahogany and rattan furnishings, a coral-encased elevator, and open-air walkways.

Probably the most unusual aspect of the Sheraton Beach Resort is its 2,000-foot boardwalk nature trail, which stretches virtually the full length of the hotel through a protected hardwood hammock. In one direction hikers may head for a lighted gazebo area and dock for views of the sunset. Or they may hike through mangroves and view environmentally protected exotic flora and fauna. The predominant species of trees in the hammock are labeled, and guests receive an annotated map so that they may further enjoy the nature trail.

In the resort's pool area, which is tucked amid the hardwood hammock, water cascades into the resort's family and adults-only pools over mounds of bougainvillea-lined coral rock. Colorful mural-covered walls surround a large hot tub. Splashes Bar and Grill provides creative gustatory comforts. Bayside, the Sheraton boasts an intimate sandy beach, a waterside tiki bar and grill, and a dive and water-sports concession (see the Recreation chapter).

The Sheraton Beach Resort Key Largo provides fitness facilities, a gift boutique, a full-service unisex salon, two lighted tennis courts, and a game room. The resort offers several on-premises dining options: Cafe Key Largo serves breakfast, lunch, and dinner; Treetops offers fine evening dining from its third-floor perch amid the leafy tops of giant gumbo-limbo trees; and Parrots Lounge provides libations at its tapas bar daily. Don't miss the Sunday champagne brunch on the cafe balcony overlooking the bay.

The 200 guest accommodations include standard and standard-deluxe bay-view, island-view, or trail-view rooms and Jacuzzi suites. All rooms have full marble baths, safes, and refreshment centers. Standard rooms are comfortably sized with a choice of one king-size bed or two queen-size beds, and each features a sleeper sofa. Double the size of a standard room, the Jacuzzi suite features a wet bar, mini-refrigerator, queen-size sleeper sofa, and long, private balconies with sweeping waterfront views. A partition divides the living and sleeping areas, where a large Jacuzzi tub, dressing room, and connecting bathroom invite guests to pamper themselves. Boaters will enjoy the 21-slip docking facilities at no extra charge.

Dove Creek Lodge $$$
MM 95 Oceanside, Key Largo
(305) 852-6200, (800) 401-0057
www.dovecreeklodge.com

The Dove Creek Lodge was established to create an atmosphere for the serious fishing person. Any type of Florida Keys fishing obsession is met here with enthusiasm because they can handle any request, can place you on the water with a guide and suggest the correct tackle to turn that passion into reality. Offering everything from fly-fishing for bonefish out on the flats, bill fishing, reef/spear fishing, snorkeling, off shore/deep sea fishing, diving, fly-fishing for beginners, eco-tours, or just exploring the backcountry, Dove Creek Lodge lives up to its reputation. For beginners or pros, they also can sign you up for all the major fishing tournaments in the Keys, which run from April through December.

The amenities on site are Lodge rooms with mini-fridge and balcony, one- and two-bedroom unit suites to luxury suites. In the luxury suites you have a full kitchen and screened patio; one of the two has an 8-foot pool table! The Lodge also houses a full tackle shop to outfit you with all the proper gear. The property sits right next door to one of the best seafood establishments in the Keys, Snapper's Waterfront Saloon and Raw Bar (see Restaurant and Nightlife chapters), where they say "our seafood is so fresh we have to change the menu daily 'cause we don't know what's coming in off the boats." You can arrive by land or sea for your stay. Dove Creek Lodge offers family packages and group rates. No pets or smoking allowed.

Ocean Pointe Suite Resort $$$
MM 92.5 Oceanside, 500 Burton Drive, Tavernier
(305) 853-3000, (800) 882-9464
www.thefloridakeys.com/oceanpointe

Directly on the Atlantic Ocean, this tropical, contemporary three-story, all-suite stilt condominium complex boasts 240 units with gingerbread-trimmed balconies facing the water. Suites at Ocean Pointe are individually owned and decorated, but, for the most part, expect to find tropical prints with wicker and rattan furnishings.

The spacious one- and two-bedroom units (two full baths) feature whirlpool tubs, complete kitchens with microwave and coffeemaker, washer and dryer, living rooms with sleeper sofas, and private balconies.

Just outside your door are nature walks, a private beach, a large heated swimming pool, barbecue grills, picnic areas, and lighted tennis courts. The 70-acre property also has a playground, a boat ramp, and a marina.

If you feel like a light bite, head for the outdoor cabana club. Kayak and canoe rentals also are available.

To reach Ocean Pointe, head toward the ocean at Burton Drive (mile marker 92.5), where signs lead to Harry Harris Park. Follow Burton Drive about a quarter mile, turn right into the Ocean Pointe complex, and pass the guardhouse. Signs will guide you to the manager's office.

Bay Breeze Motel $$-$$$$
MM 92.5 Bayside, 160 Sterling Road, Tavernier
(305) 852-5248, (800) 937-5650
www.baybreezemotel.com

Bay Breeze Motel enjoys three acres of primo bayfront property, planted with palms and bougainvillea, and features a large beach area peppered with chaise lounges and barbecue grills, Adirondack beach chairs, and hammocks. Unique to this property is a special feature of Florida Bay called the "deep hole," where depths drop dramatically to 20 feet right off-shore. A coral rock ledge shelters lobsters and starfish and a regiment of sergeant-major fish, which keep company with mangrove snappers and parrotfish. This assortment of marine life as well as a sunken Haitian raft makes for dynamic snorkeling.

The Bay Breeze Motel offers 15 units, all with full kitchens or kitchenettes for self-catering convenience, and hardwood or tile floors. The units are tropically furnished with colorful upholstered rattan and wicker. The three Caribbean suites, which have kitchenettes with microwaves and small refrigerators and private decks, are closest to the beach.

The Caribbean cottages are a little farther back from the water and enjoy views of either the heated swimming pool or Florida Bay. Each cottage has a full kitchen, living room, and separate bedroom with a king-size canopy bed. One-bedroom efficiencies are housed in a two-story, motel-style building toward the back of the property. Each unit has a full kitchen, living room with futon, and a separate bedroom with a king-size bed or twin beds.

Bay Breeze maintains two boat ramps and a 100-foot dock. Boat dockage and use of the boat ramp is available to guests at no extra charge.

Guests enjoy complimentary use of rowboats and paddleboats during their stay. To find Bay Breeze Motel, turn onto Sterling Road at mile marker 92.5 and proceed toward Florida Bay.

Lookout Lodge Resort **$$-$$$**
MM 87.7 Bayside, Islamorada
(305) 852-9915, (800) 870-1772
www.lookoutlodge.com

Situated next to Marker 88, one of the Upper Keys' most distinguished restaurants (see the Restaurants chapter), Lookout Lodge is a clean, modestly priced motel of Spanish-influenced architecture. The resort's nine basic rooms—featuring decidedly '60s decor and amenities—come in four styles: studios with one double and one twin-size bed; studios with two double beds and a patio; and one- and two-bedroom suites. Suites each include a queen-size sleeper sofa. Cribs, side rails, and rollaway beds are provided at no additional cost. All suites have kitchenettes, tile floors and baths, voice-mail telephones, and ceiling fans. Three afford full water views. A limited number of small pets are allowed.

Steps lead from the resort's raised man-made beach to the bay for swimming and snorkeling. The property features gas grills, picnic tables, a thatched-palm chickee, and lounge chairs, but no swimming pool. Dock space, available at an additional fee, is limited and must be reserved in advance. A dive/snorkel boat on premises takes guests to the reef.

Two weeks' advance cancellation is required.

Pelican Cove Resort **$$$-$$$$**
MM 84.5 Oceanside, Islamorada
(305) 664-4435, (800) 445-4690
www.pcove.com

Perched beside the Atlantic Ocean, Pelican Cove Resort—constructed in concrete with a tin roof and Bahamian shutters—ensures an ocean view from almost every room.

The resort offers a choice of accommodations ranging from standard rooms with one or two queen-size beds, mini-refrigerators, and coffeemakers, to efficiencies and one-bedroom hot tub suites, each with its own balcony. Efficiencies and suites have full modern kitchens with curved breakfast bars and either two queen-size beds or a queen-size bed and sleeper sofa. Some hotel rooms and suites connect, and all units feature tropically inspired furnishings.

Behind the resort, steps connect the raised man-made beach to the ocean, where dredging for a once-used quarry has caused waters to run 30 feet deep. A swimming pool with sundeck, outdoor cabana bar and cafe, poolside hot tub, volleyball net, playground, and water-sports concession all front the beach.

Complimentary coffee and juice are offered in Pelican Cove's office 24 hours a day, and a complimentary continental breakfast is served daily. Children younger than age 17 stay free at Pelican Cove. Sandbox toys for children are available in the office.

Limited boat dockage is available to guests at an additional fee. Reservations must be made in advance.

Chesapeake Resort **$$$-$$$$**
MM 83.4 Oceanside, Islamorada
(305) 664-4662, (800) 338-3395
www.chesapeake-resort.com

The elegant Chesapeake Resort hugs the Atlantic on six and a half acres of lushly landscaped grounds. This pristine three-story, 65-unit resort sports two heated pools, a hot tub, tennis courts, on-site laundry facilities, and an outdoor gym as well as a 700-foot sunning beach and a saltwater lagoon.

Accommodations are offered in a variety of styles, from the garden-view standard to villas and oceanfront suites. Some connecting rooms combine to provide 1,000 square feet of living space. Suites and villas offer full kitchens and have balconies or screened porches.

The higher-priced units also feature whirlpool bathtubs, king-size beds, queen-size living-room sleepers, two televisions, and wet bars. The one- and two-bedroom suites even have a Jacuzzi in the bedroom.

Fishing, snorkeling, diving, and parasailing excursions can be booked on the premises as well as sunset cruises. You can rent kayaks and powerboats of up to 33 feet. Chesapeake also provides a boat ramp and boat dockage.

Chesapeake provides a playground for children, who can stay for free if they are younger than age 13.

Casa Morada **$$$-$$$$**
MM 82.2 Bayside, 136 Madeira Road, Islamorada
(305) 664-0044, (800) 881-3030
www.casamorada.com

Tucked on the shores of Florida Bay, out of the fray of U.S. Highway 1 on a residential street, this all-suites hotel exudes the charm of a Mediterranean villa. The 16 suites, each unique, have private terraces or semiprivate gardens overlooking the water and are decorated with a mixture of wrought iron and mahogany furniture, which was exclusively created for Casa Morada. Unusual memorabilia from throughout the world accent the rooms. Rooms have cable TV, phones with modem ports, refrigerators, electric kettle coffee/tea setup, electronic safes, and hair dryers.

Opened at the end of 2000, the two-acre property showcases lush tropical gardens, which were redesigned in 2002 by Key West architect Raymond Jungles. Cross a small, ca.-1950 bridge to a private island and you'll find a sandy playground with a pool, secluded cabana, and terrace with breakfast, lunch, and beverage service.

To find Casa Morada, turn in at the Lorelei restaurant sign and follow Madeira Road into a quiet, residential neighborhood.

Cheeca Lodge & Spa **$$$$**
MM 82 Oceanside, Islamorada
(305) 664-4651, (800) 327-2888
www.cheeca.com

Majestically sprawling amid 27 manicured, tropical acres with more than 1,100 feet of beachfront, Cheeca Lodge & Spa creates a vacation enclave you may never want to leave. Follow the winding drive through splashes of bougainvillea beneath towering coconut palms, stroll across the courtyard between an avenue of date palms, and enter an island lobby alive with bromeliads and potted palms. This elegant main building, tiled with Key Largo limestone and peppered with stone pillars, houses the famed Atlantic's Edge Restaurant as well as the casually laid-back Ocean Terrace Grill. The Curt Gowdy Lounge, which offers cocktails and light fare, is wallpapered with photos of celebrity anglers, including former president George H. W. Bush, for Cheeca hosts many a prestigious fishing tournament in the Florida Keys (see the Fishing chapter).

All 203 spacious guest rooms and one- or two-bedroom suites sport tropical themes and colors that reflect the sun and the sea of the Florida Keys. Tennis Villas, Golf Villas, Lake Villas, and Ocean Villas offer full kitchens.

Four Jacuzzis are sprinkled around the property, tucked privately amid lush tropical foliage. Many rooms have balconies that overlook the ocean or across the grounds of the resort; some units have screened porches.

Focused on fishing, families, and the environment, Cheeca Lodge & Spa offers an overflowing cache of recreational options. A saltwater lagoon is stocked with tropical fish for easy on-site snorkeling. A fishing pier juts out into the ocean, where guests can dock boats with up to a 3-foot draft or just drop a line and try their luck. Two pools grace the premises, a freshwater option to the sand beach and seductively salty Atlantic.

Guests enjoy Cheeca's par-3, nine-hole golf course, designed by Jack Nicklaus, and six Har-Tru tennis courts. Nature trails wind throughout the property. Cheeca watersports offers envirotours of the Everglades, as well as kayaking and windsurfing.

The state-of-the-art luxury Avanyu Spa was completed in 2001 This 5,000 square-foot health spa and fitness center, whose name means "plumed water serpent," features four massage therapy rooms, two facial rooms, one wet treatment room for mud wraps, and a 1,200-square-foot, mirrored exercise room. You'll also find both a men's and a women's steam room here.

The award-winning children's club, Camp Cheeca, keeps the kids happily occupied with specially designed, environmentally inspired activities (see the Kidstuff chapter). Note that Cheeca Lodge & Spa charges a daily resort fee that covers housekeeping gratuity, in-room coffee and tea, in-room bottled water, use of Avanyu Spa Fitness Studio, daily newspaper, fishing poles for the pier, golf clubs, sea kayaks, bikes, pool floats, cabanas, use of tennis courts and racquets, local phone calls, 800 calls, and incoming and outgoing faxes.

The Moorings Village Resort $$$-$$$$
MM 81.5 Oceanside, 123 Beach Road, Islamorada
(305) 664-4708
www.themooringsvillage.com

The Florida Keys may be Paradise, but The Moorings Village is utopia. The 18 cottages and homes are peppered throughout 18 acres of a former oceanfront coconut plantation; hammocks laze between majestic palms; winding, floral-draped trails emit the essence of gardenia; and canoes and skiffs dot the 1,100-foot white sand beach as if guests simply washed ashore. The exquisitely elegant Moorings Village maintains a low, laid-back profile, creating an inimitable tropical ambience not readily found in the Florida Keys.

Cottages range from one to three bedrooms with one to three-and-a-half baths. The four original cottages, which have been completely renovated, date from the 1930s; newer buildings were completed in 1992. All are white with Bahamian shutters and trimmed in bright Caribbean colors. The cottages, which are named for some of Islamorada's pioneers, feature complete kitchens, telephone and television, and bathrooms with hand-painted tiles. Most units have plantation-style porches as well as washers and dryers. The newer cottages offer luxurious soaking tubs and oversize shower stalls. Only the four original Moorings cottages can be rented by the night (two-night minimum). The rest require a one-week minimum stay.

Guests enjoy use of sailboards and kayaks, a 25-meter lap pool, and tennis court. Citrus trees are sprinkled about the lush bougainvillea-bedecked grounds. Pristine and private, the Moorings Village rates as one of the best-kept secrets in the Keys.

Kon-Tiki Resort $$-$$$
MM 81.2 Bayside, Islamorada
(305) 664-4702
www.kontiki-resort.com

Kon-Tiki's pebbled walkways, private patios, and cottages consistently attract anglers and families alike. The resort's quiet, U-shaped property boasts a shuffleboard court, chickee, pier, private beach on Florida Bay, park benches, and a brick barbecue. The primary attraction here, though, is the saltwater pond stocked with all sorts of tropical fish. Guests are invited to don snorkel and mask and take an underwater look-see.

Accommodations feature bright, clean, and comfortable motel units, fully equipped efficiencies, and one-bedroom apartments, most of which have private patios or screened porches. Two-bedroom, two-bath apartments and three-bedroom, three-bath villas, priced according to size, accommodate as many as six.

Kon-Tiki offers a heated pool and a boat ramp and dockage for vessels up to 24 feet long at no extra charge.

Hampton Inn & Suites **$$$-$$$$**
MM 80 Oceanside, Islamorada
(305) 664-0073, (800) 426-7866
www.keys-resort.com

The Hampton Inn & Suites, constructed in 1997, adds a touch of class to the Atlantic shore. Situated directly at ocean's edge, it offers 59 suites, 16 standard rooms, and 4 wheelchair-accessible rooms with vistas of our endless sparkling sea.

Suites feature one or two bedrooms, one or two baths, sleeper sofas in the living rooms, and full kitchens (coffee and popcorn are supplied every day). Satellite television with HBO and pay-per-view movies entertains in each unit; suites have two televisions, which are equipped with VCRs. The fresh furnishings of the Hampton Inn reflect island ambience with fabrics of pastels and teal amid light rattan.

The common lobby area of the Hampton sports a fishing theme—giant mounted dolphin, wahoo, and tarpon; carved wood piscatory reliefs; bronze game-fish sculptures. Tables and comfy chairs flank a keystone fireplace, which is more decorative than functional, given the balmy Keys weather. A complimentary continental breakfast buffet is served here daily.

Outside, guests enjoy a heated pool and spa, tiki bar, and palm-laden, sandy sunning area. A dock jutting out into the Atlantic affords boat dockage for small vessels, but be aware that depths fall to a scant 18 inches at low tide. You'll find a complete selection of water sports on premises, including snorkel or dive excursions, parasailing, and fishing charters. The popular Outback Steak House (305-664-3344) also is on the premises.

Breezy Palms Resort **$-$$$**
MM 80 Oceanside, Islamorada
(305) 664-2361
www.breezypalms.com

Quaint coral buildings with turquoise doors, trim, shake roofs, and screened porches mark Breezy Palms Resort, a cozy place nestled on 320 feet of oceanfront. The brightly wallpapered motel rooms, efficiencies, apartments, and cottages are clean, spacious, and well appointed, featuring rattan furniture and colorful island floral prints.

Chickees and copious coconut palms pepper the property, which sits directly on the Atlantic Ocean and sports a sandy beach as well as a swimming pool. A brick barbecue, picnic table, and volleyball net add to the amenities; dockage is available for an additional fee. No straight inboards or personal watercraft, such as JetSkis or WaveRunners, are permitted.

Breezy Palms is accessible by boat. Children younger than age 13 stay free.

Matecumbe Resort **$$**
MM 76.5 Oceanside, Islamorada
(305) 664-8801

The sprawling Matecumbe Resort—31 fully equipped apartments in four two-story buildings—provides the perfect family vacation setup. The reasonably priced units, which are constantly updated, range from one- or two-bedrooms to efficiencies, and all have complete kitchens. A range of bedding options is available (doubles, queen-size, and king-size), and most baths have been modernized with fresh tile and appointments. Units vary in decor and layout, but all sport tropical pastels and have some sort of eat-in dining arrangement. Televisions with cable hookup are standard.

The grounds feature a heated pool and a man-made beach with chaise lounges and chickees. A sand volleyball court, horseshoes, and shuffleboard provide entertainment for adults while two children's play areas beckon the kiddies. The expanses of trees and coconut palms are peppered with grills and picnic tables.

Matecumbe Resort offers the use of its boat ramp to guests and provides free boat dockage as well as boat rentals.

White Gate Court **$$-$$$**
MM 76 Bayside, Islamorada
(305) 664-4136, (800) 645-4283
www.whitegatecourt.com

A touch of understated European elegance marks the restored villas and bungalows at White Gate Court, situated on three acres abutting the placid Gulf of Mexico. These 1940s-era Conch cottages survived the hurricane of 1961 and decades of neglect before receiving tender loving care from owner Susanne Orias DeCargnelli, a native of Hungary who spent many years in South America. Painted cheerful yellow and white inside and out, the seven private units—completed in 1997—exude a rustic Old World charm. Spacious interiors feature rough-plastered walls; fresh tile and lightly stained wood-plank floors; fully equipped, stylistically European white kitchens; and sparkling modern bathrooms. Beds are covered with exquisite individualized quilts. All units have covered porches and outdoor tables and chairs. Some even feature rope hammocks.

White iron gates guard this tropical hermitage, fronting a long, narrow driveway lined with palm trees, oleanders, and white coach lamps. Lounge chairs pepper a 200-foot white-sand beach where guests enjoy swimming and snorkeling in the sandy-bottom Gulf; White Gate Court does not have a pool. A finger dock stretches into the water for fishing, and tiki torches and barbecue grills are available for an evening cookout. A guest laundry also is provided. Pets and children are welcome.

Coral Bay Resort **$$$$**
MM 75.6 Bayside, Islamorada
(305) 664-5568
www.thecoralbayresort.com

Renovated in 1997, Coral Bay Resort's three motel rooms, eleven efficiencies, and two villa suites are secreted away in white-trimmed, pastel pink, air-conditioned Conch-style cottages, each with a lazy-days front porch. A painted icon distinguishes each unit, creating a virtual school of tropical fish.

The fresh interiors sparkle with light furniture, pastel fabrics, and tile floors. A selection of South Florida art adorns the walls. A variety of bedding options is available. The efficiencies feature full kitchens, and each villa suite also provides a living area with a sleeper sofa.

You'll enjoy Coral Bay's heated pool as well as the sandy beach on the Gulf of Mexico that is peppered with lounges and chickees. Fishing and snorkeling in the 14-foot-deep saltwater tidal pool are excellent. The pier itself has built-in seating and a fish-cleaning station. Guests can dock their own vessels for free or use the resort's paddleboat for exploration. Waters beyond the dock are illuminated at night so the seaside fun doesn't have to end at sunset.

Topsider Resort **$$$**
MM 75.5 Bayside, Islamorada
(305) 664-8031, (800) 262-9874
www.topsiderresort.com

The 20 octagonal, elevated time-share villas at Topsider Resort flank a wood boardwalk that marches from the secluded parking lot to the crystalline waters of the Gulf of Mexico. Ablaze with gumbo-limbos, crotons, and bougainvillea, the grounds of the Topsider effect a rainforest mystique, even though the resort itself is right off the Overseas Highway.

Consult these Web sites for more lodging information: www.thefloridakeys.com and www.fabulousvacations.com.

Units are identical in layout. Each features two bedrooms, two baths, a dining area, living room, and full kitchen. Ceiling fans, washer and dryer, and ground-level storage are standard. The units are updated on a rotating basis. Be sure to inquire as to when your unit was last renovated before booking.

Guests at Topsider Resort enjoy an elevated pool and spa, a tennis court, children's swings and slides, grills, picnic tables, and bayfront wood lounges for sunning on the sandy lagoonside beach. Free boat dockage is available on Topsider's long pier. Minimum stay here is three nights, but most guests opt for a week's sabbatical.

Caloosa Cove Resort Condominium **$$$**
MM 73.8 Oceanside, Islamorada
(305) 664-8811
www.caloosacove.com

An irregularly shaped condominium complex set apart from civilization on a 10-acre parcel of prime oceanfront property, Caloosa Cove offers 30 spacious, light, and bright efficiencies and one-bedroom suites. Suites offer eat-in kitchens, spacious bedrooms, and living rooms with sofa beds. Each efficiency is a large one-room unit with an eat-in kitchen, queen-size bed, and love seat. All are decorated with tropical rattans and pastels. A covered deck that looks directly at the Atlantic fronts every unit.

Caloosa Cove's large irregular-shaped pool, surrounded by extensive decking and thatched-palm chickees, sits directly on the ocean's edge, affording endless vistas of the beyond. The grounds encompassing the coral-laden exterior of Caloosa Cove burgeon with mature tropical plantings.

Activities and amenities on condo premises include shuffleboard and basketball courts, a barbecue area, lighted tennis courts, a full-service marina, fishing charters, and boat and bicycle rentals. The nearby Safari Lounge serves your choice of cocktails.

Middle Keys

The Middle Keys, known locally as the "heart of the Keys," stretch from the Long Key Bridge to the Seven Mile Bridge. Long, Conch, Duck, and Grassy Keys lead the way to the string of bridge-connected islands known as the incorporated city of Marathon.

Basing your accommodations in the Middle Keys offers some distinct advantages. The barrier reef sheltering the prolific fishing waters of the Atlantic supports a plethora of marine life and harbors a number of primo shipwrecks for divers (see the Diving and Snorkeling chapter). Fishing in the Middle Keys rivals that of the famed Islamorada, a well-kept secret. From flats to backcountry, bluewater to bridges, you won't hear too many tales of the "one that got away" here (see the Fishing chapter).

Marathon currently offers one golf course, the 9-hole Key Colony Beach public course. Active, ongoing tennis programs with drills, round-robins, and lessons are available at Lighthouse Cay Club Resort.

Marathon has a movie theater, too (cinemas are few and far between in the Keys). This quirky little theater, which shows first-run movies that change weekly, seats viewers in movable, swivel barrel chairs that surround small round tables designed to hold your popcorn and soda. (See the Recreation chapter for details on golf, tennis, movie theaters, and more.)

The Dolphin Research Center on Grassy Key is a must-do regardless of where your accommodations might be. And in Marathon, Crane Point will captivate the whole family, as will historic

Pigeon Key, at the end of a length of the old Seven Mile Bridge accessed at mile marker 47 (see the Attractions chapter). Sombrero Beach in Marathon, a very nice man-made public beach, provides endless ocean vistas to all.

Needless to say, like the rest of the Keys, this whole area is packed with recreational water options from party fishing boats and glass-bottomed reef excursions to personal watercraft and sea kayak rentals. Parasailing and ultralight rides are available here as well (see the Recreation chapter).

The pace is less tiki-bar frenetic here than in the Upper Keys. The sidewalk rolls up at a relatively early hour. But this area will appeal to families with children as well as serious anglers and divers who, after a day on or under the water, relish a relaxing dinner at one of the many top-notch restaurants and then a nocturnal refueling of energy for whatever tomorrow may bring.

Lime Tree Bay Resort **$$-$$$**
MM 68.5 Bayside, Layton, Long Key
(305) 664-4740, (800) 723-4519
www.limetreebayresort.com

Wiggle your toes as you laze in one of the string hammocks tied among the copious palms surrounding Lime Tree Bay Resort. Perched on the shores of Florida Bay, this resort—which features a variety of overnight options—tucks chickees and lounge chairs amid lush tropical vegetation so that your escape from the workaday world is complete. An elevated pool and heated hot tub extend over a wood boardwalk at water's edge. Accommodations range from waterfront motel-style rooms and efficiencies to one- and two-bedroom apartments. Rooms have been renovated throughout the years but span the decor of several decades. If a recently updated room is your desire, be sure to inquire.

Water sports and boat and personal watercraft rentals are within walking distance. Guests may dock their own boats at no extra charge (up to 28 feet; 3-foot draft at low tide), but Lime Tree Bay has no boat ramp, so boats must be launched at nearby Seabird Marina near Fiesta Key. Shuffleboard, a horseshoe pit, and one tennis court stand ready in case you feel like a little exercise. Children younger than age eight stay free. The Little Italy restaurant is adjacent to the property (see the Restaurants chapter).

Bay View Inn and Marina **$$-$$$**
MM 63 Bayside, Conch Key
(305) 289-1525, (800) 289-2055
www.bayviewinn.com

Located in the heart of fishing island Conch Key, with views of the Gulf of Mexico, the Bay View Inn and Marina is a quiet retreat from the busy crowds of larger resorts. The inn offers a variety of accommodations: rooms, efficiencies, and family suites. Some of the efficiencies and rooms are situated at the waterfront on the marina and have individual grills for that daily catch or late night dining. Regular rooms come with refrigerators, cable TV, and two queen-size beds. The efficiencies, which also sleep four, come with kitchenettes to support family-style vacations. The Bay View Inn and Marina can arrange for a boat slip in their deep water lagoon, or reservations can be made for boat rentals during your stay.

Conch Key Cottages **$$-$$$$**
MM 62.3 Oceanside, Walker's Island
(305) 289-1377, (800) 330-1577
www.conchkeycottages.com

Step back in time as you drive across the narrow causeway from the Overseas Highway into Keys past. Lovingly restored beyond their former grandeur, the pastel, gingerbread-trimmed Conch Key Cottages—like an upended basket of Easter eggs—are as unique as the conch shells for which they're named.

The wood-paneled Coquina, resting at water's edge, provides king-size beds in each of its two voluminous bedrooms. A walled patio with a hot tub and gas grill maximizes your privacy, and the sizable, well-equipped kitchen might even entice you to cook during your holiday. The largest cottage, the King's Crown, is about 1,200 square feet of living space, with a king-size bed in one bedroom and two queen-size beds in the other, plus a living room, dining room, kitchen, and one and a half baths. The Whelk, Queen, and Fighting Conch cottages each fringe the living/dining/kitchen combo room with a queen-size bedroom, one bathroom, and a massive, screened porch overlooking a primo bonefish flat. The honeymoon cottage, the Baby Conch, miniaturizes the features of the others, but the custom-painted lamps and specially made furnishings mirror the details of its more capacious relatives.

Periwinkle, Seahorse, and Horse Conch cottages were constructed in 1997. Grabbing a coveted ocean view, these two-bedroom, two-bath units feature full kitchens, living and dining areas, two cable televisions (one with VCR), and every amenity imaginable for a luxurious vacation stay. The Sand Dollar motel efficiency is the least expensive accommodation at Conch Key Cottages. Located in a fourplex building, the efficiency includes a kitchenette, king-size bed, and dinette as well as a barbecue grill and picnic table outside.

A small swimming pool nestles amid towering palms, and several varieties of bananas hang at the ready for guest consumption. Plantings reflect the owners' philosophy of growing old-fashioned vegetation that attracts birds and butterflies.

Conch Key Cottages maintains a boat ramp and marina that can accommodate an 8-foot draft. Guests may dock their vessels at no extra charge. So you are sure to bring those freshly caught snappers to the table, there is a fish-cleaning station complete with water and electricity. Guests enjoy the use of a complimentary two-person kayak for the entire duration of their stay.

Hawk's Cay Resort **$$$-$$$$**
MM 61 Oceanside, Duck Key
(305) 743-7000, (888) 443-6393
www.hawkscay.com

Step through the pink portico of Hawk's Cay to the strains of a disembodied steel drum. A pith-helmeted doorman sporting a riotously colored shirt bids you welcome. Mount the steps to the tiled veranda, its Bahama fans slowly stirring the subtropical air over the wicker settees. Pass into the palm-filled lobby and out the other side to . . . the West Indies? Like Alice passing through the looking glass, you will adjust your perspective, slow down, kick back, and recharge your batteries at this rambling Caribbean-style resort. Gracious yet low-key, opulent but subdued, Hawk's Cay's 60-acre facility encompasses one of the five islands of the Duck Key configuration.

Accommodations in the hotel building include standard rooms with two full-size beds; captain's suites, each with a king-size bed and a sleeper sofa in a separate seating area; and large penthouse suites with two bedrooms, one and a half baths, a living room, dining room, and private rooftop sundeck with hot tub. All rooms have balconies, mini-refrigerators, and coffeemakers.

The Villas at Hawk's Cay—completed in 1999 and 2000—offer guests the option of self-contained vacation homes. These two-story, Key West–style abodes all offer full kitchens, living rooms, covered porches, washers and dryers, ceiling fans, and televisions with VCRs. The Bungalow units feature two bedrooms and one and a half baths. Conch villas have two bedrooms and two baths. The more spacious Cottages offer two bedrooms, a den, and two-and-a-half baths as well as an optional private tropical spa pool on a porch overlooking a canal. The 18 older Marina Villas each have two bedrooms and two baths. All are individually owned and decorated with tropical Keys furnishings.

Unique to this Keys property is the saltwater lagoon, belted by a man-made, sandy beach, which borders the canal entrance to Hawk's Cay Marina boat basin (see the Cruising chapter).

When you've had enough of doing nothing at all—lazing around the lagoon, the family or adults-only pools, or the hot tub—check out the diversions. Observe the ongoing dolphin discovery program at Dolphin Connection (see the Attractions chapter). Book a fishing or diving charter or a sunset sailing cruise. Sign up for parasailing or sailing instruction, or rent a sea kayak for a self-guided ecotour through the backcountry waters (see the Fishing, Recreation, Boating, and Paradise Found chapters). Work out at the Indies Club recreation and fitness center. Or swing your racquet in the tennis garden, participating in lessons, round-robins, or just whacking returns at the ball machine.

In 2003, Hawk's Cay opened Indies Spa, a 7,000-square-foot spa with a sauna, whirlpool, and steam room. Among services offered are massages, facials, seaweed wraps, and loofahs.

The five popular restaurants on the premises whet any appetite: Palm Terrace for breakfast; Cantina or Indies Grille for poolside light bites; Porto Cayo for eclectic Italian; and the WatersEdge for steaks and seafood (see our Restaurants chapter). Children fare equally well at Hawk's Cay. The Little Pirates and Island Adventure Clubs guarantee that Mom, Dad, and the kids all find a holiday wonderland (see the Kidstuff chapter).

Grassy Key Beach Motel & Resort $$$
MM 58.2 Oceanside, Grassy Key
(305) 743-0533
www.thekeysresort.com

Literally wedged on a narrow strip of land between the Atlantic and US 1, Grassy Key Beach Motel and Resort, completed at the end of 2001, offers an up-close ocean vista across a 200-foot white-sand beach.

All 10 units enjoy the spectacular ocean views as well as private covered parking. The units, which surround the swimming pool, come in two plans—the 1,000-square-foot Dolphin and the 1,200-square-foot Manatee. Both styles feature two bedrooms, one bath, and fully equipped kitchens that include refrigerator, self-cleaning oven, microwave oven, and all the cooking utensils and linens you could ever need. All units feature a 50-inch big-screen television in the living room and a second TV in the master bedroom. Laundry facilities are on-site. The living room has a sleeper sofa.

Although their nightly rate puts them in our three-dollar-sign price-code range, each unit at Grassy Key Beach Motel & Resort accommodates a maximum of six people, making this new addition to the Grassy Key strip of lodgings a good value.

Rainbow Bend Resort $$$-$$$$
MM 58 Oceanside, Grassy Key
(305) 289-1505, (888) 929-1505
www.rainbowbend.com

Fire up a 15-foot Boston Whaler and head for the flats, for at Rainbow Bend each day of your stay entitles you to four free boating hours. Use of sailboats, canoes, kayaks, and paddleboats is also complimentary. Stretched across two and a half acres of palm-speckled oceanfront beach, Rainbow Bend presents a mixed bag of accommodations, ranging from large sleeping rooms and efficiencies to oceanfront one- and two-bedroom suites.

Relax under chickees on the lounges and Adirondack chairs that pepper the beach. If fresh water appeals to you, dip into the large pool and hot tub that edge the property. A long, wooden pier extends into the shallow ocean waters, where you can drop a line or dock your own small watercraft for the duration of your stay.

Small pets are allowed for an additional fee.

The Hideaway Restaurant, which overlooks the beach, offers dinner nightly. A complimentary breakfast is served here each morning.

White Sands Inn $-$$$
MM 57.6 Oceanside, Grassy Key
(305) 743-5285
www.whitesandsinn.com

Hugging a prime piece of direct ocean frontage on Grassy Key, White Sands Inn was lovingly refurbished in 1999. The pale-pink-and-white inn houses seven one-room units—four efficiencies and three sleeping rooms—and the Tree Top Terrace suite, which has two bedrooms with two singles and a king-size bed, living room, full kitchen, and a private deck. The other units have tile floors and remodeled bathrooms, two queen-size beds, and crisp bedding. The rooms are air-conditioned, and some sport ceiling fans as well. Efficiencies feature fully equipped kitchens, but even the sleeping rooms are fitted with mini-refrigerators, coffeemakers, and microwaves so you can self-cater if you wish.

The Sunrise Beach House is a three-unit house at ocean's edge that enjoys sweeping vistas of the Atlantic and the new heated and air-conditioned (!) swimming pool. One unit features three bedrooms, one bath, a living room with queen-size futon, and a fully equipped kitchen. The second unit features a king-size bed, bath, and mini-refrigerator, microwave, and coffeemaker. The third unit offers a queen-size bed, a full kitchen, and a sitting area with a queen-size futon.

The White Sands Inn nestles amid towering coconut palms at water's edge, where sparkling white imported sand forms a beach. Grills are available, and a large picnic table rests under a thatched chickee. The ambience at this intimate hideaway is casual and friendly.

A long, curved pier stretches out into the ocean, where kayaks, a rowboat, and a paddleboat are docked for free usage by guests. At low tide the nearshore waters abutting the inn recede, forming a natural sandy beach. You can walk for miles along the sandy flats. And rumor has it that bonefish lurk at the edge of the flat.

Cocoplum Beach and Tennis Club **$$$$**
MM 54.5 Oceanside, 109 Coco Plum Drive, Marathon
(305) 743-0240, (800) 228-1587
www.cocoplum.com

If you want quiet, quiet, quiet, find the elusive Cocoplum Beach and Tennis Club. Hidden among 53 varieties of palm trees and other tropical plantings, the pod of 20 three-story, art deco-colored "mushrooms" bestows a true island ambience. The endless ocean stretches to tomorrow, ribboned in a blue-to-green prism.

Each octagonal villa—ringed with sliding doors to a wraparound deck and screened porch—houses two bedrooms, two baths, and a family room with sleeper sofa, wet bar, two TVs, VCR, two telephones, and an answering machine. Each unit has a dining room and a full-size kitchen, complete with a microwave oven, blender, and coffeemaker. Guests enjoy use of a private utility room and washer and dryer on the lower level of each unit.

Cocoplum Beach and Tennis Club has planted a fruit-and-spice park that sports 10 varieties of banana trees, 16 types of citrus, and 4 kinds of key limes. Guests are invited to freely pick any of the ripe fruit and enjoy the tastes of the tropics.

Loll by the illusion-edge swimming pool, which was built in 1999 and is surrounded by paver-stone decking. Or pop into one of the blue cabanas sprinkled about the sandy beach area that now is much larger than it was, thanks to 1998's Hurricane Georges. The hot tub awaits your tired muscles after a few hours of spirited tennis or beach volleyball. Or just fold yourself into one of the many secluded hammocks and take a snooze.

Reservations require a three-night minimum and a full week for Christmas and New Year's. Prices vary by proximity to the ocean. Weekly discounts are available in certain periods.

Sea Isle Condominiums **$$-$$$**
MM 54 Oceanside, 1101 West Ocean Drive, Key Colony Beach
(305) 743-0173
www.sea-isle-kcb.com

The sandy beach and ocean views distinguish this 24-unit condo resort. Three tri-level, white buildings, one behind another, line Sea Isle's narrow strip of Key Colony Beach. Built in the late 1960s and individually owned and decorated, the furnishings of these spacious two-bedroom, two-bath apartments swing widely among styles of ensuing decades.

Nevertheless, all necessities for a sun-filled, fun-filled vacation are provided: a heated swimming pool, shuffleboard, gas grills, picnic tables, lounge chairs, and chickees. Stroll down Key Colony's "condo lane" to the public golf course and tennis courts or head into Marathon for a selection of boating, fishing, and diving activities (see chapters devoted to those subjects).

Reservations require a one-week minimum stay.

Continental Inn **$$-$$$**
MM 54 Oceanside, 1121 West Ocean Drive, Key Colony Beach
(305) 289-0101, (800) 443-7352
www.marathonresort.com
Don your mask, fins, and snorkel, because a small, rocky formation at the edge of Continental Inn's beach supports an aquarium of marine life. Located on the coveted sandy stretch of Key Colony Beach, this condominium resort, with its white-stone balustrade, looks faintly Mediterranean. Gulls and terns dart about the oceanfront chickees as guests drink in the limitless vistas of the Atlantic.

These individually owned, simply decorated, one-bedroom efficiencies flank a large, heated swimming pool. A small kitchen/dining/sitting area adjoins each bedroom and bathroom unit. Two 2-bedroom apartments, each of which has a full living room with a sofa and a full eat-in kitchen, provide more spacious quarters for up to four people.

You can play the links at the nearby public golf course, head for the tennis courts, or take your kids to a nice playground (see the Recreation chapter). No boats or trailers are allowed.

Key Colony Beach Motel **$**
MM 54 Oceanside, 441 East Ocean Drive, Key Colony Beach
(305) 289-0411, (800) 435-9811
www.floridakeys.com/marathon
Sitting proudly beside the ocean in Key Colony Beach—often called "condo row"—the modest Key Colony Beach Motel provides simply furnished rooms, each featuring two double beds, a refrigerator, and a primo location. A lovely, palm-lined, sandy beach fronts this two-story white motel, which also has a heated swimming pool. All you need here is a towel, some sunscreen, and a good book.

Holiday Inn & Marina **$$-$$$**
MM 54 Oceanside, Marathon
(305) 289-0222, (800) 224-5053
www.spottswood.com/holidayinn
One of the few national chain hotels in Marathon, this property is owned by a local family, and the service you'll receive here has a Keys-friendly touch. The rooms are pleasantly furnished with the expected Holiday Inn amenities: coffeemakers, cable TV, hair dryers, in-room safes, and phones with voice mail.

Outside, you can enjoy the waterfront swimming pool and kiddie pool or rent a boat, personal watercraft, or a bicycle. The Marathon Holiday Inn is located on a cut that leads from the Atlantic to the Gulf of Mexico.

Coral Lagoon Resort **$-$$**
MM 53.5 Oceanside, Marathon
(305) 289-0121, (866) 613-9330
www.florida.keys.hotelguide.net
The 18 duplex-cottage efficiencies of Coral Lagoon Resort—swaddled in trailing purple and red bougainvillea—flank a quiet, dead-end, deepwater canal. Each unit opens onto a private, canalside wooden deck, where you can lounge in a hammock strung between the posts of your own private canvas-covered chickee. Dock your boat (up to 30 feet) at the palm-lined bulkhead in front of your room for easy access out Vaca Cut to the ocean.

The units vary in size, but each one features a compact living room, dining area, and kitchen as well as a king-size bed or two twins. Most have a sleeper sofa. Each duplex shares a barbecue grill.

Complimentary use of tennis racquets, fishing equipment, and a built-in wall safe adds an extra touch of hospitality.

Tropical Cottages **$$$**
MM 50.5 Bayside, Marathon
(305) 743-6048
www.tropicalcottages.com

Built in 1952, Tropical Cottages considers itself a "vintage Florida Keys resort." This enchanting hideaway caters to adults, honeymooners, weddings, reunions, and small groups (no one under the age of 18). Nestled in a tropical cove that opens into the Gulf of Mexico, the location provides a kayak launch area, boat ramp, and dockage. It is adjacent to the Florida Keys Land and Sea Trust, offering kayak trails, which makes for quiet exploring of backcountry and calm waters. (Don't forget to put snorkeling on your list as well.) Each cottage becomes your personal hideaway, complete with private bath and dressing area and landscaped lanai with outdoor shower and patio for dining. Units are nicely decorated with wicker/rattan furniture, king- or queen-size canopy beds, and ceiling fans. There is also, if you must, air-conditioning. You may book by the night, week, month, or season. Included in your dream vacation at Tropical Cottages are fresh flowers and chilled champagne (upon arrival with reservations), daily housekeeping (upon request), and complimentary use of the resort's bikes, rowboats, canoes, and sea kayaks. Also, one of their special touches is a treasure map to help you uncover natural bathing beaches, scenic bike paths, and picnic spots, with a bonus of restaurant and shopping tips. The memories of your stay will be anything but concrete and neon, but at least this place has electric lights and running water, along with lots of laid-back charm.

The Reef Resort **$$-$$$**
MM 50.5 Bayside, Marathon
(305) 743-7900, (800) 327-4836
www.thereefresort.com

As you drive through Marathon, you may spot what looks like a cluster of beige spaceships hugging Florida Bay. No, the aliens have not landed. These 22 octagonal villas, suspended on "landing" shaft stilts, actually provide a luxurious Keys getaway.

Each villa features the same floor plan—two bedrooms, two baths, a full kitchen, and living room with sleeper sofa. The open ceiling vaults around a spoked, central fulcrum. Each unit has a washer and dryer. Lushly landscaped grounds on six acres, surrounding the two tennis courts, belie the fact that The Reef Resort borders the Overseas Highway.

Bicycles, canoes, paddleboats, and rowboats are available at no extra charge for guests who can tear themselves away from the swimming pool. Picnic tables, grills, and chickees on the waterfront inspire a cookout at sunset. The Reef Resort's marina offers dockage for your boat of 25 feet or less (5-foot draft at low tide). Minimum stay at the Reef Resort is three nights.

Lighthouse Cay Club Resort and Marina **$$-$$$**
MM 50 Oceanside, 19 Sombrero Boulevard, Marathon
(305) 743-2250, (800) 433-8660
www.cayclub.com

Cay Clubs International purchased this prime piece of Marathon real estate in 2006. Except for the name change, Cay Clubs have kept the former Sombrero Resort and Lighthouse Marina intact. Flanking Boot Key Harbor and an adjoining inland canal, Lighthouse Cay Club Resort and Marina offers efficiencies and condominium accommodations with all the amenities of a resort. Though not on the ocean, this destination resort, located in the heart of Marathon between the Overseas Highway and the oceanfront Sombrero Beach, allows you to be within steps of all the action, yet bathed in a laid-back and relaxing atmosphere.

The 99 suites and efficiencies are situated in two three-story white buildings with covered parking beneath (first-come, first-served). A typical one-bedroom condominium is light, bright, and clean, featuring a living room with sleeper sofa, dining area, kitchen, bedroom with a king-size bed, and a full bathroom with shower. Some units have two double beds. Connecting doors may be opened between units if desired.

A keystone deck surrounds the large swimming pool, complete with tiki bar for that midafternoon tropical libation. A game room, also poolside, will amuse the kids with billiards, table soccer, and video arcade games. You'll be able to improve your tennis on the four lighted courts under the expert tutelage of Tim Wonderlin. Lessons, round-robins, and group drills are scheduled on a regular basis. Or get pampered at Allegro Spa & Salon. Complimentary morning coffee is served daily in the lobby. Marathon Pizza & Pasta is located on the premises.

Lighthouse Cay Club maintains a marina and a boat ramp. Guests may launch their boats at their ramp and secure dockage at one of the slips for an additional fee per day based on availability. Boats and trailers may be kept in the parking lot.

Banana Bay Resort & Marina $$-$$$
MM 49.5 Bayside, Marathon
(305) 743-3500, (800) 226-2621
www.bananabay.com

This dazzling 10-acre plantation-style resort on Florida Bay acquired new owners in 2006. The current management is keeping Banana Bay Resort and Marina true to its reputation of a popular destination. As we go to press, they are restoring the marina on the property, which should be operational in the near future.

The spacious rooms of the two residential areas—Island House and Marina Bay House—feature upscale island-style rattan furnishings and Bahama shutters. The grounds are ancient: gnarled trunks of massive royal poinciana trees, 20-foot traveler's palms, and mature bird-of-paradise plants. And don't miss the bananas, 15 varieties tucked between towering scheffleras and gumbo-limbos, papayas, and staggering banyan trees. A resident hawk makes regular passes at the small goldfish pond, hoping for an unsuspecting appetizer.

Don't let this quiet island charm fool you. There is plenty to do besides loll by the L-shaped swimming pool or soak in the hot tub. Banana Bay offers an on-premises playland: tennis, parasailing, sea kayaking, sailboarding, or rentals of personal watercraft, sailboats, and powerboats from Rick's Watercraft Rentals.

Banana Cabana Restaurant, on the premises, is conveniently open for lunch and dinner daily. A complimentary continental buffet breaks the day poolside each morning.

Banana Bay offers popular island wedding packages, including a choice of romantic settings for the ceremony.

Marathon Key Beach Club $$$
MM 49.5 Bayside, Marathon
(305) 743-6522
www.marathonkeybeachclub.com

All the comforts of home await you at the Marathon Key Beach Club. Each of these 1,300-square-foot time-share condominiums features two bedrooms, two baths, a living room with queen-size sleeper sofa, dining alcove, a complete kitchen, and washer and dryer. A screened porch off the living room nestles in a canopy of mature trees on the shores of Florida Bay.

Gas grills and picnic tables are sprinkled throughout the property. Guests at Marathon Key Beach Club share all the facilities of the adjoining Banana Bay Resort (see separate listing in this chapter), including pool, hot tub, tennis, sandy beach, and Banana Cabana Restaurant.

Marathon Key Beach Club rents by the week.

The Blackfin Resort $-$$$
MM 49.5 Bayside, Marathon
(305) 743-2393, (800) 548-5397
www.blackfinresort.com

Accommodations at the 35-unit Blackfin Resort fall into a number of comfortable, affordable configurations: doubles, each of which features a queen-size bed and small sitting area; singles, which are

If you are not staying at one of the large resort properties in the Keys, no big deal! Their restaurants and bars still offer an excellent atmosphere for socializing. Typically, establishments have casual eats at an outside bar, and in many cases reservations are not necessary.

smaller rooms than the doubles but still are equipped with queen-size beds; and king rooms, which have king-size beds and love seats. Some mini-refrigerators are available for these rooms.

Blackfin Resort also offers six cozy single efficiencies, queen-size bedrooms with kitchenettes that are comfortable for two adults; two large efficiencies, each of which features a big kitchen, dining area, and two queen-size beds; and one very large two-bedroom apartment, a 1,600-square-foot unit that offers a separate kitchen and dining room, two baths, and a porch.

The Blackfin Resort sits on four and a half acres abutting the Gulf of Mexico. The grounds are peppered with poinciana, gumbo-limbo, and strangler fig trees and curving coconut palms. Stone paths wind through gardens of tropical flora. On a remote point of land at the end of the marina marked by a miniature lighthouse, guests enjoy a 600-foot, man-made, sandy beach sprinkled with lounge chairs, picnic tables, barbecue grills, and a thatched chickee. A freshwater pool overlooks the Gulf. The placid waters of the Gulf shelter a potpourri of tropical fish, a virtual aquarium for anglers and snorkelers.

A large marina accommodates guests' vessels at an additional charge. The resort lies just 2 nautical miles from the Seven Mile Bridge for easy access to the Atlantic for fishing or diving. Benches and a fish-cleaning station at the marina are well utilized by anglers. Personal watercraft and kayak rentals are available on-premises. Also on the premises are Hurricane Grille restaurant and a jazz/blues bar with live entertainment.

Crystal Bay Resort **$$-$$$**
MM 49 Bayside, Marathon
(305) 289-8089, (888) 289-8089
www.crystalbayresort.com

The best-kept secret in Marathon is hereby out of the bag! Situated in the heart of the city on the Gulf of Mexico, Crystal Bay Resort offers a primo location and reasonably priced lodging in Conch-style bungalows. Jack and Veronica Leggett, who bought the property in 1999, have lovingly transformed the old buildings into bright, light, modern accommodations, the likes of which are rare in the Middle Keys.

Crystal Bay Resort has 26 units, which include spacious sleeping rooms, efficiencies, a studio, and a full apartment. The bungalows and guest rooms, with many bedding configurations, are a vision of whites and pastels and feature tile floors, new or updated baths and kitchens, and stenciled walls.

Dotted with hammocks, coach lights, and a gazebo, the grounds stretch from the Overseas Highway back to the placid waters of the Gulf. Children enjoy an extensive sandbox play yard complete with state-of-the-art, climb-upon equipment. Adults like the picnic area, which is peppered with brick barbecue grills. And everyone loves the free-form swimming pool and waterfall. Equipped with fiber-optic lighting, the waters change colors in the evening, creating a kaleidoscopic effect that carries on where the spectacular sunset left off.

Chaise lounges and chickees are sprinkled about the water's edge, and a small marina basin allows easy access to explore surrounding waters. Guests may launch their boats here; dockage is an extra fee. A fishing pier, complete with cleaning station, juts offshore.

Tranquility Bay Beach House Resort **$$$$**
MM 48.5 Oceanside, Marathon
(305) 289-0888, (866) 643-5397
www.tranquilitybay.com

Brand-new in 2005, Tranquility Bay Beach House Resort is owned and operated by the Singh Company. This company has developed some of the most successful properties in the Florida Keys, and this location is yet another jewel in their crown. Combining vacation-home ownership or weekly rentals with luxury resort surroundings (see Close-Up, Vacation Rentals and Real Estate chapter) is just one of the highlights of this beautiful resort. Built on 12 acres overlooking the aquamarine Gulf of Mexico, Tranquility Bay is your own little "private island." Magnificent palm trees appoint the sand dunes, where sea oats sway in warm breezes. A two-and-a-half-acre white sandy beach sparkles in the sunlight. The beach houses are decorated with tropical cottage flare, offering a choice of two or three bedrooms. The floor plan has great rooms, one and a half baths, gourmet kitchens, two porches, and plasma TVs. Twenty-four-hour room service and daily maid service are available.

Tranquility Bay can help you produce the wedding of your dreams, assisted by their specialists on staff. You can hold a reception or meeting on their 3,000-feet "Great Lawn" or have an intimate dinner for two. In their Butterfly Café, breakfast, lunch, dinner, and Sunday brunch are offered (see Restaurants chapter). Part of your stay should include their Island Spice Private Spa. This pampered service is offered in-house. Be sure and catch a sunset or two at their Turtle Bar, which is perched on the beach.

Tranquility Bay has a supervised children's program. Upon check in let the Adventure Concierge create an outing that offers everything under the sun and sea! This is a non-smoking resort property.

Blue Waters Motel $-$$
MM 48.5 Bayside, Marathon
(305) 743-4832,
(800) 222-4832 (reservations only)
www.thefloridakeys.com/bluewaters

You'll enjoy a Mediterranean feeling here at Blue Waters Motel, for the white-stucco buildings, gray-tile roofs, and bright, turquoise-blue doors evoke visions of Greece. Two banks of motel units, some with efficiency kitchens, flank the parking lot. The rooms feature two double beds or a king-size bed.

A raised swimming pool affords a view of a small boat basin on the Gulf where guests may dock their boats for a small additional charge per day.

The Hammocks at Marathon $$$
MM 48.2 Bayside, Marathon
(305) 289-1525, (800) 456-0009
www.bluegreenrentals.com

Perched in lush tropical foliage with the Gulf of Mexico at your doorstep, The Hammocks at Marathon offers you an escape from the real world. Wildlife of parrotfish, tarpon, and lobster are in the clear waters of the lagoon. You glimpse egrets, pelicans, and herons among the mangroves. Palm trees and tiki huts dot the landscape, which also features a pool and hot tub to take you away. Lodging options include studio rooms (without kitchens); one bedroom, one bath, and kitchen; or two bedrooms, $1^1/_2$ baths, and kitchen. On the property, Barnacle Barney's Tiki Bar overlooks the marina, with full bar and menu to satisfy. Be sure to order the Lobster Reuben, their specialty. Barney's also celebrates the famous Florida Keys sunsets with the firing of a cannon as the sun sizzles into the cool Gulf waters. Water sports and fishing abound to keep your appetite humming. Sorry, no dock space; neither boat parking nor trailers permitted.

Lower Keys

The Lower Keys, sleepier and less densely populated than the Middle or Upper Keys, distinguish themselves with acres and acres of shallow-water turtle-grass flats and copious uninhabited mangrove out-islands. This is a gunk-holing bonanza. The Lower Keys are surrounded by the Great White Heron National Wildlife Refuge, a large area in the Gulf of Mexico encompassing tiny keys from East Bahia Honda Key to the Content Keys to Cayo Agua and the Bay Keys. Big Pine Key is the home of the National Key Deer Refuge, a preserved area of wilderness sheltering our diminutive key deer.

Fishing is outstanding here, though ocean access is more limited. The Lower Keys can also boast of the Looe Key National Marine Sanctuary, one of the best snorkeling and diving reefs in the world. (See the Paradise Found and Diving and Snorkeling chapters for details.)

Accommodations are scattered throughout the Lower Keys, where campgrounds tend to predominate (see the Campgrounds chapter if you'd like to camp in the area). Most of the accommodations here started as fishing camps decades ago and have been updated to varying degrees. Several wonderful bed-and-breakfast inns are tucked away on a little-known oceanfront road, offering seclusion, privacy, and limitless vistas of the sea.

Crowning the assets of Lower Keys accommodations is Little Palm Island, a premier resort that rules in a class by itself. Whatever your lodging choice in the sanctuaries of the Lower Keys, your proximity to Key West more than makes up for any tourist attractions or nightlife that may be lacking here.

Barnacle Bed & Breakfast $-$$
1557 Long Beach Drive, Big Pine Key
(305) 872-3298, (800) 465-9100
www.thebarnacle.net

Isolated from the clot of autos percolating down the Overseas Highway toward Key West, the Barnacle Bed & Breakfast lolls on a serene stretch of beach on an elbow of oölite extending into the Atlantic. Constructed as three rotated, star-shaped levels, the Barnacle is a study in contradictions.

The generous Tarpon and Dolphin rooms on the second level, with two queen-size beds per room, open to a foliage-filled atrium that houses the hot tub. Comfortably furnished with ceiling fans, a sofa, television, table, and chairs, the atrium serves as a common room. Guests meet here each morning for a complimentary breakfast buffet. The Blue Heron cottage perches in an outbuilding, its stained-glass windows lending a romantic perspective. Both the Blue Heron and the Ocean room (which nearly rests on the sand) have kitchens, living rooms, private entrances, and patios.

A circular stairway crawls to the Crow's Nest, a cozy little room located above the atrium with a skylight window.

Guests enjoy use of kayaks, bicycles, snorkeling gear, and barbecue grills. Children younger than age 16 are not permitted. Smoking is permitted only outside the guest rooms.

Finding Long Beach Road is a little tricky: Turn left at Big Pine Fishing Lodge, mile marker 33, oceanside, and proceed about 2 miles.

Casa Grande Bed & Breakfast $$
MM 33 Oceanside, 1619 Long Beach Drive, Big Pine Key
(305) 872-2878
www.floridakeys.net/casagrande

The architecture of this mission-style hacienda harks back to the roots of the Spanish conquistadores who once settled in the Keys. The second of a trio of bed-and-breakfast inns along oceanfront Long Beach Drive, Casa Grande exudes a reserved, almost mystical charm. Owner Kathleen Threlkeld recycled the foyer light fixture and stained glass from a demolished church in New York City; from Maryland she salvaged the clanging old mission bell on the red-tile roof.

All three airy bedrooms with combination louvered and paneled doors feature both Bahama fans and individually controlled central air-conditioning. Queen-size beds and private baths grace the nicely appointed rooms, and each is equipped with a small refrigerator, television, and sofa. You can watch television by the seldom-needed fireplace in the common room or hop into the hot tub on the deck. Bicycles, sailboarding, kayaks, and snorkeling equipment afford you a little exercise if you are between books. The hostess serves a full breakfast at 8:30 A.M. daily in the garden patio.

If you'd like to bring your boat, Casa Grande's canal will accommodate craft up to 26 feet in length. Children are not allowed at Casa Grande. There is a two-night minimum and reservations are essential.

To find Long Beach Road, turn left at Big Pine Fishing Lodge, mile marker 33, oceanside, and proceed about 2 miles.

Deer Run Bed & Breakfast $$
MM 33 Oceanside, Long Beach Drive, Big Pine Key
(305) 872-2015
www.floridakeys.net/deer

The diminutive key deer really do have the run of this Florida cracker-style home, for they stroll the grounds like boarded guests. Owner Sue Abbott met the herd years ago when she first bought the property, and they've remained fast friends ever since. Staying at Deer Run is akin to vacationing in a nature preserve. Self-proclaimed the "Mother Teresa of wildlife," Abbott hand-raises macaws, and at least half a dozen cackle in a wild cacophony around the property.

If you love animals and eccentricity, the three diverse units at Deer Run emanate a homey, folksy appeal. Two of the three rooms have a private entry and bath. A king-size bed fills the lower-level oceanfront room, which sports a large screened porch. A small, affordable room-without-a-view is accessed from the side yard. And in the upper level of the main house, a queen-size bed distinguishes the oceanfront third bedroom. Bathroom facilities are the conventional hallway variety.

The peaceful beach, only 50 feet beyond a raised hot tub, fronts a productive bonefish flat. After you've visited with the animals, wade out and spot a tailing fish. Breakfast is served on the veranda, overlooking the ocean.

Deer Run caters to adults. Smoking is not permitted. A three-night minimum is required on holidays. Payment must be made in cash or traveler's checks; credit cards are not accepted. To find Long Beach Road, turn left at Big Pine Fishing Lodge, mile marker 33, oceanside, and proceed about 2 miles.

Old Wooden Bridge Fishing Camp $$
MM 30.5 Bayside, 1791 Bogie Drive, Big Pine Key
(305) 872-2241

Since the 1950s, this family-owned/operated marina and fishing camp has been a haven for locals and visitors alike. The Old Wooden Bridge Fishing Camp is tucked away at the foot of the bridge that connects Big Pine Key to No Name Key. The bridge was wooden when the camp was built, but it has since been replaced with a concrete structure. Hurrah for progress, but "insiders" are happy some things do not change—like the utter authenticity of old Florida Keys flavor in this family-friendly camp.

The Old Wooden Bridge Fishing Camp sits on Bogie Channel, where you can access both the Gulf of Mexico and the Atlantic Ocean. There is nothing fancy or pertinacious about this place. There are 14 one- and two- bedroom cottages, with tile floors. Cottages are decked out in wicker furniture; finishing out the floor plans are kitchens with stoves, microwaves, and utensils; cable TV; Internet access; and air-conditioning. On the property there are campsites and picnic and BBQ areas where Key deer roam free. The full-service marina supplies folks with gas, tackle, bait, and rental boats. New to the Old Wooden Bridge Fishing Camp is a family-size swimming pool, along with game and recreation rooms. You can also check on the availability of their RV and tent campsites.

Parmer's Resort **$-$$$**
MM 28.5 Bayside, 565 Barry Avenue, Little Torch Key
(305) 872-2157
www.parmersplace.com

Originally a fishing camp in the 1930s, Parmer's Resort is something of an institution in the Lower Keys. The 43 units in 13 buildings sprinkled over the five-acre property have copped the monikers of the fish, birds, and flora populating the Florida Keys.

From the Grunt, Hibiscus, and Flamingo to the Permit, Spoonbill, and Jasmine, the homey 1960s-style units differ widely in both size and amenities. Small, medium, and large motel rooms, standard and small efficiencies, cottages, and one- and two-bedroom apartments are all clean and simple.

Fronting Big Pine Channel, Parmer's offers boat dockage at a small additional fee, but there is no beach. A free-form swimming pool anchors the center of the property. You'll need to use a pay phone to call the office, and you must pick up after yourself or pay a fee for maid service. But you can always stoke up the barbie, because Parmer's loans small gas grills to cook your catch of the day. A complimentary continental breakfast is served daily.

Little Palm Island **$$$$**
MM 28.5 Oceanside, Little Torch Key
(305) 872-2524, (800) 343-8567
www.littlepalmisland.com

Superlatives fall short of describing Little Palm Island, because this tiny slice of Paradise soars off the charts. An exquisite resort encapsulated on its own five-acre island, 3 miles offshore from Little Torch Key, Little Palm is the centerpiece of the jeweled necklace of the Florida Keys. And like all really fine gems, a stay here carries a hefty price tag. But if you just won the lottery, gave your final answer on *Who Wants to Be a Millionaire,* or simply want to splurge on the experience of a lifetime, read on.

Elevated, thatched-roof bungalows, reminiscent of the South Pacific, shelter Little Palm's privileged guests. The one-bedroom suites (two under each thatch) are exquisitely designed in three predominant themes: Indonesian, Polynesian, and British colonial. But no matter what the ambience, you will be pampered with opulence. Each villa has an elegant yet cozy sitting room, complete with a stocked minibar. The bedroom's king-size bed is romantically draped in mosquito netting. A Guatemalan lounger and polished wicker-and-rattan writing desk adorn the room. A lavish dressing room with vanity and a luxurious terra-cotta-tile bathroom sporting an indoor whirlpool and privately fenced outdoor shower complete the suite. To top it all off, add optional massages, facials, pedicures, manicures, and body treatments, either in your suite or in the Island Spa. Two Island Grand Suites provide the ultimate creature comforts—his and hers bathrooms, slate floors, sweeping front porch, and a private outdoor hot tub that looks out at the placid surrounding waters.

The island restores your soul as well. Television sets, telephones, and alarm clocks are banned, ensuring your escape from reality. Curving coconut palms and flourishing flora pepper the grounds surrounding the villas. At Little Palm Island you can elevate doing nothing at all to an art form. The unhurried pace encourages serious lounging beside the free-form pool, atop the crystal sand beach, or enveloped in a two-person hammock. You'll find a life-size chess set (the pieces are lighter than they look) nestled between the bungalows and a peaceful, meditative Zen garden secreted away deep within the island. If the sun is too much for you, stop in at the 600-volume reading library, find a good book, and sit a spell.

When you've unwound at last and you're ready to function vertically once again, the island offers a cornucopia of diversions. Play with Little Palm's complimentary toys—surf bikes, day sailers, kayaks, canoes, a Hobie Cat, and snorkeling and fishing equipment. Rent a pontoon boat or a nifty Sun Cat motorized lounge chair and gunkhole around the surrounding miniature mangrove islets. Dive Looe Key National Marine Sanctuary or hire a backcountry guide and fish for tarpon, permit, or bonefish. Head offshore with a sportfishing captain and catch that marlin. And if you are really adventurous (and your pocketbook is limitless), Little Palm will shuttle you to a deserted island by seaplane for a tropical tryst.

Access to Little Palm Island is provided from its mainland substation at Little Torch Key. A pair of Grand Craft launches—the *Truman* and *Miss Margaret*—ferry you and your worldly possessions to this very civilized outpost. Meals are taken in the outstanding gourmet dining room (see the Restaurants chapter). Choose one of three dining plans while on the island: The Modified American Plan (most popular option) provides a choice of any two meals per day; the Full American Plan supplies breakfast, lunch, and dinner; the European plan allows guests to order a la carte.

Once a fishing camp called Little Munson Island, this quiet hermitage has hosted the nation's movers and shakers, such as presidents Roosevelt, Truman, Kennedy, and Nixon. Little Palm Island still attracts a tony clientele. Such notables as Al and Tipper Gore and Joan Lunden, formerly of *Good Morning America,* found the lifestyle irresistible. In 2005 famed golfer Tiger Woods rented the entire 5½ acres for a weekend stay with his wife with a ticket price of $1 million. Now that is romance with a capital R!

A Noble House resort, Little Palm Island and its restaurant garner myriad awards and accolades from rating services and publications all over the world, consistently ranking in the top 10. But Insiders know Little Palm Island is Number One in the Florida Keys. (Children younger than age 16 are not permitted.)

Caribbean Village **$-$$**
MM 10.7 Bayside, Big Coppitt Key
(305) 296-9542

Each evening, tiny ground lights illuminate the white-trimmed pastel clapboards of the Key West–style Caribbean Village. Basic, clean, and inexpensive, Caribbean Village offers 32 units that range from a sleeping room with an outside bathroom to rooms with private baths in two floating houseboats. Some feature an efficiency kitchen in addition to a sleeping room and bath and have a metal spiral staircase that can connect the lower quarters to another unit above.

Only 6 miles from Key West, Caribbean Village offers the best of both worlds: It is close to the action of Key West at a fraction of our southernmost city's lodging prices. Prices at Caribbean Village do go up during special-event weekends in Key West.

KEY WEST

This diverse, charming, historic city is considered one of the nation's top travel destinations. Key West's accommodations range from the comfort of a standard motel room to the luxury of a private suite in a historic inn. In this section we escort you through a variety of facilities. Our selections are based on attributes of rooms, service, location, and overall ambience. All facilities have air-conditioning, cable television, and telephones unless stated otherwise.

PRICE-CODE KEY

$	**$100 to $150**
$$	**$151 to $200**
$$$	**$201 to $300**
$$$$	**$301 and higher**

Daily rates for the high season (mid- to late December through early to mid-April) for double occupancy are categorized in the price code. Because many facilities offer a variety of accommodations within one property, we have provided a range, the first to indicate the rate for a typical room and the second for more complex units, such as apartments and suites. Prices indicated in the key do not include the 11.5 percent room tax, room service, or added fees for phone calls, rollaway bed, crib rentals, and other incidentals. In most cases an additional per-person charge is levied when occupancy exceeds two. Off-season rates are typically lower, and in some cases dramatically less.

Off-street parking is usually available for guesthouses at about $5.00 per day.

Motels, Hotels, and Resorts

Motels often cater to families, Europeans, last-minute travelers, spring breakers, and active, outdoorsy types. Count celebrities among those who enjoy our full-service resorts. While filming the movie *True Lies* in the Florida Keys, Arnold Schwarzenegger chose the Pier House; *Good Morning America* host Charles Gibson and former cohost Joan Lunden stayed at the Key West Hyatt. Couples often opt for romantic weddings and honeymoons at hotels that offer tropical breezes, lush foliage, crystalline seas, and magnificent sunsets. And when spring break rolls around, college students from all over the country head for Key West's less expensive hotels, motels, and chains.

Hotels, motels, and resorts on this island tend to be so pricey that it is difficult to find a room for less than $100 during the high season (mid- to late December through early to mid-April). During Fantasy Fest (see the Annual Events chapter) in October and Christmas week, rates jump even higher.

Some chains and individually owned motels along North Roosevelt Boulevard offer waterfront accommodations. Those accommodations near the city's shopping centers and fast-food restaurants in New Town are somewhat removed from the charm of the city's historic district, the hustle and bustle of Duval Street, and public beaches.

Consult these Web sites for more lodging information in Key West: www.keywestinns.com and www.keywestforyou.com.

MOTELS

Best Western Hibiscus Motel **$–$$**
1313 Simonton Street
(305) 294-3763, (800) 972-5100

As Best Westerns go, this independently owned affiliate is small and understated. It is also one of few chains or franchises within Key West's historic Old Town. Of concrete-block construction, the Hibiscus has 61 units, including standard rooms and five one-bedroom efficiencies.

Standard rooms are relatively large with two queen-size beds, while efficiencies offer separate bedrooms and kitchens. Decor is bright and clean and features wood furnishings, carpeting, and coordinating wallpaper and bedspread patterns. All units overlook either the motel's heated swimming pool and hot tub or the street and a variety of palms. Bicycles are available for rent, and cribs are an additional cost per night.

Four people can share a room at the given rate. Breakfast is included.

Blue Marlin Resort Motel **$–$$**
1320 Simonton Street
(305) 294-2585, (800) 523-1698
www.bluemarlinmotel.com

With its reasonable rates, heated swimming pool, and off-street parking spaces that allow you to pull the car fairly close to your door, the Blue Marlin is a good choice for families who want to be near the action but don't want to pay dearly for the privilege. This two-story, pink cement-block structure is not luxurious, but the 54 rooms—all of which overlook the pool—are carpeted, clean, bright, and spacious. All rooms come equipped with a refrigerator; 10 have kitchenettes.

The best thing about the Blue Marlin, perhaps, is its location. It's tucked just a block off Duval Street on the Atlantic side of the island. The Southernmost Point and South Beach are about 3 blocks away; other downtown attractions such as the Hemingway House, Key West Lighthouse, and even Mallory Square (on the Gulf side of the island) are within a reasonable walking distance. There's no restaurant on the premises, but several reasonably priced eateries, including a 24-hour Denny's, and a convenience store are located nearby.

No more than four people may occupy a room here. No cots are available.

Comfort Inn at Key West **$-$$**
3824 North Roosevelt Boulevard
(305) 294-3773, (800) 228-5150
www.thefloridakeys.com/comfortinn

Guests at the two-story Comfort Inn have a choice of 100 rooms housed in three buildings. Options include a room with two double beds or a few larger rooms with king-size beds. The rooms are carpeted and have comfortable furnishings; rollaways are provided upon request to a limited number of rooms. Smoking and nonsmoking rooms are available, as are wheelchair-accessible facilities.

The motel is less than half a mile from the Stock Island Bridge and is across the street from the Gulf of Mexico. Rooms face either the pool or the parking lot. Those on the second floor share a common balcony.

The motel offers complimentary continental breakfast and maintains a large outdoor swimming pool surrounded by concrete decking. Scooter rentals are on the premises, and public transportation is available. Complimentary hot and cold beverages are served in the lobby throughout the day. Children younger than age 17 stay free. Comfort Inn proprietors also own the Radisson Hotel Key West (see listing in this section) next door, where a poolside tiki bar, 24-hour restaurant, and coin-operated laundry are available.

Fairfield Inn by Marriott **$-$$**
2400 North Roosevelt Boulevard
(305) 296-5700, (800) 228-2800
www.fairfieldinn.com/eywfi

Fairfield Inn's easygoing prices and comfortable, well-kept facilities make this one of Key West's popular choices with vacationers. The motel offers 100 standard rooms and 32 suites throughout three two-story buildings. Standard rooms primarily are furnished with two double beds; suites with varying amenities, including kitchens or kitchenettes and king-size beds, are other options.

Fairfield Inn offers contemporary furnishings and attractive decor, two swimming pools, gas grills, a tiki bar, volleyball court, and guest laundry facilities. A separate concessionaire offers on-premises scooter rentals.

Complimentary continental breakfast is offered daily, and covered parking spaces are available. The inn has smoking and nonsmoking rooms.

Radisson Hotel Key West **$-$$**
3820 North Roosevelt Boulevard
(305) 294-5511, (800) 333-3333
www.floridakeys.net/radisson

Next door to the Comfort Inn (see listing in this section) is the six-story Radisson Hotel Key West offering 145 rooms with two double beds or king-size beds. Suites and efficiencies also are available. When the hotel became a Radisson in 1999, all of the rooms underwent extensive renovation. Decorated in the traditional tropical style—pastel prints and white walls—they feature refrigerators, coffeemakers, and hair dryers. All of the rooms overlook either the Gulf of Mexico or the swimming pool.

On the premises at the Radisson are an outdoor swimming pool, a lobby bar, a tiki bar by the pool, and a 24-hour coin operated laundry. A 24-hour

Denny's is conveniently located next door. There is plenty of parking, but public transportation is easily accessed from here, too. In addition, front desk personnel will assist you with sightseeing and sporting excursions.

Wheelchair-accessible facilities and smoking and nonsmoking rooms are available.

Southernmost on the Beach $-$$$$
508 South Street
(305) 296-6577, (800) 354-4455
www.oldtownresorts.com

So you want to stay right on the beach? This property offers an affordable way to do just that.

Built in the 1950s and completely renovated in 2002, this two-story, 48-unit motel sits on a peninsula overlooking the water. As waterfront properties go, it provides an incredible value, with virtually all of its rooms offering a full ocean view. Carpeted rooms decorated in florals and pastels primarily feature king-size and double or queen-size beds, and all rooms have coffeemakers, refrigerators, and paddle fans.

Southernmost on the Beach also has an Olympic-size swimming pool, a tanning pier, and a sandy beach. The motel offers limited parking, but its owners and managers also operate the Southernmost Hotel (see listing in this section), which provides additional spaces.

Southernmost Hotel in the USA $-$$$
1319 Duval Street
(305) 296-5611, (800) 354-4455
www.oldtownresorts.com

Gingerbread architectural detail and native flora all come together at Southernmost Hotel, reminding visitors that they have reached an eclectic city on an island. Situated just across from Southernmost on the Beach, Southernmost Hotel's six buildings are surrounded by ample parking and are trimmed with exotic plants, flowers, and trees. One of the hotel's two swimming pools sits in the center of the parking lot, concealed by lush greenery and a wall.

The courtyard features the main pool, surrounded by decking, and a hot tub. Each pool has its own outdoor tiki bar.

The 127 guest rooms have either two double beds or a king- or queen-size bed; some rooms include sleeper sofas. A large room with two double beds and a kitchen serves as the facility's one and only efficiency. Some rooms have private balconies.

Scooter and bicycle rentals and concierge services are available. The tiki bars serve light bites for breakfast and lunch. Southernmost Hotel is wheelchair accessible and offers smoking and nonsmoking rooms.

HOTELS

Best Western Key Ambassador Resort $$
3755 South Roosevelt Boulevard
(305) 296-3500, (800) 432-4315
www.keyambassador.com

The Best Western Key Ambassador Resort consists of a cluster of two-story buildings scattered across seven acres of profuse tropical gardens punctuated by palm trees and hibiscus across the road from the Atlantic Ocean. Every room has a private balcony, and all 100 units have pleasant views of the garden, the harbor, the pool, or the ocean.

Rooms are decorated in "Key West tropical"—light wood furnishings and floral bedspreads and drapes—and the walls are hung with the works of local artists. Floors are a combination of tile and pastel carpeting, and guests have a choice of two double beds or a king-size bed. Each unit is equipped with a mini-refrigerator.

Central to Best Western Key Ambassador and overlooking the ocean is an elevated (heated in winter) swimming pool with a sundeck. A small bar and grill sits beside it. For do-it-yourselfers, a cookout area offers barbecue grills and outdoor tables and chairs. Other amenities include guest laundry facilities and a daily complimentary continental breakfast.

From Best Western Key Ambassador

it's a 10-minute walk to Smathers Beach and 2 miles to historic Old Town. Scooter rentals are available next door or the front desk staff can arrange for a trolley tour. Pets are not permitted here.

Crowne Plaza Key West La Concha **$$-$$$$**
430 Duval Street
(305) 296-2991, (800) 745-2191
www.laconchakeywest.com

If you truly want to stay where the action is, you can't do better than this. Not only is La Concha the tallest building on the island of Key West, but it's also situated smack-dab in the center of the busy Duval Street scene.

Originally opened to great fanfare in 1926, La Concha has, throughout the years, played host to a wide variety of guests, including royalty, presidents, and Pulitzer Prize-winning authors. Hemingway mentions it in one of his novels, and Tennessee Williams completed the award-winning play *A Streetcar Named Desire* while in residence here.

Like the island itself, La Concha has weathered many changes and has undergone numerous face-lifts. Today its 150 guest rooms and 10 suites have a casual yet elegant feel. Each is furnished in 1920s art deco style, with wicker chairs, poster beds, floral bedspreads, lace curtains, and period antiques. Many rooms overlook either the never-ending parade of activity on Duval Street or the pool terrace. The spacious pool, set amid lush island foliage, features a multilevel sundeck and tiki bar serving snacks and tropical libations.

The hotel's Crown Room Pub, which opens directly onto Duval Street, serves breakfast, lunch, and dinner and features nightly entertainment. Two gift shops are on the property, as well as bicycle and scooter rental and concierge service. The Old Town Trolley stops at the door of La Concha, and the island's favorite haunted attraction, Ghost Tours of Key West, leaves nightly from the lobby (see the Attractions chapter).

This hotel's most notable feature, perhaps, is its seventh-floor wraparound observation deck. The Top not only offers a bird's-eye perspective on downtown Key West, but it is also one of the best places in town to view the sunset. You're well away from the craziness down at Mallory Square and while you're drinking in all that beauty, you can be drinking a cocktail, cold beer, or soda as well. A small bar at the Top is open limited hours around sunset each evening.

The Inn at Key West **$$$**
3420 North Roosevelt Boulevard
(305) 294-5541, (800) 330-5541
www.theinnatkeywest.com

With close to four million dollars in dazzling landscaping and interior decorating, using a tropical theme in their rooms and suites, The Inn at Key West has set the stage for your enchanting vacation plans. The Inn is conveniently located along North Roosevelt Boulevard and only 3 miles from Duval Street. Designed with 105 rooms, this complex can accommodate a getaway for two or a family reunion for 20. All rooms have cable TV, climate control, and luxurious bathrooms. Choice rooms offer private balconies where you can take in a wandering tropical breeze from the Gulf of Mexico. On premises is the largest tropical freshwater pool in Key West. Creatively landscaped foliage and vegetation surrounds a lively full-service Tiki bar. The Inn at Key West houses a casual open-air cafe for breakfast, lunch, or Sunday brunch. Concierge services are available for booking everything from sightseeing tours to sports activities. Just minutes from US 1 and the Key West airport, this hotel is a great choice for business or pleasure.

Pegasus International Hotel **$-$$**
501 Southard Street (corner of Duval)
(305) 294-9323, (800) 397-8148
www.pegasuskeywest.com

Located on a busy corner in the heart of downtown Key West, Pegasus International Hotel is reminiscent of Miami's famed South Beach district. This pink-stucco structure claims to be the only art deco property in the Florida Keys.

Pegasus offers 30 rooms with various bedding combinations, including two double beds, a queen-size bed, or a king-size bed. The rooms are tastefully appointed in tropical decor. Rates are reasonable, especially considering the hotel's prime location, which is within easy walking distance of Mallory Square and the restaurants and bars on lower Duval Street, plus the fact that parking is free.

Amenities here include a swimming pool, hot tub, and sundeck, all located on the second floor and all overlooking bustling Duval Street. There are no on-premises food outlets at Pegasus; however, several restaurants are conveniently located within a block or two.

Pelican Landing Resort & Marina **$$$$**
915 Eisenhower Drive
(305) 296-9090, (888) 822-5840
www.keywesthideaways.com

You've found your home away from home in the inconspicuous gulfside Pelican Landing, a concrete-block condominium and marina complex on Garrison Bight. Among the 32 units, guests are offered a choice of standard rooms with two double beds or one-, two-, or three-bedroom suites. All accommodations are decorated according to the taste of their individual owners.

Suites have balconies overlooking the marina, and those on the fourth (top) floor are duplex style with either loft bedrooms or two enclosed, second-story bedrooms. Large sliding glass doors with vertical blinds lead to furnished balconies, and all suites have washer-dryers. Suites have king-size beds in the master bedroom, two double beds in the second and third bedrooms, and queen-size sleeper sofas. Some suites have hot tubs. A one-bedroom penthouse suite is among the most romantic.

Pelican Landing's heated swimming pool is surrounded by a sundeck. Gas barbecue grills and a fish-cleaning station are available for guests. The facility is boat accessible by powerboat only, because a fixed bridge offers only an 18-foot clearance. The marina offers 15 boat slips accommodating vessels up to 35 feet with a 12-foot beam. All guests have off-street parking. Charter fishing boats are just across the dock.

FULL-SERVICE RESORTS

The Casa Marina Resort **$$$-$$$$**
1500 Reynolds Street
(305) 296-3535, (800) 626-0777
www.casamarinakeywest.com

Construction of the Casa Marina Hotel dates from 1918, after railroad magnate Henry Flagler had envisioned a resort hotel for wealthy snowbirds. Made of poured concrete and featuring walls 12 to 22 inches thick, the hotel has hosted many prominent guests, including baseball legend Lou Gehrig and President Harry Truman.

The original structure is one of three buildings that now make up the resort, and its Old-World-style lobby is lined with old photos of Flagler, Gehrig, Truman, and others. Lobby walls, floors, and columns are made of Dade County pine, and an expansive mahogany front desk with marble top accommodates seven check-in terminals.

The Casa Marina's three- and four-story buildings are set on the Atlantic Ocean, offering a total of 311 standard rooms and suites. Rates increase from the standard non-oceanview to the standard oceanview and from non-oceanview suites to oceanview suites. Standard rooms hold two double beds or one king-size bed. Each suite has a king-size bed in the bedroom and a double sleeper sofa in the living room. All suites have sliding glass doors and private balconies. Floors are carpeted, and rooms have stocked minibars, hair dryers, irons, and ironing boards. Suites also have two televisions, mini-refrigerators, and ceiling fans.

The Casa's Sunday brunch, which is served on the terrace overlooking the ocean, is legendary. The Casa Marina also has two swimming pools—one lap pool and the other designated for, but not restricted to, children. Both pools and a hot tub are surrounded by a concrete sundeck with ramps leading to the resort's private beach, the largest such beach in Key West. The pools and hot tub are open 24 hours. During the day, poolside concierge service is available with complimentary fresh fruit and frozen "drinks of the day" from the poolside tiki bar.

A concession stand rents scooters, bicycles, personal watercraft, and Hobie Cats. Parasailing, sunset cruises, and fishing, snorkeling, and diving excursions can also be arranged through this concession. On the premises is a fitness facility with dry or wet sauna, and masseuse services are offered on a large lawn beneath magnificent palm trees or in the privacy of your room.

Three hard-surface tennis courts on the property are lighted, and equipment and lessons are available. The Casa Marina offers concierge services, valet laundry, and complimentary shuttle service to and from Key West International Airport.

Casa Marina rates are structured on a per-room basis. Children younger than age 19 stay free when accompanied by an adult. The Casa Marina offers organized activities for children; most are free of charge (see the Kidstuff chapter).

Doubletree Grand Key Resort $$$–$$$$
3990 South Roosevelt Boulevard
(305) 293-1818, (888) 844-0454
www.doubletreekeywest.com

Just when locals thought the island of Key West could simply not support one more hotel, along comes this new luxury resort. Grand Key Resort boasts 216 guest rooms in a variety of configurations, from connected double queen-size rooms to luxurious suites. The property is tucked between two condominium complexes on the north side of the island, not far from Key West International Airport. Rooms overlook the parking lot on one side and the salt ponds that border the airport on the other; if you're lucky enough to be on one of the upper floors, you might have a pretty decent view of the Atlantic Ocean and Smathers Beach in the distance.

Everything at Grand Key is, of course, brand spanking clean and bright. All of the rooms are appointed in the casually elegant tropical style that has become the hallmark of upscale hotels in Key West. All of them feature a full complement of guest amenities, including minibars, coffeemakers, hair dryers, in-room safes, ceiling fans, bathrobes, Sony PlayStations, cable TV with HBO, and in-room movies. A focal point in the lobby is the 25,000-gallon aquarium that stretches from floor to ceiling and is filled with the kind of colorful fish you would likely see in their natural habitat on a trip to the reef.

The Palm Haven Restaurant, which overlooks the pool at the far end of the lobby, serves island fare. Snacks and tropical libations are available at an open-air bar positioned poolside. A large deck and plenty of white rocking chairs beckon sun worshipers.

An on-premises gift shop, meeting facilities, and concierge services are available. Children are welcome here. In fact, those younger than age 18 stay free with parents, and nature-based programs are planned to keep them entertained.

Hyatt Key West Resort & Marina $$$–$$$$
601 Front Street
(305) 296-9900, (800) 554-9288
www.keywest.hyatt.com

Fronting on the Gulf of Mexico, the five-story Hyatt Key West is a three-building, 120-unit complex of standard rooms, junior suites, and standard suites, all with sliding glass doors and private balconies. Rooms overlook the city, pool, or Gulf of Mexico.

Fully carpeted except for tile entranceways, standard rooms generally face the city and have one king-size bed or two double beds, fully stocked minibars, hair dryers, coffeemakers, irons, and ironing boards. Some have ceiling fans, and bathrobes are provided upon request. A variety of suites feature panoramic views of the Gulf.

Junior suites (L-shaped with a small sitting area and no dividing walls) and standard suites (one-bedroom units with a door separating the bedroom from the living area) are all fully tiled and boast the same amenities as standard rooms. Junior suites also have whirlpool tubs. Furnishings all are primarily light oak accented by wicker and rattan; bed coverings and draperies are in tropical prints. Wall hangings feature colorful local and Caribbean scenes.

Hyatt has an outdoor swimming pool and hot tub, two restaurants, a small health club, two dive boats, a charter fishing boat, and a 68-foot sailing yacht for afternoon snorkeling and early-evening sunset sails. Also available are water sports, scooter and bike rentals, and the hotel has a small private beach.

A three-tier sundeck overlooks the beach, and the resort's own Nicola Seafood (see the Restaurants chapter) is a great place to enjoy the sunset. Concierge, room service, and laundry valet are available, as is a resident masseuse, who will provide a massage in your room at an additional cost.

The Hyatt has smoking and nonsmoking rooms and wheelchair-accessible facilities. Children younger than age 18 stay free. The resort offers special packages throughout the year, so inquire when you call to make reservations. Rates are based on double occupancy; each additional person is charged an additional fee per night.

The Westin Key West Resort and Marina **$$$-$$$$**
245 Front Street
(305) 294-4000, (866) 837-4250
www.westin.com/keywest

The bayfront Westin was designed so all rooms provide views of the pool, the bay, or the marina and its surrounding waters. Guests here also are provided launch service to a relatively secluded beach at Sunset Key (see separate listing).

The two buildings that make up the Westin have 178 rooms; one structure has only nonsmoking rooms. The three-story building overlooks the marina; the other, a four-story structure, sits adjacent to Mallory Square. Situated in historic Old Town near the old Custom House (see the Attractions chapter), the Westin and its grounds are surrounded by brick walkways. Sliding glass doors framed by wooden shutters open onto private terraces. Textured interior walls boast sconces; floors feature stone tiles. Bleached oak and stone furnishings and handpainted walls welcome visitors to the hotel lobby.

On-premises are a swimming pool, hot tub, and sundeck area, fitness facilities, a restaurant offering indoor and outdoor dining, and a sunset deck and lounge. Meeting space is available for large groups.

Ocean Key Resort and Spa **$$$-$$$$**
Zero Duval Street
(305) 296-7701, (800) 328-9815
www.oceankey.com

Part of the Noble House family of resorts, Ocean Key is a large resort with an intimate flavor. From their rooms and balconies, Ocean Key guests can see the water, our famous sunsets, and offbeat Mallory Square entertainers, all without the hassle of crowds.

Among the 100 units in this five-story resort are guest rooms and one- and two-bedroom, two-bath suites furnished with laminated wood and other lightweight furnishings. Ceiling fans are standard. Standard guest rooms all feature tiled floors and one queen-size bed, plus a queen-size pullout sofa in the sitting area. Kitchens and living rooms in all suites are tiled, and bedrooms are carpeted. Other features include oversize baths and private hot tubs, kitchens, living rooms with sleeper sofas, and private balconies.

One-bedroom suites have a king-size bed. Two-bedroom units have a king-size bed in the master bedroom and a queen-size bed in the second bedroom. Penthouse suites, the most expensive units in the facility, feature full kitchens with microwaves, washers, and dryers.

On the premises are Billyfish Bar & Grill on the Sunset Pier, the Hot Tin Roof restaurant, a waterfront swimming pool, and a marina with fishing, snorkeling, dive charter boats, and a glass-bottomed tour boat. A highlight of Ocean Key Resort is its sunset pier overlooking both the harbor and Mallory Square (see the Attractions chapter). Other amenities include valet laundry, room service, and concierge service. The hotel honors requests for nonsmoking rooms. Children younger than age 12 stay free when accompanied by an adult. Ocean Key Resort does not provide cots. Cribs are provided free upon request.

Ocean Key Resort and Spa offers its tranquil Spa Terra for its guests. This serene escape is a 2,550-square-foot Indonesian-inspired spa. The theme of this facility originated at the sister property, famed Little Palm Island Resort (see listing in this chapter) located on Little Torch Key.

Pier House Resort and Caribbean Spa **$$$-$$$$**
1 Duval Street
(305) 296-4600, (800) 327-8340
www.pierhouse.com

Portions of the Pier House are on the grounds of Key West's former Porter Dock Company and Aeromarine Airways Inc., two companies that played significant roles in the city's illustrious shipping days. The Pier House, which completed a $4.5 million renovation in 2002, offers 126 luxurious, tropically appointed standard rooms with one king-size bed or two queen-size beds and 16 suites. All have views of the Gulf of Mexico, the swimming pool, or the city.

Rooms overlooking the pool and the Gulf have sliding glass doors and private balconies, and those facing the water may look out on topless sunbathers along a portion of the resort's private beach. Standard in all rooms are minibars, coffeemakers, and hair dryers. Lush tropical foliage and brick paving surround the swimming pool and outdoor hot tub. The resort's beach and a secluded island glisten in the distance.

The Pier House is noted for its full-service spa, which offers fitness facilities, facials, massages, and hair and nail care. Room service is available and a concierge will arrange for additional needs. The hotel features three restaurants and several bars, including the Chart Room Bar, Zero Duval, and Havana Docks Sunset Deck.

Off-street parking is abundant. Rates are based on double occupancy; each additional person is charged an additional fee per night. Children younger than age 17 stay free when accompanied by an adult.

The Reach Resort **$$$-$$$$**
1435 Simonton Street
(305) 296-5000, (800) 874-4118
www.reachresort.com

Splendor by the sea is what visitors to the Reach Resort will discover. The resort boasts the only natural sand beach on the island of Key West.

All 150 rooms within the resort feature Spanish-tile floors and soothing tones of cream, purple, teal, yellow, and orange, combining a Caribbean twist with Southwestern appeal. Standard rooms, junior suites, and one-bedroom executive suites offer either island or ocean views. Standard rooms have either one queen-size bed or two double beds, and those with queen-size beds also have queen-size sleeper sofas.

Junior suites are large, L-shaped studios with queen- or king-size beds and queen-size sleeper sofas. King-size beds and pullout sleeper sofas are standard in all executive suites. Each room at the

For information about accommodations in Key West—whether you're looking for a quaint guesthouse or a full-service resort—call the Key West Information Center at (305) 292-5000 or The Accommodation Center at (305) 296-7701, (800) 732-2006, www.accommodations keywest.com. These services are free.

Reach Resort has a ceiling fan, private balcony, wet bar, minibar, hair dryer, terrycloth robes, iron/ironing board, and coffeemaker.

The resort has an outdoor swimming pool, hot tub, and full water-sports concession for rafts, parasailing, personal watercraft rentals, and more. The Sand Bar, a casual poolside bar and restaurant, provides full service from 7:00 A.M. to 9:00 P.M.

An on-premises gift shop carries a wide variety of items, and a salon offers haircuts, colorings, facials, and body wraps. Enjoy a massage beneath an outdoor gazebo or in the privacy of your room, or head for the fitness center with sauna and steam room.

Room service, valet laundry service, and concierge services are available, along with complimentary transportation to and from Key West International Airport.

Tennis facilities at the neighboring Casa Marina Resort are open to all guests, as are the Casa's magnificent beach and two pools (see separate listing). *NOTE:* RV campers will not fit under the resort's enclosed parking garage.

Sheraton Suites Key West $$$-$$$$
2001 South Roosevelt Boulevard
(305) 292-9800, (800) 452-3224
www.sheratonkeywest.com

Situated across from Smathers Beach, the Conch-style, three-story, 180-unit Sheraton is a luxurious all-suite facility built around an expansive concrete sundeck and a swimming pool. The roomy (550 square feet) suites here are decorated in relaxing tropical teals, peaches, and lavenders and are furnished in colorful wicker.

Walls feature bright Caribbean-colored borders; floors are carpeted, and rooms are furnished with refrigerators and wet bars, minibars, microwaves, and coffeemakers. Most offer king-size beds and whirlpool tubs, and those facing the pool and ocean have sliding glass doors leading to furnished balconies. Suites have irons and ironing boards, built-in hair dryers, and two televisions—one in the bedroom and another in the living room.

The Beach House restaurant offers breakfast, lunch, and dinner poolside or indoors. A hot tub by the pool accommodates eight, and lounge chairs and pool towels are provided. Sheraton Suites offers guests complimentary shuttle service to and from Key West International Airport as well as hourly transportation to Mallory Square (see the Attractions chapter) between 10:00 A.M. and 10:00 P.M.

The staff at the guest activities desk will assist you in planning fishing and diving excursions, restaurant bookings, and more. On the premises are a fitness center, 1,100 square feet of banquet meeting space, and a gift shop. Guest laundry facilities are available, and off-street parking is plentiful. The Sheraton Suites is a pet-friendly resort as well. Animals weighing less than 80 pounds are welcome. Call for details.

Sunset Key Guest Cottages $$$-$$$$
245 Front Street
(305) 292-5300, (888) 477-7786
www.sunsetkeycottages.hilton.com

Billed as the ultimate island hideaway, the guest cottages at Sunset Key are an extension of the Key West Hilton Resort and Marina, tucked away directly across the harbor from the main hotel, overlooking Mallory Square. Access is strictly by private launch, which operates 24 hours a day between Sunset Key and the Hilton marina.

Nestled amid swaying palms and lush flowering hibiscus, the cottages offer an opportunity to truly get away from the hustle and bustle of Duval Street, yet still enjoy the heart of Key West. You may come and go from Sunset Key at will, of course, but you truly never have to leave at all. The emphasis here is on privacy and service; if whatever you require is not on the island, rest assured that it can be delivered posthaste from Key West.

Cottages feature a beachfront, ocean view, or garden view, with beachfront being the most expensive. Rates are structured on a per-cottage basis, and up to six guests may share a single cottage. Interiors feature separate living and dining areas and bedrooms with either double or king-size beds; every bedroom has its own bath stocked with hair dryer, bathrobes, and plush, oversize towels. The decor has a distinctly Caribbean flavor—ceramic tile floors, pastel accents, ceiling fans, and comfortable, casual, whitewashed furnishings. Every cottage features a CD player, state-of-the-art stereo system, and VCR.

Airy living rooms open onto private verandas, and kitchens are fully stocked with select foods and beverages and the requisite utensils for preparing and serving your own meals. Each has a microwave/convection oven, coffeemaker, toaster, refrigerator, and dishwasher. Guests will find a limited selection of groceries at the island outpost market; however, grocery delivery service from Key West is also offered for more extensive orders. If you'd prefer to leave the cooking to someone else, simply walk a few steps to the full-service gourmet restaurant, Latitudes (see the Restaurants chapter), or arrange for a private chef to prepare a meal in your own kitchen. Room service is also available, and a complimentary breakfast basket of muffins and freshly squeezed orange juice is delivered daily, along with the newspaper, to your doorstep. In 1998, mega-celebrity Oprah Winfrey rented all of Sunset Key to host her 44th birthday party. Famous faces were everywhere in Key West that weekend.

In addition to a white-sand beach, the island features a freshwater pool, hot tub, two tennis courts, and a health club. No cars are permitted on Sunset Key. However, parking is available in the Key West Hilton garage.

Reservations for specific cottage assignments are accepted but not guaranteed; cottages are assigned on a first-come, first-served basis upon arrival. All cottages are nonsmoking. Guests must be older than age 25 unless accompanied by an adult. Children younger than age 18 stay free with parents or grandparents.

Bed-and-Breakfasts, Inns, and Guesthouses

Key West's Conch-style mansions and captains' and cigar-workers' homes date from the 1800s, and many have been marvelously restored to accommodate a thriving tourist industry. Close to 100 intimate hideaways are tucked along the streets, avenues, and lanes of Key West's Old Town, and these charming, romantic inns, bed-and-breakfasts, and guesthouses provide a sense of history, tranquillity, and intimacy within the active city.

The inns, which are within walking distance of Duval Street, offer spacious rooms that often showcase high ceilings, fine antiques and reproductions, and ornate woodwork. Renovations have brought about modern amenities: private baths, air-conditioning, telephones, and cable television with remote control. In some cases guest rooms may share bathroom facilities in the European tradition.

You'll find few waterfront or water-view guesthouse accommodations. Rather, rooms enjoy tranquil garden views or views of the often ever-changing, active, streetfront. French doors tend to lead to private verandas with picket fences overlooking lush courtyards where deluxe continental breakfasts, full breakfasts, and afternoon cocktails frequently are served beside tranquil swimming pools, goldfish ponds, or hot tubs. Some guesthouses

i ***Many full-service resorts offer free shuttle service to and from Key West International Airport. Be sure to ask about shuttles when you make your reservations.***

provide passes that allow use of beach, spa, and fitness facilities at some of the island's full-service resorts.

Ideal for those seeking a quiet escape accessible to restaurants, bars, theater, and water sports, these facilities are run by gracious innkeepers who pay careful regard to detail: Fresh flowers, terry-cloth robes, and other amenities often are provided in each room, cottage, and suite; continental breakfast and sometimes even afternoon cocktails are included in the price of the accommodation.

Key West welcomes diversity, and some guesthouses cater primarily or exclusively to gay travelers. Others are considered all-welcome or gay-friendly. In a separate section at the end of this chapter, we highlight primarily and exclusively gay retreats, many of which maintain clothing-optional policies. Some straight guesthouses and inns also have begun to incorporate a clothing-optional policy. But unlike gay accommodations—where if you disapprove of the policy, you shouldn't stay there—heterosexual guesthouses may require clothing upon complaint.

Rates quoted by inns typically are based on double occupancy, and additional guests pay anywhere from $10 to $50 extra per night. Rooms do have a maximum capacity. Inquire about this and all other details when you call to make reservations. If you are certain you'll need full telephone service in your room, check, too, to determine if your service is designed both for call-ins and call-outs.

Pets tend to be more welcome in Key West guesthouses than in hotels or other accommodations throughout the Florida Keys and Key West, but be sure to ask when making your reservation. We will note where pets are permitted. A flat fee or refundable deposit may be required.

As a general rule, guesthouses are for adults only. If a particular property welcomes children, we'll tell you. Otherwise, you may assume that you should either leave the kids at home or look elsewhere in this chapter for kid-friendly accommodations.

The city's high season is typically December through April, and room rates are even higher—with minimum stays required—during special events and holidays. If you come to Key West for Fantasy Fest in October or during Christmas week in December, the minimum stay may be set at six to seven nights. If you plan to be in Key West at either of these times, you should call and reserve your room at least six months to a year in advance.

At last count, the Key West phone book had listings for close to 100 guesthouses and inns. We have done our best to provide a representative sampling. For a complete list of accommodations, contact the Key West Information Center at (305) 292-5000 or the Key West Chamber of Commerce at (305) 294-2587 or (800) 527-8539.

Almond Tree Inn **$$-$$$**
512 Truman Avenue
(305) 296-5415, (800) 311-4292
www.almondtreeinn.com

The Almond Tree Inn sits at the historic crossroads of Truman Avenue and Duval Street in Old Town Key West. Lush tropical landscaping surrounds the 22 elegant, amenity-filled rooms. A tranquil waterfall is on the property and sundecks surround the pool. Private, off-street parking assures convenience away from the well-traveled Old Town location. All rooms have TV, voice mail, coffeemakers with gourmet coffee, mini-refrigerators, and microwave ovens. A complimentary continental breakfast is served daily, and beer and wine are offered in the afternoon underneath the pavilion. Some rooms are deluxe king, some rooms are premium king, with a king-size bed and a sleeper sofa, and oversize guest rooms have two queen-size beds and a sleeper sofa. All rooms are nonsmoking and guests must be age 25 or older unless accompanied by an adult.

Ambrosia House **$$-$$$$**
622 Fleming Street
(305) 296-9838, (800) 535-9838
www.ambrosiakeywest.com

As its name implies, Ambrosia is like a deliciously flavored tropical oasis. This delightful bed-and-breakfast compound is really a combination of six restored properties on two acres.

The compound consists of six carefully restored buildings nestled among lush tropical landscaping and clear, cool ponds. Located in the heart of Old Town Key West, just a block and a half off Duval, Ambrosia is convenient to shopping, restaurants, and nightlife. The accommodations include suites, town houses, and a stand-alone cottage. Town houses have full living rooms, complete kitchens, and spiral staircases leading to master suites with vaulted ceilings and private decks. The cottage, which overlooks a dip pool, is a perfect family retreat; it has two bedrooms, two baths, a living room, and full kitchen. Honeymoon suites have four-poster canopy beds and in-room Jacuzzis.

All rooms and suites feature individual entrances with French doors opening onto private verandas, patios, or gardens. The walls are adorned with the original works of Key West artists; the beds are dressed in designer linens. Guest amenities include refrigerators, coffeemakers, portable phones, computer modems, ceiling fans, and cable TV. Large sunning areas, a lap pool, and hot tub are also available.

Children are welcome, as are pets.

Andrews Inn **$$-$$$**
Zero Whalton Lane
(305) 294-7730, (888) 263-7393
www.andrewsinn.com

You might have to search a bit to find this place, but once you do we guarantee you won't want to leave. After a day at the beach or a night on Duval, this tiny inn offers a welcome little slice of tranquillity that is tough to beat. Andrews Inn is practically in Hemingway's backyard. You'll find it tucked behind his former house—the only thing that separates the two is a brick wall—on a shaded narrow lane between Duval and Whitehead Streets.

Guest rooms here are named for settings in Hemingway's books, such as Paris and Pamplona.

They all have vaulted ceilings, a queen- or king-size bed, remote-control TV, phones, and private bath. Just outside your door, you'll find a lush tropical garden and comfortable lounge chairs situated around a cool, refreshing pool. You're assured of privacy here all right, but we should warn you about the neighbors because you're almost certain to have a visit from at least one of them. A representative from that gang of six-toed cats that reside next door at the Hemingway House is likely to wander over to say hello.

Andrews Inn offers a complimentary champagne continental breakfast each morning and cocktails by the pool every afternoon. If you're lucky and you're able to snag one of the inn's limited off-street parking spaces, you can just abandon your car for the full length of your stay. Andrews Inn is within easy walking distance of most Key West restaurants, bars, and attractions.

The Artist House **$-$$$$**
534 Eaton Street
(305) 296-3977, (800) 582-7882
www.artisthousekeywest.com

With the addition of guest suites a block away from the original property, Artist House now offers accommodations at two levels—in a charming turn-of-the-last-century Victorian mansion and in modern, tastefully appointed villas. The one you choose is a matter of personal taste.

What the Artist House Guest Villas

might lack in Old-World charm, they more than make up for by being exceptionally bright and roomy. Each of the six suites includes a fully equipped kitchen with microwave, stove, and refrigerator and a separate bedroom with a queen-size bed and cable TV. Private sundecks, a heated swimming pool, and a reserved parking space for each guest round out the amenities.

Accommodations in the old house do not sparkle like those in the villas, but all are quite charming and spacious, with 14-foot-high ceilings, private baths, and ceiling fans. Rooms have various antique furnishings and wallpaper patterns and large windows with lace curtains. The parlor suite on the first floor features a four-poster, queen-size bed and has a sitting area with Chippendale couch and Oriental rugs over wood floors. The Turret Suite, on the second floor, offers a dressing room and a winding staircase that leads to a cupola, or circular, loft-style room with daybed. Four of the six guest rooms have working fireplaces, and three have claw-foot tubs.

Legend has it that this 1890 Victorian mansion, formerly the home of Key West painter Eugene Otto, is haunted by the ghost of Otto's deceased wife, whose burial place in the Key West cemetery lacks a tombstone. Some guests claim they have seen Mrs. Otto on a winding staircase in a room on the second floor.

If you'd care to learn more about this somewhat peculiar family, you will find Eugene Otto's paintings on display at the East Martello Museum. At the Key West City Cemetery (see the Attractions chapter), the former artist's tombstone is surrounded by those of his pet Yorkshire terriers.

Ironically, pets are not allowed at the Artist House or Villas these days. However, children age 10 and older are permitted.

Authors of Key West Guesthouse **$-$$**
725 White Street
(305) 294-7381, (800) 898-6909
www.authors-keywest.com

Visiting writers to Key West often select this private three-building compound as their outpost. Each has his or her favorite room, and each room is named for one of Key West's legendary authors, such as Ernest Hemingway or Tennessee Williams. Look for memorabilia on the author of your choice.

The main two-story, eight-room house is tucked neatly behind a cement wall. Lined with lush tropical foliage, it boasts a two-sided sundeck. Two poolside Conch houses, built around the turn of the 20th century, are available for rent; these one-bedroom homes feature queen-size beds and full kitchens. Both have small private porches.

Rooms within the main house are equally diverse, offering views of the street, the sundeck, or the gardens.

Continental breakfast is served daily in the lounge or by the swimming pool. The inn provides off-street parking, and bicycles are available for rent. Pets are not permitted. Children age 13 and older are allowed. Note that the entrance to Authors is on Petronia Street.

The Banyan Resort **$$$-$$$$**
323 Whitehead Street
(305) 296-7786, (800) 853-9937
www.banyanresort.com

The Banyan Resort is a collection of eight beautifully preserved and refurbished Conch-style homes, five of which are listed on the National Register of Historic Places. One of these buildings formerly served as a cigar factory.

The homes boast 38 contemporary studios, suites, and duplexes, with full kitchens. Some units have been sold as condominiums; others are available as time-shares and guest accommodations. Studios are least expensive, and rates increase with size: one bedroom, one bath; two bedrooms, one bath; and two bedrooms, two baths. All accommodations have French doors leading to private patios and verandas that overlook award-winning gardens. Included among the gardens are jasmine, frangipani, hibiscus, ixora, rare orchids, palm and fruit trees, and two magnificent 200-year-old banyan trees. Bicycle rentals are available on the premises.

Children, with restrictions, are permitted. Limited off-street parking is available at an additional charge.

Blue Parrot Inn **$-$$$**
916 Elizabeth Street
(305) 296-0033, (800) 231-2473
www.blueparrotinn.com

Built in 1884 with wood pegs that are more hurricane friendly than nails, the Blue Parrot Inn offers nine guest units. Rooms vary in size, number of beds, and decor. The only blue parrot in residence here is a stuffed one; however, the cats you'll see wandering the grounds are very much alive.

A large Irish room with two double beds features Celtic prints and green accessories; the flamingo room, with a queen-size bed, is flocked with feathers and photographs of the famed Floridian birds. Still others remain true to this guesthouse's name through parrot-print bedspreads. All rooms have phones and most have mini-refrigerators.

Out back, a heated swimming pool surrounded by extensive decking sets the scene for a leisurely continental breakfast consisting of fresh fruit, bagels, English muffins, and home-baked quiche or fruit breads served every morning. A tremendous staghorn fern strung along branches of a gumbo-limbo tree makes a magnificent garden centerpiece.

The atmosphere at the Blue Parrot is friendly and intimate. Guests must be at least 16 years of age. Curbside parking is free; off-street parking is available for an extra charge.

Center Court Historic Inn & Cottages **$-$$$$**
915 Center Street
(305) 296-9292, (800) 797-8787
www.centercourtkw.com

Center Court is a fine example of the historic preservation for which Key West is so justly famous. Nestled on a quiet, inconspicuous lane just half a block from Duval Street, the main guesthouse, constructed in 1874, is surrounded by a collection of former cigar-makers' cottages. Owner-operator Naomi Van Steelandt enrolled in construction courses so she could carry out the restoration, which won two Historic Preservation Awards of Excellence in 1994.

Walls are pastel-colored and feature original local art. Guest rooms are cozy and sleep two to six. Rooms are stocked with beach bags, beach towels, and other goodies. Each cottage has its own bright and cheerful personality, as well as a fully stocked kitchen, barbecue grill, and private hot tub.

The main building houses a spacious, airy breakfast room; dining takes place out on the back porch overlooking a swimming pool, spa, and exercise pavilion. Two cottages are set beside a lily pond. A spiral staircase alongside one of these cottages leads to a clothing-optional sundeck. Breakfast is complimentary for guests in rooms; cottage guests have the facilities to fix their own.

Children are allowed in the cottages and suites. Pets are permitted for an additional fee per night.

Van Steelandt also performs and coordinates weddings and makes honeymoon arrangements. For information, call her at the numbers shown above.

Chelsea House **$$-$$$**
707 Truman Avenue
(305) 296-2211, (800) 845-8859
www.chelseahousekw.com

Built in 1870 for a British ship captain who hauled tobacco from Havana and later became the first general manager of Duval Street's La Concha Hotel, Chelsea House was later converted to a guesthouse by the captain's grieving widow to provide lodging to Key West's military visitors. Later, Chelsea House became an apartment complex. In 1985 massive renovations included the addition of private baths throughout and the conversion of the carriage house into guest accommodations.

The Conch-style mansion serves as the main guesthouse. And with the addition of a pool house, garden rooms, and suites building, the total number of units now stands at 19. Each has 10-foot-high ceilings and individualized decor. Guest rooms in the main house feature hardwood floors and heavy mahogany and oak period furnishings. Pool-house rooms open directly onto the sundeck, and the garden rooms feature raised decks with rocking chairs for lounging. All rooms are furnished with antiques and feature private baths, ceiling fans, refrigerators, and complimentary bath amenities. Some have private or shared porches, oversize tubs, and cathedral ceilings.

Unlike The Red Rooster (Chelsea House's more casual sister hotel, described later in this chapter), this is co-owner Jim Durbin's showpiece, boasting four-poster beds and armoires plus nightly turndowns and fresh pool towels.

A full acre of property, shared with the neighboring Red Rooster, is likely the largest of all of Key West's guesthouse properties. Here, a private garden with massive palms and flowering plants forms an L-shaped alcove visible from the windows, French doors, and balconies of some rooms in the main house. Every room at Chelsea House either has a balcony or opens onto the pool area.

A daily continental breakfast is served in an enclosed poolside cafe, and clothing is optional on a secluded elevated sundeck. Also available for topless lounging at this adults-only inn are the gardens, deck, pool, and cabana areas. Off-street parking provides a space for every guest.

With prior approval, pets are accepted.

The Conch House Heritage Inn $-$$$
625 Truman Avenue
(305) 293-0020, (800) 207-5806
www.conchhouse.com

Since the 1800s, this historic two-story estate has been passed on from generation to generation. The current owners are Sam Holland Jr. and his mother, Francine Delaney Holland. She is the great-granddaughter of Cuban émigré Carlos Recio, a close friend of Cuban revolutionary Jose Martí.

The inn is listed on the National Register of Historic Places and was restored in 1993 to combine Old-World decor with modern amenities. The five bedrooms in the main house feature high ceilings, wood shutters, wraparound porches, and picket fences. A poolside cottage offers three guest rooms decorated with Caribbean prints and wicker. Guests may have their continental breakfast in the dining room or on the veranda.

Children older than age 12 are permitted at the inn.

Cuban Club Suites $$-$$$$
1102 Duval Street

La Casa De Luces $-$$$
422 Amelia Street
(305) 294-5269, (800) 833-0372
www.cubanclubsuites.com

Both Cuban Club Suites and La Casa De Luces share guest check-in and lobby facilities on Amelia Street, but Cuban Club Suites is actually in a separate building at 1102 Duval Street. These two-story luxury suites are condominiums occupying second and third floors above boutiques that are open to the public.

A large living area, full kitchen, bath, and bedroom with a queen-size bed occupy the main level of the two-bedroom suites. An oversized loft area above the main level is furnished either with a queen- or king-size bed and features a second bath and a small private sunning deck. One-bedroom suites have a large living area, full kitchen, and half bath on the first floor; the second-floor loft has a queen-size bed, full bath, and small sunning deck. All suites have washer/dryers and are furnished primarily with light wicker furnishings or heavy wood furnishings accented by antique reproductions.

At the less exclusive La Casa De Luces (English translation: house of lights) are eight units ranging from two small rooms sharing a bath to large garden suites with king-size bed, living room, washer-dryer, and full kitchen. Most rooms are furnished with lightweight wicker furnishings and tropical prints; all have exterior access via private verandas. Complimentary continental breakfast is delivered to guest rooms each morning, and within the La Casa De Luces lobby is a small museum illustrating the rich Cuban history of both buildings. Neither facility has a swimming pool, but guests are provided passes to a nearby resort.

Off-street parking is available. Families are welcome. Dogs are permitted if management is notified at the time the reservation is made.

Curry Mansion Inn $$-$$$$
511 Caroline Street
(305) 294-5349, (800) 253-3466
www.currymansion.com

Curry Mansion Inn's chief claim to fame is its location on the grounds of the estate that once belonged to the Currys, Florida's first homegrown millionaire family. Situated on Caroline Street, just a few steps off Duval, the 22-room mansion was begun by William Curry in 1855 and completed by his son Milton in 1899. Innkeepers Al and Edith Amsterdam purchased the property in 1975. Curry Mansion is today a museum, housing a selection of turn-of-the-20th-century furnishings and memorabilia from Key West's heyday as the richest city in America (see the Attractions chapter). It is also the centerpiece for a guesthouse that is consistently rated among the best in Key West.

Guests at the Curry Mansion Inn do not actually stay in the mansion; they do, however, have full access to it. Guest accommodations consist instead of 28 rooms adjacent to the mansion, most of which open onto a pool and all of which are surrounded by the lush foliage that characterizes the Curry estate. All of the rooms feature wicker furnishings, antiques, and ceiling fans; the beds are draped in handmade quilts. Modern amenities include private baths, wet bars, small refrigerators, air-conditioning, cable television, and telephones.

A complimentary breakfast buffet is offered poolside each morning; complimentary cocktails are served each evening from 5:00 to 7:00. The inn's heated pool and hot tub are open 24 hours. Ask about beach privileges at nearby oceanfront resorts; Curry Mansion Inn has agreements with several.

A particularly appealing feature of this guesthouse is its location—right in the heart of downtown Key West. The restaurants, bars, shops, and other Duval Street attractions are just steps away; parking is plentiful.

Cypress House $-$$$$
601 Caroline Street

Cypress House Guest Studios $-$$$
613 Caroline Street
(305) 294-6969, (800) 525-2488
www.cypresshousekw.com

The 40-foot heated lap pool surrounded by lush tropical gardens on the grounds of this 100-year-old mansion is among the largest at any of Key West's inns. The New England–style, three-story home, constructed of cypress, is listed on the National Register of Historic Places and is a noted attraction along the Conch Train tourist route (see the Attractions chapter).

Rebuilt in the wake of the fire of 1886 that consumed much of Key West, the facility was originally owned by Richard Moore Kemp, a shipbuilder and naturalist credited for the discovery of the ridley turtle (now known as the Kemp's ridley turtle). Twenty years after Kemp built his own home, he added another house to the property for his daughter and son-in-law, a pioneer Key West sponger.

Connected by a wooden fire escape, the two homes share a sundeck. Rooms throughout the structures feature 12-foot-high ceilings and wood floors with area rugs. In-room telephones allow for outside calling, and most rooms have queen-size beds and ceiling fans. Six of 16 rooms have private baths. A hand-painted floral ceiling border accents one room, and all are furnished with period antiques.

Porches on the first and second floor are accessible to guests. A breakfast buffet featuring home-baked goods is served poolside, as is a nightly complimentary cocktail hour with beer, wine, and snacks.

Formerly an exclusively gay guesthouse, Cypress is now an all-welcome, adults-only facility. Pets are not permitted, but you are invited to pet the resident dog and cat in case you miss your own.

Four luxury suites and two guest rooms distinguish Cypress House Guest Studios (formerly William Anthony House), located three doors up the street at 613 Caroline Street. Amenities include sitting and dining areas, private baths, kitchenettes, air-conditioning and heating, cable TV, and phones. The facilities were completely renovated in 1994.

However, it's not the usual amenities that will draw you in to the aura of idyllic retreat, but the spa, pond, deck, and delightful gardens. This facility offers a complimentary continental breakfast and wine at social hour. One room is wheelchair accessible.

Douglas House $$-$$$$
419 Amelia Street
(305) 294-5269, (800) 833-0372
www.douglashouse.com

Douglas House is a collection of six Victorian homes, four of which are more than 100 years old. Each house contains two to five spacious units for a combined total of 15.

Standard rooms and one-bedroom suites are furnished with a queen-size bed or two double beds; suites have a full kitchen. All units have private baths and outdoor entrances, and each unit is furnished differently. Some are carpeted with standard wood furnishings; others have hardwood floors and wicker furnishings. Suites have French doors opening to a private deck, patio, or balcony. Some suites have loft-style bedrooms.

Within the compound are two swimming pools and a hot tub surrounded by gardens. Continental breakfast is served poolside each morning, and coffee perks throughout the day.

Pets are permitted. Children younger than age 12 are not allowed during the high season.

Duval House $$-$$$$
815 Duval Street
(305) 294-1666, (800) 223-8825
www.duvalhousekeywest.com

This two-story inn may be set on busy Duval Street, but its pigeon plums, banyans, heliconia, and hibiscus successfully guard it from intrusion. Lounge poolside amid traveler's palms and light jazz music, linger on a shady hammock, or chat with others in a gazebo by the fishpond. The inn's breakfast room maintains a library of books, board games, magazines and newspapers, and a weather chart listing temperatures throughout the world.

In the 1880s Duval House was inhabited by cigar workers. Today the 30 standard and deluxe rooms and apartments are furnished with English antiques, white wicker, and wooden French doors. All are air-conditioned. Locally made frangipani soap is placed in each bathroom.

Most rooms have color television, and some feature elegant poster beds and private porches. All except the two apartments and two front rooms look out onto the gardens.

If you visit Duval House, look for Mush, the resident cat, who receives letters from former guests throughout the world.

Eaton Lodge Historic Inn & Gardens $-$$$
511 Eaton Street
(305) 292-2170, (800) 294-2170
www.eatonlodge.com

Built in 1886, the treasure that is Eaton Lodge was owned by one of Key West's first physicians, Dr. William Warren. His wife, Genevieve, founded the Key West Garden Club. Notice her intricate designs for the home's diverse courtyard, which features a fountain, fishpond, Spanish lime tree, jacaranda, and more.

Present owners Carolyn and Stephen West have painted the inn's shutters to match the lavender jacaranda and have preserved all historic appointments within the home's interior, adding a courtyard hot tub.

Eaton Lodge's main house served as both home and office for Dr. Warren. Its elegant living room features Oriental and Turkish carpets over wood floors, a Venetian glass chandelier, and an antique fireplace; bookshelves pose as inconspicuous doors to divide the living room and kitchen.

All 13 rooms and suites, including those within the carriage house next door, vary in size, decor, and view. The two-story, garden-view accommodations in the carriage house connect to create duplexes.

With their high ceilings and original moldings, rooms and suites in the main house feature 18th-century furnishings (the Palm Room), an antique brass bed (the Eaton Room), picket-fence porches, and private terraces (the Anniversary and Sunset Rooms). The unique Sunset Room has a raised bathroom and a terrace that sides a three-story cistern.

All rooms feature watercolor and oil paintings by local artists and wood-plank or parquet flooring with area carpets.

Homemade tropical breads and fresh fruits are served on the patio each morning, and an open-bar afternoon break is offered on the brick patio. A courtyard garden sports chaises for sunning around the Jacuzzi spa.

There are a number of exotic caged birds on the property, so Kuma, the inn's docile Akita, is the only pet allowed. Smoking is permitted outside only.

Eden House **$–$$$$**
1015 Fleming Street
(305) 296–6868, (800) 533–5397
www.edenhouse.com

For years Eden House was known as a no-frills, low-budget hangout for writers, intellectuals, and Europeans. Over the past few years, owner Mike Eden has added several enhancements.

When producers of the movie *Criss-Cross* scouted Key West locations, they opted for this facility. With the enhancements, the circa-1924 building was too polished for the film's needs. They "roughed it up" a bit cosmetically and sent Goldie Hawn here to portray the movie's main character. Rest assured, once the film was completed, Eden House was quickly restored to its vintage art deco grandeur.

Constructed of wood and concrete, the facility categorizes units by luxury rooms and efficiencies (two of them have sleeping lofts); private rooms and efficiencies with bath or shower; semiprivate rooms with shared baths; and European rooms with double or twin-size beds, a sink, and a bath and shower in the hall. Most other units feature queen-size beds. Prices descend respectively.

Accommodations are decorated in light, subdued colors and tropical prints and furnished with a mix of wicker and rattan. Many units have French doors leading to porches and decks near the center of the facility, where gardens surround a swimming pool, hot tub, and gazebo.

Children are permitted, but pets are not. Bicycle rentals are available and guests are treated to a cold drink at check-in. Be sure to check out the elevated sundeck and hammock area, but tread softly. Those tanning bodies are likely to be sound asleep.

Eden House is a smoke-free facility.

The Frances Street Bottle Inn **$–$$**
535 Frances Street
(305) 294–8530, (800) 294–8530
www.bottleinn.com

Tucked away in a quiet residential neighborhood on the edge of Old Town, this charming inn takes its name from the owner's collection of antique bottles and cobalt-blue glassware displayed in every window and along several interior shelves. The trim, white frame structure, once a corner grocery store and boardinghouse, has a unique place in recent Key West history, too. It was the set for the *Meteor* newspaper office in the short-lived television series *Key West.*

The atmosphere here is quiet and intimate. The Bottle Inn has just seven guest rooms, each with private bath, air-conditioning, and color television. White wicker chairs line a gracious porch across the front of the house, and in the lush tropical gardens, a complimentary continental breakfast is served each morning under the poinciana trees. Concierge service is available. Although the grounds are too small to allow for a pool, there is a hot tub.

If you're looking for a guesthouse experience well removed from Duval, yet still within walking distance of most Old Town attractions, you'll find excellent value here.

The Gardens Hotel **$$$$**
526 Angela Street
(305) 294-2661, (800) 526-2664
www.gardenshotel.com

In 1930 the late Key West resident Peggy Mills began collecting various species of orchids from Japan, Bali, and other exotic parts of the world. As neighboring homes were placed on the market, Mills would purchase and level them, adding to her garden until it encompassed a full city block.

Before she passed away, the Mills garden gained the attention of botanists worldwide and national magazines. These gardens have been restored to much of their original splendor by Bill and Corrina Hettinger, owners and operators of The Gardens Hotel, a member of Small Luxury Hotels of the World.

A complex of five guesthouses and a carriage house, the hotel offers 17 units, including a pair of two-bedroom suites, set around a tiki bar, swimming pool, hot tub, fountain, and a winding path of bougainvillea, orange, jasmine, palm, mango, breadfruit trees, and more. The architecture is classic, and rooms are furnished with mahogany reproductions from Holland and floral chintz.

InStyle magazine once described The Gardens Hotel as being like a secluded European inn. Famous guests here have included actors George Clooney and Mickey Rourke and singer k. d. lang.

Floors are hardwood, bathrooms marble with whirlpool tubs and telephones, and walls are decorated with original Key West scenes painted by equestrian Peter Williams. All rooms have garden views, and fountains throughout the grounds enhance the sense of tranquillity. Each room has a television, coffeemaker, minibar, and private porch. All except the historic rooms and the master suite have separate entrances and private porches.

Heron House **$$-$$$$**
512 Simonton Street
(305) 294-9227, (888) 861-9066
www.heronhouse.com

Centered on a 35-foot swimming pool, decorated with a mosaic of a heron, and a Chicago brick patio and sundeck, every one of the 23 rooms at the Heron House features unique woodwork and stained glass created by local artists.

Platform-style oak beds are handcrafted, and all accommodations have French doors leading to private porches or balconies overlooking the English-style country gardens. This historic facility was built prior to the turn of the last century. It offers basic, upper-standard, and deluxe rooms. All are spacious with incredibly high ceilings and double, queen-size, or king-size beds. Deluxe rooms and junior suites have wet bars, futon sitting areas, and mini-refrigerators.

Coffee is served in the breezeway. A private sundeck is clothing optional.

Heron House accepts children older than age 15.

Island City House Hotel **$$-$$$**
411 William Street
(305) 294-5702, (800) 634-8230
www.islandcityhouse.com

At Island City House, two 1880s homes and a cypress wood house designed to resemble a cigar factory encompass an Old-World-style enclave lined with brick walkways and lush tropical gardens. Wood decking surrounds the hot tub and swimming pool tucked neatly at one end of the compound; the swimming pool has a tiled alligator motif at the bottom.

Central to Island City House is its charming courtyard patio, where antique iron benches and bistro-style tables are set around a fountain and fishpond. This is the setting for the daily continental breakfast.

Island City House itself is a Conch-style mansion originally built for a wealthy merchant family. Here, guests choose from 12 one- and two-bedroom parlor suites with kitchens and antiques that provide a New England maritime feel. The Arch House, the only carriage house in Key West, maintains six studio and two-bedroom suites decorated with casual furnishings of rattan and wicker. At the Cigar House, built on a cistern and the former site of a cigar factory, spacious suites feature plantation-style decor that combines antique furnishings with wicker and rattan. The homes have hardwood floors throughout, and many rooms feature French doors leading to private patios and decks.

Children are permitted; those younger than age 12 stay free. Bicycle rentals are available on the premises, and a complimentary breakfast is served in the garden each morning.

Key West Bed & Breakfast,
The Popular House **$-$$$**
415 William Street
(305) 296-7274, (800) 438-6155
www.keywestbandb.com

When strong winds blow through the city of Key West, you can feel the three-story Key West Bed & Breakfast move with them, for this 1890 home was built by shipbuilders skilled in crafting structures able to weather any storm. Step inside from the front porch and you likely will be greeted by Dave, the inn's resident golden retriever.

With the exception of one suite, all of the inn's eight guest rooms feature a mix of bright colors, elegant Victorian furnishings, exposed Dade County pine, and 13-foot ceilings. Most have queen-size beds, and third-floor suites in the dormered attic offer a choice of two magnificent views. The back suite has French doors leading to a private deck and is decorated in more muted tones because it gathers color from the backyard's flowering trees, including a wild orchid tree that produces rich purple flowers. The suite at the front of the house is noted for its 5-foot arched Palladian window, which provides a view of the sunset above the city's rooftops and trees.

Continental breakfast, including freshly baked goods and freshly squeezed orange juice, is served outdoors, where tables and chairs line the backyard wood deck. All rooms are air-conditioned, and most have ceiling fans. The inn has no televisions or telephones except for a community telephone to which all guests are provided access.

Owner Jodi Carlson is an artist who weaves, and her bright yarns provide added color to the inn's community room where magazines, Florida Keys-related books, and an extensive CD collection and player are available to guests. Two of the inn's four porches are furnished with a swing and double hammock, and the oversized backyard hot tub is also used as a dip pool.

La Mer Hotel **$$-$$$$**
Dewey House **$$-$$$$**
504/506 South Street
(305) 296-6577, (800) 354-4455
www.oldtownresorts.com

La Mer and Dewey House are Key West's only oceanfront bed-and-breakfasts. They have the same owner, but they are marketed as individual luxury getaways with distinctly different names and ambience.

La Mer is actually a turn-of-the-20th-century Conch house with 11 rooms decorated with wicker furnishings and light, tropical prints. Most rooms, which feature king- or queen-size beds and private baths, also offer a private balcony or patio. One room has two twin beds; some rooms have sleeper sofas.

If this is not luxurious enough for your taste, the eight-room Dewey House offers decor in rich greens and golds with heavy draperies, fine antiques, whirlpool bathtubs, and French doors leading to private balconies and patios. Named for its original owner, philosopher and educator John Dewey, the house is joined to La Mer by a lush tropical garden.

Rooms at both facilities have high ceilings with ceiling fans, minibars, and Italian marble bathrooms with built-in hair dryers. Rooms have king- or queen-size beds, and some have fully equipped kitchenettes with microwaves.

In addition to a deluxe continental breakfast of freshly baked breads and coffee cakes, plus croissants, English muffins, and fresh fruits, the inn serves tea, crumpets, fresh fruits, and cheeses at 4:30 P.M. daily. *USA Today* is delivered to the door of each guest room. An 8-square-foot hot tub is set among beautifully landscaped gardens, and La Mer and Dewey House guests are allowed access to pool facilities at their owner's Southernmost and South Beach Oceanfront motels. Pets are not permitted.

Guests must be 18 years of age or older. Guests enjoy resort privileges at Southernmost Hotel.

The Lightbourn Inn **$$–$$$**
907 Truman Avenue
(305) 296-5152, (800) 352-6011
www.lightbourn.com

Owners-operators Kelly Summers and Scott Fuhriman have drawn upon sojourns in Europe and Asia in decorating rooms in their classic Conch-style mansion, which is listed on the National Register of Historic Places.

All 10 guest rooms within the Lightbourn Inn feature antiques, Key West wicker, and signed celebrity memorabilia. A complimentary breakfast, including hot entrees, is one of the inn's most popular features. Three levels of private decking overlook the pool area.

Because the owners reside on the property, holidays always include home-away-from-home celebrations.

Lighthouse Court **$$$**
900 Whitehead Street, Key West
(305) 294-9588, (877) 294-9588
www.lighthousecourt.com

Established as a guesthouse in 1984, the Lighthouse Court is a historic compound of 10 Conch houses dating from 1820 to 1920. Covering half a city block in Old Town, the location of this compound is ideal for sightseeing. It is directly next door to the Lighthouse Museum, across the street from the Ernest Hemingway house, and a block away from lively Duval Street. The half-acre grounds of the property offer many relaxing spaces to explore. Snuggle on a swing on one of the quaint porches, or follow the charming brick paths to find tree swings and hammocks. Chaise lounges and a sundeck beckon you out of the heat of the tropical sun. All of this, with the Key West Lighthouse as a backdrop. Here on the property you will find the Lighthouse Café. Open from 8:30 A.M. to 4:00 P.M., the Café offers a full breakfast and lunch fare, served poolside. There is a complimentary fitness center to help you work off your indulgence as well.

The accommodations of the Lighthouse Court are Key West charming. All are tailored to couples, with room offerings of full-, queen-, and king-size beds. The room decorations are embellished with tropical colors and open onto the courtyard. If you really want to embody the aura of old Key West, reserve the Hemingway Retreat. The penthouse at the Lighthouse Court is named after their famous neighbor and overlooks his Key West home. This suite has views of the lighthouse from the living room, sundeck, and bedroom. One thousand square feet of space houses a plasma TV, gourmet kitchen, dining area, and loft bedroom. All of the suites are nonsmoking. This is a beautiful sanctuary when only the best will do.

The Marquesa Hotel $$$–$$$$
600 Fleming Street
(305) 292-1919, (800) 869-4631
www.marquesa.com

This cluster of homes dates from the 1880s. Each standard room, deluxe room, junior suite, standard suite, and terrace suite is furnished with ceiling fans and an eclectic collection of antique English and West Indian reproductions that evoke the ambience of an exquisite English plantation.

Accommodations are spacious, with oversize marble baths. Many rooms feature French doors and private porches overlooking two pools and the garden. At the east end of the garden, brick steps accented by a fountain lead to a newer building of complementary architecture.

Breakfast (available for a nominal fee) includes a feast of baked goods fresh from the oven of the highly praised Cafe Marquesa (see the Restaurants chapter).

The Palms Hotel $$
820 White Street
(305) 294-3146, (800) 558-9374
www.palmshotelkeywest.com

Completely restored in 1995, the main Conch-style house with its wraparound porches was built in 1889. It features Caribbean influences and is listed on the National Register of Historic Places. In the 1970s the hotel added an L-shaped structure built in a complementary style, around a large heated swimming pool.

All 20 rooms are painted in pastels and furnished with wicker and Caribbean-style decor; rooms in the main house have separate access to the porch. Most have queen- or king-size beds or two double beds. Some floors are carpeted, some are tiled, and several rooms in the main house feature all-wood flooring. Private entrances, private baths, and ceiling fans are standard.

For a real Old-World-style getaway, ask for the minisuite with turret, where a king-size bed is surrounded by windows and walls of exposed Dade County pine, and the downstairs living area features hardwood floors. This suite can be connected to a guest room with queen-size bed to accommodate larger parties.

A deluxe continental breakfast is served each morning at the full-service poolside tiki bar, and the large heated swimming pool is open around the clock.

The Palms has a small parking lot on the street directly behind the hotel; on-street parking is also available. Children are permitted; pets are allowed with advance approval.

The Paradise Inn $$$$
819 Simonton Street
(305) 293-8007, (800) 888-9648
www.theparadiseinn.com

Style and distinction mark the 15 suites and 3 cottages of the Paradise Inn. Two of the three cottages are refurbished Conch houses; the rest are recently built two-story buildings of coordinating architecture.

Painted white with Caribbean-blue Bahamian shutters, all units have high ceilings, large marble baths, natural oak flooring, and unique window dressings that combine stagecoach and handkerchief valances with wood mini-blinds. French doors lead to outdoor porches in all but one cottage, and the interior decor features distressed pine, botanical prints, and pale shades of tan. Rooms have queen- and king-size wrought iron and California sleigh beds.

The inn's diverse gardens, designed by award-winning landscape architect Ray-

i ***Dade County pine is a dense, termite-resistant species of the slash pine family. The unusual amount of resin in the wood makes it very hard and heavy, unlike most pines. A drawback: It's extremely difficult to drive a nail through Dade County pine. You'll find Dade County pine in many Key West inns and gatehouses.***

mond Jungles of Coral Gables, feature Barbados cherry and avocado trees and bromeliads. Even the pool and hot tub, separated by a lily pond, evoke luxury.

Children are permitted. A complimentary breakfast is served in the lobby.

Pilot House Guesthouse $$-$$$
414 Simonton Street
(305) 293-6600, (800) 648-3780
www.pilothousekeywest.com

Restored in 1991, this 100-plus-year-old Conch-style home provides rooms and suites that mix antique furnishings with functional pieces and tropical rattan prints.

Once a three-bedroom home, the guesthouse's floor plan has been altered so the first-floor library and dining room now accommodate a guest room and two 2-bedroom suites. Suites on the second floor are furnished with its original family in mind.

Built by the late Julius Otto, son of a prominent Key West surgeon, the 3,000-square-foot mansion served as a winter retreat. Julius's brother Eugene inherited The Artist House (see listing in this chapter) around the corner, and the yards of the two Otto homes almost back each other. Here in the gracious Pilot House, curved archways lead from one room to another, and moldings are massive but not overpowering.

Frangipani and royal poinciana trees thrive in the yard, and a gumbo-limbo grows through the roof of what is known as this facility's spa building. Set along the brick-patio backyard is a Spanish-style stucco cabana building that offers six suites with queen- and king-size beds, full kitchens, and in-room hot tubs. Furnishings in the cabana are contemporary white wicker amid adobe-colored walls. Mirrors are abundant, and 6-square-foot open showers have sleek European-style showerheads jutting from the ceilings.

Passageways rather than doors create privacy for each area of these suites, and all entrances face the swimming pool.

Most rooms in the main house have balconies but are accessed through a formal entrance, and all rooms have kitchenettes, ceiling fans, and private baths. The inn does not provide breakfast, but restaurants are nearby.

The backyard swimming pool, at 15 feet by 30 feet, is larger than most in Key West, and an in-ground spa for 12 is sheltered from the sun by a tin roof with lattice and the aforementioned gumbo-limbo tree that grows through the roof. Clothing is optional at the spa. No off-street parking is provided.

The Red Rooster Inn $-$$
709 Truman Avenue
(305) 296-6558, (800) 845-0825
www.redroosterinn.com

Built in 1870 by the Delgato family, The Red Rooster is considered Truman Avenue's oldest house. At the time, the street was called Hard Rock Road. It later became Division Street, and during the 1950s Truman era it received the name Truman Avenue.

In the early 20th century, this private house was converted to apartments to house the U.S. Coast Guard; then it was converted to provide casual, low-end guest accommodations. Left to disrepair, the home was purchased by Jim Durbin and Gary Williams, owners of the exclusive Chelsea House next door (see listing in this chapter), and renamed The Red Rooster. Colorful stories about the home tell of a scandalous past, including illicit use by prostitutes and drug dealers. According to local legend, Mrs. Delgato murdered her husband and buried him beneath a concrete porch along the front of the building.

The 18 carpeted rooms, all with private, renovated bathrooms, exude an eclectic flavor, and all but one of the rooms are accessible via exterior doors. Most have queen-size beds, and some are incredibly spacious, with fireplaces and French doors leading to a front veranda. Others are small but cozy.

This reasonably priced, liberal adult guesthouse shares a yard and outdoor facilities with The Chelsea House, and clothing is optional in designated outdoor areas. A coffee bar at the entrance doubles as space for the desk clerk and evokes a European atmosphere. Continental breakfast is served here daily. Impromptu cocktail hours provide a partylike atmosphere.

Pets are welcome; children are not.

Simonton Court Historic Inn and Cottages **$-$$$**
320 Simonton Street
(305) 294-6386, (800) 944-2687
www.simontoncourt.com

Situated on two acres of property that once boasted a cigar factory, Simonton Court offers 10 varied structures among a number of buildings. The inn's four outdoor swimming pools once served as cisterns. Simonton Court's original building is a Victorianesque mansion with maritime influences, including a widow's walk. Built by a judge in the late 1880s and known as the Mansion, it now houses the most luxurious rooms and suites on the property.

Some of Simonton Court's guest rooms are furnished in period antiques and have green marble bathrooms and large terraces; others offer Caribbean-style decor. One has a spa tub and includes the widow's walk.

A two-story clapboard building with porches, once the actual cigar factory, is now known as the Inn. Within the Inn today are nine rustic old Key West-style rooms paneled with Dade County pine and featuring high ceilings and heavily shuttered windows. When closed, the shutters effectively bar the heat. Rooms here range from basic units with king-size beds to a triplex with kitchen, bedroom, and living-dining area. All rooms at the Inn have hardwood floors and private baths.

On the "rustic" side are Simonton Court's two-story cottages. Decorated with antique bamboo furnishings and brightly colored handmade fabrics, interiors are bright and airy. The first floor of each cottage has a kitchenette with microwave (no oven) and a queen- or king-size bed. Attic-style lofts with skylights are furnished with two double beds.

Still another building, known as the Manor House suite, offers a spacious two-bedroom complex with full kitchen and living room and a private outdoor pool. Simonton Court's two-story Townhouse Suites are extremely plush, decorated in Grand Floribbean-style antiques and white linens. The first floor has a living room, a bedroom with queen-size bed, a private patio, and a bath with shower. A similar floor plan upstairs is enhanced by vaulted ceilings, skylights, and a spa tub. Both floors have separate entrances via a private balcony or brick patio so that only half the townhouse can be rented if desired. Townhouse guests enjoy their own semiprivate swimming pool.

Simonton Court's tropically landscaped gardens, antique brick pathways, swimming pools, and hot tub all come aglow at night, when lighting emphasizes all the right places.

An expanded continental breakfast is served poolside daily at this adults-only facility. Inn and townhouse guests who visit during high season are greeted by a complimentary bottle of wine and treated to a nightly turndown.

Southernmost Point Guesthouse **$-$$$**
1327 Duval Street
(305) 294-0715
www.southernmostpoint.com

Throughout Key West, you will discover all

kinds of things dubbed "the southernmost"—a southernmost hockey rink and Southernmost Motel, for instance. The Southernmost Point Guesthouse, across from the Southernmost House, is a showy, three-story, Conch-style mansion built in 1885 for E. H. Gato Jr., son of Key West's first cigar manufacturer.

The home is notable for its wraparound porches and private balconies, some of which afford partial ocean or garden views. Rooms come in varying sizes, but all have private entrances, private baths, and ceiling fans. The Ernest Hemingway suite is a deluxe efficiency, with two double beds, designed with a jungle-like theme in honor of the legendary author's ardor for hunting, but most rooms are furnished either with queen-size or double beds and antiques with a tropical flair.

Some rooms have kitchenettes, and the largest of all is the two-bedroom master suite with queen-size bed in the master bedroom, with a pullout sleeper sofa and a private balcony that offers a partial view of the Southernmost Point (see the Attractions chapter). Suite No. 6 is a duplex composed of portions of the home's second and third floors, and suite No. 5 features a king-size bed and a private porch with a swing.

All guests are given a key to the hot tub (large enough for 12 people). Lounge chairs are provided amid the guesthouse's tropical gardens of banana, coconut palm, breadfruit, and mango trees.

Continental breakfast includes fresh-baked goods and cold cuts, cheeses, and boiled eggs. Children younger than age 12 and accompanied by an adult stay free, and guests with pets are charged an additional nominal fee per night. Rollaway beds are available, and cribs are complimentary. Other thoughtful amenities include wine, mints, and fresh flowers placed in each room prior to a guest's arrival.

Speakeasy Inn **$-$$$**
1117 Duval Street
(305) 296-2680, (800) 217-4884
www.speakeasyinn.com

Casa 325 **$$-$$$**
325 Duval Street
(305) 292-0011, (866) 227-2325
www.casa325.com

The Speakeasy, a turn-of-the-20th-century inn, offers spacious rooms in its main Duval Street house plus three spacious suites in a back-alley building along Amelia Street. The original building was the home of Raul Vasquez, a cigar selector at the Gato cigar factory whose true passion was rum-running between Key West and Cuba.

The newer building, built as a residence for the owner's stepdaughter, offers what is referred to as the Gallery Suite, considered to be the best offering in the house. The large, apartment-size unit has a queen-size bed and sleeper sofa and features beamed ceilings, hardwood floors, track lighting, and patio doors leading to a private deck and yard. This and other rooms at Speakeasy also are appointed with private tiled baths, refrigerators, wet bars, and ceiling fans.

First-floor rooms feature queen-size beds and private patios. Those on the second floor offer queen- or full-size beds but lack a wet bar. And room No. 2 in the main house features an elegant claw-foot bathtub.

Casa 325 offers one- and two-bedroom suites in a vintage Victorian building that has been recently restored and decorated in a tropical island theme. Suites feature queen-size beds, kitchenettes with refrigerators, microwave, wet bar, and ceiling fans. A center courtyard showcases gardens and a swimming pool.

Limited passes to the Reach Resort pool, spa, and fitness facilities are provided on a first-come, first-served basis. Children and small pets are allowed; large pets must be kept in kennel carriers.

Travelers Palm Tropical Suites $-$$$
915 Center Street
(305) 294-9560, (800) 294-9560
www.travelerspalm.com

Travelers Palm Tropical Suites encompasses two secluded little retreats on two Key West streets—Catherine and Newton. Both are operated under the auspices of their sister inn, Center Court Historic Inn & Cottages (see listing in this chapter). Each of the guesthouses is surrounded by a large tropical garden (the travelers palms at the Catherine Street guesthouse are the largest stand on the island).

Each of the suites at Travelers Palm Tropical Suites is unique. The decor is eclectic; rattan furnishings and tropical prints reflect a casual island lifestyle. Specific features vary from one property to another, but most include a heated pool, outdoor gas grill, blender, coffeemaker, toaster, microwave, stereo with CD player, hair dryer, iron and ironing board, and cable television. Suites at the Catherine Street guesthouse feature a full-size refrigerator and kitchenette, plus private courtyards with grills, hammocks, and picnic tables. Breakfast is included at the White and Newton Streets locations.

Children and pets are welcome. A small additional fee is charged for each pet. The check-in office is located at Center Court Inn, 915 Center Street. Smoking is not permitted inside any of the guesthouses.

The Watson House $-$$$$
525 Simonton Street
(305) 294-6712, (800) 621-9405
www.keywestvacations.com/watsonhs.html

Though modified, the original portions of this two-story, three-room Bahamian-influenced Conch house were built in the mid-1800s. A detached kitchen with connecting breezeway has been enclosed and extensions added to the home.

Named for the home's original owners, William and Susan Watson, this guesthouse features three suites, each decorated in a distinctive style. Tastefully appointed with lots of lace and white Ralph Lauren wicker furnishings, the Susan Suite evokes a feminine, turn-of-the-20th-century feeling. The William Suite has a four-poster, queen-size bed and items reminiscent of a ship captain's bunk. The William and Susan Suites feature wainscoting and period hand-silkscreened wallpapers and, when combined to form the Watson Suite, become a two-bedroom/two-bath unit. A third suite, referred to as the Cabana Suite, is really a fully equipped home that features a light and airy tropical decor and a triple set of French doors leading to the pool.

All suites have ceiling fans and telephones with private numbers. A heated, two-tiered backyard pool creates a centerpiece waterfall effect for lush tropical gardens and a hot tub. Continental breakfast is catered to each room, and limited off-street parking is available.

Weatherstation Inn $$-$$$$
57 Front Street
(305) 294-7277, (800) 815-2707
www.weatherstationinn.com

Nestled deep within one of Key West's premier residential communities, Weatherstation Inn could easily be considered one of this town's best-kept secrets in luxury guesthouse accommodations. Guests here are just two blocks off bustling Duval Street, but they'd never know it. Rarely does any sound intrude.

Opened in 1997, this two-story, eight-room guesthouse sits on the grounds of the Old Navy Yard inside the gated Truman Annex compound and just down the street from Harry Truman's Little White House. The beach at Fort Zachary Taylor is a short walk away (see the Attractions chapter). Motorized access is limited to the residents of the Annex, and so within these gates, life is always quiet and serene.

With its glistening hardwood floors

Most of Key West's hotel chains and budget motels are along North Roosevelt Boulevard, either on the Gulf of Mexico or on dry lots across the road. Getting from this part of town to Old Town, Duval Street, and public beaches requires a moped, scooter, bicycle, or car.

and elegant island furnishings, the inn calls to mind the plantation homes of days gone by in the British and Dutch West Indies. The balconies and decks overlook lush tropical landscaping, and from the second-floor rooms guests can catch an occasional glimpse of the cruise ships arriving in the harbor just beyond. Amenities here include a heated pool, concierge service, and complimentary continental breakfast.

Westwinds Guesthouse **$-$$**
914 Eaton Street
(305) 296-4440, (800) 788-4150
www.westwindskeywest.com

This complex encompasses a 22-room, two-story New England-style home, two-story Conch houses, and poolside cottages. The majority of guests are couples. Room decor is wicker throughout, with queen-size beds in suites, private entrances to the cottages and Conch houses, and some furnished private and shared porches.

Painted in various shades of pastels, all rooms provide a feel of tropical ambience, with ceiling fans and carpeted floors. Some rooms in the main house share a bath. Suites include one-bedroom cottage and Conch units with kitchenettes and kitchenless accommodations that sleep several guests.

In back of the compound, brick walkways wind through gardens of hibiscus, bromeliads, and other flowers and shrubs, and the kidney-shape swimming pool with waterfall is sizable. Continental breakfast is served poolside.

Children younger than age 12 are not permitted.

Gay Guesthouses

Alexander's Guesthouse **$$-$$$**
1118 Fleming Street
(305) 294-9919, (800) 654-9919
www.alexghouse.com

The main three-story building of Alexander's, a Conch-style design, was built around the turn of the past century and has since been renovated. Two additional two-story Conch houses combine for a total of 17 guest rooms. This guesthouse, which attracts both gay men and women, is gay owned and operated.

The rooms at Alexander's are relatively basic, equipped with queen-size beds. All rooms have private baths, and two share shower facilities. Deluxe rooms, some with private porches and patios, have king-size beds. For larger accommodations, opt for a more luxurious suite with king-size bed and queen-size sleeper sofa. Some rooms feature hardwood floors, while others are completely carpeted. Throughout the inn, eclectic local art mixes with poster prints. Many units offer VCRs.

A highlight is the cobalt-blue, tiled swimming pool surrounded by lush tropical flora. Second- and third-level tanning decks are clothing optional. An expanded continental breakfast is served by the pool each morning; wine and cheese are offered every evening.

Atlantic Shores Resort **$-$$**
510 South Street
(305) 296-2492, (800) 547-3892
www.atlanticshoresresort.com

Atlantic Shores bills itself as an adult alternative resort. It's not exclusively gay, but then it's not what you would call straight either. Atlantic Shores is somewhere in between. If you choose to stay here, you will almost assuredly find it quite an experience . . . no matter which way your sexual preferences lean.

Situated at the end of Simonton Street, on the oceanside of Key West, the Shores boasts 72 rooms. The decor is not particularly remarkable, but the accommodations are always clean and quite affordable; they also fill up fast. If you have your heart set on staying here at a particular time, it would be best to book early. This is one popular place.

If not the accommodations, then what draws people to Atlantic Shores? The clothing-optional pool, for starters. This is where locals and visitors alike flock on sunny afternoons to work on "real tans"—the kind that aren't defined by lines. They come to see and be seen, to meet and mingle—sans suits—while they sip frozen drinks and munch on standard fare like burgers, grilled chicken, and fries from the Pool Bar and Grill.

Regular events such as the Sunday-night tea dances and Cinema Shores (Thursday-night movies by the sea) really bring in the locals. So does Diner Shores, a full-service restaurant offering breakfast, lunch, and late-night munchies.

Big Ruby's Guesthouse $$–$$$
409 Applerouth Lane
(305) 296–2323, (800) 477–7829
www.bigrubys.com

Formerly the home of a sea captain, the main guesthouse at Big Ruby's, like its two additional on-premises structures, is New England–style clapboard architecture on the outside with contemporary styling on the inside.

Seventeen rooms of varying sizes and decor feature clean lines, hardwood floors, and Simmons Beautyrest mattresses in a variety of sizes. Refrigerators, ceiling fans, robes, and beach towels are standard in all rooms.

All three buildings of this exclusively gay male and female property share a clothing-optional sunning yard and swimming pool. An outdoor rain-forest shower amid the vines allows for rinsing before and after swimming.

Continental and full cooked-to-order breakfasts are served poolside, as are wine and juice in the early evening. Big Ruby's is set back about 20 feet from the narrow, one-way lane through which it is accessed, and all three buildings are surrounded by orchids and bougainvillea. Balconies on the third floor are set amid the trees, and the grounds are so lush that the second-floor porch does not even allow a view of the street.

Limited off-street parking is provided on a first-come, first-served basis.

Equator Resort $$–$$$
818 Fleming Street
(305) 294–7775, (800) 278–4552
www.equatorresort.com

Opened in 1998, Equator Resort is one of the more recent additions to Key West's gay guesthouse scene. The building that houses this state-of-the-art, all-male resort looks as though it might have been around for a while, but it is new. It was simply designed to blend with the surrounding structures in this Old Town neighborhood. When it came to guest rooms, the architects opted for upscale with no attempts at conserving space. All 18 rooms are bright and spacious, each featuring Mediterranean tile floors, incredibly comfortable beds, in-room refrigerators, genuinely ample closets, and plenty of walking-around space. Some have special luxuries like wet bars and two-man whirlpool bathtubs.

Common areas are equally well appointed, with a clothing-optional pool, eight-man outdoor whirlpool, lush tropical gardens, a sundeck, and covered patio.

A complimentary full breakfast is served daily; complimentary cocktails and snacks are offered every evening except Sunday. All guest rooms are nonsmoking; however, most of them open directly to private decks or balconies where smoking is permitted.

Oasis Guesthouse and Coral Tree Inn $$-$$$
822 and 823 Fleming Street
(305) 296-2131, (800) 362-7477
www.coraltreeinn.com

With its Main, Lopez, and Margaret Houses, the Oasis offers 20 guest rooms on three fronts that share a yard: The Main House faces Fleming Street; Lopez House faces Lopez Lane; and Margaret House looks toward Margaret Street. Guests at the facility, which caters to gay men, check in at Main on Fleming.

Oasis offers a range of accommodations, including standard rooms with one queen-size bed or two double beds, poolside rooms with queen-size beds and living rooms, and a penthouse on the second, and top, floor of Margaret House. All rooms feature updated furnishings and custom drapes and matching bedspreads in tropical or paisley prints. Some rooms have baths with whirlpool tubs; still others share a bath. The pool and the sundeck surrounding it are clothing optional.

Also owned by Oasis proprietors is Coral Tree Inn across the street. This handsome 11-room facility is designed to reflect an upscale European retreat. Catering to gay men, Coral Tree Inn is a tranquil setting in Old Town. Rooms here feature a queen-size bed or two double beds. They have porches and balconies facing either the pool or Fleming. Penthouse suites are on the third floor.

The clothing-optional Coral Tree Inn has a 24-man hot tub and sunning area, and guests here and at Oasis share facilities.

Both establishments are known for hospitality. A bottle of wine welcomes guests upon arrival; continental breakfast is served each morning. Tropical cocktails are offered by the pool each afternoon, and wine and hot hors d'oeuvres are served in the evening.

Pearl's Rainbow $-$$$
525 United Street
(305) 292-1450, (800) 749-6696
www.pearlsrainbow.com

Lesbian owned and operated, Pearl's Rainbow is one of only a handful of exclusively female resorts in Key West. Men, children, and pets are not permitted here.

Expanded in 1998 to incorporate the property next door, which had been The Pines, a gay male guesthouse, Pearl's Rainbow now includes two clothing-optional swimming pools, two hot tubs, and 38 guest rooms.

All standard guest rooms at Rainbow House feature queen-size beds, private baths, color TV, air-conditioning, and ceiling fans. The priciest accommodation is a deluxe poolside suite consisting of a king bedroom, private bath, and separate living room with big-screen TV.

Pearl's Rainbow is located half a block off Duval on the oceanside of the island. Shops, bars, and restaurants are within a reasonable walking distance.

Hostels

Hostelling International Key West Youth Hostel $
718 South Street
(305) 296-5719
www.keywesthostel.com

If you want to save money on accommodations in Key West, one very inexpensive option is Hostelling International Key West. The facility has 10 air-conditioned, dormitory-style rooms with bunk beds and separate baths. The hostel accommodates as many as 96 guests for as little as $19.50 per night (nonmembers pay $3.00 more) and is near Old Town and beaches along the Atlantic.

Each of the 10 motel rooms at the Sea Shell Motel—the hostel's affiliate in the same building—has two double beds, a private bath, and a mini-refrigerator. Each room sleeps four, and rates are very reasonable, especially in the off season. A common kitchen is open to all hostel and motel guests for food preparation between the hours of 8:00 A.M. and 9:00 P.M., and a common dining area is in the courtyard. Laundry facilities and lockers are available within this wood structure.

Popular with Europeans, students, and adventurous adults, the Hostelling International Key West, like other hostels worldwide, provides travelers with low-cost, friendly accommodations and an ideal means of meeting a diverse group of individuals. Bicycle rentals and snorkeling, scuba, and sunset excursions (see our Recreation and Diving and Snorkeling chapters) all are offered at rates that are discounted as much as 20 percent.

The hostel is open 24 hours a day. Reservations should be made at least one week in advance. No dorm reservations are accepted in March.

VACATION RENTALS AND REAL ESTATE

Most snowbirds and full-time residents of the Florida Keys (except for the native-born Conchs) first rented homes, condominiums, or mobile homes while on vacation in Paradise. Seduced by our ocean breezes, beguiling sunshine, percolating waters, and sensational sunsets, we all decided to buy a piece of the Rock. Throughout the Florida Keys, rentals primarily are classified as short-term and long-term. Short-term rental agreements range from a weekend to six months; anything exceeding six months is considered a long-term rental. However, to preserve the integrity of our residential communities, the Monroe County Planning Commission has prohibited short-term rentals of 30 days or less throughout residential areas of unincorporated Monroe County. Incorporated areas such as Islamorada, Layton, Key Colony Beach, Marathon, and Key West can opt for differing regulations. The bottom line for vacationers is this: Fewer short-term rental options are currently available in the Florida Keys, and the competition is fierce for those that are. The best advice we can offer in this ever-changing environment is to work through a rental agent who knows what's legally available and always book your accommodation early.

Unlike long-term tenants, short-term tenants are required by the state of Florida to pay an 11.5 percent sales tax. Generally not incorporated into the price quoted for short-term rentals, this tax includes the same tourist bed tax charged by hotels, motels, inns, and resorts for maintaining, advertising, and promoting our facilities and attractions. Quotes for short-term rentals do, however, typically include furnishings and utilities, with the exception of long-distance phone calls.

The Role of Real Estate Agents

Real estate agents handle most short-term rental properties. The exceptions are condominiums that act as hotels and employ on-site managers (see the Accommodations chapter) and homeowners who market rentals on their own. Because of changes in laws as indicated above, the latter choice is becoming more and more scarce.

Depending upon its size and specialty, an agency that handles rentals may list anywhere between 10 and 200-plus short-term rental options. Most large agencies employ sales associates who specialize in short-term rentals. Except for Key West, where agents handle much of the entire island, Florida Keys agents typically specialize within the region of their office (see the Real Estate Companies section in this chapter).

Finding a rental property through an agency has its advantages. Rental agencies almost always offer descriptions and photographs of available properties and advice on the best option for your needs and desires. Most of them, in fact, maintain Web sites, which allow you to peruse the options at your leisure and, in most cases, actually see the property you are booking. Agents ensure that a home is clean and that its grounds are maintained.

In order to manage short-term rentals for stays of fewer than 30 days, real estate agencies and/or property owners and managers of condominium complexes must be licensed by the state of Florida. Units rented for fewer than 30 days are considered resort dwellings, and agents and/or owners and managers must therefore abide by a Florida statute that applies to hotels and restaurants. Depending upon the category of accommodation (condominium or single-family home, for instance), safety and health standards set by this statute may require fire extinguishers, electric smoke detectors in sleeping areas, mattress covers on all beds, and deadbolt locks on doors.

Seasonal Rates

As Old Man Winter rolls around, travelers flock to the Florida Keys seeking respite from cold and snow. Referred to locally as "snowbirds," these visitors drive rental rates up between the months of December and April, the high season.

Summertime is when diving is typically best (see the Diving and Snorkeling chapter). It's also the time of year when residents throughout Florida head to the Keys for the relief of the ocean breezes. However, the rest of the mass market moves back home, so rents may be a bit lower than high season during the months of May through August.

September through November is relatively quiet, tourism-wise, because autumn is the prime season for hurricanes in the Florida Keys. During this period you'll find reduced rates, and, as long as you keep a watchful eye on the forecasts, you'll be able to enjoy uncrowded shops, attractions, and streets.

Minimum Stays

Most short-term tenants rent a home or condominium in the Florida Keys for a week to three or four months. The bulk of the short-term rental market consists of two-week vacationers, but our islands are also popular with northern residents and retirees who retreat here for the winter. Virtually no private homes are available for rent on a daily basis (see the Accommodations chapter).

During holidays, such as Christmas and Easter, and special events, including sport lobster season and Fantasy Fest, minimum stays range from four days to two weeks. Individual property owners establish these policies. Inquire of your rental agent or property owner/manager.

Options and Restrictions

Owners designate their rental properties as smoking or nonsmoking. The number of nonsmoking properties is growing.

Children are generally welcome, but some condominium complexes restrict the number of children allowed in a single unit. One adults-only facility, Silver Shores, a mobile-home park in Key Largo catering to senior citizens, exists in the Florida Keys.

Condominiums typically do not allow pets, but some single-family homes and mobile-home parks do accept them. An additional security deposit or a fee (sometimes both) is often required. The fee covers the cost of spraying the home for fleas, which ensures accommodations free of pesky insects. Tending to pets outside the rental facility, however, is the owner's responsibility, and fleas can be abundant on hot and humid days.

Reservations and Payment Options

Naturally, the most desirable rental properties tend to book the earliest, and many tenants book the same home for the same weeks year after year. To achieve the greatest selection of rentals, we suggest that you reserve at least six months to a year in advance. During holidays, the demand for short-term rentals can exhaust the supply. If you plan to travel to the Florida Keys during the high season (December through April) and holidays (especially Christmas week or

Want to vacation in a private historic home, grand estate, or condo? Go to www.HistoricHideaways.com and see what is available in Key West. Many properties, complete with photos, are on their Web site to entice you. Renting one of these tropical havens is one way of feeling the true ambience of this unique city.

during Fantasy Fest), you would be wise to reserve one to two years in advance.

Payment options vary according to how far in advance you book and when you check in. Typically, an initial deposit of 10 to 25 percent of the total rental cost, made with a personal check or a credit card, will hold a unit. If you book a rental unit one year in advance, you frequently can opt for an installment plan. The balance typically is paid 30 to 60 days prior to your arrival. Some agents allow you to pay with cash or credit card upon arrival, provided that you check in during office hours, which vary from agency to agency. Ask about these specifics when you call.

When you book a unit, your real estate agent will mail you a lease application and reservation agreement that must be completed and returned with a rental deposit. Reservation agreements will list the address and telephone number of the property so you can notify family and friends accordingly.

Security Deposits

Your rental agreement holds you responsible for any damage to the dwelling and its contents. Security deposits provide the homeowner with added protection and a means of paying any telephone charges not billed to your credit card. As a general rule, count on supplying 50 to 75 percent of one week's rent (slightly more for a monthly rental). Security deposits on large homes with expensive furnishings can be much higher.

If you have opted for an installment plan, you will pay the security deposit with your final payment when you check in. The deposit often is returned in the mail two weeks to one month after your departure, or after the homeowner's telephone bill is received and a damage assessment completed.

Cancellation Policies

Homeowners set monetary penalties for cancellations anywhere between 30 days in advance of reservations, with a nominal cancellation fee for administrative services, to 60 days in advance, with a full refund. Don't assume that an impending hurricane or other emergency beyond your control will warrant a refund of your payment. In such cases, some homeowners may be generous in providing full or partial refunds or offering credit toward accommodations at a future date—but don't bank on it. Generally, you forfeit your deposit when weather emergencies cancel your vacation plans.

Refund policies are negotiated among the tenant, real estate agency, and property owner and usually are not included in lease agreements. Many real estate agencies sell trip insurance, whereby a third party will refund the full cost of a vacation rental for which you have paid a portion but not used. These policies typically cost 5 percent of the total dollars at risk.

THE FLORIDA KEYS

Owning a parcel of Paradise in the Florida Keys can be summed up in two words: very expensive. Real estate prices in the Florida Keys depend largely upon access to the water. Direct oceanfront or bayfront property garners the highest prices, followed by property on a canal with an ocean or bay view, and by property on a

canal with access to the ocean or bay. Other areas, such as Ocean Reef, Duck Key, and Sunset Key, have special features that make homes desirable—such as gated security, golf courses, swimming pools, strict building covenants, and other community amenities—and owning a home there is pricey, indeed.

Some relief in the cost of owning a Keys home is available for certain owners in the form of a homestead exemption. In Florida this exemption allows $25,000 of the assessed value of a house purchased as a primary residence to be exempt from property tax. Real estate taxes in Monroe County are based on a millage rate that changes annually with the county budget and are some of the highest in the state. In addition, besides homeowner's insurance, homeowners must factor in the cost of windstorm and flood insurance to guard against our ever-threatening hurricanes.

Those of us who have chosen to live in the Florida Keys think the price of Paradise is worth it. To assist you in your search for a piece of the Rock, we provide you with a general overview of the communities of the Florida Keys, as well as the types of homes you'll encounter in our neighborhoods. At the end of the chapter, we include listings of real estate professionals who can assist you in finding a rental property or a home of your own. Look to our Key West section of this chapter for vacation rental and real estate information in our southernmost city.

Community Overviews

UPPER KEYS

Key Largo

Key Largo is popular with divers interested in the abundant reefs within John Pennekamp Coral Reef State Park and the Florida Keys National Marine Sanctuary. And because Key Largo is within 20 miles of the mainland, property here often is in great demand by weekday commuters and South Floridians purchasing weekend retreats. In real estate terms, Key Largo generally includes the exclusive, members-only Ocean Reef subdivision at the extreme northeast edge and encompasses all land southwest to Tavernier.

Ocean Reef

A luxury subdivision in North Key Largo, Ocean Reef is a private, all-inclusive gated community of large single-family homes, condominiums, and town houses. Properties here attract buyers seeking privacy, exclusivity, and the opportunity to fish, dive, snorkel, swim, shop, and dine out without ever leaving the complex. This community has three golf courses, a marina, and other amenities open only to residents.

Tavernier

Toward the southern end of Key Largo is Tavernier, one of the Florida Keys' oldest settlements. Some Tavernier homes date from the early farming settlements at the turn of the past century. Plantation Key (its northern end also maintains a Tavernier postal designation) has a wide range of real estate opportunities, with single-family subdivisions primarily bayside. The Snake Creek Drawbridge makes Plantation Key an ideal homesite for owners of large yachts and sailboats.

Islamorada

Islamorada, which was incorporated in 1998, stretches from Plantation Key to Lower Matecumbe. Lot sizes in Islamorada typically are larger than those in other areas of the Florida Keys, a factor intended to attract builders of large, impressive homes. Upper Matecumbe Key is the heart of Islamorada, commercially developed but with homes tucked along the waterfront in quiet residential areas. Lower Matecumbe Key is Islamorada's predominantly residential island, with a bike path, tennis club, and private beach.

Layton

The late Del Layton, a Miami grocery store owner, developed tiny Layton into a subdivision in the 1950s. Later he incorporated it as the Florida Keys' smallest city. Except for several oceanfront homes, all single-family residences in Layton are on oceanside canals, with the nearby Channel 5 Bridge allowing access to the bay. Fifteen miles from Marathon and Islamorada, Layton is largely a community of retirees, with a population of approximately 250.

MIDDLE KEYS

Duck Key

Duck Key is composed of five islands connected by white Venetian-style bridges. A series of flow-through canals encircle each island, ensuring that nearly half the homes or lots offer canalfront dockage or open-water views. The uniquely situated islands allow direct access to both the ocean and the Gulf of Mexico. The Duck Key Property Owners Association, an active group, maintains rights-of-way and public area plantings, has established distinctive signage, and sponsors social events throughout the year. Duck Key Club, a private swim and tennis club, is located on Center Island and also sponsors myriad social activities for its members. Residents pay a small out-of-pocket tax to employ a private security firm to supplement county services. Hawk's Cay Resort is on the first island, Indies Island, which is zoned differently from the rest. The other four islands—Center, Plantation, Harbour, and Yacht Club—are designated for single-family residential housing only. All homes must be of concrete-block-style (CBS) construction.

Grassy Key

Grassy Key, a sleepy, rural island with a few oceanfront bungalow courts and several restaurants, is distanced from Marathon by preservation lands. With no canals on Grassy Key, there is no pricing middle ground. The area has single-family homes on dry lots or waterfront estates along the Gulf of Mexico and the Atlantic. Grassy Key is now a part of incorporated Marathon.

Key Colony Beach

Incorporated in 1957, Key Colony Beach—a 285-acre peninsular finger surrounded by incorporated Marathon—developed its property with a row of condominiums directly on the Atlantic and single-family homes built on a series of canals. Key Colony Beach employs its own police and enforces its own signage and zoning ordinances. Accessed by a causeway from U.S. Highway 1, Key Colony Beach has a post office and a few small shops and restaurants.

Marathon

Marathon was heavily developed in the 1950s, when dredging was relatively commonplace. This area probably has more canals and waterways—and thus more canalfront properties—than any other region of Monroe County; however, with no active zoning ordinances for all these years, in some neighborhoods it is not uncommon to find a run-down mobile home situated next to an upscale canalfront dwelling. Marathon was incorporated in 1999 and now has its own mayor and city commission, as well as the ability to levy citywide property taxes. Marathon is the commercial hub of the Florida Keys, featuring supermarkets, a movie theater, Home Depot, Office Depot, Kmart, and other shops and restaurants.

LOWER KEYS

Big Pine Key

This rural, semi-isolated island has acres of open space and limited development potential. Home to the National Key Deer Refuge, this island is popular with many Key West and Marathon workday commuters. This area probably offers the best value for the money in affordable housing.

Little Torch and Ramrod Keys

Little Torch Key and Ramrod Key have a rural feeling, with homes on both the Atlantic and the Gulf of Mexico as well as on dry lots. These communities aren't far from Key West.

Summerland, Cudjoe, and Sugarloaf Keys

Heading closer to Key West and into the more exclusive subdivisions of Summerland, Cudjoe, and Sugarloaf Keys, you'll find luxurious properties. Summerland features a number of waterfront homes, along with a small airstrip that allows residents to park their private airplanes directly beneath their homes.

Baypoint, Shark Key, Big Coppitt, and Key Haven

Shark Key is a gated community developed with strict architectural guidelines. Large open-water lots on Shark Key are beautifully landscaped, and houses set on them typically are very expensive. Baypoint, Big Coppitt, and Key Haven are in demand for their convenient location, only minutes from Key West.

Kinds of Properties

CONDOMINIUMS

Condominiums are scattered throughout the Upper and Middle Keys, and many home buyers find them to be a low-maintenance way to keep up a part-time residence. For full-time residents, condos commonly offer amenities not always available in a single-family home, such as swimming pools, fitness facilities, saunas, hot tubs, boat dockage, and covered parking.

During our peak tourist season (generally December through April), condominiums often are teeming with activity, affording residents the opportunity to meet renters from across the country. When the low season rolls around and occupancy typically drops to 30 percent or less at any given time, full-time residents have the facilities nearly all to themselves. If you plan to become a full-time Florida Keys resident in a condominium, be sure to check on whether the complex you have your eye on maintains an active rental program. You may not enjoy living alongside transient residents.

If you rent a condominium unit anywhere in the Florida Keys, remember the water-to-wallet ratio: The closer the accommodation is to the water, the higher the rental price is likely to be.

What you'll pay for a condo depends on the size of the unit, its location, and its view. You also need to factor monthly maintenance fees into the overall cost; these increase with unit sizes and cover maintenance of the common area, a reserve account for future major repairs, and insurance for damage by flood, wind, storm, peril, and salt air. (See the Close-Up in this chapter.)

MOBILE HOMES

First the good news: A mobile home is the least expensive real estate you can buy in the Florida Keys. The bad news? Most vulnerable to hurricane damage, mobile homes are the first properties ordered for evacuation during severe-storm watches in the Florida Keys. Zoning ordinances restrict mobile homes to specific communities.

Often the least expensive mobile homes are those that have existed in residential subdivisions since before zoning ordinances were established. These mobile homes, which have individual septic tanks, lack the recreational and service-oriented amenities typically offered in mobile-home communities here.

Buyers who purchase property in a mobile-home community pay more but frequently enjoy a clubhouse atmosphere complete with a swimming pool, shuffleboard court, boat ramp, dockage, on-site manager, sewage treatment, and a convenience store. The price of any mobile home increases with a concrete or wood-frame addition—an elevated Florida room, built-up gravel roof, poured concrete slab, and other features.

SINGLE-FAMILY HOMES

Dry-lot homes—those not fronting a water view or canal—are the least expensive single-family home option in the Keys. Canalfront homes generally sell for much more, with homes on the open water usually in the millions. Because many real estate purchases here are made by boaters, homes that sit closer to a bridge—providing access to both the ocean and the bay—sell more quickly.

Since 1975, the county has required that most homes be constructed of concrete block, be positioned on stilts, and have hurricane shutters. Nonconforming structures built before the 1975 ordinance took effect have been grandfathered, but, if 50 percent or more of the dollar value of a nonconforming use structure is destroyed and requires rebuilding, new zoning laws and building restrictions apply.

Much of a buyer's decision to purchase a home in the Florida Keys depends upon the structure's ability to withstand a hurricane. Concrete-block-style (CBS) homes are considered more solid than those made of wood. Most are elevated on stilts to avoid potential flooding. CBS stilt homes typically cost more than ground-level CBS homes of comparable sizes. CBS homes typically command higher prices than all-wood frame structures.

A large percentage of Lower Keys homes are factory-built, wood-frame modulars. Because they are constructed under controlled circumstances and designed to withstand 135 mph winds, some homeowners believe they're stronger than wood-frame homes built on the site.

If you are considering buying a home in the Florida Keys, landscaping also may influence your decision. Some buyers prefer intricate vegetation, which requires costly irrigation, while others want low-maintenance pearock and xeriscaping (landscaping using indigenous plantings that require no irrigation).

Real Estate Companies

Though all Florida Keys agents share a multiple listing service (MLS) with properties available throughout Monroe County, each agency tends to specialize in its own territory. We describe some of the largest agencies for sales and rentals in the sections that follow. This is not meant to be a comprehensive listing by any means. For a complete list, consult the Yellow Pages for the appropriate communities, or pick up copies of the many real estate guides available free of charge at supermarkets and other locations throughout Monroe County. See our Key West section for real estate companies in that city.

UPPER KEYS

Century 21 Prestige Group
MM 101.9 Oceanside
Tradewinds Shopping Plaza, Key Largo
(305) 451-4321, (800) 210-6246

MM 91.8 Bayside, Tavernier
(305) 852-5595, (800) 850-7740

MM 86 Bayside, Islamorada
(305) 664-4637, (800) 541-5019
www.c21keysearch.com

With three offices in the Upper Keys, on-site rental offices in Landings of Largo and Buttonwood Bay condominium complexes in Key Largo, and offices all the way to Key West, Century 21 Prestige Group has the vacation home rental market covered.

Coldwell Banker Schmitt Real Estate Co.
MM 100 Bayside, Key Largo
(305) 451-4422, (877) 289-0035

MM 85.9 Oceanside, Islamorada
(305) 664-4470, (800) 207-4160
www.realestatefloridakeys.com

Coldwell Banker Schmitt covers the Florida Keys' real estate sales and rental market from one end of US 1 to the other. In addition to these two offices, which serve the Upper Keys, the firm also maintains offices in Marathon, Big Pine Key, and Key West (see separate listings below).

MARR Properties
MM 100 Bayside, Key Largo
(305) 451-2100, (800) 277-3728
www.marrproperties.com
Serving the Keys since 1965, this office offers sales of commercial and residential properties and a knowledge of the upper Keys real estate market.

Prudential Keyside Properties
MM 91.5 Oceanside, Tavernier
(305) 853-1100, (800) 663-9955

31 Ocean Reef Drive North, Key Largo
(305) 367-2336, (800) 692-7653
www.floridakeys-realestate.com
Prudential Keyside Properties covers the Florida Keys from the top of Key Largo (Ocean Reef) to Key West. Located in the private Ocean Reef Community, the North Key Largo office focuses exclusively on the gated community of Ocean Reef. The Tavernier office covers both residential and commercial properties from Key Largo to Marathon. Both the Old Town and New Town offices of Prudential Knight Keyside Properties in Key West cover real estate from Key West to Marathon (see the Key West section of this chapter for a separate listing).

Exit Realty Florida Keys
MM 91 Oceanside, Tavernier
(305) 852-4442, (888) 881-3948

MM 50 Bayside, Marathon
(305) 743-9292, (888) 825-9292

MM 31 Bayside, Big Pine Key
(305) 872-1133, (888) 825-9292
www.exitfloridakeys.com
Residential and commercial sales are the thrust of this company. They also offer annual and vacation rentals as well as property management services.

Freewheeler Realty
MM 85.9 Bayside, Islamorada
(305) 664-4444, (305) 664-2075 (rentals)
www.freewheeler-realty.com
Freewheeler deals in property management and sales and is a primary rental agent for the Palms of Islamorada and Summer Sea condominiums.

At www.fkren.com you can find your piece of paradise! With this Florida Keys real estate network, you can find properties for sale and rent, or receive help in finding a Realtor in the Realtor directory.

American Caribbean Real Estate Inc.
MM 81.8 Bayside, Islamorada
(305) 664-4966 (sales), (305) 664-5152 (rentals)
www.americancaribbean.com
American Caribbean handles real estate from Islamorada to Key Largo.

MIDDLE KEYS

Duck Key Realty
MM 61 Oceanside, 796 Duck Key Drive, Duck Key
(305) 743-5000
www.duckkey.com
Duck Key Realty handles sales and rentals in Duck Key and Marathon.

The Waterfront Specialist
MM 54 Oceanside, 80th Street Station, Marathon
(305) 743-0644, (800) 342-6398
www.waterfrontspecialists.com
Despite its name, this agency can direct you to sales and rental opportunities both on and off the water.

Keys Island Realty
MM 53.5 Oceanside, 309 Key Colony Beach Causeway, Key Colony Beach
(305) 289-9696 (rentals),
(800) 874-3798; (800) 253-8677 (sales)
www.flkeys.com
Check here for Marathon-area sales and rentals, especially in Key Colony Beach.

Century 21 Prestige Group
MM 53 Bayside, Marathon
(305) 743-3377, (800) 451-4899
www.c21keysearch.com

Century 21 Prestige serves the Middle Keys from Islamorada to Big Pine. Although the primary focus is on residential sales, vacation and long-term rentals are available here, too.

Coldwell Banker Schmitt Real Estate
MM 52.5 Bayside, Marathon
(305) 743-5181, (800) 366-5181
www.realestatefloridakeys.com
Sales and vacation rentals in the Middle Keys are the focus at this office of a firm that covers the real estate market from one end of the Keys to the other (see other listings in this section).

American Caribbean Real Estate Inc.
MM 52 Oceanside, Marathon
(305) 743-7636, (800) 940-7636
American Caribbean specializes in Middle Keys sales and rental properties from Islamorada to Marathon.

All-Pro Real Estate
MM 50 Bayside, Marathon
(305) 743-8333, (800) 766-3235
www.allpro-realestate.com
Established in 1990, All-Pro has a good handle on the Marathon sales and vacation rental market.

RE/MAX Key to the Keys
MM 49.5 Bayside, Marathon
(305) 743-2300, (800) 743-2301
www.wilkinsonteam.com
Agents handle sales and rental properties from Long Key to Big Coppitt.

LOWER KEYS

Century 21 Prestige Group
MM 30.5 Bayside, Big Pine Key
(305) 872-2296, (800) 637-7621

MM 24 Bayside, Summerland Key
(305) 744-3337, (800) 741-6263

MM 17 Bayside, Sugarloaf Key
(305) 745-1856, (800) 745-8610
www.c21keysearch.com
With three offices in the Lower Keys, Century 21 Prestige Group helps find the right property to rent or buy between Big Pine and Sugarloaf.

Coldwell Banker Schmitt Real Estate
MM 30.5 Oceanside, Big Pine Key
(305) 872-3050, (800) 488-3050
www.realestatefloridakeys.com
Sales and vacation rentals in Big Pine and the Lower Keys are the focus of this office.

ERA Lower Keys Realty
MM 30 Oceanside, Big Pine Key
(305) 872-2258, (800) 859-7642
www.eralowerkeysrealty.com
This establishment deals with sales and rentals in the Lower Keys.

Action Keys Realty, Inc.
MM 24.8 Oceanside, Summerland Key
(305) 745-1323, (800) 874-1323
www.actionkeysrealty.com
In addition to residential sales throughout the Lower Keys, this agency handles vacation rentals, primarily on Summerland, Ramrod, and Little Torch Keys.

KEY WEST

Despite the fact that Key West is heavily developed, with both old and new homes on generally small lots throughout the city, real estate agents report that the demand for homes far outstrips the island's supply. Also, while waterfront property is a prime attraction for home buyers throughout the rest of the Florida Keys, it is rarely found in Key West, because commercial development lines all waterfront areas. Nevertheless, real estate in the southernmost city is expensive.

The island of Key West is an incorporated city governed by local elected representatives as well as by Monroe County. Consequently, the property tax structure here includes both city and county government expenses. Key West has its own land-use plan with zoning ordinances, permitting units, density requirements, and building height and setback minimums. Within the historic district of Old Town,

another layer of control and review exists. The five-member Historical Architecture Review Commission (HARC) reviews applications for improvements and new construction. Established in 1986, HARC works to ensure the integrity of the historic district.

Key West offers a selection of styles in single-family homes, town houses, and condominiums (see the Key West Architecture Close-up in our Attractions chapter). The island has few mobile home parks, and the only mobile-home communities here are small and hidden away. There are also several on Stock Island.

Town houses, typically adjoining structures with a common wall, allow homeowners to own the ground beneath them. The center of the common wall is the dividing line, and party wall agreements determine who maintains responsibility in cases of repair or destruction.

If you wish to purchase beachfront housing, owning a condominium is without a doubt the way to go. Along the south side of Key West are several relatively new, multistory beachfront condominiums with elevators, enclosed parking, pools, tennis courts, and hot tubs. Units range in size from one bedroom, one bath to three or four bedrooms and two or three baths. Only a few units have waterfront or partial water views, however.

The majority of single-family homes in Key West are in areas known as Old Town, Mid Town, and New Town, and real estate agents further break two of these regions into "old" and "new" Old Town and "old" and "new" New Town. Boundaries are roughly established, with some overflow, and within all Key West areas you'll discover a diverse array of properties dating from between the early 1800s and the late 1900s.

Convenience to the water or to touristy Duval Street is not usually a factor in the cost of Key West property. Rather, prices generally depend on the size and condition of the house, its lot, and its location. The island itself is only 2 miles long by 4 miles wide, so beaches and harbors are never far away. Some home buyers seek property as far from the busy roadways and attractions as possible.

Community Profiles

OLD TOWN

Settled in the early to late 1800s and the early 1900s, Old Town is characterized by large wood-frame houses of distinctive architectural styles (see our Key West Architecture Close-up in our Attractions chapter). Typically built by shipbuilders and carpenters for New England sea captains, many of these homes feature Bahamian and New England influences and high ceilings. Several historic district homes are now exquisite guesthouses (see the Accommodations chapter).

In addition to its obvious aesthetic qualities, Old Town is desirable because it is within walking distance of just about everything Key West has to offer, including shops, restaurants, nightlife, and galleries. Among the community's residents are a large number of artists and writers. Toward the southern end of Whitehead Street and west of Duval on Petronia Street, about a block from the Ernest Hemingway Home and Museum, lies Bahama Village. This community now is undergoing gentrification as home buyers purchase and renovate existing properties here.

One of Key West's more recent developments in Old Town is Truman Annex, where private homes, town houses, and condominiums all boast features of Key West's distinctive architecture. This self-contained development once was an extension of the island's Bahama Village section and later a portion of the Key West naval base. Truman Annex was constructed and renovated according to a unified plan reminiscent of Old Town but with more green space and winding streets. Because of the charm that this gated development exhibits, even the hubbub created by large cruise ships entering the nearby harbor does not affect its pricey real estate values. Condominiums in the

Recycling in the Florida Keys is vital for all who inhibit this fragile place. Because of the coral reefs and wildlife, keeping the Florida Keys safe from harm and retaining its beauty is a tremendous responsibility for residents and visitors alike. For details about our recycling program and obtaining a recycling bin, call (305) 296-8297. Aluminum and metal cans, glass bottles and jars, plastic containers, and newspapers are all recyclable.

Harbour Place complex of Truman Annex are almost directly on the water and are well in seven figures. Single-family homes are in the multimillion-dollar price range.

MID TOWN AND NEW TOWN

Stretching from White Street all the way east to Kennedy Boulevard, Mid Town boasts a mix of wood-frame and concrete-block ground-level homes built in the late 1950s and 1960s. New Town, developed a bit later, spreads out along North Roosevelt Boulevard, and is largely commercial on its perimeter.

Recently completed in the Mid Town area is Roosevelt Annex, a gated community of 25 single-family homes and town houses fronting the Gulf of Mexico on the former county fairgrounds along North Roosevelt Boulevard. Billed as the last developable site in Key West with open-water views, Roosevelt Annex was constructed by the developer of Truman Annex and the Key West Golf Club.

The Key West Golf Club community, on Stock Island, looks a lot like Truman Annex. Here, single-family homes, townhouses, and condominiums display elements of Conch-style architecture. Each residence overlooks the Florida Keys' only 18-hole public golf course, along with surrounding lakes and ponds. If you are not in the market to buy at this time, a variety of long-term rental options is available. All residents have free access to tennis courts, nature walks, several swimming pools, and, of course, golf.

SUNSET KEY

If you would truly like to live on a secluded island—but not too far from civilization—consider a home on Sunset Key. Formerly known as Tank Island (the navy once stored its fuel in huge tanks here), Sunset Key is just a stone's throw across the harbor from Mallory Square. About half of the island is devoted to guest cottages and a beachfront restaurant-bar operated by the Westin Key West Resort and Marina (see the Accommodations chapter); the rest is reserved for single-family homes. Interior building lots begin at one and a half million. In addition to fabulous open-water sunset views, homeowners on Sunset Key enjoy such amenities as a health club, pool, tennis courts, and putting green. Their cars, however, must remain behind at the Westin parking garage on Key West; only golf carts and bicycles are permitted on Sunset Key. Regular ferry service is available from the Westin Marina.

Real Estate Companies

We describe some of the largest Key West agencies for sales and rentals in this section. However, this is not meant to be a comprehensive listing. For a complete list, consult the Yellow Pages.

Bascom Grooms Real Estate
1102 White Street
(305) 295-7511, (888) 565-7150
www.keywesthomes.cc
In addition to residential sales, this agency also handles commercial properties and vacation rentals.

Beach Club Brokers Inc.
1106 White Street
(305) 294-8433, (800) 545-9655
www.kwreal.com
Specializing in residential sales, Beach

Club Brokers also has a separate rental division, Rent Key West Vacations Inc. (see separate listing).

Century 21 Prestige Group
701 Caroline Street
(305) 294-6637, (800) 654-2781
www.c21keysearch.com
Century 21 Prestige Group deals with real estate sales in our southernmost city.

Coldwell Banker Schmitt Real Estate
1201 White Street
(305) 296-7727, (800) 598-7727
www.realestatefloridakeys.com
Sales and rentals in Key West are the focus of this office.

Compass Realty
201 Front Street, Building 45
(305) 296-7078 (sales), (305) 292-1881 (rentals), (800) 884-7368

1 Golf Club Drive
(305) 292-0020 (sales), (305) 292-1480 (rentals), (888) 721-7368
Compass Realty sells property throughout Key West but also focuses on the sale of Truman Annex properties as well as those in the Key West Golf Club and Roosevelt Annex communities. A separate division handles rentals of the three developments.

Island Group Realty
3436 Duck Avenue, Key West
(305) 295-7110, (800) 225-4277
www.isellkw.com
This real estate company offers any of the services you might need for relocating to the Florida Keys. If your needs are residential, commercial properties, or rentals, the sales associates at Island Group Realty can assist with your request.

Key West Realty Inc.
1109 Duval Street
(305) 294-7253, (305) 294-7368, (800) 654-5131
www.keywestrealty.com
In addition to real estate sales, this agency is very heavily into the rental business with a wide variety of vacation options.

i

Be sure to ask about parking when making your reservation for a rental property in Key West. On some Old Town streets, cars bearing non-Monroe County plates may be ticketed or towed.

Preferred Properties of Key West, Inc.
526 Southard Street
(305) 294-3040, (800) 462-5937
www.realkeywest.com
This agency offers residential and commercial property sales as well as vacation rentals, investment properties, and long-term property management.

Prudential Knight-Keyside Properties
336 Duval Street
(305) 294-5155, (800) 843-9276

3332 North Roosevelt Boulevard
(305) 294-4949, (877) 294-4949, (305) 292-0040 (Shark Key sales)
www.floridakeys-realestate.com, www.pruknight.com
A part of the quartet of Prudential Keyside Properties offices, Prudential Knight concentrates sales efforts on properties from Key West to Marathon. The Key West site handles rental listings.

The Real Estate Company of Key West Inc.
701 Simonton Street
(305) 296-0111
www.oldkeywest.com
Specializing in sales and rentals of upscale residential properties, the staff here includes a full-time property manager who oversees luxury vacation rentals ranging from cottages to multibedroom estates.

Rent Key West Vacations Inc.
1107 Truman Avenue
(305) 294-0990, (800) 833-7368
www.rentkeywest.com
A division of Beach Club Brokers Inc., this agency handles rentals exclusively. Rent Key West offers extensive listings, with properties ranging from studio apartments to four-bedroom homes.

CLOSE-UP

Spell That, Please

"Condotels" is not a word you will find in any dictionary. This new term is especially relevant in the Florida Keys because the landscape is changing from mom-and-pop motels, campgrounds, mobile-home parks, marinas, and even large hotel properties to condotels. In 2005, properties began to change hands, one after another. Major investors converged on the Keys, paying huge amounts of money for property they plan to redevelop into very upscale condominiums—units that are suites, owned by private parties and then rented out like traditional hotel or motel rooms (but for a lot more money). Each week there is another headline of yet another property going the way of this conversion craze. In September 2005, the Monroe County Tourism Development Council issued a report concluding that more than 2,076 units had been tagged for condominiums or condotels. This represents more than 20 percent of the Key's total hotel, motel, recreational vehicle, and campground space. In the Upper Keys, 75 percent of campground and RV units are being converted, mostly to residential condominiums.

On the plus side, the units will certainly be newer and larger than traditional hotel/motel rooms. On the negative side, some feel that the Keys will lose its laid-back/quaint atmosphere. Some also believe that only the wealthy will be able to live here. They fear this will drive out the infrastructure of service people who are the backbone of the Keys community and who help make any tourist destination successful.

Only time will tell what impact these condotels will have on this string of islands. Folks joke that someday the Florida Keys may be a gated community beginning in Key Largo—or, worse yet, a Disney theme park of what the Keys *should* look like! What price "Paradise"?

Truman and Company
1205 Truman Avenue
(305) 292-2244
www.trumanandcompany.com
This is a highly professional company with a great knowledge of the Key West and Monroe County real estate market. Most of the principals in this company are long-time residents and handle with first-hand knowledge the unique residential and commercial aspects of buying and selling property in the Florida Keys.

CAMPGROUNDS 

Close your eyes and concentrate on this vision: The turquoise waters shimmer like a '57 T-bird. The sun melts like orange sherbet on a hot summer day. The stars sparkle like a gilded mosaic.

Jimmy Buffett has nothing on you when you are camping in the Florida Keys.

Whether you enjoy pitching a tent or traveling with a self-contained motor home, the campgrounds of the Keys offer a reasonably priced alternative to motels and resort accommodations. However, you will find that camping rates in the Florida Keys are generally much higher than in other areas of the United States. But all our recommended campgrounds have water access, and many are perched at the edge of the Atlantic or the Gulf of Mexico.

A wide range of amenities distinguishes each campground, but one thing is certain: If you wish to camp in the Keys during January, February, or March—those winter months when the folks up north are dusting off their snow boots—you must reserve your site a year in advance. The Keys have a second high season in the summer months, when Floridians locked into triple-digit temperatures head south to our cooling trade winds and warm, placid waters. During sport lobster season, the last consecutive Wednesday and Thursday of July, it is standing room only in the Keys.

We have listed our recommended campgrounds and RV parks by descending mile marker beginning in Key Largo and ending at Stock Island. Key West devotes its land use to megahotels and quaint guesthouses, presenting a dearth of recommendable campgrounds.

If you think you might fancy a really unusual camping experience, be sure to see Camping in the Beyond in this chapter for information on camping in the Dry Tortugas National Park or Everglades National Park.

You may assume that all our inclusions maintain good paved interior roads, clean restrooms and showers, laundry facilities, and 20- and 30-amp electrical service. Most campgrounds accept pets if they are kept on a leash at all times and walked only in designated areas and never on the beach. Exceptions will be noted. Most campgrounds enforce a quiet time from 10:00 or 11:00 P.M. to 7:00 A.M.

Rates vary by the type of site you secure. Most campgrounds offer a range of options: tent sites, with or without electricity; RV sites with electricity and water; sites with electricity, water, and sewer. Waterfront sites or sites with boat dockage will be more costly. Extra people or vehicles at a site will incur additional per-diem charges. All water is municipal, piped down to the Keys from Miami. Cable television and telephone hookups are noted when applicable. Back-in and pull-through dimensions vary. Call the campground if this is critical for your rig. Toll-free telephone numbers, when stated, are for reservation purposes only.

PRICE-CODE KEY

Our listings rate campgrounds according to a four-symbol price key, representing average site cost per night during the high season.

$	**$20 to $40**
$$	**$41 to $60**
$$$	**$61 to $80**
$$$$	**More than $81**

Rate ranges are based on a per-diem stay during high season without the 11.5 percent state tax. High season is considered December 15 through Easter. Some campgrounds also consider the summer months as high season. Weekly and monthly rates are usually available at a reduced cost; be sure to inquire when you make your reservation. Major credit cards are accepted unless noted to the contrary.

THE FLORIDA KEYS

Upper Keys

John Pennekamp Coral Reef State Park **$**
MM 102.5 Oceanside, Key Largo
(305) 451-1202
(800) 326-3521 (reservation line)
www.dep.state.fl.us/parks
www.reserveamerica.com (reservation Web site)

Aesthetically, the gravel sites at John Pennekamp Coral Reef State Park don't begin to compare with their waterfront siblings at the Keys' other two state parks, Bahia Honda and Long Key, but a canopy of mature buttonwoods shades most of the sites. The wide range of fabulous recreational opportunities within Pennekamp and its proximity to the nightlife in Key Largo more than make up for any lack of romantic oceanfront ambience (see Beaches and Public Parks in the Recreation chapter).

John Pennekamp Coral Reef State Park, like Bahia Honda State Park and Long Key State Park, follows a strictly regimented reservation policy (see the Making Reservations for State Park Campsites section in this chapter). If you have a guaranteed reservation at Pennekamp and you will be arriving after 5:00 P.M. you must call before 4:00 P.M. on the day of your arrival to obtain a site assignment and the combination to open the park's front gate. To cancel your reservation, you must call by 5:00 P.M. of the day before your scheduled arrival or you will be charged for one night's camping. The park opens at 8:00 A.M. and closes at sundown daily. You may stay a maximum of 14 days. The per-night camping fee includes all taxes and allows four people and one vehicle per campsite. Pets are not allowed in the campground. Intoxicants are forbidden anywhere in the park. Water and electric (30/50 amp) are available at all sites.

If you are a Florida resident age 65 or older or 100 percent disabled, you will pay substantially discounted per-diem camping fees at John Pennekamp Coral Reef State Park, Long Key State Park, and Bahia Honda State Park.

Key Largo Kampground and Marina **$-$$**
MM 101.5 Oceanside, Key Largo
(305) 451-1431, (800) 526-7688
www.members.tripod.com/klkamp

Croton and bougainvillea hedges separate the sites in this villagelike campground laden with palm trees. Chickees line the arterial canal that connects the marina to the shallow oceanic bonefish flats beyond. About one-third of the condo campsites, with full hookups and free cable television, are available for overnighters. Some sites front the canal and have boat slips. Two beaches look out on Newport Bay, and a heated swimming pool and kiddie pool, shuffleboard, horseshoe pits, and volleyball add to the fun. John Pennekamp Coral Reef State Park is only a mile north of the 40-acre campground.

Rates are based on four people (two adults and two children younger than age six) and one camping unit per site.

Fiesta Key Resort KOA Kampground **$$-$$$$**
MM 70 Bayside, Long Key
(305) 664-4922, (800) 562-7730
www.koa.com/where/fl/09250.htm

Surrounded by the warm waters of the Gulf of Mexico, which we call "bayside" here in the Florida Keys, Fiesta Key KOA Kampground enjoys a tropical milieu and the famed Keys sunsets. Hot pink oleander hedges lead to the 35-site tent village, and more than 300 campsites welcome RVs. Most of the sites are shaded with large palms or leafy trees and sport a cement patio.

Fiesta Key really does resemble a resort: Diversions are endless. A waterfront pub offers libations and relaxed dining. You will enjoy the Olympic-size, heated swimming pool and two hot tubs. The children probably will prefer to camp out in the game room, on the playground, or the basketball court. On-premises rentals expand your horizons beyond the campground. Pontoon boats, runabouts, and center consoles take you over the calm Gulf waters. Fishing rods stand ready should you care to try your luck with a lure. A full marina provides a boat ramp and slips if you want to bring your own craft.

Rates are quoted for two people; children younger than age six stay free.

Middle Keys

Long Key State Park **$**
MM 67.5 Oceanside, Long Key
(305) 664-4815
(800) 326-3521 (reservation line)
www.dep.state.fl.us/parks
www.reserveamerica.com (reservation Web site)

Every site is oceanfront when you camp at Long Key State Park. The sandy sites took quite a beating from Hurricanes Georges and Irene in recent years, destroying most of the vegetation, but you can't get closer to the ocean than this camping in the Florida Keys. Half the 60 sites offer water and electric, and all have picnic tables fronting the shallow saltwater flats. The paved road into the campground parallels the Overseas Highway on one side and the ocean on the other. Each deep site runs from the park road to the ocean.

Like John Pennekamp Coral Reef State Park and Bahia Honda State Park, Long Key State Park follows a strictly regimented reservation policy (see the Making Reservations for State Park Campsites section in this chapter). Rates are based on four people, one vehicle per site, and include all taxes. Only one camper and one small tent or two small tents are allowed per campsite.

The park opens at 8:00 A.M. and closes at sunset. Pets are not allowed in the camping areas, beaches, or concession areas of the park.

Knight's Key Park Campground & Marina **$-$$**
MM 47 Oceanside, Marathon
(305) 743-4343, (800) 348-2267

This family-oriented campground, started by three Kyle brothers more than three decades ago, occupies the land once called Knight's Key Junction at the foot of the Seven Mile Bridge. The tracks of Flagler's Railroad ended here. The train unloaded its cargo, which was stowed on ships heading to Key West or Cuba, and then Keys or Cuban cargo was placed aboard the train, which turned around and chugged back north. The deepwater canal and swimming area, with waters 30 feet deep, remain from that bygone era when Knight's Key hummed with ship traffic.

Knight's Key Park Campground has a man-made beach, and, during the winter season, a stone aquarium near the canal is stocked with fish. From December 15 through March 30, the Kyle Inn, a pub-style restaurant with a Chicago-brick floor, provides meals, libations, bingo, cards, and billiards.

Unique to Knight's Key, you can dock your boat behind your camper at the harborside marina sites. Knight's Key maintains a pump and dump station but offers no sewer hookups. Electricity of 20, 30, and 50 amps is available, but don't expect cable TV or telephone hookups.

Rates are based on two occupants. Minibikes and motorcycles are forbidden on park roads.

Friends of a Feather

The sun streams in through an open window, and a mild breeze blows in off the Gulf of Mexico on a perfect day. All of a sudden, a dark shadow covers this brightly lit moment. Look toward the sky, and your eyes spot a *buzzard!* Just like us, these huge birds like the climate in the Florida Keys.

Bird-watching in Paradise (October through March) offers birders a unique opportunity to see more than 200 species. There are also more than 60 species that breed this far south in the winter season. Songbirds (buntings, orioles, tanagers, vireos, warblers, and doves) and raptors (swansons, hawks, and broadwings) are spectacular to view in swarms as they follow weather fronts. Buzzards can be seen without binoculars. They are on the ground, feasting on their meal or hanging out behind stores, frolicking in the dumpsters doing what buzzards do best—keeping our environment clean. Go to www.birding.com or www.keysbirdingfestival.com for more information.

Lower Keys

Sunshine Key RV Resort and Marina **$-$$$**
MM 39 Bayside, Ohio Key
(305) 872-2217, (800) 852-0348
www.rvonthego.com

Sunshine Key RV Resort and Marina occupies an entire key, officially named Ohio Key. This bustling place, with nearly 400 sites, is more like a small midwestern town than a camping resort in the Keys. The 75-acre Sunshine Key, with its winding sign-posted streets and myriad amenities, is friendly and family-oriented. The ocean-side portion of Sunshine Key has not been developed. It remains a tangle of mangroves, buttonwoods, and palm trees that shields a feathered montage of wildlife popular with bird-watchers.

You will have to rise early to pack in all you can do in a day on Sunshine Key. The large marina, which even has a fishing pier, will shelter your boat, and the experts at the bait and tackle shop will put you on the fish. Tennis courts, a heated swimming pool, volleyball, horseshoes, and a full schedule of adult activities in the clubhouse keep things hopping. A game room, basketball courts, a playground, and watersports occupy the children.

Rates are based on two adults and their accompanying children younger than 12. Sunshine Key considers its high season November 15 through April 15.

Bahia Honda State Park **$**
MM 37 Oceanside, Bahia Honda Key
(305) 872-2353
(800) 326-3521 (reservation line)
www.dep.state.fl.us/parks
www.reserveamerica.com (reservation Web site)

Claiming the Florida Keys' best natural beach (2½ miles long), the 524-acre Bahia Honda State Park offers campers three kinds of sites but no pull-through sites. The roomy sites at Buttonwood can accommodate large motor homes; Sandspur is limited to tents, vans, and pop-ups. Because these sites sit deep in a tropical hardwood hammock, the park is very selective as to which rigs are allowed to camp here. Only one car and one tent per site are permitted. All these sites have water, and more than half offer electricity. Bayside campsites, accessed by a road passing under the Bahia Honda Bridge, are restricted to tents or small pop-ups.

The bridge provides only a 6-foot, 8-inch clearance. These campsites provide water but no electricity.

Three large cabins, each a heated and air-conditioned, two-bedroom duplex with a fully equipped kitchen, a full bathroom, and all linens, literally perch on the water near the bayside campsites. You can throw a baited hook from your front porch, rock a little in the old rocker gracing the deck, and catch your dinner without missing the sunset. Each cabin will sleep six, but you'll have to rough it without television or radio. No pets are allowed in the cabins, which must be reserved in person, by telephone, or online (see the Making Reservations for State Park Campsites section in this chapter) up to 11 months in advance. A two-day deposit by credit card, check, or cash will secure the cabin reservation if it's received within 10 days of your making the reservation.

All campsites at Bahia Honda State Park provide a grill and picnic table. The park has a boat ramp, so you may bring your own craft and try your luck at catching a tarpon under the Bahia Honda Bridge, noted as one of the best tarpon-fishing areas in the state (see the Fishing chapter).

"You really don't even have to know what you are doing," counsels the assistant park manager. "Put a live mullet on the end of a line and the tarpon will bite."

Like John Pennekamp Coral Reef State Park and Long Key State Park, Bahia Honda State Park follows a strictly regimented reservation policy (see the Making Reservations for State Park Campsites section in this chapter). Rates are based on four-person occupancy and include all taxes. Maximum stay at a Bahia Honda campsite is 14 days. Pets are not allowed.

Big Pine Key Fishing Lodge **$**
MM 33 Oceanside, Big Pine Key
(305) 872-2351
www.gocampingamerica.com/bigpinelodge

The Big Pine Key Fishing Lodge abuts a natural oceanside inlet that was a by-product of the dredging of Spanish Harbor Channel for Flagler's Railroad. The sites range from rustic grass or dirt tent sites without water or electricity to dockside sites with full hookups.

The boat basin, a part of the Big Pine Fishing Lodge since the late 1950s, accommodates small fishing boats up to 25 feet long for a per-foot daily charge. Ample fish-cleaning stations are provided so you can ready the spoils of the day for the frying pan. The lodge has an oval swimming pool sunken in a raised deck overlooking a peppering of statuesque coconut palms, all grown from seed.

Rates are based on one or two occupants with one vehicle and one camping unit. Children younger than age six stay free. Air-conditioning, phone outlets, and cable hookups are included in the camping fee. No dogs are allowed in the campground.

Sugarloaf Key Resort
KOA Kampground **$$-$$$$**
MM 20 Oceanside, 251 County Road 939, Summerland Key
(305) 745-3549, (800) 562-7731
www.thefloridakeys.com/koasugarloaf

Pelicans perched in mangroves near thatched chickees on a palm-speckled beach creates an island ambience in this comprehensive KOA on Summerland Key. Nearly 200 gravel, grass, or dirt sites offer a choice of hookups, but no pull-throughs are available. Optional cable hookup is available at an additional charge.

The facility offers what you have come to expect from a KOA Kampground—all the necessities plus the amenities of a resort. A full marina covers the gamut of boating and fishing needs. A large heated pool, hot tub, minigolf, horseshoes, and bicycle rentals offer landlubbers relaxing diversions. Volleyball, a game room, and a playground amuse the children. Social activities, crafts, and special events are scheduled during the winter season. Only 20 miles from Key West and near Looe Key National Marine Sanctuary, Sugarloaf Key KOA Kampground is close to all the action.

Rates are based on two occupants; children younger than age six stay free. Some RV trailers are available for rent; call to inquire about amenities and pricing.

Bluewater Key RV Resort **$$$**
MM 14.5 Oceanside, Sugarloaf Key
(305) 745-2494, (800) 237-2266
www.bluewaterkey.com
As simple and elegant as a sophisticated ball gown, Bluewater Key RV Resort oozes class. The 80 spacious gravel sites feature metered utility hookups, including telephone and cable television. Uniquely angled toward the water and buffered with palms and shrubbery, each privately owned site has a stone patio with benches and a round cement table. No tents, popups, or vans are allowed at Bluewater Key. All units must be self-contained RVs.

A clubhouse hosts table tennis or informal card games, and the swimming pool attracts sun worshipers from up north. Oceanside flats and deepwater canals surround the property, affording primo fishing for anglers. And if you want a little action at the end of your day of quiet solitude, you are but 14½ miles from the center of Key West. Need we say more?

Those reserving waterfront or canal sites may secure their small boats to the floating docks or bulkhead. The high season at Bluewater Key RV Resort is considered December 15 to April 15. Although the resort accepts reservations for one day or one week to a month or more depending upon availability, we suggest you book at least a year in advance if you'd like a waterfront spot. Bluewater Key RV Resort has an on-site manager and is protected from intrusion by a 24-hour, phone-operated security gate.

Geiger Key Marina and Campground
MM 10.5 Oceanside, Geiger Key
(305) 296-3553
Nestled in the mangroves on the back side of "Paradise," you'll discover Geiger Key Marina and Campground. The setting on the Atlantic Ocean is what makes this quiet location a hidden gem. Great white herons patrol the grounds in search of pilchards and pinfish. Pelicans look like ornaments in the mangrove branches as they keep a sharp lookout for snapper, grouper, and parrot fish. Geiger Key Marina and Campground is only 15 miles north of Key West, yet it seems a million miles away with its laid-back 1950s aura. The property has all the updates, however, with RV hook-ups, laundry facilities, ocean-view private tent sites, transient boat slips, kayak rentals, and fishing charter boats. Their popular Tiki Bar cooks up pig roasts on Saturday night; on Sunday, they whip up a chicken and ribs BBQ. Live music is part of the bar's attraction on Friday, Saturday, and Sunday night. You can get to this jewel by RV or boat. The marina monitors VHF channel 79 for water-mode arrivals.

Boyd's Key West Campground **$$-$$$**
MM 5 Oceanside, 6401 Maloney Avenue, Stock Island
(305) 294-1465
www.gocampingamerica.com/boydskeywest
Although its brochures state a Key West address, Boyd's is actually on Stock Island, just outside the Key West city limits. Most of the level, shaded sites have cement patios. Bordering the ocean, Boyd's offers a boat ramp, a small marina, extensive dock space, and a heated swimming pool. The four bathhouses were renovated and updated in 2000. You can catch the city bus into Key West for unlimited diversions, hang out at Boyd's game room, or watch the large-screen television, which is tucked in a tiki hut near the pool.

Rates are based on two occupants and one camping unit per site. Small dogs are permitted in hard-shell campers only. Fifty-amp service and modem hookup is available.

CAMPING IN THE BEYOND

If there is a little part of you that longs to forge through uncharted territory and live off the land (or the sea), you can fulfill your fantasies here. Everglades National Park and Dry Tortugas National Park, both day-trip excursions from the Florida Keys, offer unique camping experiences for the adventuresome spirits among you.

Everglades National Park

Canoe or commandeer a small motor craft into the backcountry wilderness of Everglades National Park. This 99-mile route, which is recommended for experienced canoeists only, connects Flamingo and Everglades City. (Allow at least eight days to complete the trip.) The charted routing through such colorfully named spots as Darwin's Place, Camp Lonesome, Lostman's Five, and Graveyard Creek encompasses 47 primitive campsites of three basic types.

Chickees: These elevated, 10-by-12-foot wood platforms with roofs are placed along interior rivers and bays where no dry land exists. A design originally used by the Miccosukee Indians, these open-air structures allow the wind to blow through, keeping the insects away. A narrow walkway leads to a self-contained toilet. You will need to have a freestanding tent, because stakes and nails are not allowed.

Beach Sites: These are set on coastal beaches that have been built up through time from a conglomeration of fragmented shells. Campers are warned that Gulf waters can become extremely rough. Loggerhead sea turtles nest on Highland Beach and Cape Sable in the spring and summer. If you see evidence of their nesting, refrain from lighting a campfire nearby. (Campfires are allowed at beach sites only.)

Primitive Ground Sites: These consist of mounds of earth just a few feet higher than the surrounding mangroves. Willy Willy, Camp Lonesome, and Canepatch are old Indian mound sites. Coastal aborigines, who lived here before the Seminole Indians, constructed mounds of shells or soil as dry dwelling sites amid the mangroves. The ground sites, along interior bays and rivers, have a heavier preponderance of insects than either the beach sites or the chickees. Always be prepared for mosquitoes and tiny biting flies called no-see-ums, especially at sunrise and sunset. Mosquito season corresponds with the rainy season, April through October. We do not recommend you try to camp in the Everglades during these months.

You will need a permit (small fee in season) to camp in one of the backcountry sites. Apply in person at the Gulf Coast or Flamingo Visitor Center up to 24 hours before your trip begins. Everglades National Park also offers camping in two in-park campgrounds. Seasonal reservations (November through April) can be made for these campsites by calling (800) 365-2267 or at the online reservations center, accessed by link from the park's Web site at www.nps.gov/ever. Reservations in the winter season are limited to 14 days at one visit, 30 days total per year.

For more information on park or backcountry camping, visit the aforementioned Everglades National Park Web site, or contact the main park number at (305) 242-7700.

Dry Tortugas National Park

Roughing it takes on gargantuan proportions when you consider camping at Dry Tortugas National Park, but it's worth the effort, because this remote bit of Paradise has been preserved in a virginal state. You'll find the 11 palm-shaded tent sites—available on a first-come, first-served basis—in a sandy area on Garden Key in front of Fort Jefferson. You must pack in all your supplies, including fresh water; only saltwater toilets, grills, and picnic

Camping and campfires are not permitted in national wildlife refuges.

Don't let the skeeters get ya! Regardless of your activities here in the Keys, mosquitoes are a problem. Be sure to buy a repellent that contains DEET for the best protection against the critters.

tables are provided. There is no food, fresh water, electricity, or medical assistance of any kind on the island.

You must take your chances on securing a campsite, because reservations are not taken for the individual sites. A small fee per person, per night must be paid upon arrival at Fort Jefferson. (The park service says securing a site usually is not a problem.) Campsites accommodate up to eight people. You can reserve a group site for as many as 15 people, however, by contacting the park service, (305) 242-7700. The staff will send you a permit application, which you must mail to: Dry Tortugas National Park, Attn.: Group Camping, P.O. Box 6208, Key West, FL 33041. The application requires the following information: name, address, day/night telephone number, group name, date of arrival/departure, number of people in group, primary activities (birding, snorkeling), and mode of transportation to the islands. If the site is available when you submit your completed application, a permit reserving the group site will be issued. You may stay up to 14 days at either individual or group sites, but keep in mind you must bring complete provisioning for the duration of your stay and pack out your trash.

You may have left the civilized world behind you in Key West, but the arena of natural splendor surrounding you in the Dry Tortugas is endless. Tour Fort Jefferson (self-guided), America's largest 19th-century coastal fort. The walls of the fort are 50 feet high and 8 feet thick.

A white coral beach, nature-made not man-made, provides a tropical backdrop for doing nothing at all. But you can snorkel just 60 yards off the beach or dive the seemingly bottomless blue waters, which, preserved as a sanctuary, are filled with fearless battalions of finfish and squadrons of crawfish that are oblivious to your presence.

Bird-watching is superb. Sooty and noddy terns by the thousands gather in the Dry Tortugas from the Caribbean, nesting on nearby Bush Key. Single eggs are laid in depressions in the sand. Parent birds take turns shading them from the hot sun. The entire colony leaves when the babies are strong enough.

Getting to the Dry Tortugas presents a bit of a challenge—and expense. Seaplane is the fastest means of transportation to the Dry Tortugas, but it's also the most expensive. You can also reach the Dry Tortugas by sea. (See the Recreation chapter for information on the Yankee Fleet Ferry to Fort Jefferson.) The National Park Service provides a list of sanctioned transportation services to the Dry Tortugas, which means they are insured and bonded and they maintain good safety records. The park service advises that the criteria are stringent and the list is constantly monitored. Contact the park service, (305) 242-7700, to get the current recommendations. The Dry Tortugas National Park Web site is www.nps.gov/drto.

MAKING RESERVATIONS FOR STATE PARK CAMPSITES

Some of the most beautiful campsites in the Florida Keys nestle in hardwood hammocks or perch on oceanfront beaches in our three state parks. The per-dollar value of these sites cannot be beat, and demand outstrips supply in all seasons. The state of Florida has developed a highly structured procedure for the fair and equitable allocation of these coveted campsites. We hope this synopsis helps you snag a small patch of Paradise for your Florida Keys holiday.

Ninety percent of the sites at John Pennekamp Coral Reef State Park, Long Key State Park, and Bahia Honda State Park are available for advance reservation. Ten percent are allotted on a first-come, first-served basis. You must reserve a campsite no more than 11 months in advance in person or by telephone between the hours of 8:00 A.M. and 8:00 P.M. by calling Reserve America at (800) 326-3521 or going online at www.ReserveAmerica.com. If you plan to reserve your site via telephone, you may begin calling at 8:00 A.M. Expect the line to be constantly busy. Just keep hitting the redial button until you get through, and be diligent. If you are unlucky on your first try and your vacation plans allow, try calling again the next day, when available sites for 11 months forward will again be allocated for reservation. (Because all campers have the option of staying for 14 days, overlap may affect availability.)

The new online reservation system allows you to see the location of available sites, as well as services and amenities, fees, and general camping rules.

Your reservation must be secured with a credit card number. If you do not have a credit card or choose not to use it, a check in the amount of one night's camping fee must be received within 10 days of the date you made your reservation. The pristine surroundings, and proximity to ocean and bay waters make the camping sites at these three state parks very desirable.

BOATING

The voice of the sea speaks to the soul, no more so than in the Florida Keys. Surrounded by the shimmering aquatic prisms of the Gulf of Mexico and the Atlantic Ocean, the Keys volunteer unlimited vistas for watery exploration. Our depths secrete famed fishing grounds (see the Fishing chapter) and unparalleled dive sites (see the Diving and Snorkeling chapter). Cruisers from around the world seek out our remote, pristine anchoring-out spots as well as our resort marinas (see the Cruising chapter). And peppering the Keys, from Key Largo to Key West, a proliferation of water-sports facilities afford anyone visiting our shores the opportunity to get out on the water via canoe, sea kayak, water skis, personal watercraft, sailboards, even paddleboats (see the Recreation chapter). The waters surrounding the Florida Keys are protected as part of a marine sanctuary, so regulations concerning the use of personal watercraft are more stringent here than in other parts of Florida. For more information, contact the sanctuary office at (305) 743-2437 or log on to www.fknms.nos.noaa.gov.

But the most popular means of wandering our aqueous acres is undoubtedly by boat. The waters encompassing the Florida Keys have been designated a national marine sanctuary since 1990, and a 1997 marine zoning plan imposes certain restrictions and responsibilities on all mariners so that our resources may be preserved for all time. (See the Florida Keys National Marine Sanctuary Regulations section of this chapter.) In this chapter we will introduce you to our waters, alert you to the rules of our hydrous highways and byways, and share some safety and navigational tips. We'll provide you with a primer of available public boat ramps, marine supply stores, boat sales and service businesses, as well as motor and sailboat rentals, bareboat charters, and other sources to enhance your time on the water. If you want to rent, buy, or sell a boat slip in the Florida Keys, visit www.findslip.com for information.

So follow our lighthouse beacon as we illuminate the joys and some of the hazards of boating in the waters of the Florida Keys. The Key West section gives you details of the boating scene in our southernmost city.

THE FLORIDA KEYS

Bodies of Water

The waters of the Florida Keys conceal multiple habitats that sustain an impressive array of sea life not encountered anywhere else in the United States. Depths range from scant inches (which often disappear altogether at low tide) in the nearshore waters, the flats, and the backcountry of Florida Bay to the fathoms of the offshore waters of the deep blue Atlantic. And buried at sea 4 to 5 miles from our shores runs the most extensive living coral reef track in North America (see the Paradise Found, Fishing, Diving and Snorkeling, and Cruising chapters for more information on these waters and the creatures dwelling within).

FLATS, BACKCOUNTRY, AND SHALLOW NEARSHORE WATERS

Perhaps the most complex of our waters are the shallows of the nearshore waters, those directly off both our coasts, which vary from a few inches to several feet in depth and sometimes stretch for a mile or more from shore. Called "skinny" waters by local captains, these "flats" of the Atlantic and backcountry waters of the Gulf of Mexico and Florida Bay (that portion of the Gulf bordered by the Upper Keys and Everglades National Park) prove a challenge to navigate. Popular with anglers searching for bonefish, permit, tarpon, redfish, snook, and sea trout and inhabited by an array of barracuda, sharks, and lobsters, the shallow waters cover meadows of sea grass punctuated with patches of sand, which also function as the nursery waters for many offshore species.

As a boater in the Florida Keys, you should familiarize yourself with the necessary nautical charts before venturing off the dock. Learn to "read" the water (see the Aids to Navigation section in this chapter) because waters are littered with unmarked shoals. Nearshore waters are best traversed in a shallow-draft flatsboat or skiff, by dinghy, canoe, or sea kayak. Operators of personal watercraft should steer clear of the flats to avoid disturbing the aquatic life dwelling below.

If you do happen to run aground here, turn off your motor immediately; the rotating propeller will kill the sea grass. Usually all you need to do is get out of the boat to lighten the load and push the craft to deeper water. Then trim up your motor and proceed. If this doesn't work, wait until the tide rises a bit and try to push off the flat again.

INTRACOASTAL WATERWAY

The primary navigable waterway in Florida Bay and the Gulf of Mexico is the Intracoastal Waterway. In the Keys it leads from Biscayne Bay at the mainland, under Jewfish Creek, and then parallels the Keys, accommodating boats with drafts of up to 4 to 6 feet. The Intracoastal runs about 2 to 3 miles off the gulfside of our islands, between shallow nearshore waters and the scattered mangrove islands that lie varying distances from the coast. The Intracoastal is well marked to about Big Pine Key, where it meets the Big Spanish Channel and heads north into the Gulf of Mexico. (Red day markers should be kept to the starboard, or right, side of the vessel when traveling down the Keys in the Intracoastal Waterway.) From the Spanish Channel to Key West, boaters must pay close attention to nautical charts to navigate safe passage. Boaters will enter Key West through the well-marked Northwest Channel.

PATCH REEFS, HAWK CHANNEL, AND THE BARRIER REEF

Between the nearshore waters of the Atlantic and the barrier reef some 4 to 5 miles offshore lies a smattering of patch reefs submerged at depths as shallow as 3 feet, with some even exposed at low tide. Surrounding waters vary in depth, but generally are much deeper than the flats and nearshore waters.

Hawk Channel—a safely navigable superhighway frequented by recreational boaters and cruisers—runs the length of the Florida Keys, bordering the reef at depths between 11 and 16 feet. Square red and triangular green day markers guide boaters through these waters; red markers should be kept to the starboard, or right, side of the vessel when traveling down the Keys in Hawk Channel.

Outside this marked area, the waters are scattered with dive sites designated with anchor buoys and red-and-white flags, as well as marked and unmarked rocks and shoals. If red-and-white diver-down flags are displayed, boaters should steer clear. These flags indicate that a diver is beneath the water. Lighthouses now mark shallow reef areas, which, at one time, claimed ships that encountered bad weather or navigated carelessly close to the coral mountains. Waters covering the coral reef can run as deep as 20 to 40 feet, but as history attests, depths can vary considerably. Always consult your nautical chart and "read" the water.

THE FLORIDA STRAITS

Outside the reef in the Florida Straits, the water depth of the Atlantic increases dramatically to as much as 80 feet, deepening further with distance from shore. Although on some days these waters are relatively calm, all offshore boaters should check wind and weather advisories before venturing out.

CREEKS AND CHANNELS

The channels, or "cuts," between our islands often have extremely strong currents that make traveling between bridge pilings a bit dicey. Current continuously flows from the Gulf of Mexico into the Atlantic because sea level in the Gulf is slightly higher than that of the ocean. Exercise caution when boating in these waters.

KEY WEST HARBOR

The southernmost city's ports have traditionally been gracious, welcoming tall ships, steamships, ferries, barges, powerboats, and seaplanes. Pirates, wreckers, spongers, shippers, naval officers, and Cuban émigrés all have found shelter here in the midst of their work, play, and quest for worldly wealth and freedom.

Key West's port, the deepest in all the Florida Keys, has a main channel depth of about 33 feet; it is even deeper on the Atlantic side. Passenger cruise ships now include this island among their ports of call. Key West is ranked among the top busiest cruise-ship ports of call in the world. Also in that ranking are the Virgin Islands, Puerto Rico, and the Caymans. Recreational cruisers often head for Key West's bustling harbor to prepare themselves and their boats for a Caribbean journey.

Like the rest of the Florida Keys, Key West is protective of its coral reefs and sea-grass beds, and despite the fact that harbors run deep, waters in the backcountry are shallow everywhere. First-time and novice boaters often run aground here and by Fleming Key and Sand Key west of the harbor.

Aids to Navigation

NAUTICAL CHARTS

Always use nautical charts and a magnetic compass for navigation when boating in the waters of the Florida Keys. Use electronic means of navigation (GPS) only for confirmation of position. Be sure your vessel is equipped with a VHF marine radio.

The U.S. Coast Guard recommends you follow charts issued by the National Oceanic and Atmospheric Administration (NOAA). To secure nautical charts for the entire Florida Keys, you'll need to purchase a chart kit that includes charts for each section. You can also purchase NOAA charts individually. For instance, to navigate the waters surrounding Key West, the U.S. Coast Guard recommends you use navigational chart No. 11441 for the approaches to Key West Harbor and chart No. 11447 for the harbor itself.

Readily available in many marine supply stores throughout the Florida Keys and Key West (see store listings in this chapter), these charts are accurate based on the date marked on them. Store personnel will be able to help you secure the proper, up-to-date chart for the area you will be exploring. Be sure you know how to read the nautical charts before you set off.

CHANNEL MARKERS

In most waters, boaters follow the adage "red, right, return," meaning that the triangular red channel markers should be kept to the right, or starboard, side of the vessel when heading toward the port of origin. This jingle is confusing at best, for in the Florida Keys it does not appear to apply. Red markers should be kept to the starboard side of the vessel when heading down the Keys, from Key Largo to Key West, through Hawk Channel on the oceanside or the Intracoastal Waterway in the Gulf. Conversely, when traveling up the Keys, in either Hawk Channel or the Intracoastal Waterway, square green markers should be kept to your starboard side; keep red markers on your vessel's port, or left, side.

When traversing creeks and cuts from oceanside to the Gulf, red markers should be kept on your starboard side, and when coming from the Gulf the opposite holds true. In any event, always consult your nautical chart to determine the channel of safe passage and the corresponding positioning of the navigational markers.

TIDE CHARTS

It's important to determine mean low tides within the waters you plan to travel so that you do not run aground. In the Florida Keys tides typically rise and fall about 1 to 2 feet. During spring, autumn, and a full moon, tides tend to rise to the higher and lower ends of this scale. Boaters should, therefore, rely on a tide conversion chart. Most marinas, bait and tackle shops, and other businesses that cater to boaters can provide tide information for specific areas in conjunction with a current tide chart available from the U.S. Coast Guard.

"READING" THE WATER

In the Florida Keys visual navigation often means "reading" the water—that is, recognizing its potential depth by knowing which colors indicate safe passage and which connote danger. As water depth decreases, its underlying sea bottom is indicated by distinctive coloration. Be aware that readings may be difficult in narrow channels and in strong currents where the waters often are murky and restrict visibility. Wear polarized sunglasses to better distinguish one color from another.

The easiest way to remember what each water color signifies is to follow some poetic, but fundamental, guidance:

- Brown, brown run aground. Reef formations and shallow sea-grass beds close to the surface cause this color.
- White, white you might. Sandbars and rubble bottoms may be in waters much shallower than you think.
- Green, green nice and clean. The water is generally safely above reefs or seagrass beds, but larger boats with deeper drafts may hit bottom. If you are renting a boat, find out what the draft is.
- Blue, blue cruise on through. Water is deepest, but changing tides may cause coral reefs to surface. Allow time to steer around them.

When You Need Help

Although the U.S. Coast Guard and the Florida Marine Patrol work closely together and will make sure you contact the proper party in any event, they do handle different aspects of our waters in the Florida Keys.

FLORIDA MARINE PATROL

The Florida Fish and Wildlife Conservation Commission's law enforcement arm is the Florida Marine Patrol. They deal with violations such as environmental crime, fish and crawfish bag limits, and illegal dumping. They also enforce boating safety laws, responding to reports of unsafe boating and wake violations as well as any perceived illegal activity on the water. You can reach the Florida Marine Patrol on a cellular telephone by dialing *FMP or on a regular telephone line at (800) DIAL FMP, (800) 342-5367. The Marine Patrol vessels also monitor VHF channel 16.

U.S. COAST GUARD

The U.S. Coast Guard maintains three bases in the Florida Keys and Key West. Their mission is to ensure maritime safety and handle life-threatening emergencies at sea, such as vessel collisions, drownings, onboard fires, or other accidents at sea. The Coast Guard monitors VHF channel 16 at all times. In an emergency call (305) 743-6388. By cell phone, call *CG. If for some reason you do not have a radio or cellular telephone on board, flag a

> *Watchword for Keys boaters: "Steer clear of a standing bird with dry tail feathers." This water will be extremely shallow and you will run aground.*

passing boat and ask someone on it to radio for assistance.

SEATOW

Run aground? Out of fuel? Motor problems? Instead of calling the Coast Guard, call SeaTow, a nationally recognized boater assistance service that maintains facilities the length of the Keys. Convey the details of your problem and what you think you need. Don't just ask for a tow if you have run out of gas or need only a minor repair. Describe your problem; the difference in cost between having gas delivered to your stranded boat and a multihour tow back to land could be a lot of money. SeaTow also will provide free advice, such as projected weather changes or directions in unfamiliar territory.

SeaTow can be reached on VHF channel 16 at sea by calling "SeaTow, SeaTow." By telephone the offices are (305) 451-3330 in Key Largo; (305) 664-4493 in Islamorada; (305) 289-2055 in Marathon; and (305) 295-9912 in Key West. Or consult their Web site at www.seatow.com.

Vessel Regulations and Equipment

Vessels must be equipped with Coast Guard–approved equipment, which varies according to the boat's size, location, and use (see the Required Equipment section in this chapter). All vessels must either be documented or registered (see below), and the appropriate paperwork must be carried on board.

Federal, state, and local law enforcement officials may hail your boat so they can come aboard and inspect it. Among their reasons for imposing civil penalties: improper use of a marine radio and misuse of calling the distress channel VHF channel 16; boating under the influence (a blood alcohol level of .10 percent or higher); and negligence. Negligence includes boating in a swimming area, speeding in the vicinity of other boats or in dangerous waters, bow riding, and gunwaling. Boaters without the required Coast Guard–approved equipment on board or with problematic boats that are considered hazardous may be directed back to port.

VESSEL REGISTRATION

Whether or not you are a resident of the Florida Keys, your vessel must be registered in the state of Florida within 30 days of your arrival if one of our islands is its primary location. Registration renewals require your old registration form and a valid Florida driver's license, if you have one; for registering new boats, bring your manufacturer's statement of origin, dealer's sales tax statement, and bill of sale. If you are registering a used boat you have just purchased, you will need a title signed over to you and a bill of sale, one of which must be notarized, and the previous owner's registration if available.

Boats must be registered annually; only cash is accepted as payment. Excluded from registration requirements are rowboats and dinghies with less than 10 hp motors that are used exclusively as dinghies. All other boats may be registered any weekday between 8:30 A.M. and 4:30 P.M. at one of the following facilities:

- Plantation Key Government Center, MM 88.7 Bayside, Plantation Key, (305) 852-7150. Head bayside on High Point Road and turn left into the government center parking lot. Boat registration is handled in the tax collector's office in the annex building.
- Monroe County Tax Collector's Office, MM 47 Oceanside, Marathon, (305) 743-5585. The office is on the Overseas Highway just past the Monroe County Sheriff's Department.
- Harvey Government Center at Historic

Truman School, 1200 Truman Avenue, Key West, (305) 295-5010. Follow the Overseas Highway until it becomes Truman Avenue. Proceed south on Truman until it intersects with White Street. The Harvey Government Center is on the corner of Truman and White. Head for the tax collector's office.

REQUIRED EQUIPMENT

The U.S. Coast Guard requires that vessels using gasoline for any reason be equipped with a ventilation system in proper working condition. With the exception of outboard motors, gasoline engines must also be equipped with a means of backfire flame control. In addition, Coast Guard-approved fire extinguishers are required for boats with inboard engines, closed or under-seat compartments with portable fuel tanks, and other characteristics. There are additional requirements for vessels of more than 39 feet and boats used for races, parades, and other specific purposes.

Personal flotation devices, night distress signals, and navigation lights are other required equipment. Contact the U.S. Coast Guard at (305) 743-6778 or (305) 664-8078 for specific requirements for your size and style of boat.

RECOMMENDED EQUIPMENT

Regardless of your boat's size, location, and use, the U.S. Coast Guard recommends that you have the following equipment on board: VHF radio, visual distress signals, anchor and spare anchor, heaving line, fenders, first-aid kit, flashlight, mirror, searchlight, sunscreen and sunburn lotion, tool kit, ring buoy, whistle or horn, fuel tanks and spare fuel, chart and compass, boat hook, spare propeller, mooring line, food and water, binoculars, spare batteries, sunglasses (polarized to see water color variations better), marine hardware, extra clothing, spare parts, paddles, and a pump or bailer.

The Florida Keys National Marine Sanctuary Regulations

The Florida Keys fall within the boundaries of the Florida Keys National Marine Sanctuary, created by the federal government in 1990 to protect the resources of our marine ecosystem. And while, for the most part, visitors freely can swim, dive, snorkel, boat, fish, or recreate on our waters, there are some regulations, as of July 1997, to guide these activities. For a complete copy of the regulations and marine coordinates of the areas, contact the sanctuary office at (305) 743-2437, or log on to their Web site at www.fknms.nos.noaa.gov.

SANCTUARYWIDE REGULATIONS

These mandates focus on habitat protection, striving to reduce threats to water quality and minimize human impact of delicate resources. The following are prohibited in our waters:

- Removing, injuring, or possessing coral or live rock.
- Discharging or depositing trash or other pollutants.
- Dredging, drilling, prop dredging, altering, or abandoning any structure on the seabed.
- Operating a vessel in such a manner as to strike or injure coral, sea grass, or organisms attached to the seabed.
- Anchoring a vessel on living coral in water less than 40 feet deep when you can see the bottom. Anchoring on hard-bottom surfaces is allowed.
- Operating a vessel at more than idle speed within 100 yards of residential shorelines, stationary vessels, and navigational aids marking reefs.
- Operating a vessel at more than idle speed within 100 feet of a diver-down flag.

- Diving or snorkeling without a dive flag.
- Operating a vessel in such a manner as to endanger life, limb, marine resources, or property.
- Releasing exotic species.
- Damaging or removing markers, mooring buoys, scientific equipment, boundary buoys, and trap buoys.
- Moving, removing, injuring, or possessing historical resources.
- Taking or possessing protected wildlife.
- Using or possessing explosives or electrical charges.
- Collecting marine life species—tropical fish, invertebrates, and plants—except as allowed by Florida Marine Life Rule (46-42 F.A.C.).

MARINE ZONING RESTRICTIONS

The sanctuary's 1997 marine zoning regulations focus protection on portions of sensitive habitats, while allowing public access in others. Only about 2 percent of the sanctuary's waters fall into the five zoning categories. All sanctuarywide regulations apply in the special zones as well as a number of additional rules and restrictions.

Western Sambos Ecological Reserve (ER)
All fishing activities, spearfishing, shell collecting, tropical fish collecting, lobstering, and other activities that result in the harvest of marine life by divers and snorkelers are prohibited. Direct physical contact with corals and anchoring on living or dead coral are also prohibited. Round yellow buoys mark the area.

Sanctuary Preservation Areas (SPA)
Eighteen small SPA zones protect popular shallow coral reefs. Spearfishing, shell collecting, tropical fish collecting, fishing, and other activities that result in the harvest of marine life by divers, snorkelers, or anglers are prohibited. Direct physical contact with corals and anchoring on living or dead coral is also prohibited. The 18 SPAs are located in portions of Alligator Reef, Carysfort/South Carysfort Reef, Cheeca Rocks, Coffins Patch, Conch Reef, Davis Reef, Dry Rocks, Grecian Rocks, Eastern Dry Rocks, Rock Key, Sand Key, French Reef, Hen and Chickens, Looe Key, Molasses Reef, Newfound Harbor Key, Sombrero Key, and The Elbow.

Round yellow buoys mark the areas of restricted access.

Wildlife Management Areas (WMA)
The 27 wildlife management areas are posted with one of the following restrictions: idle speed only/no wake, no motor, a buffer of no access, or limited closures. The WMAs include portions of Bay Keys, Boca Grande Key, Woman Key, Cayo Agua Keys, Cotton Key, Snake Creek, Cottrell Key, Little Mullet Key, Big Mullet Key, Crocodile Lake, East Harbor Key, Lower Harbor Keys, Eastern Lake Surprise, Horseshoe Key, Rodriguez Key, Dove Key, Tavernier Key, Marquesas Keys, Mud Keys, Pelican Shoal, Sawyer Keys, Snipe Keys, Tidal Flat South of Marvin Key, Upper Harbor Key, East Content Keys, West Content Keys, and Little Crane Key.

Existing Management Areas (EMA)
Sanctuary regulations complement those of existing management areas: Looe Key and Key Largo Management Areas; Great White Heron and Key West National Wildlife Refuges; and all the state parks and aquatic preserves. Operating a personal watercraft, airboat, or water-skiing is prohibited in these waters.

i

Both boat safety and personal watercraft (PWC) safety courses are offered online by the Florida Fish and Wildlife Commission. The courses teach boat safety and Florida boating laws. Upon successfully completing a course, you will receive a Florida Boating Safety Education ID card, which will make you eligible for a discount on boat or PWC insurance. For more information: www.boat-ed.com/fl.

Special Use Areas
Four areas are designated "research only" sites and may be accessed only by specifically authorized personnel with valid permits. They are closed to the general public. The areas are in the vicinity of Conch Reef, Tennessee Reef, Looe Key (patch reef), and Eastern Sambos Reef. Round yellow buoys mark the areas.

Public Boat Ramps

If you trailer your boat to the Florida Keys, you can launch it at any number of public ramps. Here is a list of boat-launching sites maintained year-round for your use. Parking is limited except at park sites. Please note that for those listings noted with a $, you must pay a launch fee.

UPPER KEYS

MM 110 Bayside, Key Largo

MM 102 Oceanside, John Pennekamp Coral Reef State Park, Key Largo, $

MM 92.5 Oceanside, Harry Harris County Park, Key Largo, $ (weekends and holidays)

MM 86 Bayside, Founder's Park, Islamorada, $ (except for locals)

MM 79 Bayside, Islamorada, Indian Key Fill

MM 71 Bayside, Islamorada

MIDDLE KEYS

MM 54 Bayside, Marathon

MM 49 Bayside, Marathon Yacht Club, 33rd Street, Marathon

LOWER KEYS

West of Seven Mile Bridge Bayside, Little Duck Key

MM 37 Oceanside, Bahia Honda State Recreation Area, $

MM 33 Bayside, Spanish Harbor Key

MM 27.5 Bayside, SR 4A, Little Torch Key

MM 22 Oceanside, Cudjoe Key

MM 11 Bayside, Big Coppitt Key

MM 10 Oceanside, Shark Key Fill

KEY WEST

MM 5 Oceanside, Stock Island

End of Route A1A, Smathers Beach

Marine Supply Stores

Marine supplies and NOAA charts recommended by the U.S. Coast Guard may be purchased at the following facilities.

UPPER KEYS

Boater's World Discount Marine Center
MM 105.6 Bayside, Key Largo
(305) 451-0025, (877) 690-0004

MM 50 Oceanside, Marathon
(305) 743-7707, (877) 690-0004

3022 N. Roosevelt Boulevard, Key Plaza
Key West
(305) 295-9232, (877) 690-0004
www.boatersworld.com
Boater's World carries a variety of items, including marine paints, fenders, fishing and tackle supplies, hardware, electrical supplies, clothing, and shoes at discount prices.

*"*FMP" is a free phone call when you are on your vessel and in need of the Florida Marine Patrol.*

West Marine
MM 103.4 Bayside, Key Largo
(305) 453-9050

MM 48.5 Oceanside, Marathon
(305) 289-1009

725 Caroline Street, Key West
(305) 295-0999
www.westmarine.com
West Marine is an expansive store that carries a variety of supplies for sailboats and powerboats. Hardware and electric, safety, plumbing, and maintenance needs can be met at West Marine.

Curtis Marine
MM 92 Oceanside, Tavernier
(305) 852-5218
Curtis Marine offers complete marine and sailing supplies as well as batteries, wire, and riggings. They can help with davit cables, and there's a nice selection in their ships store.

MIDDLE KEYS

See Boater's World and West Marine entries in the Upper Keys section for their Middle Keys locations.

LOWER KEYS

Keys Sea Center
MM 29.5 Oceanside, Big Pine Key
(305) 872-2244
www.keysseacenter.com
Keys Sea Center offers boat sales, services, and supplies, including hardware, electric, and maintenance needs.

KEY WEST

Key West Marine Hardware Inc.
818 Caroline Street
(305) 294-3425, (305) 294-3519
This is the place to go for every cleat, bolt, snap, or thingamajig your powerboat or sailboat requires, because Key West Marine Hardware has it all. You'll find the complete set of official NOAA nautical charts to the Keys and Caribbean waters along with cruising, fishing, and sailing publications of every description. The stock of fishing tackle is limited, but you really can dress your boat in style with all the add-on amenities offered here. You can also dress yourself. Key West Marine carries a large selection of stylish boating togs.

Boat Sales, Repairs, Fuel, and Storage

Facilities throughout the Florida Keys carry a wide variety of new and used boats. For boat owners, most of these sales centers provide all the necessary services, including local hauling, repairs, bottom painting, and fuel.

UPPER KEYS

Travis Boating Center
MM 106.2 Bayside, Key Largo
(305) 451-3398
www.travisboatingcenter.com
Travis Boating Center carries Wellcraft, Larson, FishMaster, Yamaha, Suzuki, and Mercury brands. The store offers a full-service repair department as well as mobile service. Travis Boating Center does not sell fuel but offers an in-water service area.

Unique Marine
MM 93 Bayside, Key Largo
(305) 451-3302
www.uniquemarine.com
For more than 10 years, Unique Marine has been the established dealer for EdgeWater, ProKat, ShreaWater, SeaQuest, Venture, and Yamaha. This dealership takes pride in educating the public about Catamaran fishing boats. They are there for you long after the sale, as they value long-term relationships with their loyal cus-

tomers. Stop in and see why Unique Marine continuously receives prestigious customer-service awards from various boat manufacturers year after year.

Caribee Boat Sales
MM 90.3 Bayside, Tavernier
(305) 852-2724

MM 81.5 Bayside, Islamorada
(305) 664-3431
www.caribeeboats.com
Offshore anglers shop at Caribee for Grady Whites, Pursuits, and Contenders 20 to 36 feet in length. For fishing the backcountry, the facility carries 16- to 21-foot Hewes, Pathfinder, and Maverick boats as well as Boston Whalers. Yamaha and Mercury engines are sold here. Indoor and outdoor storage is available, and certified mechanics are on duty seven days a week. Bottom painting and boat hauling are provided; Caribee carries 89 octane fuel and sells live bait, frozen bait, and ice. Mobile service is available.

Plantation Boat Mart & Marina, Inc.
MM 90 Bayside, Tavernier
(305) 852-5424, (800) 539-2628
www.plantationboat.com
Plantation Boat Mart sells Glacier Bay, Palmetto Custom, Jupiter, Sea Pro, and Hydrasport brand boats and is a Hurricane dealer. You may also buy Yamaha, Johnson, and Evinrude engines here. Plantation Boat Mart maintains a full-service repair department.

MIDDLE KEYS

The Boat House
MM 53.5 Oceanside, Marathon
(305) 289-1323
In 2006, the Boat House was completely updated with a new, state-of-the-art boat storage facility. Dry slips can accommodate boats up to 36 feet in length and can be rented or purchased with unlimited in/out launches. The Boat House still offers a full-line marine store with bait, tackle, ice, and fishing licenses.

Quality Yacht Service
MM 52 Bayside, 10701 Fifth Avenue, Marathon
(305) 743-2898
www.wecleanfuel.com
Quality Yacht Service offers marine fuel cleaning and tank cleaning for both diesel and gasoline engines. It provides mobile service.

Inflatable Boats of the Florida Keys
MM 48.5 Oceanside, Marathon
(305) 743-7085, (888) 207-0011
www.keysinflatables.com
Buy, sell, or repair your inflatable boat here, for Inflatable Boats can take care of your needs. The establishment offers Achilles, Caribe, Avon, AB, and Nautica inflatable boats as well as Tohatsu outboards and preowned boats. The shop also stocks parts, supplies, and accessories. You'll find life rafts here, too.

Keys Boat Works Inc.
MM 48.5 Bayside, 700 39th Street, Marathon
(305) 743-5583
Keys Boat Works provides a comprehensive range of services for boats up to 67 feet in length and maintains 15-ton and 50-ton travel lifts. This full-service yard offers fiberglass work, carpentry, and Awlgrip topside painting. The six on-premises businesses contribute to the one-stop shopping for boat service: diesel mechanics, an electronics specialist, a yacht refinisher, sign painter, and fiberglasser. Keys Boat Works can store vessels up to 60

Before venturing into the Great White Heron National Wildlife Refuge, secure a Public Use Regulations Map from the Lower Keys Chamber of Commerce, MM 31 Oceanside, Big Pine Key, (305) 872-2411. Obey no-entry, no-motor, and idle-speed zones.

If you see a red-and-white diver-down flag displayed while you are boating, stay at least 100 feet away. Divers or snorkelers are in these waters. Motoring between 100 feet and 300 feet from a diver-down flag must be at idle speed.

feet, either in or out of the water. The facility has a capacity for 180 boats.

Marathon Marina
MM 47.5 Oceanside, 1021 11th Street, Marathon
(305) 743-6575

This full-service boatyard offers the option of transient dockage at one of its 80 slips (dockage up to 110-foot length, 11-foot draft). You'll find fresh water, laundry, showers, bathroom facilities, and both 30- and 50-amp power. A ship's store is on the premises. The yard maintains a 50-ton travel lift and dry storage for up to 130 boats with 24-hour security. The Marathon Marina offers boat cleaning and detailing, preventive maintenance, bottom sanding and painting, woodwork, plumbing and electrical services, fiberglass and epoxy work, and mechanics' services. The first marina on the Boot Key Channel (Marker No. 9), Marathon Marina maintains an easily accessible fuel dock.

Turn Key Marine
MM 61 Oceanside, Duck Key
(305) 289-0161

MM 47.5 Bayside, Marathon
(305) 743-2502
www.turnkey.com

Turn Key Marine is a sales and service dealer for Yamaha and Mercury outboard engines, and Cobia and Action Craft boats. At the marathon site, a 12-ton boat lift facilitates vessel storage, both inside and outside. Bottom painting is also available here.

LOWER KEYS

Skeeter's Marine
MM 30.5 Bayside, Big Pine Key
(305) 872-9040, (800) 771-2628
www.skeetersmarine.com

Skeeter's sells new boats manufactured by SeaStrike, Stamas, Shamrock, Rampage, and Talon Flats Boats. Full engine services are available here as well as mobile marine service to your boat. Skeeter's is a dealer for Mercury, Yamaha, and Yanmer engines. Hauling, dry storage, and bottom painting are also available. Skeeters has added a second location, MM 90.1 Bayside, which sells Stamas yachts and Shamrock boats.

Keys Sea Center
MM 29.5 Oceanside, Big Pine Key
(305) 872-2244

Keys Sea Center carries new ProLines and Angler and services Johnson and Evinrude engines. Bottom painting and limited boat hauling are available. The facility carries 93 octane fuel and maintains a complete marine store with parts and accessories.

KEY WEST

Andrew's Propeller Service
5600 3rd Avenue, Stock Island
(305) 296-8887

Need a propeller for your boat? Come to Andrew's to find a large selection of new and rebuilt aluminum and bronze propellers—up to 64 inches in diameter. Andrew's also specializes in expert propeller repairs and shaft straightening.

Garrison Bight Marina
Garrison Bight Causeway
711 Eisenhower Drive, Key West
(305) 294-3093, (305) 294-5780
www.garrisonbightmarina.net

This full-service marina offers both long- and short-term dry or in-water storage. Unleaded fuel may be purchased here, too. Garrison Bight Marina also rents powerboats (15 to 22 feet) by the hour, half day, full day, or full week. Garrison Bight Marina is a sales and service dealer for Yamaha, Johnson, and Evinrude engines.

Murray Marine
MM 5, Stock Island
(305) 296-0364,
(305) 296-9555 (service)

Stop here to buy a boat, dock it, fuel it, fix it, store it, buy stuff for it, and put it in the water. Offering a full-service marina, storage, fuel, a service department, engine sales, boat sales, a ramp, and a convenience store, Murray Marine defies easy categorization. This facility is an authorized dealer for Wellcraft, Bayliner, Robalo, and Action Craft skiffs, as well as being a Johnson and Mercury Outboards dealer.

Oceanside Marina
5950 Peninsula Avenue, Stock Island
(305) 294-4676
www.oceansidemarina.com

Oceanside Marina is a kind of one-stop storage and service facility for boaters. Outside dry storage and inside storage is available. Oceanside sells fuel and has a mechanic on staff, a fully stocked tackle shop, a pump-out facility, and a bathhouse.

Prop-Tec
MM 5 Oceanside, Stock Island
(305) 292-0012

The owners of Prop-Tec go by the creed of "boats need to be on the water, not out of the water." A lot of boat owners know that if you shear a prop or damage it by striking something, you could be landlocked for weeks. Now at Prop-Tec, you can be back on the high seas in a few days. They do all the work themselves on Stock Island and do not send the repairs to the mainland. You can call them and they will send a driver out to the marina to pick up the damaged prop and bring it back to you, sometimes in only a matter of hours. Prop-Tec can also handle shafts, struts, and rudders. They plan on keeping you fishing!

Powerboat Rentals

The following rental facilities offer U.S. Coast Guard-approved, safety-equipped vessels complete with VHF marine radios. Rental boat sizes vary from 15 to 27 feet, in a number of configurations: center consoles, bowriders, cuddy cabins, and pontoon boats. The boats feature options such as compasses, depth finders, Bimini or T-tops, dry storage, swim ladders, and dive platforms. You can rent a powerboat for either a half day or full day. Call the establishments to inquire about specific boats offered, their features, and prices. (Prices are usually quoted without tax or gasoline.)

Purchase the nautical chart you need (see the Aids to Navigation section in this chapter) and bring it with you to the boat rental facility of your choice. Most facilities will provide you with an operational briefing and a nautical chart review before you set off. Some of these facilities require that you remain within a specific locale at all times; others base this decision on weather conditions.

UPPER KEYS

Robbie's Boat Rentals & Charters
MM 77.5 Bayside, Islamorada
(305) 664-9814, (877) 664-8498
www.robbies.com

One of the Florida Keys' more interesting boat rental facilities, Robbie's is behind the Hungry Tarpon Restaurant. Visitors come to Robbie's just to feed the many tarpon that lurk close to shore (see the Kidstuff chapter). Boat rentals, too, are popular, since Robbie's is only half a mile from historic Indian Key (see the Attractions chapter). Robbie's rents boats from 14 feet to 27 feet in length.

Caloosa Cove Boat Rental
MM 73.5 Oceanside, Islamorada
(305) 664-4455
Caloosa Cove rents 16-foot and 18-foot powerboats.

KEY WEST

Garrison Bight Marina and Boat Rental
711 Eisenhower Drive (corner of Palm Avenue and Eisenhower Drive)
(305) 294-3093
www.garrisonbightmarina.net
Open seven days a week, Garrison Bight Marina and Boat Rental offers a modern fleet of boats ranging from 15 to 22 feet. They rent by the hour, half day, or full day; weekly charters with guides are also available. You can rent diving equipment here too as well as fish finders and GPS for your boat. Happy boating!

Key West Boat Rentals
617 Front Street
(305) 294-2628, (888) 288-8395
You can rent Wahoos and Wellcrafts of 20 to 26 feet, as well as Jet Boats and Jet Skis. Navigational charts are provided and reviewed, along with an overview of local waters and suggestions (based on weather conditions) of directions to take and places to see. A questionnaire and verbal review ensure that boaters are experienced. Jet Ski tours are also available.

Sailing

With an abundance of protected anchorages, harbors, and marinas and warm tropical waters, the Florida Keys are often described by sailors as the "American Caribbean." Our offshore barrier reef provides protection from swells. Our bayside is so sheltered that many skippers with low-draft boats (typically catamarans or small, monohull sailboats) can trim up their sails and guide their crafts through the Intracoastal Waterway. Catamarans and monohulls with drafts of 4 or 5 feet fare best along the sometimes shallow Intracoastal; monohulls with 6-foot drafts have difficulty getting out of bayside marinas. These boats may also run aground here. Most oceanside marinas and harbors typically run deep enough to accommodate virtually any type of sailboat (see the Cruising chapter).

Within the Florida Keys, local sailing clubs organize their own informal races. Sailing in the Florida Keys can include cruising, limited bareboat charters, and a combination of snorkeling, fishing, diving, or gunkholing. Many head out simply to enjoy the sail. In order to sail the diverse waters of the Florida Keys, however, boaters must know a rig from a right-of-way.

SAILING COURSES

Several facilities throughout our islands offer sailing courses for beginner through advanced levels, along with bareboat certification and brush-up sessions. Prices vary greatly depending upon the duration and complexity of the courses and the number of people participating. Be sure to ask about all your options when you call to book your instruction.

International Sailing Center
MM 104.3 Bayside, Rick's Place, Key Largo
(305) 451-3287
www.catsailor.com/isc.html
From basic sailing instruction through advançed race training, International Sailing Center shares their many years of expertise with Keys sailors and visitors from throughout the country. Instruction commences on small monohulls and catamarans. International Sailing Center is affiliated with the American Sailing Association and the U.S. Sailing Association. The center offers a full-day course for one to two people with boat and instructor or a two-and-a-half day certification course, which includes instructional material, boat, instructor, and certification.

Offshore Sailing School
MM 61 Oceanside at Hawk's Cay Resort, Duck Key
(305) 743-7000, (888) 454-8002
www.offshore-sailing.com

Earn your U.S. sailing certification aboard a Colgate-26 with a Learn to Sail course from Offshore Sailing School. The Offshore Sailing School, which has nine locations across the United States, is operated by Olympic and America's Cup sailor Steve Colgate and his wife, Doris. Colgate designed the vessel upon which you will learn to sail. (In 1999 this vessel design was chosen as the official U.S. Naval Academy training boat.)

Learn to Sail courses are offered at Hawk's Cay Resort from Wednesday through Sunday. You'll have classroom instruction in the mornings and practice your skills on the water in the afternoons. The Learn to Sail course is the prelude to any advanced sailing courses.

Offshore Sailing School also offers a Liveaboard Cruise, where you can earn your cruising certification. Here, aboard a Hunter 460 with four private cabins, four students go on a six-day cruise to Key West and back, anchoring each night. You'll have drills and instruction daily, receiving hands-on experience in engine mechanics, advanced anchoring techniques, docking, meal preparation, going aground, radio skills, weather safety procedures, navigation, dinghy safety, and yacht handling. Your week of intensive learning culminates when you drop off your instructor and head out on your own for a 24-hour mini-cruise. The Liveaboard program runs from Sunday through Saturday. The cost includes hotel accommodations at Hawk's Cay Resort for one night, the week's instruction, and all meals and beverages except two dinners (no alcoholic beverages provided). You must have basic sailing experience to participate.

If you haven't sailed before and want to do the Liveaboard Cruise, you can sign up for the Fast Track to Cruising class. This 10-day experience includes a three-day Learn to Sail course, immediately followed by the Liveaboard experience. Fast Track runs from Friday through the following Saturday. Offshore Sailing School also offers a three-hour introduction to sailing course on the Colgate-26.

There's no need for you to own or charter a yacht. Sailshare can make your dream of being aboard a yacht come true for less. Log on to www.sailshare.com.

Florida Keys Sailing
Lighthouse Cay Club Resort and Marina
MM 50 Oceanside, 19 Sombrero Boulevard, Marathon
(305) 289-9519
www.lighthousecayclub.com

You'll find a wide variety of sailing operations at Florida Keys Sailing, located at Lighthouse Cay Club Resort. The sailing school offers everything from half-day and full-day day-sailing classes to advanced bareboat sailing courses, and almost everything in between.

The basic introductory three-day, Learn-to-Sail keelboat course is designed to provide the new sailor with a solid foundation. In the basic cruising course, students learn to responsibly skipper and crew an auxiliary-powered cruising sailboat within sight of land in moderate wind and sea conditions. Bareboat cruising is the advanced cruising course.

Racing clinics aboard J/24 sloops are offered on short windward-leeward courses. Students learn the techniques of starting, luffing, positioning on the racecourse, covering an opponent to win, and defending position.

Bareboat rentals also are available. Boats include a 14-foot Day Sailer, J/24 Race Ready, Irwin 34 Basic Cruiser, and a Catalina 30-foot Keys Cruiser.

BAREBOAT CHARTERS

If you already know how to sail or you prefer to explore our waters on your own, the Florida Keys also offers captained and bareboat charters for anywhere from two hours to several weeks. Prices vary depending upon the size of the vessel and the length of the bareboat excursion.

Treasure Harbor Marine Inc.
MM 86.5 Oceanside
200 Treasure Harbor Drive, Islamorada
(305) 852-2458, (800) 352-2628
www.treasureharbor.com
Treasure Harbor maintains a fleet of 12 sloops and ketch rigs ranging in size from 19 to 41 feet by Cape Dory, Watkins, Hunter, and Morgan. Skilled sailors can charter any one of these boats on their own, and written and verbal "exams" will test your sailing experience. Professional captains will provide nautical charts, overviews of Florida Keys waters, and suggestions of places to visit from John Pennekamp and the Everglades to Key West and the Bahamas. Skippers are available. A two-day minimum is required for all boats greater than 25 feet in length. Security deposits are required. Power trawler yachts are also available.

Treasure Harbor Marine also offers charters on an Antigua 37 catamaran or a 47-foot Marine Trader, which must be rented with an accompanying captain. Advance reservations for all vessels are suggested.

Southernmost Sailing
Oceanside Marina, 5950 Maloney Avenue, Stock Island
(305) 293-1883
www.southernmostsailing.com
Southernmost Sailing maintains a fleet of charter catamarans and monohull sailboats, including Hunter, Ticon, Jeanneau, Gemini, PDQ, Tobago and J/24. They range in size from 24 to 42 feet. Qualified sailing captains are permitted to sail virtually anywhere except Cuba, including Shark River, Florida's west coast, the Marquesas, and the Dry Tortugas. A charter-boat captain is available at an additional cost.

If boats are not out on a multiday charter, customers may rent them for a per-diem cost or charter them with captain for the additional fee. All boats are equipped for cruising and have auxiliary engines that reduce fuel consumption.

Reservations are recommended. In the off-season you probably won't have any trouble securing a boat as little as one week out. However, for high-season sailing, make your reservations at least three to six months in advance.

SAILING CLUBS AND REGATTAS

Avid sailors throughout our islands have formed sailing clubs, which sponsor casual regattas. These are not your upscale yacht clubs, but membership does have its privileges—discounted race entry fees and dinners, and the opportunity to meet individuals who share your interests.

Upper Keys Sailing Club
MM 100 Bayside, 100 Ocean Bay Drive, Key Largo
(305) 451-9972
Established in 1973, the Upper Keys Sailing Club is based in a club-owned house on the bay and comprises Upper Keys residents of all ages. Races on Buttonwood Bay are held on a regular basis. Spectators watch from clubhouse grounds. Two offshore races take place over a two-week period.

As a community service, members provide free two-day sailing seminars four times a year. Seminars combine two hours of classroom instruction with extensive time on the water aboard the club's 19-foot Flying Scots. Boaters with Sunfish and Hobie Cats are welcome. Membership requires a onetime initiation fee and annual dues.

Key West Sailing Club
Sailboat Lane, off Palm Avenue
Garrison Bight Causeway, Key West
(305) 292-5993
www.keywestsailingclub.org
Key West Sailing Club is a private organization open to anyone for membership. The club itself is located at the base of the Garrison Bight Bridge. The club has four Sunfish boats and a Hobie Cat, as well as four Optimists, two lasers, a Snipe, an American Day Sailer, and a Cape Dory. In addition, a sizable fleet of privately owned JY15s is available for members to use on race days. The club sponsors monthly offshore races for boats 20 feet and larger; call for more information. During daylight saving time, small boat (20 feet or less) races are held every Wednesday at 6:00 P.M. Group and private instruction is available for both adults and juniors (younger than age 18). Dates and times of courses change seasonally; call for details.

Membership requires a onetime initiation fee and annual dues. The membership year begins in January, but dues are prorated so anyone who joins later doesn't pay for a full year. A membership entitles members to use club facilities seven days a week between 6:00 A.M. and midnight. Membership also grants possible dockage in a wet or dry slip; rates are based on boat length. Information on courses, boat races, and membership is available on the club's information line listed above.

Marathon Sailing Club
(305) 743-4917
The Marathon Sailing Club, a young, informal group, meets the second Wednesday of each month. Typically the club holds monthly regattas on courses around Marathon. The club's three major regattas each year attract sailors from across the Keys: Marathon to Key West; a two-day Sombrero Cup race; and the bay-to-ocean race, a course running bayside from Marathon to Channel Five and then back oceanside. A Lady Skipper's trophy puts only women at the helm. Membership requires annual dues. Call Bruce Palmenberg for meeting locations and more information.

The Florida Circumnavigational Saltwater Paddling Trail was inaugurated in the Florida Keys in 2006. The 26 segments allow kayakers to explore waters from Big Lagoon State Park, south of Pensacola, around the Keys, to Fort Clinch State Park, north of Jacksonville—with a kayak support network, recommended campsites and motel stays. For more information, visit www.dep.state.fl.us/gwt/paddling/saltwater.htm

SAILMAKERS

Sail lofts throughout our islands will repair or replace your tattered sails; some even have on-staff riggers. You can satisfy your hardware and electrical needs as well.

Upper Keys

Calvert Sails
MM 81.5 Oceanside, 200 Industrial Drive, Islamorada
(305) 664-8056, (866) 664-8056
www.calvertsails.com
You can count on Calvert Sails for fast repairs for any size of sailboat. Calvert offers sails for performance boats and cruisers and specializes in multihull boats. Custom hardware supplies and services also are provided. The decades-old business, which began as a small, two-man operation of hand-designing and sewing sails, has since evolved into a state-of-the-art business that uses computers in design and manufacture.

Middle Keys

Abaco Sails
MM 53 Oceanside, Marathon
(305) 743-0337

BUI stands for "boating under the influence." In the state of Florida, BUI penalties include fines of up to $2,500, imprisonment of up to one year, nonpaid public service work, and mandatory substance abuse counseling. If a drunken operator causes serious bodily injury or kills another person, the penalties increase.

As long as your boat has a mast, Abaco can accommodate it. Sails here are made to order. A rigger on-premises handles all wiring needs, and the facility carries mast and used boat hardware.

Lower Keys

A T B Canvas Designs
MM 33 Bayside, Big Pine Key
(305) 872-1500

The nice folks here are ready to take your canvas order. They specialize in custom fabrication for powerboats. A T B takes great pride in making seat covers, Bimini tops, and anything in between for your boat.

Key West

Geslin Sailmakers
201 William Street, The Loft, Key West
(305) 294-5854

Although primarily occupied with repairs on boat sails, awnings, and Biminis, this business will also repair "anything you can think of that has to do with boats and needles and thread." You can order a new sail here, and although the sail will be made outside the country (because it's cheaper), the measurements, weight, and material requests will be taken here. Geslin Sailmakers is located at Key West Seaport.

Meloy Sails
6000 Peninsula Avenue, at Peninsular Marina, Stock Island
(305) 296-4351

Offering full-service work on sails and marine canvas, Meloy Sails will repair damaged sails or make new ones according to your specifications. Meloy is a Doyle Sailmakers affiliate.

Royal Canvas Connection
5950 Peninsula Avenue, Stock Island
(305) 295-0944

Royal Canvas Connection operates out of a 2,000-square-foot loft at Oceanside Marina and has a fully equipped mobile van that services the Lower Keys. Royal Canvas specializes in custom boat canvas, cushions, upholstery, and sail repairs. The folks here also design stainless-steel and aluminum framework for Bimini tops, dodgers, and spray hoods, and have even been known to stitch up a tent or two for Renaissance festivals and awnings for homes and businesses. If it's anything to do with canvas, they'll make it.

Houseboat Rentals

Florida Keys houseboats provide all the comforts of home combined with a camp-like experience. Whether you seek a weekend excursion or a gently rocking place to spend your vacation, these rentals may very well float your boat.

Houseboat Vacations of the Florida Keys
MM 85.9 Bayside, Islamorada
(305) 664-4009
www.thefloridakeys.com/houseboats

Houseboat Vacations of the Florida Keys offers live-aboard vessels that range from two 42-foot-long catamarans that sleep six or eight adults to a 44-foot-long houseboat that accommodates eight. You must have some boating experience to rent one of these floating homes. Boaters must venture no farther than 8 miles offshore along 25 miles of surrounding coastline in Florida Bay. You may not take the houseboats into the ocean. Each houseboat offers a full galley and air-conditioning and features a gas grill on deck. There is a three-day minimum; weekly rentals are available. Call for current pricing.

Everglades National Park Houseboat Rentals
Flamingo Marina
(239) 695-3101; (800) 600-3813

You can explore the uninhabited Wilderness Waterway and Whitewater Bay in Everglades National Park aboard a 40-foot pontoon houseboat rented from the park concessionaire (four available). The aluminum pontoon boats, with a 100-hp outboard and 12-volt electrical system, reach a top speed of 6 knots. The boats are not air-conditioned and have no observation deck but offer spacious sleeping quarters, easily accommodating six adults. They are equipped with propane stove/ovens and refrigerator/freezers, charcoal grills, full heads with shower, and 120 gallons of fresh water.

Rental prices include propane, linens, cookware, flatware, dishes, safety equipment, and charts. Actual fuel consumed is an additional charge. The winter season is most popular because it is most apt to be insect-free. Call up to a year in advance to secure the houseboat of your choice for desired excursion dates.

CRUISING

Put on that string bikini. Throw your necktie in the Dumpster. And don't you dare bring your shoes. You are cruising the Florida Keys, and you must obey the dress code.

Regarded as America's out-islands by seasoned cruisers of motor and sailing yachts, the Florida Keys can justifiably boast about the sheltered harbors and easily navigated waters enveloping the serpentine stretch. Our waters are well marked; our charts, up to date; and the U.S. Coast Guard keeps channels dredged to the proper depth. The Atlantic's Hawk Channel runs along the oceanside of the Keys, protected by the only coral reef in the continental United States. The Intracoastal Waterway—called the Big Ditch in the North's inland waters—cuts through the causeway from the mainland at Jewfish Creek and then parallels the Keys through Florida Bay and the Gulf of Mexico. Keys' waters are most accessible to boats with drafts of up to 4½ feet, but you can cruise the Keys with 5½- to 6-foot drafts if you're careful.

If you covet first-class creature comforts, put into one of our comprehensive marinas and enjoy the perks of staying at a luxury resort. Do you relish seclusion? Anchor out on the leeward side of a remote, uninhabited key. Or take the best of both worlds and plan a combination of the two.

i

Never anchor on a reef. Your anchor will destroy the living coral. Drop anchor only in sandy areas. A sandy sea bottom appears white. Use mooring buoys wherever offered.

To help you plan your Keys cruising adventure, we guide you on a tour of our preeminent marinas and little-known anchoring-out destinations (in descending order from the Upper to Lower Keys). Be sure to read our Key West and Beyond section, where the junket continues.

THE FLORIDA KEYS

Marinas

All marinas listed in this chapter take transient boaters, but we suggest you make reservations at least a month in advance during the popular winter season from December through March. You may assume unless otherwise stated that all our recommended marinas supply hookups for both 30-amp and 50-amp service as well as fresh water. You'll find that provisioning is easy along the 120-mile stretch of the Florida Keys. Most marinas have ship's stores or are within walking distance of a convenience market. The occasional exception is noted.

The marinas keep an active list of expert marine mechanics who are generally on call to handle any repair needs that might develop during your cruise. We highlight fuel dock facilities and availability of laundry, showers, and restrooms. We also point out restaurants and the hot spots for partying while ashore.

There are no restrictions against bringing children and pets unless specifically noted. Keep your pet on your vessel or on a leash at all times.

Dockmasters monitor VHF channel 16, but they will ask you to switch channels once you've established contact. They will give you detailed directions to the marinas.

Marina Del Mar
MM 100 Oceanside, 527 Caribbean Drive, Key Largo
(305) 451-4107, (800) 451-3483
www.marinadelmarkeylargo.com
Plan ahead if you want to stay at one of the 137 slips at Marina Del Mar marina, which lies within the underwater boundaries of John Pennekamp Coral Reef State Park and the Key Largo National Marine Sanctuary. All but a select few are usually booked far in advance from January through March, so plan ahead. The slips will accommodate vessels with a 6-foot draft (mean low tide) and up to 70 feet in length, but depth at the mouth of the channel drops drastically at low tide, to about 4½ feet, so exercise caution. A short walk to the Overseas Highway will satisfy provisioning requirements. Laundry, shower, and restroom facilities are provided on the premises. Marina rates do not include water and electricity; a minimum daily charge will be levied. Marina Del Mar Resort (see the Accommodations chapter) has tennis courts, a swimming pool, and a hot tub for your use. Gorge yourself at the hotel's continental breakfast for a nominal charge. And don't miss Coconuts, a popular restaurant and percolating nightspot.

Marina Del Mar is accessed via Hawk Channel, Marker Red No. 2.

Watermark Marina of Snake Creek
MM 85.4 Oceanside, Islamorada
(305) 664-3380, (888) 232-6287
www.watermarkmarina.com
Fishing and family fun in the sport-fishing capital of the world is what Watermark Marina of Snake Creek has created. With a new face-lift in 2006, this marina offers a first-class facility with wet slips, dry boat storage, ship's store, barbecue areas, fish-cleaning stations, and, to top it all off, breathtaking views! An interesting eco-friendly walkway will eventually be completed; it will "snake" through mangrove wetlands, allowing the visitor an uninterrupted view of the beautiful Florida Keys.

Watermark Marina of Islamorada
MM 80.5 Bayside, Islamorada
(305) 664-8884, (888) 232-6287
www.watermarkmarina.com
Facing Florida Bay, the location of Watermark Marina of Islamorada provides clear passage into the flats and bay of the Florida Keys, Everglades National Park, and the Atlantic Ocean. If you are water-oriented to fishing, kayaking, or just pure enjoyment, then this marina is for you. Premiering late in 2006 will be the Watermark Fishing Club. This feature will be just one of the many new additions this company plans for this desirable marina.

Plantation Yacht Harbor Marina
MM 87 Bayside, Islamorada
(305) 852-2381
You can grab a slip close to the Keys' fabled backcountry at the bayside Plantation Yacht Harbor, a municipal marina located at Islamorada Founder's Park (see the Recreation chapter). This 88-slip marina can accommodate vessels up to 60 feet in length, drawing 5 feet. Mobile marine mechanics are on call to service needy vessels, and a fuel dock supplies both diesel fuel and gasoline. Plantation Yacht Harbor does not have a ship's store, but a 1-mile walk up the Overseas Highway will put you at a convenience store. You may use the on-site laundry, showers, and restroom facilities. Tennis courts, a swimming pool, a small beach, skate park,

---

i

Due to the city of Key West's bay-bottom lease, cruise ships may only dock at Mallory Square Pier 12 times a year during sunset. The ships must either moor elsewhere the rest of the year or leave at least one hour before sunset so as not to block the view!

> *Contact the U.S. Coast Guard in the event of life-threatening emergencies such as an accident at sea, or to report a drowning or onboard fire. The Coast Guard monitors VHF channel 16 at all times. From a cell phone dial *CG.*

playground, dog park, and sports field await your pleasure.

Plantation Yacht Harbor Marina is accessed via the Intracoastal Waterway, between Markers No. 78 and No. 78A, or via Snake Creek from the Atlantic.

Hawk's Cay Marina
MM 61 Oceanside, Duck Key
(305) 743-7000, (800) 432-2242
www.hawkscay.com

Probably the best all-around marina in the Keys, Hawk's Cay offers a totally protected boat basin and all the amenities of its fine resort hotel (see our Accommodations and Restaurants chapters). Dock your boat at one of the 53 full-service marina slips (5-foot draft), or if you come in a vessel less than 35 feet, you can dock it at one of 32 small-boat slips and stay at the hotel. These slips have no shore power, and you may not stay aboard your boat overnight. Rates will be the same as for the other transient slips, except there is no minimum.

Hawk's Cay maintains an extensive list of qualified marine mechanics in the area and has divers on call. The full-service ship's store sells everything, including groceries, fine wines, boating hardware, fishing tackle, clothing, and paperback books. It also offers video rentals. A full-service fuel dock pumps regular and premium gasoline and diesel fuel. Showers and restrooms are in the ship's store, and the marina is equipped with a pump-out station at the fuel dock. Laundry facilities are coin-operated. Cable television hookup is available at an extra fee.

Hawk's Cay Marina is accessed via Hawk Channel at Marker No. 44 when traveling down the Keys or at Marker No. 45 when approaching from Key West.

Dolphin Marina
MM 28.5 Oceanside, Little Torch Key
(305) 872-2685, (800) 553-0308
www.dolphinmarina.net

Quiet Little Torch Key is the safe harbor for this delightful marina. Dolphin Marina offers not only boat rentals and dockage but also quaint lodging. The lodging quarters consist of small cottages, overlooking Newfound Harbor, and cozy apartments with one or two bedrooms. All offer refrigerators, coffeemakers, and cable TV. You do not have to enjoy fishing or water activities to stay here! Just minutes from luxurious Little Palm Island (see Accommodations chapter), this down-to-earth marina offers all you need for a day afloat on the open waters of the Atlantic. Dolphin Marina has a fleet of Angler boats that you can rent. Alternatively, you can venture out in your own vessel with an experienced fishing or diving guide. The marina and ship's store can stock you with all the supplies for your outing. Boat launching and trailer storage are available if you tow your own boat. Located at 24.39.95 north latitude and 81.23.28 west longitude.

Little Palm Island
MM 28.5 Oceanside, Little Torch Key
(305) 872-2524, (800) 343-8567
www.littlepalmisland.com

Arriving at Little Palm Island by sea, you will be certain you missed your tack and landed in Fiji, because this exquisite jewel is more reminiscent of the South Seas than South Florida. Little Palm Island, the westernmost of the Newfound Harbor Keys, lies 4 nautical miles due north from Looe Key Light. And while the average bank account strains at the tariffs charged for villa accommodations on the island (see the Accommodations chapter), staying at the marina is a real deal, even though it is the most expensive marina in

The Florida Marine Patrol

The Florida Marine Patrol (FMP) enforces state marine resources laws. They deal with violations such as environmental crime, exceeding fish and crawfish bag limits, and illegal dumping. The FMP also enforces boating safety laws, responding to reports of unsafe boating and wake violations as well as any perceived illegal activity on the water. You can reach the Florida Marine Patrol on a cellular telephone by dialing *FMP or on a regular telephone line at (800) DIAL FMP, (800) 342-5367. The Marine Patrol vessels occasionally monitor VHF channel 16, but your best bet is to contact it at one of the other numbers.

the Florida Keys. As marina guests you're invited to use all the recreational facilities: sailboards, day sailers, fishing gear, canoes, snorkeling gear, beach, lagoonal swimming pool, and the sauna.

Little Palm's marina, though small, maintains slips on Newfound Harbor for boats up to 120 feet in length, with a draft up to 6 feet. Smaller boats can be accommodated at 575 feet of dock space on a protected lagoon. The controlling depth coming into the harbor is 6 feet, but the dockmaster will help you navigate around the tides. The dockmaster monitors VHF channels 9 and 16 at all times. Dockhands are available to assist with lines. Hookup for one 50-amp service is included in dockage fees; additional connections depend upon availability. Boats docked at the T-dock enjoy 100-amp service.

Because you're staying on an out-island, offshore from the contiguous Keys and their more plentiful water supply, you will be allowed only one gallon of water per foot per day. However, the resort offers you use of guest showers and restrooms in the quarterdeck and a laundry facility during your stay, so this water conservation is not a hardship.

Little Palm Island's renowned gourmet restaurant welcomes you for breakfast, lunch, and dinner. You may choose to cook aboard your vessel, but be advised that you're prohibited from consuming your own food or beverages in island public areas. Children younger than age 16 are not permitted at Little Palm Island; nor are villa guests allowed to bring pets. Little Palm does accommodate pets of overnight marina guests, but you must keep them on a leash and walk them only in designated areas. In keeping with the tranquil ambience of the island, motorized personal watercraft also are banned. Discounts are offered to members of Boat US.

Little Palm Island is accessed via the Atlantic at the entrance to Newfound Harbor, Marker Red No. 2.

Anchoring Out

Fancy yourself more Robinson Crusoe than Aristotle Onassis? Then you'll discover that anchoring out in the pristine waters lacing the Florida Keys approaches nirvana. From the northernmost keys of Biscayne Bay to Loggerhead Key at the end of the line, remote havens remain unspoiled, many reachable only by boat. Ibis, white pelicans, and bald eagles winter among select out-islands, and whole condominiums of cormorants take over the scrub of tiny mangrove islets. Gulf waters simmer with snapper, redfish, lobster, and stone crabs. The Atlantic Ocean sparkles with the glory of the living coral reef beneath. So pack up and push off for an Insiders' bareboat cruise of the Florida Keys, from top to toe.

ELLIOTT KEY

On the eastern side of Biscayne Bay, the island of Elliott Key, which has the ranger station for Biscayne National Park, guards a complex ecosystem from the ocean's battering winds. Anchor on the leeward side of Elliott Key just off the pretty little beach north of Coon Point. This anchorage—good in northeast to east to southeast winds—is usually accessed via the Intracoastal Waterway.

A strong current rushes through the shallow channel between Sands Key and Elliott Key, and small-boat traffic is heavy on weekends. Although the fishing and diving here are first rate, take care. At the southern tip of Elliott Key, Caesar Creek—named for notorious pirate Black Caesar, who dipped in to stay out of sight in the 1600s—offers dicey passage to Hawk Channel for boats carefully clearing a 4-foot draft at high tide. The more forgiving Angelfish Creek, farther south at the north end of Key Largo, is the favored route from Biscayne Bay to the ocean in this wild and deserted area. Angelfish Creek is the Intracoastal Waterway's last outlet to the ocean until after Snake Creek Drawbridge for large boats or those heading for Hawk Channel.

Remember "red, right, return"—that granddaddy of navigational rules? Sometimes the concept of going and coming makes no sense at all. It may be helpful to recall that, when in the Intracoastal Waterway, return is toward Texas. Now which way is Texas? When in doubt, read your navigational charts thoroughly.

PUMPKIN KEY

Safe anchorage surrounds Pumpkin Key, making this island an ideal choice for winds coming from any direction. Be sure to test your anchorage, because Pumpkin Key's waters cover a grassy sea bottom. Nearby Angelfish Creek—filled with grouper, snapper, and angelfish—almost guarantees dinner. Scoot out the creek to take advantage of the diving at John Pennekamp Coral Reef State Park. Approachable from Hawk Channel or the Intracoastal, this area remains virginal even though it rests in the shadow of Key Largo.

BLACKWATER SOUND

As you anchor in the placid ebony waters of Blackwater Sound, the twinkling lights of Key Largo remind you that civilization is but a dinghy ride away. Anchor along the southeast shoreline of Blackwater Sound for a protected anchorage in east to southeast winds. The Cross Key Canal, which connects Blackwater Sound to Largo Sound, passes under a fixed bridge at the Overseas Highway in Key Largo. If your boat clears 14 feet safely, traverse the canal to dive or snorkel in John Pennekamp Coral Reef State Park.

TARPON BASIN

Enter Tarpon Basin through Dusenbury Creek or Grouper Creek. Both passages teem with snapper and grouper.

LARGO SOUND (JOHN PENNEKAMP CORAL REEF STATE PARK)

John Pennekamp Coral Reef State Park and the adjacent Key Largo National Marine Sanctuary encompass the ocean floor under Hawk Channel from Broad Creek to Molasses Reef. Exit the Intracoastal Waterway at Angelfish Creek and enter Hawk Channel to proceed to Largo Sound. Enter Largo Sound through South Sound Creek. Park staff supervise this anchorage, which is completely sheltered in any weather. Call on VHF channel 16 to reserve a mandatory mooring buoy in the southwest portion of the sound; anchoring is prohibited. A nominal fee for the moorings entitles boaters full use of park facilities and its pump-out station.

The reefs of John Pennekamp Coral Reef State Park shine brighter than others in the Keys. The bulk of Key Largo's landmass has inhibited development of the erosive channels that cut between the other Keys, preserving shallower waters. More sun filters through the shallow water, causing the coral to flourish. Much of this reef breaks the surface of the water during low tide.

BUTTERNUT KEY AND BOTTLE KEY

Don't worry. Those baby sharks you see in the waters surrounding Butternut Key won't hurt you. The skittish infants leave this nursery area when they reach 2 to 3 feet in length. Prevailing winds will determine anchorage sites near these islands, which offer good holding ground. On the Florida Bay side of Tavernier, Butternut Key and Bottle Key showcase voluminous birdlife. Roseate spoonbills breed on Bottle Key, feeding upon the tiny killifish of the flats. A pond on the island attracts mallard ducks in the winter. And amid this gunkholers' paradise, the elusive bald eagle rewards the patient observer with a fleeting appearance.

COTTON KEY

Approach Cotton Key from the Intracoastal Waterway. This anchorage, protected from north to southeast winds, offers the best nightlife in the Keys north of Key West. Take your dinghy around the entire island of Upper Matecumbe and the community of Islamorada. Catch the action at Papa Joe's, the Lorelei, or Atlantic's Edge at Cheeca Lodge (see the Restaurants chapter). Check out the fishing charters at Bud n' Mary's Marina (see the Fishing chapter). Stop in at the Islamorada Fish Company and take ready-to-eat stone crabs back to your boat for a private sunset celebration (see the Seafood Markets and Specialty Foods chapter). Dinghy through Whale Harbor Channel to the Islamorada Sand Bar, which at low tide becomes an island beach. And, if you'd just like to commune with nature, the forested northeast section of Upper Matecumbe Key hosts a rookery for good bird-watching. *NOTE:* There is a no-motor zone on the tidal flat.

LIGNUMVITAE KEY

Government-owned Lignumvitae Key stands among the tallest of the Keys, at 17 to 18 feet above sea level. A virgin hammock sprinkled with lignum vitae trees recreates the feeling of the Keys of yesteryear, before mahogany forests were cut and sold to Bahamian shipbuilders. From 1919 to 1953 the Matheson family, of chemical company notoriety, owned the island, where they built a large home and extensive gardens of rare plantings.

Hug the northwest side of the island for good anchorage in east to southeast winds. Dinghy to the Lignumvitae Key dock for guided tours conducted by the state park service. You can also dinghy through Indian Key Channel to historic Indian Key (see the Attractions chapter). Nearby Shell Key almost disappears at high tide, so exercise caution. Pods of playful dolphins romp in Lignumvitae Basin, and a sighting of lumbering sea turtles is not unusual. But be sure to bait a hook—fishing is prolific.

MATECUMBE BIGHT

If winds are not good for anchoring near Lignumvitae, Matecumbe Bight provides good holding ground, except in a north wind. Two miles south, Channel Five—east of Long Key—offers a good crossover between Florida Bay and Hawk Channel for large sailboats. Strong currents run in the channel beneath the bridge, which is a fixed span with a 65-foot overhead clearance.

Traveling the Intracoastal Waterway

Jewfish Creek Drawbridge (11-foot clearance when closed) marks the point where the causeway of the 18-mile stretch from Florida City makes landfall on Key Largo. When traveling the Intracoastal Waterway, be aware that the bridge opens only on the hour and on the half hour Thursday through Sunday and on federal holidays. During the week you may seek passage on demand. A 1- to 2-knot current courses through Jewfish Creek. Note the direction to allow plenty of time if you have to wait for the bridge to open. Sailors take note: A mast taller than 80 feet will not be able to pass beneath cables near the bridge.

LONG KEY BIGHT

Anchor in Long Key Bight, which is accessed via Hawk Channel oceanside or through Channel Five from the Intracoastal Waterway. Bordering Long Key State Park—a 300-acre wilderness area with a good campground, tables, and grills—the Bight is protected yet open. Dinghy through Zane Grey Creek for good gunkholing. Legendary author Zane Grey angled at the former Long Key Fishing Club during the days of Flagler's Railroad. Beachcomb for washed-up treasure on the southeast shores of Long Key.

BOOT KEY HARBOR

Boot Key Harbor in Marathon serves as a good, safe port in a bad blow, but, crowded with live-aboards, it is a bit like anchoring out in Times Square. Enter this fully protected harbor from Sister's Creek or at the western entrance near the beginning of the Seven Mile Bridge.

NOTE: Moser Channel goes under the hump of the Seven Mile Bridge, creating a 65-foot clearance. The draw-span of the old bridge has been removed, but the rest remains. A portion on the Marathon end now functions as the driveway to Pigeon Key (see the Attractions chapter). A stretch on the Bahia Honda end is maintained for bridge fishing and is referred to locally as the "longest fishing pier in the world." The Moser Channel and the Bahia Honda Channel (with 20-foot clearance) are the last crossover spots in the Keys. You must decide at Marathon if you will travel the Atlantic route or via the Gulf to Key West. If you need fuel, note that the marina at Sunshine Key is the last bayside marina until Key West.

BIG SPANISH CHANNEL AREA

Leave all traces of civilization behind and head out the Big Spanish Channel toward the out-islands. Proceed with care, for this remote sprinkling of tiny keys is part of the Great White Heron National Wildlife Refuge. Before venturing into this backcountry area, secure a Public Use Regulations Map from the Lower Keys Chamber of Commerce (305-872-2411, 800-872- 3722). Obey no-entry, no-motor, and idle-speed zones. Get your Florida bird guide out of the cabin and count the species. Then treat yourself to a swim with the dolphins, which travel in pods throughout these Gulf waters.

LITTLE SPANISH KEY

The western side of Little Spanish Key provides the best protection from northeast to southeast winds. Explore the surrounding clear waters by dinghy where the endangered green turtles, which weigh between 150 and 450 pounds, have been spotted feeding on seagrass. Catch your limit in snapper and share your bounty with the friendly pelicans.

NEWFOUND HARBOR

Newfound Harbor—formed by the Newfound Harbor Keys and the southern extension of Big Pine Key—stars as the premier oceanside harbor between Marathon and Key West. Dinghy to exquisite Little Palm Island, the setting for the film *PT-109,* the story of John F. Kennedy's Pacific experience during World War II. Newfound Harbor lies within easy reach of Looe Key National Marine Sanctuary, a spur and groove coral reef ecosystem popular with divers and snorkelers.

KEY WEST AND BEYOND

Welcome to the ultimate cruising destination: Key West. Full of history and histrionics, this vibrant, intoxicating port pumps the adrenaline, pushes the envelope, and provides a rowdy good time for all. And when you signal a turn back into the slow lane again, dust off your charts and head out to the wild beyond of the Dry Tortugas, the end of the line.

Marinas

All of our suggested marinas take transient boaters, but the multiplicity of celebrated special events in Key West dictates that you prudently reserve a slip as far in advance as possible. You may assume unless otherwise stated that all our recommended marinas supply hookups for both 30-amp and 50-amp service as well as fresh water. Some marinas impose a minimum charge. Key West offers extensive self-provisioning facilities ranging from supermarkets to gourmet take-out shops (see the Seafood Markets and Specialty Foods chapter). The city also supports a variety of good marine mechanics, which the marina dockmasters will contact on your behalf should the need arise.

Contact the dockmaster on VHF channel 16 for directions and read your charts closely.

A&B Marina
700 Front Street
(305) 294-2535, (800) 223-8352
www.abmarina.com
A&B Marina is situated in the heart of Old Town, right in the middle of all the action. Most of its 50 transient slips will accommodate vessels with up to 7-foot drafts. A&B offers dockage for vessels up to 140 feet in length. Cable television hookup is included in dockage fees. A&B maintains a diesel fuel dock.

A $3.5 million renovation of the marina, completed in 2000, gave A&B quite a face-lift. They've added a convenience store, air-conditioned shower facilities, a laundry room, a 24-hour (10 months of the year) bar and grill, and the Commodore Waterfront Steakhouse and Alonzo's Oyster Bar. A&B Lobster House, upstairs, has been feeding hungry cruisers since 1947, and still welcomes one and all. And people-watching is great from the dockside bar.

A&B Marina is accessed from the Atlantic via the Main Ship Channel (S.E. Channel), at Markers Nos. 24 and 25. From the Gulf take the N.W. Channel to the Main Ship Channel.

The Galleon International Marina
619 Front Street
(305) 296-7711, (800) 544-3030
www.galleonresort.com
Cruisers love the Galleon, probably the most popular of Key West's marinas. The carbonated excitement of Duval Street pulsates only a few blocks away, but the ambience at the Galleon remains unhurried and genteel. The 91 dockage slips will accommodate vessels up to 140 feet, 9-foot drafts. One 50-amp service is included in the daily dockage rate, but you can secure another for an additional fee. Cable and

telephone hookups are available for a minimal charge. Fuel is available in Key West Bight or at Conch Harbor Marina.

The Galleon indulges you with all the amenities and then some: shower and restroom facilities, a laundry, pump-out station, deli, swimming pool, tiki bar, private beach, fitness center, sauna, patio, and picnic tables. And if that is not enough, book an afternoon of snorkeling at the on-premises dive shop or plan a fishing expedition with one of the charter boats at the dock. Rent a moped or bicycle and explore Key West, or just kick back and relax on the sundeck.

Pets are welcome in the marina but not on the adjoining resort property.

The Galleon is accessed via the Main Ship Channel at Marker No. 24.

Key West Bight Marina
Key West Historic Seaport,
201 William Street
(305) 296-3838
www.keywestcity.com/depts/port/kwb/index.html

Situated in the heart of the Key West Historic Seaport, Key West Bight Marina has 33 deepwater transient slips that will accommodate vessels up to 140 feet in length with a maximum draft of 12 feet. Dockage includes 30-, 50-, and 100-amp power; cable TV, water, and phone hookups; 24-hour security; a pump-out station; trash removal; ice; and bath, shower, and laundry facilities. Docking rates are the most reasonably priced in Key West. Key West Bight Marina is accessed by entering Key West waters via the N.W. Channel to the Main Ship Channel to Marker Red No. 4 from the Gulf of Mexico, or from the Atlantic via Hawk Channel to the Main Ship Channel to Marker Red No. 4.

The Westin Key West Resort and Marina
245 Front Street
(305) 292-4375
www.westin.com/keywest

The Westin Key West Resort and Marina offers transients all the perks of its lavish property: pool, hot tub, and weight room as well as Bistro 245 restaurant and Latitudes restaurant on Sunset Key. About one-quarter of the marina's dock space is available to transients. The south basin offers floating slips that accommodate vessels with 30-foot drafts; the north basin's 600 feet of rigid dock space handles craft with 15-foot drafts or less.

Make reservations up to six months in advance to dock at the Westin Key West Resort and Marina. Only 1 block off famed Duval Street, its location can't be beat and it fills up quickly. In addition to daily transient rates, a power fee is levied. Cable television hookup is included in the dockage fee, and the requisite laundry, shower, and restroom requirements are supplied on the premises. Fuel may be obtained half a mile up the channel at Key West Bight.

The Westin Key West Resort and Marina owns the private offshore Sunset Key. Guests of the hotel or marina may take a day trip to the island and enjoy its pristine beach, away from the fray of Key West.

The Westin Key West Marina is accessed via the Main Ship Channel at Marker Red No. 14 if coming from the south, or, from the north, via the N.W. Channel at Marker Green No. 17.

Oceanside Marina
5950 Peninsula Avenue, Stock Island
(305) 294-4676
www.oceansidemarina.com

This top-drawer marina, occupying a finger of Stock Island, offers a Key West alternative for peace and solitude, for it is tucked far away from the fray. Its slips will accommodate vessels up to 80 feet in length with 12-foot maximum drafts. Access to the marina is directly from Hawk Channel. Reservations are suggested 30 days in advance during the winter season. Gas- and diesel-qualified marine mechanics work on the premises. Oceanside provides all the essentials: gas and diesel fuel dock, ship's store and tackle shop, laundry, showers and restrooms, and free cable hookups. An additional charge is levied for telephone hookup. Your pet is welcome if kept on a leash.

Oceanside Marina is accessed via the Atlantic at the entrance to Safe Harbor Channel, Marker Red No. 2.

Anchoring Out

The highway may stop in Key West, but the path to adventure continues into the sunset. The Dry Tortugas, the brightest gems in the necklace, mark the real end of the line in the Florida Keys. Once you leave Key West Harbor, you join the ranks of the swashbucklers who have abandoned the safety of civilization to explore the vast unknown.

Be sure you know the range and capabilities of your craft, because only self-sufficient cruising vessels can make the 140-nautical-mile trek to the Dry Tortugas and back. There is no fuel, fresh water, provisioning, or facilities of any kind once you leave Key West. Unpredictable foul weather could keep you trapped at sea for days, so make sure you are fueled for 200 miles, and stock the larder for extenuating circumstances.

KEY WEST

If you want to anchor out in busy Key West Harbor, look for a spot west of Fleming Key in about 10 to 15 feet of water. You'll find less current, good holding ground, and less fishing-vessel traffic than around Wisteria Island. The municipal dinghy dock at the foot of Simonton Street is the only official place to land your dinghy, but you might want to arrange secured short-term dockage for your dinghy from one of the marina dockmasters.

BOCA GRANDE KEY

A string of shoals and keys snakes west from Key West, offering unparalleled diving and fishing opportunities. Beyond Man and Woman Keys—popular snorkeling spots—Boca Grande Key offers a good day anchorage on the northwestern side with a beautiful white-sand beach. The current is too swift to anchor overnight, but snorkel the small wreck visible just north of the island. Be alert to the constantly shifting shoals around the entrance channel. Note also that this island is a turtle nesting ground—all or parts of it are off-limits during specific times of the year, and fines are possible.

MARQUESAS KEYS

About 24 miles from Key West, a broken collar of low-lying, beach-belted islands forms the Marquesas Keys. If you pass Mooney Harbor Key on your way into the inner sanctum, watch for coral heads about 1,100 yards offshore. Prevailing winds will determine at which side to anchor, but you should be able to achieve a protected anchorage. Many a ship crashed on the coral heads in this area, leaving interesting wrecks, but check with the Coast Guard before you dive, because the U.S. Navy has been known to use the area west of the Marquesas as a bombing and strafing range. Explore the big rookery of frigatebirds or take aim with a little spearfishing. *NOTE:* A 300-foot no-motor zone is established around the three smallest islands, a 300-foot no-access buffer zone is established around one mangrove island, and an idle-speed-only/no-wake zone is established in the southwest tidal creek. This pit stop on the way to the Dry Tortugas rates as an end point in itself.

DRY TORTUGAS

Open water stretches like a hallucination from the Marquesas to our southernmost national park, the Dry Tortugas. Ponce de León named these islands the Tortugas—Spanish for "turtles"—in 1513, presumably because the waters teemed with sea turtles, which he consumed as fresh meat. Lack of fresh water rendered the islands dry.

The first sight of the massive brick fortress of Fort Jefferson, the colorful history of which began in 1846, is breathtaking (see the Attractions chapter). The best deep anchorage is usually directly in front of the entrance to the fort on the southeast side of Garden Key, but, depending upon the weather, you may want to check with the ranger first.

Unparalleled diving exists in these unsullied waters. Colors appear more brilliant because the waters are clearer than those bordering the inhabited Keys. The entire area is a no-take zone, so don't be alarmed if you spot a prehistoric-size lobster or jewfish. Be sure to snorkel the underwater nature trail. From your dinghy, watch for the nesting sooty and noddy terns in their Bush Key sanctuary (landing is forbidden).

LOGGERHEAD KEY

Just beyond Garden Key dozes Loggerhead Key, called the prettiest beach in the Keys by those in the know. A good day anchorage with a legion of interesting coral, this is literally the end of the line for the Florida Keys. Nothing but 900 miles of water lies between this point and the Mexican coast. Hope you remembered to fuel up in Key West!

FISHING

Angling in the Florida Keys approaches a religion to many. The very essence of the Keys is embodied in gleaming packages of skin and scales, for a day fishing the cerulean waters that lap our islands creates a sensory memory not quickly forgotten. Long after the last bait is cast, tales of captured prizes or the ones that got away evoke visions of the sun, the sea, and the smell of the salt air.

Anglers fish here with an intensity rarely seen anywhere else in the United States . . . the world, even. Eavesdrop on a conversation anywhere in the Keys, and someone will be talking about fishing. As you drive down the Overseas Highway and look out at our acres of shimmering waters, you will feel an overwhelming urge to join in the battle of power and wits—fish against angler—that makes the Keys so special.

The Florida Keys has more than 1,000 species of fish; most are edible, all are interesting. Six of them—bonefish, permit, tarpon, redfish, snook, and sailfish—have earned game-fish status, meaning they may not be sold. To pursue these and other species, you will need a saltwater fishing license (see the Fishing Licenses section in this chapter). You must obey catch and season restrictions and size limits. These regulations change often. Ask for an up-to-date listing when you purchase your fishing license.

The Florida Keys falls within the boundaries of the Florida Keys National Marine Sanctuary, created by the federal government in 1990 to protect the resources of our marine ecosystem. And while, for the most part, visitors freely swim, dive, snorkel, boat, fish, or recreate on our waters, some regulations took effect in July 1997 to guide these activities. Refer to our Boating chapter for information on these regulations before you venture into our waters. For a complete copy of the regulations and marine coordinates of the areas, contact the sanctuary office, (305) 743-2437, or check their Web site, www.fknms.nos.noaa.gov.

CATCH-AND-RELEASE ETHICS

Preserve our natural resources. "A fish is too valuable to be caught only once," the U.S. Department of Commerce, the National Oceanic and Atmospheric Administration, and the National Marine Fisheries Service maintain. We agree. The spirit behind the catch-and-release policy is to enjoy the hunt and the score, but take a photograph of the fish home with you, not the quarry itself. Taxidermists do not need the actual fish to prepare a mount for you; they only need the approximate measurements. Take home only those food fish you plan to eat.

To properly release a fish, keep the fish in the water and handle it very little whenever possible. Dislodge the hook quickly with a hookout tool, backing the hook out the opposite way it went in. If the hook can't be removed quickly, cut the leader close to the mouth. Hold the fish by the bottom jaw or lip—not the gills—with a wet hand or glove so that you don't damage its mucus or scales. Have your photo taken with the fish, then cradle the tired fish, rocking it back and forth in the water until it is able to swim away under its own power. This increases the oxygen flow through its gills, reviving the fish and thereby augmenting its chances for survival against a barracuda or shark.

WHERE TO FISH

To introduce you to our complex watery ecosystem and the species of fish dwelling therein, we have divided fishing destinations into four distinct sections: the flats, the backcountry, the bluewater, and the bridges.

The Flats

The continental shelf is nature's gift to the Florida Keys. Stretching from the shoreline like a layer of rippled fudge on a marble slab, it lingers for many shallow miles before plunging to the depths of the bluewater. In the Keys we rather reverently call this area the flats. Waters ranging from mere inches to several feet in depth cover most of the flats, but some areas completely surface during low tide, exposing themselves to the air and intense sunlight. Changing winds, tides, temperatures, and barometric pressure ensure that conditions in the flats fluctuate constantly.

An unenlightened observer might think the flats uninteresting, for most of this watery acreage is covered with dense turtle grass, shell-less sand, or muddy muck. But far from being a wasteland, the flats are the feeding grounds and nursery for a city of marine families whose members inspire dramatic tales of daring and conquest from every person who has ever baited a hook here.

The 4,000 square miles of flats—from Key Biscayne to Key West and beyond—yield a trio of prize gamefish—bonefish, permit, and tarpon—which, when caught in one day, we refer to as the Grand Slam. And keeping company in the same habitat are the bonus fish—barracuda and shark—that regularly accommodate anglers with exciting runs and fights. Fishing the flats is really a combination of angling and hunting, for you must first see and stalk the fish before you ever cast the waters. The hunt for bonefish, permit, and tarpon requires patience and unique angling skills, but most essentially, you must be at the right place at the right time.

We cannot even begin to teach you how to fish for these formidable fighters of the flats in this chapter. You should hire a professional guide, for which there is no substitute—at least while you are a novice. Guides know the local waters well and keep detailed records of where to find fish under every condition, saving you precious hours and money in the pursuit of your mission (see the Guides and Charters section of this chapter). But we will introduce you to the exciting species you will encounter on our flats, relate their personalities, tattle about their habits, and point you in the right direction so you can learn all you wish to know and share in the angling experience of a lifetime: fishing the flats in the Florida Keys.

First in the see-stalk-cast sequence so important in fishing the skinny waters of the flats is the visible interpretation of the watery hallucination under the surface. To see the fish of the flats, you must have polarized sunglasses to cut the sun's glare so you can concentrate on looking through your reflection on the top of the water, to the shallow bottom. Under the water, fish often look like bluish shadows, or they may appear as indistinct shadings that simply look different from the waters surrounding them.

Most waters of the flats in the Keys are fished from a shallow-draft skiff, or flatsboat, although you can wade out from shore in many areas if you prefer. Never motor onto a flat; the fish can hear the engine noise and spook easily. Use an electric trolling motor or, better yet, pole in, using a push pole. A push pole is a fiberglass or graphite dowel, 16 to 20 feet long with a V-crotch on one end, for traversing the soft bottom of the flats and a straight end on the other, for staking out.

i

Tune in to local radio stations for fishing forecasts and catch-of-the-day reports. For a list of local radio stations, refer to the Media chapter.

Using it requires body power and coordination and more than a little practice. A flatsboat has a raised poling platform that gives the poler or guide a height advantage to more readily distinguish the fish from its shadowy surroundings, in preparation for an accurate cast.

At the turn of the tide, the fish begin to move into the flats, grazing like sheep in a pasture. Guides know where the fish congregate during an incoming (flood) tide and an outgoing (ebb) tide. While it may prove dangerous for the fish to come up on the flats—they expose themselves to predators—the concentration of food is too enticing for them to resist. The fish prefer feeding during the low, incoming tide; the food is still easy to find, but they won't risk becoming stranded on the flats.

BONEFISH: PHANTOM OF THE FLATS

A sighting of the glistening forked tail of the Gray Ghost—alias of the famed bonefish (*Albula vulpes*) haunting our flats—has been known to elevate the blood pressure of even the most seasoned Keys angler to celestial heights. This much-respected, skittish silver bullet is considered the worthiest of all opponents, a wily, suspicious street fighter, here one moment, gone the next. The bonefish's superior eyesight, acute hearing, keen sense of smell, and boundless speed routinely befuddle anglers, some of whom dedicate their lives to thwarting the fish's Houdini-like escape attempts.

You can spot a bonefish three ways: tailing, mudding, or cruising. When the slender, silvery bonefish feeds, it looks like a washerwoman leaning over to get her laundry out of the basket—head down, bottom up. The fork of the tail will break the surface of the water—a tailing fish. The bonefish feeds into the current because its food source is delivered in the drift. As the fish puts its mouth down into the sand and silt, rooting around on the bottom of the flats, looking for shrimps, crabs, and other crustaceans, the water clouds up. This is called "making a mud." As the mudding bonefish continues feeding, the current takes the cloudy water away so it can see its prey once again. Bonefish require water temperatures of 70 degrees and higher for feeding on the flats.

Spotting a cruising fish takes some practice. Look for "nervous water." The bonefish pushes a head wake as it swims, which sometimes shows as an inconsistency on the surface of the water. On other occasions, a mere movement by the fish under water will cause the surface water to appear altered. Most of the time that the bonefish is cruising, however, it is swimming in deeper water; you will have to spot it. The back and sides of the bonefish are so silvery they act as a mirror. The fish swims right on the bottom of the flats in 8 or more inches of water. The sun shining through the water causes the bottom to reflect off the sides of the fish. So if you think you have seen a ripple of weeds, the image may actually be a bonefish.

The best bait for bonefishing is live shrimp. A guide with an experienced eye will put you on the fish by calling out directions like the hands of a clock. The bow of the boat will always be 12 o'clock. You will be instructed by the guide to look in a direction—for instance, 2 o'clock—and, at a specified distance, to spot the bonefish in preparation for a cast. The cast is the most crucial part of successfully hooking a bonefish. You should be able to cast 30 feet quickly and accurately. A cast that places the bait too close to the fish will spook it and cause the bonefish to dart away at breakneck speed. If the bait is cast too far away, the fish won't find it at all. The bait should land 2 to 3 feet in front of the fish and be allowed to drift to the ocean floor.

Many times the bonefish will smell the bait prior to seeing it because the fish is downcurrent of the bait and swimming into the current. The bonefish begins to dart back and forth and goes in circles, looking for the scented prey. Once the fish locates the source of the scent, it tends to suck in the bait. You, the angler, must make sure there is no slack in the line and that your rod tip is low to the water. Then firmly but gently lift up to set the hook. Hold on tight and raise your rod straight up in the air, holding your arms as high above your head as possible. Once the fish realizes something is wrong—that it's hooked—it will peel away in an electrifying run, taking out 100 to 150 yards of line in a heartbeat. This whole process—from sighting to hooking—explodes in adrenaline-pumping nanoseconds. Ten to 30 minutes later, after the bonefish makes several pulse-pounding sprints, you can reel in the tired fish to the side of the skiff, where the guide will photograph both victor and spoils. Then quickly release the bonefish so that it may rest up and thrill another angler on yet another day (see the previous section in this chapter on Catch-and-Release Ethics).

Bonefishing is a major playing card of the fishing deck we so lavishly deal here in the Florida Keys. Bonefish usually range in size from 5 to 10 pounds, but the size of this fish belies its strength. A 5-pound bonefish fights like a 20-pound wannabe. The Keys are the only place in the continental United States where an angler can fish for bonefish. Locals boast that the Keys have the biggest and best-educated bonefish this side of the Gulf Stream. Expect bonefish to grace our flats during April, May, June, September, October, and occasionally into November. Cool weather and cold fronts push them into deeper waters from December through March. The hot weather of July and August drives them to cooler, deeper waters as well, although some will stay all year.

i

Please watch for manatees in the waters of the Florida Keys. If you see one of these gentle creatures and it appears to be injured, call 800-Dial-FMP, *FMP, or use VHF channel 16. Stay in deep water and avoid running your motor over seagrass beds. Obey speed zone and sanctuary signs. Look, but don't touch; please do not feed or give the manatees water. For more information, visit www.savethemanatee.org.

PERMIT: ULTIMATE FLATS CHALLENGE

Though sharing the same waters as the bonefish and stalked in the same manner, the permit (*Trachinotus falcatus*) proves to be a more elusive catch. Spooky, skittish, and stubborn, this finicky eater, which can take out line like a long-distance runner, is so difficult to catch that most anglers never even see one. Three or four times the size of a bonefish—averaging 20 to 30 pounds—the silvery, platter-shaped permit forages in the safety of slightly deeper waters, not risking exposure of its iridescent blue-green back. Its sickle-shaped, black-tipped tail pokes out of the water as it feeds on bottom-dwelling crabs and shrimps, often tipping off its location. The permit's shell-crushing jaws, rubbery and strong, can exert 3,000 pounds of pressure per square inch, enabling it to masticate small clams and crustaceans and dash many an angler's expectations.

The permit will tail or mud like a bonefish. In fact, both fish have been known to rub their snouts so raw from repeatedly rooting around in the mud, looking for food, that they caricature W. C. Fields. But unlike a bonefish, the permit is often spotted lazily cruising near the surface of the water. Many times its wispy black dorsal fin will break the water, looking like a drifting piece of weed.

The best days to find permit are those glorious, cloudless sunny smiles from Mother Nature, cooled by a slight ocean breeze. Schools of permit will graze the top of the flats and near rocky shorelines in higher tides and poke around in basins and channels during low tides, searching for a meal of small crabs and crustaceans. They often hover above submerged objects such as lobster pots. If you pass above an area littered with sea urchins, be on the lookout for permit searching for gourmet fixings.

Not easily duped, a tailing permit will make you forget all about a bonefish because, if you manage to hook one, you've got a street brawl on your hands that could last an hour or more. When hooked, the permit instinctively heads for deeper water. In the transition zone between the flats and the bluewater, the permit will try to cut the line by weaving through coral heads, sea fans, and sponges. The fish will pause in its run to bang its head on the bottom or rub its mouth in the sand to try to dislodge the hook. If you manage to follow the permit through this obstacle course, you may actually catch it a quarter mile from where you hooked it.

TARPON: THE SILVER KING

It is little wonder that the tarpon (*Megalops atlanticus*) is dubbed the "silver king," for it wins 9 out of every 10 encounters with an angler. The tarpon's lunglike gas bladder allows it to take a gulp of atmospheric air from time to time, enabling the fish to thrive in oxygen-depleted water. This magnificent superhero of the sea, ranging in size from 50 to 200 pounds, will break the surface and "roll" with a silvery splash as it steals an oxygen jolt and powers on for an intensified fight. The tarpon frequents the deeper flats of 4 to 8 feet or hangs out in the rapidly moving waters of channels, or under one of the many bridges in the Keys. Live mullet, pinfish, and crabs will entice this hungry but lazy despot, which faces into the current, effortlessly waiting for baitfish to be dragged into its mouth. The tarpon's toothless lower jaw protrudes from its head like an overdeveloped underbite, filled with bony plate that crushes its intended dinner.

The successful angler will use heavy tackle and a needle-sharp hook. Hold the rod with the tip at 12 o'clock and wait. When the fish strikes and eats the bait, let the rod tip drop with the pressure, giving minimal resistance. When the rod is parallel to the water and the line is tight, set the hook through the bony structure with a series of short, very strong jabs. Once hooked, the stunned fish runs and leaps repeatedly, with reckless abandon, entering the water headfirst, tail-first, sideways, belly-flopped, or upside down, an Olympian confounding its rod-clutching judge. It is important to have a quick-release anchor when fishing for tarpon because, once the action starts, you must be on your way, chasing the cavorting fish. (See the Local Secrets for Tight Lines Close-up, in this chapter.) Be prepared to duke it out, for it is often a standoff as to who tires first, the angler or the tarpon.

Exciting to catch on light tackle is the schooling baby tarpon, which, at up to 50 pounds, sprints and practices its aerobatics like its older siblings. Look for baby tarpon in channels and in harbors.

Tarpon season generally begins in April and continues until mid-July. Because the tarpon is primarily a nocturnal feeder, the best fishing is at daybreak and dusk or during the night.

This magnificent creature grows very slowly, not reaching maturity until it is at least 13 years old. Since the tarpon is not an edible fish, some people consider killing it akin to murder.

If you want a simulated mount of your catch, take an estimate of the length and girth for the taxidermist, take a photograph with your prize, and release the fish quickly and carefully.

BARRACUDA: TIGER OF THE FLATS

Look for the barracuda (*Sphyraena barracuda*), which packs a wallop of a fight, anywhere the water is about 2 feet deep, especially grassy-bottom areas. This toothy, intelligent predator has keen eyesight and moves swiftly. The barracuda's inquisitive nature causes it to make investigative passes by your boat, where it is oft tempted to sample your baited offerings intended for other species. Pilchards make good bait for catching barracuda. Cut off part of the tail fin of a pilchard before baiting the hook. This injury causes the bait to swim erratically, attracting the insatiable 'cuda. When casting to a barracuda, your bait should land at least 10 feet beyond the fish and be retrieved across its line of sight. A cast that lands the bait too close—5 feet or less—will frighten the 'cuda into deep water. If you are using artificial baits such as a tube lure, be sure to retrieve the bait briskly to pique the barracuda's interest.

Humans eat barracuda in some tropical areas, but not in the Keys. The flesh is sometimes toxic, and it is not worth the risk. You are better off quickly releasing the fish so that it might fight another round.

SHARKS

Several shark species (order Selachii) roam our flats looking for a free meal. Sand sharks and nurse sharks are relatively docile, but bonnetheads and blacktip sharks readily will take a shrimp or crab intended for a bonefish or permit, putting up a determined fight. If you happen to catch a shark, wear heavy gloves and cut the leader with pliers. The shark will swim away and will be able to work the hook loose from its mouth. Digestive acids and salt water will corrode the hook in mere days, causing the fish no permanent harm.

The Backcountry

When Mother Nature bestowed the prolific oceanside saltwater flats on the Florida Keys, she didn't stop at our rocky isles. As the Gulf of Mexico meets mainland Florida, a lively ecosystem flourishes in a body of water known as Florida Bay. Hundreds of tiny uninhabited keys dot the watery landscape, referred to locally as the backcountry. Loosely bordered by the Keys—from Key Largo to Long Key—and Everglades National Park, backcountry waters offer a diverse habitat of sea grass or mudflats, mangrove islets, and sandy basins. The southernmost outpost of the Everglades National Park is at Flamingo, which maintains a marina, boat rentals, houseboats, and guide services.

You'll usually be able to find snappers, sheepshead, ladyfish, and the occasional shark along the grass-bed shorelines, the open bays, and in the small creeks flowing out of the Everglades. And the silver king, the mighty tarpon, frequents backcountry creeks and channels, flats, and basins and is rumored to be particularly partial to the Sandy Key Basin in the summer months. But beckoning anglers to these skinny waters is another sporting trio—redfish, snook, and spotted sea trout—which when caught in one day is boasted far and wide as the Backcountry Grand Slam.

REDFISH, AKA RED DRUM

The coppery redfish, or red drum (*Sciaenops oceallatus*), all but disappeared in the 1980s from overfishing, but conservation measures by the state of Florida and the federal government caused a rebirth. This fast-growing fish migrates offshore to spawn when it reaches about 30 inches (four years). It is a protected species in federal waters. Regulations open a scant 9-inch window for anglers to keep one captured redfish per day, which must measure between 18 and 27 inches. All redfish measuring less than 18 inches or more than 27 inches must be released, always. Because it grows so rapidly, the redfish is exposed to harvest for only one year of its life.

As with fishing for bonefish or permit, you will look for redfish on an incoming tide, when they will be rooting for crabs on the shoals and flats. As the water gets higher, the fish work their way up on the flats. You will want to use a shallow-draft boat with a push pole or electric trolling motor and be prepared with polarized sunglasses for enhanced vision in spotting a tailing fish. You'll hear experienced anglers say, "A tailing red is a feeding red." The reddish, squared-off profile of the redfish's tail can be spotted from several hundred feet. When the fish is really hungry, you may see its entire tail exposed, even the shady eyelike spot at the base. Cruising redfish will push a head wake similar to that of a bonefish.

Although a redfish isn't nearly as easily spooked as a bonefish, you should still stay as far away from the fish as possible while still casting a right-on winner. Live shrimps or crabs will entice the fish, which, with poor eyesight, hits almost any bait coming its way. The hooked redfish often sticks around and puts up a hard fight. Attracted to its discomfort, other redfish swim to the scene of the accident. You can often catch another redfish if you can get another baited hook into the water fast enough. The redfish is highly coveted for eating, put on the culinary map by New Orleans's Chef Prudhomme and his famed Cajun blackening process.

The backcountry of the Florida Keys is one of the few places in the world where you can fish for redfish year-round, although they prefer cooler waters. It is illegal, however, to buy or sell our native redfish, and they must be kept whole until you reach shore. You are forbidden to gig, spear, or snatch the red drum.

SNOOK

The second member of the Backcountry Grand Slam, the snook (*Centropomus undecimalis*) likes to tuck against the shady mangrove shorelines to feed on baitfish that congregate in the maze of gnarled roots. A falling tide will force the baitfish out of their rooted cages and into deeper holes where the snook can get at them. But the baitfish aren't the only ones getting snookered. This cagey, sought-after game fish, once hooked, has buffaloed many an angler, vanishing back into the mangroves and snapping its tenuous connection to the rod-wielder like a brittle string. If you win the battle of the bushes or find the snook pushing water in the open or at the mouth of a creek, you still haven't won the war. Once hooked, the snook thrashes about violently, trying to dislodge the barbed intruder. Its hard, abrasive mouth and knife-sharp gill covers can dispense with your line in a flash.

This silvery, long-bodied fish—thickened around the middle—faces its foes with a depressed snout and a protruding lower jaw. A distinctive lateral, black racing stripe extends the length of its body, all the way to its divided dorsal fin. The snook is unable to tolerate waters lower than 60 degrees. And while some anglers feel snook is the best-tasting fish in the Keys, Florida law mandates that in Monroe County you may not fish for snook from December 15 through January 31, nor in the months of May, June, July, and August. The fish must measure between 26 inches and 34 inches. Limits are one snook per person, per day. Snook may not be bought or sold, and you must purchase a $2.00 snook stamp for your saltwater fishing license in order to fish for them.

SPOTTED SEA TROUT, AKA SPOTTED WEAKFISH

Even though this backcountry prize is called a weakfish, it can be a challenging catch. The weakfish moniker derives from its clan's easily torn mouth membranes. The spotted sea trout (*Cynoscion nebulosus*)—actually a member of the fine-flavored drum family—nevertheless resembles a trout, with shimmering iridescent tones of silver, green, blue, and bronze.

The sea trout's lower jaw, unlike a true trout's, projects upward, and a pair of good-sized canine teeth protrude from the upper jaw. These predatory, opportunistic feeders enjoy a smorgasbord of offerings but are particularly fond of live shrimp. The sea trout makes a distinctive splash and popping sound when it feeds on a drift of shrimp. These weakfish are easily spotted in the shallow backcountry waters, popular with light-tackle enthusiasts who enjoy the stalk-and-cast challenge.

Sea trout prefer temperatures between 60 and 70 degrees. Each must measure at least 12 inches to be fished, and the catch is limited to four fish per person, per day. They are highly ranked as a table food because they are so delicately flavored, but the flesh spoils rapidly. Ice it quickly, and fillet the fish immediately upon returning to shore.

The Bluewater

The Gulf Stream, or Florida Current, moves through the Florida Straits south of Key West and flows northward, along the entire coast of Florida, at about 4 knots. This tropical river, 25 to 40 miles wide, maintains warm temperatures, hosting a piscatorial bounty from the prolific Caribbean that constantly restocks the waters of the Keys. The bluewater encompasses deep water from the reef to the edge of the Gulf Stream and is particularly prolific at the humps, which are underwater hills rising from the seafloor. The Islamorada Hump is 13 miles offshore from Islamorada. The West Hump lies 23 miles offshore from Marathon and rises from a depth of 1,100 feet to 480 feet below the surface.

Bluewater fishing is synonymous with offshore fishing here in the Keys. To an angler, it means big game: tuna, billfish, dolphin, cobia, wahoo, and kingfish. Also offshore, at the edge of the coral reef and the nearshore patch reefs, you will find a palette of bottom fish, snappers, and groupers coveted more for their table value than their fighting prowess, and a grab bag of bonus fish—some good to eat, all fun to catch.

Until you are experienced in our waters, you will need a guide. To troll for big game fish in the bluewater, you should book a private charter, which will put you on the fish and supply everything you need, including the professional expertise of the captain and mate, who know when to hold 'em . . . and when to fold 'em. These charters usually accommodate six anglers and though pricey, provide the most instruction and individual attention. You can divide the cost with five other anglers or join with another party and split the tab (see the Guides and Charters section of this chapter).

Alternately, sign on to a party boat, or head boat, which usually accommodates 50 or more anglers. These boats usually take anglers to the reef for bottom fishing, where you can drop a line and try your luck for snapper, grouper, and even kingfish and some of their sidekicks. Mates on deck untangle lines, answer questions, and even bait your hook. And although it is a little bit like taking the bus during rush hour instead of a limousine, at $30 to $40 per day—rods, tackle, and bait included—a party boat remains the most economical means of fishing offshore.

BILLFISH: BLUE MARLIN, WHITE MARLIN, SAILFISH

Before you head out to the bluewater to hunt for sailfish and marlin, you might want to have a cardiac workup and check your blood pressure because, if your trolled bait takes a hit, it will prove a battle of endurance.

The cobalt-blue marlin (*Makaira nigricans*), largest of the Atlantic marlins, migrates away from the equator in warmer months, enigmatically gracing the Keys waters on its way northward. Females of the species often reach trophy proportions—1,000 pounds or more—but males rarely exceed 300 pounds. Tuna and bonito provide the mainstay of the blue marlin's diet, but some blue marlin have been found with young swordfish in their stomachs. Anglers trolling ballyhoo or mullet have the chance of latching onto a blue marlin, especially in tuna-infested waters. A fighting blue marlin creates a specter of primitive beauty: A creature the size of a baby elephant plunges to the depths, then soars in gravity-defying splendor, only to hammer the water once again and shoot off in a torpedolike run.

Less often caught in our waters is the white marlin (*Tetrapturus albidus*), which is much smaller than the blue, averaging 50 to 60 pounds and rarely exceeding 150 pounds. Both marlin use their swordlike bills to stun fast-moving fish, which they then consume. Unlike other members of its family, the dorsal and anal fins of the white marlin are rounded, not sharply pointed. The upper portion of its body is a brilliant green-blue, abruptly changing to silvery white on the sides and underslung with a white belly. White marlin will strike trolled live bait, feathers, and lures, hitting hard and running fast with repetitive jumps. The white marlin begins its southward migration as the waters of the North Atlantic cool in the autumn.

A shimmering dorsal fin, fanned much higher than the depth of its streamlined steel-blue body, distinguishes the sailfish (*Istiophorus platyperus*) from its billed brethren. Fronted with a long, slender bill, this graceful creature—averaging 7 feet long and 40 pounds in Florida waters—is meant to be captured and released but stuffed no more. Probably the most popular mount of all time—the flaunted mark of the been-there, done-that crowd—the sailfish, at least in the Florida Keys, is generally allowed to entertain, take a bow, and go back to the dressing room until the next show. Taxidermists now stock fiberglass blanks, so you need only phone in the prized measurements to receive your representative mount.

The migration of the sailfish coincides with that of the snowbirds, those northerners who spend the frigid months in the balmy Florida Keys. In late autumn and early winter, the sailfish leave the Caribbean and Gulf waters and head up the Gulf Stream to the Keys. A fast-growing fish—4 to 5 feet in one year—the sailfish seldom lives more than five years. Feeding on the surface or at mid-depths on small fish and squid, the sailfish also is amenable to trolled appetizers of outrigger-mounted live mullet or ballyhoo that will wiggle, dive, and skip behind the boat like rats after the Pied Piper. The sailfish, swimming at up to 50 knots, will give you a run for your money, alternating dramatic runs and explosions from the depths with catapults through the air. The sailfish delights novice and expert alike. The inexperienced angler can glory in the pursuit with heavy tackle, while the seasoned veteran can lighten up, creating a new challenge. Both will savor the conquest.

Dispose of your garbage back at the boat dock. Be careful that trash does not blow out of the boat. Do not leave anything behind that cannot be immediately consumed by the ecosystem.

Florida law allows you to keep one billfish per day and mandates size limitations. Sailfish must be at least 63 inches; blue marlin, 99 inches; and white marlin, 66 inches. We recommend, however, that you follow the ethical considerations of catch-and-release, recording your conquest on film instead.

BLACKFIN TUNA

Highly sought by anglers and blue marlin alike, the blackfin tuna (*Thunnus atlanticus*) is set apart from the other six tunas of North America by its totally black finlets. Rarely exceeding 50 pounds, this member of the mackerel family is not as prized as the giant bluefin of North Atlantic waters, but Keys anglers still relish a substantial battle and the bonus of great eating. Primarily a surface feeder, the blackfin terrorizes baitfish from below, causing them to streak to the surface and skitter out of the water like skipping stones, a move that attracts seabirds. A sighting of diving gulls will tip off the presence of tuna at the feed bag. Blackfin tuna are partial to a chumming of live pilchards but will also attack feathers and lures trolled at high speeds. Tuna fishing on the humps is usually good in the spring months.

DOLPHIN: SCHOOLIES, SLAMMERS, AND BULLS

Anyone who has ever seen a rainbow of schooling dolphin (*Coryphaena hippurus*) knows the fish's identity crisis is unfounded. Nothing about this prismatic fish suggests the mammal sharing its name. The dolphinfish resembles a Technicolor cartoon. Its bright green, blue, and yellow wedgelike body looks like the fish just crashed into a paint cabinet, and its high, blunt, pugnacious forehead and Mohawk-style dorsal fin evoke a rowdy, in-your-face persona not wholly undeserved. Once out of the water, however, the brilliant hues ebb like a fading photograph, tingeing sweet victory with fleeting regret.

Second only to billfish and tuna, dolphin are prized by bluewater anglers. Frantic fights follow lightning strikes, and the dolphin often throws in some aerobatics besides. This unruly fighter rates as a delicacy at the table as well, celebrated as moist white-fleshed dolphin fillets in the Keys and South Florida, but marketed as mahimahi elsewhere. Dolphinfish are surface feeders, attracted to the small fish and other tasty morsels associated with floating debris or patches of drifting sargassum weed. Flying fish, plentiful in the Gulf Stream waters, form a large portion of their preferred diet. A school of dolphin will actually attack a trolled bait of small, whole mullet or ballyhoo, streaking from a distance in a me-first effort like schoolboys to the lunch gong. It is not unusual for three or four rods to be hit at one time, an all-hands-on-deck effort that approaches a marathon. And as long as you keep one hooked dolphin in the water, alongside the boat, its buddies will hang around and wait their turn for a freshly baited hook.

Dolphin are a rapidly growing fish, living up to five years. The young are called schoolies, generally in the 5- to 15-pound range. Slammers make an angler salivate, as they each weigh 25 pounds and more, and an attacking school can get your heart pumping. Doing battle with the heavyweight, the bull dolphin, quite often happens by accident while you are trolling for some other species. But the bull can hold his own in any arena. Dolphin season is generally considered to be from March until August, but the fish tend to stay around most of the year. Limit is 10 per person, per day.

COBIA: THE CRAB EATER

The cobia (*Rachycentron canadum*), the orphan of the piscatory world, enjoys no close relatives and is in a family by itself. Excellent on the table or on the troll, the adult cobia is a favorite bonus fish, often caught during a day in the bluewater looking for sailfish. Particularly partial to crabs, the cobia also feeds on shrimp, squid, and small fish. The young cobia is found often in the flats of nearshore bays and inlets around the mangroves and around buoys, pilings, and wrecks.

WAHOO

A fine-eating bonus fish, generally caught by fortunate accident while trolling for sailfish or kingfish, the wahoo (*Acanthocybium solandri*) is far from an also-ran. One of the fastest fish in the ocean, the wahoo is a bona fide member of the mackerel family, similar in many ways to the Spanish mackerel. Its long, beaklike snout and slender silver-and-blue-striped body contribute to its prowess as a speed swimmer, for when hooked, the wahoo runs swiftly, cutting and weaving like a tailback heading for a touchdown. This loner rarely travels in schools. Wahoo season is in May, but the fish are here year-round.

KINGFISH, AKA KING MACKEREL

Here in the Florida Keys, we call the king mackerel—which goes by assorted aliases in other parts of the country—the kingfish. At the turn of the 20th century, kingfish was the most popular catch off the Keys. Sailfish, then unrevered, were considered pests because they crashed the kingfish bait. The streamlined kingfish (*Scomberomorus cavalla*) travels in large schools, migrating up and down the coast in search of warm waters. Kingfish commonly frequent the waters of the Keys during the winter months, heading north in the spring.

Kings can be caught by drift fishing, where anglers cut the boat's engines and drift, fishing over the schools. Alternately, you can troll for kingfish with whole mullet or ballyhoo. Some captains prefer to anchor and chum, lacing the slick from time to time with live pilchards. Any method you use, a wire leader is essential when angling for kingfish because the fish displays razor-sharp teeth it is not reluctant to use. Kingfish caught in our waters commonly weigh in at about 20 pounds, although the fish have been recorded reaching upward of 40 pounds. The kingfish is a good sport fish and also makes a fine meal. Limit is two per person, per day.

AMBERJACK

When all else fails in the bluewater, you can always find a deep hole and battle an amberjack (*Seriola dumerili*). This powerful, bottom-plunging fish—nicknamed AJ—guarantees a good brawl. Bringing in an amberjack is like pulling up a Volkswagen Beetle with light tackle.

THE REEF ELITE: GROUPER, SNAPPER, AND THE MACKERELS

Inhabiting the edge of the barrier reef that extends the length of the Florida Keys and in the smaller patch reefs closer in to shore, several finned species noteworthy for their food value coexist with the brightly painted tropicals and other coral-dwelling creatures. Like a well-branched family tree, these fish encompass many clans, all entertaining to catch and most delectable to eat. Startled anglers have even brought in permit while fishing the wrecks along the reef line. The brooding presence of the barracuda is always a strong possibility on the reef because the 'cuda is partial to raw snapper "stew" or grouper "tartare" when given the opportunity. It thinks nothing of stealing half the hooked fish in one mighty chomp, leaving the angler nothing but a lifeless head.

You will need a boat at least 20 feet long to head out to the reef, some 4 to 5 miles offshore. But with a compass, your NOAA charts, a GPS, tackle, chunked bait, and some information gathered locally at the nearest bait and tackle shop, you should be able to find a hot spot on your own. Then all you need to do is fillet the captives, find a recipe, and fry up the spoils.

More than 50 species of grouper are found in the Florida waters, but three stand out in the waters of the Florida Keys. The black grouper (*Mycteroperca bonaci*) has been known to reach 50 pounds and 3 feet in length. Distinguished from other groupers by the black blotches and brassy spots mottling its olive or gray body, the black grouper is, nonetheless, often confused with the gag grouper. Large, adult black groupers are found on the rocky bottom in deep water, although the youth hang out close to shore. Limit is two per person, per day.

The aforementioned gag grouper (*Mycteroperca microlepis*) reaches a length and proportion similar to that of the black grouper, but its body is a uniform gray color with dark wormlike markings on its sides. The red grouper (*Epinephelus morio*), so named because of its brownish-red pigmentation and scarlet-orange mouth lining, lives on rocky bottoms at medium depths. This makes it an accessible catch for anglers using small boats and light tackle. Limit for both red and gag grouper is also two per person, per day.

All groupers are hermaphrodites, meaning they possess both male and female reproductive organs. The young are females that change into males as they mature. Fond of small fish and squid, groupers can be enticed to hit chunked ballyhoo, mullet, and pilchards as well as shrimp.

You will need a stout rod, a heavy leader, and a heavy sinker because the grouper will head for the rocks once it comprehends the insult of the hook. The ensuing fight is not for the fainthearted. You will have to horse the fish out of the rocks and corals, where the grouper will make every attempt to cut your line.

Recipe for Yellowtail Chum Balls

Take one bag of good-quality chum (packed from a commercial fish market in clear plastic, not a box). Allow chum to defrost overnight. Drain liquid. In a large container, mix chum with an equal portion of fine-grained mason's sand. Add flour, oatmeal, and glass minnows. Mix together well and form into solidly packed 2-inch balls (much as you would a snowball). Add more flour to the mixture if the balls do not hold together. Bait a hook (size 4 to size 1) with 1-inch, cut-up pieces of ballyhoo or mackerel. Bury the hook and bait inside the chum ball. Your hook should be tied directly to the line—no leader, no swivels, no double lines, and no sinkers. The weight of the chum ball will carry your bait to the bottom.

Open the bail on your reel or set your reel to free spool and drop your baited hook in the water. As it goes down to the bottom, bits of the chum ball will break off. When it hits the bottom, the chum ball will break up completely, freeing your baited hook. The cloud of swirling chum will attract the yellowtails. Keep your line in free spool until the yellowtail grabs the bait and peels off line. Close the bail and set the hook. The rest is history.

The snapper family is a popular bunch in the Florida Keys. The prolific cousins—all pleasurable to eat, delightful to catch, and kaleidoscopic to see—confuse northerners with their dissimilarity. Snappers travel in schools and like to feed at night. Most common on the Keys table is probably the sweet, delicate yellowtail snapper (*Ocyurus chrysurus*), which usually ranges from 12 to 16 inches in length. Big yellowtails, called flags, approach 5 to 6 pounds and 20 inches in length and are prevalent from late summer through October. The yellowtail's back and upper sides shade from olive to bluish with yellow spots. A prominent yellow stripe begins at the yellowtail's mouth and runs midlaterally to its deeply forked tail, which, as you would expect, is a deep, brilliant yellow. The yellowtail is skittish, line-shy, and tends to stay way behind the boat. The fish's small mouth won't accommodate the hooks most commonly used in the pursuit of the other snappers. Successful anglers use light line, no leaders, and small hooks buried in the bait (see the Close-up Recipe for Yellowtail Chum Balls, above).

The mangrove snapper, or gray snapper (*Lutjanus griseus*), though often haunting the coral reef, also can be found inshore in mangrove habitats. Grayish in color with a red tinge along the sides, the mangrove snapper displays two conspicuous canine teeth at the front of the upper jaw. The mangrove is easier to catch than the yellowtail or the mutton snapper. Live shrimp and cut bait, added to a small hook, will induce these good fighters to strike. Anglers enjoy taking the mangroves on light tackle.

The brightly colored mutton snapper (*Lutanus analis*) shades from olive green to red, with a bright blue line extending from under its eye to its tail and a black spot below the dorsal fin marking its side. Mutton snappers are most often caught in blue holes, so called because the water color of these deep coral potholes appears bluer than the surrounding waters. You will also find muttons in channels and creeks and occasionally even on a bonefish flat. The fish range in weight from 5 to 20 pounds. Mutton snappers are rumored to be shy and easily spooked by a bait that is cast too closely, but they love live pilchards. Usually caught in cloudy, churned-up water, the muttons provide a fierce confrontation. Limit for snappers is 10 per person, per day.

Ergonomically designed for speed, the torpedo-shaped Spanish mackerel (*Scomberomorus maculatus*) distinguishes itself from the king and the cero with a series of irregular, buttercup-yellow spots on its stripeless sides, which look like the freckles on the Little Rascals. Cherished by light-tackle enthusiasts, the Spanish mackerel averages less than 2 pounds and 20 inches in length. Its razorlike teeth dictate you carefully consider your choice in terminal tackle, for slashing your line rates at the top of the Spanish mackerel's getaway tactics. Spanish mackerel migrate into Florida Bay in February. Limit is 15 per person, per day.

Larger than its Spanish cousin, the cero mackerel (*Scomberomorous regalis*) displays yellow spots above and below a bronze stripe that runs down its silvery sides, from the pectoral fin to the base of its tail. The cero is the local in our visiting mackerel lineup, not straying far from the waters of South Florida and the Keys, where it feeds on small fish and squid. The cero makes excellent table fare when consumed fresh, but fillets do not freeze well.

You may encounter the tripletail (*Lobotes surinamensis*) if you fish around wrecks, buoys, or sunken debris. Nicknamed the "buoy fish," the tripletail has been known to reach 40 pounds and a length of 3 feet. The fish's dorsal and anal fins are so long that they resemble two more tails, hence the name *tripletail*. The tripletail is a mottled palette of black, brown, and yellow, looking like an autumn leaf. Young tripletails, which like to stay close to shore in bays and estuaries, often are spotted floating on their sides at the surface, mimicking a leaf on the water. The tripletail will put up a valiant fight, and, though not seen on a restaurant menu, it will make a tasty dinner. You must catch tripletail with a hook and line only, no snatch hooks.

The Bridges

The bridges of the Florida Keys attract fighting game fish and flavorful food fish like magnets draw paper clips. The state of Florida replaced many of the original bridges of the Overseas Highway with wider, heavier spans in the late 1970s and 1980s, subsequently fitting many of the old bridges, no longer used for automobile traffic, for use as fishing piers. These bridges are marked with brown-and-white signage depicting a fish, line, and hook. (Many of the old bridge structures have been closed because lack of maintenance has left them unsafe. Be sure to fish only from those bearing the county signage.) The fishing bridges offer the general public free fishing access to many of the same species that frequent more far-flung areas of our waters. Parking is provided at the fishing-pier bridges. The Seven Mile Bridge, the Long Key Bridge, and the Bahia Honda Bridge have been designated historical monuments.

The waters beneath the bridges host a lively population of tarpon, mangrove snappers, snook, baby groupers, and yellowtails (see the Flats, Backcountry, and Bluewater sections of this chapter for information on these fish). Grunts (*Haemulon plumieri*) also are commonly caught at the bridges. Though little respected in other Keys waters, this small, bluish-gray fish is, nevertheless, fun to catch and makes a tasty meal. The grunt's name is derived from the sounds escaping the fish's bright orange mouth when it is captured. This grunting sound is actually the grinding of the pharyngeal teeth, which produces an audible noise amplified by the air bladder.

Night fishing is popular from the bridge piers, too. An outgoing tide with a moderate flow inspires the fish to continue feeding after dark. Baitfish and crustaceans, a temptation too great for many of the finned predators to pass up, are funneled through the pilings and out to sea.

Stop in at one of the local bait and tackle shops to get rigged out for bridge fishing. The local fishing experts working in these shops are encyclopedias of knowledge and will be able to guide you as to times, tides, and tackle. Locals recommend you use stout tackle when fishing from one of our bridges. You not only have to retrieve your catch while battling a heavy current, but you also must lift it a great distance to the top of the bridge.

Live shrimp, cut bait, or live pinfish will attract attention from at least one of the species lurking below. You will need to keep your shrimp alive while fishing from the bridge. Put the shrimp on ice in a five-gallon bucket with an aerator or in a large Styrofoam cooler with an aerator. You can also lower a chum bag (filled with a block of chum, available at all bait shops) into the water. Tie a couple of dive weights to a long rope, lower the chum bag down the surface of a piling on the downcurrent side of the bridge, and tie it off to the railing. Then fish the slick. The chum will drift with the current, attracting sharks and any finfish in the neighborhood.

You will need sinkers on your line in order for your baited hook to drop to the bottom because a swift current pulses under the bridges. Don't launch your cast away from the bridge. Drop your bait straight down, near a piling or downcurrent, at the shoreside of the bridge. Rubble from past construction sometimes piled here creates a current break, allowing the fish a place to rest, feed, or hide in the swirls or eddies. Don't forget to buy a fishing license.

FISHING LICENSES

Florida law states you must possess a saltwater fishing license if you attempt to take or possess marine fish for noncommercial purposes. This includes finfish and such invertebrate species as snails, whelks, clams, scallops, shrimps, crabs, lobsters, sea stars, sea urchins, and sea cucumbers.

Exempt from this law are individuals younger than age 16 and Florida residents age 65 and older. You are also exempt if you are a Florida resident and a member of the U.S. armed forces not stationed in Florida and home on leave for 30 or fewer days, with valid orders in your possession.

Florida residents who are fishing in salt water or for a saltwater species in fresh water, from land, or from a structure fixed to land need not purchase a license. Land is defined as "the area of ground located within the geographic boundaries of the state of Florida that extends to a water depth of 4 feet." This includes any structure permanently fixed to land such as a pier, bridge, dock or floating dock, or jetty. If you use a vessel to reach ground, however, you must have a license. And if you are wading in more than 4 feet of water or have broken the surface of the water wearing a face mask, you also must have one.

You are not required to have a license when you fish with one of our licensed captains on a charter holding a valid vessel saltwater fishing license or if you are fishing from a pier that has been issued a pier saltwater fishing license. Other, more obscure exemptions also apply. Check www.floridafisheries.com for more information.

A Florida saltwater fishing license is available from most bait and tackle shops and from any Monroe County tax collector's office. You can also obtain a license over the telephone by dialing (888) 347-4356. Licenses are now available online at www.wildlifelicense.com. Residents and nonresidents pay differing amounts for this license. The state defines a resident as anyone who has lived in Florida continuously for at least six months; anyone who has established a domicile in Florida and can provide evidence of such by law; any member of the U.S. armed forces who is stationed in Florida; any student enrolled in a college or university in Florida; or an alien who can prove residency status.

Residents pay $13.50 for one year and $61.50 for five years. Applications for the five-year license may be obtained from the tax collector's office. Nonresidents must pay $6.50 for a three-day license, $16.50 for seven days, and $31.50 for one year. This price includes a $1.50 tax collector processing fee. A fifty-cent surcharge is added if you purchase your license at a location other than the tax collector's office. The processing fee is $3.95 if you purchase your license using the 888 phone number, $2.25 if you purchase the license via the Internet. If you wish to take snook or lobster, you must add the appropriate stamp to your Florida saltwater fishing license. Each stamp costs $2.00.

Florida residents may purchase a lifetime saltwater fishing license. If you are between the ages of 13 and 64, the cost is $301.50; for those younger than age 13, rates are less. Lifetime licenses are available at the county tax collector's office. No snook or crawfish stamps are required. If you are a Florida resident and are certified as totally and permanently disabled, you are entitled to receive, without charge from the county tax collector, a permanent saltwater fishing license.

The penalty for fishing without the required license or stamps is $50 plus the cost of purchasing the proper documentation. A $51.50 tarpon tag is required if you insist upon keeping and therefore killing a tarpon instead of releasing it (see the Catch-and-Release Ethics section in this chapter).

TOURNAMENTS

If you're an angler who would like to compete against your peers instead of just yourself, the Florida Keys offers a plethora of exciting tournaments—more than 50 a year—encompassing most of the finned species enriching our waters. These tournaments, scheduled year-round from Key Largo to Key West, award prizes, cash, or trophies in a variety of categories ranging from heaviest or longest to most caught and released in a specified time period.

Generally, the tournaments fit into one of three categories, although some tournaments have multiple divisions. The billfish tournaments—white marlin, blue marlin, and sailfish—are the most prestigious and the most expensive. Billfish tournaments are catch-and-release events. Proof of the catch usually requires a photograph and a sample of the leader, which will be tested for chafing. Scoring follows an intricate point system. A catch of a white marlin, a blue marlin, and a sailfish in one day—not your average day, even in the Keys—constitutes a slam.

Dolphin tournaments are more family-type competitions. Anglers use their own boats without guides, and if the dolphin exceeds prespecified poundage, it may be brought in and weighed. Anglers can keep the fish, which are excellent eating.

Flats tournaments—tarpon, bonefish, and permit—are always catch-and-release, usually scored by a point system. A catch on a fly rod scores more points than one retrieved on light tackle. The fish must be measured, a photo must be taken, and the process must be witnessed. We recommend you book one year in advance for tarpon tournaments.

Some of our tournaments are restricted to a specific category of angler—women only or juniors only, for instance—or to a particular type of tackle, such as light tackle or fly rods. Others award a mixed bag of catches ranging from gamefish to groupers to grunts. Many of the tournaments donate at least a portion of their proceeds to a charitable organization.

In the following section we introduce you to a sampling of the most important fishing tournaments held annually in the Keys. For a complete listing, call Florida Keys Fishing Tournament Administrator Christina Sharpe at (305) 872-2233 or check the Web site www.fla-keys.com and follow the fishing icons.

Coconuts Dolphin Tournament
Key Largo
(305) 453-9794

The largest dolphin tournament in the Florida Keys, Coconuts Dolphin Tournament at Marina Del Mar in mid-May regularly hosts more than 700 anglers. This three-day tournament, which awards cash prizes, runs from 8:00 A.M. to 3:00 P.M. each day. You can book a charter to fish the tournament or use your own boat. The director says there has been no proven advantage to having a charter. Scoring is determined by weight of the fish. Since this is a food-fish tournament, anglers may bring in all dolphin of more than 10 pounds.

The most famous blue-water angler in Key West's collective consciousness remains Ernest Hemingway, who augmented his famous writing with a passion for fishing these waters. Photographs of Hemingway with his prized, monster-size tarpon and sailfish cause many a covetous angler to turn green with envy.

Don Hawley Invitational Tarpon Tournament
Islamorada
(305) 664-2444

The oldest tarpon-on-the-fly tournament in the Keys and the first all-release tournament, the Don Hawley event is a five-day fishing extravaganza of all-fly, all-tarpon, and all-release. Anglers are awarded 1,000 points for a catch-and-release on 12-pound tippet; 750 points on 16-pound. Winners amassing the most points secure original Keys art by such notables as Al Barnes, Bill Elliott, and Kendall Van Sant. Proceeds of the tournament benefit the nonprofit Don Hawley Foundation, which supports the study of tarpon fishery and preservation in the Florida Keys and provides assistance to guides and their families in time of need. The tournament, held in early June, is limited to 25 anglers.

George Bush/Cheeca Lodge Bonefish Tournament
MM 82 Oceanside, Islamorada
(305) 517-4456
www.cheeca.com

Perhaps the most prestigious of all tournaments in the Florida Keys is the George Bush/Cheeca Lodge Bonefish Tournament, held in autumn. The former president, George Bush himself, competes in this event. Preceded by a kickoff meeting, two days of intense fishing are followed by an awards banquet at Cheeca Lodge. Fifty boats participate, two anglers per boat. Other than those included in the most-catches category, bonefish must weigh at least eight pounds to qualify. All must be released. Trophies are awarded to winners. Proceeds benefit a variety of Keys environmental groups.

Key West Fishing Tournament
Key West
(305) 745-3332, (800) 970-9056
www.keywestfishingtournament.com

This unusual tournament must have been designed for the angler who just can't fish enough. It lasts seven months, from April to late November, and encompasses a potpourri of divisions and species. Both charters and individuals can register for the tournament and also participate in a two-day kickoff tournament-within-a-tournament, which in itself awards cash prizes. Anglers weigh their food-fish catches or record their releases at participating marinas and are awarded citations for their efforts. At the grand finale of the tournament, the tabulated results are announced, and all prizes are presented.

Ladies Tarpon Tournament
Marathon
(305) 743-6139

The waters under the Seven Mile Bridge and the Bahia Honda Bridge are invaded by tarpon-seeking women each year in late April or early May in this ladies-only tarpon tournament. The number of tarpon caught and released in the two-day tournament determines the winners of a cache of rods and reels, trophies, and an assortment of jewelry. Points are awarded for catches on 12-pound test and 30-pound test.

Mercury Baybone Celebrity Tournament
Sheraton Beach Resort, Key Largo
(305) 664-2002
www.redbone.org

Event No. 2 in the Celebrity Tournament Series, the prestigious catch-and-release Baybone tournament in late September or early October, run by Gary Ellis, benefits cystic fibrosis research. Ellis is particularly interested in this worthy cause because his daughter, Nicole, has cystic fibrosis. The Celebrity Tournament Series, which includes the Redbone and the Mercury S.L.A.M., donates 100 percent of its proceeds to the Cystic Fibrosis Foundation for research. The stalked catch for the Baybone is bonefish and permit, which are photographed against a measuring device and released. Points are awarded for catches on fly, spin/plug, or general bait; nothing heavier than 12-pound test may be used in all divisions. An intricate point system determines the winners, who receive original paintings and sculptures as prizes. Anglers can fish as a two-person team, or one angler can be paired with a celebrity.

Mercury Cheeca/Redbone Celebrity Tournament, Islamorada
(305) 664-2002
www.redbone.org

Third in the Celebrity Tournament Series and cosponsored by Cheeca Lodge, the prestigious Redbone (first held in 1988) attracts anglers in competitive search for bonefish and redfish, in late November or early December. Also benefiting cystic fibrosis research, the Redbone follows the rules and regulations of the other two tournaments in the series. Many anglers try to fish all three tournaments. The grand champion of the series wins a gold Rolex Yachtmaster watch. Again, Gary Ellis is the one to call for more on this tourney.

Mercury Little Palm Island Grand Slam
Little Torch Key
(305) 664-2002
www.redbone.org

This small and select two-day tournament in late August or early September, with a kickoff and awards banquet at the elite Little Palm Island, is a catch-and-release event in search of the elusive Grand Slam: tarpon, bonefish, and permit in two days. Winners of the 30-boat event (two anglers per boat) receive original paintings, limited-edition prints, and pieces of sculpture. Proceeds of this tournament, like the Celebrity Tournament Series, benefit research by the Cystic Fibrosis Foundation.

Mercury S.L.A.M. Celebrity Tournament
Key West
(305) 664-2002
www.redbone.org

First in the Celebrity Tournament Series each year is the S.L.A.M. (Southernmost Light-tackle Anglers Masters) event in early September, directed by Gary Ellis, for the benefit of cystic fibrosis research (see the Baybone and Redbone tournament events). Participants in this two-day fishing event angle to score a Grand Slam: the catch and release of a bonefish, permit, and tarpon in two days. Points are awarded for each release in categories of fly, spin/plug, and general bait. Each release is photographed against a measuring device.

Like the other two tournaments in this series, the S.L.A.M. awards original art and sculpture to its winners. Anglers can fish as a two-person team, or one angler can opt to fish with a celebrity.

Scientific Anglers Women's World Invitational Fly Championships—Bonefish Series, Islamorada
(305) 664-5423

This late-September event, open to both men and women, cashes in on the growing popularity of saltwater fly fishing. Participants will be fishing for bonefish on a fly only. Photographs and regulation measuring sticks will provide proof of the catch in this release tournament. Prizes include original art pieces, fine crystal, and tackle. The director will book you a guide if desired. A portion of the proceeds benefits environmental scholarship funds. Contact Sue Moret for more information.

Never discard your fish line in the water. It can injure marine life, sea turtles, or seabirds.

Scientific Anglers Women's World Invitational Fly Championships—Tarpon Series
Islamorada
(305) 531-1233, (305) 664-2080
This ladies-only, three-day, tarpon catch-and-release tournament is limited to 30 anglers, one per boat. The tarpon must be taken on flies only and measure at least 4 feet. Touching the leader is a catch in this tournament. Regulation measuring sticks and the honor system determine size of the catch. Winners are awarded original artwork of the Keys, crystal trophies, and an assortment of rods and reels. This non-profit tournament, held in mid-June, awards a scholarship to a local high school student who will pursue studies in environmental or marine science, thereby giving back the gift of knowledge to the Keys. There is usually a waiting list for this tournament.

Shell Key West Classic
Key West
(305) 294-4042
www.shellkeywestclassic.com
Big money can be won in this late-April tournament, which holds a large pot spread over a variety of categories. The major targets are blue or white marlin, sailfish, tarpon, and permit, all catch-and-release except for fun-fish. All boats registered in other divisions can participate in the fun-fish categories, which award cash prizes for the heaviest dolphin, tuna, and wahoo weighing in at more than 20 pounds. Proceeds benefit the National Mental Health Association.

GUIDES AND CHARTERS

Nearly 1,000 charter captains and guides—be it flats, bluewater, or backcountry—do business in the Florida Keys. Our guides are the most knowledgeable in the world—licensed captains who maintain safe, government-regulated watercraft. Hiring a guide allows the first-time visitor or the novice angler an opportunity to learn how to fish the waters of the Florida Keys and catch its bounty without having to spend too much time learning about the fish's habits. And guides will be your best teachers, for they usually have a lifetime of experience. Once you fish our waters, however, you will be the "hooked" species, for this unforgettable angling experience is addictive.

Book a guide as soon as you know when you are coming to the Keys, because the guides here book up quickly, especially during certain times of the year. If you hope to fish our waters with a guide during tarpon season, especially the months of May and June, plan a year ahead. Holidays such as Christmas and New Year's book up quickly also. Traditionally, the months of August through November are a bit slower. You may be able to wing it during those months, but we wouldn't advise it. Even if you don't take a charter trip, stop at a fishing marina about 4:00 P.M. and check out the catch of the day.

Bluewater or offshore fishing charters can accommodate six anglers. The captain guides the vessel to his or her favorite hot spots, which are anywhere from 6 to 26 miles offshore and usually closely guarded secrets. Often he or she will stop on his bluewater trek so the mate can throw a cast net for live bait. The mate will rig the baits, ready the outriggers, and cast the baited hooks for you. Big game fish are usually stalked by trolling, as are dolphin. You need do nothing but relax, soak in the sea air, and wait for the call, "Fish on!" Then the action is up to you.

Bluewater charter boats range in size from 35 to 50 feet. Each generally has an enclosed cabin and a head (toilet) on board. Everything you need for a day's fishing is provided except your refreshments, lunch, and any personal items you may need. It is customary to tip the mate 10 to 15 percent in cash if you have had a good day.

Guides for flats fishing or backcountry angling usually take a maximum of two anglers per boat. The guide will pole the skiff or flatsboat through the skinny water, attentively looking for fish from atop the poling platform. This sight fishing dictates both guide and anglers stand alert, all senses engaged. The angler, whether fly fishing or spin casting, casts to the desired location directed by the guide.

Flatsboats measure 16 to 18 feet. They are not outfitted with any shading devices, nor do they have a head. Be aware, you may have to use rather primitive facilities. Many of the guides will dip into shore for a pit stop, but others will not, so inquire before you leave the dock. All fly or spin rods, reels, tackle, and bait are provided. Some guides even tie their own flies, providing special furry or feathery creations proven to entice the fish. It is customary to tip the guide 10 to 15 percent in cash if you were happy with the excursion.

When booking a charter, inquire about penalties for canceling your reservations. No-shows frequently will be charged the full price.

Always bring sunscreen, polarized sunglasses, a cap with a long bill lined with dark fabric to cut the glare, and motion-sickness pills (even if you've never needed them before). Anglers are responsible for providing their own lunches and refreshments. Keys tradition is to bring lunch for the captain and mate on a bluewater charter or for the guide on a flats trip.

Many guides are known only on a word-of-mouth basis, but we have compiled a source list of fishing marinas and outfitters you may call to secure an offshore charter or flats or backcountry guide. The chambers of commerce in Key Largo, Islamorada, Marathon, the Lower Keys, and Key West also act as referral sources (see subsequent listings).

Perhaps even more than the rest of the Keys, you'll need a guide to find the fish in the waters surrounding Key West. A busy harbor for centuries, Key West's marinas and bights are a bustling maze to the uninitiated. Many of the more than 60 charter boats in the Key West fleet dock at the City Marina at Garrison Bight, which is accessed on Palm Avenue, just off North Roosevelt Boulevard. This marina is locally referred to as Charter Boat Row. From 7:00 to 7:30 A.M. and 3:30 to 5:00 P.M. the captains are available at their vessels to take direct bookings. You can meet them and their crews, see the offshore vessels, and save money to boot. Booking a charter directly with the captain instead of a charter agency nets you a sizable discount. Other charter boats dock at Key West Bight, in the Key West Historic Seaport.

Some guides are willing to captain your private vessel at a much-reduced charter rate. If this interests you, inquire when you call one of these booking sources. Often hotels maintain a source list of guides or charter captains they will recommend. Inquire when you reserve your accommodations.

Offshore and Backcountry Guide Booking Sources

Establishments acting as booking services will determine your needs and book your flats/backcountry guide or bluewater/offshore charter directly. Cancellation policies vary and change from year to year, so be sure to inquire about procedures and penalties before you book your charter. The top guides in the Florida Keys book out of the establishments listed below. Be sure to log on to their Web sites to find out more information on the guides they represent.

UPPER KEYS

Whale Harbor Dock & Marina
MM 81.9 Oceanside, Islamorada
(305) 664-4511

Sandy Moret's Florida Keys Outfitters
MM 81.9 Bayside, Islamorada
(305) 664-5423
www.floridakeysoutfitters.com

World Wide Sportsman Inc.
MM 81.5 Bayside, Islamorada
(305) 664-4615, (800) 327-2880
www.worldwidesportsman.com

Bud n' Mary's Fishing Marina
MM 79.8 Oceanside, Islamorada
(305) 664-2461, (800) 742-7945
www.budnmarys.com

More than 10 percent of the International Game Fish Association (IGFA) saltwater line-class and fly-fishing world records have been set in the Florida Keys.

Papa Joe's Marina
MM 79.7 Bayside, Islamorada
(305) 664-5005, (800) 539-8326
www.papajoesmarina.com

MIDDLE KEYS

Hawk's Cay Marina
MM 61 Oceanside, Duck Key
(305) 743-9000
www.hawkscay.com

Captain Hook's Marina
MM 53 Oceanside, Marathon
(305) 743-2444, (800) 278-4665
www.captainhooks.com

World Class Angler
MM 50 Bayside, Marathon
(305) 743-6139
www.worldclassangler.com

LOWER KEYS

Strike Zone Charters
MM 29.5 Bayside, Big Pine Key
(305) 872-9863, (800) 654-9560
www.strikezonecharter.com

Sea Boots Outfitters
MM 30 Bayside, Big Pine Key
(305) 745-1530, (800) 238-1746
www.seaboots.com

KEY WEST

In addition to the limited number of fishing marinas and outfitters booking guides or charters, Key West's fishing excursions are put together by charter agencies operated out of booths peppering Mallory Square, Duval, and other major streets of Key West. You also can book party boats at these booths.

Oceanside Marina
MM 5, 5950 Peninsula Avenue, Stock Island
(305) 294-4676
www.oceansidemarina.com

The Saltwater Angler
Key West Hilton Resort & Marina
243 Front Street, Key West
(305) 296-0700, (800) 223-1629
www.saltwaterangler.com

CHAMBERS OF COMMERCE

Key Largo Chamber of Commerce & Florida Keys Visitor Center
MM 106 Bayside, Key Largo
(305) 451-1414, (800) 822-1088
www.keylargo.org
This chamber will provide names of guides who either belong to the Key Largo Chamber of Commerce or those from other areas of the Keys who pay a fee to the Florida Keys Visitor Center for representation.

Islamorada Chamber of Commerce
MM 82.5 Bayside, Islamorada
(305) 664-4503, (800) 322-5397
www.islamoradachamber.com
This chamber maintains an active list of guides in the Islamorada area.

Greater Marathon Chamber of Commerce
MM 53.5 Bayside, Marathon
(305) 743-5417, (800) 262-7284
www.floridakeysmarathon.com
Upon request, this chamber will send you a list of guides belonging to the Marathon Guides Association. (The list is also posted on their Web page.) The list specifies the guide's name, address, telephone number, type of fishing (such as bluewater or flats), fishing specialties (spin or fly), and size and make of boat. If you don't have time to wait for this list by mail, the chamber will provide several selections over the telephone. The visitor center maintains a reservation line at (877) 934-FISH.

Lower Keys Chamber of Commerce
MM 31 Oceanside, Big Pine Key
(305) 872-2411, (800) 872-3722
www.lowerkeyschamber.com
The Lower Keys Chamber goes beyond its membership list to refer you to a wide range of guides and captains in the area.

Key West Chamber of Commerce
402 Wall Street, Mallory Square, Key West
(305) 294-2587, (800) 648-6269
www.keywestchamber.org
The staff at the Key West Chamber of Commerce will mail you a list of guides or captains who are chamber members.

Party Boats

Party boats, sometimes called "head boats," offer a relatively inexpensive way to fish the waters of the Keys. The party boats, U.S. Coast Guard-inspected and certified vessels, generally hold 50 passengers or more, but most average no more than 25 to 30 anglers. Party boats take anglers out to the reef, where they anchor or drift and bottom fish for more than 40 species of fish. Spring and summer seasons sport a plethora of groupers, snappers, dolphinfish, and yellowtails, while kingfish and cobia are more apt to make an appearance in the winter months. Porgies, grunts, and some species of snappers and groupers show up all year. Occasionally even a sailfish or a big shark has been caught from a party boat here.

The party boat offers rod and reel rental at a nominal fee per trip. This includes your terminal tackle—hook, line, and sinker—and all bait. If you bring your own fishing gear, bait is included in the excursion fee. You do not need a fishing license on a party boat. While most party-boat information mentions your license is included in the excursion fee, this actually is only a temporary license, good for the duration of your fishing trip only. Two or more mates will be working the boat, helping you bait hooks, confiding fishing tips, and untangling the inevitable crossed lines.

Most of the party boats have seats around the periphery of the lower deck and a shaded sundeck up top. You are advised to wear shorts rather than swimsuits and durable sneakers or deck shoes, not thongs or sandals. Remember, there will be a lot of anglers and many flying hooks on the boat. Put some sturdy cloth between your skin and that accidental snag. Most captains recommend bringing a lightweight long-sleeved shirt for protection against the sun and a jacket to ward off cool breezes. Bring sunglasses, sunscreen, a hat, and motion-sickness pills (many people who never suffered from seasickness before find drifting in the swells causes them *mal de mer*). Also bring a fishing rag or towel to wipe your hands on during the day.

After you land a fish, a mate will help you take it off the hook and will check the

i

For information on flats fishing guides in Key West, call the Key West Guide Service, (305) 745-4634.

i ***Keep your rod and reel clean. Rinse them with fresh water and spray with WD-40 after each saltwater usage.***

species to make sure it is not one of those protected by law, such as Nassau grouper. The mate then will measure the fish to ensure it meets the required size limit, tag it with your name, and place it on ice. At the end of the fishing trip, you may reclaim your catch. The mate will clean your fish, usually for tips. Party boats with a set cleaning-fee policy will be noted in the descriptions. Mates work for tips aboard party boats, the standard tip being 10 to 15 percent if you had a good day and if the mate was helpful.

The following party boats may be booked for day or evening charters. It is always a good idea to arrive at the docks 30 minutes before departure to stow your gear on the boat and secure a good position on deck. All boats have restrooms on board. Most have an enclosed cabin and offer a limited snack bar, beer, and soda. Exceptions will be noted.

In all cases, you are allowed to bring your own cooler filled with lunch and refreshments. All party boats recommended in this section take credit cards unless otherwise stated. Children's rates for youngsters age 12 and younger are often available.

UPPER KEYS

Sailor's Choice
Holiday Inn Marina, MM 100 Oceanside, Key Largo
(305) 451-1802
www.sailorschoicefishingboat.com
Sailor's Choice, a 65-foot, aluminum, custom-built craft with an air-conditioned lounge, offers plenty of shade and seating for anglers on its daily fishing excursions. Children are welcome on both day and evening trips. During the day, they can easily see the big fish in the water and seabirds, porpoises, and sea turtles.

The two daily excursions are from 9:00 A.M. to 1:00 P.M. and 1:30 to 5:30 P.M.

Captain Michael
Holiday Isle Resort, MM 84.5 Oceanside, Islamorada
(305) 664-8070, (877) 664-8498
www.robbies.com
If you just can't get enough fishing, the *Captain Michael* offers a money-saving option: Fish the morning excursion, and go out again in the afternoon at a reduced price. Rates for children younger than age five, who will only be "assisting" Mom and Dad, are further reduced. The 65-foot *Captain Michael,* with spacious decks and an air-conditioned cabin, is available for private charters, sunset cruises, and wedding receptions.

Daily trips are from 9:30 A.M. to 1:30 P.M. and 1:45 to 5:45 P.M. The evening excursion is from 7:30 P.M. to 12:30 A.M.

Miss Tradewinds
Whale Harbor Marina, MM 83.5 Oceanside, Islamorada
(305) 664-8341 (dock), (800) 883-5336
www.misstradewinds.com
Docked at Whale Harbor Marina since 1973, *Miss Tradewinds* makes a quick 30-minute trip to the reef so you can maximize a full three hours of fishing time. The captains of *Miss Tradewinds,* each with more than 15 years' experience fishing the Keys' waters, offer you a great advantage.

Two daily excursions are available, from 9:30 A.M. to 1:30 P.M. and 1:45 to 5:30 P.M. The evening trip takes place from 7:30 P.M. to 12:30 A.M.

Gulf Lady
Bud n' Mary's Marina, MM 79.8 Oceanside, Islamorada
(305) 664-2461, (800) 742-7945
www.budnmarys.com
Mates are stationed at the bow and at the stern of the *Gulf Lady* and the captain also works the boat, so you'll get plenty of assistance on this fishing trip. If you bring

your own tackle, the captain recommends you have both 12-pound and 20-pound test. This 65-foot vessel also is available for private fishing charters and wedding receptions.

Daily trips are from 9:30 A.M. to 4:30 P.M.

MIDDLE KEYS

Marathon Lady
Marathon Lady Dock at the Vaca Cut Bridge, MM 53 Oceanside, Marathon
(305) 743-5580
www.fishfloridakeys.com/marathonlady

Children fish for significantly reduced rates aboard the *Marathon Lady.* Inquire when you make your reservations. If you rent a rod and reel for the excursion, your tackle is included, but if you prefer to bring your own gear, terminal tackle is available for a nominal fee. The mates will clean your catch for a small fee. A cooler with lunch and refreshments is allowed on all-day winter excursions. However, on summer evening excursions, which replace the all-day winter ventures, the captain prefers you bring your refreshments in a plastic bag; the crew will put them on ice for you.

From October through May, daily trips are conducted from 8:30 A.M. to 12:30 P.M. and from 1:30 to 5:30 P.M. From June through August, daily trips run from 8:30 A.M. to 12:30 P.M. and from 6:30 P.M. to midnight. *Marathon Lady* does not run during the month of September.

Keys Fisheries Market and Marina
MM 49 Bayside, at the end of 35th Street, Marathon
(305) 743-4353, (866) 743-4353
www.keysfisheries.com

Join the crew of a commercial lobster boat for an exciting half-day at sea. Six people are accommodated on the three-and-a-half-hour excursion. Besides your tasty catch of lobster or stone crabs, you'll be treated to the captain's stories of local history, sites, and legends. After your return, the dockside restaurant will prepare your catch—or you can have it packed and shipped home. The trips are seasonal, so it is best to call prior to your visit to the Keys.

When you see a boat being propelled by someone pushing it with a pole, please give that boat wide berth. These anglers are stalking gamefish in the shallows of the flats. The sound of an engine will frighten all the fish.

KEY WEST

Key West party boats are docked at Charter Boat Row on Palm Avenue off North Roosevelt. You can call the numbers listed to make reservations, book a space at one of the booths on Duval Street and in the Mallory Square area, or simply come down to the docks and make arrangements directly with the captain. Vessels usually operate at far less than maximum capacity during most seasons, so finding a spot should not present a problem.

Capt. John's *Greyhound V*
Charter Boat Row, City Marina, Garrison Bight
(305) 296-5139

Daily trips are from 11:00 A.M. to 4:00 P.M. Passengers who would like to ride along and use the sundeck instead of fishing may do so for a lesser charge.

In July and August two excursions are offered daily: 8:30 A.M. to 1:00 P.M. and 3:00 P.M. to 8:00 P.M. The party boat does not operate in the month of September. Mates charge a nominal fee to clean your fish.

Gulf Stream III
Charter Boat Row, City Marina, Garrison Bight
(305) 296-8494, (888) 745-3595
www.keywestpartyboat.com

The *Gulf Stream III* provides a full-service lunch counter offering sandwiches, beer, and soda. Ever prepared, the crew will provide free motion-sickness pills if the need arises. The mates will clean your catch for a small fee.

Daily excursions, September through June, are from 9:30 A.M. to 4:30 P.M. Evening outings are conducted in July and August only, from 6:30 P.M. to 1:00 A.M. Sunbathers may come along on this party boat for half price.

OUTFITTERS

Upper Keys

Boater's World Discount Marine Center
MM 105.6 Bayside, Key Largo
(305) 451-0025, (877) 690-0004

MM 50 Oceanside, Marathon
(305) 743-7707, (877) 690-0004

3022 N. Roosevelt Boulevard, Key Plaza
Key West
(305) 295-9232, (877) 690-0004
www.boatersworld.com

Boater's World Discount Marine Center is a large chain of marine stores offering marine supplies, gear, and clothing. The salespeople are knowledgeable and can special order items not in stock. Boater's World carries most popular brands of men's and women's clothing: Columbia, Sebago, and others.

Sandy Moret's Florida Keys Outfitters
MM 81.9 Bayside, Islamorada
(305) 664-5423
www.floridakeysoutfitters.com

This shop made *Field and Stream's* top-10 list as selected by the magazine's editors. The focus here is on fly fishing, and this outfitter's personnel rank as some of the most experienced in the sport. You'll find such brands as Orvis, Sage, G. Loomis, and Scott fly rods and Tibor, Orvis, and Abel fly reels, plus a wide selection of flies and fly-tying materials. In addition to Columbia, Sage, Patagonia, and Orvis clothing, Florida Keys Outfitters sells Teva sandals and Sebago and Columbia boat shoes.

Put your catch on ice immediately either in the fish box or in an insulated cooler.

World Wide Sportsman Inc.
MM 81.5 Bayside, Islamorada
(305) 664-4615, (800) 227-7776
www.worldwidesportsman.com

Anglers will discover nirvana at World Wide Sportsman, a 29,000-square-foot super store in Islamorada (see the Shopping chapter). Owned by Johnny Morris of Bass Pro Shops, World Wide is stocked to the rafters with a wide assortment of fishing tackle, such as Billy Pate, Tibor, Penn, Sage, Daiwa, Shimano, Orvis, and many more. You'll find fly-tying materials and a huge assortment of flies here. A rod and reel repair center is on premises. Ex Officio, Woolrich, Bimini Bay, Sportif, Tarponwear, and Columbia fishing clothes for both men and women are just a few of the many brands offered.

The facility also features a full-service marina of 40 to 50 slips, accommodating boats up to 42 feet in length. Many of the area guides launch from these facilities. The marina offers a fuel dock (both gas and diesel) as well as frozen, live, and fresh bait. All things considered, this fishing emporium is every angler's dream store.

Bonefish Bob's
MM 81 Bayside, Islamorada
(305) 664-9420
www.bonefishbob.com

This unique outfitter carries all kinds of tackle but specializes in fly-fishing gear and collectibles. Bob stocks Thomas & Thomas and Winston rods and a large selection of collectible reels, such as Wedding Cake Fin Nors. You can find fly-tying supplies here, too. Bob sells more than

400 used rods and maintains a collection of antique fishing memorabilia, including everything from old books to bamboo poles. Expert advice is free for the asking. The store is closed on Wednesday.

Middle Keys

World Class Angler
MM 50 Bayside, Marathon
(305) 743-6139
www.worldclassangler.com
World Class Angler sells anything and everything you'll need for saltwater fishing, stocking 37 brand names of reels, rods, and fishing gear. The facility specializes in the tarpon worm lure, a must-have if you are lucky enough to witness the annual worm hatch in our waters. The tarpon worm hatches at night for two nights in a row, and then in two weeks another worm hatch takes place. No one can predict exactly when the hatchings will happen, usually in June, but the tarpon go wild over the worms. So, we are told, do the anglers.

Lower Keys

Sea Boots Outfitters
MM 30 Bayside, Big Pine Key
(305) 872-9005, (800) 238-1746
www.seaboots.com
This fantastic, friendly, family-owned-and-operated outfitter is a Pro Fly Shop featuring the ultimate assortment of flies, including the famous Lefty's Deceiver for tarpon, designed by world-famous angler Lefty Kreh. You'll find G. Loomis and Sea Star spin or fly rods, Penn reels, and Islander fly reels here. You'll also find a wide selection of Columbia, Kahala, and Rum Reggae fishing togs and Sebago deck shoes. Sea Boots sells the entire Scientific AnglersMastery Series fly line.

You'll also find the complete Sportsman Collection of Florida Keys fishing videos here, so you don't have to wait for that Saturday-morning television show to get the best advice on how to fish like a real pro.

Key West

Conchy Joe's Marine & Tackle, Inc.
1970 North Roosevelt Boulevard
(305) 295-7745
www.conchyjoeskw.com
New to the Key West outfitter scene, Conchy Joe's offers Biscayne, Diamondback, Falcon, and Star rods, as well as Billy Baits and Chaos Lures. You'll find Daiwa, Penn, and Shimano reels and fly fishing supplies. On-site rod and reel repair is also available.

The Saltwater Angler
Key West Hilton Resort & Marina
243 Front Street
(305) 296-0700, (800) 223-1629
www.saltwaterangler.com
The Saltwater Angler specializes in fly tackle. Look for Sage, G. Loomis, Orvis, and Scott rods and Orvis, Lamson, Sage, Loop, Fin-Nor, Tibor, and Abel reels. The store also stocks a full assortment of flies and fly-tying materials. You can also select from a complete line of top-brand fishing apparel by Ex Officio, Orvis, Patagonia, and Columbia. Books and artwork with an angling theme round out their offerings.

i

Commercial shrimping is big business in Key West bluewaters, and the bonito and tuna like to follow these boats, scavenging the smorgasbord the shrimpers leave behind.

FLY-FISHING SCHOOLS

Sandy Moret's Florida Keys Fly Fishing School
MM 81.9 Bayside, Islamorada
(305) 664-5423
www.floridakeysoutfitters.com

Founded and directed by veteran saltwater fly fisherman Sandy Moret, this school brings freshwater fly-anglers back to school in droves to learn saltwater fly-fishing skills and techniques. Moret, who also owns and operates Florida Keys Outfitters, is a multi-time grand champion of the Gold Cup Tarpon Tournament. With more than a dozen fly-rod Grand Slams and four world records to his credit, he has assembled an outstanding team of world-renowned anglers to teach both novices and veterans the tricks of the trade.

DIVING AND SNORKELING

The greatest treasure of the Florida Keys, the most extensive living coral reef system in North America, lies approximately 4 to 5 miles offshore beneath the sea, hidden but not yet lost (see the Paradise Found chapter).

Ranking as the third largest reef system and one of the most popular dive destinations in the world, the Florida Keys' reef runs 192 miles from Virginia Key in Biscayne Bay all the way to the Dry Tortugas in the Gulf of Mexico. A fragile symbiotic city of sea creatures crowds our reef—fish, sponges, jellyfish, anemones, worms, snails, crabs, lobsters, rays, turtles, and, of course, both soft and stony corals—sometimes mixing it up with sunken bounty of a different kind: shipwrecks of yesteryear.

Although our coral reef appears sturdy and, indeed, has proved intractable to the many unfortunate wooden-hulled vessels it has so callously pierced throughout the centuries, this toothsome barrier is actually made up of colonies of tiny living animals. These coral polyps secrete calcium carbonate, developing so slowly it can take years for some species to grow just 1 inch. The careless toss of an anchor can destroy decades of coral growth in just seconds. Even the gentle touch of a finger can kill the delicate organisms instantly. When polyps are damaged or killed, the entire colony becomes exposed to the spread of algae or disease, and the reef is at risk.

To protect and preserve our marine ecosystem, Congress established the Florida Keys National Marine Sanctuary in 1990, signed into law by former president George Bush. Extending on both sides of the Florida Keys, the 2,800-square-nautical-mile sanctuary is the second largest marine sanctuary in the United States (see the Paradise Found chapter). The sanctuary encompasses two of the very best diving areas in the reef chain of the Keys: the Key Largo National Marine Sanctuary, established in 1975, which in turn envelops John Pennekamp Coral Reef State Park; and the Looe Key National Marine Sanctuary, formed in 1981. The proliferation of marine life, corals, and finfish is incomparable anywhere on this continent.

The state of Florida adjusted its offshore boundaries from 7 miles to 3 miles. This means many of the underwater dive and snorkel sites that used to be referred to as John Pennekamp Coral Reef State Park are now actually part of the Key Largo National Marine Sanctuary. Many dive operators and much promotional literature still refer to diving and snorkeling in Pennekamp Park. The actual boundaries of the park are much smaller than they used to be. To clear up the confusion, remember: Key Largo National Marine Sanctuary encompasses the waters of John Pennekamp Coral Reef State Park, but Pennekamp is not synonymous with the sanctuary.

In this chapter we provide you with a rundown of great reef and wreck dives and snorkel adventures from Key Largo to the Dry Tortugas. Our reefs are not within swimming distance of the shore, so you will need to make your way by boat. If you plan to venture out on your own craft or in a rental boat, be sure to stop at a dive center or marine supply store and purchase a nautical map that denotes the exact coordinates for dive and snorkel sites (see the listings in this chapter). Motor to the reef only if you know the waters, are an experienced boat handler, and can read the nautical charts well. You are financially liable for damage to the

In case of a decompression illness, call 911 and get the victim to the nearest emergency room as rapidly as possible.

reef, so always anchor only at mooring buoys when provided or on sandy areas of the sea bottom. Florida law dictates you fly the diver-down flag, which is red with a diagonal white stripe, to warn other boaters that divers are under water within 100 feet of your craft.

Probably the most popular and hassle-free way to dive or snorkel in the Florida Keys is to go out with a dive charter. Most reputable dive centers in the Keys belong to the Keys Association of Dive Operators, which sets standards of safety and professionalism. Crews are trained in CPR, first aid, and handling dive emergencies. Emergency oxygen supplies are kept on board. The dive captains, who must be licensed by the U.S. Coast Guard, judge weather conditions and water visibility each day and select the best sites suited to your experience level. Often their coveted knowledge of little-visited patch reefs and wrecks affords you an experience you could not duplicate on your own. We offer you a guide to dive centers, noting the comprehensive services ranging from instruction and underwater excursions to equipment rentals and sales.

In the Florida Keys, usually neither the crew nor the dive master accompanies divers in the water. Divers spread out across a shallow reef, two by two, swimming in a buddy system. The dive master stays on board and watches everyone from the boat. You must prove your experience level by showing current dive certification and your dive log before you may go out on a dive charter. If you have not made a comparable dive within the past six months, you must hire an instructor to accompany you in the water. Be sure you are comfortable with the sea conditions and that they are consistent with your level of expertise. If this is your first dive, alert the crew so they can help you.

Whether you dive on your own or go out to the reef with a charter, you should be aware of the strong current of the outgoing tidal flow and in the Gulf Stream. It is easy to overlook the current in the fascination of your dive until, low on both energy and air, you must swim against it to get back to the boat. Begin your dive by swimming into the current. To determine the direction of the current, watch the flow of your bubbles or lie back into a float position and see which way the current carries you.

Be careful around bridges. The tremendous energy of the tides passing through the pilings of our bridges creates coral outcroppings that would not normally be so close to shore. Divers and snorkelers without boat transportation to the patch reefs or the Gulf waters like to take advantage of this underwater terrain to look for lobsters. Be forewarned: It is very dangerous to dive or snorkel under and around our bridges. The currents are swift and the tidal pull is strong. Boat traffic is often heavy. If you do decide to dive or snorkel here, be sure to carry a diver-down flag with you on a float, and follow the buddy system. The best and safest time to tackle these turbulent waters is just before slack tide, during slack tide, and immediately following slack tide. The time of this cycle varies with wind, the height of the tide, and the phase of the moon.

With the privilege of diving and snorkeling in our waters comes responsibility. We sprinkle Insiders' Tips throughout this chapter because we know you also would like to preserve our fin-tastic coral reef for all time.

For the most part, visitors freely can swim, dive, snorkel, boat, fish, or recreate on our waters, but there are some Florida Keys National Marine Sanctuary regulations that took effect in July 1997 to guide these activities. Refer to our Boating chapter for information on these regulations before you venture into our waters. For a complete copy of the regulations and marine coordinates of the areas, contact the sanctuary office at (305)

743-2437 or log on to their Web site: www.fknms.nos.noaa.gov.

Whether you'd like to spend a few hours, days, weeks, or a lifetime exploring our coral reefs and wrecks, you'll find in this chapter all you need to know to "get wet," as divers like to say, in the Florida Keys.

IN EMERGENCIES

Divers in the Florida Keys are in good hands in the face of a recompression emergency. The Florida Keys Hyperbaric Center (305-853-1603) is located at Mariners Hospital in the Upper Keys (see the Health Care chapter).

Dive shop personnel, instructors, dive masters, and boat captains have joined with members of the local EMS, U.S. Coast Guard, Marine Patrol, NOAA, Monroe County Sheriff's office, and the Florida State Highway Patrol to develop a coordinated evacuation program to get injured divers off the water and to the hyperbaric chamber quickly. In case of a decompression injury, call 911 and get the victim to the nearest emergency room as rapidly as possible.

The Keys to the Reef

Most diving and snorkeling takes place on the barrier reefs of the Florida Keys. These linear or semicircular reefs, larger than the inner patch reefs, have claimed a graveyard of sailing vessels, many laden with gold and silver and other precious cargo. Salvaged by wreckers for centuries, the remains of these wrecks entice experienced divers, some of whom still hope to discover a treasure trove. Lighthouses were erected on the shallower, more treacherous sections of the barrier reef during the 19th century as an aid to navigation. They now also mark popular dive and snorkel destinations.

The coral reef system of the Florida Keys is distinctively known as a spur-and-groove system. Long ridges of coral, called spurs, are divided by sand channels, or grooves, that merge with the adjoining reef flat, a coral rubble ridge on the inshore edge of the reef. The ridges of elkhorn coral thrive in heavy surf, often growing several inches a year. The spurs extend 100 yards or more, with shallower extremities sometimes awash at low tide while the seaward ends stand submerged in 30 to 40 feet of water. Small caves and tunnels wind through to the interior of the reef, home to myriad species of marine plants and animals. The white grooves separating the spurs are covered with coarse limestone sand, a composite of coral and mollusk shell fragments and plates from green calcareous algae. The wave action passing between the spurs of coral creates furrows in the sand floor of the grooves.

Generally, the shallower the reef, the brighter the colors of the corals, because strong sunlight is a prerequisite for reef growth. Legions of fish sway back and forth keeping time with the rhythm of the waves. While deep dives yield fascinating discoveries—such as long-lost torpedoed ships—for those with advanced skills, sport divers will not be disappointed with the plethora of sea life within 60 feet of the surface. Night dives reveal the swing shift of the aquatic community. While the parrotfish may find a cave, secrete a mucous balloon around itself, and sleep the night through, sparkling corals blossom once the sun sets, and other species come out of hiding to forage for food.

Supplementing our coral barrier and the broken bodies of reef-wrecked ships, artificial reefs have been sunk to create underwater habitats for sea creatures large and small. The Florida Keys Artificial Reef Association, a nonprofit corporation of Keys residents, banded together in 1980 to capitalize on putting to use the many large pieces of concrete that became available during the removal of some of the old Keys bridges. More than 35,000 tons of rubble were deep-sixed throughout the Keys' waters between 1981 and 1987, creating acres of artificial reefs.

In recent years, steel-hull vessels up to 350 feet long have been scuttled in stable sandy-bottom areas, amassing new communities of fish and invertebrates and easing the stress and strain on the coral reef by creating new fishing and diving sites. You'll find a comprehensive list of the artificial reef locations at the Florida Fish and Wildlife Conservation Commission Web site: www.state.fl.us/fwc/marine.

Always use a mooring buoy if one is available. The large blue-and-white plastic floats are drilled directly into the sea bottom and installed with heavy chains or concrete bases. They are available on a first-come, first-served basis, but if you are a small craft, it is courteous to tie off with other similar boats, allowing larger vessels use of the mooring buoys. Approach the buoy from downwind against the current. Secure your boat to the pickup lines using a length of your own rope. Snap shackles provide quick and easy pickup and release. Large boats are advised to give out extra line to ensure a horizontal pull on the buoy. If no mooring buoys have been provided, anchor only in a sandy area downwind of a patch reef, so that your boat's anchor and chain do not drag or grate on nearby corals.

DIVE SITES

In the Keys parts of this section, we highlight 21 of the better-known and most enchanting dive and snorkel sites, listed in descending order from the top of the Keys in the Key Largo National Marine Sanctuary to the Looe Key National Marine Sanctuary in the Lower Keys.

In Key West our coral reef system heads west into the sunset as it swings by Cayo Hueso into the untamed and isolated but charted waters leading to the Marquesas and the Dry Tortugas. (The half-day dive excursions based in Key West do not venture as far as these outer, uninhabited Keys. You will have to charter private overnight dive excursions or travel the distance in your own motor or sailing yacht if you wish to explore these waters; see the Cruising chapter.) In the Key West and the And Beyond parts of this section, we highlight 19 of the most interesting dive and snorkel sites from Key West to the Dry Tortugas National Park.

Look but don't touch the coral. The sensitive polyps will die. Do not be tempted to take a piece of our coral reef as a souvenir. It is illegal to harvest coral in Florida.

Upper Keys

CARYSFORT REEF

Situated at the extreme end of Key Largo National Marine Sanctuary, Carysfort Reef appeals to both novice and intermediate divers. British vessel HMS *Carysfort* ran aground here in 1770. The reef, now marked by the 100-foot steel *Carysfort* Lighthouse, undulates between 35 and 70 feet. Lush staghorn corals, which look like bumpy deer antlers, and masses of plate coral, which overlap each other like roofing tiles, cascade down the 30-foot drop to the sandy bottom. Schools of algae-grazing blue tang and pin-striped grunts circulate among the coral heads of a secondary reef. The HMS *Winchester*, a British man-of-war built in 1693, hit the reef in 1695 after most of her crew died of the plague while en route from Jamaica to England. The wreck, discovered in 1938, was cleaned out by salvagers in the 1950s. It rests southeast of Carysfort Light in 28 feet of water. Location: North Carysfort: Lat. 25° 13.80, Long. 80° 12.74; South Carysfort: Lat. 25° 13.00, Long. 80° 13.06.

THE ELBOW

Aptly named, the Elbow looks like a flexed arm as it makes a dogleg turn to the right. Prismatic damselfish and angelfish, so tame they will swim up and look you in the eye, belie this graveyard of sunken cargo ships, the bones of which litter the ocean floor. The 191-foot *Tonawanda*, built in 1863 in Philadelphia, ended its short career as a tug and transport vessel in 1866 when it stranded on the reef. The ca. 1877 passenger/cargo steamer *City of Washington,* cut down and sold as a barge, piled up on the Elbow Reef in 1917 as it was towed by the *Edgar F. Luchenbach.* Dynamited so it would not impede navigation, the barge's scattered remains rest near the *Tonawanda* in about 20 feet of water covered with purple sea fans and mustard-hued fire coral trees. The unidentified Civil War wreck, now nothing more than wooden beams held together by iron pins, sits in 25 feet of water. A search of the area may yield a sighting of an old Spanish cannon, probably thrown overboard to lighten the load when one of the ships ran aground. The Elbow, marked by a 36-foot light tower, provides good diving for the novice. Depths at this spur-and-groove reef range between 12 and 35 feet, and currents vary. Location: Lat. 25° 08.82, Long. 80° 15.19.

CHRIST OF THE DEEP STATUE

Perhaps one of the most famous underwater photographs of all time is of the *Christ of the Deep* statue, which stands silhouetted against the sapphire-blue ocean waters bordering Key Largo Dry Rocks. This 9-foot figure of Christ, arms upraised and looking toward the heavens, was donated to the Underwater Society of America by Egidi Cressi, an Italian industrialist and diving equipment manufacturer. Designed by Italian sculptor Guido Galletti and cast in Italy, the statue is a bronze duplicate of the *Christ of the Abysses,* which stands under water off Genoa. Surrounded by a flotilla of nonchalant skates and rays, the statue's left hand appears to be pointing to the massive brain corals peppering the adjoining ocean floor. With depths ranging from shallow to 25 feet, snorkeling is outstanding. Schools of electric-blue neon gobies congregate in cleaning stations, waiting to service other fish that wish to be rid of skin parasites. A slow offer of an outstretched arm may net you a goby-cleaned hand. Location: Lat. 25° 07.45, Long. 80° 17.80.

GRECIAN ROCKS

This crescent-shaped patch reef, which ranges in depth from shallow to 35 feet, ranks as a favorite among snorkelers and novice divers. Colonies of branched elkhorn corals, resembling the racks of bull moose or elk, provide a dramatic backdrop for the curious cruising barracudas, which often unnerve divers by following them about the reef but rarely cause a problem. Colossal star corals dot the area, which is populated by a rainbow palette of Spanish hogfish and a scattering of protected queen conch. An old Spanish cannon reportedly is concealed in one of the more luminous of the star coral, placed there some time ago by rangers of John Pennekamp Coral Reef State Park. Look for a small patch of reef near Grecian Rocks where old cannon and fused cannonballs litter the landscape. At low tide this reef rises out of the water. Location: Lat. 25° 06.70, Long. 80° 18.55.

USS *SPIEGEL GROVE*

The USS *Spiegel Grove,* a decommissioned landing ship dock (LSD 32), was scuttled as an artificial reef in May 2002 in the waters off Key Largo. The largest vessel ever sunk as an artificial reef in the United States, the *Spiegel Grove* did not go down without a fight, however. The ship unexpectedly began to sink ahead of schedule, turtling and sinking upside down and at an angle that kept it from completely submerging. The ship's bow stuck up out of the water for three weeks before a Resolve Marine Group salvage crew rolled it onto its starboard side, allowing it to sink completely on June 10, 2002. The *Spiegel Grove* rests at a depth of 130 feet, midway between the *Benwood* wreck and the Elbow reef.

BENWOOD WRECK

The English-built freighter *Benwood*, en route from Tampa to Halifax and Liverpool in 1942 with a cargo of phosphate rock, attempted to elude German U-boats early in World War II by running without lights. Unfortunately, the American freighter *Robert C. Tuttle* also took a darkened route. In their ultimate collision, the American ship ripped the *Benwood*'s starboard side open like a can opener. As it limped along, a fire broke out on deck and attracted a German U-boat, which finished her off with two torpedo hits. A memorable first wreck for novice divers, the bow of the ship remains in about 50 feet of water, while the stern rests in but 25 feet. It lies in line with the offshore reef about 1½ miles north of French Reef. Location: Lat. 25E 03.16, Long. 80E 20.02.

FRENCH REEF

Even novice divers can negotiate the caves at French Reef. Swim through the 3- to 4-foot limestone ledge openings or just peer in for a glance at the vermilion-painted blackbar soldierfish, which often swim upside down, mistakenly orienting themselves to the cave ceilings. Limestone ledges, adorned with tub sponges, extend from the shallows to depths in excess of 35 feet. Follow the mooring buoys for the best route. A mountainous star coral marks Christmas Tree Cave where, if you swim through the two-entrance passage, trapped air bubbles incandescently flicker in the cave's low light. Hourglass Cave sports a shapely column of limestone that divides the space in half, and White Sand Bottom Cave, a large swim-through cavern, shelters a potpourri of groupers, dog snappers, moray eels, and copper-colored glassy sweepers. Location: Lat. 25° 02.06, Long. 80° 21.00.

WHITE BANK DRY ROCKS

A garden of soft corals welcomes snorkelers and novice divers to these patch reef twins. With calm waters and depths ranging from shallow to 25 feet, White Bank Dry Rocks extends north and south along Hawk Channel at the southern end of Key Largo National Marine Sanctuary. You will feel as if you are swimming in a giant aquarium, for the lacy sea fans, feathery sea plumes, and branching sea whips create surreal staging for the fluttering schools of sophisticated black-and-yellow French angelfish. Bring an underwater camera. Location: 1¼ miles inshore of French Reef.

MOLASSES REEF

Shallow coral ridges of this well-developed spur-and-groove reef radiate from the 45-foot light tower that marks Molasses Reef. Mooring buoys bob in deeper water, about 35 feet. Just off the eastern edge of the tower lies a single windlass, all that remains of the so-called Winch Wreck, or Windlass Wreck. Look for Christmas tree worms among the masses of star coral. The conical whorls, resembling maroon and orange pine trees, are actually worms that reside in living coral. If you slowly move a finger toward these faux flowers, they will sense your presence within half an inch and disappear like Houdini into their coral-encased tube homes. Location: Lat. 25° 01.00, Long. 80° 22.53.

USCG *BIBB* AND USCG *DUANE*

Advanced divers will relish the exploration of the two U.S. Coast Guard cutters sunk as artificial reefs 100 yards apart near Molasses Reef. Both these vessels, ca. mid-1930s, saw action in World War II and the Vietnam War. Both did search and rescue in their later peacetime years and were decommissioned in 1985. A consortium of dive shops and the Monroe County Tourist Development Council bought the cutters, which were subsequently stripped of armament, hatches, and masts, then cleaned. In 1987 the Army Corps of Engineers sank the 327-foot vessels on consecutive days. The *Bibb* rests on her side in 130 feet of water with her upper portions accessible at 90 feet. The upright *Duane* sits in more than 100 feet of water, but you can see the wheelhouse at 80 feet and the crow's nest in 60 feet of water. Location: *Bibb*—Lat. 24° 59.71, Long. 80° 22.77; *Duane*—Lat. 24° 59.38, Long. 80° 22.92.

PICKLES REEF

Pickles Reef got its name from the coral-encrusted barrels strewn about the ocean floor near the remnants of a cargo ship, called the Pickles Wreck, that carried them to their demise. The kegs are said to resemble pickle barrels, hence the name of the reef, but more likely were filled with building mortar bound for burgeoning construction in Key West. Look for the distinctively marked flamingo tongue snails, which attach themselves to swaying purple sea fans, grazing for algae. Flamboyantly extended around the outside of the flamingo tongue's glossy cream-colored shell is a bright orange mantle with black-ringed leopardlike spots. Don't be tempted to collect these unusual creatures, for the colorful mantle is withdrawn upon death. With depths between 10 and 25 feet and a moderate current, Pickles Reef is a good dive for novice to intermediate skill levels. Location: Lat. 24° 59.23, Long. 80° 24.88.

CONCH REEF

Dive charters usually anchor in about 60 feet of water at Conch Reef, but the area actually offers something for everyone. With depths ranging from shallow to 100 feet and currents varying from moderate to strong, beginners as well as intermediate and advanced divers will be entranced here. The shallow section, festive with swirling schools of small tropicals, extends for a mile along the outer reef line. Conch Wall steeply drops from 60 to 100 feet, where sea rods, whips, fans, and plumes of the gorgonian family's deepwater branch congregate with an agglomeration of vaselike convoluted barrel sponges. The coral of Conch Reef was nearly decimated by heavy harvesting in bygone eras; dead stumps of pillar corals can still be seen. Location: Lat. 24° 57.11, Long. 80° 27.57.

HENS AND CHICKENS

A brood of large star coral heads surrounds a 35-foot U.S. Navy light tower within 7 feet of the water's surface on this inshore patch reef, bringing to mind a mother hen and her chicks. Less than 3 miles from shore, this easily accessed 20-foot-deep reef remains popular with novice divers. Plumes, fans, and candelabra soft corals intermingle with skeletons of the coral graveyard (almost 80 percent of the reef died in 1970 after an unusually cold winter). Jailhouse-striped sheepshead mingle with shy notch-tailed grunts and the more curious stout-bodied groupers, but don't be tempted; spearfishing is not allowed here. Remains of the Brick Barge, a modern casualty, and an old steel barge torpedoed during World War II lie among the coral heads. Location: Lat. 24° 55.9, Long. 80° 32.90.

EAGLE

In 1985 an electrical fire disabled the 287-foot *Aaron K,* a freighter that carried scrap paper between Miami and South America. Declared a total loss, she was sold to the Monroe County Tourist Council and a group of local dive shops and then scuttled for use as an artificial reef. The vessel was renamed the *Eagle* after the Eagle Tire Company, which provided much of the funding for the project. A must-do for advanced divers, the *Eagle* landed on her starboard side in 120-foot waters, though her upper portions lurk within 65 feet of the surface. Densely packed polarized schools of silversides flow and drift within her interior. The tiny fork-tailed fish will detour around divers swimming through the school. Location: Lat. 24° 52.18, Long. 80° 34.21.

Middle Keys

ALLIGATOR REEF

Launched in 1820 in Boston, the USS *Alligator* hunted pirates in Florida as part of the West Indies Squadron. A 136-foot light tower now marks her namesake, Alligator Reef, which claimed the copper- and bronze-fitted warship in 1825. The navy stripped the ship's valuables and blew her up. The *Alligator* rests offshore from the 8- to 40-foot-deep reef, now a bordello of brilliant tropicals, corals, and shells. Location: Lat. 24° 51.07, Long. 80° 37.21.

AMERICAN, MARYLAND, AND PELICAN SHOALS

American, Maryland, and Pelican shoals lie just off shore of the Saddlebunch Keys. They are east of Summerland and Cudjoe Keys where dive boats depart. Teeming with fish, these reefs are less visited than others in the Florida Keys.

COFFINS PATCH

Gargantuan grooved brain corals join staghorns and toxic fire corals at Coffins Patch, a 1½-mile reef popular with Middle Keys divers. A drift of yellow-finned French grunts and festive angelfish join an escort of mutton snappers, each distinctively branded with a black spot below the rear dorsal fin, as they guard the remains of the Spanish galleon *Ignacio,* which spewed a cargo of coins across the ocean floor in 1733. Location: Lat. 24° 40.60, Long. 80° 58.50.

THUNDERBOLT

In 1986 the artificial reef committee bought the *Thunderbolt,* a 188-foot cable-laying workboat, from a Miami River boatyard. The vessel was cleaned and her hatches removed. She then was towed south of Coffins Patch, where she was sunk as an artificial reef. Sitting majestically upright in 115 feet of water, the *Thunderbolt*'s bronze propellers, cable-laying spool, and wheelhouse are still recognizable. A stainless-steel cable leads from the wreck to a permanent underwater buoy. Current is strong at this wreck. Clip a line to the eye on the buoy and walk down the line. This dive is suitable for those with advanced certification. Location: Lat. 24° 39.48, Long. 80° 57.90.

DELTA SHOALS

This shallow 10- to 20-foot shoal claimed many an unsuspecting ship through the centuries. Perhaps the most colorful history is that of an old vessel that ran aground in the 1850s. The ship yielded no treasure, but recovery of unique relics and elephant tusks led to the name Ivory Wreck. Among the wreckage were leg irons and brass bowls, leading historians to believe this was a slave ship from Africa. Location: Lat. 24° 37.78, Long. 81° 05.49.

SOMBRERO REEF

A 142-foot lighthouse tower marks this living marine museum. Coral chasms, ridges, and portals support a proliferation of fuzzy, feathery, or hairy gorgonians as well as a salad bowl of leafy lettuce coral. A battalion of toothy barracuda swims reconnaissance, but don't be alarmed. You are too big to be considered tasty. Location: Lat 24° 37.50, Long. 81° 06.50.

Lower Keys

LOOE KEY NATIONAL MARINE SANCTUARY

In 1744 Capt. Ashby Utting ran the 124-foot British frigate HMS *Looe* hard aground on the 5-square-mile Y-shaped reef now bearing her name. Remains of the ship are interred between two fingers of living coral about 200 yards from the marker in 25 feet of water. The ballast and the anchor remain camouflaged with centuries of vigorous coral growth. Preserved as a national marine sanctuary since 1981, the 5- to 35-foot-deep waters surrounding Looe Key protect the diverse marine communities from fishing, lobstering, or artifact collecting, all forbidden.

The sanctuary, like Key Largo National Marine Sanctuary in the Upper Keys, offers interesting dives for novice, intermediate, and advanced divers alike. The spur-and-groove formations of Looe Key National Marine Sanctuary are the best developed in the Keys, and you can observe a complete coral reef ecosystem within the sanctuary's boundaries (see the Paradise Found chapter).

Take a laminated reef-creature guide sheet (readily available in dive shops) on your dive to identify the senses-boggling array of sea life at Looe Key. Look for some of these interesting species: The yellowhead jawfish excavates a hole in the sand with its mouth and retreats, tail-first, at the first sign of danger. The wary cottonwick sports a bold black stripe from snout to tail. The prehistoric-looking red lizardfish rests camouflaged on rocks and coral. The occasional blue-spotted peacock flounder changes color, chameleon-like, to match its surroundings.

Commercial dive charters provide excursions to Looe Key from Big Pine Key, Little Torch Key, and Ramrod Key. Location: Lat. 24° 32.70, Long. 81° 24.50.

THE *ADOLPHUS BUSCH*

Scuttled in 1998 between Looe Key and American Shoal, this 210-foot freighter is named for one of the founders of the brewing industry. The *Adolphus Busch* sits upright in 100 feet of water. A tower comes within 40 feet of the surface and can be penetrated. *Adolphus Busch* is rapidly becoming a thriving tenement of fish and marine organisms. Location: Lat. 24° 31.81, Long. 81° 27.64.

Key West

EASTERN SAMBO

An underwater ridge at 60 feet dropping off sharply to the sand line at 87 feet goes by the name of Eastern Drop-off in this immensely popular reef area southeast of Key West. Reddish-brown honeycomb plate corals encrust the sloping reef face while boulder corals pepper the base at the outer margin of the reef. The Hook, a long spur-and-groove canyon, extends south from the Eastern Sambo reef marker. Look for cruising tarpon during the summer months. West of Eastern Sambo is a site commonly referred to as No. 28 Marker, where sea turtles and nurse sharks make their rounds of the elkhorn coral. Location: Lat. 24° 29.50, Long. 81° 39.80.

MIDDLE SAMBO

Coral heads and soft corals cover the sand beneath the 30- to 40-foot depths of Middle Sambo. You won't be alone as you observe the prolific lobsters haunting this area, especially in the summer months. Look for squadrons of tarpon and snook. Location: Lat. 24° 29.71, Long. 81° 41.79.

WESTERN SAMBO

Mooring buoys mark this popular reef area with a variety of dives to 40 feet. Fields of branch coral stretch into the blue infinity while mountains of sheet, boulder, star, and pillar corals cover the dramatic drop from 28 to 40 feet. Small yellow stingrays, which are actually covered with dark spots and can pale and darken protectively when the environment dictates, lie on the bottom with their stout, venomous tails buried in the sand. In the protected midreef area of the Cut, goggle-eyed blennies mill about with a colony of yellowhead jawfish, retreating tail first into their sand holes when frightened.

Half a mile south of Western Sambo, the remains of the *Aquanaut,* a 50-foot wooden tugboat owned by Chet Alexander, was scuttled in 75 feet of water as an artificial reef. Scattered about amid drifts of mahogany snappers and nocturnal glasseyes, the wreck is alive with spider-like yellow arrow crabs. Location: Lat. 24° 29.38, Long. 81° 42.68.

A Natural Aquarium

As you crest the Bahia Honda Bridge at MM 35, while heading down the Keys, look for The Horseshoe, or Cuban Quarry, on the bayside. During the building of the Bahia Honda Bridge years ago, the fill formed a jetty-lined lagoon that is now a natural aquarium. A shallow sandbar keeps barracudas and sharks at bay (no pun intended), protecting a menagerie of marine life. To find The Horseshoe, turn right at the first opportunity after crossing Bahia Honda Bridge when heading down the Keys. Follow the dirt road past the stack of leftover bridge pilings to the water's edge. No camping or overnight stays by RVs are allowed.

CAYMAN SALVAGER

The 187-foot-long, steel-hulled buoy tender *Cayman Salvager,* built in 1936, originally sank at the Key West docks in the 1970s. Refloated and innards removed, she went back down in 1985 for use as an artificial reef, coming to rest on her side. Hurricane-force waves later righted her, and she now sits in 90 feet of water on a sandy bottom. Look for the fabled 200-pound jewfish and 6-foot moray eel residing in her open hold. Location: 6 miles south of Key West, 1 mile southwest of Nine Foot Stake, which is 1 mile west of No. 1 Marker.

JOE'S TUG

Sitting upright in 60 feet of water, *Joe's Tug,* a 75-foot steel-hulled tugboat, was scuttled as an artificial reef in 1989. The boat rests inshore from the *Cayman Salvager* on a bed of coral. This is one of the most popular wreck dives in the Key West circuit. Look for Elvis, the resident jewfish, who hangs out at the tug with yet another large moray eel. Location: 6 miles south of Key West.

EASTERN DRY ROCKS

Shells, conchs, ballast stones, cannonballs, and rigging of disintegrating wrecks litter the rubble zone, coral fingers, and sand canyons of Eastern Dry Rocks. With depths between 5 and 35 feet and only light current, this dive is suited to novices. Location: Lat. 24° 27.50, Long. 81° 50.44.

ROCK KEY

Twenty-foot cracks barely as wide as a single diver distinguish Rock Key from nearby cousins at Eastern Dry Rocks. A 19th-century ship carrying building tiles from Barcelona went aground on Rock Key, scattering her bounty about the ocean floor. Tiles carrying the Barcelona imprint are reportedly still occasionally recovered. Location: Lat. 24° 27.21, Long. 81° 51.60.

STARGAZER

Billed as the "world's largest underwater sculptured reef," Stargazer stands 22 feet below the surface, 5 miles off Key West between Rock Key and Sand Key. The creation of artist Ann Lorraine Labriola, Stargazer mimics a primitive navigational instrument, its giant steel sections—ranging between 2,000 and 8,000 pounds—emblazoned with constellation symbols and emblems. A "mystery chart" sends divers on an underwater treasure hunt with a series of puzzles that require a certain amount of celestial knowledge to solve. Location: Lat. 24° 27.49, Long. 81° 52.09.

SAND KEY

Originally called *Cays Arena* by early Spanish settlers, Sand Key, 6 miles south of Key West, is partially awash at low tide. Topped by a distinctive 110-foot red iron lighthouse, Sand Key's shape, composed of shells and ground coral, changes with each hurricane and tropical storm. Sand Key shines as a good all-weather dive and, with depths ranging to 65 feet, appeals to all skill levels. The shallows of the leeward side provide good snorkeling. In spring and summer the Gulf Stream movement over the shallows provides great visibility and vibrant colors. You can easily reach Sand Key on your own in a 17- to 18-foot boat on a calm day. Location: Lat. 24° 27.19, Long. 81° 52.58.

TEN-FATHOM BAR

Advanced divers peruse a gallery of deep dives on the western end of the outer reef system, which is nearly 4 miles long. The southern edge, Fennel Ridge, begins at about 60 feet deep, giving the site its name, then plunges to the sand line, undulating between 90 and 120 feet. Encrusted telegraph cables at 45 to 55 feet, apparently snaking a line to Havana, cut across the eastern end of the Ten-Fathom Bar, competing with man-size sponges and dramatic black coral.

Near the cable, Eye of the Needle sports a plateau of coral spurs. Deep, undercut ledges shelter the spotted, white-bellied porcupinefish. Divers can swim under a ledge and up through a broad "eye" to the top of the plateau. Depths max out at 120 feet, but you'll see much more between 40 and 80 feet. Be prepared for a sea squadron of fin-driven tropicals to shadow your every move. Location: Half a mile due south of Sand Key.

WESTERN DRY ROCKS

Experts will love the unusual marine life at Western Dry Rocks. Novices and snorkelers will, too, because this site ranges in depth from 5 to 120 feet, averaging 30 feet with lots of light. Coral fingers with defined gullies and coral formations laced with cracks and caves showcase species normally found more in the Bahamas than in the Keys. The deep-dwelling candy basslets hide themselves away at 90 feet, while their more gregarious cousins, the orangeback bass, hang out in the open. The dusky longsnout butterflyfish prefer dark recesses, though they will sometimes curiously peer out to see what's happening. Sharks have been witnessed regularly enough to prompt advice against spearfishing. Location: 3 miles west of Sand Key.

ALEXANDER'S WRECK

Commercial salvor Chet Alexander bought a 328-foot destroyer escort from the U.S. Navy at the bargain price of $2,000 and sank her (still sporting her deck guns) in about 40 feet of water west of Cottrell Key as an artificial reef in 1972. Though the current fluctuates from moderate to strong, the relatively shallow depths here allow conscientious novices a chance to swim among fascinating sea creatures: The bodies of the prison-bar-striped spadefish resemble the spade figures in a deck of playing cards. Zebra-striped sheepshead are so curious that if you remain stationary, they may come over to investigate. The flashy metallic gold- and silver-striped porkfish is apparently the victim of a cruel creator—two bold, black, diagonal bands slash across its glittery head. Location: Lat. 24° 36.97, Long. 81° 58.91.

COTTRELL KEY

A snorkeler's paradise at 3 to 15 feet, Cottrell Key, on the gulfside, saves the day for divers when the weather is foul on the Atlantic. The grassy banks of the adjoining lakes protect the reef in east-southeast to southwest winds. Ledges and solution holes run for several miles amid intermittent coral heads and swaying gorgonians.

The pits, crevices, and coral caves hold great treasures: encrusting orange sponges, which look like spilled cake batter; lustrously mottled cowries camouflaged by their extended mantles; the Florida horse conchs, which will venture out of their long conical spire if you wait patiently; and the spindle-shaped freckled tulip snails. Location: Gulf side, 9 miles out of N.W. Channel.

And Beyond

THE SHIPWRECKS OF SMITH SHOALS

Between June and August 1942, four large ships met their demise near Smith Shoals, apparent unwary victims of American military mines. USS *Sturtevent*, a 314-foot-long four-stack destroyer, was only two hours out of port escorting a convoy when two consecutive explosions ripped her apart. She rests in 65 feet of water. The 3,000-ton American freighter *Edward Luchenbach,* en route from Jamaica to New Orleans with a cargo of tin, zinc, and tungsten, joined the *Sturtevent* after hitting the same minefield. The *Bosiljka* also made a navigational misstep, succumbing to an American mine as she carried her pharmaceutical cargo from New Orleans to Key West. Groupers, jewfish, snappers, and cobia populate the sunken 277-foot Norwegian ship *Gunvor*, taken by a mine on her way to Trinidad from Mobile, Alabama. The wreckage is scattered in 60 feet of water. Location: Lat. 24° 45.30, Long. 81° 01.18.

Discovered in 1960 in Hawk Channel near Indian Key, the San Pedro Underwater State Park makes a great shallow dive. This site is a shipwreck of a 287-ton, Dutch-built ship that was part of a Spanish flotilla that left Cuba for Spain. She was sank by a hurricane in 1733. For more information, visit www.flheritage.com.

MARQUESAS KEYS

This group of 10 mangrove islands surrounded by shallow waters has alternately been called the remains of a prehistoric meteor crater and an atoll. The ring of keys was named for the Marquis de Cadierata, commander of the 1622 Spanish fleet that included the wrecks *Atocha* and *Santa Margarita.* The wrecks were partially salvaged until 1630 by the Spanish, who enticed slave divers to search the remains, promising freedom to the first diver to recover a bar of silver from the site. Mel Fisher rediscovered the ships in 1985. Fisher, the famous 20th-century salvor, found a mother lode of treasure in the holds. The islands evidence little human influence, for they remain uninhabited. Clusters of coral heads shrouded in groupers and snappers mark the southern edge of the islands. Twenty-five miles from Key West, the Marquesas appeal to divers cruising in their motor yachts or on an overnight charter or to hale and hearty day-trippers. West of the Marquesas several wrecks dot the sub-oceanic landscape. Exercise caution before diving, however, because the U.S. Navy has been known to use them as bombing and strafing targets from time to time. Before you strap on your tanks, check your radio for a Coast Guard bulletin regarding this area. Location: 25 miles west of Key West.

NORTHWIND

The *Northwind,* a large metal tugboat belonging to Mel Fisher's Treasure Salvors Inc., tragically sank in 1975 while working on the *Atocha* project. Said to have a malfunctioning fuel valve and a leaky bulkhead, the *Northwind* capsized while at anchor, taking Fisher's son and daughter-in-law to a watery grave. The vessel lies on her side in 40 feet of water 3½ miles southwest of the Marquesas.

COSGROVE SHOAL

A 50-foot skeletal lighthouse marks the northern edge of the Gulf Stream, 6 miles south of the western Marquesas. This rocky bank runs for miles, a prehistoric dead reef where caves and ledges support gardens and forests and social clubs of marine fin and flora. A contingent of giant barracuda patrols the shallows, and black coral grows up from the depths, which extend beyond recreational diving capacities. Be sure to take the strong outgoing tide into consideration before you dive here. Location: 6 miles south of the western edge of the Marquesas.

MARQUESAS ROCK

Moderate to strong currents and depths to 120 feet dictate that this dive is only suited to advanced skill levels. A can-buoy marks the rocky plateau of Marquesas Rock, the cracks and crevices of which reveal a potpourri of sea life. A school of jacks, apparently attracted by your bubbles, may make a swing past. Saucer-eyed reddish squirrelfish, with elongated rear dorsal fins resembling squirrel tails, mind their own business in the shaded bottom crevices. Occasional sightings of sailfish, sperm whales, and white sharks have been reported. Keep in mind that when diving at Marquesas Rock you are 30 miles from the nearest assistance.

DRY TORTUGAS NATIONAL PARK

The end of the line in the Florida Keys, the Dry Tortugas lie some 60 miles beyond Key West. Small boats are discouraged from making the trip because strong tidal currents flowing against prevailing winds between Rebecca Shoals and the reef of the Tortugas can be treacherous. There is no fuel, fresh water, or facilities offering provisions, nor will you find any emergency assistance. Nonetheless, if your vessel is self-sufficient, if you are with a charter out of Key West, or you have traveled to the Dry Tortugas by seaplane or ferry to camp on Garden Key (see the Recreation and Campgrounds chapters), you are in for the treat of a lifetime.

The eight-island chain is guarded as our southernmost national park. All living creatures below are protected from collection or capture, so a virtual mega-aquarium exists beneath the sea. The constant Gulf Stream current cleanses the waters, allowing visibility of 80 to 100 feet over the 100-square-mile living coral reef. Just off the beach on the west side of Loggerhead Key slumbers a snorkelers' paradise. About a mile offshore lies the remains of a 300-foot, steel-hulled French wreck. Divers report that a monster-size jewfish estimated to be 150 years old resides under the wreck. Other wrecks are littered about the ocean floor, claimed by the reef during centuries past.

DIVE CENTERS

As you drive down the Overseas Highway from Key Largo to Key West, you will notice banner-size, red-and-white diver-down flags heralding one dive shop after another. More than 100 such establishments are listed in the phone book alone. To help you navigate this minefield of choices, we supply you with the best ammunition: information.

Many of the dive operations offer the same basic services and will take you to similar, if not the same, spots. But each also differs in many ways. Snorkelers and divers often are taken to the reef in the same excursion, for the varied depths of our spur-and-groove reefs can be experienced with multiple levels of expertise. Snorkel-only trips also are an option. The size of dive excursions varies greatly, ranging from 20 individuals or more to a small-boat group called a six-pack.

Dive rates are based on a two-tank, two-site daylight dive. If you don't have your own equipment, full-gear packages—generally including two tanks, buoyancy compensator, weight belt, regulator, octopus breathing device, gauges, and occasionally mask, fins, and snorkel—are available. A wet suit (only needed in the winter months) will cost between $10 and

CLOSE-UP

Diving for Lobster

Umm, umm good. Lobster.

Now, you easterners may conjure up scarlet visions of the mighty Maines, but when we say lobster here in the Florida Keys, a totally different creature comes to mind. Equally delectable and much in demand, the Florida lobster, or spiny lobster, is actually a crustacean whose relatives include crabs, shrimp, and crawfish. Unlike its Down East cousin, the Florida lobster is clawless. Ten spiderlike legs support its spiny head and hard-shell body, and radarlike antennae make up for bugged eyes and weak eyesight. But its best defense, and the one most coveted by hungry humans, remains its powerful tail muscle, which propels the lobster backward at breakneck speed.

Diving for lobster is a popular sport in the waters of the Florida Keys. Like any other hunt, you will need to understand your intended prey, for self-preservation will be their only consideration. Nocturnal feeders, spiny lobsters hide underwater in crevices, between rocks, in caves, under artificial reefs, near dock pilings, or in dead coral outcroppings during the day. They are not easy to spot. They occasionally peek out from their protective holes, but most often only a single antenna will be visible. The good news is that a whole gang may be hiding out together.

So how do you catch these potentially tasty morsels locals call "bugs"? We have found a few basic tools—and tricks—to help swing the scales in our favor. You will need a pair of heavy-duty dive gloves, for the two large horns on the lobster's head and the sharp spines of its whipping tail can draw blood. To store your captive prizes, get an easy-to-open mesh game bag that has a fastener that you can hook to your weight belt. Be sure this bag does not drag over the reef, which would damage coral and other marine life. A probe, or "tickle stick," which is a long metal or fiberglass rod with a short, 90-degree bend on one end, allows you to wisely restrain from poking your arm into a crevice or hole in order to coax out a lobster. That hole could just as easily house a moray eel as a lobster. (This toothsome green eel has been known to clamp its enormous mouth firmly and painfully into many an unsuspecting diver's arm.) And finally, a lobster net is a must if you hope to capture the tickled lobster.

Florida law mandates lobster hunters carry a device to measure the carapace of each lobster. (The carapace is that portion of the lobster shell beginning between the eyes and extending to the hard end segment just before the tail.) The carapace should measure at least 3 inches; otherwise the lobster—deemed a "short"—must be returned to the sea. The measuring device is most often made of plastic or metal and can be attached to a string and secured to your game bag. Measure the lobster before you put it in your bag; do not bring it to the boat to be measured.

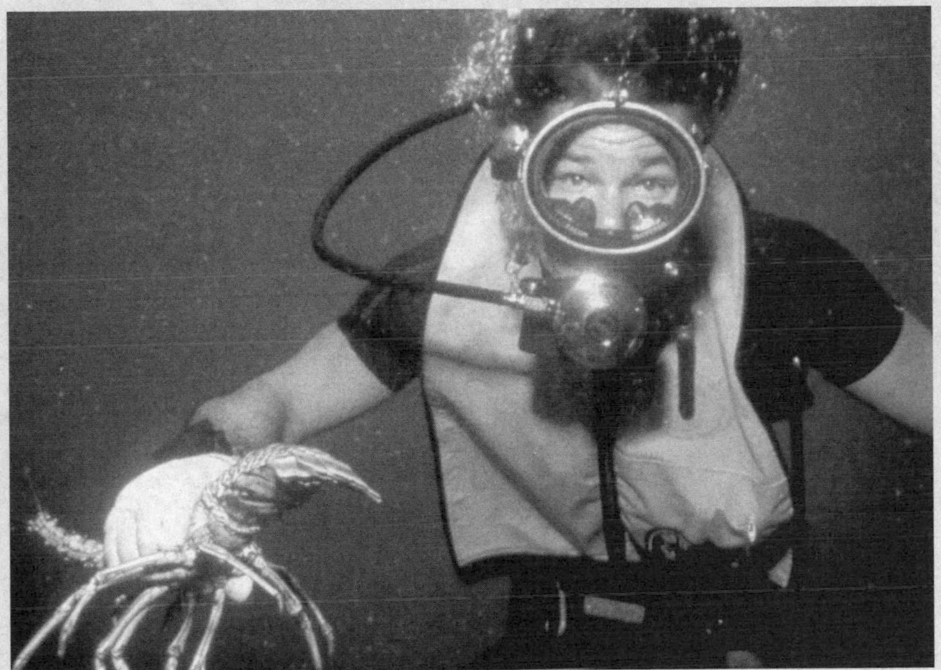

Sport diving for lobster is popular in Florida Keys waters. PHOTO: WAYNE MOCCIA

To harvest lobsters in the Florida Keys recreationally, you must possess a valid Florida saltwater fishing license with a current crawfish stamp (see the Fishing chapter).

Look for lobsters in the patch reefs on the oceanside. Patch reefs can usually be found by using the NOAA navigational charts. Look for relatively shallow areas (15 to 20 feet) surrounded by deeper water (25 to 30 feet). If your boat is equipped with a chart recorder, use this device to detect bottom contours and the presence of fish. Look for irregular bottom areas, which will usually mean coral outcroppings and sponges. When you find the suspected patch reefs, check them out with a quick dive to the bottom before anchoring your boat. You will need to scuba dive for lobsters in the patch reefs.

Alternately, look for lobster "holes" in the shallow gulfside waters and, wearing mask, fins, and snorkel, free-dive for the crustaceans—a one-breath challenge for sure. These areas will appear as patches of brightness in the turtle-grass floor as you skim across the water in your skiff. Sandy sea bottom looks bright also, so you must slow to idle speed and look for a hunk of coral. It helps to throw a buoy marker at this spot (connect a dive weight to a Styrofoam buoy with a length of line), because these coral outcroppings are few and far between. Send a dive scout over the side to bird-dog the outcropping for antennae, and with a little luck, the hunt will begin.

You have displayed your diver-down flag. You're equipped. You're psyched. You're under water. Now what? Stay cool and calm. Move slowly. These crusty crustaceans are a wily group. When frightened, the lobster will contract its powerful tail and propel itself like a bullet backward to the far recesses of its shelter or deep into the sea grass. Tickle your way to victory. Slowly slide your tickle stick behind the lobster and tap its tail. Bothered from behind, the lobster is persuaded to slowly leave its shelter to investigate. Once the lobster is out of the hole, place the net behind (yes, behind!) the lobster with the rim firmly resting on the sandy bottom if possible. Tap the lobster's head with the tickle stick. This time, irritated, the lobster will propel backward into your net. Quickly slam your net down on the seafloor so the lobster cannot escape. Then secure the net closed with your other hand. The lobster may thrash and become tangled in the net.

Holding the netted lobster firmly with one hand, measure the carapace. Carefully remove the lobster from the net. If the lobster is a short, release it to be captured another day. If it is legal size, place it securely in your game bag, tail-first. One thrust of the vigorous tail could negate all your efforts. Also, be careful not to release any other "bugs" you have already bagged. If you see a dark spot or reddish orange nodules under the tail, this lobster is an egg-bearing female. By Florida law you must release her.

Place your captured lobsters in the saltwater-filled bait well of your boat or store them on ice in a cooler with a lid. Do not wring the tails from the lobsters until you get back to shore. It is against Florida law to separate the tail from the body while on Florida waters. Once on dry land you may pull the tails, which by law must measure more than 5½ inches. There is negligible meat in the body of the Florida spiny lobster, so it may be discarded unless you want to boil it to make lobster stock. After wringing the tail, break an antenna from the severed body of the crawfish. Insert the antenna, larger end first, into the underside base of the tail and then pull it out. The spiny thorns of the antenna will snag the intestinal tract, which will be removed with the antenna. If you wish to freeze the lobster tails, place several in a small plastic zipper bag, fill the bag with fresh water, and place the bags in the freezer for up to six months.

We think the best way to cook Florida lobster tail is on the grill. First, with a sharp knife or kitchen scissors, butterfly the tail by cutting through the outer shell and meat. Spread the tail open and sprinkle with melted butter, salt, pepper, and onion powder or garlic powder if desired.

Place the tail on a double-thick piece of aluminum foil and fold the foil envelope style, sealing tightly. Grill over hot coals for 15 to 20 minutes or until the shell is bright red and the meat is no longer translucent. Serve grilled lobster tail with clarified butter or a slice of key lime.

Sport Lobster Season
Sport lobster season takes on festival proportions in the Florida Keys, but the competition is keen. Previewing the official opening of lobster season, the last consecutive Wednesday and Thursday in July are a designated sport season in the state and federal waters for the nonprofessional spiny lobster hunter. Every motel, hotel, and campground in the Florida Keys is filled beyond capacity. Divers are allotted six lobsters per person per day; sunrise to sunset is considered a day. Diving at night is not permitted. John Pennekamp Coral Reef State Park is closed to lobstering during the sport season. Contact the Florida Keys National Marine Sanctuary at (305) 743-2437 or their Web site, www.fknms.nos.noaa.gov, for more information on sport lobster season rules and restrictions.

Regular Lobster Season
Regular season, which is when commercial lobstermen begin putting out their traps, commences in early August and ends in late March. Rules differ slightly in state and federal waters. The bag limit in state waters is six lobsters per person per day, or 24 per boat, whichever is greater. State waters surround the Florida Keys out to 3 miles oceanside and 9 miles on the Gulf. You may dive for lobster at night in state waters during regular lobster season.

Areas of John Pennekamp Coral Reef State Park restricted from lobstering include Turtle Rocks, Basin Hills North, Mosquito Bank North, Three Sisters North, Higdon's Reef, Basin Hills East, Mosquito Bank Southeast, Three Sisters South, Cannon Patch, and Basin Hills South. Lobstering is prohibited year-round in Everglades National Park, Biscayne Bay/Card Sound Spiny Lobster Sanctuary, and Dry Tortugas National Park. Three areas of the Florida Keys National Marine Sanctuary are no-take areas, marked by 30-inch-diameter round yellow boundary buoys: Sanctuary Preservation Areas (SPAs), Special-use Research Only Areas, and Ecological Reserves. See the sanctuary's Web site for more information: www.fknms.nos.noaa.gov.

Those waters beyond the state limits are deemed federal waters; see a NOAA chart for the official boundary lines. The bag limit in federal waters is six lobsters per person per day, or six per person per trip when the trip is longer than one day. The per-boat quota does not apply in federal waters. You may not combine the federal bag limit with the state bag limit.

Words to the Wise
- Always display your diver-down flag when you are diving or snorkeling for lobster.
- Be careful not to damage coral while you are harvesting lobster.
- Anchor in the sand or use a mooring buoy.
- Use an official NOAA navigational chart when navigating our waters.
- Do not molest, damage, or take lobster from traps. It is a felony offense in Florida.
- You may not use spears, hooks, or wire snares to capture or dismember lobsters.

$15 extra. Always ask exactly what is included if you need a full-gear package. All our recommended dive centers make a one-tank, night-dive excursion on request unless otherwise specified.

Snorkel-only rates, which often include equipment, run between $25 and $40. Children usually are offered a reduced fare. Bubble Watchers, those who'd like to come along for the ride and watch their companions dive or snorkel, will pay between $15 and $25. You may assume that snorkelers and Bubble Watchers can accompany divers unless otherwise stated.

Virtually all of our listed dive centers offer optional dive packages, either for multiple days of diving or for hotel-dive combinations. If you plan to dive on several days of your holiday, you will save money with a package, but you will be limited to diving with one exclusive dive center.

You may assume, unless otherwise noted, all featured dive centers rent full equipment and maintain a retail dive shop where you can purchase equipment, accessories, and underwater camera housings if needed. You may also count on the fact that all recommended dive centers offer a one-day "let's give it a try" resort course (it ranges between $150 and $175) and a basic open-water certification course ($350 to $425). These courses are based on participation of two or more people. Private courses also are available at a considerably higher fee. Many of our recommended dive centers offer a wide selection of PADI, NAUI, and other advanced classes.

You will be required to show your certification card and logbook, and you must wear a buoyancy compensator and a submersible pressure gauge. Snorkels are required equipment for all divers. To dive deeper than 60 feet, considered a deep dive, you must hold advanced certification or a logbook entry showing dives to equivalent depths within the last six months. If you cannot meet these specifications, you will be required to be accompanied by an instructor or guide, which often requires an additional fee. You must wear an octopus (an emergency breathing device to share air with your dive buddy) or carry spare air for a deep dive, and you must be equipped with a depth gauge or a timing device. You do not need advanced certification to participate in a night dive, but you must own or rent a dive light and carry a Cyalume stick as a backup lighting system.

All dive centers request you check in at least 30 minutes prior to the excursion's departure. Allow even more time if you are renting a full-gear package. We list the dive centers in descending mile marker order from Key Largo through the Lower Keys to Key West, where the listings are alphabetical.

Upper Keys

Captain Slate's Atlantis Dive Center
MM 106.5 Oceanside, 51 Garden Cove Drive, Key Largo
(305) 451-1325, (800) 331-3483
www.pennekamp.com/atlantis

You can watch Captain Slate feed baitfish to a barracuda, mouth to mouth, and see him cuddle with a moray eel on the weekly Friday-morning "Creature Feature" dive trip with Captain Slate's Atlantis Dive Center, when the captain himself performs these fearless feats under water. Divers from all skill levels enjoy outings with the Atlantis Dive Center. Snorkelers can make a snorkel-only excursion to one destination aboard a glass-bottomed boat at 9:30 A.M., 12:30 P.M., and 3:30 P.M., or they can accompany divers to two reef locations. Snorkeling rates here include mask, fins, snorkel, and safety vest. Dive departure times at Captain Slate's are 8:30 A.M. and 1:00 P.M.

A special feature of Captain Slate's is the custom underwater wedding package. Divers are married in front of the *Christ of the Deep* statue at Key Largo Dry Rocks. Vows are made via underwater slates as guest-divers watch the ceremony from the ocean floor and guest-snorkelers view the proceedings from overhead. Guest-landlubbers are accommodated in the glass-bottomed boat, where the perspective varies yet again. Videos and still-photography of the blessed event are also available.

Kelly's on the Bay and Aqua-Nuts Dive Center
MM 104.2 Bayside, Key Largo
(305) 451-1622, (800) 226-0415
www.kellysonthebay.com
www.aqua-nuts.com

At Kelly's on the Bay, you can literally step off the boat and fall into bed, because this dive operation is a complete waterfront resort. Aqua-Nuts takes divers to all the popular reefs in Key Largo National Marine Sanctuary and John Pennekamp Coral Reef State Park, including *Christ of the Deep* statue, the wreck of the *Benwood,* Molasses Reef, the Elbow, the *Duane,* the *Spiegel Grove,* and even to Conch Reef. And unlike most dive shops, you can rent its gear without booking onto one of its charters—a real plus if you are venturing out on your own. Dive and snorkel departures are at 8:30 A.M. and 1:00 P.M. Night dives are regularly offered on Tuesday, Friday, and Saturday, and other times upon request.

Amy Slate's Amoray Dive Resort
MM 104.2 Bayside, Key Largo
(305) 451-3595, (800) 426-6729
www.amoray.com

From this resort, you can hop out of bed onto the deck and take off for a scuba excursion. The Amoray Dive Resort's villa lodging options, complete with hot tub and pool, cater to your every diving whim (see the Accommodations chapter). Amoray's catamaran will whisk you to the reefs of the Key Largo National Marine Sanctuary for a two-tank dive. Dive and snorkel departures are at 8:30 A.M. and 1:00 P.M. Night dives are regularly scheduled on Thursday and Saturday.

Silent World Dive Center Inc.
MM 103.2 Bayside, Key Largo
(305) 451-3252, (800) 966-3483
www.pennekamp.com/sw

Remember, queen conch is a protected species in the Florida Keys. (All conch you see offered on restaurant menus or in seafood markets is imported.) Please respect our queen of the Conch Republic.

Silent World regularly visits the Elbow, Key Largo Dry Rocks, the *Benwood,* French Reef, Carysfort Reef, and other popular sites within Key Largo National Marine Sanctuary. Dive and snorkel departures are at 9:00 A.M. and 1:00 P.M.

John Pennekamp Coral Reef State Park Boat Rentals & Dive Center
MM 102.5 Oceanside, Key Largo
(305) 451-6322, (877) 538-7348
www.johnpennekamp.com

Pennekamp State Park Dive Center prides itself on being the "only authorized dive center" in John Pennekamp Coral Reef State Park, although all the Key Largo dive centers advertise themselves as diving Pennekamp State Park. The only dive center actually situated inside Pennekamp's grounds, this company's scuba shuttles regularly visit such novice sport dives as Molasses Reef, French Reef, Christmas Tree Cove, the wreck of the *Benwood*, and the *Christ of the Deep* statue. All dives are less than 60 feet, and certification requirements are stringent. If you have not dived in the past two years, you must hire a guide. If you have not dived in three years, you will have to take a review course. Dive departures are at 9:30 A.M. and 1:30 P.M. Pennekamp does not offer night dives.

Coral Reef Park Company
MM 102.5 Oceanside, John Pennekamp Coral Reef State Park, Key Largo
(305) 451-1621
www.johnpennekamp.com

Snorkel-only excursions in John Pennekamp Coral Reef State Park leave the docks three times daily. The shallow-reef sites vary, depending upon where the least current, least wave action, and best visibility conditions exist. The snorkel trip

> **i** ***The Florida Keys National Marine Sanctuary has devised a Shipwreck Trail that directs you to nine historic shipwreck sites along our coral reef. Underwater site guides for each of the wrecks are available at local dive shops. The guides provide shipwreck and mooring-buoy positions, history of the wrecked ships, a site map, and information on marine organisms you may encounter.***

lasts two and a half hours, with an hour and a half of actual snorkeling time at Molasses Reef, White Bank Dry Rocks, Grecian Rocks, Key Largo Dry Rocks, or Cannon Patch. Departures are 9:00 A.M., noon, and 3:00 P.M. There is a $5.00 charge for equipment.

Another option is a four-hour sail and snorkel aboard a 38-foot catamaran, which leaves daily at 9:00 A.M. and 1:30 P.M. If you want to stay close to shore, you can rent mask, fins, and snorkel for $10 and paddle around in the water off Cannon Beach, where, yes, there really are a couple of sunken cannon and ancient anchors.

Ocean Divers
MM 100 Oceanside, 522 Caribbean Drive, Key Largo
(305) 451-1113, (800) 451-1113
www.oceandivers.com

Each day of diving with Ocean Divers brings a different adventure, because this company tries to maintain a rotating schedule of set dive sites if conditions allow. Visiting the popular sites within the Key Largo National Marine Sanctuary, Ocean Divers slips into Eagle Ray Alley and Fire Coral Cave at Molasses Reef, and between the stands of the rare day-feeding pillar coral. Divers who enjoy wreck dives can visit the *Bibb,* the *Duane,* and the *Spiegel Grove.* Regular dive and snorkel departures are at 8:00 A.M. and 1:00 P.M. Night dives are regularly offered on Tuesday, Thursday, and Saturday, and other times upon request.

Ocean Divers is adjacent to Marina Del Mar Resort. It maintains two dive shops. The second is located at MM 105.5 Bayside, Key Largo.

Rainbow Reef
MM 100 Oceanside, Key Largo

MM 85 Oceanside, Islamorada
(305) 451-5533, (800) 457-4354

Rainbow Reef, with two locations, offers extensive dives to coral and artificial reefs, ledges, walls, and centuries-old wrecks. Oh, and don't forget the fish! Depths range from 18 feet to 120 feet, with each dive site offering its own unique qualities. The charters hit all the spectacular spots from Pennekamp State Park down to Alligator Reef. Rainbow Reef has small (12 persons max) boats to help make your dive personal and pleasurable. They are a full-service PADI 5 Star Gold Palm Instructor.

See you beneath the sea!

Tavernier Dive Center
MM 90.7 Oceanside, Tavernier
(305) 852-4007, (800) 787-9797
www.tavernierdivecenter.com

Tavernier Dive Center will take you as far north as French Reef and all the way south to the wreck of the *Eagle* or the *Spiegel Grove* or to Alligator Reef. While the center caters to all skill levels, if you want a three-tank dive or an all-day charter, this outfit will accommodate you. Regular departures are 8:30 A.M. and 1:00 P.M. daily. Night dives depart at 5:15 P.M. Snorkelers may accompany divers to reef destinations.

Florida Keys Dive Center
MM 90.5 Oceanside, Tavernier
(305) 852-4599, (800) 433-8946
www.floridakeysdivectr.com

The Florida Keys Dive Center offers two-location reef dives between Key Largo and Islamorada as well as combo wreck/reef dives. A dive to the 100-foot-deep *Duane* is followed by a shallower dive at Molasses or Pickles Reef; an excursion to the *Eagle* is followed by a trip to

Crocker or Davis Reef. Departures are 8:30 A.M. and 1:00 P.M.

Florida Keys Dive Center will video your adventure or arrange for Nikonos or video rentals if you want a do-it-yourself setup. The center offers a discount diving package with accommodations at several local resorts and motels. Consult their Web site for more information.

Middle Keys

Tilden Scuba Center
MM 61 Oceanside, at Hawk's Cay Resort, Duck Key
(305) 289-4931, (877) 386-3483

MM 49.5 Bayside, at The Blackfin Resort, Marathon
(305) 743-7255, (877) 386-3483
www.tildensscubacenter.com

Long known as a top-notch dive center in the Florida Keys, Tilden's now has two locations, at Hawk's Cay Resort on Duck Key and at the Blackfin Resort in Marathon. Tilden's heads to such reef locations as Coffins Patch, Porkfish Reef, and Shark Harbor and takes advanced divers on guided excursions to the *Thunderbolt* and the *Adelaide Baker* wreck. Tilden's reports that the Middle Keys reef tracts are very healthy. Tilden Scuba Center operates the largest dive vessels in the Middle Keys—it's licensed to carry 40 passengers—but limits its excursions to 24 divers and snorkelers. Departures are at 8:00 A.M. and 1:00 P.M.

Abyss Dive Center
MM 54 Oceanside, at the Holiday Inn Marina, Marathon
(305) 743-2126, (800) 457-0134
www.abyssdive.com

The Abyss Dive Center in Marathon subscribes to the less-is-more theory of diving, which guarantees lots of personal attention. The company takes a maximum of six divers or snorkelers to 48 sites spread over the reefs at Sombrero Key, Coffins Patch, Yellow Rocks, and Delta Shoals. Abyss will take you to the *Thunderbolt* if your certs are current or your dive experience warrants, or you can hire an instructor and explore the wreck with a guide. Departures are at 8:30 A.M. and 12:30 P.M.

Hall's Diving Center
MM 48.5 Bayside, Marathon
(305) 743-5929, (800) 331-4255
www.hallsdiving.com

If you are an advanced certified diver or have an 80-foot dive under your weight belt, head out to the *Thunderbolt* with Hall's. Divers of other skill levels will enjoy diving the Middle Keys' 25- to 90-foot reef specialties, from Looe Key to Coffins Patch and especially around Sombrero Reef. Dive excursions depart at 9:00 A.M. and 1:30 P.M. Snorkelers may accompany divers at shallow reef locations.

In addition to standard equipment, a deluxe full-gear package, featuring top-of-the-line Nitrox clean gear, is available. Hall's also rents and provides certification in the use of a rebreather and offers such specialty dives as marine interaction dives and diver propulsion vehicles. Or you can rent mask, fins, and snorkel and explore the shallow Gulf waters or the Atlantic Ocean off Sombrero Beach with a buddy.

Hall's Diving Center offers multiple-day dive/lodging packages in conjunction with Faro Blanco Marine Resort.

Lower Keys

Underseas Inc.
MM 30.5 Oceanside, Big Pine Key
(305) 872-2700, (800) 446-5663
www.courtesyfloridakeys.com/diving.htm

In the Lower Keys, when you've said "Looe Key National Marine Sanctuary," you've said it all. And when you need a dive center, Underseas will take you to depths to satisfy all levels from snorkelers and novice divers to those with advanced skills. Looe Key is endlessly fascinating. Departures are at 8:30 A.M. and 1:30 P.M.

Spearfishing

One of the oldest methods for securing food from the sea was with a spear. Originally, this weapon was used at the water's surface while the hunter stood near or on the shore. Today divers equipped with scuba gear and spear guns spearfish underwater, which equalizes the sub-oceanic playing field.

The 3-foot to 6-foot stainless-steel shaft of the spear gun is operated with a system of rubber slings. At the end of the arrow is a sharp barb. You must first commence the hunt. Be sure not to spearfish near any other divers. Swim very quietly and peer over every rock and ridge of the outer edges of the reef until you find the fish. Reef fish are territorial, seldom found far from their habitual hiding place. (Mutton snappers and black groupers are considered prizes.) Move slowly and carefully as you stalk the fish until it is in range. Lead the fish as you would if you were hunting with a rifle and try to hit its head.

Once you spear a fish, it thrashes about in agony and causes justified commotion. Blood will be released into the surrounding waters and may attract sharks cruising the area. Be alert to their presence. While they will be after the injured fish, not you, the sharks may not readily make the distinction.

Be sure to check The Florida Keys National Marine Sanctuary Regulations section of the Boating chapter for restrictions before spearfishing in our waters.

The fish in our waters know the rules. Do you? You may not spearfish:

- Within 100 yards of a public swimming beach, a commercial or public fishing pier, or any part of a bridge from which public fishing is allowed.
- Within 100 feet of any part of an above-surface jetty, unless the final 500 yards of the jetty extend more than 1,500 yards from shore.
- In state waters (from shore to 3 miles out) from Long Key Bridge north to the Dade County line.
- In Key Largo National Marine Sanctuary, Looe Key National Marine Sanctuary, Everglades National Park, Dry Tortugas National Park, or in any body of water under the jurisdiction of the DEP's Division of Recreation and Parks.
- Without a valid Florida saltwater fishing license.
- For redfish (red drum), jewfish, billfish (all species), shark, spotted eagle ray, sturgeon, bonefish, Nassau grouper, pompano, tarpon, spotted sea trout, African pompano, permit, manta ray, snook, weakfish, tripletail, blue crab, stone crab, or lobster.
- For families of ornamental reef fish: puffers, parrotfish, angelfish, trunkfish, squirrelfish, trumpetfish, surgeonfish, butterflyfish, cornetfish, damselfish, pipefish, porcupinefish, or sea horses.

Strike Zone Charters
MM 29.6 Bayside, Big Pine Key
(305) 872-9863, (800) 942-5397
www.strikezonecharter.com
Docked out back and ready to transport you to the Looe Key National Marine Sanctuary for a spectacular two-tank dive, Strike Zone Charter's glass-bottomed catamarans depart at 9:30 A.M. and 1:30 P.M. Strike Zone now also visits one of the Keys' newest artificial reefs, the *Adolphus Busch.*

Looe Key Reef Resort & Dive Center
MM 27.5 Oceanside, Ramrod Key
(800) 942-5397, (800) 566-3539
www.diveflakeys.com
The friendly crew at Looe Key Reef Resort whisks you off to the Looe Key National Marine Sanctuary, where you will visit three sites with at least an hour bottom time at each location. On Wednesday and Saturday divers visit two reef sites plus the wreck of the *Adolphus Busch.* The other days divers will visit three reef sites. Snorkelers may accompany divers. The excursion runs from 10:00 A.M. to 3:00 P.M.

Looe Key Reef Resort and Dive Center offers dive/lodging packages at its adjoining motel. The dive boat leaves from its mooring directly behind the motel so schlepping your gear is not a burden here.

Key West

Captain's Corner Dive Center
125 Anne Street
(305) 296-8865, (305) 296-8918
www.captainscorner.com
Captain's Corner Dive Center's reef and snorkel excursions leave at 9:30 A.M. and 1:30 P.M. Wreck and reef dives and double wreck dives are available by special arrangement.

During daylight saving time months you can dive the twilight wreck and reef dive on Tuesday, Thursday, and Saturday.

i

Jules' Undersea Lodge in Key Largo offers certified divers the opportunity to stay at the only underwater hotel in the world. Located 30 feet beneath the surface of the Emerald Lagoon at Key Largo Undersea Park, guests scuba dive to reach the submarine-style lodge. Contact the lodge at (305) 451-2353 or check out their Web site at www.jul.com.

First you dive a wreck, then watch the sunset from the deck of the boat. After dark, experience the after-hours sea life during a reef dive.

Private trips may be booked to the wreck of the *Señora Nuestra de Atocha,* 30 miles west of Key West. Captain's Corner always has instructors in the water with you, so you can sign on even if you are a novice diver. The boat departs from 631 Greene Street, corner of Greene and Elizabeth Streets at the Conch Republic Seafood Restaurant.

Dive Key West Inc.
3128 N. Roosevelt Boulevard
(305) 296-3823, (800) 426-0707
www.divekeywest.com
Dive Key West offers "reef du jour," customizing the schedule based on diver demand and weather conditions. It concentrates on the 30-foot reef lines where the light is better and the colors are more brilliant, allowing you more bottom time. The inner reefs have large stands of coral and a high concentration of tropical fish, while at the outer reefs you will see less coral, more big sea fans, sponges, and larger finfish. For your two-dive combo you can choose between a wreck and a reef or two reefs. Dive Key West visits the wrecks of the *Cayman Salvager, Joe's Tug,* and the *Alexander* wreck, which, at 90 feet, 60 feet, and 30 feet, respectively, offer a skill level for everyone. Regular departures are at 9:00 A.M. and 2:00 P.M.

If you do not have the skill level for the wreck dive of your choice, you may hire an instructor to accompany you. Snorkelers will be custom-fitted with gear at no extra charge, and free instruction is available. Night dives, scheduled upon request, are always accompanied by an instructor. Departure times for the night dive vary by daylight saving time.

Key West Diving Society
951 Caroline Street
(305) 292-3221, (866) 593-4837
www.keywestdivingsociety.com
Catering to small groups, Key West Diving Society semicustomizes their dive excursions between two reef sites or a wreck and a reef. They visit such popular sites as *Joe's Tug, Cayman Salvager,* and the Western Sambos. Departures are at 8:30 A.M. and 2:00 P.M. Snorkelers may accompany divers on reef dives.

The Key West Diving Society offers technical divers the opportunity to book private charters to the *Wilkes-Barre* wreck or the Curb. All dive masters at KWDS have a specialty, so you can arrange special-interest dives such as spearfishing, lobstering, photography, and more. The dive boat is located at Conch Harbor Marina in the Historic Seaport, on the corner of Caroline and Grinnell Streets.

Lost Reef Adventures
261 Margaret Street on Key West Bight
(305) 296-9737, (800) 952-2749
www.lostreefadventures.com
Lost Reef Adventures customizes its dive trips one day before departure based upon the skill levels and dive-site desires of interested divers. Excursions visit the celebrated *Joe's Tug, Cayman Salvager,* and *Alexander* wreck sites and reefs from the Western Sambos to the Western Dry Rocks. The dive and snorkel excursions depart at 9:00 A.M. and 1:30 P.M. Lost Reef offers night pilgrimages seasonally. First you can pay homage to the sun as it sinks into the water; then you will take the plunge for a one-tank twilight dive.

Subtropic Dive Center
1605 North Roosevelt Boulevard on Garrison Bight
(305) 296-9914, (800) 853-3483
www.subtropic.com
Mornings find Subtropic's dive boat exploring two wrecks or two reefs. Wrecks visited include *Joe's Tug,* the *Cayman Salvager,* and the *Alexander* wreck, whose shallower depths invite exploration by those of all experience levels. These dives depart at 9:00 A.M.

Subtropic offers trips to a wreck and a reef or two reefs in the afternoons. These reef/reef trips and the reef-dive portion of the wreck/reef excursions visit the Sambos, Rock Key, Sand Key, and the Dry Rocks. Departure is at 2:00 P.M. Snorkelers are welcome on the afternoon reef/reef diving excursions, or they may opt for a snorkel-only trip, which is offered daily at 9:00 A.M. and 1:00 P.M. Night dives are offered regularly.

RECREATION

If you want to scuba dive, fish, sail, or motor in our abundant waters, see the related chapters in this book. For a plethora of other stimulating diversions, read on. We show you where the action is—from skydiving, parasailing, and water sports to sunset cruises, gunkholing ecotours, and bicycling. You'll find out about our beaches and public parks in this chapter. And if the weather isn't fine—which is rare—or you would just like to stay indoors, look here, too, for billiards, bowling, bingo, and movie theaters.

Expect to pay a fee for your recreational choices. We will indicate which diversions are free. Recreation facilities are organized by category from Key Largo to Key West.

AIR TOURS AND SKYDIVING

Middle Keys

History Flight
MM 52 Bayside, Marathon
(888) 743-3311
www.HistoryFlight.com

Dust off that leather bomber jacket and climb into the cockpit of a real WWII 6 Warbird. With dual controls and no flying experience needed, you can channel your own version of the Red Baron. History Flight offers introductory flights, aerobatics, combat maneuvers, or just a gentle spin in the sky. The "top gun" instructors custom-tailor the trips to your preferences. Up, up, and away. . . .

Keys Flying Boats
MM 50 Oceanside, Marathon
(305) 731-7472
www.flyingboatadventures.com

Marathon residents Bob and Kim Tilman have managed to excite adventuresome souls with a combination of sea and air travel in their Keys Flying Boats business. The "flying boats" are ultra-light aircraft that utilize the water for takeoffs and landings. They cruise at 38 knots and have a glide ratio of 6 to 1. These unique crafts can be rented for lessons, offering you a trip to view coastal areas, but they can also be purchased. The Tilmans can tailor flights for special customers; flights are offered on most weekends and holidays, depending on weather conditions.

Lower Keys

Fantasy Dan's Airplane Rides
MM 17 Bayside, Lower Sugarloaf Airport, Sugarloaf Key
(305) 745-2217
www.sugarloaflodge.com/airstrip.htm

Fantasy Dan takes passengers in his Cessna 182 on 15- to 45-minute flights, 500 feet over the Florida Keys. Excursions, which cover areas from the Seven Mile Bridge to Key West, operate from 9:00 A.M. to sunset. Air tours, which are priced per plane, accommodate a maximum of three people. Call in advance or stop by the airport. To reach Lower Sugarloaf Airport, turn toward the bay at the paved road bordering the west end of Sugarloaf Lodge.

Skydive Key West
MM 17 Bayside, Lower Sugarloaf Airport, Sugarloaf Key
(305) 745-4386, (800) 968-5867
www.skydivekeywest.com

"Skydive from a perfectly good airplane!" Try tandem skydiving from 10,000 feet over the Lower Keys and Key West with Skydive Key West. First-timers are welcome. Allow one hour per person for this venture, including training and the jump. Soft landings are provided on Lower Sugarloaf Key. Skydive expeditions aboard a Cessna 182 depart Sugarloaf Airport

The gumbo-limbo tree is also known as "the tourist tree" because the red, peeling bark looks akin to visitors who stayed in the sun too long. Sunscreen, a hat, and sunglasses are a must here in the Keys. Even on cloudy, overcast days, the tropical sun burns hot and deep. Frequent and even application of your sunscreen is every bit as important as its SPF. Do not venture into the hot, intense Florida sunshine without sunscreen protection, and if you get wet, be sure to reapply it.

between 10:00 A.M. and sunset seven days a week. Skydivers are advised not to scuba dive for 24 hours before their jump. Videos and photographs are available for purchase as souvenirs. Jumps are by reservation only, and you must be at least 18 years of age to take the plunge.

Key West

Island Aeroplane Tours
Key West International Airport, 3469 South Roosevelt Boulevard
(305) 294-8687

For a bird's-eye view of Key West and beyond, take a ride in a vintage open-cockpit biplane. Island Aeroplane Tours sightseeing biplane rides take you over the coral reef, to view shipwrecks in Fleming Key Channel, along the south shore of Key West, to Boca Grande Key, across the backcountry waters, and up the Keys as far as Little Palm Island (see the Accommodations chapter). Tours range from six minutes to more than an hour. Prices are based on two people riding in the front seat. Island Aeroplane Tours also offers aerobatic rides.

Seaplanes of Key West
3471 South Roosevelt Boulevard, Key West International Airport
(305) 294-0709, (800) 950-2359
www.seaplanesofkeywest.com

There is simply no faster, easier, more incredible way to reach Dry Tortugas National Park—70 miles due west across open water from Key West—than via seaplane. With Seaplanes of Key West, everyone on board gets a window seat for the 45-minute flight to Fort Jefferson. In addition to navigating the skies, your pilot will point out the sights as you glide just 500 feet above the emerald waters of the Gulf of Mexico. Along the way, you're likely to spot sea turtles, rays, dolphins, and a shipwreck or two.

Seaplanes of Key West offers half-day (morning or afternoon) and full-day trips to Fort Jefferson. Children younger than age two fly free. Fare includes soft drinks and snorkeling equipment, but if you want lunch, you'll have to pack your own.

A drop-off/pickup service is provided for campers at an additional cost. Campers must carry everything, including water, into and out of the park; the extra charge covers the cost of transporting their gear. Weight allowance is restricted to 40 pounds per camper; no dive tanks are permitted.

A maximum of nine passengers can be accommodated per plane trip, and reservations are required. Allow plenty of lead time for reservations, especially during high season.

BEACHES AND PUBLIC PARKS

LIFE'S A BEACH, the T-shirts say, but first-time visitors to the Keys who expect to find soft, white, endless sand along the ocean are bound to be disappointed. The coral reef protects the Keys from the pounding surf that grinds other shorelines into sand, and so most of ours must be carted in by the truckload. Nevertheless, if stretching out in the sand tops your recreational must-do list, humans and nature have teamed up here to bring you a stretch or two. Some of our parks and beaches charge admission fees, and most have specific hours of accessibility.

Keys beaches do not maintain lifeguard stations. Riptides are rare here, but jellyfish are not. Swim at your own risk and never venture out alone or after dark.

Upper Keys

Dagny Johnson Key Largo Hammock Botanical State Park
MM 106 Oceanside, Key Largo
(305) 451-1202
www.floridastateparks.org/keylargohammock

Situated on nearly 2,500 acres and stretching for nearly 11 miles of north Key Largo this state park is a jewel. The park is located in a tropical jungle of mangrove swamp, coastal rock barren, and a rockland hammock. Some of the resident species are rare tree snails, the Schaus swallowtail, the silver-banded hairstreak, and mangrove and hammock skippers. There is a guided walk every Thursday and Sunday on a beautiful half-mile nature trail. A backcountry permit, obtained at the John Pennekamp Coral Reef State Park (see listing below), gives you access to an additional 6 miles of tranquil Keys flora and fauna.

John Pennekamp Coral Reef State Park
MM 102.5 Oceanside, Key Largo
(305) 451-1202
www.pennekamppark.com

Well known to divers and snorkelers as the first underwater state park in the United States, John Pennekamp also serves a wide palette of diversions within its land-based boundaries. You can explore most of the fascinating habitats of the Florida Keys here (see the Paradise Found chapter). Enjoy campfire programs, guided walks, and canoe trips. The park offers a nature trail, beaches, picnic areas, campsites (see the Campgrounds chapter), restrooms, showers, and water-sports concessions (see listings in this chapter) where you can rent any equipment you might desire, from scuba gear to sailboats.

Expect to pay a nominal admission fee per person and per vehicle. The park is open from 8:00 A.M. to sunset.

Friendship Park
MM 101 Oceanside, Key Largo

This park sports a playground, a Little League field, swings, and a basketball court. It's perfect for those lazy afternoons with children in tow, and it's especially inviting for picnics. The park is open from 8:00 A.M. until dusk or when a Little League game is scheduled. Admission is free.

Key Largo Community Park
MM 99.6 Oceanside, Key Largo
www.fla-keys.com/keylargo/children.htm

This huge community park offers playgrounds, ball fields, and tennis and volleyball courts and is co-located with Jacob's Aquatic Center (see listing in this chapter). A new addition in 2006 is a skate park for the young and the young-at-heart. Opened in 2006 and managed by the Key Largo Family YMCA, this brand-spanking-new facility was created after hundreds of families signed petitions asking for this type of park to be built. The Woodward Ramps and Rails are known worldwide as a leader in all types of skateboarding, in-line, and BMX equipment. The park is free but you must have a permission slip signed by the Key Largo Family YMCA to skate here.

Founders Park
MM 87 Bayside, Plantation Key
(305) 853-1685
www.islamorada.fl.us

Islamorada, Village of Islands, is proud of its green spaces. One of its gleaming examples is the 40-acre municipal Founders Park on Plantation Key. This multi-purpose park offers fun for the entire family—including the family dog! The park features playgrounds, sandy beaches, a dog park, baseball diamonds, picnic areas, an Olympic-size pool with restrooms, bocce ball and tennis courts, a vita course with 18 exercise stations, a skate park, and unforgettable views of the Gulf of Mexico. Various community events

***Celebrated American author Zane Grey discovered the Florida Keys in early 1900. Staying at the posh Long Key Fishing Club (now Long Key State Park), he fished the waters of Long Key, Duck Key, and Grassy Key. It was in this tropical setting that Gray wrote* Wild Horse Mesa, Code of the West, *and* Tales of Fishes.**

are held here throughout the year, so check local publications. Some fees may apply to some areas.

Harry Harris Park
MM 92.5 Oceanside, Tavernier
(305) 852-7161
Bring the kids along to Harry Harris, where a small beach fronts a tidal pool protected by a stone jetty. You'll find a playground, ball field, volleyball net, in-line skating park, and picnic grounds. Restrooms are available. To reach the park, follow signs leading toward the coast along the oceanside by mile marker 92.5 (Burton Drive). Stay on Burton Drive about 2 miles and follow the signs to the left. Admission is free, except on weekends and federal holidays when nonresidents (persons residing outside Monroe County) must pay a per-person admission fee as well as a docking fee to use the boat ramp. The park is open from 8:00 A.M. to sunset.

Beach Behind the Library
MM 81.5 Bayside, Islamorada
This stretch of beach has no more official name than its general location, but it does offer a playground, restrooms, and showers. There is no admission charge.

Indian Key Beach
MM 78 Oceanside, Islamorada
Although there isn't much of a beach here, a swimming area and boat access are available. Admission is free.

Anne's Beach
MM 73.5 Oceanside, Islamorada
At low tide, tiny Anne's Beach holds enough sand to accommodate several blankets, but it attracts sun worshipers by the dozens. Swimming waters are shallow. A wooden boardwalk meanders for about 0.3 mile along the water, through the mangroves. Five picnic pavilions jut out from the boardwalk. Parking is limited. To find Anne's Beach, slow down along the Overseas Highway southwest of Caloosa Cove Resort and look toward the ocean for two small parking lots. The boardwalk connects the lots. Blink and you'll miss it. There is no charge.

Long Key State Park
MM 67.5 Oceanside, Long Key
(305) 664-4815
www.dep.state.fl.us/parks
A long, narrow sand spit makes up the "beach" at this state park, which is fronted by a shallow-water flat. This park was once the site of the Long Key Fishing Club. This area was a magnet for the world's finest saltwater fishermen during Henry Flagler's era, which ended with the hurricane of 1935 destroying both club and railroad. Today, you can rent a canoe and enjoy the calm, easily accessible waters while you bird-watch and fish in ideal conditions. The picnic area is equipped with charcoal grills. Long Key State Park offers superb oceanfront campsites (see the Campgrounds chapter), restrooms, and shower facilities. Expect to pay a nominal admission fee per person and per vehicle. Long Key State Park is open from 8:00 A.M. to sunset.

Middle Keys

Curry Hammock State Park
MM 56.2 Oceanside, Marathon
(850) 245-2157
The newest addition to the state park scene in the Florida Keys is Curry Hammock, at Little Crawl Key just north of Marathon Shores. Exuding an untouched charm all its own, the park offers a mix of tropical hammock, mangrove swamp, and

a wide expanse of the coral rock sand that passes for a beach in the Keys. Grills and picnic tables abound, many tucked beneath shady buttonwood trees. The kids will enjoy the swings and slides. And anglers will like the shallow, productive bonefish flat that fronts the shoreline. A cut of deeper water on the north side of the park affords the chance for a "real" swim and maybe some snorkeling as well. Changing rooms and restrooms are fresh, clean, and new. A number of roofed pavilions protect picnic tables and grills from the elements. A nominal fee for entry is charged by honor system. Camping is not allowed here. So far, this little gem remains relatively undiscovered.

Sombrero Beach
MM 50 Oceanside, Sombrero Beach Road, Marathon
(305) 289-3000
This spacious, popular public beach offers a picnic area, playground, and sweeping views of the Atlantic. Swimming waters run deep off Sombrero Beach. Restrooms are available. Marathon Chamber of Commerce, and volunteer organizations, work to keep this gem of a beach in pristine condition. There is no admission charge, and parking is plentiful.

Marathon Community Park
MM 49 Oceanside, Marathon
The city of Marathon boasts a new 14.8-acre public park, which offers two softball fields, four tennis courts, a playground, picnic area, three basketball courts that are also used as a roller hockey rink, a jogging path, a pavilion, and restrooms. City officials say it is only phase one of the park project. Phase two will add 8.9 more acres and include a band shell and more playgrounds. The park is free.

Lower Keys

Little Duck Key Beach
MM 39 Oceanside, Little Duck Key
With restrooms and picnic shelters, this beach makes for an ideal lunch spot. The small beach provides a swimming area but no lifeguards. Open from 8:00 A.M. until dusk, the beach is free to the public. And don't be confused by the name. This beach is on Little Duck Key, not Duck Key. You will find it on the left side of the Overseas Highway, just this side of Bahia Honda, as you are traveling south toward Key West.

Bahia Honda State Park
MM 37 Oceanside, Bahia Honda
(305) 872-2353
www.dep.state.fl.us/parks
Across the Seven Mile Bridge from Marathon, Bahia Honda State Park sparkles like a diamond and boasts the best natural beach in all of the Florida Keys. Narrow roads wind through the mangrove thickets, many of which have been fitted as campsites (see the Campgrounds chapter). Tarpon fishing beneath the Bahia Honda Bridge attracts seasoned anglers and novices alike, and the park has its own marina with boat ramps and overnight dockage.

At the dive shop in the concession building, you can rent snorkeling equipment or book a trip to Looe Key National Marine Sanctuary. Groceries, marine supplies, and souvenirs are sold here, too.

Bahia Honda offers picnic facilities, restrooms, guided nature walks, and charter boat excursions. Expect to pay a nominal admission fee per person and per vehicle. The park is open 8:00 A.M. to sunset.

Key West

Bayview Park
Truman Avenue and Jose Martí Drive
You will definitely notice Bayview Park if you are driving into Key West on North Roosevelt Boulevard, which becomes Truman Avenue. On your left as the road narrows and you head into Old Town, Bayview Park is one of the few free green spots still left in Key West. Look for the

gazebo. Several picnic tables are strewn throughout the park and come highly recommended for a shady afternoon lunch.

Fort Zachary Taylor
Truman Annex at the end of Southard Street

Look to the left of the brick fort for a pleasant, although rocky, beach with picnic tables and barbecue grills. The locals call this place "Fort Zach"; this is where they come in droves to sunbathe and snorkel. The water is clear and deep, and you're likely to see many colorful fish congregating around the limestone-boulder breakwater islands constructed just offshore. When it gets too hot on the beach, head for the shade—there's plenty of it available under the lofty pine trees in the picnic area. The beach area is open 8:00 A.M. to sunset. An admission fee to the park is charged.

Higgs Beach and C. B. Harvey Rest Beach
Atlantic Boulevard

These twin beaches are so close together they are often mistaken for each other. Higgs Beach offers a playground, picnic tables, and nearby tennis courts. It is between White and Reynolds Streets on Atlantic Boulevard. The beach is open sunrise to 11:00 P.M. Admission is free.

Rest Beach is smaller than Higgs Beach and is dwarfed by the massive White Street Pier. This pier is a favorite with anglers and dog walkers and is sometimes called the "unfinished road to Cuba." Rest Beach has the same hours as Higgs Beach. Right across the street is an extensive playground called Astro City, a favorite with the kids.

Smathers Beach
South Roosevelt Boulevard

Across from Key West International Airport, Smathers is a long strip of sand that bustles with food vendors, water-sports concessions, and beautiful bods in itsy-bitsy, teeny-weeny suits. Smathers underwent extensive renovation in spring 2000 so now, or at least until the next hurricane blows through, it looks like what you'd expect a Florida beach to look like.

Admission here is free, but bring plenty of quarters for the streetside parking meters. If you don't mind carting your beach gear a few extra yards, free parking is available on the far side of South Roosevelt. The beach is open sunrise to 11:00 P.M.

BICYCLING

You'll be able to get a "wheel" deal when you rent a bike and cycle the Keys. Rentals are offered by the day (9:00 A.M. to 5:00 P.M.), 24 hours, multiple days, week, or month. Most of these establishments sell parts and new bicycles, do repairs, and rent helmets and other gear. Remember, Florida state law requires helmets for cyclists younger than age 16.

Upper Keys

Among the best places to bike the Upper Keys are Harry Harris Park, where bicycle lanes are provided, and on the bicycle paths in the median and along the oceanside of the Overseas Highway in Key Largo. Down the Keys, you may safely cycle through Islamorada's Old Highway, which borders the Overseas Highway on the oceanside. A bike path on the bayside finishes a tour through Upper Matecumbe Key and on through Lower Matecumbe Key, thereby making it possible to safely cycle from about mile marker 90 to approximately mile marker 72.

B & D Bikes
MM 103.5 Bayside, Key Largo
(305) 393-2453

Located in the U-Haul complex, B & D Bikes sells, repairs, and rents all sorts of bicycles, as well as skateboards.

Tavernier Bicycle and Hobbies
MM 92 Bayside, Tavernier
(305) 852-2859
Tavernier Bicycle and Hobbies rents cruisers (one-speed bicycles) for men, women, and children by the day, week, or month Per-day prices decrease with multiple-day rentals.

Middle Keys

In Marathon you'll need to cycle on the old Seven Mile Bridge to Pigeon Key (a good 2-mile-plus jaunt), use the Key Colony Beach bicycle lane (turn onto the Key Colony Causeway at mile marker 53.5 to get to Key Colony), or pedal along the relatively traffic-free streets of the Sombrero residential area (turn onto Sombrero Beach Road, MM 50, next to Kmart).

Equipment Locker Sport & Bicycle
MM 53 Bayside, Marathon
(305) 289-1670
Equipment Locker rents beach cruisers by the 24-hour period or by the week. The store also offers 21-speed hybrid bikes. Here, too, you can rent in-line skates with complete gear, knee boards, water skis, or towable tubes. The store is open daily.

Lower Keys

The Lower Keys span 30 miles, but toward the end of the Keys you will have the best luck finding rental bikes on Stock Island and Key West (see section below).

Big Pine Bicycle Center
MM 31 Bayside, Big Pine Key
(305) 872-0130
This is the best source for bicycle rentals in the upper portion of the Lower Keys.

Key West

Adventure Scooter & Bicycle Rentals
2900 North Roosevelt Boulevard
Key Plaza Shopping Center
(305) 293-9933
Adventure has seven locations in Key West and offers conch cruisers with locks and adjustable padded seats.

The Bicycle Center
523 Truman Avenue
(305) 294-4556
The Bicycle Center offers single-speed bicycles with coaster brakes, locks, and baskets.

The Bike Shop
1110 Truman Avenue
(305) 294-1073
The Bike Shop rents one-speed cruisers with baskets and locks.

Island Bicycles
929 Truman Avenue
(305) 292-9707
Island Bicycles offers a full selection of bicycles for sale and rent. Repairs and accessories are also available here.

Moped Hospital
601 Truman Avenue
(305) 296-3344
Moped Hospital rents single-speed bicycles with coaster brakes, baskets, high-rise handlebars, soft seats, balloon tires, and locks by the hour, day, and week.

A great way to see the colorful street life of Key West is to go on a biking or walking tour. Visit www.seekeywest.com for Island City Strolls. Once you're in Key West, you can call (305) 294-8380 to arrange a jaunt.

CLOSE-UP

Gunkholing in Arsnicker Keys

Birding always conjures up visions of stealthily creeping through the forest at daybreak with a walking stick and a pair of binoculars in the pursuit of a tiny, elusive winged creature that will undoubtedly fly away the moment we come near.

So it is with great surprise that for this, our first look at a wading-bird rookery in the Florida Keys, we hop into a shallow-draft boat with two other adventurers and Capt. John Skidmore, our guide. And before you can say, "Bald eagle at 10 o'clock," we are skimming across the nearshore waters of Florida Bay at 35 knots, headed for the area's best-kept secret junket—a gunkholing expedition in the great beyond.

"In the Florida Keys," Captain John informs us, "gunkholing means more than just bird-watching." The unique, uninhabited red mangrove islands that pepper the Gulf of Mexico and Florida Bay serve as the cornerstones of the food chain for the entire tropical ecosystem here. The red mangrove thrives in salt water. It grows prop roots that drop down from its branches like stilts, catching sediment and decaying organic material. These islets feed and house a virtual aviary of indigenous or wintering winged creatures as well as a natural aquarium of fish, marine organisms, and other exotic underwater natives.

We head at breakneck speed toward the Arsnicker Keys, about 7 miles northwest of Lower Matecumbe, in Florida Bay. Our craft skims across the shallows, drawing only 8 to 10 inches. Captain John maneuvers the boat through the skinny water like a Formula One driver racing the Le Mans course. We slalom between red and green navigational markers, upon which ubiquitous brown pelicans and laughing gulls loiter and an occasional osprey nests. Black magnificent frigatebirds—which have a wingspan of 7½ feet and a distinctively forked tail—glide on the thermals overhead.

As we approach the Arsnicker Keys, Captain John cuts the engine, raises it out of the water, and climbs atop an elevated poling platform at the rear of the craft. With the 22-foot-long graphite push pole in hand, he maneuvers us through 10-inch-deep shallows toward a tiny group of islands about 50 yards away that appear to be sprinkled with a mass of white blobs.

A glance into the crystal-clear water, which is constantly cleansed by the flow and ebb of the tides, reveals darting nurse sharks and the lazy flapping of a stingray. The sandy seafloor is littered with soft sponges, spiny sea stars, and delicate algae. Turtle-grass beds camouflage the creatures at the base of the food chain—worms, snails, and crabs—which attach themselves to the grass's long, flat, wide blades. The decomposing detritus of the mangroves also forms peat. The peat dissolves the limestone under the sediment layer on the sea bottom, and, when exposed to the air, releases sulfuric acid. This is the rotten-

The red mangrove islets in the backcountry waters of Florida Bay support rookeries of brown pelicans, white herons, and cormorants. PHOTO: VICTORIA SHEARER

egg smell encountered near the mangrove swamps in the Florida Keys at low tide.

As we round the first mangrove islet, our noses detect a smell unlike rotten eggs, but equally as odiferous. Guano! The mangroves are frosted with the sticky, white droppings, the calling cards of the winged creatures that dwell within. Our boat soundlessly glides around the curve of the island, and suddenly we spy hundreds of white pelicans peacefully fishing a cove.

White pelicans, the true Florida snowbirds, winter at Arsnicker from December through March, after which they head north to summer in the Missouri River area of Montana. They are regal-looking albescent birds, showier yet more reserved than their fish-begging brown cousins. The span between their black-tipped wings exceeds 10 feet. White pelicans are cooperative feeders. They congregate on the water in large groups—300 or more are usually found in the Arsnicker Keys. Encircling schools of fish, the pelicans herd their aquatic prey into a concentrated mass that leads to their ultimate demise. Noting our approach, the shy and skittish white pelicans begin swimming away from our boat.

A sneeze from one of the gunkholers frightens the white pelicans into flight, a glorious mass of yellow beaks and black-tipped wings. The birds don't go far, just around the island out of our sight range, but they initiate a near riot. All but invisible upon our arrival, a rookery of double-crested cormorants roosts atop the mangroves. Frightened by the flap of the white pelicans, the entire colony attempts to flee like a rock-concert audience during a fire alarm, with varying degrees of success.

Cormorants are large, heavy-bodied black birds that are relatives of the pelicans. Like wide-bodied jets, the birds need a long runway to become airborne. Hundreds of black missiles simultaneously take off from the treetops, most belly-flopping first on the water before finally finding their wings. They fly about 100 yards offshore, congregating on the shallow flats in a cackling cacophony like merrymakers at a company holiday party.

Our cover is blown. The natives recognize the aliens among them. But some species here in the backcountry remain little bothered by our presence. Still perched in the mangroves are a smattering of great white herons, great blue herons, great egrets, and snowy egrets, South Florida's indigenous wading birds.

The herons and egrets breed between November and July in the Keys, building nests in the mangroves. We pass by the camouflaged nest of a great white heron, startling the sitting female, which flies away with a disgusted squawk. Captain John spots two fluffy baby herons peeking out of the nest, feathers spiked like punk rockers. We take turns scrambling up on the poling platform to garner a glimpse of the nursery.

Suddenly a bald eagle soars overhead, its distinctive white head shimmering, wings held rigidly flat. With a collective gasp we catch our breath. We had flushed it from its nest with our clamorous maneuvers. Paired eagles will use the same site year after year, adding material each year until the nests are very large. (Florida supports the largest resident bald eagle population of the lower 48 states.)

Reluctantly, we stow our cameras and binoculars, returning the privacy of the Arsnicker Keys to its winged residents and their underwater compatriots. It is little wonder that The Nature Conservancy considers the Florida Keys one of the "Last Great Places." Rachel Carson most eloquently revealed its special essence when she wrote in *The Edge of the Sea:* "I doubt that anyone can travel the length of the Florida Keys without having communicated to his mind a sense of the uniqueness of this land of sky and water and scattered mangrove-covered islands."

BILLIARDS, BINGO, AND BOWLING

Yes, we do occasionally have inclement weather here in the Keys, but we never let rainy days and Mondays get us down. In addition to the three indoor leisure pastimes described in this section, the Florida Keys has a busy bridge league schedule. For dates, times, and locations of weekly games with the American Contract Bridge League, see the Retirement chapter. *NOTE:* Indoor activities may not be offered year-round. Phone ahead before venturing out.

Upper Keys

St. Justin Martyr Catholic Church Bingo
MM 105.5 Bayside, Key Largo
(305) 451-1316

Bingo is usually on Tuesday night. Call for times.

Key Largo Lion's Club Bingo
MM 99 Oceanside, 232 Homestead Avenue, Key Largo
(305) 451-1271
Bingo is usually on Thursday night. Call for times.

Fish Bowl
MM 83.2 Bayside, Islamorada
(305) 664-9357
Extensively renovated in 2000, the Fish Bowl—the only bowling alley in the Keys—offers 12 bowling lanes, glow bowling, billiards, an arcade room, and an ice-cream parlor.

Middle Keys

Loyal Order of Moose Lodge 1058 Bingo
MM 54 Bayside, Marathon
(305) 743-6062
Bingo is usually held on Monday and Thursday. Call for times.

San Pablo Catholic Church Bingo
MM 53.5 Oceanside, 670 122nd Street, Marathon
(305) 289-0636
Bingo is usually held on Tuesday. Call for times.

Disabled American Veterans Chapter 122 Bingo
MM 52 Bayside, Marathon
(305) 743-4705
Bingo is usually held on Friday. Call for times.

Elks Club BPOE 2139 Bingo
MM 51.5 Oceanside, Marathon
(305) 743-2652
Bingo is usually held on Friday and Sunday. Call for times.

American Legion Post 154 Bingo
MM 48.5 Oceanside, Marathon
(305) 743-4783
Bingo is usually held on Wednesday. Call for times.

Key West

Down Under Sports Bar
1970 North Roosevelt Boulevard
(305) 294-1970
This sports bar features billiard tables, darts, pinball machines, video games, and half a dozen televisions that offer satellite programming. Play billiards at Down Under free of charge.

Stick and Stein Sports Rock Cafe
Key Plaza Shopping Center, North Roosevelt Boulevard
(305) 296-3352
At Stick and Stein 11 billiard tables are set around 4 bars with sports playing on 80 large- and small-screen televisions. Billiards is free with a food or beverage purchase from 11:00 A.M. to 4:00 P.M. (unlimited number of players). After 4:00 P.M., you pay an hourly fee (see the Nightlife chapter).

BOAT EXCURSIONS, SUNSET CRUISES, AND GAMBLING JUNKETS

Our crowning glory rests in our encompassing waters. Explore the backcountry and the waters of the Everglades National Park on group gunkholing ecotour expeditions (see the Paradise Found chapter) or take a glass-bottomed boat trip to the reef to view the fascinating creatures residing there. Relax aboard a sunset cocktail cruise or fire up for a casino cruise. Expect to pay a fee for all these adventures.

Upper Keys

John Pennekamp Coral Reef State Park
MM 102.5 Oceanside, Key Largo
(305) 451-1621
www.johnpennekamp.com

i ***The weather in the Florida Keys can change suddenly, so before heading out on the water, be sure to check the forecast. All radio and TV stations give updates, as does www.nws.noaa.gov.***

Pennekamp's glass-bottomed catamaran, the *Spirit of Pennekamp,* carries as many as 150 people on two-and-a-half-hour tours of the reef. Tours are offered three times daily. The 38-foot catamaran *Salsa* departs the park marina twice daily for a sailing/snorkeling adventure..

Capt. Sterling's Everglades Eco-Tours
MM 102 Bayside, Dolphin Cove, Key Largo
(305) 853-5161, (888) 224-6044
www.pennekamp.com/sterling
Venture 17 miles into the waters of the Everglades National Park, in and around mangrove and bird rookery islands (see the Paradise Found chapter) aboard a 23-foot pontoon boat. Tours are limited to six passengers and depart twice daily. The Key Largo Flamingo Express charter takes you through Crocodile Dragover, the Dump Keys, and 38 miles to Flamingo in Everglades National Park. And then there's the Crocodile Tour, a nighttime adventure that takes you in search of the elusive Florida saltwater crocodile.

African Queen
MM 100 Oceanside, Holiday Inn Docks, Key Largo
(305) 451-4655
Board the legendary *African Queen*—featured in the Humphrey Bogart and Katharine Hepburn movie of the same name—in Key Largo for daily one-hour cruises and sunset or charter excursions during the autumn and winter months.

***Key Largo Princess* Glass Bottom Boat**
MM 100 Oceanside, at the Holiday Inn Docks, Key Largo
(305) 451-4655
This princess carries passengers on narrated two-hour tours that drift above the reef. A full bar is on board, and guests can buy hot dogs and snacks. *Key Largo Princess* tours are offered three times daily. Family rates and private charters are available. The boat is wheelchair accessible.

***Quicksilver* Catamaran**
MM 100 Oceanside, Holiday Inn Docks, Key Largo
(305) 451-0105, (800) 347-9972
www.quicksilversnorkel.com
Daily sails through the sanctuary waters of John Pennekamp Coral Reef State Park vary with the season aboard this 50-foot catamaran, *Quicksilver.* Discounts and family rates are available on snorkel/sunset sail combinations. Private and group charters also can be arranged. Gear rental is extra.

SunCruz Casino
MM 100 Oceanside, Holiday Inn, Key Largo
(305) 451-0000, (800) 474-3423
www.suncruzcasino.com
Sports betting, blackjack, slot machines, dice, roulette, and video poker are among the many diversions on board *SunCruz Casino.* A full bar and a la carte sandwich menu satisfy hungers of another kind; a welcome-aboard cocktail and hors d'oeuvres are served to all free of charge. Guests at Key Largo's Holiday Inn, Ramada, or Marriott sail for free as often as they desire. The general public may board the more-than-100-foot vessel's gambling sails for a small admission fee. The actual casino is moored each day 3 miles offshore in federal waters. Water taxis take guests to and from the casino vessel every two hours.

Caribbean Watersports Enviro Tours
MM 97 Bayside, at the Sheraton Beach Resort, Key Largo
(305) 852-4707, (800) 223-6728
www.caribbeanwatersports.com

Glide through the Everglades with Caribbean Watersports' two-hour guided Hobie Sailing Safaris and explore uninhabited mangrove islands all along Florida Bay. Environmental gunkholing tours (see the Paradise Found chapter) provide the same guided ride in a 17-foot rigid inflatable Zodiac that has a fiberglass hull, stabilizing inflatable side pontoons, and a quiet electric trolling motor. Tours are limited to six people; you must call ahead to reserve a spot.

Middle Keys

Hawk's Cay Resort and Marina
MM 61 Oceanside, Duck Key
(305) 743-7000
Sail aboard the 40-foot custom sailing catamaran at up to 20 knots or sign on for a more leisurely sunset cruise. Or rent a sea kayak for a self-guided ecotour of the out-islands near Duck Key. All these excursions may be booked at Hawk's Cay.

Many other water-related activities are available at Hawk's Cay, including chartered fishing excursions to the backcountry or the reef. For those with other interests, many other amusements are available, including personal watercraft and small-boat rentals, water-skiing, pontoon party barge rentals, and parasailing.

Keys Limey Charters
MM 61 Oceanside, Duck Key
(305) 289-0318
This is the only private gunkholing charter that will whisk you away at 35 knots into the backcountry waters of Florida Bay to the Arsnicker Keys, 7 miles northwest of Lower Matecumbe, to see the fabulous white pelicans (see the Close-up, Gunkholing in Arsnicker Keys, in this chapter). These ultimate snowbirds winter in the Keys from November until about the end of March. The flock often numbers 500 or more around the tiny islets of the Arsnicker. Capt. John Skidmore stealthily poles his flatsboat through the shallows so as not to alert the birds to your presence. Bring your camera! Captain Skidmore is also an expert flats fishing guide, specializing in bonefish, permit, tarpon, redfish, snook, and other backcountry species. You can combine the bird-watching gunkholing excursion with some guided backcountry fishing if you like.

Malabar X
MM 47.5 Oceanside, Marathon
(607) 535-5253
www.senecadaysails.com
Originally built in 1930, the Malabar X won the Bermuda Race in both 1930 and 1932. This magnificent vessel, built by John Alden, is the shining example of a fine wooden racing/cruising schooner. Let her carry you away for a morning, afternoon, or sunset cruise on board this vintage yacht. The crew encourages passengers to try the helm, trim the sails, or just sit back and fantasize about historical times on a yacht with a historical past.

***Spirit* Catamaran Charters**
MM 47.5 Oceanside, 56223 Ocean Drive, Marathon
(305) 289-0614
A 40-foot catamaran named *Spirit* takes passengers snorkeling to popular Middle Keys reefs twice a day, makes family charter cruises to Pigeon Key, offers marine biology tours with classrooms of children, and sets off for a daily sunset cruise at the end of the day. Call in advance to make reservations.

i

Anyone for tennis in the tropics? There are two locations in Key West to enjoy this sport for free. Across from Higgs Beach is Astro Park, where you will find six unlighted courts, and Bayview Park, where there are five lighted, hard-surface courts. (See listings for both in this chapter.)

Lower Keys

Strike Zone Charters Island Excursion
MM 29.5 Bayside, Big Pine Key
(305) 872-9863, (800) 654-9560
www.strikezonecharter.com

This five-hour, backcountry out-island excursion, which includes a fish cookout on a secluded island, will entice your entire family (see the Kidstuff chapter for more details and see the Diving and Snorkeling chapter for Strike Zone's underwater offerings).

Key West

Adventure Charters
MM 5.5 Oceanside, 6810 Front Street, Safe Harbor Marina, Stock Island
(305) 296-0362, (888) 817-0841
www.keywestadventures.com

Looking for an alternative to the traditional party-boat booze cruise? Adventure Charters offers half-day snorkel cruises, half-day backcountry nature excursions, and full-day backcountry adventures that combine kayaking, snorkeling, fishing, and beachcombing through tidal streams and along mangrove islands that are unreachable by larger boats. To find Adventure Charters, turn at MacDonald Avenue near Chico's Cantina.

***Appledore* Charter Windjammer**
201 William Street
(305) 296-9992

Daily snorkel trips aboard this 85-foot, oak-framed pine schooner head for the reef. The excursion includes a full lunch, a fruit platter, snacks, and beverages, plus beer and wine for after-snorkeling libation. Gear is provided, and passengers need bring only towels and sunscreen. A nightly sail-only excursion includes beer and wine (champagne during sunset).

During the high season the *Appledore* fills up quickly; call with a credit card to confirm reservations in advance. The *Appledore*, which has circumnavigated the world, summers in Maine, and is in Key West October through May.

Danger Charters
231 Front Street, at the Hilton Resort & Marina
(305) 304-7999
www.dangercharters.com

Don't let the moniker fool you: *Danger* and *Danger Cay* are the names of the two Chesapeake Bay Skip Jack sailboats, not any situation you will encounter on this adventurous charter. Up to six people board the skipjack and right away owner and captain Wayne Fox assigns one of his new crew as first mate. The fun begins as the new mate learns the intricacies of tending to a sailboat and tacking into the wind. The boat soon travels to the backcountry, where the crew disembarks into three double kayaks and journeys through the mangrove islands. Then the sailboat moves to another location, where snorkeling gear is donned. Finally, after much adventure, the boat sails back home. Excursions last about five hours. Full-day trips, sunset cruises, and specialized bird-watching trips are also available. Call for details and pricing. In 2002, Danger Charters added *Roamer* to their fleet. This traditional wooden power yacht takes you to a pristine reef, where the staff serves you a picnic lunch. Kayak to an out-island in the backcountry and enjoy your yacht-for-a-day.

Dream Catcher Charters
5555 College Road, Bayside, Key West
(305) 292-7702, (888) 362-3474
www.gotothekeys.com

How romantic for a couple or great fun with a group of six—cruising the Key West harbor in your own personal 29-foot power boat. Your captain handles all the navigating as you enjoy the company and the lovely view of Key West from the water. The trip is approximately two hours. Sodas and water are provided. The sunset is free!

Fury Catamarans
201 Front Street
(305) 294-8899, (800) 994-8898
www.furycat.com

Climb aboard one of Fury's 65-foot catamarans for a sail by day or night. Fury offers two three-hour trips to the reef daily for snorkeling—one in the morning, one in the afternoon—plus a two-hour champagne sunset sail each evening. You can buy separate tickets for day snorkeling or sunset sailing, or purchase a combination snorkeling/sunset sail ticket. Fury also offers snuba excursions. (Snuba, a cross between scuba diving and snorkeling, involves a cylinder of compressed air attached to a raft and connected to two 20-foot-long regulator hoses that participants use for breathing.) Beer, white wine, sodas, and snorkeling/snuba gear are included in the price of your ticket. In addition, Fury offers parasailing as well as a land/sea excursion package that includes a trip to the reef and a tour of Key West aboard either the Conch Tour Train or Old Town Trolley.

A Key West Reef Trip
MM 5.5 Oceanside, 6810 Front Street, Safe Harbor Marina, Stock Island
(305) 292-1345
www.reefchief.com

Board a classic wood sailing schooner for dive and snorkel trips to Sambo Reef or for leisurely day, sunset, and evening sails. Sailing lessons and music cruises are also available on the 65-foot schooner *Reef Chief,* a classic Chesapeake Bay–style schooner. Ask about special activities such as full-moon sails, Sunworship Sundays, Turtle Watch Tuesdays, and wild-dolphin-watching.

Key West Stargazer Cruise
202 William Street, Key West
(305) 292-1766
www.keyweststargazer.com

As the sun sets in the Florida Keys, it's hard to avoid gazing skyward. The Key West Stargazer Cruise is a fully narrated, 90-minute cruise aboard the historic schooner *Western Union,* the last working coastal schooner, which was built in Key West in 1939.

As you cruise tropical waters off Key West, astronomer Joe Universe will be your guide to the history and mythology of the constellations. The Key West Stargazer cruises nightly, weather permitting, from the historic seaport area. Refreshments are served on board.

Liberty Fleet of Tall Ships
245 Front Street, at the Hilton Resort & Marina
(305) 292-0332
www.libertyfleet.com

The 80-passenger schooner *Liberty* now resides full time in Key West, offering two-hour morning, afternoon, and sunset sails year-round. Sunset sails include complimentary beer, wine, and champagne. Passengers are invited to participate in hands-on sailing, but it's perfectly okay if you just want to sit back and let the captain do all the work.

The 125-foot, 115-passenger *Liberty Clipper* plies the waters off the Florida Keys and Dry Tortugas from November through May. On Tuesday, Thursday, and Sunday nights, passengers can dine on Caribbean-style favorites while they listen to reggae music and watch the sun sink into the Gulf. During the summer months, the *Liberty Clipper* offers a variety of adventure cruises along the Atlantic coast. Check the Web site for details.

***Mangrove Mistress* Eco-Charters**
MM 5, Murray Marine, Stock Island
(305) 745-8886
www.floridakeys.net/mangrovemistress

Gunkhole within the Great White Heron Natural Wildlife Refuge aboard the 30-foot river cruiser *Mangrove Mistress,* a 1930s-style, smooth-riding wood craft. Snorkel gear is on board, including equipment for children. Captain Lynda Schuh guarantees "no seasickness" on the two half-day trips she offers daily. If a half-day cruise is too long, try a serene sunset or sunrise voyage through the mangroves. Customized charters and full-day cruises are also available.

Mosquito Coast Island Outfitters
310 Duval Street
(305) 294-7178
www.mosquitocoast.net

Full-day kayak trips depart Key West by van for Geiger Key or Sugarloaf Key, where guided backcountry tours include a narration of the trees, birds, fish, coral, sponges, sea grass, and sea creatures (see the Paradise Found chapter). Single and double kayaks are available; half the trip is devoted to snorkeling. Gear, snacks, and bottled water are included in the fee. Children are welcome but must be at least nine years old to participate.

Rumrunners Casino Boat Inc.
245 Front Street at the Hilton Marina
(305) 295-7775

On the good ship *Rendezvous*, you'll find plenty of opportunities to take your chances—slots, blackjack, roulette, and stud poker during the day, plus dice games at night.

Day cruises leave from the Hilton Marina Thursday through Saturday at 1:00 P.M. Sunday through Thursday the casino boat is at sea from 7:00 P.M. to 11:30 P.M. On Friday and Saturday nights it returns at midnight.

Sebago Catamarans
328 Simonton Street
(305) 294-5687, (305) 292-4768
www.keywestsebago.com

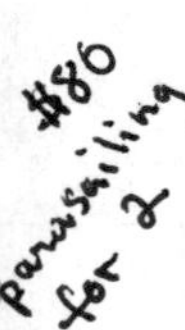

Head out to the reef for a snorkeling/sailing adventure aboard Sebago's 60-foot catamaran or cruise Key West Harbor at sunset. Complimentary drinks are served on both excursions. Sebago also offers parasailing as well as a six-hour "Island Ting" trip that includes kayaking, snorkeling, and sailing, plus a luncheon buffet. Call for details.

Stars & Stripes Catamaran Tours
Key West Historic Seaport
(305) 294-7877, (800) 634-6369
www.adventurekeywest.com

The 53-foot catamaran *Gold Coast* is equipped to carry as many as 49 passengers but typically takes smaller groups. Sandwiches, salads, and beverages are included in the per-person price for the all-day cruise. The sunset cruise offers beer, wine, mimosas, and nonalcoholic beverages. If you take the all-day excursion, you can get a sizable discount on the sunset cruise for another night of your visit.

Sunny Days Catamaran
Key West Historic Seaport
(305) 292-6100 (ferry), (305) 296-5556 (reef cruises), (800) 236-7937
www.sunnydayskeywest.com

Sunny Days could once boast of having the only "high-speed catamaran service" to Dry Tortugas National Park. Although that's no longer true, with the launching of its *Fast Cat II* in May 1999, Sunny Days does continue to have the fastest ferry service. The 100-passenger, high-speed *Fast Cat II* makes the voyage from Key West to Fort Jefferson in just less than two hours. As a result of the time saved, passengers aboard *Fast Cat II* can get in a little extra snorkeling at Garden Key or even squeeze in a snorkeling side trip to the Windjammer wreck (there's an extra charge per person for the side trip).

Fast Cat II leaves from its berth at the foot of Elizabeth Street at 8:00 A.M. A continental breakfast and lunch are included in the fare, along with snorkeling gear and instruction and a guided tour of Fort Jefferson. Campers pay an extra fee to accommodate their gear.

In addition to its daily run to Fort Jefferson, Sunny Days also offers twice-daily cruises aboard their new cat, *Caribbean Spirit*. The excursions go to the reef for snorkeling, a combination snorkeling/sunset cruise, and a champagne sunset cruise. Prices vary depending on the length of the cruise and the time of day.

Western Union
202 William Street
(305) 292-9830
www.schoonerwesternunion.com

A sail aboard the 130-foot schooner *Western Union* is truly a voyage back in time.

Built and berthed in Key West, the *Western Union* was launched off Simonton Beach in 1939 as a working schooner. Until 1974 it sailed the Caribbean and South Atlantic, logging more than 30,000 miles and maintaining thousands of feet of communications cables for the Western Union Company. In 1997 it returned to Key West to begin its second career as a passenger vessel.

From its slip next to Schooner Wharf Bar at the foot of William Street, the *Western Union* offers two-hour afternoon sails and sunset and starlight cruises; it is also available for private charters and other seafaring adventures. The sunset sails include music and complimentary beer, wine, and champagne.

Yankee Fleet Ferry to Fort Jefferson and Dry Tortugas National Park
Key West Historic Seaport
(305) 294-7009, (800) 634-0939
www.yankeefreedom.com

A voyage to Dry Tortugas National Park, 70 miles west of Key West, requires a full day. But if you have the time, be sure to include the adventure in your itinerary. Not only is this a spectacular ride back in history, it's a chance to experience what the Florida Keys are truly all about.

Ponce de León named the seven islands *Las Tortugas* (the Turtles) in 1513. The word Dry was later incorporated into the title to let seafarers know that there is no fresh water available here.

You'll be able to take a tour of the massive and historical Fort Jefferson on Garden Key and enjoy calm seas, pristine natural sand beaches, and some of the best snorkeling anywhere. The protected waters surrounding the Tortugas sparkle with all the sea creatures of the coral reef, plus a few shipwreck remains. And because this area has been designated a no-take zone, the creatures you see get a chance to grow larger than those you might otherwise encounter. Do remember, however, that there is no food, fresh water, electricity, or medical assistance at Fort Jefferson.

The *Yankee Freedom II*, a 100-passenger, high-speed catamaran, whisks passengers from Key West to Fort Jefferson in less than two-and-a-half-hours. *Yankee Freedom II* departs promptly at 8:00 A.M. and returns at 5:30 P.M. daily. Fare includes round-trip transportation; snorkeling gear; en route commentary by a naturalist-historian; a 45-minute guided tour of Fort Jefferson; continental breakfast of bagels, doughnuts, cold cereal, and juice; and lunch consisting of cold salads and a make-your-own sandwich bar. Coffee, iced tea, and water are complimentary; you can buy sodas, beer, wine, and mixed drinks on board. Passengers are not permitted to carry alcohol to the Dry Tortugas.

Only campers staying the night on Garden Key may bring large coolers (see the Campgrounds chapter). Campers pay slightly higher fees for passage aboard *Yankee Freedom II* to accommodate their gear.

There are six beaches in the Key West area. They are South Beach: end of Duval Street and the Atlantic Ocean (no facilities); Dog Beach: next to Louie's Backyard restaurant (no facilities); Higgs Beach: end of Reynolds Street (facilities); Rest Beach: home to White Street Pier (facilities within walking distance); Smathers Beach: South Roosevelt Boulevard (facilities); and Fort Zachary Taylor: entrance through Truman Annex at Southard Street (facilities).

GOLF AND TENNIS

Putters and players drive the Keys links, and racqueteers of all ages love our courts. Read on and be on the ball. Expect to pay for court time by the hour. Greens fees are reasonable at the public course in Marathon, but very, very pricey at the public course in Key West. If you belong to a country club back home, be sure to contact Sombrero Country Club to see about reciprocal privileges.

Upper Keys

Islamorada Tennis Club
MM 76.8 Bayside, Islamorada
(305) 664-5340

This facility maintains four clay and two hard courts, five of which are lit for extended play into the evening hours. Private lessons, clinics, round-robins, and tournaments are offered to the general public, and Islamorada Tennis Club will arrange games at all levels. A pro shop and boutique are on premises. Same-day racquet stringing is available.

Middle Keys

Key Colony Beach Golf and Tennis
MM 53.5 Oceanside, Eighth Street, Key Colony Beach
(305) 289-1533

Greens fees at Key Colony Beach's nine-hole, par-3 public course are a real deal. And you can rent clubs and a pull cart inexpensively as well. Tee times are not required. The course is open 7:30 A.M. to sunset. Key Colony Beach Golf Course is the only public course in the Keys outside Key West.

Tennis players can enjoy the two lit hard courts, which are open from 8:00 A.M. to 9:00 P.M.

To find the golf course, turn toward the ocean onto Key Colony Beach Causeway at the traffic light at MM 53.5.

Wonderlin Tennis
MM 50 Oceanside, 19 Sombrero Boulevard, at Lighthouse Cay Club Resort and Marina, Marathon
(305) 743-2250, Ext. 526

Marathon's favorite pro, Tim Wonderlin, together with Lighthouse Cay Club Resort, offers a tennis package that is difficult to beat. A per-day guest fee entitles you to unlimited tennis and pool privileges at the resort; you can also purchase a seasonal membership. The four hard courts are lit so play commences at 7:00 A.M. and can continue until 10:00 P.M. During the high season (November 15 through April 15), Wonderlin offers morning two-hour special clinics and organized round-robin play: women's day, men's day, or mixed doubles. Expect to pay an additional charge for these events. Private lessons may be scheduled.

Key West

Bayview Park Tennis
1310 Truman Avenue
(305) 294-1346

The tennis courts at Bayview Park are open to all on a first-come, first-served basis. Reservations are neither required nor accepted. There are no court fees, and courts are lit until 10:00 P.M.

Key West Golf Club
MM 5 Bayside, Stock Island
(305) 294-5232

The only public 18-hole course in the Keys, this par-70 course designed by Rees Jones offers a clubhouse, pro shop, and lessons. Greens fees are hefty in high season but about a third less in the off-season. For late-afternoon golfers, special "twilight" fees are available after 2:30 P.M. Monroe County residents receive discounts, but you must reside here year-round to qualify. Call for details.

Key West Tennis Too
811 Seminole Avenue
(305) 296-3029

Affiliated with the Casa Marina Resort and adjacent to it, Key West Tennis Too utilizes the hotel's three hard-surface courts. Tournament lights make nighttime play possible. A pro offers lessons by appointment, you can rent a ball machine, and a complete pro shop carries top-brand racquets and offers in-house stringing. Guests of the Casa Marina or Reach Resort play for about half the court fees that the public pays. Tennis clinics are held daily.

WATER SPORTS

Pick your pleasure and make a splash—parasailing, waterskiing, and kayaking. You'll find personal watercraft and paddleboat rentals in this section. For a rundown of scuba diving/snorkeling trips to the reef, see our Diving and Snorkeling chapter. Expect to pay a fee for these watery endeavors.

Upper Keys

It's a Dive Watersports
MM 103.8 Bayside, Marriott Key Largo Bay Beach Resort, Key Largo
(305) 453-9881, (800) 809-9881
www.marriottkeylargo.com

It's a Dive offers personal watercraft and kayak rentals. Parasailing, waterskiing, and scuba instruction are available, and snorkeling trips aboard a glass-bottomed boat depart twice daily.

Coral Reef Park Company
MM 102.5 Oceanside, John Pennekamp Coral Reef State Park, Key Largo
(305) 451-1621
www.johnpennekamp.com

Coral Reef Park Company rents snorkeling equipment at Pennekamp Park for unguided exploration of the nearshore Pennekamp waters off Cannon Beach, or you can sign on with one of the snorkeling tours to the reef (see the Diving and Snorkeling chapter for details). Rent canoes or kayaks here and paddle the mangrove water trails. Small boats also are available for hire.

Jacob's Aquatic Center
MM 99.6 Oceanside, Key Largo
(305) 453-7946
www.jacobsaquaticcenter.org

Jacob's Aquatic Center is a 3-pool complex with a 25-meter, 8-lane competition pool and contiguous diving pool with 1- and 2-meter diving boards. This facility is suitable for scuba and Red Cross certification, synchronized swimming, youth swim teams, masters swimming, swim lessons, water aerobics/Pilates, gymnastics, and water polo. They also have a interactive pool/water park featuring a pirate ship, "spray" gym, and "beachfront" entry. Co-located with the Key Largo Community Park (see listing in this chapter)

Caribbean Watersports
MM 97 Bayside, at Sheraton Beach Resort, Key Largo
(305) 852-4707, (800) 223-6728
www.caribbeanwatersports.com

Caribbean Watersports carries Hobie Cats and sailboats and provides a refresher course or an overview of how to sail before you head out on the water. You'll find parasailing (try the tandem flight with a friend) every hour and snorkeling trips twice daily. Caribbean Watersports offers kayak, sailboard, and five-passenger Jamaican bobsled (long, inflated pontoon-style kayaks pulled by powerboats) rentals, as well as personal watercraft. For all these water sports, call ahead for reservations.

Extreme Sports Florida Keys
MM 85 Oceanside, Windley Key
(305) 664-4055
www.extremesportsfloridakeys.com

Located on the premises of Coconut Cove Resort on Windley Key, Extreme Sports offers a variety of thrilling activities. You can get ultralight flight instructions here as well as kiteboarding lessons, sign up for guided or self-guided ecotours, or rent a JetSki/Waverunner or boat.

Splash Watersport Rentals
MM 84.5 Oceanside, at Pelican Cove, Islamorada
(305) 664-4435, (800) 445-4690
www.pcove.com

i

Many recreational activities are available just outside the Keys. For instance, KeysGate Community offers a golf course that is open to the public, and NASCAR racing is in nearby Homestead.

On the beach at Pelican Cove, Splash rents personal watercraft and 16-foot skiffs for round-trip visits to the Sand Bar (a popular snorkeling and swimming site). A reef boat takes snorkelers on excursions, and 16-mile, guided personal watercraft tours depart before sunset and head through the backcountry.

Florida Keys Kayak & Sail
MM 77.5 Oceanside at Robbie's Marina, Islamorada
(305) 664-4878
Explore the backcountry waters by kayak or rent an 18-foot day sailer or 22-foot Catalina from Florida Keys Kayak & Sail. You can paddle into the unknown by yourself or take one of several guided tours through mangrove canals, to Lignumvitae or Indian Key (see the Attractions chapter), or across the saltwater flats at sunset.

Middle Keys

Hawk's Cay Resort and Marina
MM 61 Oceanside, Duck Key
(305) 743-7000
www.hawkscay.com
The water-sports facility at Hawk's Cay offers parasailing, pontoon or center-console boat rentals, personal watercraft, and kayak rentals, as well as water-ski and wakeboard rentals and instruction. A sailing school is also on the premises.

Rick's Watercraft Rentals Inc.
MM 49.5 Bayside, at Banana Bay Resort, Marathon
(305) 743-7298, (800) 775-2646
www.rickswatercraft.com
Rent a personal watercraft from Rick's for a half hour or hour. Try the two-seater Yamaha IIIs, or rent your own 20-, 22-, or 23-foot boat for the day.

Lower Keys

Big Pine Kayak Adventures
MM 31 Bayside, at Old Wooden Bridge Fishing Camp, No Name Key
MM 28.5 Bayside, at Parmer's Place, Little Torch Key
(305) 872-7474, (877) 595-2925
www.keyskayaktours.com
Kayak tours through the Lower Keys backcountry waters of the Great White Heron Refuge make for superb gunkholing (see the Paradise Found chapter). Skiff tours take up to four people and their kayaks deeper into the backcountry waters. Custom backcountry tours can also be arranged, and guided ecotours on sit-atop kayaks are an option. If you prefer to head out on your own, you'll be given operational and chart instructions and suggestions of where to explore. Kayak reservations are required. Contact Capt. Bill Keogh if you're interested in a fishing charter, by kayak or skiff.

Reflections Nature Tours
Big Pine
(305) 872-4668
www.floridakeyskayaktours.com
Reflections Nature Tours is a mobile nature tour company that trailers their kayaks to a number of tour locations in the Lower Keys to take advantage of the tides and the prevailing winds. With more than 20 favorite kayaking spots, they can always find a favorable paddling site in any wind condition. Marine life, birds, plant life, and indigenous Keys animals can be viewed up close and personal. Guides will teach you kayaking techniques and give you the lowdown on the flora and fauna of the Keys.

Key West

Island Watersports
245 Front Street, Hilton Resort & Marina
(305) 296-1754, (888) 382-7864
www.island-watersports.com

Classes, Clubs, and Courses

Stretch your mind, body, and spirit! Your visit to the Florida Keys is the perfect time to renew an old passion, or try something new. Call to join the following classes/groups, or if your time here is short, ask about dropping in. Salsa Dance Lessons, (305) 296-6348; Tea Dance at Atlantic Shores Resort (see the Accommodations chapter), (305) 296-2491; Belly Dance Classes, (305) 774-3370; Painting Classes, (305) 745-2795; Key West Southernmost Runners Club, (305) 745-3027; Hares and Hounds Fun Run, (305) 292-2962; Florida Keys Community College Swim Classes, (305) 296-9081 ext 362; Community Pool, (305) 292-8248; Tai Chi on Sugarloaf Key, (305) 745-2811; Tai Chi for Adults, (305) 295-9622; Writing Course at Tropic Cinema, (305) 292-0482; Yoga College of India, (305) 292-1854; Tennis at Bayview Park, (305) 294-1346; and Meeting of Key West Writers Guild, (305) 293-8484.

Personal watercraft and Jet boats are available for rental by the half hour or hour. This business also boasts the largest riding area in Key West. If you like, wet suits and goggles are also offered. The guided tour aboard a personal watercraft offers you one and a half to two hours of island sightseeing.

Key West Water Sports
714 Seminole Street, at The Casa Marina Resort
(305) 294-2192

A wide variety of water-sports gear is ready and waiting for you here. Feel like a lazy afternoon just drifting? Try a Sun Cat floating lounge chair. Or maybe a Sea Peeper—a two-person glass-bottomed boat—is more your style. Key West Water Sports is also home to high-performance shortboards and quality sailboarding equipment. If you've never tried the sport before, climb aboard the Cat Surfer—the folks here guarantee that anyone can learn to sailboard on this baby. Hobie Cats, personal watercraft, baby-seat bikes, double-seater scooters, waterskiing, and parasailing are also available.

The Keys to Key West
5555 College Road, Bayside, Key West
(305) 292-7702, (888) 362-3474
www.gotothekeys.com

The Keys to the Keys claim they throw the largest island party in the Keys. This inclusive package is billed as "do it all in one day" and even their Web site comes with a warning label: "This trip will wear you out!" The package trip involves Wave Running, sunfish sailboating, banana boat rides, kayaking, knee boarding, snorkeling, windsurfing, and parasailing. Trips are from 10:00 A.M. to 4:00 P.M. with lunch, sodas, and water served. Be sure and eat a hearty breakfast before this outing!

Parawest Watersports Inc.
700 Front Street at A&B Lobster House
(305) 292-5199

This enterprise prides itself on offering excursionists the most free falls and dips in Key West. Regular rides of 8 to 10 minutes include heights of 300 feet with one free fall and one dip; longer, higher rides of 10 to 12 minutes reach 600 feet and include several free falls and dips. Most parasailing is done behind Christmas Tree Island and Sunset Key. Single and double personal watercraft also are available for rent. Renters must remain within a limited riding area.

Sunset Watersports
Smathers Beach
(305) 296-2554
This outfit offers something for everyone. Parasailing, Hobie Cats, kayaks, and sailboards are all provided on Smathers Beach. For an all-inclusive day trip, take the "Do It All." From the Key West Seaport, a 44-foot catamaran takes you out about 3 miles to a shallow wreck. From there, take turns exploring with personal watercraft, waterskiing, and just about anything else they can imagine.

Tropical Sailboats
Higgs Beach
(305) 296-0423

Smathers Beach
(305) 296-4185
Two locations provide an extensive list of water-sports rentals. Choose from Hobie Cats, sailboards, kayaks, rafts, and snorkeling equipment. Both locations offer free instruction, and both are authorized Hobie Cat dealers. Rentals are available by the hour or half day.

LET'S GO TO THE MOVIES

Cinema buffs can screen the latest flicks here. The theaters offer matinees on Saturday and Sunday and sometimes on weekdays at a reduced ticket price.

Middle Keys

Marathon Community Cinema
MM 50 Oceanside, Marathon
(305) 743-0288
This is no average movie theater. Owned and operated by the Marathon Community Theater, the cinema is small and intimate, although the screen is large. Seating is informally arranged in comfy barrel chairs around cocktail-style tables. A single movie is shown twice nightly. Matinees are offered on Saturday and Sunday. The theater is tucked behind Marathon Liquors.

Key West

Cinema Shores
510 South Street, Atlantic Shores Resort
(305) 296-2491
Enjoy a movie under the stars every Thursday night (weather permitting), beginning at 9:00 P.M. Atlantic Shores Resort shows a new feature each week, downstairs from the pool in the parking lot area. Call for details. Recent offerings have included adult-oriented short subjects, foreign films, and popular feature flicks you may have missed on the big screen. Ticket prices include popcorn. Cocktails are available for purchase. In case of rain, the film is usually postponed until Friday night.

Regal Cinema 6
3338 Roosevelt Boulevard, Searstown Shopping Center
(305) 294-0000
Six movies run concurrently at the Florida Keys' only multiplex cinema. All tickets for shows before 6:00 P.M. are discounted. Listening devices for the hearing impaired are available here as well.

Tropic Cinema
416 Eaton Street, Key West
(305) 294-5857
www.tropiccinema.com
This movie theater is a show unto itself. Historical and beautifully renovated, with loving care to detail (see Arts and Culture chapter), this is one magical setting for any film being shown. Tropic Cinema houses three screening rooms. The largest features independent films and first-run features; the second rolls classic and repertory films, and the third is used for conferences and seminars.

PHYSICAL FITNESS

Upper Keys

Curves
MM 101 Oceanside, Key Largo
(305) 451-1972

MM 50 Oceanside, Marathon
(305) 289-3211

1101 Key Plaza (Kmart Shopping Center)
(305) 293-8777
www.curvesinternational.com
Curves is a worldwide fitness and weight-loss franchise with three locations in the Keys. They offer a 30-minute workout program for women. The facility is focused on providing exercise and nutritional guidance. A one-year membership in the club will allow you the privilege of using any Curves location.

Froggy's Fitness
MM 91.8 Bayside, Tavernier
(305) 852-8623
Froggy's Fitness is a 6,500-square-foot fitness center that features state-of-the-art weight-training equipment, cardio machines, and rubber-coated weights. In addition to customized personal training, Froggy's offers yoga, Pilates, and aerobics classes as well as indoor cycling. The center provides individualized diet and nutrition plans and body-fat testing. You can purchase gym wear, aerobics footwear, and vitamins, protein supplements, and other health foods here, too.

Middle Keys

Nick's Fitness Express
MM 53 Bayside, Town Square Mall, Marathon
(305) 743-7618
Patrons work out in this full-service gym with free weights and weight machines, and cardiovascular equipment including treadmills, step machines, and stationary bikes. Weight management, body-fat testing, and certified personal trainers are other features here. This facility is open daily.

Keys Fitness Center
MM 49.5 Oceanside, Marathon
(305) 289-0788
www.keysfitnesscenter.com
Offering state-of-the-art fitness equipment by Paramount, Life Fitness, and Nautilus, Keys Fitness Center also sports a separate free-weights room for the serious workout addict. The facilities offer private showers and a relaxing sauna. Personal trainers are bilingual. Keys Fitness Center is open daily from 6:00 A.M. to 9:00 P.M.

Image Appeal
MM 24.9 Oceanside, Summerland Key
(305) 744-9995

3706C North Roosevelt Boulevard, Key West
(305) 293-1113
This fitness center promises "no mirrors and no men." Image Appeal is a ladies-only center for workouts, massages, facials, waxing, sauna, cellulite treatments, and tanning. In other words—head to toe—they cover just about all of you. Choose one treatment or treat yourself to all of them.

Lower Keys

Sugarloaf Fitness Resort
MM 19 Bayside, Sugarloaf
(305) 745-2289
If you want to work out in a tranquil setting, come to Sugarloaf Fitness Resort. The club is situated 1 mile off U.S. Highway 1 where there's not one shopping mall in sight. The resort offers a full gym, aerobics studio, clay tennis courts, volleyball leagues, heated pool and Jacuzzi, wellness and massage center, and a restaurant with a full bar.

Key West

Body Zone South
2740 North Roosevelt Boulevard, Overseas Market
(305) 292–2930
Key West's largest gym offers something for everyone. A full range of exercise equipment is available, including Nautilus equipment, treadmills, stationary bikes, stair climbers, and plenty of free weights. Exercise programs come in all shapes and sizes, from those for children to seniors and from low impact to hard core. Personal training and massage are available. The juice bar and play care for children are both convenient services. Body Zone South is open daily.

Club Body Tech
1075 Duval Street, Duval Square
(305) 292-9683
Some of the most high-tech equipment in the fitness industry, including the David 900 Series machines, is available at Club Body Tech. Stationary bikes, stair climbers, and free weights also are available. The center offers classes in aerobics, step, abdominals, and back and leg. Check here, too, for personal training and massage services. This facility is open daily.

Coffee Mill Cultural Center
916 Pohalski Street
(305) 296-9982
This local center promotes good health. It's the home of the Key West Dance Theatre and also offers many workout opportunities. Get ready for some yoga meditation in the morning, or opt for aerobics, dance, Pilates, or martial arts. Classes are held daily, and visitors are welcome. Attend a single class or sign up for a month's worth.

Iron Bodies Nutrition Center and Gym
1010 Truman Avenue
(305) 296-3250
If you're in the market for a low-impact, highly social fitness experience, you won't find it here. Iron Bodies is a no-nonsense, get-down-to-business, sweat-and-burn kind of gym. Think no pain, no gain and you've got the picture. In addition to a full range of Nautilus equipment and more than 10,000 pounds of iron, this place also features a full boxing ring, plus all the accoutrements—gloves, speed bags, jump ropes—that pugilist training requires. The gym's Bubba Boxing team practices here five days a week.

Iron Bodies opens at 6:00 A.M. daily (Sunday, too!). Memberships are available in a variety of terms and price ranges. But beware: Apply only if you're serious about your workouts. Casual exercisers won't feel comfortable here.

Paradise Health and Fitness
1706 North Roosevelt Boulevard
(305) 294-4120
If you've ever feared walking into a health club because you think everyone else will be perfectly toned and attired in the most fashionable exercise togs, fear no more. At Paradise Health and Fitness, all your lumps, bumps, and comfy old clothes are welcome.

In addition to a full-circuit weight room featuring Hoist equipment, Paradise offers a wide range of group classes, including yoga, tai chi, cardio kick-boxing, toning, low-impact, and step, for all ages and fitness levels. If you'd like some individual attention, Paradise has five personal trainers on staff to assist you; they even make home visits if you're so inclined.

Short- or long-term memberships as well as daily rates are available.

Yoga College of Key West
812 Southard Street
(305) 292-1854
This is the real thing and is not for wimps—yoga with an attitude. Renowned yoga experts often give seminars here, expounding upon what they call "Rambo Yoga." Classes are held daily; call for details.

JUST PLAIN FUN

YMCA Daily Grind Skateboard Park
Corner of Flagler Avenue and Kennedy Drive behind the fire station, Key West
(305) 295-9622

At last, something new for Key West kids to do. Built by the city of Key West and operated by the YMCA, the YMCA Daily Grind Skateboard Park offers thrills and spills aplenty. It opened to great fanfare in 2000 and is available to in-line skaters and skateboarders only; no BMX bikes allowed.

Hours vary depending on the season. The skateboard park is open daily in the summer and from Wednesday through Sunday when school is in session. A yearly membership fee is charged and there is also a nominal fee levied for each three-hour skating session. Pads and helmets are required; if you don't have your own, you may rent them. The YMCA requires release forms, signed by parents, for all skaters and skateboarders.

Even if you don't plan to skate, do stop by and watch. The ramps make for amazing acrobatic feats. You won't believe what some of these kids can do!

ATTRACTIONS 

Our landmass is but a drizzle of frosting across our seas, but this yummy confection of coral yields some tantalizing attractions. Don't wait for a rainy day (you might not have one) to explore our historical sites, out-islands, museums, nature preserves, and marine research centers.

We've organized the attractions described in this chapter by mile marker in descending order down the Keys, beginning in Key Largo. You'll find the majority of our most popular land-based diversions bordering the Overseas Highway, for our string of islands is not very wide. In our Key West section, we offer several categories of attractions scattered throughout our southernmost city. Many are free or charge a nominal amount for admission.

Don't miss this chapter's final section, "And Beyond . . . ," where we reveal the hidden treasures of our three nearby national parks.

So put on your sandals, grab your hat, and look for those car keys. Dally with us on an Insiders' tour of Paradise's distractions.

PRICE-CODE KEY

This code is based on adult admission.

	(FREE)
$	**$5.00 or less**
$$	**$6.00 to $10.00**
$$$	**$11.00 to $20.00**
$$$$	**$21.00 and higher**

THE FLORIDA KEYS

Upper Keys

Dolphin Cove **$$$$**
MM 101.9 Bayside, Key Largo
(305) 451-4060, (877) 365-2683
www.dolphinscove.com

Dolphin Cove, situated on a five-acre lagoon in Key Largo, offers an in-water encounter with bottlenose dolphins in addition to myriad other water activities. The dolphin program is offered daily. Participants must be age 7 and older and, if younger than age 18, must be accompanied by an adult. The encounter is preceded by a 30-minute boat ride in the waters of the backcountry, where you will receive an orientation briefing about the dolphins and about the interactions you will experience.

Dolphin Cove also offers Natural Swim dolphin encounter, which is a freestyle snorkel program. In this unstructured encounter, the dolphins do not exhibit trained behaviors, instead choosing to freely swim and interact with human participants. Participants must be at least age 8 for this encounter, and a participating adult or guardian must accompany anyone younger than age 13. Participants ages 13 to 17 must be observed by a parent or guardian.

Dolphin Cove also offers guided ecological tours of the Everglades National Park backcountry waters and Florida Bay, where you'll learn the mysteries of the mangrove habitat and probably encounter many of the species of birds and sea life discussed in our Paradise Found chapter. Other interesting trips into Florida Bay are offered on request, such as guided snorkel trips, kayak tours, sunset cruises, and even a private nighttime crocodile search in the nearshore waters of the Everglades. Call Dolphin Cove to arrange one of these customized trips.

Dolphins Plus Inc. **$$$$**
MM 100 Oceanside, Ocean Bay Drive, Key Largo
(305) 451-1993, (866) 860-7946
www.dolphinsplus.com

This marine mammal research and education facility offers you the opportunity to learn the fascinating habits and lifestyles of the bottlenose dolphin and enter its world for a compatible swim. The two-and-a-half-hour natural swim, offered twice daily, teaches you all about dolphins, including their social pod structure, communication methods, and anatomy. You'll learn how to conduct yourself in the water for your 30-minute swim with the dolphins. Participants must be comfortable in water above their heads and know how to use a mask, fins, and snorkel. Participants who do not wish to swim are also welcome. Individuals age 8 and older may swim with the dolphins, but a participating adult must accompany those younger than age 13. Participants ages 13 to 17 may swim alone but must be accompanied by an observing parent or guardian.

Dolphins Plus also offers a two-hour, structured interaction program three times daily where you can be in the water and involved directly with the dolphins. After an educational briefing, you will experience a structured water session encompassing platform behaviors and in-water behaviors. Interaction varies in each session, depending on the dolphin and the instructor. Sessions for the structured orientation program are offered daily. Participants must be age 7 or older, and a participating parent or guardian must accompany anyone younger than age 13. Pregnant women may not participate in either program.

Twice daily, from Monday through Friday, participants age 7 years and older can swim with sea lions for an hour. This program includes a 30-minute introduction as well as hands-on behaviors with a sea lion.

Nonswimmer admission for both programs is $10.00 for adults and $5.00 for ages 7 to 17; children younger than age 7 are admitted at no charge. Participants in all programs must call for reservations. Directions to Dolphins Plus are complicated. Call the center or check the Web site for detailed instructions.

Florida Keys Wild Bird Center **$**
MM 93.6 Bayside, Tavernier
(305) 852-4486, (888) 826-3811
www.fkwbc.org

Dedicated to the rescue, rehabilitation, and release of ill, injured, and orphaned wild birds, the Florida Keys Wild Bird Center will fascinate visitors of all ages. Artificial environmental hazards such as entanglement with anglers' lines or fishhooks also can render the birds injured and helpless. This rapid-care aviary treats the wounds, supervises the convalescence, and releases the birds back into the wild. Meanwhile, you may walk along a boardwalk path through the birds' natural habitats, which have been discreetly caged with wire enclosures. Signage and brochures provide environmental education of Keys habitats.

The Wild Bird Center is open daily during daylight hours. The center is funded by public donations; there are no admission fees. Look for the FLORIDA KEYS WILD BIRD CENTER signs as you drive down the Keys.

Windley Key Fossil Reef
State Geologic Site **$**
MM 85.5 Bayside, Windley Key
(305) 664-2540

Quarried long ago by workers building Flagler's East Coast Railroad Extension, the fossilized coral reef that forms the bedrock of the Keys (see the Paradise Found chapter) is exposed here for all to see. Borrow the in-house trail guide, which interprets what you'll discover on Windley Key's four trails.

The state site is open Thursday through Monday. Guided tours are offered at 10:00 A.M. and 2:00 P.M.

Theater of the Sea **$$$-$$$$**
MM 84.7 Oceanside, Islamorada
(305) 664-2431
www.theaterofthesea.com

With continuous performances offered daily, Theater of the Sea is the Florida

Keys' showiest marine entertainment facility. The natural saltwater lagoons, created by excavations for Flagler's Railroad, are home to a potpourri of popular marine creatures: dolphins, stingrays, sharks, sea turtles, game fish, and more.

Special programs are offered for an additional fee, which includes park and show admission. The Trainer-for-a-Day program, open to those age 10 and older, allows you to assist the trainers in feeding and caring for the dolphins and sea lions. You'll learn about nutrition and food preparation behind the scenes, then interact with the mammals in this three-hour session, but you will not swim with the dolphins or sea lions.

The Swim with the Dolphins program and Swim with the Sea Lions sessions are offered to visitors ages five and older. (Children ages five to seven must have a parent or legal guardian swim with them.) The programs include 30 minutes of instruction and 30 minutes in the water snorkeling and swimming with the dolphins or the sea lions. The Swim with the Stingrays program includes 15 minutes of instruction and 30 minutes in the water snorkeling with the stingrays, sea turtles, and other marine life. Swimmers must be age five and older to participate. (Minors must be accompanied by a parent or legal guardian in the swim area.)

Youngsters age three and older will enjoy the Wade with a Dolphin program. The one-hour session includes an orientation and thirty minutes interacting with a dolphin while standing in shallow water. Interaction includes such dolphin behaviors as cradles and kisses.

Participants in the special swim programs must be competent swimmers, must not be pregnant, and must speak and understand English. Call for reservations.

Pioneer Cemetery (FREE)
MM 82 Oceanside, at Cheeca Lodge, Islamorada

Their gravestones defiled in the hurricane of 1935, the founding fathers and mothers of Islamorada—the Parkers, Pinders, and Russells—still rest in the Pioneer Cemetery, now a part of the extensive grounds of Cheeca Lodge. A schoolhouse and the Methodist church, both destroyed in the hurricane, once bordered the cemetery. The angel statue marking the grave of Etta Dolores Pinder was found on the highway, miraculously intact except for a broken arm and wing. In 1989 Cheeca Lodge and University of Miami historian Josephine Johnson researched the cemetery, leading to the designation of the Pioneer Cemetery as a historical site by the Historical Association of Southern Florida. A plaque at the cemetery gate commemorates the event. You'll find the tiny Pioneer Cemetery surrounded by a white picket fence near the beach on the Cheeca Lodge grounds. The cemetery is open for free viewing by the general public.

Hurricane Monument (FREE)
MM 81.6 Oceanside, Islamorada

Honoring the hundreds of residents and railroad workers in Islamorada who lost their lives in the Labor Day hurricane of 1935, this monument depicts the fury of nature's elements with a bas-relief of high seas and wind-battered palm trees. Carved out of local coral limestone, the Hurricane Monument may be freely viewed just off the Overseas Highway.

Indian Key State Historical Site $
MM 77.5 Oceanside, Indian Key
(305) 664-2540

A colorful history paints Indian Key, a 10-acre, oceanside island about ¾ of a mile offshore from Lower Matecumbe Key. Now uninhabited, this tiny key has yielded archaeological evidence of prehistoric Native American cultures. Once visited by Spaniards and pirates alike, the island was purchased in 1831 by Jacob Housman, who established a thriving settlement. Indian Key became the Dade

County seat in 1836. Physician Henry Perrine sat out the Second Seminole War here, which proved a misguided decision, for Indians attacked the island in 1840, and he lost his life after all. Fires destroyed all the structures except for the foundations. Although some people returned after the assault, by the early 1900s the key supported only burgeoning vegetation.

Indian Key is accessible only by boat. Limited private dockage is available for small boats, but the site has no restrooms or picnic facilities. The historical site is open from 8:00 A.M. to sundown. Ranger-led tours are at 9:00 A.M. and 1:00 P.M.

Robbie's Marina, MM 77.5 Bayside, (305) 664-9814, or www.robbies.com, offers the only regularly scheduled tour transportation to the island. Tours depart Thursday through Monday to Indian Key and Lignumvitae Key (see the following write-up). No tours are given on Indian Key on Tuesday or Wednesday, but the island is open to those with their own transportation. The boat shuttle to Indian Key departs Robbie's docks at 8:30 A.M. and 12:30 P.M. The launch will carry you to Lignumvitae Key at 9:30 A.M. or 1:30 P.M. Admission to the islands is included in the tour price. Reservations are preferred. And while you are waiting for the boat, buy a cup of bait and feed the tarpon that come around the docks regularly.

Lignumvitae State Botanical Site $
MM 77.5 Bayside, Lignumvitae Key
(305) 664-2540

Named for the lignum vitae tree, Lignumvitae Key—our highest island at 17 feet above sea level—supports one of the best examples of a virgin hardwood hammock in the Florida Keys (see the Hardwood Hammock section in the Paradise Found chapter). Also on the island is the 1919 home of the Matheson family, of chemical company fame, who owned the island for many decades. The stilt-style home sports two storm hatches—bedroom and porch—so doors would not be blown off their hinges in a bad blow. The screened porch enabled the Mathesons to leave via the hatch, keeping the mosquitoes at bay.

One-hour ranger-guided walks at 10:00 A.M. and 2:00 P.M. allow visitors to tour the house and the hardwood hammock. You may not enter the hammock unless accompanied by a ranger. Park officials suggest you come equipped with mosquito repellent and sturdy shoes. Like Indian Key, Lignumvitae Key may be accessed only by boat, and limited private dockage for small craft is available (see previous write-up for information on Robbie's Marina, which offers transportation to the key). Lignumvitae Key is closed Tuesday and Wednesday.

Middle Keys

The Dolphin Connection $$$$
MM 61 Oceanside, at Hawk's Cay Resort, Duck Key
(888) 814-9154
www.dolphinconnection.com

Dolphin Connection's Dolphin Discovery provides an interactive, 25-minute, in-water encounter with the most famous of our Florida Keys marine creatures, bottlenose dolphins. You will not actually swim with the Connection's dolphins, but you'll get to know them up close and personal. You'll be able to touch, feed, pet, and play with them from the security of a submerged platform (great for nonswimmers or those people with physical limitations).

After a short classroom orientation reviewing dolphin and people etiquette, you will sit in the water on a shallow platform, where the trainer will familiarize you with the dolphin's anatomy. Trainers enlighten participants about the dolphins and their marine environment as well as the Florida Keys' ecosystem. From the submerged platform you will move to the deep area, standing in water 3 feet deep. Here you will play games with the dolphins, which will jump, splash, fetch, and thoroughly entrance you. (Other special guidelines apply.)

The 45-minute Dolphin Discovery program is open to participants who are 4 feet, 6 inches or taller. The encounters are held several times daily. There is a maximum of six people per program, with the intimate ratio of three people to one trainer and one dolphin.

Adults who do not wish to get wet in the Discovery program can participate in Dockside Dolphins, as can pregnant women, who are not allowed to join in the in-water Dolphin Discovery. Dockside Dolphins is a 30-minute, behind-the-scenes look at dolphin training sessions. Participants learn how the professionals at Dolphin Connection train the dolphins and then, from the dock, take part in an actual training procedure. You'll be able to feel, feed, and pet the dolphins but not have to get into the water. Adults and children love this experience (children age five and younger must be accompanied by a paying adult). Dockside Dolphins is offered daily.

Kids have a ball as participants in the unique 30-minute Dolphin Detectives program. From the dry docks, the children learn how to be dolphin trainers. (Children age five and younger must be accompanied by a paying adult.) The kids learn the trainer's hand signals and get to try them out on the playful dolphins during a supervised training session. The participants are taught how to feed the dolphins—touching, weighing, and preparing those fish the mammals like so much.

Dolphin Detectives kicks off daily. Advance reservations are required for all programs. Bookings are accepted up to three months in advance.

Dolphin Research Center $$$–$$$$
MM 59 Bayside, Grassy Key
(305) 289-1121,
(305) 289-0002 (reservations)
www.dolphins.org

Look for the giant statue of a dolphin and her calf that heralds the Grassy Key home of the Dolphin Research Center. Once the lodging for Flipper, the famed television star of yesteryear, the Dolphin Research Center offers a variety of fascinating encounters with these smart marine mammals.

One-hour, narrated walking tours introduce you to the dolphins in their natural environments, where you'll witness their training sessions. Walking tours are offered five times daily. Children younger than age four are admitted free with a paying adult.

The half-day Dolphin Encounter enables you to learn how people interact with the dolphins. You'll attend a workshop, take the walking tour, and then spend 20 minutes in the water with two dolphins and up to five other people. The ratio of people to dolphins is never more than three to one. Children ages 5 to 12 must be accompanied in the water by a paying adult. Life jackets will be supplied to participants of all ages who desire them. This program is very popular, and access is limited. For reservations, you must call on the 1st or 15th day of the month preceding the month you'd like to swim. (For example, call October 1 if you'd like to reserve a dolphin swim from November 1 to November 14; call October 15 if you'd like a reservation from November 15 to the end of the month.)

In the DolphinSplash program, you can meet the dolphins in the water without swimming. Participants stand on a submerged platform, waist-deep in water, and the dolphins swim up to say hello. You'll receive 15 minutes of instruction, enjoy 15 minutes in the water, and then take one of the guided walking tours. Make reservations following the same procedures as Dolphin Encounter. For DolphinSplash, however, a few spots are saved every day for walk-ins, so you might get lucky. Participants must be at least 44 inches tall; children below this height must be held in the arms of a parent or guardian. Children younger than age three are admitted free. A participating adult must accompany children younger than age eight.

New programs at the Dolphin Research Center include Meet a Dolphin, where you can observe a dolphin behavior session and then join the trainer at the dock for a personal introduction to the dolphin; and Paint with a Dolphin, where you can help a dolphin actually paint a T-shirt for you in your choice of two colors. Unlike the other interactive programs at the center, you can purchase tickets for these after you arrive.

On Wednesday afternoons you can participate in Tursiops Training, where you will learn the principles of dolphin behavior training and the signals used to elicit certain dolphin behaviors. On Friday afternoons in the Bottlenose Babies program you will receive private instruction about the DRC's dolphin youngsters from the "staff only" boardwalks, then participate in an actual data collection session. The half-day sessions are open to participants age 12 and older. Reservations are suggested although walk-ins are accepted on a space available basis.

You can immerse yourself in a dolphin world and earn college credit at the one-week DolphinLab, a series of dolphin behavior seminars and hands-on encounters. You'll live on the premises in the center's dormitory and enjoy side trips to Key West and snorkeling at Looe Key National Marine Sanctuary. Summer programs for middle school, junior high, and teens are also available. Call for more information.

Museums of Crane Point **$$**
MM 50.5 Bayside, Marathon
(305) 743-9100
www.cranepoint.org

The small, interesting Museum of Natural History and the adjoining Florida Keys Children's Museum (see the Kidstuff chapter) sit on the skirt of the Crane Point hammock, which covers a bit of history in itself. The museum houses a potpourri of Keys icons and exhibits. Creatures of the reef have been authentically re-created in tropical splendor and are accompanied by an audio of the sounds of the deep. You'll see the inhabitants of the pinelands habitat—slash pines, red mangroves, silver buttonwood, key deer, and miniature raccoons; ancient shipwreck memorabilia; shells of giant sea turtles; tree snails of the tropics; even a stuffed osprey, great white heron, egret, frigatebird, and the like.

Come to the Museums of Crane Point on the second Saturday of each month and meet Mike Price, owner of Bee's N the Keys. He will be talking about the new honeybee exhibit at the Cracker House (behind the Museum) and giving presentations on every aspect of honey bees. Mike has the only honey processing plant in the Keys (located on Cudjoe Key).

Between the two museum structures, a fish-filled lagoon attracts fin fanciers, and the wild-bird rescue flight cage fascinates bird lovers of all ages. You'll see a Caribbean-style sailing canoe, paddled here in 1989 by three Guatemalan refugees, and an authentic Cuban freedom raft. Children enjoy the outdoor osprey nest exhibit, in which they really get a bird's-eye view of the museum. They can climb right up into the nest. Guided tours of the museum are offered weekdays from December through April.

After you tour the exhibits, traipse down the nature trails that loop through Crane Point hammock, which is named for the Cranes, who owned the property until the early 1970s. The Cranes protected the area from development and preserved the forested land as a good example of our rare hardwood hammock habitat (see the Paradise Found chapter). A ¼-mile boardwalk trail, which leads through a mangrove habitat, was created in 2000.

The museum provides a self-guided tour pamphlet that also lists some of the unusual tropical hardwoods you'll see along the nature trails. The Adderley House walk, about half a mile long, leads to the restored Bahamian-style house built around 1905 by George Adderley, a black Bahamian settler of the Middle Keys. The concretelike walls of the one-room structure are constructed from ground shells.

Crane Point is open daily. One admission charge allows access to both trails and museums. Children age six and younger get in free.

Pigeon Key National Historical Site $$
Old Seven Mile Bridge, Bayside, Pigeon Key
(305) 289-7178,
(305) 743-5999 (gift shop)
www.pigeonkey.org

Though undoubtedly Pigeon Key was known to Native Americans and Bahamian fishermen in the early days of the Keys, it was Henry Flagler's East Coast Railroad Extension that put the tiny five-acre key on the historical map. And it is the volunteer-staffed Pigeon Key Foundation that keeps it there. The island is connected to the mainland by a bridge that was originally built for the railroad and which served as a construction and maintenance site for the railroad from 1908 to 1935. The hurricane of 1935 flooded Pigeon Key and caused so much damage to the railroad that the company decided not to rebuild (see the Historical Evolution chapter). When the Seven Mile Bridge was built over the railroad spans in the late 1930s, Pigeon Key became headquarters for the Bridge and Toll District.

Over the ensuing decades the key was used as a fishing camp, a U.S. Navy site, a park, and a marine biology center for the University of Miami. In 1982 the new Seven Mile Bridge was constructed, bypassing Pigeon Key from auto traffic. The Pigeon Key Foundation, a nonprofit local organization with the stated mission "to preserve the history and environment of the Florida Keys" was established in 1993, securing a long-term lease to the island from Monroe County.

Pigeon Key is a living testament to the Florida Keys of 1912 to 1940. The foundation has restored eight of the island village's buildings dating from the early 1900s. Automobiles are not allowed on the Old Seven Mile Bridge. A trolley shuttle leaves every day on the hour from 10:00 A.M. to 4:00 P.M. from the Pigeon Key Visitor Center, which occupies a quaint old railway car that still rests on Flagler's tracks at MM 47 Oceanside, Knight's Key.

Once on the island, the trolley driver conducts a 20-minute guided tour of Pigeon Key. You may return on any shuttle you wish; the last one leaves the island at 5:00 P.M.

Visitor fees include shuttle service. You can get out to Pigeon Key under your own steam, if you'd rather. The 2 miles of renovated bridge make for a good workout via walking, jogging, in-line skating, or biking. Stop by the visitor center to purchase tickets before your trek through history. Pigeon Key hosts a number of festivals and special events each year, which require a separate admission charge (see the Annual Events chapter).

Lower Keys

The Blue Hole (FREE)
MM 30.5 Bayside, Key Deer Boulevard, Big Pine Key
(305) 872-2411

You may wonder why all those cars are parked on the side of Key Deer Boulevard, for from the roadside the area looks like an uninhabited stand of slash pines. Park your vehicle and join the crowd. A few steps into the thatch palm understory you'll see a large, water-filled barrow pit, known as The Blue Hole. Inhabiting this incongruous water hole are a couple of resident alligators, the only known 'gators in the Keys. If you're lucky, you may catch a glimpse of one of these elusive reptiles.

Ducks and wading birds stay out of the alligators' path. The Blue Hole is ¼ mile north of the intersection of Key Deer and Watson Boulevards. There is no charge for visiting The Blue Hole.

National Key Deer Refuge and Watson Nature Trail (FREE)
MM 30.5 Bayside, Key Deer Boulevard, Big Pine Key
(305) 872-2239

The National Key Deer Refuge protects the pineland habitat frequented by the key deer, a small species—not much larger than a German shepherd—that is found nowhere else in the world (see the Paradise Found chapter). Some areas of the refuge, which encompasses a large portion of Big Pine Key, are off-limits to visitors and are so marked. National wildlife refuge signs, depicting a flying bird, mark the boundaries of the refuge, which is open for daytime public access on designated trails.

You can find the ⅔-mile Watson Nature Trail 1.3 miles north of the intersection of Key Deer and Watson Boulevards. The trail winds throughout the pineland habitat of the refuge (see the Paradise Found chapter). The short Mannillo Trail, a fifth of a mile, traverses pine rockland and freshwater wetland habitats.

The key deer are protected by law—even feeding them is a misdemeanor offense. Roadkill remains a primary hazard to the key deer. Speed limits on U.S. Highway 1 through Big Pine Key are reduced to 45 mph during the day and 35 mph at night and are strictly enforced. The best time to look for key deer is early in the morning or at dusk.

You can sometimes spot key deer beside US 1, but you are more likely to see them along the back roads and especially on No Name Key, where there are fewer human inhabitants. To reach No Name Key, turn right at the intersection of Key Deer and Watson Boulevards. The road will take you through a residential neighborhood and across a cement bridge to No Name Key, ending abruptly at a pile of boulders.

Perky Bat Tower (FREE)
MM 17 Bayside, Sugarloaf Key

Richter Perky may have had bats in his belfry in 1929 when he decided to build this Sugarloaf Key tower, but such are dreams that lay the foundations for legends. Perky believed that the uniquely designed, louvered pine tower, when laced with the proper bait, would attract a Keys population of mosquito-loving bats, thus solving his insect-infestation problem. Alas, the nocturnal fliers bypassed his offering, and Perky had to go back to the drawing board. The structure has withstood the tests of time and the elements, however. Perhaps Perky should have called it a hurricane shelter.

To find Perky Bat Tower, turn right (bayside) at the SUGARLOAF AIRPORT sign just beyond Sugarloaf Lodge when heading down the Keys. When the road forks, bear to the right.

KEY WEST

Key West's historic Old Town district is perfect for a leisurely stroll to take in the history and eccentricity of this tiny island. How about visiting an aquarium, a cemetery, or a garden? Or maybe a tour of haunted houses or an old wrecker's house filled with antiques? We've checked out all the high points for you, including a few "only in Key West" attractions guaranteed to keep you entertained.

Key West attractions have been divided into three categories: Historic Homes and Museums, One of a Kind, and Guided and Self-Guided Tours. Within each category, attractions are listed in alphabetical order.

Historic Homes and Museums

Audubon House & Tropical Gardens $$
205 Whitehead Street
(305) 294-2116, (877) 281-2473
www.audubonhouse.com

It was 12 years before the house was built, but in 1832 John James Audubon did spend time on the grounds of John Geiger's huge garden. Legend has it that Audubon sketched the white-crowned pigeon and the geiger tree he found in the garden here. During his stay in the

CLOSE-UP

Passport to Adventure
Getting Hitched in Paradise, 24/7

Jet skiing, sky diving, a horseback ride, scuba diving, yachts and schooners, atop a lighthouse, sunset on the beach, historic sites, a private garden, fabulous mansions, dressing in a theme (as pirates, Civil War characters, you name it), or whatever your dream fantasy might be! This might sound like a delightful tour of the Florida Keys, but actually these are places where you can be married and activities you can enjoy while tying the knot.

The Keys are filled with wedding planners who will orchestrate a "destination wedding" you and your wedding party will always remember. Whether you are getting married or renewing your vows, using the Florida Keys as a backdrop will be a day like no other—in more ways than one. Most wedding coordinators offer free consultations and will help orchestrate such details as locations, tropical florists, photographers, creative caterers, personalized vows, magical music, or wedding accessories that you might have forgotten (jewelry, veils, bridal gifts). They can even arrange for a gown presser who is insured by Lloyds of London to come to you! The laid-back ambience of the Keys allows everyone attending the wedding to enjoy the days prior to the big day hanging out at the beach, fishing, or just relaxing. Most couples say that when the wedding invitations note that the wedding is being held in the Florida Keys, no one refuses! To marry in the Keys you must be 18 years of age. Out-of-state residents don't have to undergo a blood test, and there's no waiting period for non-Florida residents or non-residents from other countries. A public notary may perform the ceremony, or arrangements can be made for a minister and a church of your choice. For more detailed information, visit www.fantaseaweddings.com, www.keysweddings.com or www.greateventscatering.com.

A beautiful dream wedding in a romantic tropical keys setting. PHOTO: HAWK'S CAY RESORT

Keys, Audubon produced 18 sketches of native wildlife. Original lithographs of these drawings are on display at the Audubon House. The house and environs, however, are more reminiscent of the family of Capt. John Geiger, a wrecker who built the house and lived here with his family. Set your own tour pace with a free pair of headphones and a tape that brings the house alive.

Audubon House is open daily. Children younger than age six are free.

Curry Mansion **$**
511 Caroline Street
(305) 294-5349, (800) 253-3466
www.currymansion.com

This imposing home evokes images of an opulent old Key West, although the three-story Conch house now serves as the focal point for a bed-and-breakfast inn and a museum. Built in 1905 by Milton Curry, Florida's first homegrown millionaire, the inn's public rooms display a selection of antiques and memorabilia. Poke around in the attic, and you'll find an 1899 billiard table among the old dresses and luggage. From the attic you can climb the widow's walk for a panoramic view of Key West Harbor. Self-guided tours are available daily. See the Accommodations chapter for information on overnight stays in the adjacent buildings.

Duval Street Wrecker's Museum—The Oldest House **$**
322 Duval Street
(305) 294-9502

Withstanding every storm since 1835, the former Watlington House has rightly earned its Key West nickname as the oldest house in the city. Captain Watlington bought the house in 1839, and it was family occupied for the next 130 years. Donated to the state of Florida in 1974, it is now the Wrecker's Museum, housing nautical photos and memorabilia from the Key West wrecking era, including an authentic wrecking (some prefer to call it salvaging) license. Highlights are a shipwreck display, which shows the location of many a wreck on local reefs; an antique dollhouse that even has a miniature Key West mural; and the detached cookhouse kitchen, separated from the main structure to safeguard against fires.

The Wrecker's Museum is open daily. The tours are self-guided, but a docent is always available on the premises to answer questions.

East Martello Museum **$$**
3501 South Roosevelt Boulevard
(305) 296-3913
www.kwahs.com

This enchanting, artifact-filled former fort will bring you up to speed on Key West history. Built during the Civil War, the brick fortress was never completely finished because the circular Martello design became antiquated before it was ever armed. Operated today as a museum and gallery by the Key West Art and Historical Society, the 8-foot-thick walls support pictures, artifacts, and historical documents. Featured in the small gallery are the charming wood carvings of Key West's Mario Sanchez and the funky welded sculptures by the late Stanley Papio of Key Largo, fabricated from bedsprings, toilet fixtures, and other so-called junk. You can climb the citadel to the lookout tower for an unobstructed view of the Atlantic coast.

East Martello Museum is open daily. Kids younger than age six get in free. Adults may purchase a combination ticket that allows admission to this museum, the Key West Lighthouse Museum, and the Key West Museum of Art and History at the Custom House (see descriptions later in this chapter). Visits to all three facilities need not be made on the same day.

Harry S Truman Little White House **$$**
111 Front Street
(305) 294-9911
www.trumanlittlewhitehouse.com

Ordered by his doctor to retreat to a stress-free climate and recover from a lingering cold, President Harry S Truman came to Key West for the first time in 1946. Like so many others, he was instantly smitten with the island and spent 11 working vacations in the commandant's quarters, dubbed the Little White House. Built in 1890, the house was renovated for its famed visitor in 1948. Opened to the general public as a museum dedicated to "Give 'Em Hell Harry" in 1991, the home has once again been restored to its 1948 splendor. You'll be able to view Truman's Winter White House as it looked when he spent his 175 working vacation days here. The family quarters, poker porch, dining room, and living room (complete with Truman's piano) are open to the public.

The guided tour takes you into the rooms and lives of Harry and Bess. The Exhibition Room displays a permanent collection of photographs of Presidents Eisenhower and Kennedy. Eisenhower spent two weeks here recuperating from his second heart attack, and Kennedy held a summit meeting here before the Bay of Pigs action. Jimmy Carter visited with his family in 1996, and Bill and Hillary Clinton spent a weekend here in 2005. A 10-minute video recounts the history of the home, and a collection of presidential memorabilia is on display in the museum gift shop.

Guided tours are conducted daily. Children younger than age four are admitted free.

Hemingway Home and Museum $$
907 Whitehead Street
(305) 294-1136
www.hemingwayhome.com

Once the home of Key West's most famous writer, Ernest Hemingway, the Hemingway Home and Museum ranks at the top of any must-do list and is Key West's most popular attraction. Built by wrecker Asa Tift in 1851, the home took on historical significance when Ernest and Pauline Hemingway moved in. Pauline spearheaded extensive remodeling, redecorating, and refurnishing and fitted her backyard with the island's first swimming pool. Hemingway wrote several of his most celebrated works, including *For Whom the Bell Tolls, Death in the Afternoon, The Green Hills of Africa,* and *To Have and Have Not,* from his pool house office out back. The Hemingways lived in this Key West home from 1931 to 1939.

Guided tours lasting approximately 45 minutes are offered every 10 minutes, daily. Children younger than age six enter free. Be sure to look for the infamous six-toed cats!

Heritage House Museum and Robert Frost Cottage $$
410 Caroline Street
(305) 296-3573
www.heritagehousemuseum.org

The memorabilia in the Heritage House Museum pays tribute to Jessie Porter, a cultured, well-traveled woman at the center of Key West society in the mid-1900s. Visitors to the house included Tallulah Bankhead, Thornton Wilder, Gloria Swanson, Tennessee Williams, Pauline Hemingway, and, of course, regular visitor Robert Frost, who stayed in the small cottage in the rear garden when he wintered in Key West, which he did off and on from 1945 through 1960. Visitors are invited to make themselves at home in the comfortable original surroundings and even to play the antique piano.

Heritage House Museum is closed Wednesday and Sunday. Heritage House is generally closed the first two weeks of September, and in summer, hours may be shortened; in either case it is best to phone ahead. Children younger than age 12 get in free.

Key West Lighthouse and Keeper's Quarters Museum $$
938 Whitehead Street
(305) 294-0012
www.kwahs.com

This 1847 structure, inland on a Key West street just across from the Hemingway Home, affords visitors a bird's-eye view of Key West from atop its 90-foot light tower (88 steps to the top). Why a lighthouse so far from the water? It was positioned here to avoid the fate of its predecessor on Whitehead Point, which toppled in a hurricane the previous year. The keeper's quarters houses maritime memorabilia and a gift shop.

The lighthouse museum is open daily for self-guided tours. Children younger than age six are free. Adults may purchase a combination ticket for admission to this museum, the East Martello Museum, and the Key West Art and History Museum at the Custom House (see descriptions elsewhere in this chapter).

The Key West Museum of Art and History at the Custom House $$
281 Front Street
(305) 295-6616
www.kwahs.com

Even if it contained no exhibits, this lovely building just off Mallory Square, where Front and Whitehead Streets come together, would be worth a stop. With its 20-foot ceilings, arched windows, 12 fireplaces, and magnificently restored staircase, the structure itself is a work of art. Designed by the renowned architect Henry Hobson Richardson and completed in 1891 at a cost of less than $110,000, the building required 917,000 bricks from New York, iron from Pennsylvania, dozens of masons from Massachusetts, and more than 100 carpenters, plasterers, and other skilled construction workers from throughout the United States. Although it was officially called the U.S. Custom House, this structure also housed the U.S. Postal Service and the U.S. District Court. Here, in the second-floor courtroom, the official inquiry into what caused the sinking of the USS *Maine* was conducted. The Custom House served the city well for four decades, but as government needs changed and the various agencies moved to larger quarters elsewhere on the island, the building was deemed "superfluous property" and abandoned in the 1960s. Fortunately, it was not targeted for demolition. Today it is on the National Register of Historic Places and remains one of the finest examples of Richardsonian/Romanesque Revival architecture in existence.

For close to 30 years, the Custom House stood empty and forlorn. In 1990 the Key West Art and Historical Society acquired the building and began a restoration that would take nine years and nearly $9 million to complete. It was finally reopened to the public as a museum of national stature in August 1999.

Inside you will find seven galleries and a gift shop. Exhibits of artwork and historical artifacts change periodically; however, those on the second floor traditionally focus on the history of Key West. Be sure to continue up the stairs to the third floor. There are no exhibit galleries here, but the works of folk artist Mario Sanchez, which line the walls between the closed office doors, are worth the climb. There's a great view from the arched window overlooking Sunset Key and the harbor here, too.

The museum is open daily. Children younger than age six enter free. Adults may purchase a combination ticket that allows admission to this museum as well as to the East Martello Museum and the Key West Lighthouse Museum (see descriptions elsewhere in this chapter).

i

Looking for a quiet, tranquil place to catch your breath? Just a few blocks off the hustle and bustle of Duval Street is the serene Stations of the Cross Gardens on the grounds of historic St. Mary's Star of the Sea Catholic Church (see Worship chapter, Close-up). This half-acre garden is open to travelers and islanders alike.

Mel Fisher Maritime Heritage Society and Museum $$
200 Greene Street
(305) 294-2633
www.melfisher.org

For 16 years, "today's the day" was the hope of treasure salvor Mel Fisher, who finally struck pay dirt on July 20, 1985. Finding the *Nuestra Señora de Atocha,* which Fisher estimated to be worth $400 million, ensured his legacy as treasure hunter extraordinaire. Heavy gold chains, jeweled crosses, and bars of silver and gold are among the artifacts on display at the permanent first-floor exhibit. Hefting a gold bar worth more than $18,000 is a highlight.

CLOSE-UP

Key West Architecture

The mix of Key West architecture, like the cultural melting pot of the 19th century, is duplicated nowhere else in the world. Self-taught craftsmen, working from their own designs, built many of the 3,000 frame structures in historic Old Town. These ship's carpenters and sea captains drew upon their knowledge of wooden vessels to construct their new homes. They were primarily influenced by the structural techniques of their homeland, the Bahamas. Several houses were actually dismantled in the Bahamas and transported to Key West, where they were reassembled.

The climate of Key West and the Bahamas is similar, so every attempt was made to capture breezes and keep the houses cool. Houses had to be built to withstand the hot sun, heavy rains, and hurricanes. Builders used hand-hewn wood instead of plaster because plaster cracks and decays in high wind and humidity. Dade County pine, when available, was imported from the Upper Keys and Pensacola. It was preferred because the heavy resin content made it dense and impenetrable to termites. But much of the time wood from wrecked ships or the cargo salvaged from them was used. Nails were scarce because they were handmade and expensive, so wooden pins held the timbers together.

Most of the houses were built on wooden posts or coral rock piers for protection from high tides and storm waters. Roofs were designed to shed heavy water, with gutters and downspouts carrying the runoff to cisterns, where it was collected for later use. The roofs featured scuppers, or scuttles, which are openings that allow the hot air from the upper stories or attics to escape. Window and door openings were protected from the sun by louvered wood blinds. Wide covered verandas protected windows and doors from rain. And the houses were trimmed with intricately carved wood molding that has come to be known as gingerbread.

The 19th-century Key West homes preserved today through ongoing restoration efforts are unique architectural mutations we call Conch houses, for the original Bahamian settlers who first designed them. These styles are often referred to as Classic Revival, Victorian, or Queen Anne.

The so-called eyebrow house is easy to spot because the sloping front roofline all but covers the upper-story windows, like bushy eyebrows over glassy orbs.

The two-story Conch temple has distinctive columns supporting roof overhangs on both levels.

The simple shotgun houses are so called because the interior rooms are lined up, one behind the other, with a hallway extending the length of the house from front to back. Hence, a bullet shot from the front door would hit no wall at all before it reached the back of the house. Most shotgun houses were built in the 1800s by cigar factories to house their workers.

You'll find other elaborate frame structures laden with capitals and pedi-

Descendants of Ernest Hemingway's famous six-toed cats still hang out at Hemingway Home and Museum in Key West. The house was built in 1851. PHOTO: FLORIDA KEYS TDC

ments, porches and bay windows, gingerbread and other decorations borrowed from styles throughout the ages, as distinctively individual as their owners and defying easy classification.

For a good, thorough look at the architecture of Key West, get a copy of *The Houses of Key West,* by Alex Caemmerer (available at Key West bookstores). Caemmerer describes the architectural styles in detail, inside and out, and gives addresses of classic examples of these private homes so all you need to do is put on your walking shoes and stroll back in time down the streets of Key West's historic district.

The road to restoration and preservation of Key West's charming architecture is paved with official actions at several levels of government. In 1965 the city of Key West established the Old Island Restoration Commission; its mission was to preserve the historic buildings in Old Town. The U.S. Congress passed the National Historic Preservation Act in 1966, creating a National Register of Historic

Buildings, Sites, and Districts. The Florida legislature created the Historic Key West Preservation Board of Trustees in 1972 to specifically deal with Key West. In 1986 the Historic Architectural Review Commission (HARC) assumed responsibility for the ongoing restoration and preservation of Key West's historic areas and does so to this day.

The second-floor exhibit changes frequently—call for details. A museum shop offers a variety of pirate and nautical gifts.

The museum is open daily. Children younger than age six are admitted free.

The Pirate Soul Museum **$$**
524 Front Street
(305) 292-1113
www.piratesoul.com

Old artifacts and new technologies meet at this handsome new museum, which brings to life the swashbuckling legends and lore of Key West. Opened in 2005, the Pirate Soul Museum depicts the era from 1690 to 1730 with over 500 artifacts, a re-created pirate ship (that you're invited to explore), and one of two authenticated pirate flags in the world. Go on your own treasure hunt using an interactive clue-filled logbook, listen to Blackbeard speak on piracy's golden age, or read part of the original journal of Captain Kidd's last voyage. Don't miss the 1696 Wanted poster for Henry Avery and the many other authentic items here, including ceramics, dishes, and rare cannonballs. Ahoy Mate!

San Carlos Institute **(FREE)**
516 Duval Street
(305) 294-3887

Founded in 1871 by Cuban exiles, the San Carlos Institute was established to preserve the language and traditions of the Cuban people. Dubbed "La Casa Cuba" by legendary poet and patriot José Martí, the institute helped unite the exiled Cuban community. The present building was completed in 1924 and operated as an integrated school until the mid-1970s, when deteriorating conditions necessitated its closing. With the perseverance of the Hispanic Affairs Commission, a state agency headed by Rafael Penalver, restoration of the San Carlos was completed and the institute reopened on January 3, 1992, 100 years to the day after José Martí's first visit in the late 19th century. Today the San Carlos Institute is a museum, library, school, art gallery, theater, and conference center. The institute is open Tuesday through Sunday. Admission is free.

West Martello Tower
Joe Allen Garden Center **$**
Atlantic Boulevard and White Street
(305) 294-3210

Built in 1862, the West Martello Tower, like the other forts on the island, was never involved in an actual war. It was, however, used for target practice by the U.S. Navy, which accounts for its somewhat shabby condition. Today the tower is also the Joe Allen Garden Center, and the Key West Garden Club operates here. Use the self-guided tour to spot local flora, including a key lime tree, or just find an inviting spot to relax.

West Martello is open Tuesday through Saturday in season. The schedule may vary; call for more information. Admission is free, but note that shirt and shoes are required.

One of A Kind

Flagler Station Over-Sea Railway Historeum **$**
901 Caroline Street
(305) 295-3562
www.flaglerstation.net

Our southernmost city can literally trace its beginnings as a tourist destination to the vision of one man—Henry Morrison Flagler—and his Key West Extension of the Florida East Coast Railroad. Flagler made his money in oil, but he made his name by building a railroad as well as luxury hotels along the east coast of Florida from Jacksonville to Miami. In 1905, at the age of 75, Flagler proposed his most daring venture to date—he instructed his engineers to extend the Florida East Coast Railroad 130 miles out to sea to Key West.

This museum, part of which is housed in an actual Florida East Coast Railroad car, celebrates Flagler's magnificent obsession, which took eight years, $30 million, and the loss of hundreds of lives to complete. Costumed "historytellers" and video footage help re-create the day in January 1912 that the Key West Extension, also known as the Over-Sea Railway, opened to great fanfare with a frail Henry Flagler himself aboard the first train to arrive in Key West. You'll see photos and memorabilia from that momentous occasion, as well as a film titled *The Day the Train Arrived,* which includes eyewitness accounts from people who were actually there and who made the trip by rail on the Key West Extension. There's an entire display devoted to the building of the Seven Mile Bridge, an amazing engineering feat even by today's standards, as well as photos and video recollections of the devastating hurricane of 1935 that took out the Over-Sea Railway.

Flagler Station is open daily.

Fort Zachary Taylor State Historical Site **$**
Truman Annex at Southard Street
(305) 292-6713

Although not fully completed until 1866, this Key West military bastion served the Union well during the Civil War, when it guarded against Confederate blockade runners. So impressive were its defenses, the fort was never attacked. It saw continuous usage by the military until the federal government deeded the structure to the state of Florida for use as a historic site. The Florida Park Service opened Fort Zachary Taylor to the public in 1985.

Today, however, much of the fort is again closed to public exploration, this time because the structure has succumbed to the ravages of time. The park service secured a $1.25 million grant, used to restore the north curtain, which is where the guns were mounted. As portions of the fort are structurally repaired, they will be reopened. At present, only the parade ground, the south curtain observation deck, and the north curtain can be toured. The museum is also closed for repairs. Exhibits have been transferred to East Martello Museum (see the Historic Homes and Museums section) until the restoration is complete.

The surrounding park offers a beach for fishing, swimming, or snorkeling, as well as picnic areas equipped with tables and grills, outside showers, snack bar, and restroom facilities. It also offers one of the best, unobstructed views of the sunset.

Fort Zachary Taylor is open daily from 8:00 A.M. to sunset. Hang on to your ticket stub; you may leave the park and return at any time throughout the same day by simply showing your ticket to the booth attendant. *Hint:* Come here to watch the sunset away from the craziness going on at Mallory Square (see description later in this chapter).

Key West AIDS Memorial **(FREE)**
Foot of White Street and Atlantic Boulevard
www.cyberconch.com

Key West has been especially hard hit by the AIDS epidemic; more than 1,000 here have died. The names of many of those victims are inscribed on this memorial, which consists of flat granite slabs embedded in the walkway approaching White Street Pier.

Built with private funds and dedicated on World AIDS Day, December 1, 1997, the memorial has room for 1,500 names. At the unveiling, it contained 730. New names are engraved annually and dedicated in a ceremony that takes place each

December on World AIDS Day. Members of a volunteer group—Friends of the Key West AIDS Memorial—maintain and protect this site.

Key West Aquarium $$
1 Whitehead Street at Mallory Square
(305) 296-2051, (800) 868-7482
www.keywestaquarium.com

Key West's oldest tourist attraction (built in 1934) and still one of the most fascinating our southernmost city has to offer, the Key West Aquarium affords you a diver's-eye view of the marine creatures of our encompassing waters. Stroll at your leisure alongside the backlit tanks re-creating our coral reefs, but don't miss the guided tours offered four times daily, when you'll witness the feeding of the species. You'll marvel at the feeding frenzy of the sharks and sawtooths; the nurse sharks and stingrays flipping and splashing for their rations; and the tarpon, barracuda, game fish, and sea turtles recognizing the hands that feed them in the outdoor Atlantic Shores Exhibit, created to look like a mangrove lagoon.

A highlight for kids is the "touch tank" just inside the front door. Here, they can reach in and grab hold of horseshoe crabs, hermit crabs, conchs, sea cucumbers, and many other creatures that populate the waters surrounding Key West. Be sure to bring your camera—you'll want to capture the expression on your child's face when the horseshoe crab in his or her hand suddenly flexes its legs.

The aquarium is open daily. Children age three and younger are admitted free. Discounts are available.

The Key West Butterfly & Nature Conservatory $$
1316 Duval Street
(305) 296-2988, (800) 839-4647
www.keywestbutterfly.com

The Key West Butterfly & Nature Conservatory was opened in January 2003 by Sam Trophia and George Fernandez, the proprietors of the perennially popular Wings of Imagination: The Butterfly Gallery. The Conservatory celebrates the lives of butterflies around the globe. Visitors first stop at the Learning Center for a brief introductory film on the wonders of the butterflies' world before proceeding to the Miracle of Metamorphosis exhibit. Here you can watch the actual butterfly-hatching process and observe the stages of development from egg to caterpillar to chrysalis. All the butterflies are bred in captivity on butterfly farms in North, Central, and South America, as well as Southeast Asia and Africa. When mature, the butterflies are released into a 5,000-square-foot glass-enclosed greenhouse featuring more than 3,500 tropical trees and plants. The gardens are a horticulturalist's nirvana—lush and tropical vegetation inhabited by 30 to 50 species of exotic butterflies, such as Blue Morpho and Emerald Swallowtail, and a myriad of birds from all over the world. A gallery displays Trophia's original butterfly designs. The Conservatory is open daily. Children younger than age four are free.

Key West City Cemetery (FREE)
Bordered by Angela, Frances, and Olivia Streets, and Windsor Lane
(305) 292-8177

Built in 1847 after the horrific hurricane the year before washed out the sand sanctuary at the island's southernmost point, Key West City Cemetery, right in the center of town, adds a human element to the history of Key West. The marble monuments of the wealthy were shipped to the island; local markers were generally produced from brick or coral-based cement. Carved with symbols and prosaic sayings, such as I TOLD YOU I WAS SICK and DEVOTED FAN OF JULIO IGLESIAS, the gravestones are a living legacy for those lying beneath. Some of the tombs are "bunked," or stacked, because digging in the coral rock proved difficult and seawater percolates just under the surface.

The Historic Florida Keys Foundation makes it easy to explore the Key West City Cemetery, which was recognized by the state as a Florida Heritage Site in

2006. The organization's self-guided tour pamphlet lists graves of 42 of Key West's most prominent or notorious deceased citizens, with brief personality profiles and a translation of the meaning of the carved symbols on the gravestones. Pick up a free Historic Key West City Cemetery Self-guided Tour pamphlet in the Florida Room at the Monroe County Public Library, 700 Fleming Street, or at the Key West Chamber of Commerce, Mallory Square.

If you'd like a little help with your meandering, an hour-long guided tour of the cemetery is available every Tuesday and Thursday, courtesy of the Historic Florida Keys Foundation. Tours leave at 9:30 A.M. from the cemetery's main gate, which is located at the corner of Margaret and Angela Streets. Reservations are required. A donation of $10 is requested. For reservations, phone (305) 292-6718.

Historic preservationist Sharon Wells also conducts cemetery tours by reservation only (see the Guided and Self-Guided Tours section of this chapter).

Key West Historic Seaport and HarborWalk (FREE)
201 William Street, at the Key West Bight
(305) 293-8309
www.keywestseaport.com

Formerly known as Key West Bight, this once-seedy piece of prime waterfront real estate was where shrimpers, spongers, and turtle traders came to unload their daily catch, tell tall tales of the sea, quaff a few brews, and just generally hang out. With the relocation of the shrimp boats to Stock Island and the demise of sponging and turtle hunting, this area has undergone a complete metamorphosis. In January 1999 it was officially opened as the Key West Historic Seaport and HarborWalk.

Tall ships still tie up here, but so do million-dollar yachts. Trendy shops, restaurants, and raw bars now line a pristine wooden boardwalk that follows the bend of the coastline here from the foot of Front Street to the foot of Margaret Street. Despite gentrification, this remains a busy, working marina. Vessels bound for the Dry Tortugas leave from here, as do many of the snorkel and sunset cruises and fishing charters (see our Recreation chapter for details). You even can catch an occasional glimpse of the old Key West in places like Turtle Kraals, a turtle-cannery-turned-restaurant, and Schooner Wharf Bar.

The seaport area bustles with activity on a daily basis; it's also home to numerous special events throughout the year. For a complete listing of seaport shops, services, activities, and attractions, pick up a free copy of the *Historic Seaport Log*. This quarterly publication can usually be found at several locations along the HarborWalk, at the Key West Chamber of Commerce on Mallory Square, and at stores throughout Key West. Look for it wherever you see stacks of free weekly newspapers.

Key West Historical Memorial Sculpture Garden (FREE)
Mallory Square
(305) 294-4142

Located on Key West's original shoreline just behind Mallory Square, this tiny fenced-in "garden" pays homage to three dozen men and women whose lives and deeds have had tremendous impact on the southernmost city. Here you will find the stories and likenesses of such former influential citizens as wreckers Asa Tift and Capt. John Geiger; Ernest Hemingway, writer; Harry S Truman, former U.S. president; railroad magnate Henry Flagler; Sister Louise Gabriel, whose Grotto to Our Lady of Lourdes is said to have protected Key West from hurricanes for more than 75 years; and Charley Toppino, land developer. All of the bronze busts, as well as the imposing wreckers sculpture, are the works of sculptor James Mastin of Coral Gables, Florida.

As you wander through the garden, be sure to look down, too—the walkways are paved with commemorative bricks purchased by individuals and families in remembrance of their friends and relatives. Proceeds from the sale of these bricks help support construction and maintenance of the garden. The sculpture garden is open daily during daylight hours; there is no admission charge.

Key West Shipwreck Historeum $$
1 Whitehead Street, Mallory Square
(305) 292-8990

Relive the days of wreckers, lumpers, and divers at the Shipwreck Historeum—part museum, part theater—where actors, video footage, and interactive presentations re-create vestiges of Key West's once-lucrative wrecking industry. During the 1800s about 100 ships passed by the port of Key West daily, many running aground on the reef. Asa Tift, a 19th-century wrecker and the original owner of what would one day become the Hemingway Home, tells his story of salvaging the goods of the SS *Isaac Allerton,* which was downed by a hurricane in 1856 (see our Kidstuff chapter).

Shows run every 30 minutes, daily. Children younger than age four are admitted for free.

Key West Tropical Forest and Botanical Garden (FREE)
5210 Jr. College Road, Stock Island
(305) 296-1504
www.keywestbotanicalgarden.org

Follow Jr. College Road, then turn right just past Bayshore Manor, to find this little-known slice of serenity tucked between the Florida Keys Aqueduct Authority plant and the Key West Golf Course. Maintained by volunteers from the Key West Botanical Garden Society and funded by donations since 1935, this 11-acre garden represents the last undeveloped native hardwood hammock in the environs of Key West. Despite its proximity to US 1 and a busy public golf course, the garden features exotic and native plants that can be viewed from a series of walking trails and is surprisingly peaceful. The garden is home to numerous birds and butterflies, especially during the spring and fall migration seasons. On any given day, you're apt to see a turtle sunning itself on a log or an egret searching for food in Desbiens Pond.

The Gardens took a hard hit from Hurricane Georges in 1998, and botanists predict that it will be many years before the foliage returns to its prestorm abundancy. Nevertheless, some rare trees still survive, including the 10,000,000th tree planted in the United States by the National Tree Trust. The garden also features a locustberry tree and a cloned champion green buttonwood that was recently planted by the Champion Tree Project.

Mallory Square Sunset Celebration (FREE)
1 Whitehead Street
(305) 292-7700
www.sunsetcelebration.org

A do-not-miss event during any visit to Key West is the famous (perhaps infamous) sunset celebration. Buskers and street players, vaudevillians and carny wannabes strut their stuff every day as the sun sinks into the Gulf of Mexico over Sunset Key off Mallory Square. Beverage and nosh vendors hawk refreshments while the entertainers compete for your attention. From fire-eaters to furniture jugglers, tightrope walkers to sword swallowers, you'll rarely see the same routine two nights in a row. A footbridge links Mallory Square to the pier at the adjacent Hilton Resort and Marina, where the likes of vaudevillian Jeep and his dog Moe and Dominique's high-flying cats delight the crowd.

This daily event, a Key West tradition since 1984, is free to all, but pack your pocket with small bills because the performers play for tips. The fun starts approximately one hour before sunset at Mallory. Check page three of the morning *Key West Citizen* for daily sunset times.

Mile Marker 0 (FREE)
Corner of Whitehead and Fleming Streets

Key West is truly the last resort and here's the proof: The official green-and-white mile marker 0 signifying the end of US 1 is posted at this corner. Have someone snap a picture of you in front of the sign that reads END—U.S. 1. It will make a wonderful reminder of that very moment you finally arrived at the end of your road . . . that's providing some souvenir hunter hasn't made off with the sign, which happens with great regularity. Tampering with highway signs (including those enticing green mile markers) is against the law, by the way. If you must own one, replicas of mile marker 0 are available for purchase in many Key West shops.

National Weather Service Station (FREE)
1315 White Street, Key West
(305) 295-1316
www.srh.noaa.gov/eyw

Weather observation in Key West dates back at least as far as 1832, when rainfall measurements were taken at the Sand Key Lighthouse. In 1870, the first observation station was opened on Duval Street. The National Weather Service relocated to different spots during the 1900s. In 2006, a new $5.1-million station opened on White Street, bringing the art and technology of weather reporting into the 21st century.

Key West sits in a prime location between the Gulf of Mexico and the Atlantic Ocean, making it an important stop along international shipping lanes. Forty percent of the world's shipping relies on the Key West Weather Station for weather data. Tours of this architectural marvel are available Monday to Friday by appointment only.

The Southernmost Point (FREE)
Corner of Whitehead and South Streets

Look for the traffic jam at the Atlantic end of Whitehead Street and you'll see the giant red, white, green, and yellow marker buoy that designates the southernmost point of the continental United States. And standing in front of it, in the street, blocking traffic trying to turn left onto South Street, preens a never-ending stream of Key West visitors, trying to capture the moment they stood closer to Cuba than anyone else in the country. Call it touristy, even tacky, if you like, but the crowds seem to love it.

Wildlife Rescue of the Florida Keys (FREE)
Atlantic Boulevard and White Street
(305) 294-1441, (888) 826-3811

On the grounds of McCoy Indigenous Park, a large, quiet park full of rare and native species of flora, lies Wildlife Rescue of the Florida Keys. Since 1993 Wildlife Rescue has released more than 2,000 healed animals back into the wild. At any given time approximately 100 animals, ranging from seabirds to raccoons to chickens, are recovering here; you can see them during visiting hours. Wildlife Rescue will rescue animals anywhere from the Seven Mile Bridge to the Dry Tortugas.

The park is open daily from sunup to sundown. Admission is free, but donations are appreciated, and volunteers are always needed.

Guided and Self-Guided Tours

Conch Tour Train $$$
301 Front Street at Mallory Square
Flagler Station, 901 Caroline Street
(305) 294-5161, (800) 868-7482
www.conchtourtrain.com

Some folks might think a narrated motor tour spells tourist with a capital T, but the quirky little Conch Tour Train is a great way to garner an overview of Key West in the shaded comfort of a canopied tram. You'll pass by most of the attractions we've written up in this chapter, sometimes twice, because in tiny Key West the train weaves a circuitous route that often changes from one hour to the next depending on road construction and special events that necessitate street closures. Regardless of the path, you're sure to enjoy the ride as your guide recounts fact and legend, tall tales, and sad stories about life in Key West.

Tours start at Mallory Square or Flagler Station on Caroline Street. Children younger than age four ride free. The tour lasts 90 minutes, with one 10-minute rest break at the Conch Tour Train ticket station, 501 Front Street. Train passengers can also get off at Land's End Village at the foot of Margaret Street to explore the historic seaport area on foot, then reboard another train to complete the tour.

Ghosts & Legends of Key West $
(305) 294-1713, (888) 419-4467
www.keywestghosts.com

Each evening at 7:00 and 9:00 P.M., Ghosts & Legends of Key West leads visitors to our southernmost city on a shadowy saunter down the narrow lanes of Old Town. The second ghostly attraction in Key West (see Ghost Tours of Key West below), Ghosts & Legends meets at the corner of Duval and Caroline Streets at the Porter Mansion. Guides share dark narratives of haunted mansions, voodoo superstitions, a secret leper colony, and pirate lore, hitting such "low" spots as the old city morgue and St. Paul's Cemetery. This 90-minute jaunt may put you in touch with Key West's restless spirits.

Ghost Tours of Key West $
(305) 294-9255
www.hauntedtours.com

Love a good ghost story? Key West's No. 1 haunted attraction, Ghost Tours, offers you the chance to get an in-depth introduction to the most famous ghosts of our island. Highlights include a visit to the city's original hanging tree. Tales of Robert, a haunted doll said to have been possessed by an evil spirit, intensify the mystery. Disbelief and awe surround the deeds of the German count who dug up the body of his true love, dressed her in a bridal gown, and serenaded her for seven years. Narrated by a spooky, caped, lantern-bearing guide, this 1-mile tour wends its way through Key West after dark and lasts about 90 minutes.

Tours leave nightly from the lobby of the Crowne Plaza La Concha, 430 Duval Street. Plan to arrive approximately 15 minutes in advance to purchase your tickets, and do bring cash or traveler's checks; no credit cards are accepted. Groups of six or more may purchase tickets in advance in the lobby of the La Concha hotel. You will need to make reservations for this popular tour. Space is limited, so book early by phoning the number shown above.

Old Town Trolley Tours $$$
3840 North Roosevelt Avenue, Key West Welcome Center
(305) 296-6688
www.trolleytours.com/keywest

Join the Old Town Trolley Tour for an informative, convenient entry into Key West. The trolley stops at most major hotels, handy if you're staying in the southernmost city. Day-trippers will appreciate the free parking at the Key West Welcome Center, where you can pick up the tour. The trolleys depart every 30 minutes, and you can get off at any of the nine stops and reboard the same day. All along the way the tour guide will treat you to a Key West history lesson, full of anecdotes and legends.

Old Town Trolley Tours run daily. For children younger than age four, it's free.

The Orchid Lady
(877) 747-2718
www.eorchidlady.com

Capture the beauty of Key West with a guided tour by the Orchid Lady. You will enjoy a leisurely stroll through historic Key West with an informative trek full of facts and beauty. Visit gardens filled with beautiful orchids and learn from an expert why these gorgeous flowers have bewitched creatures for centuries.

Pelican Path (FREE)
Old Island Restoration Foundation
(305) 294-9501

Visitors who like to wander on their own should be sure to first pick up a copy of the Pelican Path brochure at the chamber of commerce on Mallory Square. This handy compact walking guide and map offers a short history of Key West as well as a suggested route that will take you past 50 of our most prominent historic structures. Most of the buildings described in this brochure are now private homes and guesthouses. Those that are open for touring are highlighted in yellow. Don't be surprised, however, if you can't spot those yellow-and-blue Pelican signs described in the brochure as path markers; many of them have disappeared over the years. Even so, the Pelican Path remains relatively easy to follow and is a great way to get acquainted with island history.

PT 728 **$$**
631 Greene Street, Key West
(305) 849-3069
www.pt728.com

The Key West Maritime Historical Society is proud to welcome back into service the 1945 Vosper Motor Torpedo Boat, PT 728. This is the last of the PT boats in the world that is still floating and certified by the U.S. Coast Guard (Most of the others have been scrapped or are in museums). This fully restored PT boat offers its 49 passengers an educational narrative by a crew wearing WWII-era uniforms. There is also a simulated torpedo run, which requires the passengers to put on helmets and man their battle stations. Tours on Historic Key West Harbor depart daily, weather permitting.

Ripley's Believe It or Not **$$**
108 Duval Street, Key West
(305) 293-9939
www.ripleysbelieveitornot.com

Ripley's Believe It or Not is world-famous for strange, fantastic, weird, and just hard-to-believe artifacts. The Ripley's museums have always been noted for oddities such as the world's heaviest man, the biggest human nose, and the person with the most tattoos. In the Ripley's Key West location, they house a Key West gallery with items from Ernest Hemingway (reading glasses, typewriter, and a shrunken torso) and Count Von Cossel (who stole the body of his beloved and kept her in the fuselage of a plane in his backyard). There is also a Boutique of Weird Clothing showing a vest made of human hair, a giant pair of shoes, and even a pair of Madonna's underwear. And if all that weren't enough, they also have a portrait of Vincent Van Gogh made from butterfly wings. You know you're not in Kansas anymore!

Sharon Wells's *Walking & Biking* Guide to Historic Key West **(FREE)**
(305) 294-8380
www.seekeywest.com

Historic preservationist Sharon Wells makes it easy for you to explore and enjoy Key West at your own pace with this superbly organized, information-packed guide. In addition to 10 self-guided tours, complete with maps and descriptions of the important structures you will see along the way, this 64-page booklet contains suggestions for nature treks in and around Key West. Best of all, it's free.

You'll find copies of Sharon Wells's *Walking & Biking Guide* at more than 200 locations in and around Key West, including the Key West Public Library, 700 Fleming Street; and the Key West Chamber of Commerce, Mallory Square. Up the Keys you'll find the guide at the chambers of commerce in Big Pine Key, MM 30.5 Oceanside; Marathon, MM 53.5 Bayside; Islamorada, MM 82.5 Bayside; and Key Largo, MM 106 Bayside.

If you'd rather not go it alone, Wells also offers personally guided tours called Island City Strolls ($$$). These include a 90-minute architectural stroll, which winds through the historic neighborhoods of Old Town, a 90-minute cemetery stroll, and two bike tours—The "Island Trek" through Key West's historic neighborhoods and the "Literary Landmarks Trail," leading past the homes of famous Key West writers. Upon request, Sharon can also put together a personalized tour for individuals or groups. Space is limited on all guided tours, and reservations are required. Call for prices and tour times.

Trails of Margaritaville **$$$**
(305) 292-2040
www.trailsofmargaritaville.com

For Jimmy Buffett fans, known as Parrotheads, a trip to Key West is akin to a religious pilgrimage. Thousands of them flock here annually to buy Buffett paraphernalia, down a few margaritas, and visit the venues where their hero played and sang before he went big-time. This 90-minute tour gives them all an officially sanctioned peek at the places and legends of Buffett's 1970s salad days in Key West.

The guides, attired in full Parrothead regalia—Hawaiian shirts, parrot hats—lead you past the former site of Howie's Lounge, the compound on Ann Street where Buffett once lived, and Shrimpboat Sound, the studio where he still records, spinning yarns about Buffett and Key West in general all along the route. The tour ends, you guessed it, at Margaritaville Cafe on Duval Street.

If you are an inveterate Parrothead, you probably won't learn anything new on this tour—you've read it all before—but you will at least see the places you've heard about. If you're not a Parrothead, you may not understand the fans' fascination with Buffett, but you'll still find this tour fun, even if it does mean that you have to walk around town with a silly-looking shark fin hat on your head.

The tour departs daily at 4:00 P.M., appropriately, from Captain Tony's Saloon, 428 Greene Street, Key West. In case you don't know it, Buffett played for Captain Tony back in the 1970s and immortalized this former Key West mayor in his song "Last Mango in Paris." Bring cash or traveler's checks; no credit cards accepted. Reservations are required. And if you have a Margaritaville passport, bring it along, too; these folks will stamp it for you.

AND BEYOND . . .

Biscayne National Park **$**
National Park Service Main Visitor Center, Convoy Point
(305) 230-7275
www.nps.gov/bisc

Only 5 percent of Biscayne National Park's 181,500 acres are above water, consisting of about 45 tiny keys and a mangrove shoreline. The crystalline depths shelter the northern portion of the Florida Keys' barrier reef and all the marine life lurking in the submerged coral nooks and crannies. Biscayne's complex ecosystem, like that of the Florida Keys, extends from the mangrove-lined shoreline to the Gulf Stream. The northernmost of the Florida Keys protects the waters of Biscayne Bay from the pounding surf of the Atlantic.

The best time to visit Biscayne National Park is from mid-December to mid-April. Unless you have your own boat, you will have to explore the park's waters by concessionaire-run cruises. You'll find glass-bottomed boats that will take you on a reef cruise or for a snorkeling or diving excursion. More than 200 species of fish, as well as spiny lobsters, crabs, shrimp, sponges, sea turtles, and other marine life, will be visible as you pass from the nursery grounds of the turtle grass at 4 to 10 feet to the deeper waters of the reef. Some of the excursions visit Adams Key, Elliott Key, and Boca Chita Key, where picnic facilities, restrooms, and nature trails have been established for visitors.

Visitors may also enjoy swimming, fishing, and bird-watching. Canoes are available for rent. Biscayne National Park is open year-round. There are no entrance fees, but concessionaire boat trips levy a charge. From Homestead, take Southwest 328th Street to the park entrance.

Everglades National Park **$$-$$$**
National Park Service Main Visitor Center, Highway 9336, Florida City
(305) 242-7700
www.nps.gov/ever

The largest remaining subtropical wilderness in North America and one of the world's richest biological preserves, Everglades National Park encompasses the eight ecosystems of the Everglades within its 1.5 million acres. Endlessly fascinating, the Everglades is so much more than the ubiquitous alligator that quickly comes to mind. From the acres of saw-grass prairie to the pinelands, the hardwood hammocks, and the mangrove-lined inland waterways, the Everglades supports a fascinating array of organisms at all levels of the food chain.

Ranger-led activities originate at the various visitor centers of Everglades National Park, located at the southern tip of the 100-mile-long stretch of the Everglades. Three centers are accessible from the main entrance: Main Visitor Center, at the park's main entrance near Florida City; Royal Palm, off the main park road a few miles inside the main entrance; and Flamingo, on the main park road at Florida Bay. Other centers include Shark Valley, at the north end of the park on U.S. Highway 41; and Gulf Coast Ranger Station, at Everglades City on Highway 29 at the northwest entrance.

You'll find naturalist-led hikes and talks, guided canoe trips, and evening programs under the stars. Also available are tram tours and scenic, narrated boat tours into the backcountry waterways of Whitewater Bay or the Gulf waters of Florida Bay. Available for rent are motorboats, canoes, kayaks, bicycles, even houseboats. Fishing is good in the waters of Everglades National Park, and bird-watching is unparalleled, for the 'Glades is home to the multispecied heron, egret, and ibis families as well as wood storks, ospreys, bald eagles, snail kites, and more. The Anhinga Trail at the Royal Palm Visitors Center teems with wading birds and alligators in January and February. Bring your camera.

The best time to visit Everglades National Park is the dry season, mid-December through mid-April, when mosquitoes are minimal. Many park activities are curtailed during the rainy season. Entrance fee is $10 per car, per week (seven-day period).

Dry Tortugas National Park
National Park Service
(305) 242-7700
www.nps.gov/drto

Visit Dry Tortugas National Park, the end of the line in the Florida Keys, for a spectacular ride back in history. Accessible only by boat or seaplane (see the Cruising, Campgrounds, and Recreation chapters for transportation options), the Dry Tortugas, 70 miles west of Key West, harbor a rich history and an even more prolific underworld. (No admission charge is levied to visit the park, but transportation charges can be substantial.)

Ponce de León named the seven islands "Las Tortugas" in 1513, presumably for the multitude of sea turtles (tortugas). The "Dry" moniker was added later to indicate the islands' lack of fresh water. You'll be able to take a self-guided tour of Fort Jefferson on Garden Key, America's largest 19th-century coastal fort, which was started in 1846 but never completed. The walls are 50 feet high and 8 feet thick. For years the fort operated as a military prison. Fort Jefferson's most famous inmate was Dr. Samuel Mudd, who was convicted of conspiracy after he set the broken leg of President Lincoln's assassin, John Wilkes Booth.

The protected waters surrounding the Tortugas sparkle with all the sea creatures of the coral reef as well as a good many shipwreck remains. With natural sand beaches and calm seas, snorkeling and swimming are a must. All the waters of the Dry Tortugas National Park are designated a no-take zone, so you may see fish and lobsters of gargantuan proportions. There is no food, fresh water, electricity, or medical assistance at Fort Jefferson. Saltwater toilets, grills, and picnic tables are provided. No lodging exists out here in the beyond, but you may camp on Garden Key if you pack in and pack out all water and supplies (see the Camping chapter). Campers pay slightly more than day-trippers for passage to Fort Jefferson, mostly to cover the cost of transporting the gear they must carry in and out.

KIDSTUFF

Get ready, get set, go! It's time to explore the alphabet soup of things to do in the Florida Keys and Key West, especially for kids. But we have to warn you. Your parents will want to come along.

We deviate from our usual geographic arrangement in this chapter, but all the attractions we list include addresses and phone numbers. Look to related chapters for a comprehensive listing of hours of operation, admission-cost ranges, and Web sites.

Tell Mom and Dad if they want to find out more details of our ABCs (and 1, 2, 3s in Key West), they can look in the Recreation and Attractions chapters, where they'll find lots more fun things to do.

THE FLORIDA KEYS

Fun from A to Z

A IS FOR . . .

affectionate sea lions that may try to kiss you at Theater of the Sea at MM 84.7 Oceanside, Islamorada, (305) 664-2431—so be prepared. You can pet the sharks in the touch tank and touch the dolphins in another tank. In the main lagoon, created by excavations for Henry Flagler's Railroad (see the Historical Evolution chapter), the dolphins put on quite a show. Watch them walk on their tails and jump high in the air. You'll see tropical fish and game fish, stingrays, and sea turtles. There is even a boat ride through the lagoon (for more on Theater of the Sea, see the Attractions chapter).

B IS FOR . . .

baiting a hook. Go fishing on one of our group party boats (see the Fishing chapter for complete information). You may catch the prismatic dolphinfish, which has a blunt forehead like Bart Simpson's. Or reel in some yellowtail snappers; they really have yellow tails. Almost certainly you'll catch grunts. They make a funny grunting sound when you take them out of the water. Keep a lookout for the playful mammal dolphins and sea turtles.

C IS FOR . . .

climbing into the osprey nest exhibit at the Florida Keys Children's Museum at the Museums of Crane Point, MM 50.5 Bayside, Marathon, (305) 743-9100. You'll really get a bird's-eye view because you'll be 3 feet off the ground. You can dress up in pirate clothes and hop aboard a pirate ship or play in a thatched chickee sandbox built by the Miccosukee Indians. You'll find a real Cuban freedom raft, a fishpond where you can feed the fish, a touch tank full of hermit and horseshoe crabs, and a huge seashell exhibit. Don't miss looking for the resident wild iguanas (for more, see the Attractions chapter).

D IS FOR . . .

"Don't touch!" If you touch the sap of the poisonwood tree when you walk through the nature trails at Crane Point, MM 50.5 Oceanside, Marathon, (305) 743-9100, it will make you itch like poison ivy does. This tropical Keys forest is full of interesting sinkholes, red mangroves, thatch palms, and lots of cool lizards, land crabs, and birds. One fee covers admission to the hammock and the Florida Keys Children's Museum. And you'll enjoy the adjoining Museum of Natural History, too (see the Attractions chapter).

E IS FOR . . .

examining the fossilized imprints of ancient shells and marine organisms you'll find in the coral quarry walls of Windley Key Fossil

Reef Geologic Site, MM 85.5 Bayside, Windley Key, (305) 664-2540. If you bring a paper and crayon, you can make a crayon rubbing (see the Attractions chapter for more on the geologic site).

F IS FOR . . .

feeding the giant tarpon that swim in the waters at Robbie's Marina, MM 77.5 Bayside, Islamorada, (305) 664-9814, (877) 664-8498. You can purchase a cup of baitfish, the tarpon's favorite snack, at the marina. These giant "silver kings" will swim in a frenzy before your very eyes, jockeying to be first in line when you throw the fish in the water.

G IS FOR . . .

grabbing some rays at the beach. Play in the sand or look for crabs and crustaceans at Sombrero Beach in Marathon, MM 50 Oceanside, Sombrero Beach Road, which even has picnic tables so you can make a day of it. There is no admission fee. Bahia Honda State Park, MM 37 Oceanside, has two beaches. A small one near the concession stand at the south end of the park is calm, sheltered, and roped off for safety. The other, the Sandspur, is much longer. You can wade in the soft sand through waters that vary from several inches to 3 feet deep looking for sea creatures and washed-up treasure (see the Recreation chapter for more on beach options).

H IS FOR . . .

hopping aboard a glass-bottomed boat for a five-hour ecological tour of the Lower Keys backcountry with Strike Zone Charters, MM 29.5 Bayside, Big Pine Key, (305) 872-9863, (800) 654-9560. You'll learn the history of the key deer and the tiny out-islands, the hurricanes, the wreckers, and the Indians. You'll see bald eagle nesting sites, great white herons, egrets, and dolphins feeding in the wild. You can snorkel and fish a little too. And to top it all off, you'll enjoy a fish cookout picnic on

Mel Fisher Maritime Museum offers a summer kids program, Mer Academy, at Fort Zachary Taylor State Park. Parents may sign their children up for one to four weeks. Class size is limited and students must have completed the fifth grade to participate. Call the Mel Fisher Maritime Museum Education Department at (305) 294-2633 for more information.

a private island (see the Recreation chapter for more information).

I IS FOR . . .

investigating the Blue Hole—but don't feed the alligators. This freshwater sinkhole at MM 30.5 Bayside, Key Deer Boulevard, Big Pine Key, is home to a couple of curious 'gators, and they'll swim almost up to the viewing platform. Keep your puppy on a leash because its barking will ring the alligators' dinner bell. You'll see turtles in the Blue Hole, and key deer come 'round at dusk. There is no admission charge.

J IS FOR . . .

jumping into a good book. Visit one of our Keys public libraries: Key Largo, MM 101.4 Oceanside, Tradewinds Shopping Center, (305) 451-2396; Islamorada, MM 81.5 Bayside, across from the Hurricane Monument, (305) 664-4645; Marathon, MM 48.5 Oceanside, next to Fisherman's Hospital, (305) 743-5156; Big Pine, MM 31 Bayside, 213 Key Deer Boulevard, (305) 289-6303; Key West, 700 Fleming Street, (305) 292-3595.

K IS FOR . . .

kicking your finned feet as you practice snorkeling in the shallow waters of the protective U-shaped jetty called The Horseshoe, MM 35 Bayside, just over the Bahia Honda Bridge as you head down the Keys (see Insiders' Tip in the Diving and Snorkeling chapter). You'll see a natural

Become a "star" of the Florida Keys Eco-Discovery Center. Your donation purchases a sea star inscribed with your name, the name of a friend, or a tribute to a loved one. It will be embedded in concrete as a permanent part of the Florida Keys Eco-Discovery Center walkway. For more information, visit www.NMSFocean.org.

aquarium of colorful tropical fish with no danger from sharks or barracuda 'cause they can't get in. It's free.

L IS FOR . . .

looking a great white heron in the eye at the Florida Keys Wild Bird Center, MM 93.6 Bayside, Tavernier, (305) 852-4486, (888) 826-3811. Although some of the birds you'll see are permanent residents at the shelter because they can't exist in the wild anymore, others are recovering from injuries and will leave the center once healed. All the birds live in natural habitats that have been enclosed by huge wire cages. You can even go into the pelican cage by yourself (see the Attractions chapter for more on the center).

M IS FOR . . .

meeting friendly dolphins up close and personal at the Dolphin Research Center, MM 59 Bayside, Grassy Key, (305) 289-1121. The dolphins' behavior trainers will put them through learning exercises in the saltwater lagoon. You can swim with dolphins in the Dolphin Encounter if you are between 5 and 12 years old and your mom or dad goes with you (see the Attractions chapter for more information).

N IS FOR . . .

navigating your way through marked mangrove trails or the Largo Sound of John Pennekamp Coral Reef State Park, MM 102.5 Oceanside, Key Largo, (305) 451-1621, in a two-person kayak rented from Coral Reef Park Company. Take a grown-up with you and then paddle the kayak and spy on all the neat fish and sea creatures that are under the water (for more information, see the Recreation chapter).

O IS FOR . . .

observing the catch of the day when you visit one of our fishing marina docks between 3:30 and 4:00 P.M. (see the Fishing chapter). That's when the charter boats come back in from offshore, and if their luck held, so will yours. You'll see giant dolphin, tuna, snapper, wahoo, grouper, and cobia. But you probably won't see sailfish and marlin because, since they aren't good to eat, we prefer to release them back into the ocean so they may continue to live. This is free fun.

P IS FOR . . .

putting a golf ball around the greens at Boondocks Mini-Golf. Located at MM 27.5 on Ramrod Key, this miniature golf park if fun for kids of all ages. Some of the larger hotels offer mini-golf for their guests, but this is the only public mini-golf course in the Keys. The 18-hole course features waterfalls, tunnels, ponds, a tiki hut, a clubhouse, and some towering, giant cavemen. Boondocks Mini-Golf is a fun place to hold birthday parties, tournaments, or fundraisers. Call (305) 872-4094 for hours.

Q IS FOR . . .

qualifying as a super sleuth when you participate in the Dolphin Connection's Dolphin Detectives Program. If you are at least five years old, you can learn how to be a dolphin trainer. You'll get your hands all fishy preparing the dolphins' food. And you might get splashed as you supervise a dolphin training session from the dry docks. You'll find Dolphin Connection at Hawk's Cay Resort, MM 61 Oceanside, (888) 814-9154 (see the Attractions chapter).

R IS FOR . . .

riding out Watson Boulevard in Big Pine

Key and crossing the bridge to No Name Key. If you come just as the sun is setting, you'll probably see our miniature key deer—they're only 3 feet tall—wandering along the roadside. To get to No Name Key, go to MM 31 Bayside. Turn right onto Key Deer Boulevard, then right onto Watson and across the bridge. This is a free ride.

S IS FOR . . .

swimming in the tidal pool at Key Largo's Harry Harris Park, MM 92.5 Oceanside, (305) 852-7161, if you get tired of swinging or playing on the slide. This state park has a small beach collared by a stone jetty so the waters are always calm. When the tide goes out, you can look for sea creatures (for more information, see the Recreation chapter).

T IS FOR . . .

taking in a movie matinee. Visit one of the Keys' cinemas: Marathon Community Cinema, MM 50 Oceanside, Marathon, (305) 743-0288; or Regal Cinema 6, Searstown Shopping Center, 3338 Roosevelt Boulevard, Key West, (305) 294-0000.

U IS FOR . . .

unlocking the mysteries of a hardwood hammock on a nature walk with a naturalist on Lignumvitae Key, (305) 664-2540. You'll have to take a boat trip from Robbie's Marina, MM 77.5 Bayside, Islamorada, (305) 664-9814, for Lignumvitae is out in Florida Bay. This is the way all the Keys looked long ago. You'll see the red bark of the gumbo-limbo tree, called the "tourist tree" because the bark peels like a sunburned vacationer. You'll also encounter leafy trees with such unusual names as mastic, strangler fig, and pigeon plum. The lignum vitae tree (its name means "wood of life") grows very slowly (see the Attractions chapter for more information).

V IS FOR . . .

visiting Perky Bat Tower, MM 17, Sugarloaf Key. Mr. Perky built this tower many years ago thinking he could attract lots of bats to eat the mosquitoes that were bothering him. His plan didn't work, but the tower is still standing. To find Perky's crazy tower, turn right (bayside) at the Sugarloaf Airport sign just beyond Sugarloaf Lodge when heading down the Keys. When the road forks, bear to the right.

W IS FOR . . .

watching skilled artisans at Bluewater Potters work the clay by hand to form creative and functional shapes for spoon rests, dinnerware, lamps, and fun decorative pieces. You'll find their studio at MM 102.9 Oceanside, Key Largo, (305) 853-0616.

X IS FOR . . .

relaXing by watching a video from Blockbuster Video, MM 100 Oceanside, Key Largo, (305) 451-1313; MM 91 Bayside, Tavernier, (305) 852-0202; MM 50 Bayside, Marathon, (305) 743-3034; and 3020 North Roosevelt Boulevard, Key West, (305) 294-4600. You can also rent games and game machines here.

Y IS FOR . . .

"Yow!" That's what you'll say when you see a shark really close up. Stop at Captain Hook's Marina, MM 53.1 Oceanside, Marathon, (800) 278-4665, and look at their 48,000-gallon outdoor aquarium. Every day at 4:00 P.M. you can watch the sharks—and lots of other big fish, too—receive their evening meal. Keep your fingers out of the tank so you don't become dessert. It's free fun.

Z IS FOR . . .

zipping across the old Seven Mile Bridge to Pigeon Key in an old-time trolley car. Or you can walk, jog, or ride a bicycle to this five-acre history-rich island. Pigeon Key was the construction camp for workers building Henry Flagler's Railroad. Now the preserved early-19th-century buildings are listed on the National Register, and you can see them and take an island tour with a volunteer. Catch the trolley shuttle at the visitor center, MM 47 Oceanside, Knight's Key, (305) 743-5999 (see the Attractions chapter for more information).

Kid-Friendly Resorts

Several of our premier resorts in the Florida Keys offer special organized programs for children, ensuring that you, Mom and Dad, have some time to pursue your own interests or just unwind and relax with a good book by the swimming pool. You will find more information about these hotels in our Accommodations chapter.

The Kids Club at Marriott Key Largo Bay Beach Resort
MM 103.8 Bayside, Key Largo
(305) 453-0000, (800) 932-9332
www.marriottkeylargo.com/kids.htm
The Kids Club offers children ages 5 to 13 the opportunity to attend a theme-of-the-day activity group from 10:00 A.M. to 4:00 P.M. from Wednesday through Sunday. Activities include arts and crafts, pool time, sports, and games. Lunch is served as well. Kids Night Out, Friday and Saturday nights from 6:00 to 10:00 P.M., gives Mom and Dad a night out as well. Kids enjoy games, arts, crafts, pizza and soda, and a full-length movie. Parents receive a 10 percent discount at Gus' Grille for dinner if their children attend Kids Night Out.

Camp Cheeca at Cheeca Lodge and Spa
MM 82 Oceanside, Islamorada
(305) 664-4651, ext. 4411,
(800) 327-2888
www.cheeca.com
While Mom and Dad are enjoying their stay, young vacationers can have a memorable time too! Camp Cheeca is a fun and energetic camp for children ages 5 to 12. Daily activities include swimming, fishing off Cheeca's pier, arts and crafts, round-robin tennis, kayaking, snorkeling, and other fun festivities. Camp Cheeca is open Tuesday through Saturday from 9:00 A.M. to 1:00 P.M. The Camp also offers "Kids Night Out" on Friday and Saturday evenings from 6:00 to 10:00 P.M., which includes arts and crafts, a pizza dinner, movies, and games. Preregistration is required.

The Casa Marina
1500 Reynolds Street
(305) 296-3535, (800) 626-0777
www.casamarinakeywest.com

The Reach Resort
1435 Simonton Street
(305) 296-5000, (800) 874-4118
www.reachresort.com
The Casa Marina and The Reach Resort offer children's activities for residents of the two properties. The interesting, fun Keys Kids projects are personalized for children, depending on ages and length of stay. As activities change daily, be sure to check their calendar of events when making your resort reservations.

Dolphin Dayz, Island Adventure Club, Little Pirates Club, Indies Teen Spa, Cove Teen Club, and Indies Club
Hawk's Cay Resort and Marina,
MM 61 Oceanside, Duck Key
(305) 743-7000, (800) 443-6393
www.hawkscay.com
Hawk's Cay ensures an exciting stay for the whole family with some great places and programs for kids of all ages. Dolphin Dayz is a fun-filled room for kids at the Indies Club. Island Adventure Club, for children ages 6 through 11, offers fun activities: nature-oriented games, arts and crafts, swimming, and sports. Children ages four through five discover the treasures of the Keys with theme-oriented activities at Little Pirates Club. Kids Night Out is for children ages 4 through 11 and includes a make-and-take craft, dinner, and a movie. Indies Teen Spa Escape is a menu of special services for the next spa generation. All services are formulated for young adolescent skin types. They offer massages and facials, and they even have a "Friend's Timeout" that encourages you to bring along a friend. All

services and clubs require prereservations and parental consent.

At the Cove, teens can enjoy a game room, dance floor, music, karaoke, and electronic games. Hours for preteens, ages 9 to 12, are 4:00 to 7:00 P.M. and for teens, ages 13 to 17, 8:00 P.M. until midnight. The Indies Club, which houses the Cove, Dolphin Dayz, and other kid activities, also offers outdoor fun just outside its doors: a family pool, kids' pirate-ship pool, tree house, basketball and volleyball courts, and a putting green.

KEY WEST ADVENTURES

Now that you have arrived in the southernmost point in the United States, let's count down the top 15 things to do on a Key West adventure!

No. 15.

Visit the tide pool at the end of Simonton Street, Oceanside, located between the Reach Resort (see the Accommodations chapter) and the Sands Beach Club. This is a really great place to walk into the water and check out the marine life.

No. 14.

Partake in some terrific programs that run yearlong at the YMCA in Key West. If you call them at (305) 295-9622, they will give you a schedule and locations for all of their fun and exciting programs. Be sure to ask about the Skate Park! There you can roller blade and in-line skate (see the Recreation chapter).

No. 13.

Hang out, enjoy the water, and watch parasailing, windsurfing, ships coming into the port of Key West (even though they are miles out to sea, because of their size they are easy to view), and kite flying at Smather's Beach. The Key West Kite Company, 408 Green Street, Key West, (305) 296-2535 (see the Shopping chapter), has kites in every size, shape, and color you can imagine!

i

Sign up for a summer Kayak Camp with Florida Bay Outfitters. These camps, beginning in June, offer kids ages 8-12 an introduction to the fun and exciting adventure of paddle sports. For more information, visit www.kayakfloridakeys.com or call (305) 451-3018

No. 12.

Enjoy ice cream at Flamingo Crossing, 1107 Duval Street, Key West, (305) 296-6124. The folks here make 150 flavors of ice cream with 32 flavors offered at a time. Some of the tempting choices are orange, blue curacao, papaya, mango, sour sop, passion fruit, cinnamon, coconut and, you guessed it, key lime sorbet!

No. 11.

Discover Wyland, the world's leading marine life artist and his life-size Whaling Wall murals, which are truly breathtaking. There are three in the Florida Keys, and two are in Key West. One is located on the building of the Waterfront Market, 201 William Street (for more on the market see the Seafood Markets and Specialty Foods chapter), and the other two are located in Marathon. The largest one is on the Kmart storefront in the Kmart Shopping Center, MM 50.5, and the smaller one is directly across U.S. Highway 1 on the front of the Museums of Crane Point (see the Attractions chapter). (See more on Wyland in the Arts and Culture chapter.)

No. 10.

Stop by the Key West Conch Baby Farm, 631 Greene Street, (305) 296-3551, and learn how the world-famous Mote Marine Laboratory is advancing the science of the sea and working to replenish conch in the waters of the Florida Keys. Capture of queen conch within the waters of the

There are rainy days in the Keys, so why not sign up at the Dance Factory, in Key West, for family dance lessons? Call (305) 296-5015 for a schedule of classes.

Florida Keys is prohibited. Conch shells used to be a form of communication, and the meat was harvested locally. Now our conch comes to us from off the waters of the Bahamas. The farm is located behind the Conch Republic Seafood Company (see Restaurants chapter).

No. 9.

Take a walking ghost tour. This is a "sight" to behold as you walk the Old Town area of Key West. The historical homes and buildings on the tour reveal exciting stories about their past (see the two ghost tours described the Attractions chapter).

No. 8.

Take art lessons. Some of the art galleries in Key West will allow you to sit in on some of their classes and take a lesson. Check out the Art Galleries section in the Arts and Culture chapter to find the right gallery for you.

No. 7.

Visit Key West Butterfly and Nature Conservatory, 1316 Duval Street, (305) 293-9258. This is a fascinating experience even if you think you don't like butterflies! The history of the butterfly and how it evolves is a fun lesson you will not soon forget. The beauty of the conservatory is a camera buff's dream and a great place to spend a rainy day because everything in enclosed in an atrium (see the Attractions chapter).

No. 6.

Head on over to the Key West Library at 700 Fleming Street for Family Hour, held every Saturday starting at 1:00 P.M. Enjoy arts and crafts and free movies. The program is available to children of all ages. Call (305) 292-3595 for information.

No. 5

Step back in time as you explore the Civil War–era fort at East Martello Museum and Gallery, 3501 South Roosevelt Boulevard, (305) 296-3913. The brick walls are 8 feet thick, and you can climb the winding steps right to the top of the tall citadel. Don't forget to tour the 100-square-foot, lavish, life-size doll house. (See Attractions chapter.)

No. 4

Climb the 88 steps to the top balcony of the Key West Lighthouse, 938 Whitehead Street, (305) 294-0012, which was built in 1847. You'll have a sweeping view of Key West and its surrounding waters from the top of this 90-foot tower. Its three red sector panels used to signal dangerous approaches to Key West Harbor. A photoelectric cell lights up in the tower when daylight fades, and the light can be seen for several miles out at sea (see the Attractions chapter).

No. 3

See all kinds of gold and silver treasure recovered from the ancient ship *Atocha,* which sank off the Marquesas in 1622, at the Mel Fisher Maritime Heritage Society and Museum, 200 Greene Street, (305) 294-2633. Every 30 minutes a documentary movie shows how Mel Fisher searched for the fortune, a task that took nearly 20 years. Examine gold coins, bars of silver, gold chains, and giant emeralds. Upstairs, the museum showcases maritime exhibits that change every six months. You can get a special guide at the front desk and if you can successfully identify the objects in the exhibit you might be awarded a small prize. Be sure to visit the Discovery Room, which has 160 drawers

CLOSE-UP

Leaping Lizards

Blink once—blink twice—Nope, you are not seeing things. That is an iguana! In some areas of Central America and the Caribbean, iguanas are considered endangered. Not so in the Keys, where these nonnative animals propagate like stray cats and are about as popular, horning in on our favorite water spots and gardens. Good swimmers, you'll see germ-laden droppings around Jacuzzis, boats, and swimming pools. They'll eat up a garden too—they're particularly fond of hibiscus and impatiens plants—then escape high into the trees using the sharp toenails that make them such sure climbers. Most iguanas are green, but as they age their color fades. Brownish to gray shades may indicate an illness or stress. Just as humans wear light or dark colors to reflect or absorb heat from the sun, the iguana regulates its body temperature by changing from light to dark. They can grow very large—there is one so large it keeps dogs at bay. While the iguana still has fans on the Keys—pet owners who show them off in public on leashes, riding in cars, draped over their bodies—many other Keys residents find them a cause for concern. Since there are no natural predators, their numbers are growing. They are huge, they are hungry, and they can bite!

Iguana. PHOTO: ROB O'NEAL

for you to open. Each drawer holds maritime artifacts that will teach you about shipwrecks and treasure salving (for more information on the museum, see the Attractions chapter).

No. 2

Deep in a dark cistern, a foot below sea level, meet a 175-year-old wrecker named Asa Tift at the Key West Shipwreck Historeum, 1 Whitehead Street at Mallory Square, (305) 292-8990. Surrounded by thick ropes, jugs, rigging, and cannonballs, he'll tell all about the wreck of the *Isaac Allerton,* the richest Key West shipwreck of all. Each exhibit has headphones you can put on to hear recorded messages chock-full of information. (See the Attractions chapter for more information.)

No. 1

Meet all the fish and sea creatures we tell

you about in our Diving and Fishing chapters at The Key West Aquarium, 1 Whitehead Street at Mallory Square, (305) 296-2051, (800) 868-7482. Be sure not to miss the guided tours—11:00 A.M. and 1:00, 3:00, and 4:30 P.M.—because you'll be able to watch the feeding sessions of the stingrays, sharks, sawfish, and barracuda. The tour guide will show you the touch tank, where you can handle the hermit crabs, horse conchs, horseshoe crabs, sea cucumbers, pencil urchins, and common starfish. Go outside to the Atlantic Shores exhibit, re-created to give you the experience of a Florida Keys mangrove habitat. You'll see huge tarpon, snook, jacks, and sea turtles swimming in the crystal-clear water. The aquarium is open daily (see the Attractions chapter).

ANNUAL EVENTS 

No one knows how to throw a party better than residents of the Florida Keys. Come dress with us in period attire as we relive eras of our past. Or join locals and folks from across the world in a challenging road race on a bridge spanning miles of open sea.

We also have boat parades, bikini contests, battle reenactments, and our own unplugged, underwater concert. Or try your angling skills in one of our many fishing tournaments (see the Fishing chapter for an expanded listing). Immerse yourself in Florida Keys arts and culture at our historical observances, music festivals, or arts and crafts fairs.

And my, how we love to eat. From Key Largo to Key West, food festivals abound. These events provide an inexpensive means of sampling incredibly fresh seafood and menu items from leading local restaurants.

The following selection of festivals and events is a sampling of what we offer annually in the Florida Keys, organized by month, from Key Largo to Key West. Additional events occur sporadically from year to year. Dates and locations often change from year to year, and admission prices vary. Call the local chambers of commerce for details: Key Largo, MM 106 Bayside, (305) 451-1414, (800) 822-1088; Islamorada, MM 82.5 Bayside, (305) 664-4503, (800) 322-5397; Marathon, MM 53.5 Bayside, (305) 743-5417, (800) 262-7284; Lower Keys, MM 31 Oceanside, (305) 872-2411, (800) 872-3722; Key West, Old Mallory Square, (305) 294-2587, (800) 527-8539. You can pick up the annual *Attractions & Events* brochure at any of these chambers. You also will find annual event information on the official Web site of the Monroe County Tourist Development Council: www.fla-keys.com.

JANUARY

Florida Keys Medieval Fest
MM 17 Bayside, Sugarloaf Key
(305) 849-2311
www.flkeysmedievalfest.org

Dedicated to the reenactment of a bygone era, the January Florida Keys Medieval Fest is an exciting way to spend a weekend. It features artisans making and selling crafts, jousting tourneys, knife throwing, fire eaters, a live-battle chess match, and live musical performances to delight the ladies, lords, and wee ones. Proceeds from the Medieval Fest benefit community organizations.

Key West Craft Show
Whitehead Street, Key West
(305) 294-2587

Key West ends the month of January with a weekend-long exhibit of original crafts. Among the one-of-a-kind items offered for sale, you'll find handmade jewelry, leather goods, wood carvings, kitchen accessories, and beach and lounge chairs. Exhibitors come from throughout the United States. The crafts show takes place in the street—on Whitehead Street between Eaton and Greene. Admission is free.

Key West Literary Seminar
516 Duval Street, San Carlos Institute, Key West
(888) 293-9291
www.keywestliteraryseminar.com

Key West's San Carlos Institute serves as the home base for these sessions. Writing workshops, tours of legendary local authors' homes, and cocktail parties also are offered to seminar participants. Included in the core seminar price, these parties offer the opportunity to mingle with panel guests. Workshops and tours cost an additional fee. The four-day event is typically held during the second week

If you are in the Keys in January, join in the fun at the annual Chef's Classic. Chefs from a dozen restaurants literally step up to the plate for this taste-of-the-islands gormandise event. Chefs compete in three categories: appetizers, entrees, and desserts. The proceeds benefit the Monroe Association for Retarded Citizens. For more information, call (305) 294-9526.

of January. Call for information on registration and workshop fees, but reserve early. These events are typically sold out up to a year in advance.

Old Island Days House and Garden Tours
Various Key West sites
(305) 294-9501, (800) 648-6269
www.oirf.org
Olde Island Restoration, a nonprofit organization that encourages preservation of Key West's many historical structures, sponsors this popular tour—spanning December, January, February, and March—to show off some of the city's finest private properties. Typically, each event features five or six privately owned homes. Tours explore shotgun-style cottages, Conch-style mansions, and everything in between (see the Key West Architecture Close-up in the Attractions chapter).

The tours are self-guided, but participants may meet at the Olde Island Restoration offices along Mallory Square and then embark on a Conch Train bound for the tour site. Scheduled dates vary from year to year. There is an admission fee.

Terra Nova Trading Key West Race Week
Waters off Key West
(781) 639-9545
www.premiere-racing.com
Sailors from throughout the world flock to Key West the second week in January for this event, the biggest annual regatta in America. More than 300 sailboats compete for no money, just glory and prestige. America's Cup teams use this event for training and to scope out the competition. Everyone who's anyone in sailing is sure to be here. The event lasts five days, with races beginning each day at around 10:00 A.M. Spectating is free. Call Premier Racing at the number above for more information.

FEBRUARY

Florida Keys Outdoor Art Show at Key Colony Beach Park
West Ocean Drive, Key Colony Beach
(305) 743-5417, (800) 262-7284
In addition to the works of artists throughout the country, local high school students display their talents at this intimate showing. Bronze, stone, and metal sculptures, oil paintings, watercolors, and other fine arts and crafts are among the items featured. Judging is held for the work of high school students only. Food, beverages, and live entertainment are offered throughout the weekend, and a raffle drawing affords you the chance to win some of the work on display. This event is usually held in late February or early March. Admission is free.

Pigeon Key Art Festival
Pigeon Key, Marathon
(305) 743-7664, (305) 289-0025
www.pigeonkey.org
More than 700 artists from throughout the country apply to display their works in this annual show, but only 70 are selected by the judges to participate, so you can be assured of the highest-quality work. The festival is generally scheduled for the first weekend in February, on the shores of Pigeon Key. At weekend's close, judges bestow awards for the best artwork in categories such as watercolor, oil and acrylic painting, jewelry, photography, sculpture, glass, pottery, and graphics. Live entertainment features the music of

steel-drum bands, jazz groups, classical ensembles, and country-and-western performers. Local restaurants sell food, and raffle drawings include original artwork donated by each participating artist.

Getting to this festival by your choice of water taxi, trolley, or Pigeon Key choo-choo is half the fun, and transportation is included in the admission price. All proceeds are donated to the Pigeon Key Foundation for restoration of the island (see the Attractions chapter). Artists pay entry fees, and half the show's work has a Florida theme.

The Winter Star Party
MM 23.8 Oceanside, West Summerland Key
(386) 362-5995
www.scas.org

Each year in February, for the last 22 years, more than 600 amateur astronomers have flocked to the Florida Keys for one of the largest stargazing gatherings in the world. The Winter Star Party, sponsored by the Southern Cross Astronomical Society, is a weeklong celebration and an opportunity to gaze at the clear skies offered here. Participants also attend lectures and workshops and learn from special guest speakers. This get-together is not just for well-versed astronomers, but also for beginners. There are no walk-in tickets, so purchase yours in advance on the Web site listed above.

Art in the Park
Fort Zachary Taylor State Park, Key West
(305) 295-3800

Every winter (February through March), Fort Zachary Taylor State Park in Key West becomes home to a wonderful sculpture exhibit known as Art in the Park. Since its inception in 1995, the annual event has provided emerging and established artists and the public the opportunity to enjoy contemporary sculpture in a breathtaking and natural setting. The artist chooses each site where sculpture is displayed. The artists work in steel, concrete, wood, marble, and other materials.

i

If you are taking a road trip south to the Florida Keys, remember that Florida's Turnpike is a toll road. If you travel on I-95 or US 1 in Florida, there are no tolls.

Old Island Days Art Festival
Whitehead Street, Key West
(305) 294-1241

If you appreciate art, your heart is bound to beat faster at the sight of several blocks of exhibits by talented local artists. Inspired by this southernmost city, they take this opportunity to showcase their vivid creations. Virtually all artistic media are represented in this prejuried, weekend-long show, including oil, watercolor, and acrylic paintings; graphics; wood, metal, and stone sculptures; glasswork; and photography. Judges provide merit awards within each category. Old Island Days Art Festival exhibits line Whitehead Street from Greene Street to Caroline and into Truman Annex. No charge for browsing.

MARCH

The Original Marathon Seafood Festival, Marathon
(305) 743-5417

Sponsored by the Marathon Chamber of Commerce and Organized Fishermen of Florida (OFF), the Original Marathon Seafood Festival features thousands of pounds of fish, including cobia ceviche, golden crabs, conch fritters, Florida lobster, and a raw bar. Landlubbers can munch on hot dogs, hamburgers, and ethnic dishes.

Pick up some of the distributed educational literature on the commercial fishing industry, and check out the Middle Keys Marine Association's festival flea market with new and discontinued marine items at below-retail prices. Rides, games, vendors, raffles, and live entertainment mean fun for the entire family. There is an admission fee.

Conch Shell Blowing Contest
Sunset Pier at Ocean Key House, Duval Street, Key West
(305) 294-9501
www.oirf.org

Feel free to toot your own horn. The Conch Shell Blowing Contest offers adults and children the opportunity to sound off. Prizes are awarded to the loudest, the funniest, and the most entertaining conch-shell blowers in several divisions. This one-day, springtime event takes place on the waterfront and on various dates each year, but usually in March or April. Participation is free.

Heritage Days at Fort Zachary Taylor State Historical Site
Truman Annex at Southard Street, Key West
(305) 292-6713

This annual festival and Civil War reenactment celebrates the unique history of Fort Zachary Taylor. Against all odds, the fort remained a Union stronghold throughout the Civil War, despite the fact that Florida had seceded from the Union. Costumed reenactors—soldiers and their families alike—stage military drills and demonstrate everyday life in a Civil War–era fort. Heritage Days is typically held the first weekend in March. The event is free with admission to Fort Zach (see the Attractions chapter).

Key West Garden Club Flower Show at West Martello Tower
Atlantic Boulevard and White Street, Key West
(305) 294-3210
www.keywestgardenclub.com

Established in 1949 by former Key West politician Joe Allen, the Garden Club organizes monthly educational seminars for the public. Plant-swapping sessions also are popular. The group holds a prejuried show every other year. Held at the Joe Allen West Martello Tower, home of the Key West Garden Club, the show features some 800 entries of floral arrangements, potted plants, palms, rare tropical flowers, and hybrids. Judges from garden clubs throughout the state of Florida award ribbons and prizes in several categories. The flower show is typically held during the spring, not necessarily always in March. There are admission costs.

APRIL

Taste of Islamorada
Islamorada
(305) 664-4503

Islamorada's most popular restaurants all come together for this annual chamber of commerce fund-raiser that lets you cast your "palate ballot" for the best appetizer, entree, dessert, low-calorie, and vegetarian selections. Booths at the event allow visitors to sample a variety of unlimited cuisines from 15 to 20 fine-dining establishments, all for one minimal cover charge. If you have never dined at Islamorada's local restaurants, this is a wonderfully inexpensive opportunity to try out several. Live entertainment and raffle prizes make this a popular family event. Locations change annually. The event is usually held in April or May. Expect to pay an admission fee.

Earth Day at Cheeca Lodge
MM 82 Oceanside, Islamorada
(305) 451-5094, (800) 327-2888
www.cheeca.com

Every year Cheeca Lodge puts on quite a spectacle in honor of Mother Earth. The big draw here is the land-based aerial display, where revelers put together the words Earth Day in huge letters made out of sand. Other events include fishing tournaments, cooking demonstrations, costume contests, live entertainment, and barbecues. Open to the public, Cheeca Lodge's Earth Day celebration raises funds for environmental causes. Admission is free.

Seven Mile Bridge Run
Marathon
(305) 743-5417

Men and women from across the world flock to this 7-mile roadway, which spans the open water between Marathon and Bahia Honda. In the wee morning hours, these spirited individuals participate in the most scenic competition of its kind: a run across one of the world's longest bridges. Organized by the Marathon Runners Club, sponsored by a number of Florida Keys businesses, and designed to raise money for local schools and youth groups, the run is said to be the only one in the world held completely over and surrounded by water. Post-race prizes are awarded in various categories, and runners gather for what is likely the world's largest early-morning celebratory bash. Usually, the run is held on the second Saturday in April and begins on the Marathon end of the Seven Mile Bridge. Expect to pay an entry fee. Spaces are limited, so if you plan to run, reserve your spot early.

Conch Republic Independence Celebration
Various Key West sites
(305) 296-0213
www.conchrepublic.com

Key West has always been marked by an independent spirit, and this 10-day festival exalts it. It officially commemorates the city's attempt to secede from the United States on April 23, 1982, after the U.S. Border Patrol established roadblocks at the end of the mainland to screen for drugs and illegal aliens. Independent Key Westers rebelled, creating their own flag and attempting to secede from the United States.

The secession fizzled, of course, but locals here find the brief attempt at independence a reason to party nevertheless. Around this same time every year, officials of the fictitious Conch Republic—secretary general, prime ministers, navy, air force, and all—host a picnic, fashion show, buffet, and pirates' ball. Events also include Conch cruiser car shows, the Red Ribbon Bed Race down Duval Street, and what has been dubbed "the world's longest parade"—spectators lining the route simply join in the fun as the floats pass by.

One final word on emancipation in the southernmost city: Duck! During the Great Battle of the Conch Republic, all forms of food whiz through the air and ultimately find their marks on participants and spectators. The battle engages the Conchs and the U.S. Coast Guard in a water fight held at sea just off Mallory Square. Conch Republic Celebration events are held throughout the island and on the water.

A Taste of Key West
Higgs Beach, White Street at Atlantic Boulevard, Key West
(305) 296-6196

"So many restaurants, so little time," is the lament we often hear from visitors to Key West. Our tiny island boasts more than 100 eateries, and on an average visit, you simply can't try them all. But if you're lucky enough to be here in April you may have the chance to sample the best of the best on one night, at one location.

A Taste of Key West, which benefits AIDS Help Inc., brings together chefs and their favorite dishes from many of Key West's finest restaurants. There is no admission charge, but you must buy tickets at a nominal cost to eat. The individual restaurants set the number of tickets you will need to sample their wares. For three tickets, you can nosh on a salad or a dessert; entrees typically cost four or five tickets. In addition to cash, be sure to bring your appetite—the portions are always generous.

The date for this annual event changes from one year to the next, but it is always held outdoors and typically on a Monday or Tuesday night.

Shell Key West Classic
Various Key West sites
(305) 294-2587

This tournament spreads a huge pot of prize money over a variety of categories—blue or white marlin, sailfish, tarpon, and permit. Proceeds benefit the National Mental Health Association.

See the Fishing chapter for details. This tournament usually occurs in late April or early May.

MAY

Key West Songwriters Fest at Hog's Breath Saloon
400 Front Street, Key West
(305) 296-4222

You may not recognize the names of the performers at this annual event, but if you're a country music fan, you'll almost certainly know their songs. This festival, launched in 1996, brings some of the country's foremost performing songwriters to the Key West stage.

Past performers have included Billy Dean, whose "Somewhere in My Broken Heart" earned a Grammy nomination and Academy of Country Music Song of the Year honors; Gretchen Peters, whose "Independence Day," sung by Martina McBride, won a Country Music Association Song of the Year Award; and Mark Selby and Tia Sellers, whose roster of hits includes the Dixie Chicks' 1999 Grammy winner "There's Your Trouble."

The four-day festival includes intimate concerts by all the songwriters, held at the Hog's Breath Saloon. Plan to arrive early for the best choice of seats.

JUNE

Don Hawley Invitational Tarpon Tournament
Islamorada
(305) 664-2444

This Don Hawley event is the Keys' oldest tarpon-on-the-fly tournament and the original all-release event. Proceeds benefit the nonprofit Don Hawley Foundation, which supports the study of tarpon fishery and preservation in the Florida Keys. See the Fishing chapter for details.

Cuban American Heritage Festival
Various locations around Key West
(305) 295-9665
www.cubanfest.com

With so many Key West residents claiming Cuban roots, this was an event just waiting to happen. Launched in 1999, this now annual, five-day festival celebrates Key West's Cuban heritage. Events include a street fair, two-day fishing tournament, cigar dinners, guided tours highlighting Key West's links to its nearest neighbor, salsa bands, and a domino tournament. Perhaps the highlight, however, is a coast-to-coast conga line stretching down Duval Street from the Atlantic to the Gulf. Everyone—Cuban or otherwise—is invited to participate.

On the more serious side, a three-day symposium at San Carlos Institute, 516 Duval Street, examines Cuba, then and now. Most festival events, including the symposium, are free.

Florida Keys Tropical Fruit Fiesta
Bayview Park, Key West
(305) 292-4501
www.floridakeystropicalfruitfiesta.com

Usually held in the month of June, the annual Florida Keys Tropical Fruit Fiesta draws large crowds excited to buy fruit trees, tropical fruit, fruit ice cream, and various prepared fruit dishes. Produced by the University of Florida's Institute of Food and Agricultural Sciences in cooperation with the Monroe County Cooperative Extension Office, this event is your chance to ask the tropical fruit experts all your horticulture questions. Although few varieties of fruit trees are native to the Keys, many tropical and subtropical species thrive and are easily grown here in pots and gardens. Jackfruit, mango, key lime, sugar apple, avocado, and banana are just a few. You can attend lectures given by the pros and enter your fruit in the home-grown fruit contest. Various vendors and nonprofits, including 4-H (with the 4-H Children's Corner), are in attendance. This is a fun day in a shady spot under big tents, where a sweet, heady bouquet fills the air.

JULY

Fourth of July Fireworks
Bayside, Key Largo
(305) 451-1414

View this 30-minute fireworks display from land or, if you are a boater, by sea. Funded by local merchants, the show typically begins at 9:00 P.M. The best coastal viewing spots are the Caribbean Club, Señor Frijoles, Sundowners, and Marriott Key Largo Bay Beach Resort. Some of these facilities host barbecues with live entertainment. Admission is free, but you must be a patron to enjoy the view from a private business. Food and drinks are sold separately.

Star Spangled Event at Sombrero Beach
MM 50 Oceanside, Marathon
(305) 743-5417

On July 4 follow a parade to the beach, where fireworks decorate the sky, and enjoy all-American hot dogs, hamburgers, and fish sandwiches. Live entertainment is provided; games are available for the kids, and an afternoon volleyball tournament welcomes last-minute sign-ups. Many people see the fireworks display from the decks of their boats, anchoring offshore for the extravaganza. The traffic jam at sea rivals the one on land. No admission or entry fee is required. Food and games are priced individually.

Underwater Music Festival
MM 31 Oceanside, Big Pine Key
(305) 872-2411

Whether you dive, snorkel, or merely swim, here is an unplugged series of concerts that beats music videos fins-down. Enjoy six hours of prerecorded, commercial-free music—from Beethoven to the Beatles to the humpback whale song—in synchronicity with tropical fish swimming across the reefs of the Looe Key National Marine Sanctuary. Dance the day away under water, and look out for surprises such as mermaids and the Keys' very own Snorkeling Elvises. Typically, the music fest runs from midmorning to midafternoon and is broadcast live on WWUS/US 1 radio, 104.1 FM. Landlubbers and those who have danced up an appetite can enjoy this same music plus a variety of foods, arts and crafts, and family games at the Lower Keys Chamber of Commerce, MM 31 Oceanside. Admission to both the concert and the food festival, usually held the second Saturday in July, is free. See Diving chapter for a list of dive and snorkel charters that will take you to the reef.

Hemingway Days Festival at Hemingway Home and Museum
907 Whitehead Street, Key West
(305) 294-2587
www.hemingwaydays.net

Celebrate the legendary author's birthday with residents of the old man's former hometown by the sea. Tours of the Hemingway Home and Museum are offered, along with a street fair, a short-story competition, and a Hemingway look-alike contest at what was one of his favorite haunts, Sloppy Joe's (see the Nightlife chapter). This weeklong event centers on the author's July 21 birthday. Fees for some events are required. Call for more information.

July 4th Fireworks
White Street Pier, White Street and Atlantic Boulevard, Key West
(305) 296-5000

The Key West Rotary Club sponsors this pyrotechnic extravaganza every July 4 beginning at 9:00 P.M. and lasting approximately 30 minutes. Best viewing spots are Higgs Beach and the Casa Marina. There is no admission charge; the fireworks are funded strictly by donations.

The Monroe County Tourist Development Council maintains an online calendar of events. For the latest month-by-month listings of festivals, gallery showings, and theater productions, click on www.fla-keys.com.

July 4th VNA/Hospice Picnic
1500 Reynolds Street, at The Casa Marina Resort, Key West
(305) 296-5000

The whole town turns out for this old-fashioned beachside picnic to benefit the Visiting Nurses Association/Hospice of the Florida Keys. You'll find plenty of hot dogs, hamburgers, watermelon, and fun for all, plus special activities for the kids, continuous live entertainment, and a raffle. The picnic begins around 5:00 P.M., but because the beach at the Casa is one of the best places to view the fireworks, you'll probably want to come early and stick around until well after dark. Admission is charged for the picnic.

Reef Awareness Week
201 William Street, at Reef Relief, Key West
(305) 294-3100
www.reefrelief.org

Reef Relief is one of the best known and largest of the organizations whose sole purpose is to protect North America's only living coral reef. And when these folks throw a party, they invite everyone. This weeklong event offers all sorts of information to those who want to learn about the coral reef. Visit the art auction and poetry readings, or become a member of this worthy organization during the kickoff week. For more information, call Reef Relief, or visit the organization's retail store at the address listed. Admission is usually free, but some events may carry an entry fee.

SEPTEMBER

Florida Keys Poker Run
Miami through Key West
(305) 292-1177

With so many magnificent bridges, the Florida Keys is extremely popular with motorcycle riders. For this event, more than 10,000 motorcyclists ride from Miami to Key West, stopping at various points within our islands to pick up playing cards. At the end of the ride, the player with the best poker hand wins, and all enjoy live bands, field events, and runs-within-a-run on Duval Street. Bikers can also get their machines blessed before returning home. Entry is free; each poker hand costs a nominal fee.

Mercury S.L.A.M. Celebrity Tournament
Key West
(305) 664-2002
www.redbone.org

First of the annual Celebrity Tournament Series is the Southernmost Light-tackle Anglers Masters (S.L.A.M). Anglers try to score a Grand Slam by catching and releasing a bonefish, permit, and tarpon in one day. Proceeds benefit the Cystic Fibrosis Foundation. See the Fishing chapter for details or contact Gary Ellis at the number listed above.

WomenFest Key West
Various Key West sites
(305) 296-2491
www.womenfest.net

They are women; hear them roar. Each week after Labor Day, thousands of women from all over the country gather in Key West for a bit of female bonding. They include women from diverse races, religions, professions, and sexual preferences; the motto is "Free to Be You with Me in Key West." Atlantic Shores Resort serves as the headquarters for this seven-day celebration, which includes women-only watersports, cocktail comedies, and concerts. Organizers host wine-tasting dinners, parties, and picnics, and women

ship off together on sunset sails.

Many events are free, including the "Sisters for Brothers" blood drive to compensate for the gay male population not being permitted to donate blood. Discounted party passes are available for groups of events that come at a cost, such as the Old Town Trolley Tour that highlights infamous Key West women.

Gay male and female guesthouses and mainstream hotels provide accommodations, and some of the island's "all-boys" houses (see the Accommodations chapter) become all-women for this week instead.

OCTOBER

Mercury Baybone Celebrity Tournament
Sheraton Beach Resort, Key Largo
MM 97 Bayside, Key Largo
(305) 664-2002
www.redbone.org

Event No. 2 in the Celebrity Tournament Series (see the September section for the first event) is a catch-and-release tournament in pursuit of bonefish and permit. Proceeds benefit the Cystic Fibrosis Foundation. See our Fishing chapter or contact Gary Ellis at the number above for more information.

Fantasy Fest
Various Key West sites
(305) 296-1817
www.fantasyfest.net

This is Key West's biggest party of the year—a citywide celebration similar to Mardi Gras in New Orleans (see the Close-up in this chapter).

Goombay Festival
Petronia Street, Key West
(305) 294-2587

Designed to showcase the cultural customs of the city's Bahamian community through food, music, and crafts, this grassroots affair has grown to include African, Filipino, and Latin traditions, too. Food booths dish up typical festival fare such as gyros, sausages, peppers, and Thai selections, but tucked among them are the treasures of this event: Jamaican jerk chicken and pork, Bahamian cracked conch, conch salad, fried fish, and pigeon peas and rice, all highly seasoned. Dance in the streets to the music of African and steel drummers or calypso bands. Stop by the simulated Nassau straw market to see straw hats and fruit baskets being woven.

The festival stretches from the corner of Petronia at Duval down to Emma Street and now encompasses many of the streets that make up a good share of the neighborhood known as Bahama Village. Held the first weekend of Fantasy Fest (see the Close-up in this chapter), Goombay sets the stage for an even wider segment of society to flaunt their heritage. There is no admission charge.

Attention parents: The Fantasy Fest Parade on Duval Street is truly an adults-only event. Unless you want your kids exposed to heavy drinking, seminudity, and the bizarre-often-bordering-on-lewd behavior of some spectators, leave the little ones at home this time.

NOVEMBER

George Bush/Cheeca Lodge Bonefish Tournament
MM 82 Oceanside, Cheeca Lodge, Islamorada
(305) 517-4456
www.cheeca.com

Former president George H. W. Bush himself participates in this, the most prestigious of all our tournaments. The tournament is usually held in October or November, depending on Mr. Bush's schedule. All bonefish must be released. Winners are awarded trophies. See the Fishing chapter for details.

Mercury Cheeca/Redbone Celebrity Tournament
Islamorada
(305) 664-2002
www.redbone.org

CLOSE-UP

Fantasy Fest

Kookier than Carnival and merrier than Mardi Gras, Fantasy Fest is Key West's own decadent decibel of dreamy delight.

Fantasy Fest was originally conceived as a way to boost tourism in an otherwise soft season. It succeeded—and how! Today, more than two decades after its conception, this event more than doubles the island's population for one week in October, culminating with the arrival of some 70,000 revelers on Duval Street for the Saturday-night parade.

Fantasy Fest is a nine-day adult Halloween celebration that commences on a Friday night with the Royal Coronation Ball, where the King and Queen of Fantasy Fest are crowned. The competition is open to all, and campaigning for the titles begins as early as late August. The winners are the ones who "buy" the most votes (translation: They raise the most money for AIDS Help Inc.). The closer it gets to Fantasy Fest, the fiercer the competition becomes and the more creative the candidates must become at finding sponsors and venues for their fund-raising efforts.

Contributions are accepted right up to the last minute when the final tally takes place at the Coronation Ball. The man and woman—or man and man-in-drag—are dubbed "royalty" only after emerging from a field of entrants whose votes have been bought and sold and bought and sold all over again. The King and Queen receive regal robes, crowns, and scepters and preside over all official Fantasy Fest events. While it's considered quite a coup to be named King or Queen, the real winners in all of this are the people served by AIDS Help Inc.

The competition doesn't end with the race for King and Queen. It continues throughout the weekend as captains seek the winner's cup in the Fantasy Yacht Race's Victory at Sea. On Masked Monday fines are imposed on anyone (including any unsuspecting tourist) who does not comply with the loony law of the land: You must be masked to meander Duval Street, or the Mask Rangers will make an example of you.

Each year, Fantasy Fest features a new theme, which is emblazoned on

Third in the Celebrity Tournament Series is the Redbone, the competitive search for bonefish and redfish, usually held in late November or early December. Proceeds in this tournament also benefit the Cystic Fibrosis Foundation. For more information, check out the Fishing chapter or contact Gary Ellis at the number listed above.

Sky Dive Marathon
MM 52 Bayside, at Florida Keys Marathon Airport, Marathon
(305) 743-5417

More than 150 skydivers from throughout the United States participate in this two-day event, typically held in November on the grounds of the Marathon Airport. Weekend activities include skydiving

At Fantasy Fest, designers vie for the most beguiling masquerade creations. PHOTO: FLORIDA KEYS TDC

posters and T-shirts promoting the events—all of which are for sale, of course. In keeping with Key West's penchant for parties, a poster-signing celebration is held on Masked Monday. The following night you can enjoy a preview of some courageous/outrageous costumes at the Masked Madness and Headdress Ball. Then on Wednesday, be sure to enter your pet (and yourself) in the Pet Masquerade and Parade. No species is excluded.

demonstrations and an air show. There is no admission fee. Food and beverages are available for purchase.

American Powerboat Association
World Championship
Waters off Key West
(305) 296-6156
www.apba-offshore.com

Just as Key West begins to recover from Fantasy Fest, the big boats roar into town to compete in a week's worth of offshore races that culminate in the naming of the world's champ. These are no little, putt-putt motorboats; they are high-performance ocean racers costing more than $1 million each and boasting speeds of 125 to 150 mph. Close to 50,000 fans line the waterfront to view the competition, which generally takes place the second week of

Each year the Key West Audubon Society does a traditional December bird count. Anyone can participate with a $5.00 donation to the National Audubon Society. The data collected from the national society, which has been compiled over decades, helps gauge the health of bird populations. For more information, call (305) 294-2116 or (877) 281-2473.

November. There's no charge to watch, and the best viewing spots are along Mallory Square and at the harborside hotels—the Pier House, Ocean Key House, Hyatt, and Hilton. Even if you're not a particular fan of powerboats, these are something to see.

Cayo Carnival
3501 S. Roosevelt Boulevard, at East Martello Museum, Key West
(305) 296-3913
This annual party to benefit Reef Relief is like a mini-Taste of Key West. Your ticket (discounted if purchased in advance) entitles you to dance the night away to more than half a dozen local bands and sample the food and drink offered by some of Key West's finest restaurants. The party always takes place on the Saturday night of the weekend before Thanksgiving in the gardens at East Martello Museum; for many Key Westers, Cayo Carnival marks the start of the holiday season.

On-site parking is limited, but free transportation is available from several locations around town, including the Key West Welcome Center, Key West High School, and Reef Relief.

DECEMBER

Christmas Boat Parade
Bayside, Key Largo
(305) 451-1592
Deck the boats with boughs of holly . . . Come watch a festive parade of between 30 and 50 lighted boats glow its way through Blackwater Sound. Prizes are awarded in various categories. At recent events, we've spotted Santa Claus catching a sailfish and Frosty the Snowman water-skiing. As with the Fourth of July Fireworks, the best coastal viewing locations are the Caribbean Club, Señor Frijoles, Sundowners, and Marriott Key Largo Bay Beach Resort. Some of these facilities host barbecues with live entertainment. Admission is free, but you must be a patron at any of these facilities to enjoy the view.

Key Colony Beach Boat Parade
MM 53.5 Oceanside, Key Colony Beach
(305) 289-1212
A more intimate, equally spectacular version of the Key Largo boat parade, this one is held along the landmark canals of Key Colony Beach. Admission is free.

Boot Key Harbor Christmas Boat Parade, Marathon
(305) 743-4011
Sponsored by the Marathon Power Squadron, this parade begins at sundown on the first Saturday in December. The best public viewing areas include Faro Blanco Marina, Boot Key Harbor Bridge, and the Dockside Lounge on Sombrero Road, where judging ceremonies are held immediately following the parade.

Christmas Around the World at Marathon Garden Club
MM 50 Bayside, Marathon
(305) 743-4971
This annual display by the Marathon Garden Club features more than a dozen Christmas trees, each decorated in the traditional style of a different country. Expect to pay an admission fee.

Key West Lighted Boat Parade
Various Key West sites
(305) 294-2587
Lighted boat parades are common throughout our islands, and Key West is no exception. In addition to the magical entourage of skiffs, schooners, and cruis-

ers, viewers may enjoy the preparade sunset activities at Mallory Square. The boat parade begins at Schooner Wharf Bar at the foot of William Street, but you can get the best view from Mallory Square and the pier beside the Hilton Resort and Marina. The boat parade is typically held on the third Saturday in December. Participation is free, but call Schooner Wharf at (305) 294-2587 to reserve your spot.

New Year's Eve on Duval Street
Key West
(305) 292-3230

Times Square has nothing on us when it comes to knowing how to ring in a new year. We close off the street and, in typical Key West style, party outdoors till the bars close down at 4:00 A.M. So come New Year's Eve, grab your hat and horn and head for Duval to watch the conch shell drop from the top of Sloppy Joe's Bar at the stroke of midnight (or the red high heel at Bourbon Street Pub). Just don't wear your best silks and satins for this celebration because it will be raining champagne for sure! Round out your New Year's revelry with an "ooh" and an "ah" as you watch the fireworks explode above Key West Harbor.

i

The Key West Holiday Parade, complete with floats, marching bands, and Santa Claus riding atop a fire truck, is usually scheduled for the first Saturday night in December. The parade follows Truman Avenue (U.S. Highway 1).

ARTS AND CULTURE 

Creative juices flow freely in the Florida Keys. Is it the sunshine? Or maybe the profusion of riotous colors everywhere you look? Perhaps our pervasive nothing-is-impossible, sky's-the-limit attitude is a contributing factor. Or maybe it's the fact that when you're in the Keys, you take the time to smell the bougainvillea.

Key West is the cultural center of the Florida Keys. This scintillating port has long attracted free spirits and adventurers—wreckers, sailors, spongers, shrimpers, and pirates—who played an enormous role in Key West's settlement and development. An enigmatic quality inherent in the essence of Key West draws fertile minds and searching souls to its inner sanctum like moths to a flame. From Ernest Hemingway to earnestly trying, Key West has hosted for a time the famous, the infamous, and the obscure.

Join us for an Insiders' look at the arts, from Key Largo to Key West, some traditional, others not so. Enjoy our music, theater, and dance while you are here and tour our myriad galleries. Or, if your timing is right, catch an arts festival, literary seminar, or theater gala for a creative night out. Be sure to check the Annual Events chapter for descriptions of special arts festivals and events.

i

A visit to the Donkey Milk House Museum, 613 Eaton Street, Key West, will take you back to the 1866 era of neo-classical architecture and furnishings. The name derives from the donkeys that carted milk from the alley behind the house to customers in Key West.

ARTS ORGANIZATIONS

The Monroe Council of the Arts Corp. is considered the official arts organization of the Florida Keys. Regional organizations offer members the opportunity to network and showcase their talents. Arts organizations are organized alphabetically.

Florida Keys Council of the Arts
1100 Simonton Street, Key West
(305) 295-4369 (Key West)
(305) 743-0079, ext. 4369 (Marathon)
(305) 852-1469, ext. 4639 (Upper Keys)
www.keysarts.com

The Florida Keys Council of the Arts acts as the "chamber of commerce" of arts throughout the Keys. The council's stated mission is "to connect artists and arts organizations with each other, with local audiences, and with the important tourism economy." They maintain an artist registry and Web site on which you'll find complete, year-round listings of the arts and entertainment events in the Keys. In addition, they get the cultural word out to the public via a weekly calendar in five local newspapers and a quarterly brochure of events.

One of the council's most prominent projects is the ongoing "Art in Public Places" program, in which the group displays the works of local artists in changing exhibits at such places as the Key West airport.

The arts council both writes and provides grants that benefit individual artists, arts organizations, schools, and libraries. It is supported by Monroe County and private donations and has several hundred members throughout the Florida Keys. A referral and support service, the arts council provides thousands of artists throughout the Keys with a means of political clout.

Lower Keys Artists Network
MM 30.5 Bayside, 221 Key Deer Boulevard, Big Pine Key
(305) 872-1828
www.artistsinparadise.com

Formed in 1994, the Lower Keys Artists Network has about 50 members, and anyone in the Lower Keys interested in art is welcome to join. Meetings are held from December to May at Artists in Paradise, a co-op gallery in Big Pine. Members assist in judging student art competitions and work with the public library to provide arts and crafts programs for children. The group raises funds for art scholarships through corporate sponsorships. Lower Keys Artists Network also provides demonstrations and seminars on all forms of art, including watercolor, wood sculpture, food sculpture, stained glass, and etching.

South Florida Center for the Arts
(305) 853-7070

After Hurricane Andrew tore through South Miami and Dade County in 1992, the South Dade Center for the Arts moved to Key Largo and established itself as the South Florida Center for the Arts (SFCA). A private, nonprofit organization, SFCA provides a community concert series and some years offers jazz and chamber music programs as well as concerts for children.

Local fund-raisers support Arts for Youth, which encourages young audiences to participate in the arts. Members also provide workshops, plays, and arts programs in local schools. Between its arts and concert association members, this organization has approximately 350 members, many of whom reside in the Upper Keys.

PERFORMING ARTS

Theater

Marathon Community Theatre
MM 49.5 Oceanside, Marathon
(305) 743-0994
www.marathontheater.org

Providing top-notch live theatrical entertainment to locals and visitors for decades, the Marathon Community Theatre annually stages four to six productions, such as *Music Man, Ravenscroft,* and *Applause!,* which each run Thursday through Saturday for a month.

Productions utilize full sets and full costuming, and actors hail from all throughout the Keys, from Key Largo to Key West. The group also hosts other productions, ranging from art shows and concerts to the Lovewell Foundation's summer theater program for children.

The theaters in Key West are small and tickets sell out quickly, but do check with the box office. A few single seats may be available at the last minute.

Red Barn Theatre
319 Duval Street (rear), Key West
(305) 296-9911
www.redbarntheatre.com

Quaint and charming, the restored carriage house that hosts the Red Barn Theatre has stood in the shadows of one of Key West's oldest houses, now the Key West Women's Club, for more than 50 years. Up from its humble beginnings as an animal stable, the building hosted the Key West Community Players for a time and also was the venue for puppet shows and piano concerts. Lovingly restored in 1980, the 88-seat structure shines with professional regional theater at its finest. And because of its size and layout, there isn't a bad seat in the house.

The Red Barn Theatre does five or six shows each year, including original comedies, musicals, and dramas by published writers. Its season runs from late November through June. Past productions have included: *I Love You, You're Perfect, Now Change; The Ride Down Mount Morgan; The Big Bang;* and *The Bathroom Plays,* by Key West's own, the late Shel Silverstein. Full sets, costumes, and orchestrated scores are featured.

Tennessee Williams Fine Arts Center
5901 West College Road, Stock Island
(305) 296-1520
www.keywesttheater.org
The Tennessee Williams Fine Arts Center (TWFAC) opened in January 1980 on the campus of Florida Keys Community College with the world premiere of Tennessee Williams's unpublished play *Will Mr. Merriwether Return from Memphis?* Named for one of Key West's most illustrious writers, this 478-seat, air-conditioned theater features a thrust stage extending 8 feet in front of the curtain line, a fly system, and a state-of-the-art lighting and sound system.

The Tennessee Williams Fine Arts Center produces a full season of dance, theater, chamber music, and shows by nationally known performing artists. It is also home to the Key West Symphony Orchestra (see separate listing later in this chapter). In-house productions involve amateur actors from the community and feature students working toward associate of science degrees in acting and theater production. Professional touring companies bring a wave of nationally and internationally recognized artists to the Florida Keys. The St. Petersburg Ballet of Russia has appeared here, as have the Irish Rovers and singer Cleo Laine with Johnny Dankworth. Chamber music concerts are sprinkled throughout the copious performance calendar of the Tennessee Williams Fine Arts Center, which runs from late November through April.

Most of the productions are held in the evening, but some events offer matinees on weekends as well. The Florida Keys Community College Chorus, which is coed, performs here three times each year, including early December and mid-to late March. (The chorus also offers a concert under the stars at Fort Zachary Taylor Historical Site in April.)

For listings of current shows in Key West, visit www.keystix.com or call (305) 295-7676. You can also purchase tickets via this service, which is sponsored by the Founders Society and Presenters of the Performing Arts for Key West.

Waterfront Playhouse
Mallory Square, Key West
(305) 294-5015
www.waterfrontplayhouse.com
Community theater at its finest shines from an unlikely thespian arena on the waterfront. Once the site of Porter's warehouse, the physical structure served as an icehouse in the 1880s, storing blocks of ice cut from New England ponds and brought to Key West as ships' ballast. The Waterfront Playhouse restored the old warehouse into the present theater, infusing the crumbly stone walls with enduring creativity and talent.

The Waterfront Playhouse, dedicated to expanding knowledge of dramatic works to the general public, presents a variety of musicals, comedies, dramas, and mysteries each season. Past productions have included *Misery, The Sunshine Boys, Six Degrees of Separation*, and Terrence McNally's *Lips Together, Teeth Apart*. The community thespians also offer a children's theater workshop in the summer and other participatory theater experiences to Key West schoolchildren throughout the year.

The performance season is from November through April.

Cinema

Tropic Cinema
416 Eaton Street, Key West
(305) 294-5857
www.tropiccinema.com
Until 1998 there was no creative film representation in the Keys. In that year the Key West Film Society formed to bring the area the best of independent, foreign, and alternative movies. Since then Tropic Cinema has shown over 150 films. Highlights have included the Cuban musical *Buena Vista Social Club,* Pedro Almodovar's Oscar-winning *All About My Mother,* and

for the avant-garde, *The Celebration*—an ultimate in contrast: no lighting, no music, and shot on video. The purpose of the Key West Film Society and Tropic Cinema is to showcase film in Key West and be a magnet for this cutting-edge art.

MUSIC

Island Opera Theatre
Various Florida Keys locations
(305) 294-0404
www.islandopera.com

Island Opera Theatre provides affordable opera and musical theater for residents and visitors. This polished company provides training for talented students and performance opportunities for local musicians and technical personnel. Island Opera Theatre performs throughout the Florida Keys to rave reviews. Their repertoire runs the gamut from serious to comedic opera and from dinner theater to musicals. Come and enjoy the wonderful world of opera in a tropical atmosphere.

Key West Symphony Orchestra
1119 Varela Street, Key West
(305) 292-1774
www.keywestsymphony.com

On a laid-back island like Key West, where Duval Street rocks until 4:00 A.M. with the beat of calypso and soca, blues and Buffett wannabes, you might not expect to find many hard-core classical music fans. But they are here, all right. And in enough numbers, it seems, to support a symphony orchestra.

Thanks to the enthusiasm, not to mention the untiring fund-raising efforts, of a small but dedicated corps of classical music fans, the Key West Symphony Orchestra made its debut in fall 1998. Under the musical direction of native Key Wester Sebrina Maria Alfonso, the orchestra plays to standing room only at the Tennessee Williams Fine Arts Center on three weekends between November and April. The critically acclaimed symphony consists of more than 40 classical musicians, many from major metropolitan symphonies throughout the United States, who come together to perform under the baton of conductor Alfonso. In addition to a regular concert series, selected members of the orchestra also participate in community outreach programs, taking their music directly into the Monroe County schools and participating in question-and-answer sessions at a variety of fund-raising events.

Performances by the Key West Symphony Orchestra take place on consecutive Friday and Saturday evenings in November, February, and April at the Tennessee Williams Fine Arts Center on the campus of Florida Keys Community College. Tickets may be purchased at the TWFAC box office.

The Middle Keys Concert Association, Inc.

Every year since 1969, the Middle Keys Concert Association has brought live concert artists to the Florida Keys for the cultural enrichment of our residents and visitors. Four to six concerts are held annually at Marathon venues, quite often San Pablo Catholic Church (MM 53.5 Oceanside). A well-balanced season of offerings includes classical and semi-classical music, encompassing voice, strings, brass, and organ.

You may purchase a subscription to all concerts or buy tickets at the door. Children are admitted for free. Pick up a current brochure at the Marathon Chamber of Commerce, MM 53.5 Bayside, (305) 743-5417 or (800) 262-7284.

ART GALLERIES

Unique galleries dot the Florida Keys, often tucked amid commercial shops in a strip mall or gracing a freestanding building off the beaten track. In Key West galleries abound along Duval Street, and you'll also find small lofts and garrets secreted off the beaten track down narrow lanes. Come along for a gallery crawl through the high spots of the Florida

Keys' art scene, from Key Largo to Key West. The Florida Keys section is organized by descending mile marker. Listings are alphabetical in the Key West section.

Consult www.keysarts.com/culture/galleries.cfm for even more information.

The Florida Keys

Bluewater Potters
MM 102.9 Oceanside, Key Largo
(305) 853-0616
www.bluewaterpotters.com

High-fire stoneware and functional pottery set the theme for Bluewater Potters. Husband-and-wife owners Corky and Kim Wagner demonstrate their work right on the premises. The Wagners' inventory includes everything from spoon rests to full dinnerware and architectural pieces. Some work is brought in by outside artists. Among the pieces offered are wine goblets and baking dishes. All glazes are oven, microwave-, and dishwasher-safe. Custom dinnerware is a specialty of the Wagners.

The Gallery at Kona Kai
MM 97.8 Bayside, Key Largo
(305) 852-7200, (800) 365-7829
www.konakairesort.com

The Gallery at Kona Kai secretes away a small yet exquisite changing exhibit of fine art treasures. The gallery showcases prominent South Florida artists such as Clyde Butcher, who is known for his hauntingly surreal black-and-white photography of the Everglades and Big Cypress National Preserve. Also featured is Gregory Sobran, a watercolorist who chronicles quintessential scenes of the Keys in a spectrum of pastel hues.

In 2000 Kona Kai Gallery partnered with a Paris gallery, so they now also represent some fine contemporary French artists whose works in oils and bronze sculptures feature interpretations of flower fields of the French countryside, landscapes of Provence, and depictions of the French people. Italian minimalist Franco Passalaqua and painters Jonny, of Venezuela, and Reuther, of Brazil, have joined the ranks of featured artists. The Gallery at Kona Kai represents these three artists exclusively in America.

Rain Barrel Village of Artists and Craftspeople
MM 86.7 Bayside, Islamorada
(305) 852-3084
www.seefloridaonline.com/rainbarrel

The Rain Barrel Village of Artists and Craftspeople is a garden complex of creativity. The 2,000-square-foot front galley is owned and operated by Carol Cutshall, Rain Barrel's founder and proprietor for more than 20 years. At the entrance to the "village," this mixed-media galley features an array of paintings, sculpture, woodwork, and decorative glass. More than 100 artists from throughout the United States are represented here. You'll find an eclectic assortment of art and craft creations, including whimsical ceramics and an expansive wind chime collection.

Showcased in the Hibiscus Gallery is Haitian and tropical art, featuring sculptures, paintings, and steel cut-outs.

The resident potter at Rain Barrel is Nancy Jefferson of Jefferson Clay Creations. She handcrafts creative vases and dinnerware in the shape of our Keys tropical fish and also works in the medium of raku. Her crystalline-glazed vases are striking. Jefferson Clay Creations also offers classes.

In the Sculpture Gallery you will behold everything from fired copper to sculptures fashioned out of a potpourri of musical instruments. Talent oozes from every corner of the expansive room.

Also with galleries in Rain Barrel are artists Dan Lawler and John David Hawver.

And if you feel like a bite to eat, stop in at The Garden Cafe (see listing in the Seafood Markets and Specialty Foods chapter), which is set in a tropical garden within the hardwood hammock that encompasses the studios of the Rain Barrel Village.

Rain Barrel Village of Artists and Craftspeople is open daily.

The Stacie Krupa Studio Gallery of Art
MM 82.9 Oceanside, Islamorada
(305) 517-2631, (305) 924-0614
www.staciekrupafineart.com
You can watch Stacie Krupa, artist in residence, as she creates her huge, vibrant, mixed-media works on canvas at this contemporary, SoHo-style gallery. A powerful combination of bright colors and massive images, some of which depict Florida Keys birds and fish, Krupa's expressive creations will knock your sandals off.

Redbone Art Gallery
MM 82 Oceanside, 200 Industrial Drive, Islamorada
(305) 664-2002, (877) 534-7423
www.redbone.org/gallery.htm
The Ellis family of Islamorada began this nonprofit organization as a means of raising funds for research for cystic fibrosis, a disease that afflicts their daughter. Each year the Ellises hold a trilogy of celebrity backcountry fishing tournaments in order to raise these funds (see the Tournaments section of the Fishing chapter), and their art gallery defrays the cost of office expenses.

The gallery sports a variety of saltwater and marine art and sculptures from local artists and others noted for their works related to sportfishing, such as Don Ray, Diane Peebles, James Harris, Jeanne Dobie, and C. D. Clarke. Redbone Art Gallery exclusively showcases the original watercolors of Chet Reneson in South Florida.

Bougainvillea House Gallery
MM 53.5 Bayside, Marathon
(305) 743-0808
A varied group of talented Marathon artists showcase their works at the Bougainvillea House Gallery, a charming cooperative gallery. Fronted by an enormous hot pink bougainvillea "tree" that intertwines through the roof of the wooden front porch, Bougainvillea House Gallery features reasonably priced prints, original watercolors, acrylics, mixed media, sculpture, decorative baskets, hand-sculpted glass, jewelry, and ceramics by local artists.

Kennedy Studios
MM 48 Oceanside, Marathon
(305) 743-2040, (877) 539-2787
Kennedy Studios frames the Keys, thanks to the steady, creative hand of owner Diane Busch. Custom framing of any and all objets d'art is the specialty of this studio, which resembles the chain—established by watercolorist Robert and oil painter Michele Kennedy—in name only. Works by both Kennedys are included in the collection here, including limited-edition prints of Pigeon Key, the Seven-Mile Grill, and the Faro Blanco Lighthouse. Also displayed are original works by such local artists as Lynn Voit, Eileen Seitz, Christi Mathews, Millard Wells (A.W.S.), and Susan Thomas.

In addition to custom framing, Kennedy Studios provides creative matting for needle arts and shadow boxes. The studio also does museum and conservation framing.

Artists in Paradise
MM 30.5 Bayside, 221 Key Deer Boulevard, Big Pine Key
(305) 872-1828
www.theartistsinparadise.com
Artists in Paradise is a cooperative gallery in Big Pine run by those artists from the Lower Keys Artists Network who use the gallery to display their work (see the listing in this chapter). More than 30 artists presently show works done in a variety of media: sculpture, oils, watercolors, acrylic, pen and ink, pottery, copper, and stained glass. The gallery is open daily.

Key West

Alan S. Maltz Gallery
1210 Duval Street
(305) 294-0005
www.alanmaltz.com
Using the mystical nature of light, Alan S.

Maltz, a world-renowned fine-art photographer, is an inspiration with his haunting and magical images. When you enter his gallery and view the art on the walls, you feel as though you are not looking at a piece of artwork hanging there but rather upon the actual scene he photographed. His pieces are large and compelling. Alan's framing technique is as unique as his talent because he has the ability to keep his audience involved in the piece as a whole. Mr. Maltz is the author of *Key West Color, Miami; City of Dreams;* and *Florida—Beyond the Blue Horizon.*

A Boy and His Dog Fine Art Gallery
826 Duval Street, Key West
(305) 296-7721
www.aboyandhisdog.net
A Boy and His Dog was established in 2003 by David Todd. His comfortable, relaxed showplace envelopes you in a homey atmosphere where you can enjoy the various works displayed. The gallery features original oils, limited editions, and photorealism of acclaimed artist Thomas Arvid. The gallery also sponsors various events throughout the year where you can meet a featured artist.

The Butterfly Boutique
291 Front Street, Clinton Square Market
(305) 296-2922, (866) 949-0900
www.wingsofimagination.com
Art really does imitate life in the case of this gallery. Raised in butterfly farms and imported from the continents of South America, Africa, and Southeast Asia, the butterflies live out their 10-day life cycle and are then shipped to the Key West production studio, where they are arranged in geometric compositions and preserved in acrylic cases. Don't miss this fruition of Sam Trophia's childhood dream, capturing the everlasting beauty of the "flowers of the sky." And don't miss the Key West Butterfly & Nature Conservatory (see our Attractions chapter).

Florida Keys Community College
5901 West College Road, Stock Island
(305) 296-9081
www.firn.edu/fkcc
Florida Keys Community College stages four art shows a year in the Library Gallery. Invitational shows are held in October and February, and the Florida Artist series is showcased in January and February. Student work is exhibited during the month of April.

The Gallery on Greene
606 Greene Street
(305) 294-1669
www.galleryongreene.com
Think you can't afford fine art? Think again. This gallery prides itself on displaying original art priced for every pocketbook—from $10 to $25,000! Among the offerings here are works by former part-time Key West resident the late Jeff MacNelly (he drew the cartoon strip "Shoe") and Henry La Cagnina, the last survivor of 12 artists brought to Key West in the 1930s by the WPA. This gallery also supports working artists. You can usually expect to find at least one artist in residence, bent over his or her work, in a corner of the gallery.

Gingerbread Square Gallery
1207 Duval Street
(305) 296-8900
www.gingerbreadsquaregallery.com
Billed as Key West's oldest private art gallery, established in 1974, Gingerbread Square Gallery on upper Duval features sculptures, art glass, one-person shows, and ongoing presentations of the highly acclaimed works of Key West's favorite artists. Sal Salinero's oils depict the treasures of the rain forest. John Kiraly's fanciful paintings capture the spirit of locales real and imagined.

Glass Reunions
825 Duval Street
(305) 294-1720

Glass is the business here, and you can get it in almost any form or color imaginable. Lamps, vases, and mirror wall hangings all showcase the talents of the various artists. For the traditionalist, a wide selection of stained-glass art is available.

Guild Hall Gallery
614 Duval Street
(305) 296-6076
More than 20 local artists display their work here, presented in a vast array of media. Most of the pieces focus on island life, with a definite Bahamian and Caribbean influence thrown in. Head upstairs for more unusual, and larger, works of art. This is Key West's original artists' co-op.

Haitian Art Company
600 Frances Street
(305) 296-8932
www.haitian-art-co.com
Bold, wild colors and primitive designs mark the artistic offerings of Haiti, displayed in the multiple rooms of Haitian Art Company. The intricate paisley-style designs often weave an image of a serpent or wild animal within the overall picture. The work of Haiti is a study of form and color not readily encountered in this country. All pieces are originals. This gallery is tucked into a residential neighborhood at the corner of Frances and Southard Streets, way off Duval, but it's definitely worth the walk.

Hands On
1206 Duval Street
(305) 296-7399
www.handsongallery.com
The loom in the front of this attractive shop says it all. Here you will find the ever-changing, always exquisite creations of owner Ellen Steiniger. Her handwoven scarves, jackets, and shawls are as beautiful to see as they are enjoyable to wear. Shop here, too, for handcrafted earrings, bracelets, and beads to accessorize your

---

Here in the Keys we have wonderful county libraries that offer a wealth of reading material. They also have fabulous programs for all family members. Check the Web site at www.keyslibraries.org for a list of events.

---

wearable art as well as an array of other fine American-made crafts.

Harrison Gallery
825 White Street
(305) 294-0609
www.harrison-gallery.com
Sculptor Helen Harrison and her husband Ben, a musician and author, have operated this charming gallery since 1986. In addition to Helen's own work, ever-changing exhibitions highlight local artists. Open daily, but please ring the bell.

Island Arts
1128 Duval Street
(305) 292-9909
www.island-arts.com
This co-op of local artists fashions itself after a Caribbean bazaar, and many of the items herein illuminate just how fertile the imagination can be. Welded sculptures created out of scrap iron, metal junk, old screws, and tools turn up as a rooster, ostrich, duck, or dinosaur. Paper Smash is sculpted recycled paper made into snakes, pelicans, fish, and manatees. You'll also find a potpourri of handpainted tiles, stained-glass pieces, and ceramics, all with an island theme.

Island Needle Point
527 Fleming Street
(305) 296-6091
www.islandpoint.com
Julie Pischke is one of a handful of needlepoint designers who specialize in tropical designs. Her award-winning creations draw from the colors and textures of her home in the Florida Keys. She

offers her art on pillows, bags, belts, shoes, rugs, and footstools. Julie's bold, bright, colorful, and eclectic motifs befit their inspiration. Long after your trip has ended, a bright, handmade memento reminds you of your hot days in the sun and your cool tropical nights in Paradise.

Joy Gallery
1124-B Duval Street
(305) 296-3039

A little sign that hangs amid the surreal paintings of out-of-body experiences by Lucie Bilodeau in the Joy Gallery reads: WARNING—THE PURCHASE OF FINE ART IS NOT NECESSARILY A LOGICAL DECISION. Bilodeau's brooding pieces are joined by limited editions by Irma Quigley and Gretchen Williams. A must see is the rooster art by Thomas Easley.

Kate's Gallery
930 Eaton Street
(305) 294-8451
www.katesgallery.com

"Art that is fun and art off the beaten path." Gallery owner Kate Peachy lives this verve. Inside this playful studio you'll find paintings, sculpture, furniture, and pottery. Looking around you'll see a fisherman painted on a piece of driftwood, a young Picasso illustrated on a four-string guitar, a 3-foot fountain crafted from chrome bumpers and artistically shaped into a dolphin, and a 3-foot sculpture made from cigarette packs. This shop gives new meaning to whimsical and fanciful.

Key West Light Gallery
534 Fleming Street
(305) 294-0566
www.kwlightgallery.com

The size of the gallery is small in comparison to the multiple offerings inside. Sharon Wells's Key West Light Gallery features exhibits of photography and original paintings, including luminous watercolors. Some pieces are so full of light you think there is special lighting behind the art. There's no limit to Sharon's talent or her themes: Key West, Cuba, architecture, cemeteries, Mexico, flowers, and more. This is a not-to-be-missed shop if you love electrifying art.

Lucky Street Gallery
1120 White Street
(305) 294-3973

Contemporary fine art of the cutting-edge variety is the focus here. Sculptures by John Martini and the works of artists Roberta Marks, Susan Rodgers, Lincoln Perry, and others are featured. New shows are staged approximately every two weeks.

Marine Wildlife Gallery
291 Front Street
(305) 296-4259, (800) 447-6999
www.marinewildlifegallery.com

Marine Wildlife Gallery focuses on the art of Guy Harvey, renowned Keys artist-angler. Always obsessed with the sea and the creatures dwelling within, Harvey taught college biology for years before becoming a full-time marine wildlife artist in 1988. In addition to original works of art, the gallery sells wearable art that features imprints of his famous paintings. Watch your back . . . or that of the next guy going down the street. Harvey's paintings are showcased on the back of many a T-shirted visitor to the Florida Keys.

Mary O'Shea's Glass Garden
213 Simonton Street
(305) 293-8822

The ancient Egyptians get credit for discovering glass fusion 5,000 years ago, but Mary O'Shea is the artist who brought it to Key West. Her gallery, opened in 1999, features a profusion of original and colorful sculpture, masks, bowls, plates, and jewelry—all made from fused glass and each taking three days to complete.

Each piece of glass must be cut and layered to form a double thickness, then melted in a kiln. The piece is then cooled for a day, melted again, transposed, and formed into the desired shape. The resulting pieces are not only beautiful but also durable, and dishwasher- and microwave-safe. Don't be afraid to touch and don't hesitate to ask Mary about custom designs.

Night on White
Various art shops on White Street
(305) 294-3973
The monthly Night on White walk takes place in one of the art districts of Key West. This three-hour stroll in and out of various art galleries lets you see the best of their offerings. The Lucky Street Gallery, White Street Healing Arts, Harrison Gallery, and The Wave Gallery are the evening's hosts.

Stone Soup
519 Fleming Street
(305) 296-2080
Facing busy Eaton Street is a quaint building housing a charming gallery and framing studio. Inside you will find paintings, sculpture, and a delightful shop owner, who shared the story of naming her establishment. Stone Soup comes from a children's book in which the soup begins with water and stones. Soon, village folks come by to add their offerings, and eventually the soup becomes so delicious that everyone starts coming by to taste the alluring concoction. Stone Soup Gallery and Framing Studio is as tantalizing as the storybook soup.

The Wave Gallery
1100 White Street
(305) 293-9428
www.thewavegallery.com
Barbara Grob is the owner of this way, way off-Duval Street gallery. You may not recognize her name, but chances are you've seen her work around town—the steel gecko sculptures for which she is justly famous. She opened this tiny shop in April 2000 to display her own work as well as that of about a dozen other artists.

Wild Side Gallery
291 Front Street, Clinton Square Market
(305) 296-7800
From carved wood walking sticks to ceramics, jewelry, and watercolors, all objets d'art in this interesting and affordable gallery depict some element of nature. Artists and craftspeople represented here are from throughout the United States.

Paintings created by inmates of the Monroe County Detention Center who participate in the Art Behind Bars program are displayed in galleries all around Key West. A share of the proceeds is pumped back into the program to purchase supplies. The rest goes directly to charity. The inmates realize no direct profit from the sale of their work.

Wyland Galleries
102 Duval Street
(305) 294-5240, (888) 294-5240

719 Duval Street
(305) 292-4998, (888) 292-4998
www.wyland.com
The first East Coast display venues of Wyland, the world's leading marine-life artist, these two Key West galleries display a wide range of the environmental artist's work. His world-renowned, life-sized whaling wall murals, one of which adorns the Kmart building in Marathon and another the Waterfront Market building at the Key West Historic Seaport, reflect Wyland's unshakable commitment to saving the earth's oceans and thereby its marine creatures. Also displayed are several paintings from the "above and below" series, for which Wyland collaborated with other talented artists to create a scene looking beneath and above the sea concurrently.

SHOPPING

Stretched along our 100 miles of Overseas Highway is every diversion imaginable for the serious (and not-so-serious) shopper. Scuba aficionados find nirvana here, reveling in state-of-the-gear offerings from our plethora of dive shops (see the Diving and Snorkeling chapter). Anglers, who may readily concede that you might be able to be too thin or too rich, staunchly maintain that you can never have too many fishing rods or an excess of tackle (see the Fishing chapter). And boaters, who all know that a vessel is really a floating hole into which you pour money, find a virtual smorgasbord of shopping options guaranteed to fertilize their needs exponentially (see the Boating chapter).

But what about the rest of us, free spirits who like to see the ocean through the rim of a glass, preferably while lying prone by the swimming pool in the shade of a coconut palm? We know we don't require much in the way of clothing here in the Keys' tropicality, just a suit (small and stringy), shoes (light and strappy), and a hat (woven and floppy), but we have pent-up shopping desires, too.

So here is the ultimate road map to the shops. We describe our favorite shops in geographic order by mile marker, from Key Largo to Key West. Our Key West section is divided into four sections. Best of Duval is organized by numerical address, from upper Duval (oceanside) to lower Duval (gulfside), so you can stroll the street and take in all the shops. Off Duval, the not-to-be missed shops on surrounding streets, is organized in alphabetical order. Lastly, we give you information on noteworthy shops Way Off Duval and in New Town. Be sure to scope out the Arts and Culture chapter for descriptions of galleries selling creative works, many by local artists. And turn to our Seafood Markets and Specialty Foods chapter to find piscatory treasures and other palate pleasers.

Many of our shops are open daily, especially in Key West, but many close on Sunday. Some close on alternate days. We will alert you to unusual hours a shop might have. But in all cases, it is best if you call before venturing out, as hours and days of operation can vary season to season.

UPPER KEYS

Island Smoke Shop
MM 103.5 Bayside, Pink Plaza, Key Largo
(305) 453-4014, (800) 680-9701
www.islandsmokeshop.com

The Island Smoke Shop offers a full line of cigars, lighters, and accessories and has one of the largest selections of pipes in South Florida as well as some wonderful house blends of tobacco. The shop also exclusively sells El Originale cigars, voted best in the United States by both *Smoke* and *Cigar Aficionado* magazines. On Saturday, Island Smoke Shop has live cigar-rolling demonstrations; the rollers come down from Miami. You can order by mail here.

The White Rhino
MM 103.2 Bayside, Key Largo
(305) 453-0065

No white elephants here! You can go "ape" because this consignment shop offers everything you'll need to "feather your nest." The shop carries a wide range of household items ranging from knick-knacks and accessories to furniture, all from someone else's "den." It's a jungle out there in the world of retail, so it's fun to check out the Rhino's catch!

Largo Cargo
MM 103.1 Oceanside, Key Largo
(305) 451-4242

The can't-miss landmark for Cargo Largo is a large cannon pointing at US 1 with "magic" smoke being propelled from the barrel. Inside this bright blue dwelling is some pretty cool stuff for your souvenir collection. They have: pirate flags and windsocks with skulls and crossbones; key lime products of juice, oils, jellies, chutneys, and BBQ sauces for culinary buffs; tropical apparel with the big favorite—men's' khaki beer-can shorts (need I say more?); nautical jewelry handcrafted from silver and sea glass; metal sculptures of fun "Pelican Pete" for your yard; and the all-time favorite, a message in a bottle—perfect to mail home (in a small box) in lieu of a postcard.

WS Kitchen Store
MM 103 Bayside, Pink Plaza Shopping Center, Key Largo
(305) 453-4890

WS Kitchen Store has small floor space but packs an array in inventory. Cuisinart, Waring, Kitchen Aid, and J. A. Henckels are just a few of the names in stock. Great quality and selection for your own home or for gift-giving. Only small appliances, accessories, and professional cookware in stock, with a knowledgeable, Keys-friendly owner.

Moore Books
MM 103 Bayside, Pink Plaza Shopping Center, Key Largo
(305) 451-1468

If reading rates a spot in your Florida Keys vacation Moore Books packs a multitude of best sellers, popular paperbacks, children's books, and specialty publications into a compact space. The shop, with friendly and helpful personnel, also carries used books at great prices.

Sandal Factory Outlet
MM 102.4 Oceanside, Key Largo
(305) 453-9644, (800) 736-5397
MM 82 Oceanside, Islamorada
(305) 664-9700

These sandal outlets allow you to fit yourself. Pick from a copious sea of ladies' sandals—strappy, sport, and utilitarian. Men and children can be accommodated here, too. You won't find every style in every size, but you can choose from hundreds of designs.

Florida Keys Gift Company
MM 102 Oceanside, Key Largo
(305) 453-4700

This bright, entertaining gift shop is loaded with a wide array of Florida Keys treasures. Dazzling glass jewelry; men's, women's, and children's island wear; hats; postcards; and T-shirts for the whole family (one comes with markers so the kids can color in a pre-printed pattern). Cute, unusual gifts with a friendly staff to make stopping here a pleasure.

World Watersports
MM 100 Oceanside, Key Largo
(305) 451-0118, (800) 243-8938

535 Greene Street, Key West
(305) 293-5122, (800) 243-8938
www.worldwatersports.com

A grand water-sports emporium, World Watersports offers everything from men's, women's, and children's clothing—swimsuits, strappy dresses, shorts, shirts, and shoes—to dive gear, kayaks, boat towables, surfboards, wakeboards, snorkeling and scuba gear, underwater photography equipment, and videos and books about the fascinating undersea world. As their business card boasts, this is the place to come for "everything you need to get wet!"

Captain's Imports
MM 99 Bayside, Key Largo
(305) 453-1800
www.captainsimports.com

There is no need for neon signs to alert you to Captain's Imports, especially at night. In front of this shop are pulsating, colorful, 24-foot palm trees! The first time you see these delightful symbols of tropical living come to life in orange, purple, red, and blue, you promise yourself you will not party so hard any more! Inside the store is equally a Technicolor joy. You'll find steel drum art and wall art featuring fish, iguanas, and seahorses. Captain's Imports also carries Talavera pottery, the beautiful art form originating in 16th-century Moorish Spain and now made in Mexico. There is one fish pattern named "Key West." This is not a store you'll find on Main Street back home.

Anthony's Women's Apparel
MM 98.5, in the median, Key Largo
(305) 852-4515

MM 50 Bayside, Gulfside Village, Marathon
(305) 743-5855
At Anthony's you can expect to find a constantly changing array of reasonably priced, casual attire in petite, junior, and misses sizes, by such manufacturers as Liz Sport and Alfred Dunner, Koret, and Lisa Int'l. The shops offer a wide variety of swimsuits and cover-ups. Anthony's sales are not to be missed.

Pink Junktique
MM 98 Oceanside, Key Largo
(305) 853-2620
You can't miss this unusual building going north on U.S. Highway 1. It is hot pink with giant flamingos out front. Inside is an inviting, nostalgic collection of vintage clothing, housewares, bedding, jewelry, and collectibles. The inventory changes constantly, so it is a great place to browse and recall those "happy days" of whatever era you remember.

Shell World
MM 97.5, Key Largo
(305) 852-8245
At Shell World, you'll think you've been beached with every type of shell in existence. Yes, they have your typical clam, oyster, and mussel shells, but they also carry a tremendous variety of other shells from throughout the world. In the aisles throughout the store are conch, abalone, cone, and nautilus, as well as wind chimes, jewelry, and flowers made from various shells. This is a great place for kids to see what nature develops under the oceans.

Key Lime Products and Tropical Gifts
MM 95 Oceanside, Key Largo
(305) 853-0378, (800) 870-1780

MM 82 Oceanside, Islamorada
(305) 517-4090, (800) 870-1780
www.keylimeproducts.com
From tangy edibles and thirst-quenching beverages, to soothing lotions and luscious bath products, Key Lime Products and Tropical Gifts offers a cornucopia of Florida Keys products at its two locations in the Upper Keys. Here at Key Lime Products you can even purchase lawn and patio ornaments as well as a Tiki Hut for your yard! Have no fear about getting this stuff home: They ship worldwide.

Island Hammocks
MM 89.2 Bayside, Tavernier
(305) 852-9222, (888) 252-5299
www.islandhammocks.net
You can really lie around in style, lazin' in the Florida Keys' sun, if you pick up a hammock from this colorful store. Chockablock with try-'em-out samples of styles by Hatteras Hammocks, Nicamaka, Pawleys Island, and more. Island Hammocks also stocks frames, ropes, fasteners, and hammock accessories.

Gerry Droney Tropical Gardens
MM 88.7 Bayside, Tavernier
(305) 852-4715
A riot of orchids, bromeliads, anthuriums, gingers, and other exotic tropical plants greets you as you wander through Gerry Droney's Tropical Gardens. This is tropical browsing at its finest. You'll find pots galore of every shape, size, and color as well as a full line of insecticides, fertilizers, and soil additives. Even if you eventually have to hop a plane for home, stop in here to see how Paradise blooms.

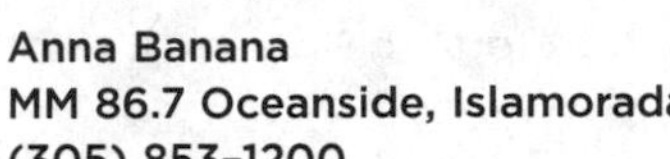

Anna Banana
MM 86.7 Oceanside, Islamorada
(305) 853-1200
Anna Banana offers draped Moroccan cottons and elegantly long casual linen dresses amid their tropical ladies' fashions. Plus sizes are available here. Look for funky costume jewelry to finish off your ensemble. Anna Banana also offers a good selection of the Harmony Kingdom collectibles.

Rain Barrel Village of Artists and Craftspeople
MM 86.7 Bayside, Islamorada
(305) 852-3084
www.seefloridaonline.com/rainbarrel
A lush, tropical hideaway greets you in this artisan village as artists and crafters work in retail shops that are peppered beneath the gumbo-limbos and amid the bougainvillea. Refer to the Arts and Culture chapter for a rundown of the galleries and studios at the Rain Barrel.

Expressions Swim N' Sun Wear, Inc.
MM 86.7 Oceanside, Islamorada
(305) 852-1155
Ladies, tropicalize your wardrobe at Expressions, which offers the wonderful Caribbean prints by Jams in a variety of comfortable styles. You'll find swimsuits and floppy hats as well as cover-ups—everything you need for a sojourn, Keys style. Men can dress down as well, finding their favorite tropical brands here.

Latitude 25
MM 82.7 Bayside, Islamorada
(305) 664-4421, (866) 664-4421
A step inside this low-lighted, paneled emporium evokes a big-game feeling. Massive mounted tarpon, blue marlin, swordfish, and jewfish adorn the walls. Latitude 25 offers upscale, popular brands of men's and women's sport togs, such as Tommy Bahama, Body Glove, and Sportif, as well as accessories and gift items. The simple, sophisticated ladies' sundresses, tops, and shorts are made of exquisitely soft cottons in muted wear-anywhere colors. You'll also find a small children's department.

All the treasures of the Keys are not in the watery deep. Three of our favorite flea markets, which are open Saturday and Sunday, are Key Largo Storage/Flea Market, MM 103.5 Bayside, Key Largo; Grassy Key Flea Market, MM 60 Oceanside, Grassy Key; and Big Pine Flea Market, MM 30 Oceanside, Big Pine Key.

Hooked on Books
MM 82.6 Oceanside, Islamorada
(305) 517-2602
Hooked on Books is filled to the rafters with used books and paperbacks. You can trade in your used paperback books two-for-one. For every two paperbacks you bring in, you can take one used paperback with you. Or for the hardback books, bring the book in for a 25 percent credit based on the publisher's price. (If the hardcover book has been printed in paperback, you will receive only a $1.00 credit.) Accumulate credits to buy other used hardcover books. This is a great deal for avid readers and book collectors.

Down to Earth
MM 82.5 Oceanside, Islamorada
(305) 664-9828
Poke around in this cute little shop on a rainy, or even sunny, day. Down to Earth stocks an eclectic selection of decorative items for the home as well as some neat gift items, such as coconut candles. You'll also find a good selection of aromatherapy items. A selection of children's clothes is also offered.

Garden of Eden
MM 82.3 Oceanside, Islamorada
(305) 664-5558
Have you noticed those manatee mail-

boxes along the Overseas Highway? Well, this is the place to find them. Garden of Eden is filled with silk flowers and arrangements, including orchids, bromeliads, and many other faux tropicals. Look for the hand-carved bottle stoppers; the caricatures are a riot and sure to remind you of someone back home.

Island Silver & Spice
MM 82 Oceanside, Islamorada
(305) 664-2715, (305) 664-2714
Billed as the Keys' department store, Island Silver & Spice offers a quality sampling of many things. The men's department is tucked away in the rear of the store, allowing the much larger ladies' section to predominate. Dressing rooms, looking like tiny pastel conch houses, are sprinkled throughout the store. Fine jewelry is offered as well as a limited selection of shoes, children's clothing, books, and games. The peach-and-green building also houses an eclectic assortment of gourmet kitchen items, bath and household accessories, and an upstairs bargain corner.

Ichthyophile
MM 82 Bayside, Islamorada
(305) 664-8960
This unique shop with an even more unique name is sure to hook your attention. Ichthyophile (one who enjoys and studies fish) is lovingly stocked with rare, historic prints of sea life that have been preserved from books that are up to 200 years old. The owner was a backcountry guide for 13 years and his interest led him to open this entertaining and interesting shop. Look for the Kids' Corner, with toys and books with a water/fish subject; it's a great way to interest kids in becoming anglers.

Angelika
MM 81.9 Oceanside, Islamorada
(305) 664-9008
Upmarket ladies' fashions with an old-fashioned twist, natural fabrics, and whimsical designs mark the merchandise at Angelika's. Look for Angelika's great hats and handbags.

Blue Marlin Jewelry
MM 81.9 Oceanside, Islamorada
(305) 664-8004, (888) 826-4424
www.bluemarlinjewelry.com
Discover gold in this interesting jewelry shop. Blue Marlin sports a great selection of gold charms, depicting most of the species of our ecosystem. Especially striking are the black coral fish. Many pieces are also offered in sterling silver.

Sunny Exposures
MM 81.9 Bayside, Islamorada
(305) 664-8445, (800) 725-0801
See suits, suits, and more suits here—for surf and sun, not the office. Ladies' swimsuits of every style and description, for every imaginable body type, join ranks with cover-ups, lotions, and sunglasses. Sunny Exposures even carries some men's and kids' suits.

World Wide Sportsman Inc.
MM 81.5 Bayside, Islamorada
(305) 664-4615, (800) 327-2880
www.worldwidesportsman.com
Don't miss a stop at World Wide Sportsman, the massive fishing emporium that is an Islamorada must-see. Housed in a former in-and-out storage building renovated with an old-fashioned, exposed-brick exterior and surrounded by native trees and shrubs, World Wide showcases the exact replica of Hemingway's 42-foot ship, the *Pilar.* Visitors can climb aboard and examine Hemingway's chair and even his typewriter. Rumor has it that he wrote at least one novel while fishing on the *Pilar.* A 6,000-gallon saltwater aquarium presents the creatures of our reef, including baby tarpon, bonefish, and redfish. A small art gallery upstairs features works of local artists.

Memorabilia aside, World Wide is stocked to the rafters with a wide assortment of fishing tackle (see the Outfitters section in the Fishing chapter), and a full line of men's and women's technical clothing is offered, including Ex Officio, Woolrich, Sportif, Columbia, and much more.

If your stamina runs out before your money does, sit a spell in one of the rocking chairs lining the back porch and watch the action on the Gulf of Mexico. Or pop up to the Zane Grey Bar; sink into a leather chair; look at the vintage fishing photos of Grey and his cronies; and sip a tall, cool one. Even if you don't like to fish, World Wide Sportsman is one place you won't want to pass by.

Eye Candy Boutique
MM 80 Oceanside, Islamorada
(305) 664-3100, (888) 868-6079
Fun with lots of genre is what Eye Candy Boutique offers you. This destination shop sells Free People, Yellow Box shoes, Paul Frank Women, Steve Madden, and more. The shop is decorated with lots of flair and personality.

MIDDLE KEYS

Bayshore Clothing and Small World
MM 52 Oceanside, Marathon
(305) 743-8430
www.bayshoreclothing.com
Bayshore caters to men's and women's tropical garment needs, a guaranteed attitude adjustment from the busy workaday world up north. The little people's shop beckons parents and especially grandparents with a cute selection of swimsuits, warm-weather togs, and toys.

Key Bana Resort Apparel
MM 53.5 Oceanside, Key Colony Beach Causeway, Key Colony Beach
(305) 289-1161
www.keybana.com
Ladies, you are sure to find a new swimsuit or tropical cotton item here that you can't pass up. And Key Bana has a roomful of shorts and shirts for men, too. Check out the solar tan-through bathing suits or the beer-can shorts.

Equipment Locker Sport & Bicycle
MM 53 Bayside, Marathon
(305) 289-1670
You'll find a great selection of bicycles and related biking gear here as well as exercise equipment and the gamut of necessities for every sport, from hoops to weight lifting to in-line skating. Top-brand athletic shoes line the walls.

D'Asign Source
MM 52.7 Bayside, Marathon
(305) 743-7130
www.dasignsource.com
This wonderful home furnishing and design center oozes class. You'll find the very latest and very best in materials, fixtures, finishes, and designs for home remodeling, building, and furnishing. Even if you aren't in the market for a home makeover, make your way to D'Asign Source's megastore, with home ideas for both indoors and out. Browsing the 25,000-square-foot showroom is an inspiration.

Wicker Web
MM 52 Oceanside, Marathon
(305) 743-3696
Across from the Marathon Airport runway, in the Southwind Building, you'll discover the Wicker Web, three showrooms chock-full of tropically inspired items for every room in your house. You'll find a wide selection of baskets, wall hangings, wicker items, lamps, plasticware, and bath accessories.

Marooned in Marathon
MM 51 Oceanside, Marathon
(305) 743-3809
Maroon (muh*roon) v.—to cast ashore, jettison. Definitely cast yourself ashore and hurry into this charming shop so you can be marooned in Marathon too! This is a fun gift shop for the young and young at heart. As they say to their customers, "everything you want, some things you need, and many things you can't live without when you're not marooned on this tiny tropical island." They offer T-shirts, kid

stuff, Atocha jewelry, Beach Bum novelties, and other things you can't live without!

Food for Thought
MM 50.5 Bayside, Gulfside Village, Marathon
(305) 743-3297, (800) 338-9495
Food for Thought is really two shops in one: half books and magazines, half health foods (see the Seafood Markets and Specialty Foods chapter). You can fuel your mind and your body at the same time. Custom orders are the norm here.

The Port Hole
MM 50.5 Bayside, Gulfside Village, Marathon
(305) 743-3552
Don't miss the Port Hole, an upmarket ladies' clothing boutique guaranteed to pry open your pocketbook. Jean and her crew keep even more temptations in the back room, so be sure to clue them in to your tastes, and they'll dress you in style. This is one of the few shops around where the clerks pamper you with service while you're in the dressing room, exchanging sizes and styles, replacing the clothes on the hangers, and suggesting smart accessories.

Goofy Gecko and Crazy Larry's Last Store
MM 50.3 Oceanside, in the Publix Shopping Center, Marathon
(305) 289-4228
This combo store, actually two stores in one rambling space, stocks unique tropical "stuff." The store meanders from room to room, chockablock with palmy treasures—furniture, rugs, pillows, items for entertaining, soaps and lotions, garden items, even swishy, Keysy clothes. You'll have a ball just looking around here, even if tropical isn't your decorating motif up north.

Keyker's Boutique & Gallery
MM 50.3 Oceanside, 67 53rd Street, Marathon
(305) 743-0107
Keyker and other local clothing designers create custom island clothing for women and children, unusual yet flattering styles using exquisitely fine cottons. You'll find them displayed at this cooperative establishment, along with interesting jewelry, accessories, craft items, and paintings.

Lazy Lizard
MM 50.3 Bayside in the Publix Shopping Center, Marathon
(305) 743-5001
Full of cool cottons, fun aprons, Keys jewelry, stationery, cards, and glassware, Lazy Lizard is a shop for all occasions. This is the place to find a campy touch of the Keys for your memory box.

Patio & Home Furniture Galleries
Original Furniture Art Gallery
MM 50 Oceanside, Marathon
(305) 743-2740

Tropical Furniture Gallery
MM 49.5 Oceanside, Marathon
(305) 289-2038

Casual Furniture Gallery
MM 48.5 Bayside, Marathon
(305) 743-2776
Sometimes we stroll through the enormous Furniture Art Gallery just to see what wild new things they've added to the collection. Besides offering the most complete selection of quality furniture in the Keys—such as Lexington, Tommy Bahama, Natuzzi Leather, and Cabana Joe—the Furniture Art Gallery peppers the showroom with accessories that range from the sublime to the outrageous. Tropical Furniture Gallery sells upmarket bamboo, wicker, and rattan furniture. The Casual Furniture Gallery is the place to go for Lloyd Flanders, Tropitone, and other outdoor patio and deck furniture. You'll find a way-out selection of only-in-the-Keys accessories here, too.

Marathon Discount Books
MM 48.2 Oceanside, Marathon
(305) 289-2066

Marathon Discount Books offers all books at 10 to 90 percent off retail prices. Selling primarily publishers' overstock, the store also offers best sellers, local-interest books, and books on tape. The staff also will place special orders. Open daily.

Golden Nugget
MM 48 Bayside, Faro Blanco Resort, Marathon
(305) 743-3059
This "gem" of a jewelry store is nestled on the grounds of the Faro Blanco Marine Resort in a floating houseboat. Golden Nugget has been here since 1971 and is the premier Rolex jeweler of the Florida Keys. Visit to discover their dazzling array of nautical-themed pieces, gold, diamonds, and more, but wear your sunglasses inside. This mother lode of glitter will take your breath away.

Pigeon Key Foundation Gift Shop
MM 47 Oceanside, Pigeon Key Visitors Center, Marathon
(305) 289-0025
Look for the old railway car, still sitting on the tracks of Flagler's Railroad at MM 47 Oceanside. Hidden unassumingly inside resides the Pigeon Key Visitor Center Gift Shop, a potpourri of Keys memorabilia and gift items. The gift shop, like everything on Pigeon Key, is run by a contingent of loyal volunteers, and all proceeds go to the Pigeon Key Foundation.

LOWER KEYS

Tiki Living Hammocks and Gifts
MM 30 Oceanside, Big Pine Key
(305) 872-2502
www.tikiliving.com
What was a weekend business at the local Big Pine Flea Market has turned into a full time business with a lovely store filled with hammocks, hanging chairs, art, and giftware from around the world. Tiki Living Hammocks and Gifts stocks the top makers of hammocks, from Pawleys Island to Hatteras Hammocks. The fun part about shopping here is that you can sit in the store's swing and relax for awhile, in addition to checking out their appealing products. Truly tropical shopping!

Not enough space in your luggage for your shopping purchases? Several mail shops in the Keys will ship your treasures home. Visit The UPS Store in Key Largo (305-453-4877), in Marathon (305-743-2005), or in Key West (305-292-4177); The Package Solution in Key Largo (305-451-5461); or The Mail Spot in Key West (305-296-5333).

The Crystal Loft
MM 29 Oceanside, Big Pine
(305) 872-9390
This is a fun shop to browse and get a hands-on feel of crystals, minerals, and gemstones. The staff is very knowledgeable, and you can spend loads of time just examining the various intriguing minerals from our earth. The Crystal Loft also sells beautiful jewelry made from items available in the shop.

Little Palm Island Gift Shop
MM 28.5 Oceanside, Little Torch Key
(305) 872-2524, (800) 343-8568
www.littlepalmisland.com
Stop at this mainland substation of Little Palm Island and visit the gift shop. You'll find interesting glassware, sculptures, and handpainted plates, in addition to upscale clothing and straw hats. If you go out to Little Palm Island itself, for lunch or dinner or to stay the night, don't miss the island shop. The tropical ambience will tempt you to discard your shorts and don an island caftan.

KEY WEST

For shoppers, Key West lives up to its reputation as Paradise. Colorful, funky, one-of-a-kind shops abound on our fair island. To aid your search-and-purchase mission, we have taken the best of Key West—a little of this, a little of that—and presented it in a simple

By Key West city ordinance, all T-shirt shops are required to post a list of prices inside the store. Be sure to confirm the total price before consenting to a purchase. If you feel you have been overcharged by any store, call Key West Code Enforcement at (305) 292-8191.

format. Our shop-till-you-drop tour of Key West begins on Duval Street with the Best of Duval section. Other little treasures are tucked in and about the narrow, quiet streets of Old Town, and although sometimes tough to find, they are definitely worth the search. We've categorized them as Off Duval. And finally, we lead you to Way Off Duval, for some interesting offerings, with a mention of New Town, where you'll find the major retail chains, which stock all the basics for living in Paradise.

The Best of Duval is arranged by numerical address order, from the Atlantic to the Gulf. Off Duval is organized alphabetically. If your tastes lean more toward original artwork and handcrafted jewelry, be sure to check the Art Galleries section of our Arts and Culture chapter for additional shopping suggestions.

Best of Duval

The Chicken Store
1229 Duval Street
(305) 294-0070
www.TheChickenStore.com

The Chicken Store is the home of the Rooster Rescue Team, a volunteer group devoted to preserving gypsy chickens that roam Key West. Here, tucked among the fine art, crafts, and world-exclusive T-shirts celebrating the gypsy chickens of Key West, you'll find the real thing. Caged roosters, hens, and chicks—some wounded, some orphans, some simply deemed neighborhood nuisances—reside in this tiny shop while they recoup (no pun intended), recover, and await relocation. Take home a brochure that tells the Key West chicken story (a 25-cent donation is appreciated) or even a live souvenir—not the bird itself but a fresh, fertilized egg and a miniature incubator to help you hatch it.

Key West Havana Cigar Company
1117 Duval Street
(305) 296-2680, (800) 217-4884
www.keywestcigar.com

Make your selection from among the many brands of quality, handcrafted cigars and accessories in this small shop that doubles as the front entry of the Speakeasy Inn. A prompt mail-order service is available, so you can readily send cigars to the folks back home.

Country Conch
1108 Duval Street
(305) 294-1452

It was only a matter of time before the country craze in decorating that swept the Midwest a few years back made its way to Key West. Shop here for household accessories that say country with a South Florida flair. Wicker and muted tropical prints abound, along with the ubiquitous chickens, manatees, dolphins, and conch shells.

Abaco Gold
1102-C Duval Street
(305) 294-7796

418 Front Street
(305) 296-0086

A honeymoon voyage to the Abaco Islands prompted owners John and Angela to dub their stores "Abaco Gold." The jewelry line here is exclusive—like no other in the Florida Keys, or elsewhere for that matter. Abaco Gold specializes in unique, nautical designs featuring mermaids, dolphins, and tropical themes. If you love jewelry, you'll love these stores.

Eye! Eye! Eye!
1102 Duval Street
(305) 292-7909
www.eyeeyeeye.com

This shop offers the best selection of designer and vintage eyeglass frames this side of Miami. Choose from Anne et Valentin, Alain Mikli, Theo, and more. This is a wonderful optical boutique that also offers small repairs for your existing eyeglasses.

Fletcher on Duval Island Furniture
1024 Duval Street
(305) 294-2032
Decorate your home with the fine-crafted furniture offered by Fletcher. The specialty here is coral keystone, wrought into strange and wonderful forms. Coffee tables with end stands of this intricate rock hold a glass top in place. Choose from a variety of artistic pedestals, fireplace mantels, and much more. Be prepared to spend a considerable amount—art like this does not come cheap.

Island Accents
912 Duval Street
(305) 296-1922
www.islandaccentskeywest.com
Spruce up you home with some handmade tropical decor. Island Accents can help you fill any room with tropical lovelies that will be sure to remind you of the Florida Keys. This store offers handmade (in Key West) tropical linens. They also carry dinnerware, silverware, lamps, candles, pillows, and bath accessories. Fun, unique, and functional pieces for anywhere you hang your hat.

Tikal Trading Company
910 Duval Street
(305) 293-0033

129 Duval Street
(305) 296-4463
Two locations hold a vast store of women's apparel. Artfully displayed flowery dresses, perfect for the warm climate of the islands, invite passersby to step inside. The same prints and styles are available in several sizes, suitable for both mothers and daughters.

Everyone knows that US 1 ends in Key West. Some folks stand on the corner of Fleming and Whitehead Streets (see Attractions chapter) to be photographed next to MM 0, but if that's not convenient, you can buy a souvenir to take home. The official Mile Marker "0" Store is located at 510 Greene Street in Key West. Everything—clothing, signage, bumper stickers, hats, glassware, and more—has the famous imprint.

Cuba! Cuba!
814 Duval Street
(305) 295-9442
Get a little *"Libre!"* in your life with this quaint little shop that espouses a passion for all things Cuban. Art is very much a part of the selection evidenced by nostalgic wood carvings, depicting a typical Cuban kitchen. Cookbooks and authentic jams and marmalades line the shelves, and guitars and maracas are just begging to be played. A selection of cigars is also on display.

Towels of Key West
806 Duval Street
(305) 292-1120, (305) 294-1929,
(800) 927-0316
www.towelsofkeywest.com
Towels in all shapes, sizes, and budgets fill this simple store. Get the best-selling, colorful print terry robe, or immerse yourself in big, warm, oversized, colorful beach and bath towels.

Key West Island Store
712-B Duval Street
(305) 292-0409
www.islandestore.com
This is the place to go for funky, psychedelic Key West gecko, flamingo, and parrot metal sculptures. Key West Island Store has one of the largest collections of Haitian metal sculptures in the United States. The store sells handpainted furni-

Take a piece of Key West with you or send it to someone. Baskets by Karem arranges beautiful Key West memories in dazzling baskets and ships them anywhere in the country. You can select custom baskets featuring tropical items or let Karem design a breathtaking one-of-a-kind Keys souvenir. For more information, call (305) 295-8326 or visit www.basketsbykarem.com.

ture, ceramics, lamps, tiles, jewelry, and home accents as well.

Island Shoe Box
712-A Duval Street
(305) 294-7420
Yes, even in Paradise, some occasions may require you to wear real shoes. And this is the place to find them. Island Shoe Box stocks hundreds of styles for men, women, and children—everything from traditional oxfords to high-heeled pumps, as well as a complete array of sandals.

Beads of Distinction
712 Duval Street
(305) 293-8840
www.beadsofdistinction.com
Walking along Duval Street you're sure to notice the window of this establishment, which shimmers and shines with colorful beads. Beads of Distinction offers beads from all over the world as well as beading supplies and unique embellished gifts. They also sell whimsical "Key West" charms or "pet" charms for that special companion in your life.

Open Minded
703 Duval Street
(305) 295-9595
Tiffany lamps of all shapes and vivid colors perch daintily in the front display window of this unusual store. Part New Age and part boutique, Open Minded caters to those who wish to decorate their lives and homes in an otherworldly manner. Colorful wall hangings, chimes, and women's apparel commingle with incense, tarot cards, and colorful serenity.

Earthbound Trading Co.
618 Duval Street
(305) 295-8484

400 Duval Street
(305) 292-8604
Semiprecious stones and minerals fill this shop, in more forms than you would think possible. Big pieces of lovely purple amethyst and golden citrine are offered in their natural forms, but you could also opt for a marble chess set, wood-carved animals, beautiful sliced opaque rock chimes, bead jewelry, or agate bookends. This is a great place to buy a toe ring, too!

White House-Black Market
621 Duval Street
(305) 292-7740
www.whiteandblack.com
You'll have no trouble deciding on the right color for your next new outfit here, because you have only one choice—black or white. Every dress, skirt, shirt, or pair of trousers in this shop is either solid black or solid white. There are simply no shades of gray. It's an unusual concept—particularly in a climate where pastels and bright prints rule—but it certainly takes the guesswork out of buying.

ACA Joe
617 Duval Street
(305) 294-1570
Need some cargo shorts? A pair of deck shoes? A lightweight jacket for your sunset cruise? ACA Joe has a wide assortment of cool, comfortable cotton clothing for men and women as well as shoes that are perfect for boating and beachcombing. You'll find a nice selection of tropical print camp shirts here, too—tasteful enough to wear even when you return home.

Hot Hats
613 Duval Street
(305) 294-1333, (800) 344-4287
www.hothatskeywest.com

If you're heading out into the midday sun, you'd best wear a hat. And you're sure to find a flattering one at this shop devoted entirely to headgear, including everything from canvas caps to straw boaters. There's even a rack full of multicolored baseball caps with propellers for catching those island breezes in a whimsical way.

Birkenstock of Old Town
612 Duval Street
(305) 294-8318, (800) 330-2475 (orders)
www.birkenstore.com

With sandals being essential apparel for island life, it makes good sense for Birkenstock to have a large, full-service store right in the middle of it all. Although Birkenstocks don't come cheap, the shoes are exceptionally durable and comfortable. Rare is the local who doesn't own at least one pair. Count on paying upward of $50 for yours, but do watch the sale rack here. You can sometimes get a pretty good deal on discontinued styles. This store also does in-house repairs.

Environmental Circus
518 Duval Street
(305) 294-6055
www.e-circuskeywest.com

A Deadhead's delight lies within this cozy store, filled to the brim with tie-dyed T-shirts, essential oils, lava lamps, dyed wall hangings, and smoking accessories.

Fast Buck Freddie's
500 Duval Street
(305) 294-2007

If there weren't literally hundreds of stores to explore in Key West and you never reached the bottom of your pockets, Fast Buck Freddie's, at the southeast corner of Duval and Fleming, would be your one-stop shop. FBF's carries men's and women's clothing in metropolitan and tropical styles. Just around the bend from the megastore's clothing section are imported items from around the world, such as clocks, candleholders, picture frames, and some of the most unusual home furnishings you'll see anywhere. Look to Freddie's kitchenware department for an extensive selection of cookbooks, gourmet kitchen accessories, herb-flavored oils, and Godiva chocolates. And be sure to check out the unusual toys, novelty items, and greeting cards in the back of the store. But beware—some may be X-rated.

See the listing later in this chapter for Half Buck Freddie's, Fast Buck Freddie's discount store.

---

i

"Shop till you drop" can be taken literally here in the tropical heat of the Florida Keys. Give yourself a gift by pampering your body with a spa treatment for an hour or a full day. Some therapist are mobile and will even come to you! The local Yellow Pages or hotel concierge can assist you in locating this service.

Margaritaville Store
500 Duval Street
(305) 296-3070
www.margaritavillestore.com

Everything here is tuned to one thing—the works of Key West's favorite son, Jimmy Buffett. All his albums are available here, along with tons of shirts, books, photos, and other Parrothead paraphernalia. Spend some time perusing the walls—they're packed with photos and memorabilia related to events in the life of the man from Margaritaville. This place is a must-stop for Buffett fans old and new.

Shades of Key West
335 Duval Street
(305) 294-0519

306 Front Street
(305) 294-0329

Protect your eyes from the intense tropical sunlight with a wide selection of brand-name sunglasses, including Oakley, Ray-Ban, Vuarnet, Armani, Arnet, and Hobie. These are not your drugstore-variety sunglasses—everything's top quality.

You may not have a need to purchase a bouquet of flowers or a tropical arrangement while visiting here, but do take the time to stroll into the florist shops that dot the Florida Keys. From Key Largo to Key West, you will be swept away by the choices of posies the talented designers use for their oh-so-magnificent designs.

Hair Wraps of Key West
310 Duval Street
(305) 293-1133
If you want to make a real statement or you just want to get your hair done in a new way, head over to Hair Wraps in the courtyard of the Garden Cafe. Tons of beads are available, and these folks have just about any color or detail you'd like.

Thomas Kinkade Gallery
305 Duval Street
(305) 292-0069
www.thomaskinkade.com
You may not know Thomas Kinkade by name, but you surely have seen his little cottages on everything from greeting cards to gift items on the shopping network, QVC. New to Key West in 2006, the "Painter of Light" has chosen Key West as the home of his 300th store. The deep-blue walls of the gallery enhance the glowing images of his work. If you don't see anything that appeals to you, look over a lovely 200-page catalog that will show you categories of his paintings. His collection is so large that none of his stores can physically handle the inventory. Kinkade's latest work is "Living Waters—Golfer's Paradise/Hole One."

Neptune Designs
301 Duval Street
(305) 294-8131
www.orchidspecies.com
Most of the jewelry filling this shop has an oceanic motif and is wrought in gold or silver. Leaping silver dolphins frolic with golden, gliding sea turtles on necklaces displayed on a black background. Noah's Ark figurines are on display—tiny ships decked with all manner of wildlife.

Congress Jewelers
128 Duval Street
(305) 296-5885
Congress Jewelers might have only a small store on Duval, but boy, do they have the jewelry. They are one of only two authorized Rolex dealers in the Keys, so if glamorous watches are your bling-bling, get your eye candy here. Congress also has breathtaking gold, silver, precious-gem, and semiprecious-gem pieces to tempt you.

Biker's Image
121 Duval Street
(305) 292-1328
Get your Harley tuned up and race over to Biker's Image, where you can splurge on your fantasies with leather, Harley T-shirts, helmets, smoking accessories, and just about anything that complements the biker lifestyle.

Off Duval

A Grande Mulher
241 Front Street (at Key West Hilton Marina)
(305) 295-8805
www.agrandemulher.com
One of the string of shops at the Hilton Marina, overlooking the Gulf of Mexico, A Grande Mulher offers clothing that's "grande" in style. The voluptuous woman will find fabulous clothing and accessories here. The shop's beautifully designed lines hint of the tropics but are practical enough to wear back home. A great staff can assist you in selecting that special outfit to make you look schön!

Assortment, Inc.
514 Fleming Street
(305) 294-4066
This chic men's clothing store, just a few steps off Duval Street, carries the latest in

men's casual fashions with a dressy flair. Handsome jackets, shirts, slacks, and shoes are tastefully displayed. Polo by Ralph Lauren, Barry Bricken, and Cole-Haan shoes are just a few of the lines you'll find here. Assortment, Inc., also offers great-looking gifts and accessories for that special guy in your life.

Becky Thatcher Designs
425 Eaton Street
(305) 296-0886
www.beckythatcherdesigns.com
If one-of-a-kind jewelry creations from unusual gemstones such as tourmaline, boulder opal, fancy sapphire, tanzanite, sugalite, and chrysocolla pique your interest, visit Becky Thatcher Designs. Set in gold or silver, the gemstones join with shells and ancient beads from around the world, creating what Becky calls "picture" necklaces and earrings that capture the essence of spirit and individuality.

Besame Mucho
315 Petronia Street
(305) 294-1928, (866) 237-2631
ww.besamemucho.net
Step into this tastefully decorated shop, and you will feel as though you have stepped back in time. Ceiling fans stir the air, and the CD playing softly in the background is reminiscent of Old Havana. The shelves are filled with items that look as though they belong on a movie set, ca. 1940. Here you'll find an assortment of picture frames, desk accessories, tableware, lucky tokens, tropical cards and books, baskets, Tahitian bath oils—in short, what the owners lovingly refer to as "essential island provisions."

Blue
718 Caroline Street
(305) 292-5172
www.blueislandstore.com
Shop here for classic linen skirts, tops, jackets, pants, and dresses that will look just as appropriate on Fifth Avenue as they do on Duval. Be sure to check out the accessories here, too. The bead jewelry is handmade, and the colors are a perfect complement to the easy-fitting, understated styles.

Clinton Square Market
291 Front Street
(305) 296-6825
Enclosed within Clinton Square Market, you'll find a diverse assortment of shops in which to browse. From men's and women's clothing, to fine jewelry, to kitschy souvenir shops, the marketplace bustles. Consult the Arts and Culture chapter for information on the art galleries in the market.

Commotion
800 Caroline Street
(305) 292-3364
www.localcolorkeywest.com
Stylish island separates that are as fun to wear as they are practical to own await you here. These natural, washable linen and flax fabrics will help you keep your cool—a definite must in the Florida Keys. Best of all, unlike some island designs that look out of place outside the Tropics, these will look just as great when you get back home.

The Dreaming Goddess Boutique
613 Ashe Street
(305) 923-9589, (866) 390-7455
www.thedreaminggoddess.com
When the owner of The Dreaming Goddess, Jasmine Sky, received a hand-painted silk scarf from her sister, a "dream" was born. The gift inspired Jasmine to leave her career and move to the Florida Keys. Today she creates hand-painted sarongs, tunics, dresses, and pants. She has a niche market for these wearable works of art, many of which can go from beach to dinner. The Dreaming Goddess also offers accessories and home decor. Call for an appointment to the studio.

Jasmine says, "the silk is magical and feels divine on your skin. Not only are the pieces beautiful but they are sensuous, practical, and comfortable." Ooh la la!

Make time to browse the gift shops at our museums and attractions, too. You might just find the perfect Keys book, trinket, or T-shirt for that special someone on your shopping list.

Duck and Dolphin Antiques
601 Fleming Street
(305) 295-0499
www.duckanddolphin.com

This elegant shop—reminiscent of the antiques shops we've seen in Europe—is filled with ornate furnishings and accent pieces that can only be called trés chic. You'll find everything from a grand piano to a crystal chandelier. These items are in mint condition, with price tags to match.

From the Ruins
219 Whitehead Street
(305) 293-0897

No one—and we do mean no one—should pass up the opportunity to experience From the Ruins, where previously owned, one-of-a-kind handmade garments and accessories make for a sweet shopping trip. Wear your heart on your sleeve with a handbag crafted in the form of your favorite dog breed, or pick up an intricate, handblown glass vase. Be sure to bring a full wallet—these one-of-a-kind artifacts have one-of-a-kind prices. Look for the cozy cottage with a white picket fence and welcoming front porch.

Half Buck Freddie's
726 Caroline Street
(305) 294-2007

Slightly dated, overstocked, or slow-moving merchandise from Fast Buck Freddie's (see earlier listing in this section) never dies. It simply ends up across Duval and down a few blocks, at Half Buck Freddie's on Caroline. Everything here, from clothing to calendars to kitchen gadgets, was once on sale at Freddie's. Now it's moved out and marked down 50 percent from its original price. The stock changes regularly, and the hours are limited. Shop for bargains here Thursday through Sunday only. Half Buck Freddie's does not have a phone number. The number listed above is for Fast Buck Freddie's; the folks there can answer all your questions.

In One Era
1118 White Street
(305) 293-0208

This tiny shop has a large selection of delightful estate jewelry, old period costumes (great for Fantasy Fest), vintage lighting, chandeliers, and small antiques. Their inventory also includes Cuban and Key West memorabilia.

Key West Aloe
540 Green Street
(305) 293-1885, (800) 445-2563 (orders)
www.keywestaloe.com

Step into Key West Aloe on Front Street for a showroom of the only perfumes, skin-care products, and cosmetics to boast a "made in Key West" label. Their products are shipped throughout the world.

Key West Hand Print Fabrics and Fashions
201 Simonton Street
(305) 294-9535, (800) 866-0333
www.keywestfashions.com

At Key West Hand Print Fabrics and Fashions, silk-screeners and seamstresses create brightly colored men's and women's fashions from more than 3,000 original designs. Copyrighted Key West prints adorn men's shirts and neckties as well as various ladies' fashions and accessories, all ready to wear for your next outing. The prints are also sold by the yard; be sure to ask for a label to sew inside your own personal creations.

Key West Island Bookstore
513 Fleming Street
(305) 294-2904

Doubled in size in 1999, this shop sells everything from the classics to the best sellers, along with topical nonfiction and the works of Florida Keys and Key West writers—often at below-market prices. This store is especially supportive of Florida authors and often hosts book-signing events that generate lots of local excitement and a party atmosphere. Carl Hiaasen, James Hall, Jimmy Buffett, Philip Caputo, James Dickey, and Thomas McGuane have all signed books here. Be sure to check the rare-book room in the back. You probably won't find a first-edition Hemingway on the shelves, but then again you might.

Key West Jewelry Station
508 Southard Street
(305) 294-0027, (800) 604-0027
www.keywestjewelrystation.com
Inside this tiny gem of a jewelry store, tucked off busy Duval Street, are some dazzling bits of body ornamentation. If you are getting married in the Keys, the Jewelry Station offers Art Carved wedding sets as well as items from the Judith Jack, Crislu, and Pandora design houses. Their prices are great and they even offer "same as cruise ship" bargains.

Key West Kite Company
409 Greene Street
(305) 296-2535
www.shopfloridakeys.com/kites
The Key West Kite Company is just waiting to make windy days wondrous with flags, banners, and flying tours. The first kite store to set up shop in all of Florida, Key West Kites offers everything from handmade to high-performance sport kites. There's a great selection of yo-yos here, too, plus juggling supplies and instructions.

Key West Winery, Inc.
103 Simonton Street
(305) 292-1717, (866) 880-1717
www.thekeywestwinery.com
This is wine like you've never tasted before. Not one variety is made from grapes! These wines live up to Key West's tropical image—laid-back, funky, and packed with pizzazz. All the wines are made from a potpourri of fruits, such as Eleganta, a semisweet red raspberry variety that won a silver medal at the Indiana International Wine Competition in 1999. Also medal winners: Hot Sun, a dry white wine with a slight tomato taste and a hint of peppers; Orange Sunshine, a semisweet wine made from 100 percent fresh-squeezed Florida orange juice; and 40 Karats, a buttery semidry white wine that is similar to a Chardonnay, but 100 percent carrot and much more flavorful. You'll find many, many more interesting fruit wines here, and best of all, you can stop in and taste as many wines as you want, seven days a week.

Kino Sandals
107 Fitzpatrick Street
(305) 294-5044
www.kinosandalfactory.com
When Roberto "Kino" and Margarite Lopez immigrated from Cuba they had no idea their Kino sandals would be so well received. Roberto had a factory in Cuba and after working several odd jobs in Key West, he opened a sandal factory here in 1966. Using his nickname, Kino, for the business, he built a lovely Cuban-style factory that is still in operation today. The high ceilings in the factory allow the heat to drift outside while the terra-cotta tiled floors remain cool. Here you pick from a variety of leathers and colors for your custom sandals. Prices are very reasonable, and they make a terrific souvenir. A constant reminder of your trip to the Florida Keys, there's nothing like happy feet!

Lazy Way Hammocks
205 Elizabeth Street
(305) 296-2246, (866) 426-2227
www.lazywayhammocks.com
You'll find woven hammocks of soft cotton or durable nylon from South and Central America at Lazy Way Hammocks, as well as rope hammocks from El Salvador, Costa Rica, Colombia, and Brazil. Hammock stands and accessories are available here also.

Looking for that one-of-a-kind gift to send home to friends or family? Ship a Key lime pie from the Blond Giraffe or Kermit's Key West Key Lime Shoppe (both are listed in our Seafood Markets and Specialty Foods chapter). While placing your order, savor their Key West versions of key lime pie on a stick—frozen key lime pie dipped in chocolate. It will be a sweet ending to a frenzied day of shopping!

Lilly Pulitzer
600 Front Street
(305) 295-0995
www.lillypulitzer.com
In 1960 a young socialite, Lilly Pulitzer, opened a juice stand in West Palm Beach. When her uniform seemed more popular than her juice, the famous "Lillys" were created. Jackie Kennedy was photographed in *Life* magazine wearing one, and from then on *EVERYONE* had to have the Florida shift. Today, Lilly Pulitzer shops offer the signature piece in tropical green and hot pink, along with bright and fun prints in various other tantalizing colors. She has also extended her line to include jewelry, shoes, home accents, and a clothing line for children.

Little Switzerland
271 Front Street
(305) 296-1998

400 Front Street
(305) 296-1907
You don't have to take a trip to the Caribbean to get "island" prices on jewelry and gifts. Little Switzerland offers fabulous discounts at their two Key West locations. The stores have all the designer names in jewelry and watches: Roberto Coin, Cartier, Mont Blanc, Tiffany and Co., Oliva, and Yvel, to name just a few. The great staff and managers are very knowledgeable about their wares and provide excellent assistance in helping you make a selection.

Local Color
274 Margaret Street,
Key West Historic Seaport
(305) 292-3635

425 Greene Street
(305) 296-0151
www.localcolorkeywest.com
The Margaret Street shop is where locals and tourists alike come to purchase the colorful, comfortable clothing that fits the Key West lifestyle. In addition to casual apparel for men and women, you'll find fun hats, handbags, and costume jewelry to complete your island look. The Greene Street location is the place to shop for inexpensive, fun jewelry to adorn your neck, ears, wrists, fingers, even ankles and toes.

Neat Stuff
3201 Flagler Avenue
(305) 296-7677
This store is jam-packed with fun and funky treasures—which is why the owners named it Neat Stuff! You can purchase just about anything with Keys' themes: clothes, hats, trinkets, jewelry. And when Fantasy Fest (see Annual Events chapter) comes around, this is where you'll find those outrageous costumes.

Off Duval
1442 Kennedy Drive
(305) 296-3317
This is a darling shop tucked in a strip mall but worth the trip to go see. Inside you will find unique gifts for the home as well as beautiful clothing for ladies. The shop also has handmade clothing for children. If you need adorable baby things and dress outfits for l'enfant, this is the place to shop.

Pelican Poop Shop
314 Simonton Street
(305) 292-9955
This eclectic collection of artwork includes originals from all over the Caribbean. If you're in the market for a life-size, stone Mayan deer dancer or a Haitian oil-drum sculpture, this is the

place to come. For a small purchase or a nominal admittance fee, you can tour the private Casa Antigua gardens out back, linked forever to Ernest Hemingway by a quirky twist of fate. He completed *A Farewell to Arms* here while awaiting delivery of his new Ford back in 1928.

Long after Hemingway left Key West, this building became a hotel, then later the island's largest brothel, and its first drag club. Today it is home to City Commissioner Tom Oosterhoudt and his mother, Mary Ann Worth. On your visit to the gardens, you will hear Tom himself recount the colorful history of the building in a six-minute audio presentation.

Reef Relief Environmental Center & Store
End of William Street
Key West Historic Seaport
(305) 294-3100
www.reefrelief.org
You can learn about our fragile coral reef here at the Reef Relief Environmental Center. Continuous videos, displays, and free information will heighten your awareness of what you can do to protect North America's only living coral reef. Merchandise on sale includes coral reef books, educational products for both adults and children, and informational videos.

The Restaurant Store
1111 Eaton Street
(305) 294-7994
www.keywestchef.com
The Restaurant Store is chock-full of kitchen and cooking gear to feed 5 or 50. You'll discover state-of-the-art utensils, pots and pans, and accessories for culinary aficionados and chefs alike. This store is nirvana for foodies.

Scrubs of Key West
720 Caroline Street
(305) 295-7232, (888) 727-8259
www.scrubskeywest.com
Scrubs are not necessarily just for surgeons anymore. Nor do the loose-fitting shirts and drawstring pants have to be hospital green. Scrubs of Key West stitches them up in all manner of tropical prints—fish, palm trees, lizards, and the like. And although plenty of local doctors, nurses, dentists, and hygienists shop here, nonmedical types have discovered that this is a great place to buy casual wear and gifts—like soft fabric handbags, keychains, and eyeglass cases.

Strunk Ace Hardware
1101 Eaton Street
(305) 296-9091
Don't let the word "hardware" fool you. Inside this lovely new building is not only one of the best places to find items to fix up a home but also one of the greatest gift emporiums in the Keys. They have all sorts of lovelies such as beautiful silk flowers, dishes, candles, and knickknacks for house, cabana, or boat. The stock is forever changing and the staff is a delight.

Whitfield Jack
200 Elizabeth Street
(305) 294-7092, (800) 845-2243
www.jewelrygenius.com
Were it not for the cases of jewelry lining the walls of Whitfield Jack, you likely wouldn't realize you are inside a store at all. Set inside a simulated tropical garden, Whitfield Jack jewelers carries original 14k designs. The gold Key West conch pendant is said to be the ultimate souvenir of Key West. Legend has it that "those who wear the conch will return again someday."

Way Off Duval

Bargain Books and Newsstand
1028 Truman Avenue
(305) 294-7446
South Florida's largest retailer of pre-read books is right here on our tiny island. Wander through room after slightly dusty room of fiction, sci-fi, romance, and other literature. A couple of cats may find your lap a cozy spot to take a nap as you sit in one of the comfortable chairs and peruse

a favorite title. If you love books and you love a bargain, you won't be disappointed. But be prepared to spend some time here. Half the fun of finding your bargain book is in the search for it.

Borders Express
2212 North Roosevelt Boulevard
(305) 294-5419
www.amazon.com

Not surprisingly, this is Key West's largest bookstore and, perhaps, its most visible. It's a stand-alone shop on US 1 with plenty of free parking. On the inside, the store looks much like every other Borders Express you've ever been in, with a notable exception: Right up front, there's a huge display of titles by Key West authors as well as an impressive array of books on a variety of Florida-related subjects. In addition to several guides to Key West and Florida Keys attractions, you'll find island cookbooks, maps, history tomes, and nature guides to help you identify our native flora and fauna. You'll also find especially helpful clerks here as well as frequent book signings and sales, the proceeds of which are often earmarked for local charities.

Consigning Adults
802 White Street
(305) 294-2125

This consignment shop is a real trip! They have everything from small household accessories to lightly worn designer clothes for men and women. The best part about the shop is their large selection of "costumes" that everyone likes to buy for Fantasy Fest (see chapter on Annual Events). The staff is loads of fun.

Lilo Surf Shop
MM 4.5 Oceanside, US 1, Stock Island
(305) 294-1800

The Keys might not be known for surfing waters, but you can still look the part. Located at the Hurricane Hole Marina (see the Restaurants chapter), the Lilo Surf Shop has the coolest selection of surf apparel. The owner stocks everything from Reef and Rainbow sandals , T-shirts, shorts, and swimsuits to skim boards, skateboards, hats, and, of course, surfboards. Just about everything for you cool surfer-dudes!

Seam Shoppe
1114 Truman Avenue
(305) 296-9830
www.tropicalfabricsonline.com

This fabric shop offers a fabulous selection of tropical fabrics for fashion, quilting, and home decor. Patterns include fish, shells, Hawaiian themes, nautical, palm trees, and tropical foliage. You'll find batiks and bark cloth here as well.

Timmy's Tuxedos
812 Fleming Street
(305) 294-8897

In spite of what you may think about the Keys dress code of flip flops and T-shirts, we do dress up occasionally, and Timmy's Tuxedos is the only formal attire shop in the Keys. Here you can buy all the "dress-up" garb you need, plus rent jackets and tuxedos. They also carry beautiful Keys prints for ties and cummerbunds, to make that formal gathering tropical.

Welcome Home
Key Plaza Shopping Center
(305) 292-4004

Just because this charming furniture boutique sits next door to Kmart, don't be fooled into thinking this is put-together furniture in a box! Be thankful there are plenty of parking spaces in the shopping mall, so you can get to this delightful shop. Inside you will find an array of beautiful home accessories, from beds to couches, end tables, pictures, and accessories. The owners say "Why drive to Miami when Miami is here in Key West?" High quality at affordable prices from delightful owners make this a must if you are looking for a great hostess gift or decorating your tropical abode.

Best of New Town

The New Town area along North Roosevelt Boulevard is often overlooked by shoppers enamored with the funky shops of Old Town. But this is where the locals shop. A series of strip malls or plazas—Kennedy, Key, Luani, Overseas Market, Searstown—are within blocks of each other and feature the staples of everyday life as offered by major retail chain stores.

RETIREMENT

If we are to believe Noah Webster, retirement means "withdrawing from active life." Not so in the Florida Keys. Our retirees are anything but retiring. Each year, about the time Jack Frost starts whistling up north, the influx of snowbirds to our sun-kissed islands begins, and the collective pulse of our communities quickens.

Unlike other retirement areas in Florida, our seniors usually don't keep to themselves in preplanned communities. You'll find them living in residential neighborhoods and condominiums, RV parks, and mobile-home villages. Our seniors contribute an added dimension to our communities. They form a much-needed core of volunteers for many of our public services, including the county libraries, local hospitals, and area schools.

The American Association of Retired Persons (AARP) accepts individuals age 50 and older into membership, which means the first wave of baby boomers have already reached "senior" status, and some are taking the Florida Keys by storm. These prime-of-lifers have taken a career-course detour, leaving that corporate 9-to-5 (or, more likely, 9-to-9) grind to venture off the track into uncharted territory.

Regardless of age, the retirees in the Florida Keys remain youthful. Our warm, tropical climate is kind to old bones (young ones, too!). The pace of our lifestyle moves to a different drummer . . . well, more of a reggae beat. Some people even feel we live longer down here . . . and they're in their 90s. Our energetic retirees enjoy fishing and scuba diving, golf and tennis, boating, and bridge. They are active in myriad special-interest organizations the length and breadth of the Keys. Many pursue artistic hobbies long put on the back burner while the rest of their lives simmered. Some go back to school, developing new skills and honing others.

At the heart of the retirement community in the Florida Keys are the senior citizen centers, which serve as cohesive units of companionship and support to retirees of all ages and circumstances. The centers were constructed and are maintained as a joint venture between Monroe County and the local chapters of AARP. The county nutrition sites are in the centers (see Nutrition Services in the Senior Services section in this chapter). Membership in AARP is not a prerequisite for most activities of the senior citizen centers, but anyone age 50 or older may pick up an application to AARP at any of the centers. Because our seniors participate in activities based all throughout the Keys, we have organized this chapter by interest group, incorporating all areas of the Keys from Key Largo to Key West.

SENIOR CENTERS

Upper Keys Plantation Senior Center
MM 88.7 Bayside, Plantation Key
(305) 852-7132

This active group of seniors in the Upper Keys has a series of fund-raisers, such as its annual rummage sale, to raise money for community organizations, including the fire department, the ambulance corps, and the local Red Cross chapter. Besides monthly meetings, this Upper Keys group enjoys bingo; members donate the money raised to Hospice. During the winter season, when the ranks swell by some 60 to 75 percent, classes such as Spanish are offered at the center. Puzzles, crafts, and cards are favorite impromptu activities.

Many of the retirees in the Upper Keys are active in conservation and preservation organizations, fraternal organizations, the

Florida Keys Fine Arts Council and the Key Players (see the Arts and Culture chapter), and human service groups such as Hospice and the Domestic Abuse Shelter.

The center is next to the sheriff's substation.

Middle Keys Levitt Senior Center
MM 48.8 Bayside, 535 33rd Street, Marathon
(305) 743-4008

This lively bunch in the Middle Keys maintains a whirlwind of activities, especially during the winter season, such as bridge, crafts, weekly bingo, and regular exercise sessions. A balanced meal is served at the center every weekday at noon. The seniors trip the light fantastic with special events, such as the Valentine Sweetheart Dance and the St. Patrick's Day party. They charter buses and go on special excursions to the Monkey Jungle or Everglades National Park, to Homestead or Miami, even an overnight to Busch Gardens in Tampa. The trips usually cost a nominal fee and include entrance fees and dinner.

The center offers Arrive Alive instruction for seniors several times throughout the year. Arrive Alive is a bookwork driving course that, when passed, nets the senior citizen a discount on auto insurance. The crafting groups hold boutiques where they display and sell their creations. The seniors have a series of yard sales throughout the year to make money to maintain the center. Volunteers also go to the elementary schools several times a week and, like grandparents, assist children in reading or math, or just talk to the child and give a hug when needed.

The Middle Keys Levitt Senior Center has a large lending library. It also has free income tax preparation when that dreaded time rolls around. Free flu shots and blood pressure checks are available on a regular basis.

The center is near the Marathon Yacht Club.

Lower Keys Big Pine Senior Center
MM 31 Bayside, 380 Key Deer Boulevard, Big Pine Key
(305) 872-3990

Not to be outdone by the other Keys centers, the seniors in the Lower Keys boogie in a bevy of activities like their compatriots up the Keys. The winter season finds them country line dancing and exercising, taking French lessons, and attending classes in hatha yoga. The center shows classic movies and hosts potlucks and bingo. The group has an active barbershop quartet and a serious chess club. Two times each month seniors can get free blood pressure checks.

The Lower Keys Big Pine Senior Center, which is right behind the Big Pine Key firehouse, is open every day for card playing and puzzle making. The seniors sponsor 55 Alive driving classes (much like the group in the Middle Keys) as well as computer instruction. During the winter season the center often holds dances, playing recorded Big Band music.

Key West Senior Center
1016 Georgia Street, Truman School at the Harvey Government Center
(305) 295-5165

The seniors in Key West often go their own way, we are told, so not as many organized activities emanate from this center as from others in the rest of the Keys. The seniors are active in the Key West Garden Club, the Art and Historical Society, the Maritime History Society, the Key West Yacht Club (see the Cruising chapter), the Power Squadron, and fraternal organizations such as Moose and Elk. More than 50 seniors regularly come to the center for the county-supplied hot meals each day (see Nutrition Services in this chapter), staying to play bingo or cards afterward. Bridge is popular, too.

COLLEGE COURSES

The Florida Keys Community College offers a selection of courses of interest to seniors, but there is no tuition break for senior citizens. Check the FKCC Web site for current course offerings and tuition charges. The academic year is divided into three terms. The fall class session runs from August through December. The spring term is January to May. Summer classes are held from the beginning of May through mid-August. Class offerings change often, so call the college branch of your choice for a course catalog and the most recent class schedule.

Upper Keys Campus
MM 89.9 Oceanside, Coral Shores High School, Tavernier
(305) 852-8007
www.fkcc.edu
Seniors and retirees particularly enjoy the computer classes offered at this branch of Florida Keys Community College. They also sign up for such classes as conversational Spanish, watercolor painting, beginning drawing, creative writing, and American and English literature.

Middle Keys Campus
MM 50 Oceanside, 900 Sombrero Beach Road, Marathon
(305) 743-2133, (305) 743-0749
www.fkcc.edu
The Middle Keys branch of FKCC offers general-interest classes in foreign language and computer science as well as more unusual fare, such as nature walks, tours of the Everglades, conservation classes, and photography instruction.

Be sure to inquire about senior citizen discounts wherever you go in the Florida Keys. You may find admission costs reduced or waived at some of our tourist attractions as well as at state and national parks. Some restaurants have early-bird specials or offer discounts to seniors.

Florida Keys Community College
5901 West College Road, Stock Island
(305) 296-9081
www.fkcc.edu
The main campus of the Florida Keys Community College offers many more classes of interest to seniors than the other branches up the Keys. Art classes in ceramics, stained glass, jewelry making, lettering and calligraphy, drawing, wheel throwing, print making, photography, graphic arts, painting, and sculpture will intrigue the artistically inclined. Courses in computerized photography and graphic arts are also offered. Many foreign languages are available, and the selection of literature courses includes one on Florida Keys writers and literature. Seniors can try their hands at creative writing and dabble in the natural sciences with marine data collection, marine archaeology, and the culture and environment of the Florida Everglades. Vocational courses include marine propulsion technology (good for those with boats to repair) and electronic engineering technology (to fix VCRs and their like).

FKCC has a beautiful swimming pool and offers classes in water aerobics and fitness swimming. Seniors can take classes as non-degree-seeking students or work toward an associate of arts or associate of science degree.

Lifelong learning doesn't necessarily mean that you must enroll in a degree program or semester-long course. FKCC also offers a variety of continuing education workshops, seminars, and classes devoted to a single subject such as stock-market investment, custom rod making, accessing the Internet, or bookbinding. These classes may meet for a single session or several weeks depending on the complexity of the subject matter. For additional information and a list of upcoming classes, contact the FKCC Continuing Education Department at (305) 296-9081, ext. 280.

PUBLIC LIBRARIES

The Monroe County libraries are popular reading-room destinations with seniors in the Keys. They all maintain ever-growing large-print collections and a wide selection of current magazines. In addition, most of the libraries have a burgeoning number of videotapes and books on tape that may be checked out. Electronic catalogs in each of the libraries list all the materials in the system. Your local library will be able to get information from other branches for you upon request. The Key West library maintains a well-stocked Florida History Room that provides a fascinating look back through the centuries in Key West and all of the Keys. Volumes of old photographs are housed here.

The libraries also host special events, such as lectures and film screenings, throughout the year. The library system has a strong volunteer program as well.

The Monroe County library system includes the following branches: Key Largo, (305) 451-2396, MM 101.4 Oceanside, Tradewinds Shopping Center, Key Largo; Islamorada, (305) 664-4645, MM 81.5 Bayside, Islamorada; Marathon, (305) 743-5156, MM 48.5 Oceanside, next to Fishermen's Hospital, Marathon; Big Pine, (305) 872-0992, MM 31 Bayside, 213 Key Deer Boulevard, Big Pine Key; and Key West, (305) 292-3595, 700 Fleming Street, Key West.

SPECIAL-INTEREST ACTIVITIES

It is not uncommon here in the Florida Keys to hear a senior citizen complain, "Since I've retired, I've never been so busy in my life!" Seniors get involved in civic clubs and fraternal organizations such as the Elks, Eagles, Moose, and Shriners. They work with human service organizations such as Big Brothers/Big Sisters, Florida Keys Children's Shelter, Domestic Abuse Shelter, and the AIDS Prevention Center. Retirees donate valuable time to the Florida Keys Council of the Arts, the American Cancer Society, and Guardian Ad Litem. And they participate in activities helping the Florida Keys themselves such as Reef Relief, Florida Keys Wild Bird Rehabilitation Center, and Friends of the Everglades.

Contact the chamber of commerce in your area for a complete listing of the special-interest organizations of the Florida Keys. Area chambers include those in Key Largo, (305) 451-1414, (800) 822-1088; Islamorada, (305) 664-4503, (800) 322-5397; Marathon, (305) 743-5417, (800) 262-7284; Lower Keys, (305) 872-2411, (800) 872-3722; and Key West, (305) 294-2587, (800) 527-8539.

Garden Clubs

Some of the most popular organizations in the Florida Keys are its garden clubs, perhaps because we have so many days of glorious sunshine or because our subtropical climate fosters the growth of such exotic flowering foliage and palms.

Upper Keys Garden Club
MM 94 Bayside, Key Largo
(305) 852-9216

The Frances Tracy Garden Center (next to the Red Cross Building) hosts members of the Upper Keys Garden Club on the third Tuesday of every month. The group often hears a lecturer speak on some phase of subtropical horticulture. They hold a Plant Ramble sale as a fund-raiser and sponsor a garden walk through lovely private gardens of the Upper Keys each year.

The Upper Keys Garden Club is affiliated with the Florida Federation of State Garden Clubs and the National Council of State Garden Clubs. Members support the community's landscaping needs by donating plants and labor in landscaping the Coast Guard Station, Coral Shores High School, and Plantation Key Elementary School.

Bingo—Bocce—Biking

The Florida Keys is not all about fishing and sunsets. If you enjoy bingo, check out the game at the 801 Club at 801 Duval or at La-Te-Da, 1125 Duval. Neither has a cover, and all proceeds go to charity. Bingo can also be played at the Key West Senior Center, (305) 295-5165, and Sons of Italy at the American Legion, (305) 294-7374.

Bocce is a game of Italian origin similar to lawn bowling. The sport is played at the Indigenous Park, and the season begins in October, (305) 294-7354.

Bike paths are plentiful in the lower Keys. Try the one at MM 17 Sugarloaf Road. You can park at the Sugarloaf Lodge, across US 1. The round-trip mileage is approximately 15 miles. MM 19.5 on Sugarloaf Key takes you on Crane Boulevard to the bay. MM 27.8 Middle Torch and Big Torch is just off US 1. Park on Middle Torch Road. The scenic trip is about 15.5 miles.

Marathon Garden Club
MM 50 Bayside, Marathon
(305) 743-4971

The Marathon Garden Club was organized in March 1955, when the Keys were in desperate need of beautification. Beginning as a small grassroots group that held meetings in each other's homes, the ranks have burgeoned. Much of the lovely landscaping gracing public areas of Marathon is the work of the Marathon Garden Club. You'll notice the group's creative handiwork at the American Legion, the chamber of commerce building, the firehouse, Fishermen's Hospital, the public library, the Key Colony Causeway, along the Overseas Highway, and at Marathon High School.

Since the 1970s the group has sponsored successful house tours, plant and crafts fairs, and flower shows. Each year in March they sponsor a house and garden tour in Marathon that is open to the public. In December they stage Christmas Around the World (see the Annual Events chapter). Garden club members take their collective expertise into the Monroe County schools, where they teach the children about plants and trees as well as flower arranging.

The Marathon Garden Club meets the third Friday of each month from October through May. The public is invited. The gift shop, which offers a changing rota of unusual specialty gift items, is open year-round from Monday through Saturday, 10:00 A.M. to 2:00 P.M.

Key West Garden Club
Atlantic Boulevard and White Street, at West Martello Tower, Key West
(305) 294-3210

The Key West Garden Club maintains the gardens of West Martello Tower, an old Civil War fort at Higgs Beach on Atlantic Boulevard. The club meets once a month for a short business meeting followed by a presentation by a guest speaker, often a visiting horticulturist. These events are open to the general public. Twice a year the group holds a plant sale at its West Martello Tower headquarters. You can walk away with beautiful plants at bargain prices and a wealth of free gardening tips and information to boot. In March of alternating years, the Key West Garden Club sponsors a garden tour during which the general public can visit five private gardens in Key West (see the Annual Events chapter for details).

American Contract Bridge League

Duplicate bridge passes muster as the game of choice among those addicts of the sport. "If there's a game in town, we'll find it," says one duplicate player. The play is recognized by the National American Contract Bridge League, and you can earn Life Master's points. The games are open to all. If you don't have a partner, don't worry; the director will pair you with a partner for the day's game. A nominal fee is charged to play.

It is best to call the director before the day of play to make sure the schedule has not been changed. The groups are listed here by location.

- Civic Club, MM 99.5 Oceanside, Key Largo. Play is year-round on Monday and Friday afternoons and on Tuesday evening.
- San Pablo Catholic Church, MM 53.5 Oceanside, 550 122nd Street, Marathon. Play is year-round on Thursday afternoons.
- Kirk of the Keys, MM 51 Oceanside, Marathon. Play is on Monday, Wednesday, and Friday afternoons.
- Senior Center, Harvey Government Center, 1016 Georgia Street, Key West. Play is on Tuesday, Thursday, and Sunday afternoons.

Golf and Tennis

Two of the most popular sports among seniors are golf and tennis. See our Recreation chapter for information on facilities in the Florida Keys.

Quilter's Club

Next to avid gardeners, bridge fanatics, loyal golfers, and tireless tennis players, quilters rank as a group prepared to go the distance. We've never known a quilter who could pass up a fabric store or a quilt shop, and it is a hobby that has burgeoned across the nation.

Totally hooked on quilting in the Florida Keys are the members of the Quilter's Club, who come from across the Keys, and even South Florida, to attend meetings at the Key Largo Library every Friday at 10:00 A.M. The group does not jury any bodies of work, but participants have a popular show-and-tell of projects in process. Each month members also hold a themed fabric exchange of 6-inch squares and a "block of the month" drawing.

Every other year the Quilter's Club has a quilt show on National Quilting Day in March, complete with national advertising. It draws a worldwide audience, we're told. Contact the Key Largo Public Library (305-451-2396) for more information and to be sure the meeting is on for a particular week. The quilters sometimes get bumped by another organization that needs the meeting space.

SENIOR SERVICES

Monroe County Social Services

The Florida Keys offers senior citizens a wide range of services through the Monroe County Social Services Agency, whose main administrative offices are in Key West. We also have listed the branch office locations in the Upper and Middle Keys and the contact numbers of each department in the individual descriptions. Note that services in the Middle Keys also include Big Pine Key, which ordinarily is included with the Lower Keys throughout the book. The rest of the Lower Keys are handled from the offices in Key West.

Alternately, you can call the Elder Helpline (800-963-5337) and describe your problem or need; you will be referred to the proper agency. Monroe County Social Services office locations include: in the Upper Keys, Plantation Key Government Center Annex, MM 88.8 Bayside, Tavernier; in the Middle Keys, Marathon

Government Annex, MM 50.5 Oceanside, 490 63rd Street, Suite 190, Marathon; and, in the Lower Keys, Public Service Building, Wing III, 5100 College Road, Key West.

To find information on Monroe County Services online, consult www.co.monroe.fl.us.

In-Home Services
Upper Keys (305) 852-7154
Middle Keys (305) 852-7154
Lower Keys, Key West (305) 292-4583
In-Home Services networks information and referrals between the private and public sector for family members, friends, and other agencies seeking services on behalf of impaired elderly persons. Participants must be at least age 60. The program is designed so the elderly may maintain quality of life while remaining in their homes.

The information and referral telephone line (800-273-2044) is staffed by case managers from 8:00 A.M. to 5:00 P.M., Monday through Friday. They will specifically target the needed assistance and refer the caller to the resources available. Case management provides a social worker to support and help those requiring assistance.

Chore services for impaired elderly who can no longer accomplish the tasks for themselves are available. These include yard work, heavy-duty cleaning services, and small minor household repairs. Homemaking support with light housekeeping, meal preparation and planning, shopping, laundry tasks, and other essential errands assist clients in need. Personal care, in-home respite aides will help with bathing, dressing, and other personal needs, providing relief for caregivers. A fee schedule assessment based on the person's income will determine what or if he or she will have to pay for these services.

Want to feel like a kid again? Even if you do not have kids or grandkids in tow while in Florida Keys, check out our chapter on Kidstuff. There are a bunch of fun and inexpensive idea (some free!) to occupy your time. Besides, it is quite delightful, every once in a while, to act your shoe size!

Nutrition Services
Upper Keys (305) 852-7133
Middle Keys (305) 743-3346
Lower Keys (305) 872-3617
Key West (305) 294-0708, (305) 295-5166
Funded by the Older Americans Act of 1960 and the Alliance for Aging for Miami-Dade and Monroe Counties, and aided with a 10 percent cash match by the Monroe County Board of Commissioners, seniors age 60 and older may take advantage of many county nutrition programs. Homebound persons can receive a daily hot meal from Meals on Wheels. The senior centers throughout the Keys offer a low-cost, noontime, complete balanced meal (see the Senior Centers section in this chapter). The midday repast is supplemented with instruction on nutrition, hygiene, health-care concerns, and hurricane preparedness, and the group also participates in card games and organized activities.

Senior Community Service Employment Program (SCSEP)
Lower Keys, Key West (305) 292-4593
The Senior Community Service Employment Program (SCSEP) is a national program funded by Title V of the Older Americans Act. It provides temporary work experience and training for persons age 55 and older who meet financial and eligibility guidelines. Most seniors living on Social Security payments alone will qualify. The training occurs at governmental and nonprofit community service agencies. Jobs include library aides, nutrition site aides, senior citizen center receptionists, or aides in the Social Security office, Job Service office, or Red Cross office. The employment prepares candidates for jobs in the private sector.

Transportation Program
Upper Keys (305) 852-7148
Middle Keys (305) 289-6052
Lower Keys, Key West (305) 292-4424
Monroe County maintains eight mini-buses throughout the Keys, providing transportation for individuals age 60 and older or those physically challenged or transportation disadvantaged (those who don't or can't have a driver's license for some reason). Travelers must be able to get to the bus unassisted, but the vehicle has a wheelchair lift to aid entry. The bus picks up and drops off at your door between 8:15 A.M. and 5:00 P.M. (last pickup is 4:30 P.M.). Seniors must call for bus service 24 hours in advance, no later than 3:00 P.M. The route is figured every day, based on the pickup times and locations requested. Riders must allow plenty of time to get to their appointments and should expect that actual pickup may be 30 minutes before or after requested pickup time.

Each of the eight buses has a set territory: The Lower Keys circuit is considered Key West to Big Pine Key. The Middle Keys territory is between Sugarloaf Key and Marathon. The two Upper Keys routes travel between Marathon and MM 72 and between MM 72 and MM 112 at the county line on the 18-mile stretch. Fees are figured on a sliding scale based on mileage. Inquire about the cost of your transport when you make your reservation. The dispatcher will compute the mileage between your pickup point and your destination.

Veterans Affairs
88820 Overseas Highway, Tavernier
(305) 852-7104

490 63rd Street, Marathon
(305) 289-6009

1200 Truman Avenue, Key West
(305) 295-5150
This office is a liaison between veterans and the veterans administration, providing services for more than 21,000 vets in Monroe County. This office helps in locating education benefits, outpatient and hospitalization needs, insurance claims, social security appeals, transportation to the Miami VA, and other services.

Welfare Department
Upper Keys (305) 852-7125
Middle Keys (305) 289-6016
Lower Keys, Key West (305) 292-4408
Monroe County, which encompasses the Florida Keys, has the highest cost of living of any county in the state of Florida. Yet no adjustment is made in eligibility requirements for aid for senior citizens, who are usually managing on fixed incomes. This county agency works with seniors on a case-by-case basis as an interim assistance agency, helping solve unexpected crises that put them at temporary financial risk. The agency also aids seniors in matters of lost checks, robbery, and fraud; provides equipment loans of wheelchairs and walkers; and helps out with short-term medical needs such as prescriptions, eyeglasses, and hearing aids. This help is designed to restore the individuals to self-sufficient status or to refer them to the appropriate state or federal agencies for more long-term support. Documentation of need is required to qualify for assistance.

ASSISTED-LIVING FACILITY

Bayshore Manor
MM 4, 5200 College Road, Stock Island
(305) 294-4966
Bayshore Manor is the oldest assisted-living facility in Monroe County and the only such facility in the state of Florida owned and operated by county government. It is staffed on a 24-hour basis by State Certified Nursing Assistants and is licensed to provide full residential care.

In addition to full-time residents, Bayshore Manor also operates the only respite/daytime program in Monroe County for elderly residents who require constant nonmedical attention at home either because of mental, emotional, or physical limitations or simply because their families are concerned about them remaining at home alone during the day. This program provides daily group activities such as field trips, arts and crafts, music, games, and simple calisthenics plus a daily hot lunch. This service is available seven days a week.

Additionally, bed space permitting, short-term admissions for up to 30 days are available for caregivers who require longer periods of time away from the person in their care. Residents live in private rooms equipped with a color television. The facility is centrally air-conditioned, and meals are served in a communal dining room. In addition to assistance with activities of daily living, Bayshore Manor provides a full laundry service.

The monthly fee for residential service is based upon the client's ability to pay, and the admission procedure is a joint process involving both the Bayshore Manor director and the Monroe County Social Services Department's social workers.

Dancing Under the Stars

This may not be "Dancing with the Stars," exactly but where else is it possible to dance *under* the stars 365 days a year? But first, a few dance lessons. The Florida Keys has a wonderful and diverse mix of cultures, so our tastes in style run the gamut from salsa to swing. On Fridays in Key West, Paradise Health and Fitness offers salsa lessons and then dinner at El Meson de Pepe. On Saturdays they offer lessons for swing, Latin, hustle, ballroom, country/western, and salsa dancing.

In Big Pine Key, on Wednesday you can enjoy line dancing at the Big Pine Senior Center on Key Deer Boulevard. In Marathon, on Monday and Tuesday at the Marathon Community Theatre, Tropical Tappers meets for classes. On the first Friday of every month, there is an open house dance party at Theo and Ganine's Dance Center, (305) 743-0660.

HEALTH CARE (H)

In case you need health care while you're here, this chapter offers a synopsis of options, listed by category in descending mile marker order from Key Largo to Key West, then alphabetically in Key West.

We have included information on health-care options, ranging from full-service hospitals and specialty care providers for patients in need of cancer or dialysis treatments to physical therapy clinics and mental health services. And don't miss the information on veterinary-care options. We care about Spot and Fluffy too!

Please be reminded, however, that this is not intended to be a comprehensive listing of all possible health services. The Florida Keys and Key West are served by physicians in nearly every specialty as well as by osteopaths, chiropractors, podiatrists, dentists, and optometrists. So if, while visiting our islands, you should develop a sudden toothache from downing one too many frozen coladas or drop a contact lens somewhere in the sand, don't despair. One of our many health-care providers will be available to help you, even on short notice. Ask your hotel concierge for a referral to the appropriate specialist or consult the Yellow Pages.

And should your situation call for medical expertise that is not available in the Florida Keys, rest assured that you will still be able to receive state-of-the-art treatment in a timely manner. The University of Miami's renowned Jackson Memorial Medical Center as well as other mainland hospitals and trauma facilities are just a helicopter ride away.

ACUTE-CARE CENTERS

Upper Keys

NOVA Care Rehabilitation
MM 100 Bayside, Key Largo
(305) 453-0409

3156 Northside Drive, Key West
(305) 292-1805
NOVA Care Rehabilitation maintains a network of therapists throughout the Florida Keys, specializing in physical, speech, and occupational therapy. Some locations also offer orthopedist, family physician, and internist referrals.

Mariners Hospital
MM 91.5 Bayside, Tavernier
(305) 434-3000
www.baptisthealth.net
Mariners Hospital, established as a nine-bed physicians' clinic in 1959, today is a state-of-the-art hospital facility, completed in the late 1990s. Among the services provided here are 24-hour emergency care, surgery (including outpatient), respiratory therapy, pulmonary rehabilitation, cardiac rehabilitation, and radiology (including MRI, CT scans, and mammography). Mariners maintains a sleep diagnostic center, laboratory, and pharmacy and has a hyperbaric, or decompression, chamber (see the Diving and Snorkeling chapter). Mariners has a helicopter pad for transfer of severe cases to mainland hospitals.

The hospital is a part of Baptist Health South Florida, a nonprofit health-care organization. Mariners Hospital also maintains and operates a state-of-the-art physical therapy center in a separate location at MM 100.3 Bayside, Key Largo, (305) 451-4398.

Middle Keys

Fishermen's Hospital
MM 48.7 Oceanside, Marathon
(305) 743-5533
www.fishermenshospital.com

The medical staff at Fishermen's Hospital offer care in the areas of cardiology, cardiac rehabilitation, family practice, general surgery, gynecology, oncology, internal medicine, neurology, pathology, radiology, rheumatology, and plastic/reconstructive surgery. A CT scanner, known as a helical scanner, provides three-dimensional images with extraordinary clarity. Emergency service and same-day surgery also are available.

A helicopter pad allows for emergency chopper services, and a hyperbaric emergency response team is on call for divers. Fishermen's Overnight Guest program provides testing and presurgery (the night prior to surgery) room and board. Also licensed to provide home health care, Fishermen's accepts most forms of insurance. Other hospital resources include a certified diabetes educator and nutritional support services. Fishermen's Hospital also offers physical therapy services at two separate locations: at MM 54, across from the Quay on Marathon Key, and at the Big Pine Key Plaza at MM 29.7. For information on either of these physical therapy centers, phone (305) 289-9950. This hospital is a for-profit organization.

Lower Keys

Big Pine Medical and
Minor Emergency Center
MM 30 Oceanside, Big Pine Key
(305) 872-3321

This emergency-care center, conveniently located on Big Pine Key, treats minor illnesses and emergencies (broken bones, cuts, insect bites, and so on). Although appointments are encouraged, walk-ins are welcome. The clinic is generally open Monday through Friday from 8:00 A.M. to 5:00 P.M. and some Saturday mornings. However, hours may vary with the season and patient demand, so it is best to phone ahead.

Key West

Fresenius Medical Care
1122 North Roosevelt Boulevard, Key Plaza Shopping Center
(305) 294-8453

This facility offers dialysis for kidney patients who would otherwise have to travel to the Upper Keys or Homestead. FMC is open during regular business hours and on Saturdays as well.

Key West Urgent Care
1503 Government Road (corner of Flagler Avenue and Seventh Street)
(305) 295-7550

Not feeling so hot? Need to see a doctor in a hurry? This is the place to go. No appointment necessary.

Treatment for minor illnesses and injuries is available six days a week, from 8:00 A.M. to 3:30 P.M., and credit cards are accepted. Some local insurance plans may also be accepted.

Keys Cancer Center
5900 Junior College Road, Stock Island
(305) 296-0021

External and internal radiation therapy for all types of cancer, including breast, skin, prostate, lung, and AIDS-related malignancies, is provided at the Keys Cancer Center. Patients are generally referred by other physicians, but walk-ins are always welcome. The center also offers state-of-the-art seed implants for prostate cancer.

The Keys Cancer Center is open Monday through Friday from 8:00 A.M. to 4:30 P.M. The staff actively work to educate and promote cancer awareness within the community, sponsoring screenings and working closely with cancer support groups.

Lower Florida Keys Health System
5900 Junior College Road, Stock Island
(305) 294-5531

Emergency Numbers

While we sincerely hope you won't ever need to use the following telephone numbers, it is a good idea to keep this information in a convenient place.

Police, fire, or rescue emergencies	911
Florida Poison Information Center	(800) 282-3171
U.S. Coast Guard Marine and Air Emergency	(305) 295-9700 CG, VH channel 16
Florida Marine Patrol	(305) 289-2320 (800) DIAL FMP; (800) 342-5367
Florida Highway Patrol	(800) 240-0453 FHP (statewide cell phone number)
Monroe County Emergency Management	(305) 289-6018 (800) 427-8340 (hurricane preparedness) (800) 955-5504 (emergency information hotline)

This accredited primary-care hospital is the only hospital in the Florida Keys to offer maternity services. Lower Florida Keys Health System maintains 169 beds, a 24-hour emergency room, a clinical lab, and a heliport. Added services include pediatrics, inpatient and outpatient psychotherapy, physical therapy, radiation therapy, chemotherapy, and cardiovascular and ambulatory care. The hospital offers substance-abuse assistance and comprehensive wellness programs.

MOBILE MEDICAL CARE

Rural Health Network of Monroe County Florida Inc. Medi-Van
1623 #4 Spalding Court, Key West
(305) 293-7570

The Rural Health Network was inaugurated in September 1999 to address Monroe County residents' need for affordable and accessible health care. Two fully equipped RVs travel up and down the Keys to provide free medical services to folks who are uninsured and might not otherwise seek primary-care treatment.

A combined effort of the Monroe County Health Department, the three Keys hospitals, the Health Foundation of South Florida, Catholic Charities of the Archdiocese of Miami, HUD, FEMA, HRSA, and the Florida Keys Area Health Education Center in conjunction with the University of Miami, this mobile medical service starts in Key Largo on Monday and finishes on Friday in Key West.

The vans are equipped like doctors' offices. Each has two small examination rooms and a cab that doubles as a triage area. Each mobile unit is staffed by a registered nurse, a nurse practitioner, and a health educator, as well as nursing and medical students. In addition, the medical director (a physician) is available from 10:00 A.M. to 7:00 P.M. for consultation. Patients needing care beyond the scope of the Medi-Van staff may be referred to specialists and area hospitals.

Appointments are available and walk-ins are welcome. The Medi-Vans charge a co-pay for their services.

Filling Prescriptions in the Keys

As is the case in so many other communities, small-town pharmacies are a thing of the past in the Keys. The national chains have taken over here. You might miss the indulgence of having a milk shake at the lunch counter while you wait for your prescription to be filled, but all the same, it is convenient to be able to fill your medical needs while on vacation. Even if you live in another state and have forgotten your meds, all the pharmacist has to do is click on the computer to call up your file from your local branch of the chain. Walgreens has five locations and CVS has seven. Some of these stores are open 24 hours.

Walgreens

Key Largo
(305) 451-4076
(305) 451-2512

Key West
(305) 292-9902
(305) 292-4936

Marathon
(305) 743-6923

CVS

Key Largo
(305) 451-3261

Islamorada
(305) 664-2576

Marathon
(305) 743-9484

Big Pine Key
(305) 872-3797

Key West
(305) 294-6693
(305) 294-2576
(305) 294-6337

HOME HEALTH SERVICES

Hospice of the Florida Keys/Visiting Nurse Association

MM 92 Oceanside, Tavernier
(305) 852-7887

MM 50.5 Oceanside, Marathon
(305) 743-9048

1319 William Street, Key West
(305) 294-8812

Hospice provides care for terminally ill patients with six months or less to live. Services are provided in private homes and nursing homes throughout the Keys by a staff of registered nurses, patient-care managers, and social workers. Certified nursing assistants tend to personal needs such as bathing, grooming, and bedding. All home-care patients must be referred to the agency by a physician. Comfort Care, which is private-duty nursing care, is also available. Hospice's purpose is to ensure patients' comfort so that the last days of their lives are quality ones.

Within this same nonprofit organization, the Visiting Nurse Association provides more aggressive home care for patients still undergoing various treatments or who need blood tests or care for wounds. This service also is provided upon a physician's request. Both Hospice and VNA are on call 24 hours a day, 7 days a week. Medicare and Medicaid are accepted.

NURSING HOMES

Plantation Key Convalescent Center
MM 88.5 Bayside, 48 High Point Road, Tavernier
(305) 852-3021

Crisis Intervention and Help Lines

Abuse Registry	(800) 96-ABUSE; (800) 962-2873
AIDS Help Inc.	(305) 296-6196; (305) 289-0055
AIDS Hotline for Counseling and Information	(800) 590-2437
Alcohol Treatment Center, 24-hour Helpline	(800) 711-6402
Alcoholics Anonymous	
Key Largo	(305) 852-6186
Marathon	(305) 743-3262
Lower Keys and Key West	(305) 296-8654
Domestic Abuse Shelter	
Key Largo	(305) 451-5666
Tavernier	(305) 852-6222
Middle Keys	(305) 743-4440
Big Pine Key	(305) 872-9411
Lower Keys	(305) 294-0824
Drug Helpline	(800) DRUGHELP; (800) 378-4435
Elder Helpline	(800) 963-5337
Hospice of the Florida Keys	
Upper Keys	(305) 852-7887
Middle Keys	(305) 743-9048
Lower Keys	(305) 294-8812
Narcotics Anonymous	
Islamorada	(305) 664-2270
Narcotics Anonymous Referral and Treatment Program	(800) 711-6375
Overeaters Anonymous	(305) 293-0070
Teenline (24-hour crisis intervention)	(305) 292-8440

This 120-bed facility specializes in long- and short-term convalescent care and physical and occupational therapy. This center and Key West Convalescent Center (see following listing) are under the same ownership.

Key West Convalescent Center
5860 West Junior College Road, Stock Island
(305) 296-2450
The 120-bed facility provides skilled and acute care as well as physical, speech, and occupational therapy. Psychologists are on staff.

MENTAL HEALTH SERVICES

The Counseling Associates
MM 99.5 Oceanside, Nationsbank Building, Suite 205, Key Largo
(305) 453-9522

MM 48 Oceanside, Fishermen's Hospital Medical Complex, Marathon
(305) 743-4748
A multidisciplinary staff, which includes a psychiatrist, psychologists, and social workers, has been providing comprehensive counseling and evaluation services for

individuals, couples, and families since 1989. Their specialties include stress management and marital counseling, hypnotherapy, psychiatric medication management, and evaluations related to learning disabilities, attention-deficit disorder, and child custody issues.

The Guidance Clinic of the Upper Keys
MM 92.5 Bayside, Tavernier
(305) 853-3284
Two psychiatrists and a psychologist provide comprehensive mental health care at this outpatient clinic. Available services include individual and group psychotherapy, marital and family therapy, and parental and child guidance. Substance-abuse counseling is also available. Clinic hours are by appointment, Monday through Friday.

The Guidance Clinic of the Middle Keys
MM 49 Oceanside, 3000 41st Street, Marathon
(305) 289-6150
This mental health facility offers primarily inpatient treatment for substance-abuse and mental illness. Other programs include day treatment, job coaching, case management, medication management, a detox unit, a crisis stabilization unit, and a residential program. The staff consists of a psychiatrist and several qualified and licensed care providers.

Care Center For Mental Health
1205 Fourth Street, Key West
(305) 292-6843
This traditional outpatient community mental health center offers psychiatric diagnosis, treatment, evaluation and testing; psychological services; substance abuse treatment services; 24-hour emergency services for those in imminent danger; crisis services during business hours on a walk-in basis; and acupuncture service.

ALTERNATIVE HEALTH CARE

Many of the people who reside full time in the Florida Keys are laid-back types who were drawn to our islands by a desire to pursue a less-than-conventional lifestyle. In many cases their approach to health care is as nontraditional as their approach to life.

The Florida Keys, and Key West in particular, boast a wealth of options in the alternative health care category. These include everything from yoga classes and massage therapy on the beach to acupuncture, homeopathic medicine, organic foods, and herbal remedies. For a complete list of alternative health care options and practitioners throughout the Florida Keys, consult the local Yellow Pages under the following categories: Acupuncture, Health Clubs, Health and Diet Food Products, and Massage Therapists.

VETERINARY SERVICES

Your four-legged friends and "family" sometimes need health care, too. These pet clinics cater to their needs from the top of the Keys to Key West.

Upper Keys

Animal Care Clinic
MM 100.6 Bayside, Key Largo
(305) 453-0044
Boarding and grooming are small parts of the operation at Animal Care Clinic. The clinic maintains oxygen-intensive critical-care units and offers surgery, lab testing, X-rays, EKG, and ultrasound dentistry, as well as emergency on-call service, 24 hours a day, seven days a week.

VCA Upper Keys Animal Hospital
MM 87.8 Oceanside, Islamorada
(305) 852-3665

This clinic provides comprehensive services for all types of animals, including dogs, cats, birds, reptiles, ferrets, and exotics. Twenty-four-hour emergency care is offered seven days a week. Boarding is provided for clients.

Middle Keys

Animal Hospital of the Keys
MM 52.5 Bayside, Marathon
(305) 743-3647, (305) 743-2287
This veterinary hospital offers a full range of services, including 24-hour emergency care and boarding. (Note that the last four digits of their telephone numbers respectively spell "dogs" and "cats.")

Marathon Veterinary Hospital
MM 52.5 Oceanside, Marathon
(305) 743-7099, (800) 832-7694
www.marathonvethospital.com
Marathon Veterinary Clinic is small, but the vets here offer full services, including 24-hour emergency care, for dogs, cats, and all exotics.

Lower Keys

Cruz Animal Hospital
MM 27 Bayside, Ramrod Key
(305) 872-2559
A variety of medical services for virtually all pets, plus 24-hour emergency service is available at Cruz Animal Hospital. Military and senior citizen discounts are available.

Doc Syn's Veterinary Care
MM 22.7 Bayside, Cudjoe Key
(305) 744-0074
At Doc Syn's the motto is "we treat your pets as if they were our own." The facility offers complete medical and surgical care for dogs, cats, birds, ferrets, and reptiles. Evening hours are available.

Key West

All Animal Clinic
5505 Fifth Avenue, Stock Island
(305) 294-5255
This clinic offers medicine, surgery, dentistry, an in-house laboratory, X-rays, and emergency care. They offer house calls by appointment and also have an air-conditioned boarding facility.

Animal Hospital of Olde Key West & Stock Island
6150 Second Street, Stock Island
(305) 296-5227
Veterinary services for dogs, cats, birds, and small exotics are provided in a modern, full-service facility that offers a yearly health-care plan. A complete boarding facility is on the premises. Twenty-four-hour emergency service is also available.

House Call Vet
(305) 294-9551
House Call Vet is exactly what this name implies! If you are visiting Key West and have a pet that needs a veterinarian, this is the doc to call. If you get a recording, leave a message and someone will get back to you to discuss your animal's needs and arrange a time to visit. Too bad we humans don't have the same service!

Lower Keys Animal Hospital
3122 Flagler Avenue, Key West
(305) 294-6335
This facility treats small exotics but mostly sees cats and dogs. The staff offer regular checkups, surgery, dentistry, vaccinations, X-rays, and general medical treatment for pets.

EDUCATION AND CHILD CARE

The Florida Keys and Key West are served by public and private schools, preschools, and a community college. Thanks to a visiting institute and college degree programs at the Boca Chica Naval Air Station in the Lower Keys, students can earn bachelor's, master's, and even doctoral degrees without ever leaving our islands. In addition, several institutions of higher education in Miami are within commuting distance.

Following the information on education options is a comprehensive look at the child-care scene in the Florida Keys and Key West. We explore traditional child-care services along with other handy (sometimes vacation-saving) options such as drop-in care, babysitting, sick-child and respite care, family child-care homes, and public after-school programs.

EDUCATION

Public Schools

The Monroe County School District oversees schools from Key Largo to Key West, including three high schools. Some elementary and middle schools within our county occupy the same building; other middle and high schools share facilities.

Upper Keys students attend Coral Shores High School in Tavernier or Key Largo Elementary and Middle School or Plantation Elementary and Middle School in Tavernier.

Students in the Middle Keys are taught at Switlik Elementary School and Marathon Middle and High School.

Lower Keys elementary-age students are taught at Big Pine Neighborhood School or the Sugarloaf Elementary/Middle School, a $16 million, state-of-the-art campus opened to students in winter 2000. High school students may choose between Key West High School and Marathon High School.

Key West elementary schools are Glynn Archer on White Street, Gerald Adams on West Junior College Road, Poinciana on 14th Street, and Sigsbee at Sigsbee Naval Base. Grades 6 through 8 are at Horace O'Bryant Middle School on Leon Street, and grades 9 through 12 are at Key West High School on Flagler Avenue.

The school system, which operates on a school year that runs from late August through early June, offers computer technology and other innovative programs, including a television production lab and theatrical program at Key Largo School and a mentoring program and a welcome package for new students at Coral Shores High School in Tavernier. Dropout prevention programs and college credit courses taught in high school are other special programs.

An elected board headed by an elected superintendent, who oversees five district representatives, governs our public schools. Board members serve four-year terms. School funding comes from Monroe County property taxes. For more information on Monroe County Public Schools, consult their Web site at www.monroe.k12.fl.us.

Private Schools

Private schools typically offer smaller student-teacher ratios and a variety of learning curricula. The following list includes private schools operating in the Florida Keys and Key West.

Montessori Island Charter School
MM 92.3 Oceanside, Tavernier
(305) 852-3482
Montessori schools across the country work on the principle of self-pacing for children. This Montessori school, established in 1996, works on the same idea of purposeful action. The school provides education for preschool through elementary children with Montessori-certified teachers.

Island Christian School
MM 83.4 Bayside, Islamorada
(305) 664-2781,
(305) 664-4933 (high school)

14 125th Street Bayside, Marathon
(305) 743-2200
Established in 1974 by a group of parents from Island Community Church, Island Christian began with 54 students. As grade levels were added and the school became accredited, enrollment increased to 300. Island Christian today teaches prekindergarten through high school students in a traditional college-preparatory curriculum that incorporates the Abeka and Bob Jones Christian teachings. The average class size is 18. The school offers a full interscholastic sports program to junior and senior high school students. Each elementary-level class has computers, and junior and senior high levels have computer labs.

Marathon Lutheran School
MM 53.3 Bayside, 325 122nd Street, Marathon
(305) 289-0700
A service of Martin Luther Chapel and the Lutheran Church Missouri Synod, a national Lutheran organization, Marathon Lutheran School offers education from kindergarten through sixth grade. Using the School of Tomorrow PACE program, Marathon Lutheran offers its students the opportunity to learn at their own speeds with several class levels combined. Established in 1987, the school requires students to attend weekly chapel service and take religion classes. Music and karate instruction also are offered here, and students work on computers at least once a day.

Grace Lutheran School
2713 Flagler Avenue, Key West
(305) 296-8262
Established in 1952 and designed for prekindergarten three-year-olds through second-graders, Grace Lutheran offers computers and teaches Spanish in all but pre-kindergarten classes. During "God Time," students learn about Christian ideals and how to live them.

Mary Immaculate Star of the Sea
700 Truman Avenue, Key West
(305) 294-1031
Mary Immaculate follows a pre-kindergarten through eighth-grade curriculum outlined by the Archdiocese of Miami, including religious instruction. The school's mission is to provide opportunities for all Lower Keys families to experience a Catholic education. Within a Christian environment, the instructors foster spiritual, academic, and social development.

Montessori Children's School of Key West
1221 Varela Street, Key West
(305) 294-5302
Montessori is designed to support a child's need for purposeful action. Here teachers guide students without unnecessary interference—all furnishings are child-size, and photos are hung at a child's viewing level. Allowed freedom within certain guidelines, Montessori children work at their own pace on their own projects. Classes are mixed in age—ages three through five and grades one through three study together. The idea is to foster learning by example and learning to share. A director and assistant director are assigned to each class of about 28 students. The school also offers summer day-care programs.

Additional Educational Opportunities

Residents and visitors to the Florida Keys may participate in a number of hands-on educational opportunities listed below.

MarineLab Marine Resources Development Foundation
51 Shoreland Drive, Key Largo
(305) 451-1139, (800) 741-1139
www.mrdf.org
Offering students an in-depth introduction to the ecology of the Keys, the nonprofit Marine Resources Development Foundation provides customized programs for students. Learn about sea life in the Emerald Lagoon or explore the MarineLab Undersea Laboratory. Customized programs can include scuba certification, coral reef ecology, mangrove ecology, or a trip to the Everglades.

Seacamp Association
MM 30 Oceanside, Newfound Harbor Road and 1300 Big Pine Avenue, Big Pine Key
(305) 872-2331
www.seacamp.org
This scuba and marine science camp for children ages 12 through 17 has been in Big Pine Key for more than 30 years. Children from across the world sign up for Seacamp's 18-day program to experience scuba diving, sailing, snorkeling, and sailboarding. Marine science classes teach about such subjects as exploring the seas, animal behavior, and Keys critters. Scuba certification is available.

The camp operates from June through August and offers a day camp in summer for resident children ages 10 through 14. In addition, Seacamp is affiliated with the Newfound Harbor Marine Institute, which hosts three-day winter field trips for teachers and students from fourth grade through high school.

i ***Run by the University of North Carolina and funded by the National Oceanic and Atmospheric Administration, the National Undersea Research Center in Key Largo operates the Aquarius Undersea Laboratory, the nation's only underwater research habitat. The center has been featured on ABC's 20/20. The Aquarius Web site (www.uncw.edu/nurc/aquarius) contains detailed information about current science projects and missions.***

San Carlos Institute
516 Duval Street, Key West
(305) 294-3887
In keeping with its century-old mission of promoting Cuban culture and democratic ideals, the historic San Carlos Institute offers Spanish-language classes for adults in two terms: winter and summer. Taught by native speakers, these eight-week sessions are available at three levels: beginner, intermediate I, and intermediate II.

Higher Education

Florida Keys Community College
5901 West College Road, Key West
(305) 296-9081
www.firn.edu/fkcc
When Florida Keys Community College (FKCC) began operation in fall 1965, it became the first institution of higher education in the Florida Keys. FKCC was established through funding provided to Monroe County by the Florida state legislature after parents and teachers had expressed concerns over the lack of a college in the Keys. Today the school boasts an enrollment of more than 6,000 and offers associate of science and arts degree programs in such fields as business administration, computer programming and analysis, nursing, multimedia technology, and marine environmental technology.

FKCC's performing and visual arts programs are enhanced by the college's Tennessee Williams Fine Arts Center (see the

Arts and Culture chapter). Its marine environmental technology and dive programs are especially popular. Certificate programs are offered at FKCC in business data processing, marine propulsion technology, small-business management, addiction studies, and more. Vocational training is also available for law enforcement and correctional officers. In 1995 FKCC opened the Mario F. Mitchell Aquatic Safety Center for dive technology and a state-of-the-art oceanfront pool.

In addition to its main campus on Stock Island, Florida Keys Community College also offers a limited number of classes at two other Keys locations: the Middle Keys Center at 900 Sombrero Beach Road, MM 50, Marathon, (305) 743-2133; and the Upper Keys Center at MM 89.9, Tavernier, (305) 852-8007.

Saint Leo College-Key West Center
718-A Hornet Street, Boca Chica Naval Air Station, Key West
(305) 293-2847
www.saintleo.edu
Saint Leo College offers the only regionally accredited bachelor's degree program in the Florida Keys. Located in Key West since 1975, Saint Leo is a private college that offers associate of arts and bachelor of arts degrees in business administration, criminology, human services, and/or human resource administration. Situated at the naval air station, Saint Leo College is open to all civilian and military personnel and their families in the Florida Keys. Classes are designed for the working adult.

CHILD CARE

Gone are the days of Ward and June, Ozzie and Harriet, and Lucy and Ricky, those televised icons of the '50s nuclear family. In their TV Land, Pop went to the office while Mom stayed home with the children. Nowadays, when fathers go off to work, most mothers are right behind them on their way to jobs; grandparents work, too. Child care has become a necessity, and the Florida Keys' scenario differs little from this national norm.

i

The Florida Keys is a destination for many international visitors. The two predominant languages spoken here are English and Spanish. In fact the words Florida and Keys (or cayos) are Spanish words meaning "flowery" and "little islands." With many countries represented on our "little islands," be sure to use your language skills when visiting. In order, here are the countries sending most visitors to the Florida Keys:* USA, Canada, Central America, United Kingdom, Brazil, Italy, Germany, Netherlands/Holland, and Venezuela.

****Monroe County Tourist Development Council***

The problem of finding good, competent child care is compounded here by a shortage of available providers at any cost. According to the National Association for the Education of Young Children, child care is the fourth-largest item in the family budget after food, housing, and taxes. Infant care (birth to age one) and weekend and evening care are in particularly short supply in Monroe County, which encompasses the Keys.

Day-to-day child care in the county generally falls into two categories: center-based care and family child-care homes.

In this section we provide information on resources, types of child-care programs, and contacts for centers that serve the Florida Keys and Key West.

Resources

Wesley House Family Services Coordinating Agency
1304 Truman Avenue, Key West
(305) 292-7150, ext. 228
www.wesleyhouse.org
With offices in Key West and serving all of the Florida Keys, Wesley House assists

families in making the best of a difficult situation. The Wesley House Resource & Referral Network is perhaps the most important resource in the Keys for parents looking for appropriate, quality child care. (Wesley House is a national division agency of the United Methodist Church and a United Way of Monroe County agency.) WHR&R acts as a link between families and the child-care services they seek. It can recommend affordable child care for children up to 5 years old and after-school and summer care for children up to 12 years old. Families may access services at three locations in the Florida Keys: 175 Wrenn Street, Tavernier, (305) 853–3518; 2796 Overseas Highway, Marathon, (305) 289–2675; and 1304 Truman Avenue, Key West, (305) 292–7150.

WHR&R offers other assistance in the forms of subsidized child care, scholarships, and help in obtaining legal aid, medical aid, food stamps, and other services. The network conducts classes for parents in money management, parenting skills, nutrition, and handling everyday pressures. It provides personal help for families with at-risk children, assisting them in filling out paperwork to meet eligibility requirements. Wesley House also offers transportation to and from child-care centers for children in at-risk situations.

Wesley House will provide referrals for families needing sick care or in-home nursing specialists. Some child-care centers will offer drop-in care.

Types of Programs

This section describes the center- and home-based child-care options available to parents in Monroe County.

CHILD-CARE/PRESCHOOL CENTERS

The minimum state licensing requirements dictate that a child-care center must hold a valid license from the Health and Rehabilitative Services Department of the state of Florida. The license must be posted in a conspicuous place within the center.

The center must adhere to the number of children for which it is licensed, and it must maintain the minimum staff-to-child ratio for each age level: Younger than age 1, one teacher for every four children; age 1, 1 to 6; age 2, 1 to 11; age 3, 1 to 15; age 4, 1 to 20; and age 5, 1 to 25. We stress that this is the minimum ratio. It may not be sufficient to give your child the level of care you desire.

Licensing standards mandate health and safety requirements and staff training requirements. These include: child abuse and neglect training, a 20-hour child-care training course, a 10-hour specialized training module, and 8 hours of in-service training annually. In addition, there must be one CPR- and first-aid-certified person on-site during business hours. Some centers are prepared to accept infants; others are not.

Some child-care centers are exempt from HRS licensing. They are accredited and monitored by religious agencies, the school board, or the military.

Unfortunately, no child-care centers are open weekends or evenings in the Keys.

Contact Wesley House for a list of HRS-licensed and license-exempt child-care/preschool centers in the Florida Keys and Key West.

FAMILY CHILD-CARE HOMES

Family child-care is considered by the state of Florida to encompass home-based child care with five or fewer preschool-age children from more than one family unrelated to the caregiver. Any preschool children living in the home must be included in the maximum number of children allowed. The adult who provides the child care is usually referred to as a family child-care home operator.

Some counties in Florida require that family child-care homes be licensed. Monroe Country, which includes the Florida Keys, requires only registration with the Department of Health and Rehabilitative

Services. Every adult in the household must be screened. Registration requires no on-site inspection of the home for minimum health, safety, and sanitation standards, however. Nor is there a requirement that the family child-care operator have CPR or first-aid training.

Military programs are exempt from this registration. They have their own accreditation procedures and are available only to family members of military personnel.

Wesley House actively recruits for and offers a three-hour course covering basic health and safety issues to persons who wish to operate registered family child-care homes.

PUBLIC AFTER-SCHOOL PROGRAMS

Many public schools in the Florida Keys and Key West run their own after-hours programs for school-age children from 2:15 to 5:30 P.M. and also on school holidays and summer weekdays. Most schools charge for this service. Contacts at the schools are: Key Largo Elementary School, MM 104.8, Key Largo, (305) 453-1255; Plantation Key School, 100 Lake Road, Tavernier, (305) 853-3281; Switlik Elementary, MM 48.8 Bayside, 33rd Street, Marathon, (305) 289-2490; Big Pine Key Neighborhood School, Palomino Horse Trail, Big Pine Key, (305) 872-1266; Sugarloaf Elementary/Middle School, 255 Crane Road, Sugarloaf Key, (305) 745-3282; Poinciana Elementary School, 1212 14th Street, Key West, (305) 293-1630; Sigsbee Elementary, Sigsbee Naval Base, Key West, (305) 294-1861 (military families only); Gerald Adams Elementary School, 5855 West Junior College Road, Key West, (305) 293-1609.

The following are phone contacts for various programs offered by Monroe County for youths and children: Boy Scouts of America, (305) 364-0020; Girl Scouts of Tropical Florida, (305) 253-4841; Boys and Girls Clubs of the Keys Area, (305) 296-2258.

BABYSITTING

Personal knowledge of the person you choose to care for your child in your absence is the best of all possible worlds, but it isn't always a reality. If you are a visitor to the Florida Keys or Key West or a newly relocated resident, you may have to take a leap of faith and entrust your child to someone you do not know. Therefore, you should check references. For referrals, contact Wesley House (see listing under Resources) or ask the concierge at your hotel.

You can also contact local chambers of commerce, which often keep lists of local residents who babysit: Key Largo, (305) 451-1414, (800) 822-1088; Islamorada, (305) 664-4503, (800) 322-5397; Marathon, (305) 743-5417, (800) 262-7284; Lower Keys, (305) 872-2411, (800) 872-3722; and Key West, (305) 294-2587, (800) 527-8539. Be sure to ask by what criteria these referrals have been checked for more insight as to who best suits your needs.

MEDIA

Even after Henry Flagler's extension of the Florida East Coast Railroad provided Florida Keys residents access to the mainland, communications on our islands were limited. To receive local news and news outside the South Florida area, residents relied on radio broadcasts from Miami, sporadic postal service, and what was probably their most effective and timely means of dispatch: word of mouth, or what is jokingly referred to as "the Conch telegraph."

Today two dailies and a contingent of weeklies and free papers tie the Keys together. Both AM and FM radio stations are still restricted by wattage, and residents must subscribe to satellite or cable service to get television reception.

NEWSPAPERS

In addition to home delivery, our newspapers are often sold in curbside vending racks, grocery stores, pharmacies, convenience stores, and bookstores. A handful of shops carry national and international newspapers. Because the Florida Keys is considered a remote distribution site, some national newspapers, such as the *New York Times,* are sold at a higher newsstand price. A rule of thumb: Get to the newsstand early. The farther you travel from the mainland, the more quickly the out-of-town papers sell out.

Dailies

Key West Citizen
3420 Northside Drive, Key West
(305) 292-7777
www.keysnews.com

In 1904 a small, weekly newspaper known as the *Citizen* appeared on the newspaper scene in Key West; it was later consolidated with the 1899 *Inter-Ocean* to form the *Key West Citizen.* Cooke Communications now owns the *Key West Citizen,* along with *Solares Hill,* the *Free Press* Community Newspapers, and Florida Keys News Service.

The *Citizen* shares editorial coverage and classified advertisements with its sister publications and features a significant amount of syndicated material and lifestyles coverage.

The *Citizen*'s editorial focus is primarily on features. *Paradise,* a tabloid appearing in Thursday's edition, is a comprehensive compendium of what's currently happening in the theaters and at the clubs and galleries around town. Free copies of *Paradise* are available at newsstands, hotels, guesthouses, restaurants, and other businesses throughout Key West. The *Citizen* also publishes "The Menu," a free quarterly guide containing menus from many area restaurants.

The *Citizen* is published daily. If you happen to be in the Keys on April 1, be sure to grab a copy of the April Fool's edition. The front page is almost believable and always a hoot!

The Miami Herald
1 Herald Plaza, Miami
(305) 350-2111, (800) 437-2535

619 Eaton Street, Key West
(305) 294-5131 (newsroom)
www.miamiherald.com

The largest-circulation daily newspaper in the southeastern United States, this Pulitzer Prize winner has maintained Key West correspondents for decades and now has a bureau in the southernmost city, Key West. *The Miami Herald* features crisp writing and tends to favor features over hard news except when issues are pressing.

The *Herald* is widely available throughout the Keys.

Weeklies and Biweeklies

The Reporter
MM 91.6 Oceanside, Tavernier
(305) 852-3216
www.upperkeysreporter.com
When the *Reporter* began in the early 1900s, the newspaper, which was based in Key Largo, was mimeographed. As the publication grew, its owners bought what was at the time a top-of-the-line printing press—a monumental event in Keys publishing, since few newspapers were actually printed in this stretch of Monroe County. The *Reporter* is now published by Knight-Ridder, which also publishes the *Miami Herald* and the *Florida Keys Keynoter.*

Published each Thursday, this tabloid packages community news from south Miami-Dade County to Marathon in a traditional black-and-white format and is available in stores throughout the Upper Keys.

***Free Press* Community Newspapers**
MM 81.5 Oceanside, Islamorada
(305) 664-2266, (800) 926-8412

MM 52 Oceanside, Marathon
(305) 743-8766
www.keysnews.com
Formerly known as the *Islamorada Free Press,* this group of weekly tabloid newspapers has grown to include five separate editions, each serving a segment of the Florida Keys population, from Ocean Reef to Big Pine Key. Owned by Cooke Communications since August 2000, the *Free Press* community newspapers cover local news and sports in each area. The newspapers are published each Wednesday and are available free in grocery and convenience stores as well as in curbside racks from Homestead to Big Coppitt Key.

Florida Keys Keynoter
MM 48.6 Oceanside, Marathon
(305) 743-5551

Key West Keynoter
2720A N. Roosevelt Boulevard, Key West
(305) 296-6989
www.keynoter.com
The *Florida Keys Keynoter* is owned by Knight-Ridder Publishing and is considered the *Miami Herald*'s sister newspaper. The *Keynoter* is Monroe County's second-oldest publication. With a weekly television news program and a separate Key West edition, the twice-weekly *Keynoter* offers comprehensive local coverage of the Florida Keys. Known for its in-depth coverage of the Keys' political scene, once a week the *Keynoter* also features "L'Attitudes," an arts and entertainment section that includes complete television listings for the area, special features, and upcoming Keys events.

This tabloid-style newspaper is published each Wednesday and Saturday and is widely available in shops, newsstands, and curbside racks throughout the Keys.

Want to know what is current in the Florida Keys? Click on www.fla-keys .com, the official tourism Web site.

Celebrate Key West
1075 Duval Street, Suite 19, Key West
(305) 295-8292
www.celebratekeywest.com
Celebrate Key West caters to the gay and lesbian population of Key West. Offering various community features along with gay-perspective editorials and stances on issues, *Celebrate Key West* provides a welcome alternative forum in Key West publishing. Of particular interest is a pull-out section listing gay-owned and gay-friendly businesses in and around Key West. This free paper is distributed throughout Key West each Friday.

El Faro
2311 Fogarty Avenue, Key West
(305) 296-3719
El Faro editor and publisher Jose Cabaleiro was working in the accounting department of a company in Cuba that printed Spanish versions of *Reader's Digest, Time,* and *Life* magazines when the Castro regime confiscated the business. Cabaleiro fled to Venezuela. In 1962 he moved to the United States, and in 1971 he established *El Faro* newspaper.

Published on the 15th and 30th of each month, this free Spanish/English newspaper covers social and political issues affecting residents of Monroe and Miami-Dade Counties.

Key West The Newspaper
422 Fleming Street, Key West
(305) 292-2108
www.kwest.net/~kwtn
Since its debut in January 1994, *Key West The Newspaper* has found its niche in the realm of politics and entertainment. While the paper boasts a hearty entertainment section full of live music listings, reviews, and local color, it is perhaps best known for its investigative reporting. This free weekly's motto is "journalism as a contact sport." It is distributed every Friday morning in Key West and Stock Island.

Solares Hill
3420 Northside Drive, Key West
(305) 294-3602
www.solareshill.com
Founded in 1971, the free weekly *Solares Hill* ceased its independent status in 1998 when it was acquired by the publishers of the *Key West Citizen* and the *Free Press* community newspapers. Although the newspaper's former slogan "the straight truth plainly stated" has been replaced with the words "the way a newspaper should be," its focus remains primarily on politics and business, along with a smattering of restaurant, theater, and book reviews. Distributed free of charge on Friday from Key West to Big Pine Key, *Solares Hill* covers the Lower Keys and Key West exclusively.

RADIO

Radio reception in the Florida Keys is heavily influenced by factors such as weather and distance from the transmitter. Clear skies and sunshine will optimize good reception; luckily, we have plenty of both most of the time.

TELEVISION

Florida Keys residents must pay for cable television service in order to receive network channels. Our cable provider is Comcast, (866) 288-3444.

In addition to national programming, local-origination programming is offered on channels 5 and 16. This public service programming includes live coverage of city commission and local political meetings, as well as real estate listings, and local-interest shows on a variety of topics such as health care and fishing. Channel 5 also offers interesting and informative infomercials during the day and evening, highlighting many of the Keys' attractions found in this book.

Satellite communication is an alternative to cable service. Check the Yellow Pages for companies offering satellite dishes and service.

WORSHIP

The Florida Keys owes much of its religious history to the Conchs, the group of seafaring settlers who emigrated from the Bahamas.

Some of the Conchs were the descendants of members of the Eleutherian Society, who left England in 1649 and 1650 to seek religious freedom. Others were descendants of loyalists who fled the Carolinas and Georgia during the American Revolution to settle in the Bahamas, which was then still controlled by England. They settled primarily in Key West, bringing with them devout religious beliefs, mostly Methodist.

Until 1881, local lay preachers filled the ministerial needs of the sparsely populated Florida Keys (except for Key West). Settlements were scattered and rustic, their inhabitants farming the unyielding coral rock with attempts at growing pineapples, tomatoes, limes, and melons. Many worked the sea as fishermen, harvesting a bounty more prolific. Two Key West ministers began making rounds of the Keys communities by boat, holding services for the next six years anywhere they could find a welcoming group of worshipers.

The main Upper Keys settlements in the late 1800s were Tavernier at the southern end of Key Largo; Planter, a mile north of Tavernier; Rock Harbor (present-day Key Largo); Newport, between Rock Harbor and Tarpon Basin; and Basin Hills, at the northern end of Key Largo. The first actual building outside Key West dedicated solely for worship services was built at Newport in 1885. Then a church was built in 1886 in Tavernier, named Barnett's Chapel in honor of its pastor. By 1887 a minister from the Florida Methodist Conference traveled a monthlong circuit of the Upper Keys, visiting Basin Hills, Newport, Tavernier, and Matecumbe. Plantation Key Methodists built their own church in 1899, and other congregations began assembling in private homes.

After the turn of the 20th century, with the advent of Flagler's East Coast Railroad Extension, the population of the Keys above Key West began to grow, and this growth spawned churches of diverse denominations. After World War II, the Florida Keys saw a further boom in population (see our Historical Evolution chapter), which spurred the construction of more churches. Unfortunately, the devastating hurricanes of 1935 and 1960 wiped out the physical church structures of the Middle and Upper Keys. None of the church buildings on these islands approach the age and stature of those of Key West.

Consult the Yellow Pages of the local telephone directory for times and locations of worship services. Florida Keys churches all welcome both visitors and new parishioners. Some of the churches offer child care during selected services or prayer groups. If this is of interest to you, call the church directly to inquire about arrangements.

KEY WEST

Earliest worship in Key West took place in the old courthouse on Jackson Square, where English-speaking persons would gather and hold nondenominational services. If a clergyman happened to be on the island for any reason, a service would be held and would be well attended by the devout of all faiths. When a group sharing the same beliefs became large enough, members splintered off and built a church of their own.

The first settlers to arrive were Bahamians who followed the Church of

The Grotto Shrine

The coral-rock grotto built in 1922 at Key West's St. Mary Star of the Sea's Convent of Mary Immaculate holds a legend. A destructive hurricane passed over the island in 1919, leaving death and property damage strewn in its wake. Sister Louis Gabriel envisioned the grotto as a shrine dedicated to protecting Key West from hurricanes. Since then, whenever a hurricane threatens, islanders flock to the grotto to say prayers and light candles. So far their faith has worked. Key West narrowly missed the hurricanes of 1935 and 1960 that hit the rest of the Keys. And although the island took a direct hit from Hurricane Georges in 1998 and hurricane Wilma in 2005, many believe there were no deaths or serious injuries and only minimal property damage because of the grotto.

England's Anglican teachings. They were seafarers, descendants from the religious dissenters who had left England more than 100 years before. They brought deeply religious convictions with them to the Keys. In March 1831 a movement started to bring a clergyman to the island of Key West on a permanent basis. It was stipulated, interestingly enough, that he would not be required to remain in the Keys any portion of August or September that he found disagreeable. These happen to be the most hurricane-prone months in the Florida Keys.

From the Bahamian root of religious conviction sprang a proliferation of church denominations in Key West, some of which still meet for worship today. Many churches in Key West are historically or architecturally significant: St. Paul's Episcopal Church, 401 Duval Street; First United Methodist (Old Stone) Church, 600 Eaton Street; St. Mary Star of the Sea, 1010 Windsor Lane; and Cornish Memorial A.M.E. (African Methodist Episcopal) Zion Church, 702 Whitehead Street.

For a complete listing of worship services in Key West each week, see the Friday edition of the *Key West Citizen*.

INDEX

A

Abaco Gold, 356
Abaco Sails, 203–4
Abbondanza, 79
A&B Lobster House, 64
A&B Marina, 213
Abyss Dive Center, 263
ACA Joe, 358
accommodations
  Key West bed-and-breakfasts, inns, and guesthouses, 145–62
  Key West gay guesthouses, 162–64
  Key West hotels, motels, and resorts, 136–45
  Lower Keys, 131–35
  Middle Keys, 122–31
  overview, 107–10, 122–23, 131–32, 135–36
  Upper Keys, 110–22
  vacation rentals, 166–68
  See also campgrounds
Action Keys Realty, Inc., 174
acute-care centers, 377–79
Adolphus Busch, The, 251
Adventure Charters, 280
Adventure Scooter & Bicycle Rentals, 273
African Queen, 278
Afterdeck Bar at Louie's Backyard, The, 103
airport limousines, 35
air tours, 267–68
air travel, 30–32
Alabama Jack's, 85
Alamo Rent A Car, 34
Alan S. Maltz Gallery, 343–44
Alexander's Guesthouse, 162
Alexander's Wreck, 253
Alice's at La Te Da, 73
All Animal Clinic, 383
Alligator Reef, 250
All-Pro Real Estate, 174
Almond Tree Inn, 146–47
Alonzo's Oyster Bar, 64
alternative health care, 382
amberjack, fishing for, 227
Ambrosia House, 147
American bald eagle, 21
American Caribbean Real Estate Inc., 173, 174
American Legion Post 154 Bingo, 277
American Powerboat Association World Championship, 335–36
American Shoals, 250
American white pelican, 17–18
Amy Slate's Amoray Dive Resort, 110–11, 261
anchoring out, 209–13, 215–16
Andrews Inn, 147
Andrew's Propeller Service, 198
Angelika, 352
Animal Care Clinic, 382
Animal Hospital of Olde Key West & Stock Island, 383
Animal Hospital of the Keys, 383
Anna Banana, 351
Anne's Beach, 270
Annette's Lobster & Steak House, 58
annual events, 325–37
Anthony's Women's Apparel, 350
Antonia's Restaurant, 79–80
Appledore Charter Windjammer, 280
Aqua-Nuts Dive Center, 261
Arsnicker Keys, 274–76
Art in the Park, 327
Artist House, The, 147–48
Artists in Paradise, 343
Art of Baking by Henrietta, The, 91
arts and culture
  arts organizations, 338–39
  cinema, 340–41
  Florida Keys art galleries, 341–43
  Key West art galleries, 343–47
  music, 341
  theater, 339–40
assisted living, 375–76
Assortment, Inc., 360–61
A T B Canvas Designs, 204
Atlantic's Edge, 51–52
Atlantic Shores Pool Bar & Grille, 103
Atlantic Shores Resort, 162–63
attractions
  beyond the Keys, 314–15
  Key West architecture, 304–6
  Key West guided and self-guided tours, 311–14
  Key West historic homes and museums, 299, 301–3, 306
  Key West one of a kind, 306–11
  Lower Keys, 298–99

Middle Keys, 295-98
overview, 292
Upper Keys, 292-95
See also children, activities for
Audubon House & Tropical Gardens, 299, 301
Authors of Key West Guesthouse, 148
Avis Rent A Car, 34

B

Baby's Coffee, 91
Bagatelle, 73
Bahama Mama's Kitchen, 84
Bahia Honda State Park, 182-83, 271
Bama Sea Products, 91
Banana Bay Resort & Marina, 129
Banana Cafe, 80
Banyan Resort, The, 148-49
bareboat charters, 202
Bargain Books and Newsstand, 365-66
Barnacle Bed & Breakfast, 132
barracuda, fishing for, 221-22
Barracuda Grill, 58
Bascom Grooms Real Estate, 176
Bay Breeze Motel, 116-17
Baypoint, 171
Bayshore Clothing and Small World, 353
Bayshore Manor, 375-76
Bayside Grille, 48
Bayside Resort, 113
Bay View Inn and Marina, 123
Bayview Park, 271-72
Bayview Park Tennis, 284
B & D Bikes, 272
Beach Club Brokers Inc., 176-77
beaches, 268-72
Beads of Distinction, 358
Becky Thatcher Designs, 361
bed-and-breakfasts. *See* accommodations
Benwood Wreck, 248
Besame Mucho, 361
Best Western Hibiscus Motel, 136
Best Western Key Ambassador Resort, 138-39
Bicycle Center, The, 273
bicycling, 272-73, 372
Big Coppitt, 171
Big John's Pizza, 73-74
Big Pine Bagel Island, 90
Big Pine Bicycle Center, 273
Big Pine Kayak Adventures, 286
Big Pine Key, 170
Big Pine Key Fishing Lodge, 183
Big Pine Medical and Minor Emergency Center, 378
Big Pine Restaurant & Coffee Shop, 61
Big Ruby's Guesthouse, 163
Big Spanish Channel Area, 212
Biker's Image, 360
Bike Shop, The, 273
billiards, 276-77
bingo, 276-77, 372
birds and birding, 17-22, 182
Birkenstock of Old Town, 359
Biscayne National Park, 314
Blackfin Resort, The, 129-30
blackfin tuna, fishing for, 225
Blackwater Sound, 210
Blond Giraffe, 91-92
Blue, 361
Blue Heaven, 64-65
Blue Hole, The, 298
blue marlin, fishing for, 224-25
Blue Marlin Jewelry, 352
Blue Marlin Resort Motel, 136-37
Blue Parrot Inn, 149
Bluewater Key RV Resort, 184
Bluewater Potters, 342
Blue Waters Motel, 131
Boater's World Discount Marine Center, 195, 240
Boat House, The, 197
boating and cruising
anchoring out, 209-13, 215-16
bareboat charters, 202
boat sales, repairs, fuel, and storage, 196-99
channel markers, 190-91
creeks and channels, 190
excursions, 277-83
flats, backcountry, and shallow nearshore waters, 188-89
Florida Keys National Marine Sanctuary regulations, 193-95
Florida Straits, 189-90
getting help, 191-92
gunkholing, 17-22, 274-76
houseboat rentals, 204-5
Intracoastal Waterway, 189
Key West harbor, 190
marinas, 206-9, 213-15
marine supply stores, 195-96
nautical charts, 190
overview, 188, 200, 206

patch reefs, Hawk Channel, and the barrier reef, 189
powerboat rentals, 199-200
public boat ramps, 195
reading the waters, 191
sailing clubs and regattas, 202-3
sailing courses, 200-201
sailmakers, 203-4
sunset cruises, 277-83
tide charts, 191
vessel registration and equipment, 192-93
See also diving and snorkeling; fishing
Bobalu's Southern Cafe, 62-63
Boca Grande Key, 215
bocce, 372
Body Zone South, 290
bonefish, fishing for, 219-20
Bonefish Bob's, 240-41
Bone Island Shuttle, 39
Boot Key Harbor, 212
Boot Key Harbor Christmas Boat Parade, 336
Borders Express, 366
BO's Fish Wagon, 65
Bottle Key, 211
bottlenose dolphin, 22
Bougainvillea House Gallery, 343
Bourbon Street Pub, 100
bowling, 276-77
Boy and His Dog Fine Art Gallery, A, 344
Boyd's Key West Campground, 184
Brass Monkey, 99
Breezer's Tiki Bar, 97
Breezy Palms Resort, 120
bridge clubs, 373
brown pelican, 17
Budget Car & Truck Rental, 34
Bud n' Mary's Fishing Marina, 236
Bull & Whistle, 101-2
Burdine's Chiki Tiki Bar and Grill, 59
bus service, 35-38
Butterfly Boutique, The, 344
Butterfly Café, 59
Butternut Key, 211

C

C. B. Harvey Rest Beach, 272
Cabot's on the Water, 59-60
Cafe Largo, 47-48
Café Marquesa, 74
Caloosa Cove Boat Rental, 200
Caloosa Cove Resort Condominium, 122
Calvert Sails, 203
Camille's Restaurant, 65
Camp Cheeca at Cheeca Lodge and Spa, 320
campgrounds
Lower Keys, 182-84
Middle Keys, 181
national parks, 185-86
overview, 179-80
reserving state park campsites, 186-87
Upper Keys, 180-81
Capt. John's *Greyhound V*, 239
Capt. Sterling's Everglades Eco-Tours, 278
Captain Hook's Marina, 236
Captain Michael, 238
Captain Run Aground Harvey's Floating Pub and Grub, 69
Captain's Corner Dive Center, 265
Captain's Imports, 349-50
Captain Slate's Atlantis Dive Center, 260-61
Captain's Three, 89
Captain Tony's Saloon, 102
Care Center For Mental Health, 382
Caribbean Club, 97
Caribbean Village, 135
Caribbean Watersports, 285
Caribbean Watersports Enviro Tours, 278-79
Caribee Boat Sales, 197
Caroline Street Parking Lot, 42
car rentals, 34-35
Carysfort Reef, 246
Casa Grande Bed & Breakfast, 132-33
Casa Marina Resort, The, 140-41, 320
Casa Morada, 118
Casa 325, 160
Cayman Salvager, 252
Cayo Carnival, 336
Celebrate Key West, 391
Center Court Historic Inn & Cottages, 149
Century 21 Prestige Group, 172, 173-74, 177
Chad's Deli and Bakery, 86-87
chambers of commerce, 112, 236-37
charters
bareboat, 202
boat excursions, sunset cruises, and gambling junkets, 277-83
fishing, 234-40
Cheeca Lodge & Spa, 118-19
Chelsea House, 149-50
Chesapeake Resort, 118
Chicken Store, The, 356

Chico's Cantina, 78
child care
babysitting, 389
child-care/preschool centers, 388
family child-care homes, 388–89
public after-school programs, 389
resources, 387–88
children, activities for
child-friendly resorts, 320–21
Florida Keys activities from A to Z, 316–20
top 15 Key West activities, 321–24
China Garden West, 82
Christmas Around the World at Marathon Garden Club, 336
Christmas Boat Parade, 336
Christ of the Deep Statue, 247
churches, 393–94
cinema (independent, foreign, and alternative), 340–41
Cinema Shores, 288
City of Key West Department of Transportation, 38
climate, 23–25
Clinton Square Market, 361
Club Body Tech, 290
cobia, fishing for, 226
Coconuts Dolphin Tournament, 231–32
Coconuts Restaurant & Lounge, 47, 97
Cocoplum Beach and Tennis Club, 126
Coffee and Tea House of Key West, The, 92
Coffee Mill Cultural Center, 290
Coffins Patch, 250
Coldwell Banker Schmitt Real Estate Co., 172, 174, 177
colleges, 386–87
Comfort Inn at Key West, 137
Commodore Waterfront Steakhouse, 69
Commotion, 361
Compass Realty, 177
Conch House Heritage Inn, The, 150
Conch Key Cottages, 123–24
Conch Reef, 249
Conch Republic Independence Celebration, 329
Conch Republic Seafood Company, 69–70
Conch Shell Blowing Contest, 328
Conch Tour Train, 311–12
Conchy Joe's Marine & Tackle, Inc., 241
condotels, 178
Congress Jewelers, 360
Consigning Adults, 366
Continental Inn, 127
Coral Bay Resort, 121
Coral Lagoon Resort, 127
Coral Reef Park Company, 261–62, 285
Coral Tree Inn, 164
cormorant, 18
Cosgrove Shoal, 254–55
Cotton Key, 211
Cottrell Key, 253–54
Counseling Associates, The, 381–82
Country Conch, 356
Cove Teen Club, 320–21
Crabby Dicks' Seafood Restaurant and Lounge, 70
Crack'd Conch, 44
Craig's Restaurant, 49
crisis intervention and help lines, 381
Crowne Plaza Key West La Concha, 139
cruising. *See* boating and cruising
Cruz Animal Hospital, 383
Crystal Bay Resort, 130
Crystal Loft, The, 355
Cuba! Cuba!, 357
Cuban American Heritage Festival, 330
Cuban Club Suites, 150–51
Cudjoe Key, 171
Curry Hammock State Park, 270–71
Curry Mansion, 301
Curry Mansion Inn, 151
Curtis Marine, 196
Curves, 289
Cypress House, 151–52
Cypress House Guest Studios, 151–52

D

Dagny Johnson Key Largo Hammock Botanical State Park, 269
Damn Good Food To-Go, 92
dancing, 376
Danger Charters, 280
D'Asign Source, 353
Deer Run Bed & Breakfast, 133
Deli Restaurant, The, 66
Delta Shoals, 250
Dewey House, 155–56
Dion's Quick Mart, 76–77
Disabled American Veterans Chapter 122 Bingo, 277
Dive Key West Inc, 265–66
diving and snorkeling
dive centers, 255, 260–63, 265–66
dive sites beyond the Keys, 254–55

diving for lobster, 256–59
getting help in emergencies, 245
Key West dive sites, 251–54
Lower Keys dive sites, 250–51
Middle Keys dive sites, 250
overview, 243–46
spearfishing, 264
Upper Keys dive sites, 246–49
See also boating and cruising; fishing
DJ's Diner and Coffee Shop, 48
Dockside Cakes Bakery & Deli, 86
Dockside Lounge, 98–99
Doc Syn's Veterinary Care, 383
Dollar Rent A Car, 34
dolphin, fishing for, 225–26
Dolphin Connection, The, 295–96
Dolphin Cove, 292
Dolphin Dayz, 320–21
Dolphin Marina, 208
Dolphin Research Center, 296–97
Dolphins Plus Inc., 292–93
Don Hawley Invitational Tarpon Tournament, 232, 330
Don Pedro's Restaurant, 56
Doubletree Grand Key Resort, 141
Douglas House, 152
Dove Creek Lodge, 116
Down to Earth, 351
Down Under Sports Bar, 277
Dream Catcher Charters, 280
Dreaming Goddess Boutique, The, 361
Dry Tortugas National Park, 185–86, 215–16, 255, 315
Duck and Dolphin Antiques, 362
Duck Key, 170
Duck Key Realty, 173
Duffy's Steak & Lobster House, 70
Duval House, 152
Duval Street Wrecker's Museum—The Oldest House, 301

E

Eagle, 249
Earthbound Trading Co., 358
Earth Days at Cheeca Lodge, 328
Eastern Dry Rocks, 252
Eastern Sambo, 251
East Martello Museum, 301
Eaton Lodge Historic Inn & Gardens, 152–53
Eden House, 153
education. *See* schools
E Fish and Seafood, 91
801 Bourbon Bar, 100
Elbow, The, 246–47
electric cars, 40, 41
El Faro, 392
Elks Club BPOE 2139 Bingo, 277
Elliott Key, 210
El Meson de Pepe, 78
El Siboney, 78–79
emergency phone numbers, 379, 381
Encore, 46
Enterprise Rent-A-Car, 35
Environmental Circus, 359
environmental organizations, 25, 28–29
Equator Resort, 163
Equipment Locker Sport & Bicycle, 273, 353
ERA Lower Keys Realty, 174
Everglades National Park, 185, 314–15
Everglades National Park Houseboat Rentals, 205
excursions, boat, 277–83
existing management areas, 194
Exit Realty Florida Keys, 173
Expressions Swim N' Sun Wear, Inc., 351
Extreme Sports Florida Keys, 285
Eye Candy Boutique, 353
Eye! Eye! Eye!, 356–57

F

Fairfield Inn by Marriott, 137
Fantasy Dan's Airplane Rides, 267
Fantasy Fest, 333, 334–35
Fast Buck Freddie's, 359
Fat Tuesday, 101
Fausto's Food Palace, 92
festivals, 325–37
Fiesta Key Resort KOA Kampground, 180–81
53rd Street Dock & Deli, 57
Finnegan's Wake Irish Pub & Eatery, 80, 103
Fish Bowl, 277
Fishermen's Hospital, 378
Fish House Restaurant & Seafood Market, The, 46, 86
fishing
amberjack, 227
in the backcountry, 222–24
barracuda, 221–22
blackfin tuna, 225
blue marlin, 224–25
in the bluewater, 224–29
bonefish, 219–20
from the bridges, 229–30
catch-and-release, 217

cobia, 226
dolphin, 225-26
in the flats, 218-22
fly-fishing schools, 242
grouper, 227-29
guides and charters, 234-40
kingfish, 226-27
licenses, 230-31
mackerel, 227-29
outfitters, 240-41
overview, 217
permit, 220-21
redfish, 222-23
sailfish, 224-25
sharks, 222
snapper, 227-29
snook, 223
spearfishing, 264
spotted sea trout, 223-24
tarpon, 221
tournaments, 231-34
wahoo, 226
white marlin, 224-25
See also boating and cruising; diving and snorkeling
Fish Tales Market & Eatery, 89-90
fitness centers, 289-90
5 Brothers, 92-93
Flagler Station Over-Sea Railway Historeum, 306-7
Flamingo Crossing, 93
Fletcher on Duval Island Furniture, 357
Flora & Flipp on Fleming, 93
Florida Keys Community College, 344, 370, 386-87
Florida Keys Commuter Bus Service, 38
Florida Keys Council of the Arts, 338
Florida Keys Dive Center, 262-63
Florida Keys Gift Company, 349
Florida Keys Kayak & Sail, 286
Florida Keys Keynoter, 391
Florida Keys Marathon Airport, 30
Florida Keys Medieval Fest, 325
Florida Keys National Marine Sanctuary, 25, 193-95
Florida Keys Outdoor Art Show at Key Colony Beach Park, 326
Florida Keys Poker Run, 332
Florida Keys Sailing, 201
Florida Keys Tropical Fruit Fiesta, 330-31
Florida Keys Wild Bird Center, 293
Florida Marine Patrol, 191, 209
Florida stone crabs, 88-89
Florida Straits, 189-90
fly-fishing schools, 242
Food for Thought, 90, 354
Fort Lauderdale-Hollywood International Airport, 31
Fort Zachary Taylor, 272, 307
Founders Park, 269-70
Fourth of July Fireworks, 331
Frances Street Bottle Inn, The, 153-54
Free Press Community Newspapers, 391
Freewheeler Realty, 173
French Reef, 248
Fresenius Medical Care, 378
Friendship Park, 269
Froggy's Fitness, 289
From the Ruins, 362
Fury Catamarans, 280-81

G

Galleon International Marina, The, 213-14
galleries, art, 341-47
Gallery at Kona Kai, The, 342
Gallery on Greene, The, 344
gambling junkets, 277-83
Garden Cafe, The, 87
garden clubs, 371-72
Garden of Eden, 351-52
Gardens Hotel, The, 154
Garrison Bight Marina and Boat Rental, 198-99, 200
geckos, 14
Geiger Key Marina and Campground, 184
George Bush/Cheeca Lodge Bonefish Tournament, 232, 333
Gerry Droney Tropical Gardens, 350
Geslin Sailmakers, 204
Ghosts & Legends of Key West, 312
Ghost Tours of Key West, 312
Gingerbread Square Gallery, 344
Glass Reunions, 344-45
glossary, Keys-speak, 2
Golden Nugget, 355
Goldman's Bagel Deli, 93
golf, 283-84, 373
Good Food Conspiracy, 90
Goofy Gecko and Crazy Larry's Last Store, 354
Goombay Festival, 333
Gotobus, 31
Grace Lutheran School, 385
Grand Café, The, 80-81

Grande Mulher, A, 360
Grassy Key, 170
Grassy Key Beach Motel & Resort, 125
great egret, 18–19
Greater Marathon Chamber of Commerce, 237
great white heron, 19–20
Grecian Rocks, 247
Green Parrot, 100
Greyhound Bus Lines, 35–37
grouper, fishing for, 227–29
guesthouses. *See* accommodations
Guidance Clinic of the Middle Keys, The, 382
Guidance Clinic of the Upper Keys, The, 382
guides, fishing, 234–40
Guild Hall Gallery, 345
Gulf Lady, 238–39
Gulf Stream III, 239–40
gunkholing, 17–22, 274–76
Gus' Grille, 45

H

habitats
  bare-mud bottom, 23
  bare-sand bottom, 23
  coral reef, 22–23
  hardbottom, 16
  hardwood hammocks, 12–13
  mangrove, 15
  pinelands, 13, 15
  sand beach, 15–16
  sea-grass, 16
Hair Wraps of Key West, 360
Haitian Art Company, 345
Half Buck Freddie's, 362
Half Shell Raw Bar, 70–71
Hall's Diving Center, 263
Hammocks at Marathon, The, 131
Hampton Inn & Suites, 120
Hands On, 345
Hard Rock Cafe, 101
Harpoon Harry's, 66
Harriette's, 48
Harrison Gallery, 345
Harry Harris Park, 270
Harry S. Truman Little White House, 301–2
Hawk Channel, 189
Hawk's Cay Resort and Marina, 124–25, 208, 236, 279, 286, 320–21
health care
  acute-care centers, 377–79
  alternative care, 382
  assisted living, 375–76
  crisis intervention and help lines, 381
  emergency numbers, 379
  home health services, 380
  mental health services, 381–82
  mobile care, 379
  nursing homes, 380–81
  overview, 377
  pharmacies, 380
Hemingway Days Festival at Hemingway Home and Museum, 331
Hemingway Home and Museum, 302
Hens and Chickens, 249
Herbie's, 57
Heritage Days at Fort Zachary Taylor State Historical Site, 328
Heritage House Museum, 302
Heron House, 154
Hertz Rent A Car, 35
Hideaway Cafe, 55
Higgs Beach, 272
history
  Bahamians, 4–5, 7–8
  cigar industry, 7
  Florida East Coast Railroad Extension, 8–10
  geologic, 11
  homesteading, 7–8
  Key West, 5
  Native Americans, 3, 4
  1930s to the present, 10
  piracy, 5
  role of the Gulf Stream, 3–4
  salt industry, 7
  Spanish explorers, 3, 4
  sponging industry, 6–7
  wrecking/salvage industry, 6
History Flight, 267
Hobo's Café, 44
Hog Heaven Sports Bar, 98
Hog's Breath Saloon, 66–67, 102
Holiday Inn Key Largo Resort and Marina, 97–98, 113
Holiday Inn & Marina, 127
home health services, 380
Hooked on Books, 351
Horseshoe, The, 252
horseshoe crab, 21
Hospice of the Florida Keys/Visiting Nurse Association, 380
Hostelling International Key West Youth Hostel, 164–65

hotels. *See* accommodations
Hot Hats, 358–59
Hot Tin Roof, 74
houseboat rentals, 204–5
Houseboat Vacations of the Florida Keys, 204
House Call Vet, 383
Hungry Pelican Motel, 114
Hurricane Joe's Bar and Grill, 71
Hurricane Monument, 294
hurricanes, 23–25
Hyatt Key West Resort & Marina, 141–42

I
Icthyophile, 352
iguanas, 323
Image Appeal, 289
Indian Key Beach, 270
Indian Key State Historical Site, 294–95
Indies Club, 320–21
Indies Teen Spa, 320–21
Inflatable Boats of the Florida Keys, 197
In-Home Services, 374
Inn at Key West, The, 139
inns. *See* accommodations
In One Era, 362
International Sailing Center, 200
Intracoastal Waterway, 189, 212
Iron Bodies Nutrition Center and Gym, 290
Islamorada, 169
Islamorada Chamber of Commerce, 236
Islamorada Fish Company, 53, 87–88
Islamorada Restaurant and Bakery, 87
Islamorada Tennis Club, 284
Island Accents, 357
Island Adventure Club, 320–21
Island Aeroplane Tours, 268
Island Arts, 345
Island Bicycles, 273
Island Christian School, 385
Island City Flying Service, 32
Island City House Hotel, 155
Island Grill, 50–51
Island Group Realty, 177
Island Hammocks, 350
Island Needle Point, 345–46
Island Opera Theatre, 341
Island Shoe Box, 358
Island Silver & Spice, 352
Island Smoke Shop, 348
Island Tiki Bar & Restaurant, The, 56
Island Watersports, 286–87
It's a Dive Watersports, 285

J
Jacob's Aquatic Center, 285
Jamaican Me Hungry, 84
Jimmy Buffet's Margaritaville Cafe, 67, 101
Joe's Tug, 252
John Pennekamp Coral Reef State Park, 180, 210–11, 269, 277–78
John Pennekamp Coral Reef State Park Boat Rentals & Dive Center, 261
Jose's Cantina, 79
Joy Gallery, 346
Jules' Undersea Lodge, 111
July 4th Fireworks, 331
July 4th VNA/Hospice Picnic, 332

K
Kaiyo, 52
Kate's Gallery, 346
Kelly's Caribbean Bar, Grill, & Brewery, 67–68
Kelly's on the Bay, 261
Kennedy Studios, 343
Kermit's Key West Key Lime Shoppe, 93–94
Key Bana Resort Apparel, 353
Key Colony Beach, 170
Key Colony Beach Boat Parade, 336
Key Colony Beach Golf and Tennis, 284
Key Colony Beach Motel, 127
Key Colony Inn, 55–56
Key Haven, 171
Keyker's Boutique & Gallery, 354
Key Largo, 169
Key Largo Chamber of Commerce & Florida Keys Visitor Center, 236
Key Largo Coffee House, 86
Key Largo Community Park, 269
Key Largo Fisheries, 86
Key Largo Kampground and Marina, 180
Key Largo Lion's Club Bingo, 277
Key Largo Princess Glass Bottom Boat, 278
Key Lime Products and Tropical Gifts, 350
key lime trees, 60
Keys Boat Works Inc., 197–98
Keys Cancer Center, 378
Keys Fisheries Market & Marina, 59, 90, 239
Keys Fitness Center, 289
Keys Flying Boats, 267
Keys Island Realty, 173
Keys Limey Charters, 279

Keys Sea Center, 196, 198
Keys to Key West, The, 287
Key West, 215
Key West AIDS Memorial, 307–8
Key West Aloe, 362
Key West Aquarium, 308
Key West Bed & Breakfast, The Popular House, 155
Key West Bight Marina, 214
Key West Boat Rentals, 200
Key West Butterfly & Nature Conservancy, The, 308
Key West Chamber of Commerce, 237
Key West Citizen, 390
Key West City Cemetery, 308–9
Key West Convalescent Center, 381
Key West Craft Show, 325
Key West Diving Society, 266
Key West Fish Cutters Restaurant and Fish Market, 90–91
Key West Fishing Tournament, 232
Key West Garden Club, 372
Key West Garden Club Flower Show at West Martello Tower, 328
Key West Golf Club, 284
Key West Hand Print Fabrics and Fashions, 362
Key West Havana Cigar Company, 356
Key West Historical Memorial Sculpture Garden, 309–10
Key West Historic Seaport and HarborWalk, 309
Key West International Airport, 30–31
Key West Island Bookstore, 362–63
Key West Island Store, 357–58
Key West Jewelry Station, 363
Key West Key Lime Pie Company, 94
Key West Keynoter, 391
Key West Kite Company, 363
Key West Lighted Boat Parade, 336–37
Key West Light Gallery, 346
Key West Lighthouse and Keeper's Quarters Museum, 302–3
Key West Literary Seminar, 325–26
Key West Marine Hardware Inc., 196
Key West Museum of Art and History at the Custom House, The, 303
Key West Realty Inc., 177
Key West Reef Trip, A, 281
Key West Sailing Club, 203
Key West Senior Center, 369
Key West Shipwreck Historeum, 310
Key West Songwriters Fest at Hog's Breath Saloon, 330
Key West Stargazer Cruise, 281
Key West Symphony Orchestra, 341
Key West Tea & Coffee, 94
Key West Tennis Too, 284
Key West The Newspaper, 392
Key West Tropical Forest and Botanical Garden, 310
Key West Urgent Care, 378
Key West Water Sports, 287
Key West Winery, Inc., 363
Kids Club at Marriott Key Largo Bay Beach Resort, The, 320
kidstuff. *See* children, activities for
kingfish, fishing for, 226–27
Kino Sandals, 363
Knight's Key Park Campground & Marina, 181
Kona Kai Resort, 114–15
Kon-Tiki Resort, 119–20
Kyushu Japanese Restaurant, 83

L

La Casa De Luces, 150–51
La Dichosa Bakery, 94
Ladies Tarpon Tournament, 232
La Mer Hotel, 155–56
Largo Cargo, 349
Largo Lodge, 111–12
Largo Sound, 210–11
La-Te-Da, 100
Latitudes Beach Cafe, 74–75
Latitude 25, 351
La Trattoria, 81
Layton, 169–70
Lazy Days Oceanfront Bar & Seafood Grill, 54
Lazy Lizard, 354
Lazy Way Hammocks, 363
Leigh Ann's Coffee House & Antipasti Bar, 56
Liberty Fleet of Tall Ships, 281
licenses, fishing, 230–31
Lightbourn Inn, The, 156
Lighthouse Cay Club Resort and Marina, 128–29
Lighthouse Court, 156–57
Lignumvitae Key, 211
Lignumvitae State Botanical Site, 295
Lilly Pulitzer, 364
Lilo Surf Shop, 366

Lime Tree Bay Resort, 123
limousines, airport, 35
Little Duck Key Beach, 271
Little Italy, 54
Little Palm Island, 134–35, 208–9
Little Palm Island Gift Shop, 355
Little Palm Island Resort & Spa, 61–62
Little Pirates Club, 320–21
Little Spanish Key, 212–13
Little Switzerland, 364
Little Torch Key, 170
Lobo's Grill, 68
lobster, diving for, 256–59
Local Color, 364
lodges. *See* accommodations
Loggerhead Key, 216
Long Key Bight, 212
Long Key State Park, 181, 270
Looe Key National Marine Sanctuary, 250–51
Looe Key Reef Resort & Dive Center, 265
Lookout Lodge Resort, 117
Lorelei Restaurant Cabana Bar and Grand Slam Lounge, 51, 98
Lost Reef Adventures, 266
Louie's Backyard, 75
Lower Florida Keys Health System, 378–79
Lower Keys Animal Hospital, 383
Lower Keys Artists Network, 339
Lower Keys Big Pine Senior Center, 369
Lower Keys Chamber of Commerce, 237
Loyal Order of Moose Lodge 1058 Bingo, 277
Lucky Street Gallery, 346

M

mackerel, fishing for, 227–29
magnificent frigatebird, 21
Malabar X, 279
Mallory Square Parking Lot, 42
Mallory Square Sunset Celebration, 310
manatee, 21–22
Mangia Mangia, 81
Mangoes, 75
Mangrove Mama's Restaurant, 62
Mangrove Mistress Eco-Charters, 281
Marathon, 170
Marathon Community Cinema, 288
Marathon Community Park, 271
Marathon Community Theatre, 339
Marathon Discount Books, 354–55
Marathon Garden Club, 372
Marathon Jet Center, 32
Marathon Key Beach Club, 129
Marathon Lady, 239
Marathon Lutheran School, 385
Marathon Marina, 198
Marathon Pizza and Pasta, 57–58
Marathon Sailing Club, 203
Marathon Veterinary Hospital, 383
Margaritaville Store, 359
Marina Del Mar Resort and Marina, 112–13, 207
marinas, 206–9, 213–15
MarineLab Marine Resources, 386
Mariners Hospital, 377
marine supply stores, 195–96
Marine Wildlife Gallery, 346
Marker 88, 49–50
marl lands, 24
Marooned in Marathon, 353–54
Marquesa Hotel, The, 157
Marquesas Keys, 215, 254
Marquesas Rock, 255
Marriott Key Largo Bay Beach Resort, 111
MARR Properties, 173
Martin's Cafe Restaurant, 81–82
Mary Immaculate Star of the Sea, 385
Maryland Shoals, 250
Mary O'Shea's Glass Garden, 346
Matecumbe Bight, 211
Matecumbe Resort, 120–21
Mattheessen and Magilner's Candy Kitchen, 94
Mattheessen's 4th of July Ice Cream Parlor, 94–95
media. *See* news media
medical care. *See* health care
Mel Fisher Maritime Heritage Society and Museum, 303, 306
Meloy Sails, 204
mental health services, 381–82
Mercury Baybone Celebrity Tournament, 233, 333
Mercury Cheeca/Redbone Celebrity Tournament, 233, 333–34
Mercury Little Palm Island Grand Slam, 233
Mercury S.L.A.M. Celebrity Tournament, 233, 332
Meteor Smokehouse, 77
Miami Herald, The, 390
Miami International Airport, 31
Michaels, 71
Middle Keys Campus, Florida Keys Community College, 370

Middle Keys Concert Association, Inc., 341
Middle Keys Levitt Senior Center, 369
Middle Sambo, 251
Mid Town, 176
Mile Marker 0, 310–11
Miss Tradewinds, 238
mobile medical care, 379
Molasses Reef, 248
Monroe County Library System, 371
Monroe County Social Services, 373–74
Montessori Children's School of Key West, 385
Montessori Island Charter School, 385
Moore Books, 349
Moorings Village Resort, The, 119
Moped Hospital, 273
mopeds, 40, 41
Morada Bay Café, 52–53
Mosquito Coast Island Outfitters, 282
motels. *See* accommodations
movies, Florida Keys as the site for, 104–5
movie theaters, 288, 340–41
Murray Marine, 199
Museums of Crane Point, 297–98
music, 341

N

National Key Deer Refuge, 298–99
National Weather Service Station, 311
Nature Conservancy of the Florida Keys, The, 25, 28
Neat Stuff, 364
Neptune Designs, 360
Newfound Harbor, 213
news media
  newspapers, 390–92
  radio, 392
  television, 392
New Town, 176
New Year's Eve on Duval Street, 337
Nichols Seafood of Conch Key, 89
Nick's Fitness Express, 289
Nicola Seafood, 75–76
nightlife
  Key West, 99–106
  Lower Keys, 99
  Middle Keys, 98–99
  overview, 97, 99
  Upper Keys, 97–98
Night on White, 347
nine one five, 76
No Name Pub, 60–61, 99
Northwind, 254
NOVA Care Rehabilitation, 377
Num Thai Restaurant & Sushi Bar, 45–46
nursing homes, 380–81
Nutrition Services, 374

O

Oasis Guesthouse, 164
Ocean Divers, 262
Ocean Key Resort and Spa, 142–43
Ocean Pointe Suite Resort, 116
Ocean Reef, 169
Oceanside Marina, 199, 214–15, 236
Off Duval, 364
Offshore Sailing School, 201
Old Island Days Art Festival, 327
Old Island Days House and Garden Tours, 326
Old Tavernier Restaurant, 49
Old Town, 175–76
Old Town Parking Garage, 42
Old Town Trolley Tours of Key West, 39, 312
Old Wooden Bridge Fishing Camp, 133
Open Minded, 358
Opera Italian Restaurant, 82
Orchid Lady, The, 312
Origami Japanese Restaurant, 83
Original Marathon Seafood Festival, The, 327
osprey, 20–21
outfitters, fishing, 240–41
Overseas Highway, 33–34

P

Palms Hotel, The, 157
Papa Joe's Landmark Restaurant, 54
Papa Joe's Marina, 236
Paradise Cafe, 68
Paradise Health and Fitness, 290
Paradise Inn, The, 157–58
Paradise Jet Support, 31–32
Paradise Pedicab, 40
Parawest Watersports Inc., 287–88
parking, 41–42
parks, 268–72
Parmer's Resort, 134
Parrotdise Bar and Grill, 61, 99
party boats, 237–40
Patio & Home Furniture Galleries, 354
Pearl's Rainbow, 164
Pegasus International Hotel, 139–40

Pelican Cove Resort, 117–18
Pelican Landing Resort & Marina, 140
Pelican Path, 312–13
Pelican Poop Shop, 364–65
Pelican Shoals, 250
Pepe's Cafe & Steak House, 68
Peppers of Key West, 95
Perky Bat Tower, 299
permit, fishing for, 220–21
pharmacies, 380
Picchi's 88 Ristorantino, 50
Pickles Reef, 249
Pier House Resort and Caribbean Spa, 103, 143
Pierre's Restaurant, 53
Pigeon Key Art Festival, 326–27
Pigeon Key Foundation Gift Shop, 355
Pigeon Key National Historical Site, 298
Pilot House Guesthouse, 158
Pink Junktique, 350
Pioneer Cemetery, 294
Pirate Soul Museum, The, 306
Pisces, 82
Pizza in the Mangroves, 49
Planet Smoothie, 95
Plantation Boat Mart & Marina, Inc., 197
Plantation Key Convalescent Center, 380–81
Plantation Yacht Harbor Marina, 207–8
Porky's Bayside, 60
Port Hole, The, 354
powerboat rentals, 199–200
Preferred Properties of Key West, Inc., 177
Prime 951, 71–72
private schools, 384–85
Prop-Tec, 199
Prudential Keyside Properties, 173
Prudential Knight-Keyside Properties, 177
PT 728, 313
PT's Late Night Bar and Grill, 77, 103
public boat ramps, 195
public libraries, 371
public schools, 384
public transit, 38
Pumpkin Key, 210

Q

Quality Yacht Service, 197
Quarterdeck Restaurant, 55
Quicksilver Catamaran, 278
Quilter's Club, 373

R

radio, 392
Radisson Hotel Key West, 137–38
Rain Barrel Village of Artists and Craftspeople, 342–43, 351
Rainbow Bend Resort, 125
Rainbow Reef, 262
Ramada Key Largo Resort and Marina, 113
Ramrod Key, 170
Reach Resort, The, 143–44, 320
real estate
- community descriptions, 169–71, 175–76
- condominiums, 171
- mobile homes, 171
- overview, 168–69, 174–75
- real estate companies, 172–74, 176–78
- single-family homes, 172

Real Estate Company of Key West Inc., The, 177
recreation
- air tours, 267–68
- beaches, 268–72
- bicycling, 272–73, 372
- billiards, 276–77
- bingo, 276–77, 372
- boat excursions, 277–83
- bowling, 276–77
- classes, 287
- fitness centers, 289–90
- gambling junkets, 277–83
- golf, 283–84, 373
- movie theaters, 288
- parks, 268–72
- skateboarding, 291
- skydiving, 267–68
- sunset cruises, 277–83
- tennis, 283–84, 373
- water sports, 285–88

Red Barn Theatre, 339
Redbone Art Gallery, 343
redfish, fishing for, 222–23
Red Rooster Inn, The, 158–59
Reef Awareness Week, 332
Reef Environmental Education Foundation, 29
Reef Relief, 28
Reef Relief Environmental Center & Store, 365
Reef Resort, The, 128
Reflections Nature Tours, 286
Regal Cinema 6, 288
RE/MAX Key to the Keys, 174

Remedy's Health Foods, 86
Rent Key Vacations Inc, 177
Reporter, The, 391
resorts. *See* accommodations
restaurants
Key West, 63–84
Lower Keys, 60–63
Middle Keys, 54–60
overview, 43–44, 63–64
Upper Keys, 44–54
Restaurant Store, The, 365
retirement and senior services
assisted living, 375–76
biking, 372
bingo, 372
bocce, 372
bridge clubs, 373
college courses, 370
dancing, 376
garden clubs, 371–72
golf and tennis, 373
nursing homes, 380–81
overview, 368
public libraries, 371
quilter's clubs, 373
senior centers, 368–69
senior services, 373–75
Rick's Key West, 102
Rick's Watercraft Rentals Inc., 286
Ripley's Believe It or Not, 313
Robbie's Boat Rentals & Charters, 199
Robert Frost Cottage, 302
Rob's Island Grill, 60
Rock Key, 252
Rooftop Cafe, 76
roseate spoonbill, 20
Royal Canvas Connection, 204
Rum Barrel, 100–101
Rumrunners Casino Boat Inc., 202
Rural Health Network of Monroe County Florida Inc. Medi-Van, 379
Rusty Anchor Fisheries, 95
Rusty Anchor Restaurant, 72

S

sailfish, fishing for, 224–25
sailing. *See* boating and cruising
Sailor's Choice, 238
Saint Leo College–Key West Center, 387
Saltwater Angler, The, 236, 241
San Carlos Institute, 306, 386
sanctuary preservation areas, 194
Sandal Factory Outlet, 349
Sand Key, 253
Sandy Moret's Florida Keys Fly Fishing School, 242
Sandy Moret's Florida Keys Outfitters, 236, 240
San Pablo Catholic Church Bingo, 277
Sarabeth's, 77–78
schools
colleges, 386–87
hands-on educational opportunities, 386
private, 384–85
public, 384
Schooner Wharf Bar, 103
Scientific Anglers Women's World Invitational Fly Championships—Bonefish Series, 233
Scientific Anglers Women's World Invitational Fly Championships—Tarpon Series, 234
scooters, 40, 41
Scrubs of Key West, 365
Sea Boots Outfitters, 236, 241
Seacamp Association, 386
SeaCoast Airlines, 31
seafood/specialty food markets
Key West, 91–96
Lower Keys, 90–91
Middle Keys, 89–90
overview, 85
Upper Keys, 85–88
Sea Isle Condominiums, 126–27
Sea Key West Express, 33
Seam Shoppe, 366
Seaplanes of Key West, 268
Seatow, 192
sea travel, 32–33
sea turtle, 21
Sebago Catamarans, 282
Senior Community Service Employment Program (SCSEP), 374
senior services. *See* retirement and senior services
Señor Frijoles, 45
Seven Fish, 72–73
Seven Mile Bridge Run, 328–29
Seven Mile Grill, 99
Shades of Key West, 359
Shark Key, 171
sharks, fishing for, 222

Sharon Wells's *Walking & Biking* Guide to Historic Key West, 313
Shell Key West Classic, 234, 329–30
Shell World, 350
Sheraton Beach Resort Key Largo, 115–16
Sheraton Suites Key West, 144
shopping
  Key West Duval Street, 356–60
  Key West off Duval Street, 360–67
  Lower Keys, 355
  Middle Keys, 353–55
  overview, 348
  Upper Keys, 348–53
Shucker's Raw Bar & Grill, 56–57
shuttle services, 35, 39
Silent World Dive Center Inc., 261
Simonton Court Historic Inn and Cottages, 159
skateboarding, 291
Skeeter's Marine, 198
Skydive Key West, 267–68
Sky Dive Marathon, 334–35
skydiving, 267–68
Sloppy Joe's Bar, 102
Smathers Beach, 272
Smith Shoals shipwrecks, 254
Smuggler's Cove, 50
snapper, fishing for, 227–29
Snapper's Waterfront Saloon & Raw Bar, 48, 98
snook, fishing for, 223
Snook's Bayside Restaurant, 47
snorkeling. *See* diving and snorkeling
snowy egret, 18–19
Solares Hill, 392
Sombrero Beach, 271
Sombrero Reef, 250
Southernmost Hotel in the USA, 138
Southernmost on the Beach, 138
Southernmost Point, The, 311
Southernmost Point Guesthouse, 159–60
Southernmost Sailing, 202
South Florida Center for the Arts, 339
Speakeasy Inn, 160
spearfishing, 264
special use areas, 195
Spirit Catamaran Charters, 279
Splash Watersport Rentals, 285–86
sponges, 21
sports. *See* recreation
spotted sea trout, fishing for, 223–24
Square Grouper Bar and Grill, The, 62
Square One, 76
Squid Row, 52
St. Justin Martyr Catholic Church Bingo, 276–77
Stacie Krupa Studio Gallery of Art, The, 343
starfish, 21
Stargazer, 252
Star Spangled Event at Sombrero Beach, 331
Stars & Stripes Catamaran Tours, 282
Stick and Stein Sports Rock Cafe, 103, 106, 277
stingray, 21
Stock Island Lobster Co., 95
Stone Soup, 347
Strike Zone Charters, 236, 265, 280
Strunk Ace Hardware, 365
Stuffed Pig, The, 58
Subtropic Dive Center, 266
Sugar Apple Natural Foods, 95
Sugarloaf Fitness Resort, 289
Sugarloaf Key, 171
Sugarloaf Key Resort KOA Kampground, 183–84
Summerland Key, 171
SunCruz Casino, 278
Sundowners on the Bay, 44–45
Sunny Days Catamaran, 282
Sunny Exposures, 352
Sunset Cove Motel, 114
sunset cruises, 277–83
Sunset Key, 176
Sunset Key Guest Cottages, 144–45
sunsets, 26–27
Sunset Watersports, 288
Sunshine Key RV Resort and Marina, 182
Sunshine Supermarket, 87

T

tarpon, fishing for, 221
Tarpon Basin, 210
Taste of Islamorada, 328
Taste of Key West, A, 329
Tavernier, 169
Tavernier Bicycle and Hobbies, 273
Tavernier Dive Center, 262
taxis, 35
television, 392
Ten-Fathom Bar, 253
Tennessee Williams Fine Arts Center, 340
tennis, 283–84, 373

Terra Nova Trading Key West Race Week, 326
Thai Cuisine, 83–84
theater, 339–40
Theater of the Sea, 293–94
Thomas Kinkade Gallery, 360
Thunderbolt, 250
Tikal Trading Company, 357
Tiki Living Hammocks and Gifts, 355
Tilden Scuba Center, 263
Timmy's Tuxedos, 366
Top, The, 101
Topsider Resort, 121–22
tournaments, fishing, 231–34
tours
  air, 267–68
  Key West guided and self-guided, 311–14
  trolley, 39, 312
Towels of Key West, 357
Tower of Pizza, 46–47
Trading Post, The, 88
Trails of Margaritaville, 313–14
Tranquility Bay Beach House Resort, 130–31
transportation
  airport limousines, 35
  air travel, 30–32
  bus service, 35–38
  car rentals, 34–35
  directions from Miami International Airport, 32
  mopeds, scooters, and electric cars, 40, 41
  Overseas Highway, 33–34
  parking, 41–42
  public transit, 38
  sea travel, 32–33
  shuttle services, 35, 39
  taxis, 35
  trolley tours, 39, 312
  walking, 40
Transportation Program, 375
Travelers Palm Tropical Suites, 161
Travis Boating Center, 196
Treasure Harbor Marine Inc., 202
trolley tours, 39, 312
Tropical Cottages, 128
Tropical Sailboats, 288
Tropic Cinema, 288, 340–41
Truman and Company, 178
Truman's at WatersEdge, 98
Turn Key Marine, 198
Turtle Hospital, 28–29
Turtle Kraals Museum, 72
Turtle Kraals Waterfront Seafood Grill and Bar, 68–69, 106
TV, 392

U

Uncle's Restaurant, 53–54
Underseas Inc., 263
Underwater Music Festival, 331
Unique Marine, 196–97
Upper Crust Pizza, 46
Upper Keys Campus, Florida Keys Community College, 370
Upper Keys Garden Club, 371
Upper Keys Plantation Senior Center, 368–69
Upper Keys Sailing Club, 202
U.S. Coast Guard, 191–92
USCG *Bibb* and USCG *Duane*, 248–49
USS *Spiegel Grove*, 247

V

vacation rentals, 166–68
VCA Upper Keys Animal Hospital, 382–83
Veterans Affairs, 375
veterinary services, 382–83
Village Cafe, 57
Village Gourmet, 87
Virgilio's, 100

W

wahoo, fishing for, 226
walking, 40
Waterfront Market, 96
Waterfront Playhouse, 340
Waterfront Specialist, The, 173
Watermark Marina of Islamorada, 207
Watermark Marina of Snake Creek, 207
WatersEdge, 54–55
water sports, 285–88
Watson House, The, 161
Watson Nature Trail, 298–99
Wave Gallery, The, 347
weather, 23–25
Weatherstation Inn, 161–62
weddings, 300
Welcome Home, 366–67
Welfare Department, 375
Wesley House Family Services Coordinating Agency, 387–88
Western Dry Rocks, 253
Western Sambo, 251

Western Sambos Ecological Reserve, 194
Western Union, 282–83
Westin Key West Resort and Marina, The, 142, 214
West Marine, 196
West Martello Tower, 306
Westwinds Guesthouse, 162
Whale Harbor Dock & Marina, 235
White Bank Dry Rocks, 248
White Gate Court, 121
White House-Black Market, 358
white ibis, 20
white marlin, fishing for, 224–25
White Rhino, The, 348
White Sands Inn, 125–26
Whitfield Jack, 365
Wicker Web, 353
wildlife management areas, 194
Wildlife Rescue of the Florida Keys, 311
Wild Side Gallery, 347
Windley Key Fossil Reef State Geologic Site, 293
Winter Star Party, The, 327
WomenFest Key West, 332–33
Wonderlin Tennis, 284
Woody's Saloon & Restaurant, 98
World Class Angler, 236, 241
World Watersports, 349
World Wide Sportsman Inc., 236, 240, 352–53
Wreck & Galley Grill and Sports Bar, The, 55
WS Kitchen Store, 349
Wyland Galleries, 347

X

X-Press to Key West, 33

Y

Yankee Fleet Ferry to Fort Jefferson and Dry Tortugas National Park, 283
yellowtail chum balls, 228
YMCA Daily Grind Skateboard Park, 291
Yoga College of Key West, 290

Z

Ziggie's Gumbo and Crab Shack, 51

ABOUT THE AUTHORS

VICTORIA SHEARER

A University of Wisconsin graduate, Victoria Shearer taught school briefly, then worked as an advertising account executive in Fairfield County, Connecticut, outside New York City. In the late 1980s she was copy editor for *COOK'S* Magazine. Her passions for travel and food were further kindled when Vicki lived in London for several years in the early 1990s. A member of the Society of American Travel Writers, she now writes feature articles on these topics for newspapers and magazines across the nation. Besides this and the previous ten editions of *Insiders' Guide to the Florida Keys and Key West,* she also is the author of *Walking Places in New England* (Out There Press, 2001). Her latest book is *Foodways to Paradise: A Florida Keys Cookbook,* published by The Globe Pequot Press. Writing from her home on Duck Key, Vicki shares the bounty of the Florida Keys with her husband, Bob, and her visiting adult children and grandchildren—Kristen, John, and Christopher, and Brian, Lisa, Bethany, Bobby, Ashleigh, and Nicholas.

NANCY TOPPINO

Nancy Toppino left the cold winters of the East Coast in 1996 for the year-round paradise found only in the Florida Keys. Since then, she has come to know this string of tiny pearl islands like the back of her hand.

She traveled extensively as a young girl and lived all over the world with her parents, instilling in her at a young age a yearning to visit new places. Knowing how important a good guidebook can be to any traveler peaked her interest in working on this guide.

She has collaborated on, revised, or updated five editions of the *Insiders' Guide to the Florida Keys and Key West.*

Nancy lives in Key West with her husband, Frank, where she most enjoys spending time with her children, Liz, Craig, David, Kim, Danny, Richard, Deborah, Ramona, and Aldo, and her grandchildren Sofia, Wil, Bingham, Olivia, John, Lindsey, Andrew, Lizzie, Anthony, and Alex.

In her words, "living in the Florida Keys makes every day seem like a Saturday." To Nancy, family is paramount; life is full; and this is the true meaning of *paradise*.